Stress Management for

Wellness

Fourth Edition

Stress Management for

Fourth Edition

Walt Schafer

California State University, Chico

THOMSON

✦

WADSWORTH

Australia • Canada • Mexico • Singapore • Spain • United Kingdom • United States

Publisher	Earl McPeek
Executive Editor	Carol Wada
Market Strategist	Kathleen Sharp
Project Editor	Elaine Richards
Art Director	David A. Day
Production Manager	Andrea Archer

Cover image: © Copyright 1998 PhotoDisk, Inc. Illustrator manipulation, David A. Day

ISBN: 0-15-507943-3

Library of Congress Catalog Card Number: 99-61921

Wadsworth Group/Thomson Learning
10 Davis Drive
Belmont CA 94002-3098
USA

For information about our products, contact us:
Thomson Learning Academic Resource Center
1-800-423-0563
http://www.wadsworth.com

For permission to use material from this text, contact us by
Web: http://www.thomsonrights.com
Fax: 1-800-730-2215
Phone: 1-800-730-2214

Printed in the United States of America
10 9 8 7 6 5

Preface

Evidence is mounting that, in several respects, Americans are becoming healthier. For example, fewer smoke and more eat low-fat diets. Still, a substantial number of Americans continue to experience a high rate of illness-induced absenteeism from school and work, feel sluggish or depressed, and see their doctors regularly for one medication or another. And, often, those who are not ill within a medical framework are not truly well either, since they are hardly maximizing their potentials, enjoying daily life, or maintaining high levels of vitality and energy.

Evidence from epidemiological and behavioral medicine studies clearly tells that wellness is largely a function of our daily habits: sleep, diet, exercise, relationships, how we handle anger, our chronic and acute tension levels, work satisfaction, and the presence or absence of energizing visions for ourselves and our world. Studies also leave little doubt that how we manage stress vitally influences the degree of wellness we experience.

This book brings together two significant and challenging topics: wellness and stress management. Both have central relevance, for the ultimate values this book intends to promote are maximization of human potential, good health, and enjoyment of daily life. This volume contains few *I's* or *me's*, but it is a very personal book; it is, first and foremost, an expression of my own learning and search for wellness through wise stress management. I have learned from many sources, which I acknowledge later. Most of all, I have integrated information from others' experience and research studies with my own search for a lifestyle of true wellness—a lifestyle with a proper balance of work and play, giving and receiving, mind and body, intensity and recovery.

There is no better time to improve stress management practices than during the college years, although, even if you are beyond that stage, it certainly is never too late. Many of my cardiac rehabilitation students in their 60s and 70s have benefited from the ideas and techniques presented here. My sincere hope is that, through this book, all will be aided in their personal quest for wellness through stress management.

Content and Approach

This book is distinctive in five main ways. First, the approach balances realism and idealism. I assume that life is and always will be difficult. There is no freedom from challenge, change, or conflict, but you can learn to confront, adapt, and grow by facing your problems. I also assume that personal change comes gradually through effort and patience. There are no magic pills or panaceas for everlasting bliss. Yet for most of us, greater happiness, vitality, and realization of potentials is possible. Idealism, in short, needs to be blended with realism.

Second, this book is distinguished by its integrated, whole-person, lifestyle approach to stress management. I believe wellness is promoted not by practicing any single stress management method (such as meditation, deep breathing, positive thinking, exercise, managing time better, or assertiveness training), but rather by integrating a number of methods to control stress and tension. It is vital to find the unique combination that works best for you. As noted above, introducing these techniques into your daily life requires time, patience, and gradualism. There are no miracles. Treat yourself as an experiment of one, and see what works best for you.

Third, the book weaves together information and application. The ultimate goal is not abstract learning for its own sake, but rather its application to the pursuit of higher-level wellness for yourself and others.

Fourth, this book's approach is constructive. Its goal is to assist you in learning to control and channel stress rather than succumb to it. Stress (arousal of mind and body in response to demands placed upon them) is unavoidable and can, in fact, be highly useful in order to meet performance demands, deadlines, and physical emergencies. This is positive stress. On the other hand, distress (harmful stress resulting from too much to too little arousal) can do untold harm to your health, career, relationships, and emotional life. It can be very costly to your family, to your employer, and to society.

Fifth, this book places personal stress within social context. You are not an island unto yourself, and your experiences with stress are not entirely unique. In many respects, they are shared with others. Furthermore, personal problems do not emerge in isolation—they are the product of larger social forces. This means that understanding the dynamic interplay between self and society is vital in managing stress. Seeking to improve social conditions out of which distress flows becomes just as important as dealing with personal problems, and caring for others becomes as valuable as caring for oneself. Thus, this book focuses on balancing self-care with social commitment.

A key assumption here is that wise stress management is a kind of preventive medicine—you will reduce the risk of illness to the degree that you succeed in harnessing stress. This book is designed to assist you in living wisely, thereby enhancing your wellness and preventing illness.

Organization of This Book

This book is organized into five parts. Part I presents an overview of stress and wellness with special applications to the college experience. Part II elaborates by presenting variations in the stress experience, the physiological dynamics of stress and relaxation, early warning signs of distress, and a review of distress-induced disorders.

Part III focuses on distress-prone and distress-resistant influences both within the person and in the external social environment. In Part IV, we turn to applications of stress management strategies and methods. Included are chapters on coping; self-talk, beliefs, and meaning; health buffers such as exercise, nutrition, sleep, and healthy pleasures; relaxation methods; managing time; giving and receiving social support; and blending personal wellness with commitment to the common good.

Changes in the Fourth Edition

Readers of the third edition of *Stress Management for Wellness* will note several key changes here. First, additional emphasis is placed on social roots of stress and wellness and on linkages of personal distress with social influences and public issues. Second, research studies are updated, especially in burgeoning fields related to mind-body-behavior interaction. Third, a number of new vignettes and examples are added. Fourth, the number of personal applications is reduced. The reader is invited to use the new *Student Manual* along with the text for a host of additional personal application exercises and suggestions. What has not changed from previous editions is the blending of learning with application. My hope is that after having used this book, you will not only have a better understanding of stress and wellness, but you will already have begun to take steps to improve your own wellness lifestyle.

Acknowledgments

I am grateful to many people for their contributions to this effort. Some who have influenced and inspired me the most have done so at a distance through their research and writing. Most important among them are the late Hans Selye, Kenneth Pelletier, Kenneth Cooper, Herbert Benson, Redford Williams, Meyer Friedman, Ray Rosenman, Robert Eliot, Donald Ardell, Joe Henderson, the late George Sheehan, Richard Lazarus, and Albert Ellis.

Ideas in this book have taken shape through my interaction with several groups of people. First, I am most grateful to former students in my Human Stress and Occupational Stress classes at California State University, Chico, with whom I have shared many of the ideas expressed here. These thousands of students have been invaluable in challenging me to formulate and present my ideas coherently and usefully.

Second, I wish to acknowledge several thousand community members with whom I have experienced reciprocal learning at the N.T. Enloe Memorial Hospital Stress and Health Center, which I founded and, for a number of years, directed. Especially useful have been my interactions with them in my five-month stress management class, Reducing Perfectionism, Irritability, and Hurry Sickness. Ranging in age from early 20s to early 80s, these co-learners have sharpened my awareness of the positive and negative features of stress, which techniques seem to be most effective, and what the personal change process   is really like.

Third, my interactions with colleagues have been rewarding and instructive. This especially includes my fellow instructors of Human Stress at California State University, Chico (Walter Zahnd, Laurie Wermuth, Robert Dionne, Sharrie Herbold-Sheley, Debbie Powers, and Janell Campbell). I also am grateful to my close colleagues and friends, Bruce Aikin, Terrence Hoffman, Darrell Stevens, David Welch, and Manuel Esteban.

In preparation of the book, I have enormously benefited from beedback, criticism, and suggestions from several exceptional reviewers: Jolynn K. Gradner, Anoka Ramsey Community College; Nolan Ashman, Dixie College; Rosemary Hornak, Meredith College; Murella Bossee, McKendree College; Neil Ramsey, Virginia Wesleyan College; and Sharon Gillespie, Andrews University.

The editorial, design, and production staff at Harcourt College Publishers have provided helpful guidance and support. Special thanks to my editor, Carol Wada, for helping to distill and integrate feedback from reviewers. David Day has created a beautiful design, and Elaine Richards, Andrea Archer, and Lisa Kelley did a marvelous job in producing and printing the text.

My daughters, Kimberly and Kristin, who were teenagers when I wrote my first book on stress more than two decades ago, have witnessed firsthand the evolution of these ideas in my own life and work. Over the years, they have participated in my personal quest for a balanced lifestyle. I am grateful for their support. My special friend, Clinton, whose amazingly effective stress management practices I have carefully watched and learned from, and who has been truly "with me" during the writing, also deserves credit.

Finally, Teresa Kludt, my wife, best friend, and kayak partner, has been a source of ideas, caring, energy, and good humor throughout this project. She has been most patient during my many days at the keyboard. She also has helped me avoid sexist language in my writing. To her I am most grateful of all. This book is dedicated to her.

Table of Contents

PART I

Stress and Wellness: An Overview

CHAPTER 1

Birds sing after a storm. Why shouldn't we?
—Rose Fitzgerald Kennedy

The Stress Experience: Myths and Reality

THE NATURE OF STRESS
Brian: A Case Study of Stress

Brian's mounting tension was increasingly apparent to him, his family, and his co-workers. His hands trembled as each day wore on, his stomach churned, his shoulders were tight, and his lower back hurt. He felt edgy and anxious and was often depressed for days at a time.

Communication became increasingly difficult, thinking more fuzzy, and speech sometimes staccato. He snapped at secretaries, boiled inside as business sales slowed, then blew up at colleagues. Working lunches usually included one or two stiff drinks to dull the tension. His wife and children became targets of irritability and short-temperedness.

Brian knew that tension was inevitable in his work. He even had found in the past that some anxiety was useful before a difficult meeting or speech. Yet chronic tension was getting out of hand. Something had to change and soon. Already his body showed signs of breakdown, his work was inefficient, his business partnership was threatened, and his family was becoming progressively alienated. Finally, his drinking was nearly out of control.

Following a series of stress-management consultations, Brian was determined to take positive steps.

During the next several months, he began a daily running and deep relaxation program. He improved his diet. He learned new techniques of mental and physical relaxation (on-the-spot tension reducers), which reduced the frequency of destructive stress build-ups. He developed new communication skills for coping with colleagues and for supervising subordinates. He decided to eliminate alcohol consumption completely for at least the next year. Finally, he learned to accept moderate tension as a fact of life and sometimes even as a positive force.

As a result of these steps, Brian's quality of life markedly improved. His energy level rose, and he felt better. His productivity increased, and his relationships at work and home improved. A key difference was his moderate reaction to stressful events, compared to his previous overreactions. These improvements were as apparent to him and others as his distress symptoms had been earlier.

Brian's experiences taught him a great deal. They also illustrate a number of key concepts related to stress. Each of these concept terms is a building block for a thorough understanding of the stress experience—including its helpful and harmful sides.

Brian's emotional and physical symptoms clearly suggest too much stress. In order to bring his stress under control, he had to learn more about it. Understanding several key terms was a first step, beginning with **stressor** and **distressor.**

Stressors and Distressors

Like you and me, Brian finds his life to be a constant process of responding to stimuli, pressures, and changes. Like Brian, you do not live in a vacuum. Rather, you are an "open system," continually exchanging energy, information, and feelings with the environment. You also place demands on yourself. Thus, you are always dealing with stressors—demands on your mind, your body, or both.

Viewed this way, stressors are ever-present. Adaptation is a continuous process. Most of the time, you respond to these demands with ease and familiarity. That is, stressors re-

Beliefs About Stress

Below are ten common beliefs about stress. With which do you agree or disagree? Later in this chapter you will read more about them.

1. All stress is bad.
2. The goal of stress management should be to eliminate stress.
3. The "good life" should be free of stressors.
4. The less the stress, the better.
5. A person can always adapt to difficult circumstances if he or she tries hard enough.
6. Some people are destined by their heritage to be highly stressed.
7. Distress has only harmful effects.
8. Physical exercise drains energy that otherwise might be used to cope with stress.
9. Meditation is cultish, anti-Christian nonsense.
10. Stress affects only adults.

main facts of life with no ill effects. But adjustment can exact a toll in wear and tear on mind or body. Physical upset or emotional turmoil often result. When this happens, stressors become distressors.

One stress expert has written, "The most elementary acquaintance with history, with anthropology, and above all, with literature—be it the Bible, the Greeks, Shakespeare, Dante, or Dostoyevski—reveals the rarity of tranquility in human existence" (Antonovsky, 1979, 87).

This rather gloomy opinion about the possibility of human peace may or may not be valid, depending on one's point of view and definition of tranquility. We do know that the history of the human species is marked indeed by considerable misery, illness, and struggle. In part, this results from humankind's continual need to adapt—to a changing physical environment, to ever-shifting technology, to neighboring tribes and nations, and to the life cycle itself. At a more personal level, human unhappiness results from sharp disagreements in points of view, from blocked-up emotions of hurt and frustration, and even from intentional acts of emotional or physical violence. In short, stressors become distressors. Demands no longer are neutral. They result in effects harmful to the individual.

Charlesworth and Nathan (1984) have presented an informative list of types of stressors:

Environmental	Chemical	Social
Commuting	Family	Pain
Physical	Decision	Phobic
Change	Disease	Work

College students deal daily with a host of stressors, including the following:

Exams	Noisy neighbors	Sexual encounters
Term papers	Conflict between job	Parental pressure
Conflicting demands	and school	College bureaucracy
Meeting new people	Parking problems	
Too little money	Career decisions	

Be aware that demands do not *cause* harmful effects. Rather, harmful effects result from the person's *interpretation* of those demands.

It is important to note here that awareness of stressors can itself be a deterrent to turning them into distressors. As Hans Selye, a pioneer in the stress field, has said, "It is well established that the mere fact of knowing what hurts you has an inherent curative value" (Selye, 1976, 406). This is illustrated by both animal and human studies showing that the greatest harm results from stressors that are unknown and therefore unpredictable. When stressors are perceived as predictable and manageable, they seem to be less threatening.

Stress Defined

Like many other ideas in the behavioral sciences, the concept of stress had its origins in the physical sciences (Hinkle, 1977). Dating back at least to the last century, *load* referred to an external force on, say, metal or wood. *Stress* was the ratio of resulting internal forces to the area over which the external force acted. The term *strain* was applied to disruption or distortion of the material being acted on, such as a building beam or a floor.

In the nineteenth century, first applications of stress to human experience began to occur in the medical literature. For example, the mind-body pioneer Sir William Osler made this comment about Jewish businessmen:

> Living an intense life, absorbed in his work, devoted to his pleasures, passionately devoted to his home, the nervous energy of the Jew is taxed to the uttermost, and his system is subjected to that stress and strain which seems to be a basic factor in so many cases of angina pectoris. (Hinkle, 1977, 30)

Note the direct connections here between mind and body and between lifestyle and health. Of course, this quote also represents a sweeping ethnic/religious stereotype that modern research has called into serious question. Nevertheless, it is an old version of the modern concept of Type A behavior (Lazarus & Folkman, 1984).

Definitions are neither right nor wrong. They are useful in varying degrees according to scope and clarity. Definitions can be inclusive or narrow, fuzzy or clear. My definition of stress has several advantages: **Stress** is arousal of mind and body in response to demands made on them.

First, the definition makes clear that stress is ever-present, a universal feature of life. Arousal is an inevitable part of living. We constantly think, feel, and act with some degree of arousal. Stress cannot and should not be avoided. Rather, it is to be contained, managed, and directed.

Second, this definition points to the multifaceted nature of stress. The stress response (arousal) involves virtually every set of organs and tissues in your body. Thoughts and feelings are clearly intertwined with these physiological processes. Anxiety and depression, for example, are not only feelings but also inseparable mental-physiological states. Body influences mind, and mind influences body. Behavior often is an outward expression of stress— for example, short-temperedness, fast talking, accidents, and harried movement.

Third, this definition is neutral. Arousal of heart rate, blood pressure, and muscle tension intrinsically are neither helpful nor harmful. Most often, arousal is simply a fact of life.

But stress can become positive or negative. This neutral feature of our definition is significant because it calls attention to a wide range of experiences with stress, from the positive tension of the Wimbledon tennis tournament finalist to the recurrent colds or flu of the unstable college student who plans time poorly.

It is useful to compare my definition of stress with two other prominent definitions in the field: one by Selye, the other by Lazarus and Folkman.

In the 1920s, the late Hans Selye, a young medical student then at McGill University, became fascinated early in his studies with the body's response to illness. He later stated, "In my second year of training I was struck by how patients suffering from the most diverse diseases exhibited strikingly similar signs and symptoms, such as loss of weight and appetite, diminished muscular strength, and absence of ambition" (Selye, 1982, 9). Selye called this generalized response "the syndrome of just being sick."

His curiosity about the "sick syndrome" led him to a detailed study of the stress response in laboratory rats. In the course of this research, Selye discovered a curious thing: Whatever "noxious agents" (stressors such as hormone and tissue extracts, electrical shocks, heat, and cold) he introduced into the bodies of rats, the response always seemed the same.

> Three types of changes were produced: (1) the cortex, or outer layer, of the adrenal glands became enlarged and hyperactive; (2) the thymus, spleen, lymph nodes, and all other lymphatic structures shrank; and (3) deep, bleeding ulcers appeared in the stomach and upper intestines. Being closely interdependent, these changes formed a definite syndrome. (Selye, 1982, 9)

Selye's well-known definition of stress, based on his research, is "the non-specific response of the body to any demand made upon it" (Selye, 1974). My definition has one important similarity to Selye's: Both have to do with the person's response to demands, rather than to the demands themselves. However, the two definitions also differ in one important respect. While Selye limits his definition to the body, mine focuses on the mind as well. By including mental arousal, we attend to a much wider range of human experience under the category of stress.

Lazarus and Folkman define stress as "a particular relationship between the person and the environment that is appraised by the person as taxing or exceeding his or her resources and endangering his or her well-being" (1984, 19). This definition is more restrictive than my definition, since it focuses on only the negative side of stress, which I define as distress later in the chapter. However, it has a number of advantages.

First, attention is directed to the interplay between the individual and the environment, rather than to the person as an isolated entity. Second, the key role of appraisal or interpretation in the person's response to demands is implied in this definition. Third, stress is seen as a dynamic process in which the human body and mind actively respond back, engaging in continuous efforts to adapt and restore balance or homeostasis. In other words, adaptation is active, not passive, and continuous, not static. Fourth, attention is directed to intervening with the environment, as well as the person, in managing stress. It becomes clear, then, why Lazarus and Folkman believe stress can best be understood from "a transactional, process, appraisal- and coping-centered approach" (1984, 19). However we define stress, its measurement presents a substantial challenge to researchers. For a comprehensive discussion of these measurement issues and for a collection of stress measures, see Cohen et al. (1998).

Three Types of Stress

Neustress

As noted at the beginning of the chapter, Brian responded neutrally to internal and external demands. His mind and body were aroused, but he moved along with little impact from these demands one way or another. In short, most of the time, his stress was neutral, neither particularly helpful nor harmful. Morse and Furst (1979) refer to this as **neustress**.

Distress

When arousal is too high or too low, **distress** ensues. The challenge is to identify your own zone of positive stress and to maintain a perspective and lifestyle that will enable you to stay within that zone most of the time.

An advantage to this definition is that it calls attention to individual meaning and perception. As Lazarus and Folkman (1984) have pointed out, whether a person experiences an event as "harmful" depends on the degree to which a stressor is perceived as exceeding her or his resources to cope with it and whether personal well-being is threatened. A theme throughout this book is that events are not intrinsically distressing. They become so only when they are interpreted that way—sometimes quite realistically, of course, when they do endanger one's well-being and one is uncertain of his or her ability to handle it.

See Application Exercise 1-1 to write about your own distressors and distress symptoms.

SYMPTOMS OF DISTRESS   The following is a sampling of common distress symptoms:

Poor concentration	Tight shoulders	Depression
Short-temperedness	Sore lower back	Fuzzy thinking
Trembling hands	Edginess	Accelerated speech
Churning stomach	Anxiety	Irritability

These distress symptoms serve as warning signs—messages that something is wrong and needs to be changed.

Minor distress signals such as trembling hands and tension headaches serve as useful early warning signs when we listen to them and respond constructively. You will read more about these and other distress symptoms in Chapter 6. Too often such symptoms remain undetected, become chronic, and turn into full-blown illnesses requiring medical attention. As we shall see in Chapter 7, a variety of health problems can follow.

STRESS-RELATED DISORDERS   Distress often leads to two types of disorders, physical and psychological. Below is a partial list of stress-related illnesses among persons referred by physicians to the Enloe Hospital Stress and Health Center for my stress management classes or for counseling.

Migraine headaches	Gastritis	Cancer
Noncardiac chest pain	Ulcers	Dizzy spells
Rheumatoid arthritis	Colitis	High blood pressure
Tension headaches	Lower-back pain	Panic attacks
Psoriasis	Heart attack	

Experts estimate that between 50 and 80 percent of illness episodes are stress related (Charlesworth & Nathan, 1984; Pelletier, 1977). The American Academy of Family Physicians estimates that two thirds of all appointments with family doctors involve some stress-related problem (*Time,* June 6, 1983). A study in a prominent medical journal identified only 16 percent of the most common symptoms among more than 1,000 patients seen by physicians at an internal medicine clinic as having a probably organic cause. The remaining 84 percent had unknown causes. The authors remarked that "it was probable that many of the symptoms of unknown etiology were related to psychosocial factors" (Kroenke, 1989).

Stress contributes to illness in four ways:

- By imposing long-term wear and tear on the body and mind, thereby reducing resistance to disease, such as catching a cold during exams or developing ulcers after years of chronic work pressure

---

Gallup Poll on Distressors and Distress

A Gallup Poll commissioned and published by *Health* magazine revealed the following responses by a nationwide random sample of adults to the question, "Which of the following sometimes or frequently cause you stress?" Note that Gallup uses "stress" in the way we use "distress" in this book. Figures are the percentages of respondents to whom the question applied.

Your job	71%
Money problems	63%
Family	44%
Housework	37%
Health problems	35%
Child care	20%

Source: Paulsen (1994, 46)

- By directly precipitating an illness such as a heart attack or tension headache
- By aggravating an existing illness such as increased arthritic pain or a flare-up of psoriasis
- By precipitating unhealthy or even illness-generating coping habits such as smoking, alcohol abuse, overeating, or sleep deprivation

Psychological distress, the other major category of stress-related disorder, can include severe depression, debilitating anxiety, disoriented thinking, paranoia, or lack of motivation to perform daily routines. The line between distress symptoms and full-blown distress illnesses is not distinct. Symptoms tend to shade gradually into more serious disturbed states. Most often, psychological distress symptoms accompany physical illness because of the intricate interplay of mind and body.

COSTS OF DISTRESS   Costs to the individual of prolonged and recurrent distress can include the following:

Decreased productivity at work or school	Wasted potential	Low self-esteem
Joylessness and meaninglessness	Lack of career advancement	Noninvolvement in public issues
Physical illness	Decreased satisfaction with life, work, and relationships	Absence of fun and play
Lowered energy		Loss of interest in sex

Unfortunately, the costs of distress do not stop with the individual. Negative energy ripples outward, affecting others. In the family, high personal distress of one member, especially a parent, can contribute to such problems as these:

Tension in the air	Low self-esteem of others in the family	Inattentiveness to emotional and physical needs of others
A damper on freedom of expression	Loss of potential earnings by an ailing family member	Family breakups
Open conflict		High health-care costs
Psychological put-downs		
Physical abuse		

Costs, too, are great in the workplace, incurred mainly through the following:

Low productivity	Conflict with co-workers	Worker turnover
Worker dissatisfaction	Absenteeism	High health-insurance costs

Matteson and Ivancevich (1987) have estimated the dollar value of these costs. The probable stress-related expenses to a hypothetical industrial firm employing 1,000 people with gross sales of about $40 million per year were estimated at $2.773 million, more than double the 3 percent profit of $1.2 million for a given year. The authors point out that if we multiply the estimated $2,773 stress-related cost per employee by 108 million workers (total estimated U.S. workforce at the time), we end up with a mind-boggling cost of stress to industry of more than $300 billion—a high cost indeed for stress-induced loss of effectiveness and efficiency. In Great Britain, stress-related absenteeism is 10 times more costly than all other industrial disputes combined (Cartwright & Cooper, 1997).

Experts have estimated that half of all hospital admissions could be prevented by changes in lifestyle habits (Charlesworth & Nathan, 1984). Many of these, such as overeating, lack of exercise, alcohol abuse, and smoking, are maladaptive coping behaviors.

Some years ago, Roglieri (1980) estimated that mismanagement of stress alone probably will contribute to more than one fourth of all deaths during a given five-year period in a typical group of white men 40–45 years old.

Costs of distress are not limited to adults. According to a news report, "The United States is raising a new generation of adolescents plagued by pregnancies, illegal drug use, suicide and violence . . ." (Associated Press, *San Francisco Chronicle,* 1990). A commission formed by the National Association of State Boards of Education and the American Medical Association concluded that "young people are less healthy and less prepared to take their places in society than were their parents." Among the statistics that "astonished" commission members were these:

- One million teenage girls—nearly 1 in 10—become pregnant each year.
- Thirty-nine percent of high school seniors reported that they had gotten drunk within the two previous weeks.
- Alcohol-related accidents are the leading cause of death among teenagers.
- The suicide rate for teenagers has doubled since 1968, making it the second leading cause of death among adolescents. One of 10 teenage boys and nearly 2 of 10 teenage girls have attempted suicide.

Since 1950, teenage arrests have increased 30-fold. Homicide arrests of youths between ages 10 and 14 increased 65 percent from 1988 to 1992 (*Time,* 1994, 61). More than half (56 percent) of American adults rank drug abuse as their prime worry about American youth (Dobbin, 1997).

According to a spokesperson for the National Association of State Boards of Education, "We are absolutely convinced that if we don't take action immediately, we're going to find ourselves with a failing economy and social unrest." In short, excessive distress is extremely costly to individuals, families, employers, schools, and the entire nation. Many experts predict these costs will rise.

DISTRESS AND DISHARMONY   By definition, distress is something to avoid whenever possible. Yet a period of distress can be transformed into a positive experience.

Distress almost always is a sign of some kind of **disharmony** among different wants or needs within the person or between the person's inner wants and needs and outside circumstances. When distressed, ask yourself these questions:

1. What is the disharmony within me or between my environment and me?
2. What can I do to resolve this disharmony?

Distress is to be avoided whenever possible. But when unavoidable, it can yield positive benefits by providing the basis for new learning, a change of direction, or resolution of disharmony.

We have focused attention here on the dark side of stress. Let us now turn to the brighter side with a discussion of positive stress.

Positive Stress

Stress involves a curious duality. On the one hand, excessive chronic arousal can seriously threaten health, productivity, satisfaction, and relationships. On the other hand, moderate, occasional elevations of anxiety can help prepare one for meetings, difficult conferences, and complex business negotiations. In short, stress can have both negative and positive faces.

EXAMPLES OF POSITIVE STRESS   **Positive stress** can be helpful in a number of specific ways, including these:

- Positive stress helps us to respond quickly and forcefully in physical emergencies, such as averting an auto collision, avoiding a dropped brick, lifting a heavy object off a child, fighting a fire, or administering cardiopulmonary resuscitation to a heart-attack victim.
- Positive stress is useful in performing well under pressure, such as in the U.S. Tennis Open, the Law School Admission Test, a job interview, or a speech.
- Positive stress helps to prepare for deadlines—a term paper, 5 p.m. clock-out time, or the income-tax filing date.
- Positive stress helps realize potential over a period of years in athletics, academics, and career.
- Positive stress adds zest and variety to daily life.
- Positive stress helps you push your limits.

> See Application Exercise 1-2 to write about personal growth through pushing your limits in your own life.

PERSONAL GROWTH THROUGH PUSHING YOUR LIMITS   Personal growth comes through sometimes pushing your limits beyond what is immediately comfortable. If you stayed in your comfort zone constantly, you would begin to stagnate. You will grow through sometimes deliberately pushing yourself in pursuit of a meaningful goal, to reach a higher level of performance than before, or to cope with an emergency. Marathon running, mountain climbing, studying very hard for a final examination, working very long hours on a project at work, missing sleep while caring for a loved one—all are examples of dedicated, meaningful efforts requiring pushing one's mental or physical limits.

If distance runners never felt physical distress, they would never approach physiological potential. Similarly, if you are never willing to work very, very hard in pursuit of a goal, you will remain half-developed. You may never know the trade-off of temporary emotional or physical pain for the joy of accomplishment and of approaching potential. I have grown through pushing my limits in a number of parts of my life over the years: tackling the academic rigors as a new student at a major university after a not-so-academic career at a small-town high school; public speaking; competitive running at the high school, university, club, and masters levels; taking communication risks in family life and friendships; writing books; assuming administrative responsibilities; and, most recently, white-water kayaking, which I began in my early 50s. In each case, I not only developed confidence in the specific realm in which I was challenged, but also that confidence spilled over into other areas of my life.

In sum, the following principles can be stated about personal growth through pushing your limits.

- Personal growth occurs through pushing your limits.
- Pushing your limits depends on positive stress—and sometimes tolerating temporary distress.

Personal growth comes from pushing your limits to meet a specific goal, like returning to school, studying for tests, and spending time with family.

- Pushing your limits will heighten confidence not only related to this specific activity but also in other spheres. Stated differently, increased confidence will likely transfer to other activity areas in your life.

These principles apply to many aspects of life—and to one's total growth as a person, as illustrated by the story by one of my middle-aged students in the box in this section.

Clearly, then, you do not want to avoid stress altogether. Without it, life would be stagnating and unsatisfying. Positive stress is vital for pushing your limits, and pushing your limits is essential for personal growth.

THE SOCIAL CONTEXT OF STRESS

Medical sociologist Aaron Antonovsky (1994, 7) recently pointed out that *"the voluminous writing [on] the holistic approach to health . . . shows a near-total absence of reference to or awareness of the larger social system in which the mind-body relationship operates. History, social structure, and even culture do not seem to exist"* (his italics). Applied to the topic of this book, the conventional view of human stress is to see it as an internal quality of the person, arising entirely from forces within the person.

This view is limited and incorrect. Just as mind-body-behavior are inextricably interlinked, so is each individual's experience interwoven with the surrounding social environment—family, friends, school or college, workplace, church, neighborhood, community, region, nation. The individual's experience with stress—whether neutral, positive, or negative—can be understood and effectively managed only by understanding the social context.

Personal Growth Through Pushing Her Limits:
A Personal Application

Below is a paper written in my Human Stress class by a college student in her 40s who had returned to school after many years.

"Personal growth through pushing your limits" is something I have been doing both physically and mentally during the last six years. This has been the most difficult effort I have ever made, but the most rewarding experience, which I wouldn't trade for anything in the world.

I am now a completely different person than I was, and it took pushing through a "brick wall" of many phobias, severe lack of self-esteem and self-confidence, Type E behavior [see Chapter 9] which was a cover-up for my insecurities, and a life-threatening disease. I came from being a "doormat," terrified of everything and everybody, to a self-confident, healthy, well-balanced individual.

In 1984, I discovered for the first time that I had some choices in my health status, started listening to my body to discover what it was telling me, and took one step at a time to make changes. As I pushed to get well, I discovered there were more steps I could take in my emotional status as well. I see the last several years as climbing a ladder, as I struggled to climb out of my pit and discover life on the outside of my "prison." Every step I took was terrifying, because it was new to me, but my survival depended on climbing out.

Gradually, I discovered I survived each step! The steps got slightly easier, and I saw it as the beginning of an adventure! Now, the adventure keeps me going, and I see the obstacles as "rocks to climb on for a better view" instead of "boulders to crush me." There is no stopping now, as I see life as an incredible opportunity to discover ever new ideas. The more I learn, the less I know, because each open door opens to many more open doors!

My life up to 1984 was extremely distressful, and for several years I had felt like my stress response was stuck on "ON." My body was continually in a state of panic. I finally depleted my energy reserve and had to rebuild my system. Now, I am distressed only occasionally, because I look for the positiveness of my situations. I no longer am terrified of being well, because I have dealt with both my internal and external barriers to wellness and have discovered it feels wonderful! The hard work of pushing to literally hundreds of unknowns has brought a life that I had never imagined. My car license plate reminds me that —I DUN IT.

John Donne's words still hold: "No man is an island entire of itself." In our case study, Brian's personal distress did not develop in a vacuum. It resulted from his efforts to adapt to changing circumstances around him, both in his immediate day-to-day environment and in the larger national and international climate. For example, Brian's business had taken a downturn in recent months in response to high interest rates, rising unemployment, and inflation. Periodically, his business faced a cash-flow crisis, a problem that seemed to correlate directly with his physical ailments and flare-ups with employees.

Beyond Self

There seems to be a growing disillusionment and backlash against narcissism in the name of health. In his article entitled "Through a Glass, Darkly," published in *Newsweek* in December 1991, the playwright and bartender Jeff Morris gave some "bartenderly advice": "Jogging, Stairmasters, aerobics classes and diets are not the answer. They only relieve the symptoms: stress, anxiety, poor physical condition. They do nothing to effect change or to alleviate the causes of our problems. All the effort that goes into focusing on one's self can be detrimental in the long run. All the energy we exert in the name of health and the glorification of the self is diverting and sapping us of all the energy we need to come to terms with what our real problems are: the economy, AIDS, human rights, the environment, education—these things can't be fixed unless people think more about other people and less about themselves."

Source: Pelletier (1994, 16)

Brian's experience was consistent with research studies showing that a deteriorating economy markedly increases rates of stress-related illness, depression, suicide, child abuse, and alcoholism. During hard times, individuals and families face twin crises. Tension mounts from too little income and job security at the very time when options for day-to-day coping decline because of limited resources—for example, options such as taking a weekend trip, eating out, beginning a new project around the home, or seeing a counselor. We all face other chronic pressures from the environment beyond economic ones—from the threat of nuclear war, air pollution, rising crime rates, traffic congestion, daily international tensions, the energy shortage, sexism and racism, urban noise, competition for grades, and more. Like Brian, each of these strains intrudes into our daily lives in a multitude of small ways. For many, the effect is a build-up of physical, psychological, and social tensions.

Looking at the same thing in the other direction, positive changes in the larger social structure affect individuals in a positive way. Srole and Fischer (1980) applied this principle to the changing role of women when they wrote that there is "a cause-and-effect connection between the partial emancipation of women from the nineteenth-century status of sexist servitude, and their twentieth-century advances in subjective well-being."

A vital implication of this social perspective toward stress is to take into account the person's social position and social characteristics in order to fully understand and address stress and distress. These need to include, for example, educational background, socioeconomic status, type of family of origin (married or divorced parents, number of siblings), ethnic background, neighborhood characteristics, religious background and affiliation, community size and characteristics, and more. Only then can one fully understand the nature and origins of the stress experience, whether in the self or someone else.

Another implication is that effective stress management needs to include not only learning to live with distressors emanating from the social environment but also becoming engaged in seeking change in that environment when needed. Alvin Toffler may well have been correct when he wrote more than two decades ago in *Future Shock*:

> The assertion that the world has "gone crazy," the graffiti slogan that "reality is a crutch," the interest in hallucinogenic drugs, the enthusiasm for astrology and the occult . . . the attacks on science, the snowballing belief that reason has failed

Social Context and Childhood Trauma

Carl Bell, a Chicago physician and mental health worker, reports that almost two thirds of an inner-city high school student sample reported they had seen a shooting and 45 percent indicated they had seen someone killed (Bell, 1997). Many of these students suffer from post-traumatic stress disorder. However, many also experience other trauma-related disorders. Here is an example, as described by Dr. Bell. This story graphically illustrates the influence of social context on one boy's personal distress.

A 10-year-old African-American male was referred for having problems with academic performance in school. For more than a year, his grades had been dropping from Bs to Cs and were currently down to Ds. The patient and his mother were at a loss as to why he had begun to do poorly in school as he had always been a B student. He reported he had not been able to concentrate on his homework due to frequently feeling sick to his stomach while studying. When asked what he thought was helping keep a B average when he had one, he revealed his father used to help him with his homework, and now his father was dead.

When asked about his father's death, the patient reported that he had been with his father when his father died. They had been getting on the elevator when two men began to argue over something, and one of the men began shooting at the other. The patient's father was shot in the stomach the elevator doors closed. His father was dead before they reached the sixth floor where they lived. He reported the smell had made him sick and he threw up.

This patient's current symptom of nausea during his study time was connected to the nausea and vomiting he experienced during his father's death. Studying was a trigger that evoked intolerable, unpleasant memories of his father's death that were not directly recognized but indirectly experienced through the symptom of nausea. Thus, the focus of therapy was to allow the patient, in a supportive relationship, to reexperience the death of his father and to grieve his loss—something he had not been able to do at the time of his father's death because of his mother's inability to tolerate her son's grief. With this grief work done, it was suggested to the patient that rather than become nauseous at the memory of his father's death, a more apt memorial for his father would be to take those feelings of remorse and transform them into some efforts at getting better grades. Gradually, the patient's grades improved substantially.

man, reflect the everyday experience of masses of ordinary people who find they can no longer cope rationally with change. (1970, 365)

Faced with challenges such as these, some people collapse, get sick, abuse others, or become seriously demoralized and resort to alcohol or drugs to numb their pain and depression. Others press onward in pursuit of their own private goals, paying little attention to the external circumstances influencing their personal distress. Some experts believe these negative tendencies are more prevalent in this country than in other industrialized nations.

Still others not only pursue their own goals but also transcend themselves to do all they possibly can to improve social conditions. Understanding that personal problems and public issues are linked, they practice **constructive maladjustment.** That is, they are appropriately indignant about social conditions they find unacceptable, and they are motivated to seek to improve these conditions. They link their *personal problems with public issues,* and they get involved. They believe in—though not by this label—**egoistic altruism,** which is self-fulfillment through promoting the well-being of others.

Effective stress management, then, includes not only self-care in pursuit of personal wellness but also includes social awareness and concern for the *common good*.

DISPELLING COMMON MYTHS ABOUT STRESS

Earlier in the chapter, you read several common beliefs about stress. As you may have concluded by now, all 10 beliefs might better be described as myths.

These and many other false beliefs about stress exist in the minds of people who know they have too much distress and are searching for what to do about it. If these beliefs remain simply beliefs, little concern need exist. However, too often they are translated into **action**—action that is destructive at worst and ineffective at best in handling stress. Therefore, it is important to dispel these common myths.

1. **All stress is bad.** Stress can be helpful as well as harmful. Positive stress can provide zest and enjoyment, as well as attentiveness and energy for meeting deadlines, entering new situations, coping with emergencies, achieving maximum performance, and meeting new challenges. In moderate amounts, stress is useful. Even in large doses, it is often appropriate and vital.
2. **The goal of stress management should be to eliminate stress.** Stress cannot and should not be eliminated. As Hans Selye, father of this field, has stated, only the dead are free of stress. Arousal is part of life. The goal of stress management should be to control stress so it turns into harmful distress as infrequently and as briefly as possible.
3. **The "good life" should be free of stressors.** Stressors, demands on mind or body, are an ever-present part of existence, just like stress. It is vital, insofar as possible, to control stressors and your interpretations of them so they are not overburdening in intensity or number. But fulfillment of human potential, in fact life itself, depends on exposure to appropriate kinds of stressors.
4. **The less the stress, the better.** Not necessarily. The more arousal the better when facing challenges or emergencies, up to a certain point. Stress mobilizes for action, shapes interpretations of events, and heightens attention. The less distress the better, since by definition distress is harmful.
5. **A person can always adapt to difficult circumstances if he or she tries hard enough.** This belief is false on two counts. First, each person has limits of adaptability. If physical, social, or psychological pressures exceed your upper stress limit for an extended period, wear and tear will lead to eventual breakdown. This state of resistance gives way to the stage of exhaustion. Second, "trying harder" is not always the answer to distress. The opposite may be true, in that activity needs to be alternated with rest and recovery.
6. **Some people are destined by their heritage to be highly stressed.** It is true that to some degree genetic and social background can affect resistance and vulnerability to pressure. But environmental and biological inheritance sets only very broad limits, except in cases of severe mental or physical handicaps. Whatever the

background, most people can take personal responsibility and constructive steps, which can dramatically increase the ability to handle and reduce stress.

7. **Distress has only harmful effects.** By definition, mental and physical distress are harmful to the self and others. Yet even intense distress can have positive side effects—learning about the self or others, a new beginning, or a renewed relationship with someone, for example. (Dafter, 1996; Remen, 1996).

8. **Physical exercise drains energy that otherwise might be used to cope with stress.** Moderate, progressive physical exercise increases energy through the body's marvelous adaptive process. The claim "I don't have enough energy to exercise; I need it to meet the demands of my life" is a hollow excuse without foundation in the reality of exercise physiology. The only exceptions are when a very hard workout might leave one temporarily too tired to cope well, when recovering from illness, or during the early weeks of exercise after a long period of sedentary living.

9. **Meditation is cultish, anti-Christian nonsense.** Some forms of meditation indeed are associated with gurus and cults. But meditation itself is a highly effective method of controlling stress by means of quieting the body (releasing the relaxation response) with a repeated mental focus, such as a silent sound, word, or thought. Research clearly shows that deep relaxation through meditation is effective in preventing and reducing stress-related illnesses and psychological disorders. It is important to assess meditation as a method separately from any persons or organizations that might promote it.

10. **Stress affects only adults.** Stress is part of everyone's life, young or old. Children and adolescents experience the same responses as adults and run the same risks of distress illnesses. Therefore, the guidelines and techniques presented in this book apply equally to persons of all ages.

A WHOLE-PERSON, LIFESTYLE APPROACH TO STRESS MANAGEMENT

From the prior discussion, it becomes clear that no single panaceas to managing stress exist. Rather, we need an integrated, whole-person, lifestyle approach. From the recent study by Kenneth Pelletier (1994) of 51 prominent, high-functioning Americans, as well as from other studies, we know that most good stress managers practice the essential ingredients of such a lifestyle.

What Do Good Stress Managers Do?

1. They anticipate, monitor, and regulate stressors insofar as possible.
2. They are aware of and control their interpretations of stressors.
3. Good copers believe they can influence events and their reactions to those events.
4. They practice daily deep relaxation in order to balance chronic excitation of the stress response with recovery, as well as to keep arousal at a lower level most of the time.
5. Effective stress managers use mental and physical on-the-spot tension reducers to control arousal when confronted with threatening stressors.
6. They maintain positive health buffers—daily exercise, good eating habits, adequate sleep and healthy pleasures—to build stress resistance and prevent stress build-up.
7. They recognize early warning signs of mental and physical distress.
5. Good stress managers develop means of mobilizing and controlling stress in performance situations.

See Application Exercise 1-3 for an assessment of your own stress management skills.

9. They use constructive reactions to distress when it does occur in order to reduce distress, rather than destructive reactions that heighten distress.
10. They develop and maintain a strong sense of meaning in their lives—meaning that provides direction and coherence in their private and public lives.
11. They get involved in contributing to the well-being of other persons, organizations, and communities.

These, then, are some of the habits of people who manage their stress well. The box "Stress Management Heroes" presents a number of college students' responses to the sentence completion: "My number one hero in managing stress is . . . because . . ." Let us now turn to a series of assumptions with which such an effective pattern of stress management can be built.

Assumptions About Stress Management

From the discussion throughout this chapter, we are led to see that stress is the experience of arousal of mind and body in response to demands made on them by stressors. Stress can be neutral, negative, or positive. What is needed is an integrated approach blending mind-body-behavior and focusing not just on the person as an isolated unit but on how she or he relates to the surrounding world. This needs to include attention to promoting the well-being of others as well as engagement in contributing to the broader common good.

As noted previously, this framework leads to a *whole-person, lifestyle* approach to stress management that is presented in the following chapters. This approach is based on several guiding assumptions.

1. **Personal Responsibility** Effective management of stress can be accomplished only by you. Your doctor, counselor, spouse, or minister cannot do it for you. They can help. You will need them as partners from time to time. But self-care rather than dependence on others is a keystone in the chapters that follow. The opposite of personal responsibility is helplessness, a bedfellow of distress.
2. **Holism** There is no single, magical way of controlling stress and minimizing distress. Regular running or swimming can help. So can improved diet, regular meditation, slowing down, expressing feelings, taking vacations, and a number of other activities.
3. **Gradualism** No one should adopt too many new stress management methods at once. If you try too hard or expect change too soon, you will be frustrated and overloaded. You must be patient. Introduce one or two new stress management methods at a time, so you can concentrate and carry through. Change comes gradually, not overnight. Wholeness is a long-term ideal, gradualism the short-run way to get there.
4. **Balance** As you search for the pace of life and daily habits that are best for managing your stress, you stand to gain from striving for balance with each of the following:

Self-interest and the well-being of others	Intensity and ease	Change and stability
	Thought and action	Stimulation and quiet
Work and play	Risk and safety	

Only you can determine the right balance for you in each of these respects—and what is right for you can change over time. You must be continually alert to internal cues that tell you what balance your body and mind need for health and growth.
5. **Rhythm** Stress and distress come and go in stages and rhythms, some of which are quite predictable. Perhaps the greatest contribution of Gail Sheehy's best-selling book, *Passages,* was the message to millions of readers that many adult crises are predictable, that many people experience the same crises, and that these crises will pass (Sheehy, 1976). The same holds for the pre-adult years and for the later years.

Stress Management Heroes

Below are excerpts from my college students who wrote, "My number one hero in managing stress is . . . because . . ."

- My number one "hero" in managing stress is my boyfriend, _____. He is always calm, cool, and collected about everything. His patience is wonderful and unbelievable. He never overreacts to situations and is a great listener.
- My number one "hero" in managing stress is: my dad. Because: He is always under a lot of stress at work but has found ways for it not to interfere too much with his "free" time. He found things that he enjoys that help to relieve him a bit.
- My number one "hero" in managing stress would have to be my mother. I have never once heard her say "I'm so stressed out." Where I, on the other hand, often feel literally sick from stress (or distress), she is very easy going. She is active in church as well as exercises daily. She just lives life, and it doesn't seem like she ever worries.
- My number one "hero" in managing stress is my sister, _____, because she is always open with her feelings and gets her problems off her chest by discussing them with someone or facing the problem head on.
- My number one "hero" in managing stress is my friend, _____. She never worries about a thing that isn't seriously important. She never does anything she doesn't want to do. She is the most carefree, happy-go-lucky girl I know. I admire this quality in her, and that's why she's my stress heroine.
- My dad would have to be my "hero" in managing stress. He has never taken his stress out on anyone else and can be very cool under pressure. Even though he is deeply hurting, he doesn't let anyone know about it.
- My number one hero in managing stress is: my mom. Because: With everything going on in her life right now, she still manages to be as positive as possible, do everything she can for my sister and me, and still have a little fun herself.
- My number one hero in managing stress is one of my friends, _____. She handles more stress than anybody I know. Not only does she handle her own stress, she helps me by listening to my problems and making light of bad situations.

Knowing that distress ebbs and flows can be reassuring. Your inner drive toward health and growth can take you from the deepest valleys to new peaks of authenticity and self-expression.

An important ingredient of wise stress management is conscious control of the rhythms of stress and distress. Daily life inevitably has stressful periods of intensity and effort. If you are to manage stress wisely, you must deliberately return your stress level to normal relatively quickly, so you can handle the next stressful event of the day.

6. **Awareness** This book emphasizes the key role of understanding stress and distress—what stressors are, what causes them, how they can play useful and harmful roles in your life, and how you can handle them. Continually increasing your understanding of both can be useful in two ways. First, awareness can be directly

useful. If, for example, you are aware that a particular mental or physical state is stress-related (and that you are not "going crazy"), your worry about it almost always will subside. Similarly, anticipating a crisis and that it might produce illness or upset can lessen the tension. In short, understanding in itself can aid in handling stress.

Second, enhancing awareness can play an indirectly useful role, by leading to coping responses that are constructive rather than irrelevant or destructive. Knowing through experience, for example, that two long nights' sleep are vital for reducing accumulated tensions can aid you in coping with depression or intense anxiety. Conversely, the awareness that simply working harder may not help can encourage you to slow down or take a vacation.

Awareness of stress often comes with **hindsight**—after-the-fact awareness. Next often comes **midsight**—for example, awareness during a destructive coping response. Finally comes **foresight**— awareness before getting into severe distress or before a harmful coping response starts.

7. **Action** Awareness by itself is only half the picture. The other half is paying attention to what you as you seek to manage stress. How you spend your time, the actions you take, what you do in relation to others and your daily tasks—ultimately these will determine how well you manage stress. Both understanding and action are necessary, but neither is sufficient alone. Action guided by informed understanding—that is the necessary and sufficient combination required for handling stress well.

8. **Experiment-of-one** People are different, and the same approach will not work for everyone. Scientists can tell us what sometimes works to improve health or reduce tension for different kinds of people. But, in the final analysis, you are unique. You have your own particular needs, you live your life in your own way, and your social setting is not exactly like anyone else's. You need to test out what fits your own body, personality, and way of living. Through experimentation, you will discover your own methods for controlling stress and preventing distress. This means that you must adopt the perspective of a scientist toward yourself—testing, observing, drawing conclusions, repeating what works, discontinuing what does not, searching for new stress methods when needed. The artful application of wisdom gained in this manner is an exciting and continuing challenge.

9. **Egoistic altruism** As noted earlier, it is vital to focus attention on promoting the well-being of others as well as improving social conditions in the surrounding environment. Stress management includes not only personal care but also caring for others. As noted, egoistic altruism is personal fulfillment through promoting the well-being of others. This can be based on focusing energy on either the micro-environment (persons and groups directly around you) or on the macro-environment (social conditions in the larger community, state, or nation). Since research shows that helping is healthy, self-transcendence results in gain for both self and others. Kenneth Pelletier (1994, 112) states, based in part on his study of intensive 51 high-functioning individuals, "Research has documented that purpose is beneficial to psychological health, in alleviating such conditions as depression and anxiety, and to physical health, in contributing to recovery from heart attacks and cancer. It has also been shown that individuals who express their purpose in life through altruism are unusually healthy and recover more quickly and fully from both major and minor illnesses."

10. **Lifelong process** Managing stress is not something you do once and then forget. Rather, in my life as in yours, managing stress is an ongoing, never-ending, some-

times joyful, and sometimes frustrating challenge. This underscores the vital importance of deeply internalizing the principles in this book, making them part of your everyday approach to time, your body, other people, and daily activities.

So you need not be helpless or overwhelmed. Your fate is not sealed at birth or by the circumstances of your life, trying as they may be. You can take affirmative steps to build personal protection against the mounting forces creating distress for millions. You can learn from those who handle life's pressures without illness or unnecessary strain. We noted that good stress managers do not rely on one single technique or approach. They weave together a blend of stress management methods. This is *a whole- person, lifestyle approach*—the theme of this book.

Stress Management for What? A Word About Wellness

The point of stress is to enhance health and well-being for the self and for others. Managing stress effectively will benefit the self by improving quality of life and decreasing risk of illness. It will benefit those in your immediate environment by improving relationships and generating caring. It will benefit the wider world by directing personal energy toward improving social conditions out of which mental and physical illness, violence, and other social problems arise. In short, the whole point of managing stress effectively is to promote wellness for the self and for others. For a formal definition and more complete explanation of wellness, see Chapter 3.

References

Antonovsky, A. (1979). *Health, stress and coping.* San Francisco: Jossey-Bass.

Antonovsky, A. (1994). A sociological critique of the "well-being" movement. *Advances, 10,* 6–12.

Associated Press (1990). Experts say new generation in trouble already. *San Francisco Chronicle,* June 9, A1.

Bell, C. C. (1997). Stress-related disorders in African-American children. *Journal of the National Medical Association, 89,* 335–340.

Cartwright, S., & Cooper, C. L. (1997). *Managing workplace stress.* Thousands Oaks, CA: Sage Publications.

Charlesworth, E. A., & Nathan, R. G. (1984). Stress management: A comprehensive guide to wellness. New York: Atheneum.

Cohen, S., Kessler, R. C., & Underwood, L. (Eds.)(1998). *Measuring stress: A guide for health and social scientists.* New York: Oxford University Press.

Dafter, R. E. (1996). Why "negative" emotions can sometimes be positive: The spectrum model of emotions and their role in mind-body healing. *Advances, 12,* 6–19

Dobbin, M. (1997). Drug abuse seen as No. 1 threat to kids, poll finds. *Sacramento Bee,* December 9, A6.

Hinkle, L. E., Jr. (1977). The concept of "stress" in the biological sciences. In Z. J. Lipowski, D. R. Lipsitt, & P. C. Whybrow (Eds.), *Psychosomatic medicine: Current trends and clinical implications.* New York: Oxford University Press, 330–339.

Kroenke, K., & Mangelsdorff, A. D. (1989). Common symptoms in ambulatory care: Incidence, evaluation, therapy, and outcome. *American Journal of Medicine, 86,* 262–266.

Lazarus, R. S., & Folkman, S. (1984). *Stress, appraisal and coping.* New York: Springer.

Matteson, M. T., & Ivancevich, J. M. (1987). *Controlling work stress.* San Francisco: Jossey-Bass Publishers.

Morse, D. R., & Furst, M. L. (1979). *Stress for success: A holistic approach to stress and its management.* New York: Van Nostrand Reinhold.

Paulsen, B. (1994). A nation out of balance. *Health, 8.* October 1994, 45–48.

Pelletier, K. R. (1977). *Mind as healer, mind as slayer.* New York: Dell.

Pelletier, K. R. (1994). *Sound mind, sound body.* New York: Simon & Schuster.

Remen, R. N. (1996). All emotions are potentially life affirming. *Advances, 12,* 23. 28.

Roglieri, J. L. (1980). *Odds on your life.* New York: Seaview.

Selye, H. (1974). *Stress without distress.* Philadelphia: Lippincott.

Selye, H. (1976). *The stress of life* (rev. ed.). New York: McGrawHill.

Selye, H. (1982). History and present status of the stress concept. In L. Goldberger & S. Breznetz (Eds.), *Handbook of stress: Theoretical and clinical aspects.* New York: Free Press, 7–17.

Sheehy, G. (1976). *Passages: Predictable crises of adult life.* New York: E. P. Dutton.

Srole, L. & Fischer, A. K. (1980). The midtown Manhattan longitudinal study versus 'The mental paradise lost' doctrine. *Archives of General Psychiatry,* 37, 209–221.

Time (1983). Stress: Can we cope? June 6, 48–53.

Time (1994). When kids go bad. September 19, 1994, 60–63.

Toffler, A. (1971). *Future shock.* New York: Bantam Books.

Application Exercise 1–1

Distressors and Distress Symptoms

This exercise is intended to assist you in identifying your goals in reading this book. In the "Distressors" column below, list several stressors you would like to handle more effectively as a result of reading this book. In the "Distress Symptoms" column, list personal symptoms of distress (emotional, cognitive, physical, or behavioral) that you would like to minimize or prevent in the future.

Distressors	Distress Symptoms
1.	1.
2.	2.
3.	3.
4.	4.
5.	5.

Additional comments:

Application Exercise 1–2

Personal Growth Through Pushing Your Limits

1. Areas of my life in which I *now* push my limits with positive stress include:

2. Areas of my life in which I *will* push my limits with positive stress include:

Application Exercise 1–3

Self-Assessment of Stress Management Skills

This exercise is intended to help you assess how you measure up on the qualities of good stress managers presented on pages 17-18.

1. Which qualities are your greatest *strengths?*

2. Which qualities are your greatest *weaknesses?*

3. Ask a friend or family member to answer the above two questions about you. Then discuss it with her or him.

When students feel that they are in control of their lives and their time, they remain eager, curious, and caring.

—N. A. WHITMAN, D. C. SPENDLOVE,
AND C. H. CLARK

Passing the Test of College Stress

Role Conflict in College

Kim is a college junior who occupies several roles: student, roommate, lover, daughter, and employee. Usually, others' expectations do not seriously conflict, but sometimes she does feel in a bind. On a recent Thursday, for example, her history professor and classmates expected her to present an oral report on the life of Calvin Coolidge at their noon class, her roommates wanted her to help clean the apartment all morning, her boyfriend wanted to have lunch with her, she felt pressured to answer her mother's letter of last week, and her boss called at 7:30 A.M. to ask her to substitute for a sick employee.

CHALLENGE AND OPPORTUNITY DURING THE COLLEGE YEARS

The college years bring to mind the Chinese writing character with a dual meaning: crisis and opportunity. Whether the new student is an 18-year-old, fresh out of high school, or a 38-year-old working-class single mother returning to school as a step toward a better life, the college journey puts him or her to personal tests that most likely are beyond anything experienced before. Challenges such as those faced by Kim can be approached as an opportunity or a threat, a chance to practice wellness or worseness.

How you respond will determine how much is gained from the college experience. Maintaining a wellness lifestyle, including turning challenges into positive stress, can facilitate your academic learning and personal development (Whitman, Spendlove, & Clark, 1984; 1986). But more, how you cope during these years can shape habits that last a lifetime, vitally influencing your well-being for years to come.

In a host of ways, the college years present a wonderful opportunity to apply many of the ideas and skills you will read about in this textbook.

To possess the *sociological imagination* is to see individual experience within a broader social context. This certainly applies to the college experience at the turn of the century.

Most students entering college in 2000 were born about 1982. As Hoffman (1989, 4) has noted, the early life experiences of this cohort took place during "a period of economic stagnation, falling expectations, and rising social dislocations."

During these years, unemployment fluctuated, and many in our nation were disillusioned by Vietnam, Watergate, and the Clinton sex scandal. The stock market experienced a mini-crash, we became a debtor nation, and our space program endured a traumatic tragedy.

We were frightened by Chernobyl, international terrorism became widespread, and AIDS created fear. Crime and drugs became everyday realities. Our national debt soared to previously unthinkable levels. The condition of the natural environment continued to deteriorate, with little evidence of social or political will to reverse the destruction.

The profit motive and self-aggrandizement took extreme forms in the rhetoric of our government leaders and in the unethical conduct of many in business. We witnessed a corresponding decline in concern with the common good.

Our rate of divorce reached a new high, with fully half of all new marriages expected to end in dissolution. A record high number of students thus entered college having grown up in a climate of separation, divorce, single-parenting, remarriage, and reconstituted families. An increasing number of students, in fact, themselves had been involved in family dissolution, often returning to college as a next step after a separation, divorce, or remarriage. Most often, at least on my campus, these are women in their late 20s to early 40s.

This period saw progress in ethnic and women's rights, yet sharp divisions emerged over abortion and freedom of choice. On many campuses, ugly incidents of racism and sexism were reported. Prejudices remained.

Economic pressures in families, combined with declining federal support, meant that financing college became a major stressor. Consequently, many students could expect to work while going to school. For millions, the four-year college experience turned into five—at the very time when, perhaps for the first time in our history, students had reason to question whether they would be better off than their parents.

To be sure, this is not a pretty picture. Yet, it is real. Hoffman recently summarized implications of this context for college students approaching the new century as follows:

> . . . the contemporary generation of students is growing up in an era which has not provided for them a sense of future possibilities, which has indeed called into serious question the legitimacy of traditionally valued institutions. Their life choices are made in an economic context which provides severe constraints on their ability to establish independent households, not to mention, for those who would so desire, forming committed relationships and their own families. Their expectations, encouraged by the affluence of many of their families of origin, are high; they are anxious about their ability to realize their expectations. The culture says of them (and they of themselves) that they are self-interested, disinclined to develop a meaningful set of principles or values beyond the self. They are a relatively small generation; their social and political influence, therefore, is not strongly felt. They, and we, are confused about how to think about their place in adult society. (1989, 7)

Given this context, it should not be terribly surprising that this generation of college students is perceived by faculty as ill-informed and uninvolved in national and international affairs (Curtis, 1989; Henry, 1989).

The social and cultural context described here also has produced a new generation, according to one observer, that "acts as if the world owes them, as if they have a right to win, as if they need whatever they want and deserve whatever they need" (Associated Press, 1990b).

Yet, some signs indicate that many college students are moving beyond self-preoccupation and political alienation to a new era of social concern and political activism. For example, enrollment in social-science and social-work undergraduate majors is up, perhaps reflecting a turn from the Me-First perspective of the Reagan years to the beginnings of a greater concern with the common good (Kleiman, 1990). This positive trend is reflected in a report about college students traveling to Florida in order to use spring break to build homes for the homeless through Habitat for Humanity, rather than to party in the sun (Associated Press, 1990a).

The college years are never easy, then, yet they become even more difficult—and potentially distressful—within the context we have described, because of added uncertainty and ambiguity.

COPING WITH STRESSORS OF THE COLLEGE YEARS

As Lazarus and Folkman (1984) have noted, the individual continually appraises stressors through time, sees some as more threatening than others, copes in ways that seem appropriate at the moment, according to available personal and social resources, and moves along to the next stressors in the process. Often, of course, these stressors confront the person in combination, even at the same time.

A study by Roscoe (1987) identified a number of serious concerns in the lives of college students, based on their reports of what was happening to them in the past week. These concerns ranged from academic pressures to illness and injuries, dating-related problems, sex/pregnancy concerns, and death in the family. In the following discussion, we will identify a number of key stressors for college students, along with suggestions for coping with each stressor.

Clustering of Life Changes

Most students face enormous **clustering of life changes.** The number of simultaneous transitions can seem awesome, illustrated by the following.

- Leaving home (parents, siblings, one's room, family routines), perhaps for the first time
- Leaving familiar friends and community surroundings
- Entering a dorm or apartment living arrangement—very different from home
- Developing new friends and acquaintances
- Becoming familiar with new ethnic and social-class groups
- Becoming accustomed to new class organization and teaching styles that are different from high school
- Confronting the need to manage one's time
- Facing greater academic competition than in high school
- Dealing with less feedback about performance
- Entering new clubs and other campus organizations
- Assuming greater responsibility for personal finances
- Making and breaking intimate relationships
- For older students, balancing new demands on time and family resources

Most students make these clustered transitions smoothly, with no ill effects. Large-scale studies of more or less normal college students suggest that four of five (around 80 percent) will experience some degree of anxiety or turmoil but will proceed along a relatively normal path of personal development, despite this clustering of change (Giddan, 1987; Giddan & Price, 1985; Katz, 1968). Yet among college students, just as with others, the higher the life-change scores, the greater the risk of illness and other difficulties (Damush, Hays, & DiMatteo, 1997).

Powell (1987) classifies student adjustment to this clustering of life changes into four categories, which vary according to success of coping style:

1. The Green Zone: Normal Adaptation
2. The Yellow Zone: Temporary Adjustment Reactions
3. The Orange Zone: Neurotic Symptoms
4. The Red Zone: Severe Maladjustments

This clustering of life changes is inherent in the very process of entering college, especially if one has left home for a campus elsewhere. Yet, distress from these multiple stressors varies a great deal among students, depending on a number of factors:

- Self-talk habits (for example, interpreting these stressors as a challenge, rather than a threat; believing the demands can be mastered; displaying hardiness)

- Social supports from family and friends (for example, isolation versus exchanging support and caring when needed; drawing on campus resources when needed)
- Health buffers (for example, exercise, nutrition, sleep habits, and healthy pleasures)
- Coping style when pressed (for example, denial, alcohol abuse, and procrastination versus careful time allocation, continuation of regular exercise, and talking about the pressure with a supportive friend)
- Relaxation practices (for example, daily deep relaxation, conscious use of deep breathing, and mental rehearsal)

See Chapter 12 for a discussion of steps for coping with clustering of life events. These apply during the college years, as well as at other times.

Separation From Parents

Concerning younger students, one of the most central factors among these clustered changes is **separation from parents.** As a student, you may be unaware that your challenge of breaking away happens at the very time your parents are going through difficult changes of their own. As Philip states:

> Parents of college age students are generally facing what has come to be called, perhaps somewhat dramatically, the mid-life crisis. Among other things, this may involve anxiety and depression at getting older, a sense that they no longer will be quite as central to their children's lives as they had been (perhaps not an unmixed blessing), a foreboding about their own future as they see the aging of their own parents and, as husband and wife, perhaps having to become reinvolved as a couple no longer having children at home to act as buffers between them. (1988, 18)

Separation from parents occurs in the context of a number of developmental tasks facing the young person. Included are these, according to Long and Long (1970, 6):

1. The development of competence
2. The management of emotions
3. The management of interpersonal relationships
4. The development of purpose
5. The development of integrity
6. The development of identity
7. The development of autonomy

In the course of curricular and extracurricular pursuits, the college student gradually progresses toward resolution of each of these issues—never reaching closure, of course, since each is a lifelong challenge.

Part of the challenge of autonomy is separation from parental control. This has not always faced young people, of course, but in the context of our society's emphasis on separate nuclear families, the decline of the extended family, and our Western tradition that once a person reaches 18 or 21, parental control should cease (or at least dramatically diminish), separation from parents becomes a central task for the young adult. The flip side of this process is individuation—becoming one's own person in terms of emotions, direction in life, and decision making.

Philips notes:

> Entering college marks the end of childhood/adolescence and the beginning of adulthood. Important aspects of this transition for freshmen include (1) leaving the family for membership in the college community; (2) new responsibilities for

decision making and caring for their own physical needs if they are living away from home; (3) mourning the losses involved in leaving home, such losses including parents, friends, and various forms of support networks. (1987, 20)

For some college youth, this transitional process goes smoothly with little disruption or tension. For others, the process is not so clean. Students sometimes are beset by loneliness, others by rebelliousness, and still others by depression. One study found 15 categories of problems in relations between college students and their parents (Anderson & Younger, 1987). These difficulties centered on lack of emotional contact, too much control, and perceived manipulation by parents. Another study (Bogat et al., 1985) found parents to be the most important source of generalized social support among college students. Yet, other researchers (Langinrichsen-Rohling, Larsen, & Jacobs, 1997) have found that the more troubled the family of origin, the greater the difficulty in adjusting to college, even controlling for high school adjustment.

On a more positive note, Fraser and Tucker (1997) recently found that the greater the individuation from parents, the better the problem-solving abilities and the less the stress among college students. They state, "Perhaps parents who allow their children to achieve optimal levels of individuation also promote a sense of responsibility, self-confidence, and optimism in their children that leads to their adeptness at problem solving (Fraser & Tucker, 1997, 465).

Using constructive coping steps is vital to turning this process of separation into one of growth and maturation, rather than one of staying stuck and dependent—or turning to alcohol, drugs, disorganization, and disarray. A key to constructive transition is maintaining contact with home through telephone calls, letters, and visits—at the same time that new, supportive friendships are developed at college.

Reintegration: Developing New Relationships

The process of developing new friendships, thereby **reintegrating** into a new social network, is an important step in the developmental process for all students. This new network can become an important source of support and well-being. One study showed, for example, that perceived social support can make a difference in problem-solving (Lakey & Heller, 1989). Another showed that the greater the social support, the more favorable the immune response (Jemmott & Magloire, 1989). It can also be a source of considerable worry and tension. As Figure 2-1 reveals, relationship conflicts are the common precipitating source of distress among a sample of college students.

In an excellent book on coping in college, *Do We Have to Know This for the Exam?*, Virshup suggests the following to new students about reintegrating into a new social-support network:

Eventually the feeling of homesickness will pass, and you will begin to establish new friends, new caring relationships. Some people seem to need a lot of friends; others need just one or two good friends with whom they can share their deepest thoughts and feelings. Whichever style fits you better is right for you. But everyone needs friends to help cope with life. Otherwise, college can be very lonely. (1987, 24)

Developing new friendships does not always just happen. You have to make it happen. A first step is to make yourself available to others, pushing through shyness if necessary. (See box on shyness.) Being with others is necessary. Greeting people gives the impression you are open to talking. You have many opportunities to meet people—in your place of residence, in classes, in study groups, in the halls, in the snack bar.

Friendships are a major contributor to success and satisfaction during the college years, yet conflict in relationships is students' most common distressor.

Figure 2-1

Distress-Symptom Score by Life-Change Score

Life-Change Score	Distress-Symptom Score				
	High	Medium	Low	Total	(N)
High	53	42	6	101	(36)
Medium	32	27	41	100	(34)
Low	14%	31%	55%	100%	(29)
P = <.001 N = 99					

Source: Schafer & McKenna (1981)

Joining an interest group is another way. Special-interest groups may be based on sports, computers, music, arts, language, politics—the list is endless. One of the best ways to meet people in a more than superficial way is to find study partners. This shared activity develops into lasting and meaningful friendships.

Appropriate self-disclosure also helps. The term "appropriate" is important to remember. The antithesis of appropriate is the "plunger," the person who too quickly and too openly shares personal experiences.

SHYNESS

My heart is pounding. I stand unable to speak.
My thoughts rushing, yet my mind feels weak.
Anxiety twisting its knife in my intestine;
All I want is a favorable impression.
Why do I feel this way; wishing to disappear
And be away from this horrible fear?
In a crowded room, no where am I so alone.
For what sins must God, in this way, make me atone?
Someone addresses me and I clutch in desperation,
At old phrases, my palms wet with perspiration.
Soon they leave and, with tears of rage,
I exit the party, my social life still an empty page.
I arrive at the safe and secure womb
That is my bedroom.
I see my books and familiar walls
Where no one ever falls,
And the words flow with passion and precision,
Never with dullness or indecision.
I lie in my bed in the position of my birth
And dream the meek inherit the earth.

Source: Gibson (1998)

One also needs to avoid "ego-speak," which is the tendency to always steer the conversation to what you want to talk about. Empathy and effective listening are absent in the student who practices ego-speak.

So, appropriate openness and honesty are important. Self-disclosure begets self-disclosure. Virshup's advice to students is worth noting.

> . . . trying to make too good an impression is obvious and puts people off. Giving people a little bit of what they expect makes them like you. Trying too hard to be what you are not makes you a phony, and that reputation is the kiss of death. There is a fine line which you mustn't cross. It is best to err on the side of authenticity, so that who you are is what you are offering, no more nor less. You must, therefore, learn candor, authenticity, and open self-disclosure; nothing less will do. You must be reasonably honest from the first encounter. (1987, 24)

Another key guideline is to be authentic. It is very easy during the early college years to try to put on an image that you think others will like but that turns out to be quite unreal. Others will see through this facade soon. Being the real you is the best way. Chances are you will be valued and accepted—not by everyone, but by some who will become your friends and support persons.

Some of the guidelines and communication methods proposed in Chapter 17 can be useful in building new social connections in college, as the bonds with parents gradually are weakened.

Love and Sex

Developing intimate relationships is another development task that becomes an important source of satisfaction and growth for the college student and, at the same time, a common source of worry, anxiety, guilt, and frustration.

We live in a culture that tells us to expect much from **love** and **sex.** We admire those who attain satisfaction in these realms. In fact, we probably share a basic psychological need for intimacy. Our physiological drive for sexual expression takes us in the same direction.

As a consequence of these social, psychological, and physiological influences, almost all students are drawn into erotic feelings during the college years. The making and breaking of intimate relationships are significant potential sources of stress.

A high percentage of students enter college already sexually experienced (Associated Press, 1990c). Many already have had a variety of sexual partners. Just as before, sex during the college years can be an authentic expression of caring and commitment or a casual, passing encounter. Uncertainty of meaning and intention of sexual attraction and sexual activities becomes a source of anxiety, especially for women.

As Virshup (1987) notes, college is a time when the individual often struggles to reach a proper personal balance between casual sex and sex based on commitment. For some, sex is disassociated from intimacy and caring. For others, intimacy and love begin with casual sex. For still others, sex only seems right as an expression of intimacy, following a period of courtship. Finding the personal balance that fits one's background, wants, needs, and ethics is a continuing issue during the college years.

The breakup of intimate relationships is a major source of upset for many students (Pistole, 1995). Many times, students overreact, upsetting their emotional life, their study habits, academic performance, and other relationships. It is important to keep the making and breaking of relationships in perspective and to avoid magnifying, awfulizing, catastrophizing—and the destructive behavior such as heavy drinking, use of drugs, procrastination, and social withdrawal that often accompany such negative self-talk.

Another common stressor for college students is long-distance romantic relation-ships. A recent study (Guldner, 1996) confirmed previous findings that about 1 in 4 students is involved in this type of relationship. These students were found to experience greater personal distress, more depression, and more "uneasiness in crowds." Female students were more likely than male to experience depression.

Possible pregnancy has always been a focus of concern for young adults, of course, and it continues. Added to that in recent years has been concern about AIDS and other sexually transmitted diseases (Speers et al., 1995). Normal anxieties associated with sexu-ality among college students thus have heightened.

Another sexual issue for many students relates to sexual orientation. Experts estimate that probably about 10 percent of college students are gay in orientation, although more than that among college men probably have had some homosexual contact (Virshup, 1987). Many struggle with the hidden identity of bisexuality. The college years often serve as the time when decisions about sexual orientation are made, or at least grappled with (Rhoads, 1995). Counseling sometimes is appropriate for students dealing with this issue.

Sexual harassment concerns most female college students at one time or another, sometimes from faculty, other times from male students. Date rape probably is more com-mon than most realize. Clear communication about intentions and limits is most important to prevent misunderstanding, exploitation, and sexual violence.

Daily Hassles

In Chapter 12, you will read about Lazarus's study on the harmful effects of **daily hassles** (Lazarus, 1981). These microstressors are the "irritating, frustrating, distressing demands that, to some degree, characterize everyday transactions with the environment" (Kanner et al., 1981, 3). The more filled people's lives are with these negative daily annoyances, the more the emotional difficulties.

As we previously noted, the presence or absence of daily hassles is not a matter of adverse circumstances alone. Such events only become "hassles" if they are seen that way. What is a neutral occurrence for one person becomes a hassle for the next if it is seen as a threat, imposition, or burden.

Following the publication of Lazarus's study, my students and I developed the **Daily Hassle Index,** a measure designed for college students. After my own students listed the 10 most frequent sources of irritation in their daily lives, they asked four of their friends to do the same. These were then codified into the 49 most common daily hassles. The re-sulting scale is presented in Application Exercise 2-2.

This scale can be used in two ways. First, comparison of individual total scores yields a measure of irritability. Second, comparison among items tells us some-thing about the "hassle ranking" of events and circumstances among respondents.

See Application Exercise 2-1 for the Daily Hassle Index, a mea-sure of irritability.

The 10 most irritating daily hassles among a sample of 185 students at Cali-fornia State University, Chico, were these:

1. Too little money
2. Too little time
3. Constant pressure of studying
4. Writing term papers
5. Taking tests
6. Future plans
7. Boring instructors
8. Getting up in the morning
9. Weight
10. Parking problems around campus

Does high irritability contribute to elevated distress symptoms and to other signs of a less satisfying quality of life, as we might expect? Figure 2-2 reveals that among my Human Stress class students, those with high irritability scores were significantly higher in distress-symptom scores. Additional analysis revealed other correlates of high Daily Hassle Index Scores:

See Application Exercise 2-2 for steps to assess the Daily Hassle Index.

- Lower levels of internal control
- More depression
- More emotional tension
- Lower life satisfaction
- Less vitality and energy
- Lower self-esteem
- Less fun and playfulness
- Lower levels of self-reported health
- Lower levels of happiness
- Lower total quality-of-life scores

This was a cross-sectional, one-time survey; we cannot know for certain what causes what. But the data are consistent with the notion that if you see events in a way that irritates you a good deal, you will experience a variety of adverse effects in terms of distress, health, well-being, and quality of life.

A recent study by Johnnie-Len Call (1990), a student at Coastal Carolina College, found a significant correlation in a sample of 95 undergraduate students between external locus of

Figure 2-2

Mean Distress-Symptom Score by Irritability

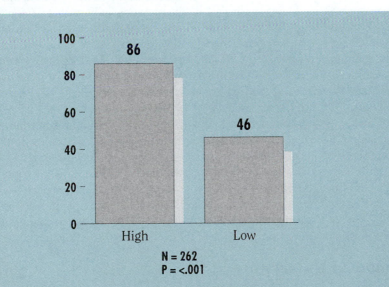

N = 262
P = <.001

MEASURES: *Distress Symptoms:* 50-Item Distress Symptom Scale
Irritability: 49-Item Daily Hassle Index

FINDING: Students with high irritability scores reported significantly higher distress-symptom scores.

Figure 2-3

Irritability by Gender

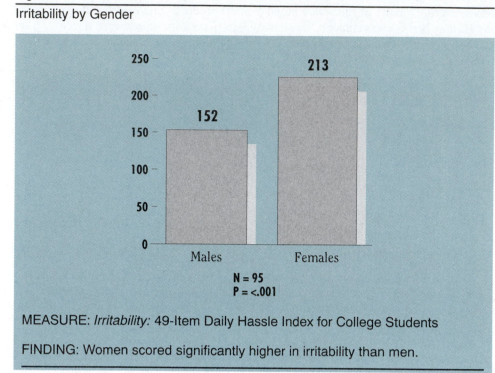

MEASURE: *Irritability:* 49-Item Daily Hassle Index for College Students

FINDING: Women scored significantly higher in irritability than men.

Source: Call (1990)

control (based on scores on the Rotter Internal-External Control Scale) and Daily Hassle Index scores. This finding is consistent with previous findings that persons with external locus of control are more vulnerable to distress because of their greater attribution of events to luck, chance, or fate—rather than to their own ability to cope (Caldwell, Pearson, & Chin, 1987; Johnson & Sarason, 1978; Sandler & Lakey, 1982; Zika & Chamberlain, 1987).

Call also found a significantly higher daily-hassle score for women than men, as shown in Figure 2-3. This finding is consistent with results each time I have administered these scales to CSU, Chico, students.

The key point about daily hassles, of course, is that nothing is inherently irritating about any of the events or experiences listed in the Daily Hassle Index. Rather, interpretation of these events determines how stressful or irritating they become. As Marcus Aurelius said, "Our life is what our thoughts make of it" (Bedford, 1980). Chapter 14 describes a number of techniques for managing your interpretations and perspectives in such a way that you can minimize irritation and upset, especially over daily microstressors.

Several of the daily hassles are not so minor for many students and represent significant stressors in their own right. One of these is financial uncertainty.

Financial Uncertainty

We noted earlier in the chapter that increasing numbers of students face financial strain, partly as the result of reductions in federal support for students in the form of grants and loans.

College students' **financial uncertainty** is quite different from low-income members of the community, in that the "plight" of students usually is temporary. For many noncollege families, low income brings not only limited money for basic needs but also limited job opportunities, poor community services, substandard schools, inadequate health care, and poor housing. Children in poor families often grow up amid insecurity, despair, anger, crime—and high stress. Poverty happens among ethnic minorities more often than among whites.

Whether white or black, rural or urban, young or old, most low-income persons face an array of stressors. Predictably, rates of stress-related illness, psychological disturbance, violence, and crime are higher among low-income persons than others. For example, African American men have very high rates of hypertension in the United States, although their difference with whites disappears when economic status is the same.

In a report to the Congressional Joint Economic Committee, Harvey Brenner (1979) identified seven indicators of social stress as statistically related to unemployment in the United States: homicide, suicide, deaths from cardiovascular disease and kidney disease, deaths from cirrhosis of the liver, total number of deaths, number of persons sent to jail, and admissions to mental hospitals.

This study suggests that the stressors of economic uncertainty affect not only those who are poverty-stricken or members of an ethnic minority. They may affect anyone faced with the threat of not being able to make ends meet. This is especially true of those on fixed incomes, such as the disabled and the elderly.

For many college students, this pressure may be temporary but nevertheless real. This takes its toll in several ways. Included are anxiety and distraction, associated with wondering about one's ability to pay the next set of bills, including registration fees, tuition, and books. Another is the need to hold one or more jobs while going to school. Students have always worked, of course, but more and more students work longer hours at more jobs in order to make ends meet. This can cause time pressure, erode sleep, and decrease time devoted to exercise, healthy play, and friendship. Academic performance and health often suffer.

This problem is especially prominent among older students returning to school, most often single mothers. Financial uncertainty combines with overload and role conflict to generate special challenges for this group.

In the face of financial uncertainty, careful budgeting (with assistance, if needed), maintaining good health buffers, social supports, self-talk habits, and coping styles become especially critical.

Grade Pressures

The reality is that grades are important—for athletic eligibility, scholarships, job applications, and more. Grades are the center of a host of complex challenges, motivations, rewards—and problems.

In many ways, our grading system serves as a reflection of the larger society. It is based on the belief that competition is intrinsically good, that rewards should be in scarce supply, that accomplishment should be attained only after an open contest and considerable hard work, that one's future—indeed, worth—should be ranked according to achievement, and that self-image should reflect one's accomplishment.

Without debating here the merits of the American grading system, it is worth noting that this system motivates many students toward higher levels of learning and achievement than they otherwise might achieve. Yet, the same system risks a great many difficulties for some students.

It is not the system, of course, that gets individuals into problems of distress; it is their interpretations and reactions to **grade pressures.** As Virshup points out,

There are many ways in college to feel good or bad about yourself. There are many ways you can decide whether or not you are a good and worthwhile person. You may believe you are only as good as your latest grade. Then that you

FEAR OF FAILING

Ellen is a college sophomore who carries an intense fear of failing from early childhood, when her parents humiliated her several times in front of friends for having gotten *C*'s on tests. This lingering memory continues to create intense anxiety every time she faces a test. Ellen is intensely afraid she will "fail" again, thereby "ensuring" rejection by others. While she is almost always well-prepared, she often underperforms because her fear creates "static" in her thinking process during exams. Moreover, she deliberately avoids challenging situations whenever possible because of this fear of failure. For Ellen, a normal desire to perform well and to avoid a poor showing has turned into an irrational, nearly debilitating fear of failure, which creates much unhappiness and threatens to stunt her continued academic and occupational progress.

must spend your life studying harder and doing better, and generally proving yourself through your performance. You may develop "test anxiety," freeze in tests, fail to measure up to your own standards, and generally feel inadequate. (1987, 16)

A key step in handling the challenge of grades is to make a dual commitment to yourself: to do your very best and to separate your self-esteem from your grades.

A central cause of grade-related distress is test anxiety. Positive stress can be very helpful in motivating you to peak performance. Yet, too much stress can interfere with your preparation, concentration, and performance. This is test anxiety. The key is to attain optimal arousal, optimal anxiety, and optimal tension.

Other common difficulties with grades are fear of failure and fear of success. **Fear of failure** is common to most of us. To fall short of our own or others' expectations in school, job, athletics, or any other activity one risks both external and internal costs: threat to academic or career prospects, disapproval, rejection, humiliation, guilt, chagrin, and a blow to self-esteem. Fear of failure, then, is perfectly natural and can help motivate you to prepare and perform well.

Sometimes, however, fear of failure becomes so extreme that it creates unnecessary emotional and physical distress.

Less common is **fear of success.** To succeed is to convey the message to others that you are capable, bright, and dependable. The natural result is that others will expect you to succeed again in the future. This is a frightening prospect for persons so lacking in self-confidence and so fearful of rejection that they do not want anyone to expect anything of them, now or tomorrow. The solution is to avoid succeeding.

Since such persons also fear failure because of the rejection that would result, they cannot risk total failure in school, job, athletic, or community situations, either. Two alternatives present themselves: Either avoid performance situations altogether, or perform in a mediocre fashion, neither clearly succeeding nor failing. Hovering somewhere between these two extremes is not very rewarding, to be sure, but it allows an individual to remain safe from the rejection inherent in either failing now or falling short of others' expectations. Those who fear success, then, usually destine themselves to a lifetime of banality, neither realizing performance potential nor enjoying the rewards of accomplishment.

Figure 2-4 shows the growing gap through time between actual performance and perception of others' expectations. The consequence is ever-mounting anxiety, despite or because of rising performance. The solution for some persons, though usually not a con-

Figure 2-4

Performance and Perceived Expectations

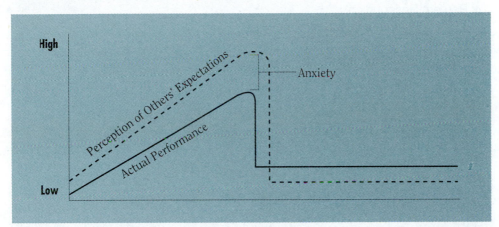

scious choice, is to fail dramatically, as in not answering any of the test questions at all, being totally unprepared for an important job meeting, going to work drunk, or oversleeping for a conference with the boss. Figure 2-4 shows that such failure quickly brings others' expectations down to a low level again. Anxiety thereby is reduced again to a tolerable level, while low self-esteem is reconfirmed. For others, the answer is to hover between success and failure, never really trying.

Role Difficulties

A number of key challenges during the college years relate to **role difficulties.** A role is a cluster of expectations associated with a given social position. For example, the position of college student brings with it a host of expectations from role partners: instructors, classmates, friends, librarians, study partners, roommates, and others. We will examine several role difficulties during the college years: role overload, role conflict, role strain, and role ambiguity. In each case, becoming aware of the stressor can be a first step to effective coping.

Role Overload

You may recall that two of the top three daily hassles reported earlier were "Too little time" and "Constant pressure of studying." In short, chronic overload is almost endemic to the college years. This probably is more true today than ever, as more and more students work part-time and more are returning to school between ages 25 and 40 (especially single mothers).

Figure 2-5 presents a picture of how a large sample of students spend their time. For many students, this adds up to too much to do in too few hours. The result can be a feeling of chronic hurry, hassle, and struggle with time or **role overload.**

Role Conflict

College students face two types of **role conflict.** One is incompatible expectations associated with two or more different roles (inter-role conflict). Examples include student-employee, student-mother, student-daughter, and student-friend. Role demands often bump into one another, as in the case of Kim, described in the box at the beginning of this chapter.

The second type of conflict is incompatible expectations from different role-partners within a single role (intra-role conflict). For example, a student's five professors each put a claim on the time and energy of the person. Three may expect her to be fully prepared

Figure 2-5

Number of Hours Students Spend Each Week on Selected Activities
(by Percent Responding)

Activity	Hours per Week						
	None	1–2	3–4	5–6	7–8	9–10	11 or More
Talking informally to other students	3	19	16	13	9	9	31
Watching television	13	22	18	14	11	8	14
Leisure reading	23	35	17	11	6	4	4
Talking to faculty members	26	56	11	4	1	1	1
Studying in the library	27	24	14	9	5	6	15
Attending campus cultural events	46	36	11	4	1	1	1
Participating in organized student activities (other than athletics)	50	26	10	6	3	2	3
Participating in intramural sports	70	16	8	3	1	1	1
Participating in intercollegiate athletics	93	1	*	*	1	1	4

* = less than 1 percent

Source: The Carnegie Foundation for the Advancement of Teaching, National Survey of Undergraduates (1984)

for midterm exams on the same day that another expects her to present a top-notch oral presentation, and the last one expects her to turn in a well-written term paper.

The result of role conflict can be confusion, anxiety, tension, underperformance, irritability, and even illness. Studies in occupational stress indicate that the greater the role conflict on the job, the lower the job satisfaction, the greater the anxiety, the higher the blood pressure, the greater the incidence of heart attacks, the higher the cholesterol, the greater the obesity, the higher the heart rate, the greater the occurrence of abnormal EKGs, the greater the absenteeism, and the greater the worker turnover (Matteson & Ivancevich, 1987). Some of the same effects are likely to occur among students when these pressures are accompanied with ineffective coping.

Potentially harmful effects of role conflict in college can be minimized by recognizing when role conflict occurs and that it can have adverse effects. Other preventive steps include proper time-management practices, careful planning and pacing, effective health buffers, and constructive self-talk.

Role Strain

Still another type of role difficulty is **role strain**—when personal desires conflict with others' expectations. Many instances can be identified in the lives of college students:

- A student wants to attend an unusually appealing Tuesday night concert, while his instructor expects him to attend his Tuesday night class.
- A student would rather watch the World Series game than attend a biology lab session.
- A student wants to take his girlfriend to a movie. His fraternity brothers expect him to attend an emergency meeting.
- A student wants to write about the Kennedy policy toward Cuba in the early 1960s. His instructor wants the paper to be limited to Central America.

Balancing personal wants and desires with others' expectations is a lifelong challenge, of course, with no single, simple formula. Awareness helps. So does having clear goals and priorities. So does having good sense as to when to compromise or accommodate. Balancing self-interest with social responsibility and concern for others is the long-run guideline to follow.

Role Ambiguity

Roles sometimes lack clarity in what is expected. That is, the guideposts by which a person finds direction may be ambiguous. Young people today face **role ambiguity** in a host of ways.

> Probably no society makes the transition from childhood to adulthood more difficult than we do in America. We have developed very few patterns that dramatize the "coming of age" of the adolescent. We have provided him with few guideposts by which to find directions. At adolescence, we expect the boy or girl to stop being a child, yet we do not expect him to be [an adult]. Any definitions he has of his changing age positions are quite inconsistent. He may drive an automobile at sixteen, leave school at eighteen, be subject to the draft at nineteen, and vote at twenty-one. He is told he is no longer a child, but he is treated like a dependent, supported by his parents, and mistrusted for the tragedies that befall some adolescents—auto accidents, juvenile delinquency, pre-marital pregnancies, and drug addiction. In a word, there are many situations in which he scarcely knows whether he is expected to act like an adult or a child. (Vander Zanden, 1975)

Role ambiguity arises from several sources, all of which can affect college students. One is rapid social and cultural change. Relationships between younger college students and their parents undergo continual redefinition, with both experiencing uncertainty as to how to make decisions, communicate, and reach a mutually agreeable accommodation in terms of autonomy and control.

A second source of role ambiguity is passage from one life-cycle stage to another. Transition from childhood into adolescence and from adolescence into adulthood are classic examples. This source relates to virtually every younger college student, especially combined with the rapid change noted.

Third, role ambiguity can result from incomplete, fuzzy, or otherwise inadequate communications from role partners. This can happen to the college student, for example, when a faculty member is not clear as to what is expected or when roommates do not develop clear understanding about noise, visitors, cooking, shopping, or housecleaning.

Whatever the cause, role ambiguity can heighten distress and increase stress-related illness, emotional disturbance, and troubled behavior. Research in the workplace has identified a wide range of negative effects of job-related role ambiguity: more job dissatisfaction, more job-related tension, lower self-confidence, higher blood pressure, lower self-esteem, greater depression, greater anxiety, and greater resentment toward the employer (Matteson & Ivancevich, 1987). College students who cope ineffectively with role ambiguity risk some of the same effects.

Effective coping with role ambiguity can occur by means of clear internal goals and priorities, assertiveness in clarifying unclear role expectations from others, constructive self-talk rather than awfulizing or negativizing, and maintaining effective health buffers.

LIFE SCRIPTS, IDENTITY FORMATION, AND CAREER CHOICE

During the college years, every student continues to deal with the questions that have been the central focus of his or her life from childhood: Who am I? Whom will I become?

Eric Berne (1964; 1972; 1976), the founder of transactional analysis, contended that nearly everyone emerges from adolescence with a **life script**—a blueprint for thinking, feeling, and living. As an actor follows a stage script, people spend their lives blindly living out their own life script. Included in the script are directions related to matters such as the following.

- How to be masculine or feminine
- How to get love and attention
- How to feel about oneself
- How to feel about others
- How to cope with stress
- How to spend time
- Whether and how to succeed or fail

Your life script emerges during childhood and adolescence out of early messages from parents and other adults and early decisions you make. Early messages—given through example, reward and punishment, and direct instruction—include attribution (you are, you aren't) and injunctions (you should, you shouldn't; you must, you must not). Because you have the power of choice, you are not merely a passive receiver of these messages. Choice is possible, including acceptance, rejection, or modification of early messages. Many people raised in destructive homes are exposed to "losing" or violent messages, yet they turn out well because they choose their own life plan.

Life scripts are inherently limited because they stifle authenticity and spontaneity. By definition, they are harmful. But they are damaging in another way as well—they often lead to distress. Life scripts can cause distress in several ways.

1. By directly calling for a life of unhappiness, failure, pity, half-effort, depression, boredom, illness, or loneliness. These are **banal life scripts.**
2. By directly calling for tragedy—suicide, a life in prison, or premature death through alcoholism, accident, or heart attack. These are **tragic life scripts.**
3. By indirectly calling for either a banal or a tragic life through inept or harmful coping responses—violence toward others, drugs, schizophrenia, impulsive spending, or compulsive overeating.

Life scripts reflect in part the norms and values of the surrounding culture and sub-culture. Yet each script is unique in many ways. Scripts maintain their lifelong hold over a person through the **repetition compulsion**—the drive to be and do what is familiar. This drive probably is stronger than the "pleasure principle." Doing and feeling what is familiar often takes priority even over enjoying life—not out of choice but out of habit. A tragic illustration of the power of the repetition compulsion is the fact that as many as 90 percent of parents who abuse their children are repeating their own histories of abuse by their parents—a pattern currently scarring the lives of as many as 2.2 million children between the ages of 3 and 17 in the United States.

Not everyone has a life script. A small minority of people are raised by parents to be *self-directed,* to make up their *own* minds about what to believe and how to live—rather than to be controlled by a script from childhood. Yet most people are bound by their script, spending their lives blindly following it or struggling somehow to break free. Many adults succeed—attaining a genuine authenticity, autonomy, and self-direction. Through aware-ness, effort, and support from others, life scripts can be left behind or at least rewritten in major ways. Full development of potential depends on script-free living.

A central challenge during the college years, then, is to become fully aware of one's life script as it has been shaped by culture, subculture, family, and the self. Simultane-ously, one must sort and select, retaining those elements we want and discarding those early decisions that no longer fit the self and the future one wants.

ANTICIPATING POST-COLLEGE CHALLENGES

The college experience is shaped by anticipation of what lies ahead as well as by pre-sent demands. Students at the turn of the century face a number of demanding challenges, including the following.

- **Selecting and starting a career.** A particularly challenging aspect of career choice is assuring that it is fully one's own, reflecting one's deepest interests and values. Often, of course, students concern themselves with pleasing parents or with expe-diency, material gain, and short-run opportunity rather than with the more impor-tant issues of values, ethics, personality-career fit, and lifestyle options. Attentive-ness to these broader concerns is vital, beginning from arrival at college all the way through choice of major, job interviews, and job choice.

- **Adjusting to career changes.** It is likely students will change jobs and even ca-reers a number of times during their working lives. Flexibility and adaptiveness are vital. This likelihood reaches back into the college years by underscoring the im-portance of developing personal adaptibility and transferrable intellectual, commu-nication and technical skills.

- **Striving for financial security.** Many students leave college with substantial debt. At the same time they face the challenge of beginning payments on these loans, they must begin to save funds for purchase and furnishing of a home, for emergencies, and for eventual college costs of children. This adjustment is easy for some, tough for others who may not have managed personal finances well during the college years. New fiscal discipline often is needed.

- **Preventing "affluenza" disease.** Affluenza is addiction to spending, consumerism, and material possession. In short, it is the never-ending struggle for the almighty "more." The engine of advertising is the driving force behind this affliction, which means it is deeply embedded in American culture. As they begin their personal financial management, students benefit from asking themselves how much they truly need for genuine life satisfaction. As a *Time* story (Pooley, 1997) recently noted, many Americans are turning to voluntary simplicity as an alternative.

- **Living lightly on the earth.** Closely related is the challenge of minimizing harmful impact on the earth's environment and resources. During the lifetimes of students entering college near the turn of the century, this no doubt will become a central personal and social challenge. As White (1997) recently noted, this is illustrated by the inherent conflict between the Kyoto Protocol, the international treaty to reduce greenhouse gases, and the driving habits of Americans. Finding a workable balance between comfort and convenience, on one hand, and protecting the environment, on the other, is a major challenge facing students as they build new lives.

- **Creating a stable and satisfying family.** Mary Pipher (1996, 4) has noted that "our culture is at war with families." She cites three main invaders of family stability: abusive and intrusive media, pop psychology which is often disconnected from "common-sense moorings," and isolating and addictive technology in the home (e.g., computer games, passive TV). Added to these problems are pervasive culturally-driven pressures noted above for ever-greater affluence, and the tensions inherent in dual careers by both parents. A substantial challenge facing students, then, as they anticipate "settling down" is to create a stable family life that is reasonably satisfying to all members.

- **Raising children.** Closely related is the challenge of raising children in a world with few guidelines as to what works at this time in history. Providing stability, nurturance, and understanding, direction, and discipline are major challenges facing young parents, made all the more difficult by personal demands from career, relationships, and internal struggles in a world of change.

- **Balancing work and family.** Among the greatest challenges students can anticipate is balancing the demands of work and family. This is especially challenging for working mothers who tend to shoulder a disproportionate share of household chores. In fact, one recent study found that physiological stress levels were higher at home than at work for employed women with children at home (Luecken, 1997). This was true whether they were single or married. With an increasing proportion of parents working full-time, these multiple demands increase. In a recent article on "daddy stress," Thomas (1997) notes that fathers feel the crunch as well.

- **Dealing with blended families.** With our high divorce rate, students face a high probability they will either create broken families that eventually will reconstitute following remarriage or they will marry into a blended family by marrying a spouse with children. This means many will need to adapt not only to a new marriage partner but to new parenting challenges as well. These new arrangements bring a host of personal and interpersonal challenges as all involved adjust to each other's styles and demands.

- **Adjusting to new friendship, work, and community networks.** As students leave the campus and begin a new life elsewhere, they adapt to a host of new social and interpersonal ties. Some make this transition easily, but others find it difficult. The success of these personal and social adjustment is influenced by internal and interpersonal adaptability skills—how readily and comfortably one can establish new ties and networks. This underscores the importance of getting involved during college in organizations and friendship networks through which these skills can flourish and grow.

- **Dealing with racial and ethnic diversity.** Living in a multiethnic/multiracial world has been part of American life from the beginning. While the challenge facing both minorities and the white majority are not new, they are still intense and real. This is especially true in those parts of the country with large numbers of immigrants such as Florida, the Southwest, and California. As Farley (1997) has noted, polls show many youth have fortunately moved beyond their parents' views of race toward greater tolerance and eagerness to get along. Still, many youth of color still experience stigma and discrimination. These challenges of dealing with racial and ethnic diversity will persist into young adulthood for both minorities and whites.

- **Coping with high-tech demands.** As we noted above, one unanticipated effect of many technological innovations is to separate family members from each other. Another is to create even more overload and an even faster pace of life. Moreover, many consumers add to their already-filled basket of frustrations with new devices they may not truly need and have great difficulty mastering. As Slone and Chmielewski (1998, F1) note, "When things don't work, or we simply can't master all the functions, we feel inadequate and stressed. The 'I'm dumb' impulse." The challenge, then, is to utilize technologies to their full advantage without allowing them to unduly clutter our lives, add to overload, or become an unnecessary source of frustration.

- **Making time for exercise, deep relaxation, and other healthy pleasures.** In a fast-paced life, it is a challenge of the first order to make time for regular exercise, deep relaxation, and other healthy pleasures—pleasures that lift the spirit and restore energy. Many students have great difficulty with these in college. If they have not mastered this challenge by graduation, they can expect event greater problems later on as the demands of work and family only intensify. Developing a wellness lifestyle during the college years is the best way to embed these positive habits to a point where they will readily continue later on.

COPING AND SUCCESS IN COLLEGE

Throughout this textbook, we note that coping with difficult events and circumstances is most usefully understood as an ongoing, transactional, fluctuating process of appraisal and response as the individual deals with the multitude of stressors in his or her life. In this chapter, we have briefly described a number of common potential distressors in the lives of college students. A number of approaches to managing stress set forth in later chapters apply here as in other stages of life. Included are:

- Awareness of the nature and effects of stress—positive, neutral, and negative
- Management of self-talk
- Practicing effective techniques for eliciting the relaxation response
- Maintaining effective health buffers (exercise, nutrition, and sleep)
- Managing time and change
- Participating in strong, stable, and supportive social networks
- Employing effective coping techniques in dealing with specific stressors

A study by DeGrauw and Norcross (1989) provides useful information about what a sample of 469 students experienced as their most distressing episode of the last three years, what they did to cope, and which coping methods were most effective.

Figure 2-6

Precipitating Event of Distress Episode

Events	Percent of Students Reporting
Relationship Conflicts	38
School-Related	20
Family Death	12
Moving/Relocation	4
Death of Friend	3
Family Illness	2
Personal Illness	2
Occupational Difficulty	0
Other	18
	99

Source: DeGrauw & Norcross (1989, 64)

Students were asked in a questionnaire to focus on their worst period of psychological distress during the past three years. They then were asked whether a particular event was associated with this period of distress. Nearly 8 of 10 reported affirmatively. Figure 2-6 presents the types of precipitating events reported by the students. It is apparent most have to do with stressors discussed previously in this chapter. Others, such as family death or illness, relate to life back home.

Next, respondents in the study were asked what specific steps they took to cope with their distress. Figure 2-7 shows the most- and least-often-used types of coping processes.

In summarizing these results, DeGrauw and Norcross state, "In other words, college students tended to lean on others, restructure their thinking and wish for a better outcome. They tended not to restructure their environments, use prescription drugs, or emotionally release their feelings" (1989, 67).

Female students were found more often to use helping relationships, catharsis, information seeking, and social support, while men were more likely to keep to themselves and to avoid other people.

Finally, the authors studied **success in coping**—what worked and what did not work in dealing with the distressing episodes. They summarized their results as follows:

The methods positively correlated with success in the present study of distressed students and previous investigations of non-students were active—problem solving, behavioral, positive focus—and interpersonal—helping relationship—in nature. Methods negatively associated with success were largely passive—wishful thinking, blame self—and avoidant—keep to self, avoidance. The recommenda-

Figure 2-7

Most and Least Used Coping Processes

Most Often Used	Least Often Used
Helping Relationship	Environmental Evaluation
Wishful Thinking	Stimulus Contro
Logical Analysis	Social Liberation
Active Cognitive Coping	Catharsis
Seeking Social Support	Medication

Source: DeGrauw and Norcross (1989, 66)

tions for student self-changers would thus be to maximize supportive relationships, maintain an optimistic attitude, employ action strategies, avoid self-recriminations, and resist the temptation to withdraw into themselves.

Walter and Siebert note that the difference between successful students and unsuccessful ones is that "successful students persist. They keep going. The less successful students give up too easily. They quit when they become frustrated, don't do well at first, or do less well than others" (1990, 30).

Walter and Siebert also state that the students who persist through times of difficulty do several things differently:

1. They practice mental rehearsal of desired accomplishments.
2. They handle the challenge and uncertainty of college by developing a healthy balance between self-reliance and acceptance of guidance.
3. They develop self-confidence and a positive self-image through a healthy balance of self-praise and self-criticism.
4. They accept nervousness, fear, and not always doing well at first as natural.

Walter and Siebert consider healthy self-esteem, self-confidence, and a positive self-image most important of all. They point out that these provide an inner stability that yields several benefits. It lets you:

Accept praise, recognition, success, and friendship as legitimate;
Examine and learn from mistakes and failures;
Not be pressured into undesirable actions or situations out of fear of being disliked;
Resist and not be manipulated by insincere flattery;
Reject undeserved criticism;
Admit mistakes and apologize to others for them;
Handle new, unexpected developments knowing you can count on yourself; and
Value yourself as a unique, special human being. (1990, 29)

Researchers recently asked nearly 2,400 graduating seniors from nine colleges what factors contributed most to their success in college. Their responses are summarized in

Figure 2-8

Percentage of Students Who Said the Factor Contributed to a Successful and Satisfying College Career

Factor	Percentage
Personal contacts with students	89
Personal contacts with faculty and staff	78
Time I have spent on special interests and activities out of class	73
Ability to organize tasks and use my time effectively	72
Work experience during college or in the summer	63
Social life on campus	62
Sense of direction; knowing why I am in college and what career I would like to work toward	56
Availability of financial resources	52

Source: Walter & Siebert (1990, 5); adapted from Willingham (1985)

Figure 2-8. Social contacts, with both fellow students and faculty/staff, are high on the list. So is organizing time well and getting involved in campus activities outside the classroom.

In the next chapter, we turn to a discussion of the nature of personal wellness and of the characteristics of social environments likely to enhance and diminish personal wellness.

REFERENCES

Anderson, W., & Younger, C. (1987). Parents as a source of stress for college students. *College Student Journal, 21,* 317–323.

Associated Press (1990a). Some college students using spring break to build up, not party down. *Chico Enterprise-Record,* March 16, 2C.

Associated Press (1990b). Study criticizes ethics of younger generation. *San Francisco Chronicle,* October 11, A12.

Associated Press (1990c). Teen sexual activity increases. *Chico Enterprise-Record,* November 8, 4A.

Bedford, S. (1980). *Stress and tiger juice.* Chico, CA: Scott Publications.

Berne, E. (1964). *Games people play.* New York: Grove.

Berne, E. (1972). *What do you say after you say hello?* New York: Grove.

Berne, E. (1976). *Beyond games and scripts.* New York: Grove.

Bogat, S. A., Caldwell, R. A., Rogosch, F. A., & Kriegler, J. A. (1985). Differentiating specialists and generalists within college students' social support networks. *Journal of Youth and Adolescence, 14,* 23–35.

Brenner, H. (1979). Mortality and the national economy. *Lancet, 2,* 568–573.

Caldwell, R. S., Pearson, J. L., & Chin, R. J. (1987). Stress-moderating effects: Social support in the context of gender and locus of control. *Journal of Personality and Social Psychology, 13,* 5–17.

Call, J. L. (1990). The relationship between daily hassles, gender, and locus of control in college students. Unpublished manuscript, University of South Carolina, Coastal Carolina College.

Curtis, D. (1989). Professors say their students are shallow. *San Francisco Chronicle,* November 7, 1.

Damush, T. M., Hays, R. D., & Dimatteo, M. R. (1997). Stressful life events and health-related quality of life in college students. *Journal of College Student Development, 38,* 181–190.

DeGrauw, W. P., & Norcross, J. C. (1989). Students coping with psychological distress: What they do and what works. *Journal of College Student Psychotherapy, 4,* 55–76.

Farley, C. J. Kids and race. *Time,* 88–91.

Fraser, K. P., Tucker, C. M. (1997). Individuation, stress, and problem-solving abilities of college students. *Journal of College Student Development, 38,* 461–467.

Gibson, G. (1998). Shyness. *Unpublished poem.*

Giddan, N. S. (1987). Coping and identity development in college students. *Journal of College Student Psychotherapy, 2,* 33–58.

Giddan, N. S., & Price, M. K. (1985). *Journey of youth: Psychological development during college.* Schenectady: Character Research Press.

Guldner, G. T. (1996). Long-distance romantic relationships: Prevalence and separation-related symptoms in college students. *Journal of College Student Development, 37,* 289–295.

Henry, T. (1989). Survey reveals young Americans turned off by politics. *Chico Enterprise-Record,* November 22, 3C.

Hicks, R. A., Grant, F., & Chancellor, C. (1986). Type A-B status, habitual sleep duration, and perceived level of daily life stress of college students. *Perceptual and Motor Skills, 63,* 793–794.

Hoffman, F. L. (1989). Development issues, college students and the 1990s. *Journal of College Student Psychotherapy, 4,* 3–12.

Jemmott, J. B., & Magloire, K. (1989). Academic stress, social support, and secretory immunoglobulin A. *Journal of Personality and Social Psychology, 55,* 803–810.

Johnson, J. H., & Sarason, I. G. (1978). Life stress, depression and anxiety: Internal-external control as a moderator variable. *Journal of Psychosomatic Research, 22,* 205–208.

Kanner, A. D., Coyne, J. C., Schaefer, C., & Lazarus, R. S. (1981). Comparison of two modes of stress measurement: Daily hassles and uplifts versus major life events. *Journal of Behavioral Medicine, 4,* 2–39.

Katz, J. (Ed.). (1968). *No time for youth.* San Francisco: Jossey-Bass.

Kleiman, C. (1990). Students abandon big bucks for social sciences. *San Francisco Examiner,* September 30, 44.

Lakey, B., & Heller, K. (1989). Social support from a friend, perceived social support, and social problem-solving. *American Journal of Community Psychology, 16,* 811–824.

Langinrichsen-Rohling, J., Larsen, A.E., & Jacobs, J. E. (1997). Retrospective reports of the family of origin environment and the transition to college. *Journal of College Student Development, 38,* 49–60.

Larimer, M. E., Irvine, D. L., Kilmer, J. R., & Marlatt., G. A. (1997). College drinking and the Greek system: Examining the role of perceived norms for high-risk behavior. *Journal of College Student Development, 38,* 587–598.

Lazarus, R. S. (1981). Little hassles can be hazardous to your health. *Psychology Today, 15,* 58–62.

Lazarus, R. S., & Folkman, S. (1984). *Stress, appraisal, and coping.* New York: Springer.

Long, N. J., & Long, J. (1970). *Conflict and comfort in college.* Belmont, CA: Wadsworth.

Luecken, L. J. (1997). Stress in employed women: Impact of marital status and children at home on neurohormonal output and home strain. *Psychosomatic Medicine,,* 59: 352–359.

Matteson, M. T., & Ivancevich, J. M. (1987). *Controlling work stress.* San Francisco: Jossey-Bass.

Philips, A. F. (1987). Parents, sons and daughters: Growth and transition during the college years. *Journal of College Student Psychotherapy, 2,* 17–32.

Pipher, M. (1996). *The shelter of each other: Rebuilding our families.* New York: Grosset/Putnam.

Pistole, M. C. (1995). College students' ended love relationships: Attachment style and emotion. *Journal of College Student Development, 36,* 53–60.

Pooley, E. (1997). The great escape. *Time,* December 8, 52–63.

Powell, D. H. (1987). Is my college student normal? *Journal of College Student Psychotherapy, 2,* 149–186.

Rhoads, R. A. (1995). Learning from the coming-out experience of college males. *Journal of College Student Development, 36,* 67–74.

Roscoe, B. (1987). Concerns of college students: A report of self-disclosures. *College Student Journal, 21,* 158–161.

Sandler, I. N., & Lakey, B. (1982). Locus of control as a stress moderator: The role of control perceptions and social support. *American Journal of Community Psychology, 10,* 65–80.

Schafer, W., & McKenna, J. F. (1981). Life change, stress and injury: A study of male college athletes. Unpublished paper.

Slone, E., & Chmielewski, D. C. (1998). High-tech stress. *Sacramento Bee,* F1.

Speers, R., Abraham, C., Sheeran, P., & Abrams., D. (1995). Students' judgments of the risks of HIV infection as a function of sexual practice, sex of target and partner, and age and sex of student. *Journal of College Student Development, 36,* 103–111.

Thomas, K. M. (1997). Daddy stress. *Sacramento Bee,* June 29, E3.

Vander Zanden, J. W. (1975). *Sociology: A systematic approach* (3rd ed.). New York: Ronald.

Virshup, B. (1987). *Do we have to know this for the exam?* New York: W. W. Norton.

Walter, T., & Siebert, A. (1990). *Student success.* Fort Worth, TX: Holt, Rinehart and Winston.

White, M. (1997). LA lifestyles, driving habits clash with global warming pact. *Chico Enterprise-Record,* December 15, 1A.

Whitman, N. A., Spendlove, D. C., & Clark, C. H. (1984). *Student stress: Effects and solu-tions.* Washington, D.C.: ASHE-ERIC Higher Education Research Report No. 2.

Whitman, N. A., Spendlove, D. C., & Clark, C. H. (1986). *Increasing students' learning.* Washington, D.C.: ASHE-ERIC Higher Education Research Report No. 4.

Willingham, W. W. (1985). *Success in college: The role of personal qualities and academic ability.* New York: College Entrance Examination Board.

Zika, S., & Chamberlain, K. (1987). Relation of hassles and personality to subjective well-being. *Journal of Personality and Social Psychology, 53,* 155–162.

Application Exercise 2-1

Daily Hassle Index

Below is a list of daily hassles that commonly irritate college students. Please indicate how often each one is an irritation to you. Use numbers as follows:

 0 Almost never an irritation to me
 5 Sometimes an irritation to me
10 Frequently an irritation to me

____ Parking problems around campus
____ Careless bike riders
____ Library too noisy
____ Roommate too noisy
____ Preparing meals
____ Too little time
____ Too little money
____ Deciding what to wear
____ Laundry
____ Materials unavailable in library
____ Getting up in the morning
____ My weight
____ Not enough time to exercise
____ Noisy neighbors
____ Conflicts with roommate
____ Instructor not available
____ Boring instructor
____ Constant pressures of studying
____ Instructor difficult to understand
____ Not enough close friends
____ Not enough time to talk with friends
____ Too few dates
____ Room temperatures
____ How I look

____ Too little intimacy
____ Other students are unfriendly
____ Getting to class on time
____ Car problems
____ Quality of meals
____ Future plans
____ Relationships at work
____ Tensions in love relationship
____ Conflict with family
____ Crowds
____ Other drivers
____ Missing my family
____ No mail
____ Being lonely
____ Being unorganized
____ Others' opinions of me
____ Roommate's messiness
____ Problems with own or roommate's pet
____ Too little sleep
____ Shopping
____ Taking tests
____ Writing term papers
____ Household chores
____ Fixing hair in morning
____ Physical safety after dark

Application Exercise 2-2

Assessing Your Daily Hassle Index Score

1. What is your Daily Hassle Index Score?

2. Is it higher than you would prefer? Explain.

3. To what degree is your score a result of objective life circumstances versus your own attitudes and interpretations? Explain.

4. What specific self-talk statements might you use to turn these daily hassles into minor irritants?

Wellness is a bridge that takes people into realms far beyond treatment or therapy—into a domain of self-responsibility and self-empowerment.

—REGINA RYAN AND JOHN TRAVIS

Wellness: Beyond Normal Health

Allison: A Model of Worseness

Allison came to California State University, Chico, as a freshman from a Bay Area high school, where she had averaged B+ grades and had been active in a number of school activities.

Slightly insecure, she immediately put out her antennae to detect what was expected around her. She was eager to please and fit in.

During the first two weeks, Allison slept about four hours a night and less on weekends. She spent lots of time sharing stories with new friends.

She went to class most of the time but missed several Thursday and Friday classes during those early weeks. She did not study much, sure that she could catch up. It had been no problem in high school.

Allison had been physically active as a high school field hockey and soccer player. But now she just could not seem to find the time to exercise here.

She missed a lot of dorm meals, especially breakfast, and she readily admitted to being hooked on junk food, especially late at night.

Allison met some very attractive young men and was sexually active—sometimes rather foolishly. She loved "partying," although she felt pretty wiped out afterward.

By the fourth week of school, she was beginning to feel lonely and slightly depressed. None of her new relationships were very meaningful or supportive. Allison missed her family but seldom called.

She awoke one morning at the end of the fifth week with a sore throat, which turned into a lingering bad cold. She missed classes for about a week. Allison virtually panicked at her first midterm exam and performed poorly.

She continued to feel lousy—out of control, lonely, overwhelmed, TATT (Tired All The Time), short of money (which she had failed to ration), behind in school, and losing confidence by the day. Allison ended that first semester with a C+, 3 C's, and a D and was put on academic probation.

Allison's story is a story of worseness.

INTRODUCTION: WORSENESS VERSUS WELLNESS

The contrasting scenarios on pages 55 and 56 describe two students with different lifestyles, including their approaches to handling pressure. Clearly, Allison lives not so well, and Jennifer lives well. The former is a poor stress manager; the latter is an effective stress manager. These stories raise an important question: Stress management for what? As suggested by the title of this book, **wellness** is the answer.

See Application Exercise 3-1 for a second look at Allison and Jennifer.

WHAT IS WELLNESS?

Americans typically have grown up with the cultural belief that if they are not ill, they must be well. This perspective is reinforced by our medical system. If I go to a typical doctor with a physical complaint and nothing is diagnosed through usual medical tests, I probably will be sent on my way with the message, "I can't find anything wrong with you. You are well. Be on your way and don't worry." While it may be true I am not *sick*,

Wellness is the process of living at one's highest possible level as a whole person and promoting the same for others.

Jennifer: A Story of Wellness

Jennifer came to California State University, Chico, from a background much like Allison's—fairly well-to-do family, a record of modest academic success, vague goals of wanting to "work with people" and to meet and marry a handsome and wealthy young man.

She, too, came to college with a certain degree of insecurity, yet she got off to a rather different start. She made two or three very good friends who were available when needed for support and fun. They also loved to exercise together, alternating running and aerobics for a total of four or five days a week.

She talked by phone each week with her parents and younger brothers. Jennifer soon became active in CAVE (Community Action Volunteers in Education), a campus-based community volunteer program.

She went to bed by a reasonable hour during the week, averaging more than seven hours of sleep per night. She ate consistently well and kept healthy snacks on hand in her room.

Jennifer studied about an hour each weekday, another two hours or so each evening, and more when needed. She was able to stay focused on her homework from the start and missed only one class during the first five weeks, because of a time conflict with her academic adviser.

At midterm time, Jennifer felt prepared and confident. She got good grades right away, which bolstered her confidence and reinforced her habit of carefully managing her time. She didn't get sick all semester and ended up with an A, 3 B's, and a B-. She was delighted and optimistic.

Jennifer's story is a story of wellness.

this does not necessarily mean I am *well*. For wellness is much more: Wellness is the process of living at one's highest possible level as a whole person and promoting the same for others.

Four elements of this definition are worth noting. First, wellness is not a state that is attained but is an ongoing, dynamic, fluid process through time. In any given time period (week, month, year), fluctuations in how well one lives will occur. Wellness is characterized by relatively continuous high-level living over the long run. Seen this way, it is a continuing challenge, rather than something attained and then forgotten.

Second, note the phrase "one's highest possible level." In my own life, I want to "be all I can be" rather than be satisfied with mediocrity or "normality." This is true not only of the physical or medical aspects of my life but also of all other aspects as well, including those noted in the later section on the wellness lifestyle.

Third, the definition focuses on the "whole person." From a conventional medical point of view, all that matters is the physical body. If illness occurs, diagnostic efforts usually are focused on the sick organ and on other parts of the body that might be involved as either the cause or effect of the sick organ. It is almost as if the body were a machine, disconnected in any way from mind, spirit, emotions, meaning, or behavior (Dossey, 1991). As noted previously, a key assumption of this book is that mind-body-behavior are interwoven into an integrated whole—and that the **whole person** is inherently interconnected with the environment.

Fourth, the definition ends with "and promoting the same for others." High-level well-being includes promoting the well-being of others as well as of the self. This means attending to the effects of one's moods and behavior on those in the immediate micro-

Low-Level Worseness				High-Level Wellness
−10 - 0 - +10				
Major Illness Signs and/or Very Unhappy	Feeling Symptoms	Feeling Just OK	Feeling Fairly Well	High Energy and Very Happy

environment—family, intimate partners, friends, teammates, roommates, neighbors, co-workers, fellow students. It also means getting involved in broader local, regional, state, or national efforts to improve social conditions in the macro-environment.

Wellness, then, is maximizing one's potentials while enjoying the process and maintaining optimal health along the way—for the self and others. As Don Ardell (1982) states, high-level wellness contrasts with low-level **worseness.** Ardell (1989, 10) proposes that we think of wellness/worseness as a continuum. A modified version of his continuum appears above.

See Application Exercise 3-2 for an assessment of where you stand on the wellness/worseness continuum.

My definition of wellness bears some resemblance to the classic 1946 definition of health from the World Health Organization (WHO): "Health is a state of complete physical, mental, and social well-being and not merely the absence of disease or infirmity" (Antonovsky, 1979, 52). However, WHO's inclusion of the term "complete" suggests that health or wellness is an achievable end-state. I suggest instead that it is a dynamic, continually improving process. Note also that this half-century-old WHO definition implies the individual is an isolated unit, not necessarily connected to or influenced by the surrounding environment. WHO's more recent definition of health omits these earlier deficiencies. "A process of enabling individuals and communities to increase control over the determinants of health" (Pelletier, 1994, 70).

Wellness and **normal health** are not synonymous. To be "well" includes more than simply being "normal" or "nonsick." To illustrate the point, it is useful to examine in Figure 3-1 contrasts provided by Harold Elrick (1980) between standards of "normal" and "optimal" health. Our concept of wellness is similar to (though more inclusive than) Elrick's notion of optimal health.

Several of these values can be debated in view of recent medical research. Nevertheless, these contrasts effectively illustrate the difference between normal health and wellness. To be well is to have the best possible test values, not just minimally acceptable ones.

The term *wellness* is hardly new. As Travis and Callander have noted (1990, AA4), the *Oxford Unabridged Dictionary* reports usage of the term dating back to the seventeenth century. For example, one D. Osborne wrote to a friend, "You . . . never send me any of the new phrases of the town. . . . Pray what is meant by wellness and unwellness?" Wrote T. Twining in 1791, "When I say 'well,' I can't be supposed to mean the wellness that one should predicate of a professor who makes those instruments his study." In 1864, Mrs. Carlyle mentioned "Some weeks of such comparative ease and well-ness."

The term *wellness* first entered modern American lexicon through lectures and a now-obscure book nearly 40 years ago by a public health professor, Halbert Dunn, called *High-Level Wellness.* He defined the term in this way:

Figure 3-1

Normal and Optimal Health Standards

Standard	Normal	Optimal
1. Diet	Calories,*	Optimal amount nutrients
	Fat,* Salt,*	
	Cholesterol,*	
	Sugar,* Protein,**	
	Fiber,** Calcium**	
2. Exercise	0–Occasional	Daily
3. Smoking	Common	None
4. Alcohol	Common	0–Occasional
5. Blood Pressure	100/70–150/95	90/60–120/80
6. Pulse	60–100	35–65
7. Body Fat (Male)	12–25%	5–10%
8. Cholesterol	150–300	125–135
9. Triglycerides	30–200	30–100
10. Uric Acid	2.5–8	2.5–6.5
11. Magnesium	20–40	40–80

*Excessive **Deficient
Source: Elrick (1980). Reprinted by permission.

High-level wellness for the individual is defined as an integrated method of functioning which is oriented toward maximizing the potential of which the individual is capable. It requires that the individual maintain a continuum of balance and purposeful direction with the environment in which he is functioning. (1961, 4)

This early definition still bears striking similarity to mine in its focus on a continuing process, on the whole person, and on the person's linkage with the surrounding social environment. His focus is only on personal well-being, whereas mine includes promoting the well-being of others as well.

One of Dunn's medical interns, John Travis, was so influenced by Dunn's perspective that he found conventional medical practice quite unsatisfying, preferring instead to devote his career to developing and promoting the wellness model (Ryan & Travis, 1981; Ryan & Travis, 1991; Travis & Callander, 1990). Travis was instrumental through his Wellness Resource Center in stimulating the growth of the wellness movement in the United States. Another key player has been Donald Ardell, especially through his seminal book, *High-Level Wellness: An Alternative to Doctors, Drugs and Disease* (1977), but also including his later books (Ardell, 1984; Ardell, 1989; Ardell, 1996; Ardell, 1999; Ardell & Langdon, 1989; Ardell & Tager, 1982) and newsletter, *Ardell Wellness Report.* The wellness movement also was given substantial impetus through the innovative student-focused wellness program at the University of Wisconsin, Stevens Point, and the annual National Wellness Conference to which it gave birth.

A final point about defining wellness. Striving to live at one's highest possible level will decrease chances of illness. But it will not guarantee you will never get sick. We all know of instances when people come down with an illness despite living very healthfully, as a result of genetic influences, accidents, contact with powerful viruses or bacteria, or simply chance and bad luck. As I have defined wellness, however, it does mean living well—mentally, spiritually, and physically—with illness, whether temporary or chronic. A recent study demonstrates that stress management training can be effective in reducing stress among adolescents with diabetes (Boardway et al., 1993).

I have friends and colleagues who live—at a very high level of wellness—with diabetes, coronary artery disease, psoriasis, rheumatoid arthritis, and migraine headaches. One of my heroes for many years was George Sheehan, a runner-cardiologist-writer. I saw him place seventh, in his age group, with an 800-meter time of 2:46 in the 1989 World Veterans Track and Field Championships in Eugene, Oregon, at the age of 71—two or three years after his cancer of the prostate had moved into his bones. He continued participating in running and triathlon events for more than four years. When he finally died in 1993 just before his 75th birthday, he was busy at work on his final book—this one about the process of dying. Dr. Sheehan lived well with disease.

A wellness lifestyle is mutually reinforcing positive habits in the following areas:
Environmental
Intellectual
Emotional
Spiritual
Physical
Social
Time

A WELLNESS LIFESTYLE

See Application Exercise 3-3 for an assessment of your wellness lifestyle strengths and weaknesses.

Environmental wellness habits include awareness of the precarious state of the global environment and of the effects of one's daily habits on the physical environment; maintaining a way of life that minimizes harm to the environment; and being involved in socially responsible activities to protect the environment.

Intellectual wellness habits include the abilities to engage in clear thinking and recall, with minimal interference from emotional baggage; to think independently and critically; to possess basic skills of reasoning; and to be open to new ideas. They also include the broadest and deepest possible knowledge of cultural heritage.

Emotional wellness habits include awareness of one's emotions at any given time; the ability to maintain a relatively even emotional state with moderate emotional responses to the flow of life events; the ability to maintain relative control over emotional states; and the ability to experience a preponderance of positive over negative emotional states.

Spiritual wellness habits include concern with issues of meaning, value, and purpose. If they are not clear or certain in these respects, they are at least attentive to their importance and a continuing quest for clarity.

Physical wellness habits include sound nutritional practices; regular exercise, including aerobic exercise several times a week; consistent and adequate sleep; nonabuse of alcohol, drugs, and tobacco; use of seat belts and cycle helmets and practice of other safe traffic measures; and, if sexually active, practice of safe sex.

Social wellness habits include sharing intimacy, friendships, and group memberships; practicing empathy and active listening; caring for others; being open to others' caring; and demonstrating an ongoing commitment to the common good of the community, the state, and the nation.

Time wellness habits include maintaining a pace of life within one's comfort zone most of the time; maintaining relative control over one's time; minimizing chronic hurry and hassle, on the one hand, and boredom and stagnation, on the other; balancing activity and rest, work and play, solitude and relationships.

At the beginning of a recent semester, students in my Human Stress class at California State University, Chico, completed a series of measures related to stress, health, attitude, and lifestyle. Included was the Distress Symptom Scale, a 50-item checklist described in Chapter 6. They also completed a comprehensive wellness lifestyle measure, TestWell. Developed by the National Wellness Institute, TestWell includes one hundred total questions in the following categories of wellness lifestyle:

Physical Fitness	Social Awareness	Intellectual Wellness
Nutrition	Emotional Awareness and	Occupational Wellness
Self-Care and Safety	Sexuality	Spirituality and Values
Environmental Wellness	Emotional Management	

It is reasonable to expect—if the theme of this book is valid—that the higher the wellness lifestyle score, the lower the distress symptom score. Figure 3-2 below shows the actual findings.

Figure 3-2

Wellness Lifestyle and Distress: Mean Distress Symptom Score by TestWell Score

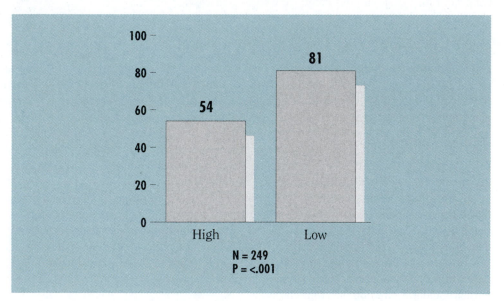

Measures: *Wellness* 100-Item TestWell

Distress Symptom Score: 50-Item Distress Symptom Scale

Finding: Students with high TestWell scores reported significantly lower distress symptom scores.

Families can contribute greatly to one's culture of wellness.

A wellness lifestyle pervades one's entire life, at work, school, home, in the community, while alone, or with others. It is a way of being and a way of relating to the world around us. A continuing challenge is to maximize one's potentials in each of these areas of wellness. As you make positive progress in one area, other areas automatically benefit, since the dimensions of wellness tend to be interrelated and mutually reinforcing.

Stress relates to wellness in two ways. On the one hand, constructive, adaptive stress habits will contribute to wellness. On the other hand, living a wellness lifestyle will help minimize distress.

The point of managing stress effectively, then, is not only to **prevent** harmful **distress**—emotional upset, headaches, or heart attacks—but also for the higher purpose of **promoting wellness**—well-being and fulfillment. Others in turn will benefit.

How and why do people develop a wellness lifestyle or a worseness lifestyle? These obviously are very complex questions with no simple answers. We do know that the likelihood of a person developing a wellness lifestyle is influenced by both social environment and personal choice. If you grew up in a home in which no one exercised, all adults smoked, high-fat foods were regularly served, people were abusive toward one another, and drugs (including alcohol) were used daily, then chances are high you will fall into the same patterns. Highly probable though such an outcome might be, this is not predetermined or inevitable, since each person possesses the ability to make independent choices about lifestyle. Social environment, past experiences in that environment, and personal choice all contribute, then, to the chances of a wellness or worseness lifestyle.

Little attention is given in the wellness movement or the wellness literature to specific qualities of the environment that are likely to enhance or detract from wellness. In Chapter 11, we will discuss the concept of "cultures of wellness," which is useful for identifying some of these wellness-enhancing characteristics of social environments. Next, however, we continue at the individual level of wellness by focusing on a vital component of wellness, personal energy.

ENERGY: A VITAL COMPONENT OF WELLNESS

A key element of wellness is possessing maximum energy for daily living. In many of my workshops and classes, I ask how many people feel tired most of the time. Consistently, 80 to 90 percent raise their hands. "General fatigue and heaviness" has been reported in studies of college professors (McKenna, 1980) and city managers (Schafer & Gard, 1988) to be the most commonly cited symptom of distress on the 50-item Distress Symptom Scale, which is presented in Chapter 6.

This need not be so. Part of a wellness lifestyle—and part of managing stress effectively—is maintaining daily practices and attitudes that promote and sustain one's energy level. Being truly well—that is, more than just nonsick—is to have energy available when needed.

Figure 3-3 suggests that perceived personal energy may help to protect against distress and may contribute to a sense of general well-being, measured with a question on happiness, among 1,171 adult participants in my community class, Reducing Perfectionism, Irritability, and Hurry Sickness.

For 10 years, I taught this 10-session community class at the Enloe Hospital Stress and Health Center. Participants completed pre- and post-questionnaires and received feed-

Figure 3-3

Distress Symptoms and Happiness by Perceived Energy

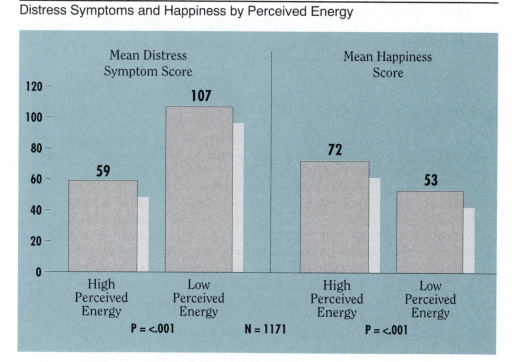

Measures: Distress Symptoms: 50-Item Distress Symptom Scale
  Happiness: 10-point scale from Quality of Life Assessment
  Perceived Energy: 10-point scale from Quality of Life Assessment

Finding: The higher the perceived energy, the lower the distress symptom score and the higher the happiness score.

back about their progress on a number of aspects of stress and health over the 20 weeks of the course. Results of these pre-post comparisons are presented in Chapter 8.

Of interest here is the statistical association of perceived energy with other factors. Participants were asked this item about energy: "Circle the number below that best describes your *sense of vitality or energy level* these days." Response options ranged over a 10-point scale, from Very Low Energy Level (1) to Very High Energy Level (10). Another 10-point item asked about "how *happy* you are these days, all things considered." In addition to these questions, the class also completed a 50-item distress symptom scale. First, Figure 3-3 shows that the higher the perceived energy, the lower the distress symptoms. Of course, causation probably runs both ways: High energy protects against distress, while high distress saps energy. Second, on a more positive note, Figure 3-3 reveals that the higher the perceived energy, the higher the happiness. Again, energy is a vital part of wellness. Being truly well includes the ability to sustain high energy for long days, long weeks, long semesters—and a long lifetime.

The cases in the box illustrate variations in energy levels. They also point to the importance of energy in health, productivity, and emotional well-being.

Energy, in fact, is a central component of wellness. With it, you can reach your highest possible levels of performance, maintain satisfying relationships, provide the basis for emotional stability, think clearly, and ensure good health. Without it, you will underachieve, become irritable, burn out, break down, and more. In short, energy is vital.

Unfortunately, many among us are chronically tired, with too little energy to meet zestfully the demands of daily living. My physician friend, a family practitioner, tells me fatigue by far is the most common presenting symptom among his patients. He and his colleagues note this in their medical charts with *TATT— Tired All The Time*. The "chronic fatigue syndrome" has become a major medical problem in this country, baffling scientific

---

College Student Energy

- José is an energetic college student who thrives under pressure, gets a great deal done in a day's time, and seldom seems tired or discouraged. He works out nearly every day, gets six to eight hours of sleep most nights, and catnaps when needed.
- Josephina pays her own way through a western university, where she carries a 3.4 grade point average. She is active in several campus organizations yet somehow finds time for her friendships, play, and her aerobics class. She seldom feels run down or fatigued. In fact, she surprises most of her friends with her apparently boundless supply of energy.
- Jennie is a community college student who feels tired most of the time. She sleeps restlessly, eats sporadically, and is either cranky or depressed most of the time. She seldom exercises—she never seems to have enough time.
- Jonathan is a likable college sophomore who moves through his days more like a turtle than a racehorse. He is quite content with his pace, and he seems to know his limits. He sleeps 9 to 10 hours most nights. Jonathan turns down many opportunities to party with his friends, preferring instead to spend time alone reading or working on computer graphics.

experts (Cowley, 1990). According to a 1993 report by the U. S. Department of Health and Human Services, fully 14 million Americans go to their doctors because of exhaustion. As Emanuel Cheraskin puts it, "Add to that the uncounted millions who seek medical adviced for other reasons but also mention significant exhaustion. And plus the fact that there are millions more who never seek help but are nonetheless tired all the time. It becomes clear that fatigue is one of the major problems in America (Gazella, 1996, 11).

Energy, Stress, and Relaxation

Energy relates to the stress response and the relaxation response in a host of ways, positively and negatively. The stress response greatly increases energy in emergencies, of course, through the fight-or-flight processes described in Chapter 4. Yet chronic stress can deplete energy. The result often is physical illness or emotional disorders.

As Kuntzleman notes, this can be avoided:

> Stress need *not* rob you of energy. The key to stress and energy is how you handle it— whether you can manage stress or allow it to manage you. And that's why trying to avoid stress just doesn't work. You can run away from it all, build a log cabin in the wilderness, and sit by the fire the rest of your life and still be plagued by stress—if you are a worrier, uncomfortable with change, and angry at the world. It's all a matter of learning how to cope with stress and understanding your place in the world. (1981, 9)

The relaxation response helps restore energy. When elicited regularly, the relaxation response can provide stress resistance in the face of challenge, change, and crisis. Yet if the relaxation response is your state of being most of the time, stagnation results.

Energy can be a vital element in stress resistance. This is consistent with the theory of generalized resistance resources by Antonovsky (1979, 1987). Implied in his formulation is that personal energy is a key ingredient to one's ability to cope effectively with potentially distressful life events.

Energy also is implicit in the theory of stress by Lazarus and Folkman (1984). As we noted in Chapter 1, Lazarus and Folkman define stress as "a particular relationship between the person and the environment that is appraised by the person as taxing or exceeding his or her resources and endangering his or her well-being" (1984, 19). They maintain that appraisal of events influences behavioral, emotional, and physical responses to events. They emphasize the ongoing, interactional process of coping through time in their effort to understand why some individuals are more effective than others in staying healthy under pressure. Among "the resources upon which people draw in order to cope with the myriad demands of living is health and energy." They point out, "A person who is frail, sick, tired, or otherwise debilitated has less energy to expend on coping than a healthy, robust person" (1984, 159). As with Antonovsky's theory, in other words, the greater the energy, the greater the resources for dealing effectively with the stressors of daily life.

Let us examine more closely the nature of energy, its various dimensions, some of the factors that influence it, and some of its effects.

The Nature of Human Energy

Defining Energy

Energy is your own perception at any given moment of your potential for action. It's your sense of what you could do if you chose to.

In physics, *energy* is defined as "the capacity for doing work and overcoming resistance" (*Webster's New World Dictionary,* 1980, 463). **Energy** in humans, too, can be viewed as potential for action. Thus, one has high energy to the degree one has high physical and emotional reserves available when needed.

While human energy can be measured physiologically, it is most useful here to conceive of it subjectively. Thus, we will follow the definition of energy by Flora Davis in her informative book about energy, *Personal Peak Performance: Making the Most of Your Natural Energy* (Davis, 1980, xxvii): "Energy is your own perception at any given moment of your potential for action. It's your sense of what you could do if you chose to."

Stated differently, perceived energy is a subjective feeling that one has the internal resources to respond to demands when needed. Davis (1980, xxx) uses the term "body truth" to describe your awareness of energy. A *body truth* is a personal, internal experience. High energy is the relative presence of such internal resources. Low energy is the relative absence.

Beliefs About Energy

Davis points out that Americans have mixed feelings about energy:

> Because we live in a highly competitive society that is very accomplishment-oriented, we value and envy people who seem to have unusual vitality. On the one hand, we sometimes denigrate them as well, insisting that if they're constantly on the go, it's because they're driven by their own private demons. "I'm not high-energy at all," one woman replied indignantly when I asked to interview her. "I'm not the nervous type." I never said she was. (1980, xxxi)

Our cultural beliefs about work and achievement usually lead us to place greater value on high energy than low energy. Most Americans equate energy with accomplishment. As one interviewee told Davis (1980, xxxi), "Energy is what it takes to do work." It apparently never occurred to her it also takes energy to play. And we sometimes forget that low energy is intrinsically no better or worse than high energy—unless it is the result of emotional impairment, irresponsibility, selfishness, or poor health habits.

Another common belief is that energy belongs more in the masculine than the feminine realm, especially energy related to accomplishment. At least traditionally, men are supposed to possess drive and vitality, while women are supposed to be more passive and subdued. Of course, neither gender is supposed to have a monopoly on sexual energy.

Two Dimensions of Energy

Energy has two key dimensions: endurance and intensity. *Endurance* refers to your ability to sustain a moderate or high level of energy over a given period. A high-energy person is someone who stays "up" without wearing down throughout the day, as energetic at 9 P.M. as at 9 A.M. You are high energy if you are as fresh Friday noon as you were Monday noon; as fresh in May as you were in September if you are a teacher or student; as active, alert, and productive at age 72 as at age 32. Endurance over the lifetime is illustrated, for example, by Paul Reece, a 73-year-old retired school administrator from Sacramento (Reese, 1990) who recently became the oldest person to *run* from coast to coast (3,182 miles in 122 days) and by 70-year-old Bert LeFevre, who in 1990 traveled 700 miles through the Far West—by mule (Gray, 1990). Thus, *endurance* refers to maintaining energy throughout the day, week, season, and lifetime.

Intensity is the second dimension of energy. High-energy persons are fully present, fully engaged, and attentive at whatever they are doing. Energy can be too intense, of course, as in persons who are "hyper." What is best is to be involved and able to concentrate when needed. Low-energy persons are detached, too tired to concentrate or to perform to their fullest.

Types of Energy People

As Davis (1980) has noted, there are several types of energy people:

- *Strollers* are low-energy types who move relatively slowly. They thrive under relatively low levels of stimulation and enjoy a slow pace of life.

Examples of Blocking Energy

Students in my Human Stress class were asked to complete the following sentence. Below is a sample of their responses.

I sometimes block my energy by:

- holding in my true feelings.
- trying to be a perfectionist and wanting the same from others.
- getting caught up in other things that aren't important.
- having low self-esteem, having a fear of failure, and sometimes having unexpressed feelings.
- anger in my relationships with my boyfriend, parents, and friends.
- being too critical of myself. I sometimes try to think of things so hard that I block the flow. I get very frustrated and therefore un-productive.
- not having enough confidence or worrying too much about what others will think.
- being so shy. I'm shy because I fear being rejected by others. If I don't open up or let my real self show, then I think they won't reject me.
- procrastinating. I have fear of success, and I don't express my emotions as much as I would like.
- not expressing my anger.

- *Joggers* move at a moderate, steady pace with a moderate and even energy level. They know their limits, are often quite productive, and know how to take care of themselves.

- *Sprinters* go very fast for brief periods, then need to come down for recuperation. Like Carl Lewis in the 100-meter dash, they can sustain their full-tilt pace for only a short while.

- *Long-distance athletes* are like joggers in that they are steady over the long haul, but they differ in that their energy is sustained at an unusually high level for a long period.

Sources of Energy

Anyone who has visited a hospital nursery knows that infants vary in energy levels in their first hours, surely the result of *hereditary* influences. Yet *social learning* affects them considerably later on. Early examples set by parents and peers, the nature of rewards and punishments, the community, region, culture, and subculture in which one lives—all play a role in determining one's energy level. Finally, *personal choice* plays a part. Whether you choose to live at a fast or slow pace; whether or not you take care of yourself by maintaining good habits of sleep, nutrition, and exercise—these, too, influence your energy level.

Energy Qualities

People vary in several **energy qualities.** Energy can be *natural* or *nervous.* Natural energy is energy that flows easily with little effort or struggle. Nervous energy comes from fear, low self-esteem, anger, or anxiety. It is marked by struggle. This distinction corresponds with Maslow's terms "deficiency motivation" and "self-actualization" (Maslow, 1962).

Energy can be *satisfying* or *unsatisfying* to the person in question. Of course, this is a matter of degree and is entirely subjective.

Energy can be distinguished by whether it is *helpful* or *harmful,* according to its effects on others.

Finally, energy can be *directed* or *wasted.* Having high energy does not necessarily mean you are productive or useful. A great many people endure lives of futility and frustration because they drift, flail, or sputter.

To live a wellness lifestyle, then, is to live so your energy is as *natural, satisfying, helpful,* and *directed* as possible. Stress can interfere with this ideal. Managing stress effectively—through wise balance of the stress response and the relaxation response—can promote it.

Blocked Energy

Blocked energy is a common barrier to reaching full potential. Energy can be blocked for several reasons: perfectionism, fear of failure, fear of success, fear of disapproval, self-doubt, and unexpressed anger or frustration from the past, either immediate (e.g., yesterday) or long-term (e.g., childhood).

You no doubt have experienced writer's block at some time in your life. You have been afraid to take a risk in this way or in other ways. In short, you have blocked your energy.

Maximizing your energy, then, includes clearing away these blockages so energy is available when needed. Sometimes therapy or other professional assistance is needed. Learning self-talk techniques such as those in Chapter 14 also can help.

Energy Rhythms

People differ in the stability and variability of their energy, or **energy rhythms,** throughout the day. Some are relatively even in physical and mental energy; others experience definite highs and lows. Some are morning persons, others are night persons, and others are in-between. A catnap, a deep relaxation break, or physical exercise can be very effective for countering down times throughout the day. One study found a 10-minute walk to be more effective than a "candy bar break" for restoring energy and reducing anxiety (Thayer, 1986).

Energy in Relationships

As Davis (1980) notes, couples sometimes vary in energy levels, creating potential for conflict. Consider the following case:

> "My husband has much more energy than I do," Amy said. "That's something that became uncomfortably obvious to me when we were on our honeymoon years ago. I was exhausted from all the wedding preparations, and I just wanted to lie on the beach and rest, but Arthur was all set to swim and play tennis, go do snorkeling and scuba diving; in the evenings he wanted to go dancing until all hours. I trailed around after him, but it was hard. In fact, I thought we were so mismatched that I was ready to leave him." (1980, 371)

Amy and Arthur are still together 12 years later, partly because it was Arthur's energy to which Amy was attracted. Yet the potential for conflict and disagreement is apparent.

Davis points out that energy gaps can be good or bad, depending on the meaning to those involved. Certainly, energy is one personal quality to be considered in selecting a partner. When serious differences do exist, several solutions are available: compromise by both, one person moving toward the other's energy level, vice versa, or learning to live with the difference.

Energy for What?

You may have lots of energy, but for what purpose? What values direct your energy? As Chapman (1986, 1987) and Tubesing (1994) have noted, it is vital to address these key

12 Steps to Wellness

Donald Ardell, who several years ago authored a pioneering book (Ardell, 1977) that helped launch the wellness movement, believes that "wellness is too important to be presented grimly." Accordingly, he has presented "12 steps to wellness." He cautions, "Like AA's steps, these are SOMEWHAT redundant, preachy and oriented to what a screw-up you've been. But, for lots of people, AA's steps worked, so who knows? Maybe these will work, too."

1. Acknowledge that you are a wimp in the face of worseness. By admitting your obsessive, chemical and spiritual abdication of responsibility to the siren song of abusive self-ruination and slovenly destructive near-term gratification of an inappropriate nature, you take the FIRST STEP to liberation by wellness. Namely, you conclude that you are a pox on the Earth, a slime-bag of a human being, but that you need not and will not stay that way.

2. Decide that you need to GAIN POSITIVE support and LOSE NEGATIVE support in getting started. Ask for the former from wellness seekers and dump your low level worseness "friends." Plant yourself in a healthful garden environment while weeding your social garden.

3. Choose yourself as guru or sovereign master for the course of your life. Make a commitment to independence and self-sufficiency tied to friendships, professional guidance and a belief in a benevolent spirit or force that wants you to live joyfully and well.

4. Conduct a searching inventory of where you are. Assess liabilities and strengths, with an emphasis on the latter. Look at extremes of past self-abuse. For instance, consider old patterns of blaming, denial, worry, anger, self-pity, and dead-end relationships and grim associations that reinforce worseness. Make a conscious decision that these kinds of patterns are no longer acceptable.

questions within a framework of spiritual wellness—that aspect of total well-being dealing with matters of value, meaning, and purpose.

We noted in Chapter 1 that personal well-being needs to be balanced with concern with the common good. I hope this book will stimulate you toward self-care, not merely as an end in itself but in order to provide more energy for contributing to the well-being of others.

Changing Energy Levels

It is entirely up to you, of course, as to whether you need to change your energy level at all. The key question is, what does your present energy level do for you and others? Is it constructive in terms of your stress and wellness? How does it affect others?

For some, reducing energy level may be needed, especially when it is now more nervous than natural, if you are setting the stage for later burnout or breakdown by imposing

5. Write out, analyze, and discuss your old profile. By disclosing who you used to be as well as what you are becoming with special wellness-oriented friends and colleagues, you put the past *in* the past, where it belongs.

6. Create a personal plan for wellness. Since the lack of wellness planning got you into a worseness frump in the first place, a written wellness plan is a sure way to lock-in that lifetime slow-fix to self-actualization.

7. Pursue realistic, worthy goals in a systematic way. Consider what you want from life and why that seems important.

8. Identify very special people crucial for your wellness quest—and include them in your support network. Avoid isolation; wellness is challenging under any circumstances. Only die-hards could sustain wellness on uninhabited land.

9. Explain your commitment to a wellness lifestyle to anyone who was a willing or other participant in your worseness past. Make amends, if necessary, in order to secure a tranquil spirit—and eliminate your guilt. Take a few disclosure chances.

10. Reassess along the way. A wellness lifestyle is never finished as long as life remains; adjustments, variations and fine-tuning are always appropriate—if you think so.

11. Add a dash of imagery, meditation or any other form of self-dialogue if doing so helps you find inner peace. There are many ways and diverse paths to deepening your spiritual reservoir and finding balance and serenity.

12. Reach out and assist others. Becoming involved, sharing insights about personal rewards and satisfactions are services to those who need support. The joy of living is potentially too great to keep to yourself. Offer to share it—without being a bore or a bothersome proselytizer.

SOURCE: Ardell (1990, 3). Donald Ardell is publisher of the Ardell Wellness Report. Copies can be obtained by writing to *Ardell Wellness Report,* 345 Bayshore Blvd. #414, Tampa, FL 33606. The first copy is free if you send a self-addressed stamped envelope.

undue wear and tear on your body, or if others are negatively affected by your present pace.

For others, increasing energy may be desirable. This probably is the most commonly perceived need. Low energy in a potentially high-energy person often results from chronic overload, chronic and unexpressed emotional tension, depression, poor sleep habits, inadequate nutrition, or lack of exercise (Chopra, 1985). Following guidelines and techniques from this textbook can help overcome these barriers to full energy.

For still others, changing energy habits might mean smoothing out erratic energy rhythms or increasing accessibility to energy reserves by removing energy blockages.

Whatever your specific energy need, awareness of your own "body truth" is a starting point. Acceptance of your own potential for modifying energy level is next.

PERSONAL BENEFITS OF WELLNESS

We have defined wellness, discussed the wellness lifestyle, explored cultures of wellness, and discussed energy as a component of wellness. Wellness as a way of living is likely to have a number of positive benefits for the individual:

- Minimal frequency of illness

- Low illness risk

- Maximum energy for daily living

- Enjoyment of daily life

- Continual development of abilities

- Contribution to well-being of those around you

- Contribution to the common good in the larger environment

The American health-care crisis—more accurately, our medical-care crisis—exists in part because of widespread unhealthy lifestyle choices. As people's energy increases, so does their illness resistance. If enough people increase energy at the personal level, demand for medical treatment services in the first place can be reduced because at the same time they will have improved their health and illness resistance.

References

Antonovsky, A. (1979). *Health, stress and coping.* San Francisco: Jossey-Bass Publishers.

Antonovsky, A. (1987). *Unravelling the mystery of health.* San Francisco: Jossey-Bass Publishers.

Ardell, D. B. (1977). *High level wellness:An alternative to doctors, drugs and disease.* Emmaus, PA: Rodale Press. Also see revised edition (1986). Berkeley: Ten Speed Press.

Ardell, D. B. (1984). *The history and future of wellness.* Pleasant Hill, CA: Diablo Press.

Ardell, D. B. (1989). *Die healthy: Sixteen steps to a wellness lifestyle.* Wellness Australia.

Ardell, D. B. (1996). *The book of wellness: A secular approach to spirit, meaning, and purpose.* New York: Prometheus Books.

Ardell, D. B. (1999). *14 days to wellness: The easy, effective, and fun way to optimum health* (2nd ed.). New York: New World Library.

Ardell, D. B., & Langdon, J. G. (1989). *Wellness: The body, mind and spirit.* Dubuque, IA: Kendall/Hunt Publishing Co.

Ardell, D. B., & Tager, M. J. (1982). *Planning for wellness.* Dubuque, IA: Kendall/Hunt Publishing.

Boardway, R. H., et al. (1993). Stress management training for adolescents with diabetes. *Journal of Pediatric Psychology, 18,* 29–45.

Chapman, L. S. (1986). Spiritual health: A component missing from health promotion. *American Journal of Health Promotion, 1,* 38–41.

Chapman, L. S. (1987). Developing a useful perspective on spiritual health: Well-being, spiritual potential and the search for meaning. *American Journal of Health Promotion, 1,* 31–39.

Chopra, D. (1985). *Creating health: The psychophysiological connection.* New York: Vantage Press.

Cowley, G. (1990). Chronic fatigue syndrome: A modern medical mystery. *Newsweek,* November 12.

Davis, F. (1990). *Personal peak performance: Making the most of your natural energy.* New York: McGraw-Hill.

Dossey, L. (1991). *Meaning & medicine.* New York: Bantam.

Dunn, H. L. (1961). *High-level wellness.* Arlington, VA: R. W. Beatty.

Elrick, H. (1980). A new definition of health. *Journal of the National Medical Association, 72,* 695–699.

Gazella, K. A. (1996). Enhancing energy. *Health Security,* January/February, 10–12.

Gray, E. (1990). LeFevre trek: Paradise to Idaho on horseback. *Chico Enterprise-Record,* August 25, 1B.

Kuntzleman, C. T. (1981). *Maximum personal energy: Unleash your energy potential and enjoy life.* Emmaus, PA: Rodale Press.

Lazarus, R. S., & Folkman, S. (1984). *Stress, appraisal and coping.* New York: Springer Publishing.

Maslow, A. (1962). *Toward a psychology of being.* New York: Van Nostrand.

McKenna, J. R. (1980). *Occupational stress and the university professor* (Unpublished masters thesis, California State University, Chico).

Pelletier, K. R. (1994). *Sound mind, sound body.* New York: Simon & Schuster.

Reese, P. (1990). Reese runs the U.S. *Run Cal,* no. 41, 8.

Ryan, R. S., & Travis, J. W. (1981). *Wellness workbook.* Berkeley: Ten Speed Press.

Ryan, R. S., & Travis, J. W. (1991). *Wellness: Small changes you can use to make a big difference.* Berkeley: Ten Speed Press.

Schafer, W., & Gard, B. (1988). Stress and California's city managers. *Western City, 64,* 13–15.

Thayer, R. (1986). Energy, tiredness and tension effects of a sugar snack versus exercise. *Journal of Personality and Social Psychology, 52,* 199–225.

Travis, J. W., & Callander, M. G. (1990). *Wellness for helping professionals: Creating compassionate cultures.* Mill Valley, CA: Wellness Associates Publications.

Tubesing, D. A. (1994). What is spiritual wellness, anyway? *Wellness Management, 4,* 6–7.

Webster's New World Dictionary (2nd College ed.); 1980.

Application Exercise 3-1

A Second Look at Allison and Jennifer

1. Make a list of all the attitudes and actions by Allison that represent worseness.

2. Make a list of all the attitudes and actions by Jennifer that represent wellness.

3. If you are a college student, which of the two patterns of attitudes and actions most closely resembles your own? Be specific.

Application Exercise 3-2

Where Are You on the Wellness/Worseness Continuum?

1. All things considered, where would you place yourself on the wellness/worseness continuum on page 57?

2. Explain with details.

Application Exercise 3-3

Strengths and Weaknesses in Wellness Lifestyle

Please use the following chart to rank yourself in the seven categories of the wellness lifestyle presented in this chapter. You might want to reread the brief description of each category on pages 59-60 as you complete this exercise.

	Very Positive	Somewhat Positive	Somewhat Negative	Very Negative
Environmental	———	———	———	———
Intellectual	———	———	———	———
Emotional	———	———	———	———
Spiritual	———	———	———	———
Physical	———	———	———	———
Social	———	———	———	———
Time	———	———	———	———

Briefly explain why you ranked yourself as you did in each category.

The area(s) I would most like to improve is (are):

PART II

More About Stress

The fact is, a person can be intoxicated with his [or her] own stress hormones. I venture to say that this sort of drunkenness has caused much more harm to society than the alcoholic kind.

—HANS SELYE

THE DYNAMICS OF STRESS AND RELAXATION

Fight-or-Flight: On the Run

During a five-mile run in the foothills where I live, my easy rhythm was severely interrupted by the sudden, silent approach of a full-grown, teeth-baring Doberman pinscher. Some months earlier the same dog had bitten my daughter, so I saw  him as a genuine threat. Already my heart had been beating at 130–140 beats per minute during the run. Suddenly it sped up, probably to 160–170 beats per minute. My breathing accelerated. My muscles tensed, my eyes dilated and opened wide. I could feel adrenaline pouring into my limbs.

My attention focused immediately on coping with this threat. I had two alternatives: fight or flee. Experience had taught me that fighting, or at least pretending readiness to fight, would prove most effective. I yelled at the dog, reached for stones on the road, and threw two or three at the ground in front of him. The dog turned tail and vanished, but it took my body several minutes to "come down" from intense arousal to its previous normal condition associated with running at an easy eight-minute-per-mile pace.

In certain respects, the experience described in the box was unique. I had never met this particular dog at this particular time of day or in this particular place. Yet the reactions in my body and mind were not at all unique. What I experienced was the stress response, a distinctive mental-neurological-muscular-hormonal-cardiovascular reaction that I had known many times before. So has everyone. And so have other animals.

My encounter with the dog was a genuine physical threat, eliciting an appropriate, useful response from my body. Arousal helped me cope. Most stressors, however, are social and psychological rather than physical. Hence, such physical arousal usually is quite useless. As we shall see, in fact, the stress response can be hazardous to well-being when chronic and unreleased. My stress response was *temporary* and intense; that is, a **maxi fight-or-flight response.** Normally, short-term arousal does no harm and, in fact, can prove helpful. But the pressures of daily living too often result in a *chronic* stress response at too high a level. In short, chronic daily hassles often produce a continuous, erosive **mini fight-or-flight response.** Its damage is cumulative and often imperceptible, like a low-grade fever.

In this chapter, you will learn more about the *stress response* and how it affects you. You also will read about its opposite, the *relaxation response,* including the role of several systems of the body. Focusing on these topics will provide an important base of understanding on which to build attitudes and practices for managing stress and maximizing wellness.

THE INTERPLAY OF MIND, BODY, AND BEHAVIOR

For most of human history, mind and body have been viewed as two separate entities. An influential spokesman for this view was the French philosopher, René Decartes (1596–1650), whose dichotomous view of humans directly influenced modern medicine. Kenneth Pelletier (1994, 21) wrote of Descartes: "His treatises characterized the body as essentially a complete machine and illness as the manifestation of a breakdown in one of the machine's parts. The role of medicine—and ultimately the physician—was to identify

---

The Human Body: A Bag of Ingredients?

Traditionally, the body has been seen as a machine. Following this logic, one person has pointed out that the body is made up in part of the following ingredients:
- Water sufficient to fill a 10-gallon keg
- Enough fat for seven bars of soap
- Enough carbon for 9,000 "lead" pencils
- Enough iron to forge a nail
- Phosphorous sufficient for 220 matches
- Enough lime to whitewash a chicken coop
- Enough sulfur to purge a dog of fleas

Source: Murchie (1978, 319)

and repair the broken part." Most medical training continues to be based on this body-as-machine model, with diagnosis and treatment directed exclusively at a particular organ or body system—and (except for psychiatry) with attention to matters of the mind left entirely to nonmedical specialists like clinical psychologists and counselors.

By contrast, a fundamental assumption of our whole-person, lifestyle approach to stress is that mind, body, and behavior are closely intertwined. In fact, they are inseparable. Cause-effect arrows depicting these **mind-body-behavior linkages** run both ways, as illustrated in Figure 4-1. These interconnections occur in response to both major events and minor daily hassles.

Physical wear and tear (body) often results from chronic mental strain (mind) associated with coping with (behavior) a difficult marriage, an unsatisfying job, or overload at school. Distress often results as mind, body, and behavior affect each other in an accelerating cycle of stress buildup.

A fascinating illustration of mind-body-behavior interplay is the change in blood pressure during conversation. Studies by James Lynch and his associates at the University of Maryland clearly show that each time a person talks (an action), his or her blood pressure goes up (physical arousal), most likely in response to thoughts and feelings (in the mind) associated with the act of communicating. When the person stops talking, blood pressure declines (Lynch, 1985).

This nearly universal pattern is illustrated in Figure 4-2 by the average blood pressure readings of six nurses before, during, and after talking.

Figure 4-1

Mind-Body-Behavior

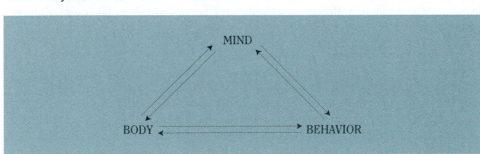

Figure 4-2

Blood Pressure and Talking

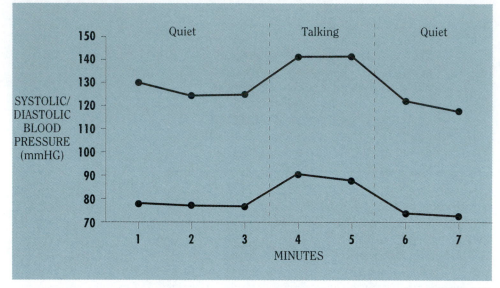

Source: Lynch (1985, 123)

Lynch has found that whether the spoken content is negative or positive, blood pressure arousal results. However, the more emotionally intense the content, the greater the arousal.

The likely mediating role of thoughts and emotions is further illustrated by Figure 4-3, which shows that reading alone elevates blood pressure somewhat but not as much as reading in someone else's presence. It also shows that reading in the presence of a "high status" person (an experimenter dressed up as a physician) raised blood pressure more than did reading in the presence of an "equal status" experimenter (a graduate student dressed casually in blue jeans, sport shirt, and tennis shoes).

This finding strongly suggests that interpretation (thoughts) affects emotions ("performance anxiety" with the physician), which in turn affects blood pressure through changes in the heart and blood vessels (body).

Here is another fascinating illustration of mind-body interaction. Phillips and King (1988; Phillips, 1990) have found in several samples that people seem able to postpone their own deaths until after a meaningful date or event, such as their own birthday, Passover, and, among elderly Chinese women, the Harvest Moon Festival.

For many years, studies of **"placebo power"** also have consistently shown that the mind can influence the body. As reported by Norman Cousins, one Harvard medical researcher concluded the following after reviewing results of 15 studies involving 1,082 subjects:

> He discovered that across the broad spectrum of these tests, 35 percent of the patients consistently experienced "satisfactory relief" when placebos were used instead of regular medication for a wide range of medical problems, including severe postoperative wound pain, seasickness, headaches, coughs, and anxiety. Other biological processes and disorders affected by placebos, as reported by medical researchers, include rheumatoid and degenerative arthritis, blood-cell count, respiratory rates, vasomotor function, peptic ulcers, hay fever, hypertension, and spontaneous remission of warts. (1979, 58)

Figure 4-3

Blood Pressure Rise in Presence of Person of Higher and Equal Status

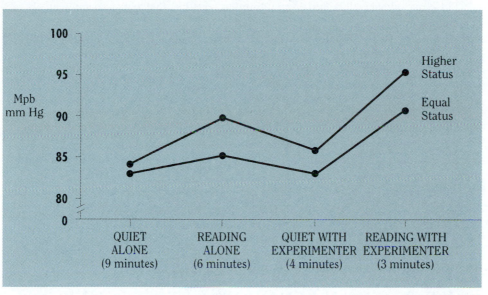

Source: Lynch (1985, 149)

Physician-writer Larry Dossey notes that one of his earliest exposures to placebo power occurred while working in a hospital pharmacology during college (1991, 163). After becoming curious to learn about the most popular medication in the hospital, he was even more puzzled when he was told it was Lipragus, a medication he had never heard about. Lipragus, he wondered? "Sugar pil(l)" spelled backward.

Another important mind-body-behavior link is that exercise (behavior) improves mental clarity and emotional stability (mind), as well as energy level and cardiovascular capacity (body).

Anxiety and the Self-Fulfilling Prophecy

A robust, middle-aged male was to undergo a cardiac catheterization as part of his evaluation for the cause of chest pain. He confessed to his cardiologist prior to the test that he felt his heart would stop during the procedure and that he would die. This revelation was made with considerable embarrassment because he took great pride in his masculinity and his ability to "take anything." The cardiologist assured him that everything would be fine and that his fear of death was for naught. However, during the procedure, which revealed relatively normal coronary arteries, the patient's heart beat began to gradually slow from 90 beats to the 50s and 40s, and then completely stopped. The man became unconscious and his electrocardiogram revealed a "straight line." Resuscitation procedures were immediately instituted, with complete and uneventful recovery. When interviewed later, he had no recall of the event, stating only that he "knew it would happen."

Source: Dossey (1991, 77)

One study found a direct link between anxiety and heart rate among U.S. Border Patrol officers participating in a simulated field shooting test. The author reports:

> Pulse rates were well within normal limits at baseline; they began to show an elevation during the control and the briefing intervals and demonstrated a dramatic rise—to nearly 150/minute—during the judgment shoot. Pulse rates began to return to normal during the debriefing session and reached normal levels once again at the second baseline period. (Rahe, 1988, 121)

A fascinating example of the mind-body linkage is that more fatal heart attacks take place on Monday than any other day of the week (Muller et al., 1987; Rabkin et al., 1980). And most of these cluster around 9 A.M. Certainly, these facts suggest a linkage with the stress of returning to work after the weekend.

Later in this chapter, you will read that mind, body, and behavior also interrelate during the relaxation response, the opposite of the stress response. You will come to understand why an integrated, whole-person, lifestyle approach to stress management is so important. As Foss (1996) recently noted, traditional, biological medicine tends to exclude attention to such mind-body and wellness factors in health and well-being.

THE STRESS RESPONSE: A PSYCHO-PHYSIOLOGICAL-BEHAVIORAL PERSPECTIVE

The integrated mind-body-behavior model of humans has implications for how we approach a wide variety of experiences: health and illness, athletic performance, intimacy, cooperation, risk-taking, and more. As noted, it also provides a useful framework for understanding the stress response and for managing stress.

The stress response is physical arousal of the body in response to a perceived threat or challenge.

This section describes the *physiology* of the stress response and its integration with thoughts, feelings, and behavior. We will approach the topic by examining the parts played by several systems of the body, beginning with the brain. In each case, the organ or system plays a useful role in enabling the person to prepare for direct physical action when needed. However, each also has the potential to generate harm—stress that turns into distress.

The Brain

The stressor-stress response link is not a direct stimulus-response connection. Intervening between the two is a distinctive, higher-level mental process: perception/interpretation/ appraisal of the stressor. For example, any of the following can be interpreted as a challenge or as a threat: rock climbing, speaking at the annual sorority alumni dinner, taking an organic chemistry exam, meeting someone for a first date, calling on a customer to sell life insurance, treating a cardiac arrest in the intensive care unit.

Humans are not unique in this respect. My dog sometimes pauses before responding to determine whether an approaching person is friend or foe. His behavior and physical response will vary markedly depending on his assessment of the situation. Similarly, the nature and strength of a person's internal reactions are affected by whether a stressor is perceived at all and, if so, how it is interpreted. As Shakespeare stated, "There is nothing either good or bad, but thinking makes it so." Norman Cousins (1989) wrote, "belief becomes biology."

When perception is aroused, the **stress response** is set in motion. For example, the simple act of listening usually elicits an increased tone on a biofeedback monitor known as the galvanic skin response, which measures electrical conduction on the skin. As you

> ## The Stress Response: An Adaptive Inheritance
>
> Today we are living in the bodies of our ancestors in a world they never dreamed would exist. We inherited the adaptive responses that enabled them to survive attacks of wild beasts, weather extremes, food deprivation, and environmental catastrophes.

Source: Eliot (1994, 22)

read earlier in this chapter, blood pressure usually rises while a person is talking and falls immediately afterward.

These are two simple illustrations of the fact that almost any perception of a stimulus elicits the stress response. In relation to stress, the important questions are how intense, prolonged, and frequent the response is and what effects it has on the body. The important question for stress management is how this response can be managed. This textbook provides guidelines and techniques for managing the stress response.

When conscious appraisal occurs, the **cerebral cortex** becomes aware of, assesses, and interprets the stress trigger (Asterita, 1985; Lovallo, 1997). The cerebral cortex is far more developed in humans than in other animals, and it allows for more thoughtful reactions to stress triggers.

> The addition of the vast number of cortical cells (in humans) allowed the development and storage of analytical skills, verbal communications, writing ability, empathy, fine motor control, additional emotion, memory, learning and rational thought, as well as more sophisticated problem-solving and survival abilities. (Girdano & Everly, 1986, 23)

For better or worse, an individual's reality can be determined by his or her interpretations. Behavior can be weighted against possible outcomes. Symbolism, goals, motivation, and anticipation become parts of the functioning human being. Unfortunately, our interpretations often distort reality, making our lives more difficult than they need be.

Human beings also are gifted with a more highly developed **limbic system** or midbrain, which is part of the of the subcortex. This further removes us from a simple stimulus-response relationship to the world around us. Among other things, the limbic system attaches feelings to pieces of information in the cerebral cortex. These feelings may include fear, anxiety, anger, joy, or pleasure. Thus, a continual interplay takes place between awareness and feeling as the cerebral cortex and limbic system exchange messages.

The **reticular activating system** (RAS) is a two-way pathway of nerve cells or neurons extending from the spinal cord up through the lower brain centers and midbrain to the cerebral cortex. Its main function is to transmit messages and impulses among different parts of the brain. These messages may be specific or general. For example, the perception of an unusual sound is transmitted via the RAS to various lower-brain and midbrain points, and this results in general attentiveness arousal. Even before the cortex appraises the situation, the limbic system may produce a feeling of fear, and the hypothalamus, which regulates various bodily processes, may send messages to the body to prepare for action. This may include tensing muscles and increasing blood flow to the limbs.

An important feature of the RAS is that when it is turned on too frequently at too high a level, it will stay aroused. It essentially says, "If you're going to ask me to turn on like this so often, I'll simply stay turned on continuously." Continuous arousal throughout the body can contribute to such stress-induced ailments as hypertension and insomnia. Recent studies by Candace Pert (Dienstfrey, 1991; Neimark, 1997; Pert, 1997) suggest that emotions might emerge not just from this portion of the brain, but from peptides circulating throughout the body.

A key link in the stress response is the **hypothalamus,** which is a virtual dynamo of potency, even though only the size of a pea. When a stress trigger enters the brain through either the conscious or unconscious appraisal pathway, the hypothalamus is stimulated. Despite its small size, it is the control center regulating both the stress response and the relaxation response.

As shown in Figure 4-4, the hypothalamus activates the body through two avenues, the sympathetic nervous system and the endocrine system.

The Autonomic Nervous System

The nervous system is divided into two main parts: the **central nervous system (CNS),** made up of the brain and the spinal cord, and the **peripheral nervous system (PNS).** The PNS consists of the **somatic network,** a series of pathways through which sensory messages are sent back and forth between the brain and the body's five senses; and the **autonomic nervous system (ANS),** which regulates such internal processes as digestion, temperature regulation, respiration, and circulation. These visceral processes normally occur automatically, without conscious thought or intent, although research during the past quarter-century strongly suggests that we have much more ability to influence activities of the autonomic nervous system than once thought, including, for example, heart rate, blood pressure, skin temperature, and gastric secretion. As Kenneth Pelletier has stated, "This discovery is one of the most profound discoveries of contemporary medicine, with far-reaching implications for the future of holistic, preventive health care" (1977, 54).

The autonomic nervous system, in turn, is divided into two parts, the **sympathetic nervous system,** through which arousal (the stress response) occurs; and the **parasympathetic nervous system,** through which quieting (the relaxation response) occurs. Later, we will examine the parasympathetic nervous system. Here, we will briefly describe the role of the sympathetic nervous system in the stress response.

When Blanca Hernandez decides it is time to check the mail outside her student apartment, she activates the **voluntary nervous system,** which controls striate, voluntary muscles throughout the body, controlling posture and movement. As she leaves her apartment, she is startled by an unfamiliar young man who suddenly appears from around the corner. Here, she activates her sympathetic nervous system, her body immediately aroused as it prepares for fight or flight.

When a stressor stimulates the brain, the sympathetic nervous system sends neurological messages to glands, organs, and tissues to arouse, to prepare for action. Our bodies cannot know what the stressor is and whether a physical reaction indeed is called for. It simply does what it is told by the sympathetic nervous system: Prepare to react, to defend by fighting or fleeing. One important unit in this activation is the **adrenal medulla.**

The adrenal glands are located just above the kidneys and are divided into two distinct parts—the adrenal medulla (inner part) and the **adrenal cortex** (larger, outer part). The medulla is stimulated during stress by the sympathetic nervous system. When this happens, the medulla secretes into the bloodstream two main hormones, adrenaline or **epinephrine** and **noradrenaline** or **norepinephrine,** which together comprise the **catecholamines.**

Adrenaline acts on the liver, which sends more glucose into the bloodstream, ensuring a quick source of energy. Adrenaline also increases carbohydrate metabolism, dilates arteries and capillaries throughout the body, accelerates heart rate, increases the amount of blood

Figure 4-4

The Stress Response

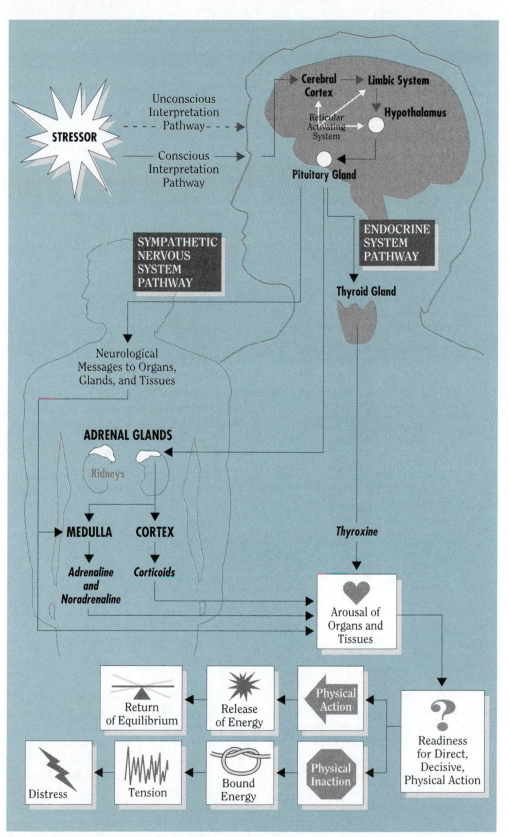

Stress and Surgical Complications

The stress response can affect the mind and body in unexpected ways. One is the risk of surgical complications.

Physicians are aware that some surgical patients recover quickly and completely, while others suffer complications. Recent evidence suggests a key factor influencing chances of complications is stress of the patient (Linn, Linn, & Klimas, 1988).

Researchers at the Miami Veterans Administration (VA) Medical Center studied 24 men, average age 59, undergoing elective hernia repair. A control group with the same average age and medical history also was followed.

Stress was measured in two ways. One was a questionnaire about recent stressful events. The second was a physical measure: reactivity of blood pressure to putting one's hand in cold water (known as the cold pressor test).

Those patients who had a high response to the cold pressor test ("hot reactors") experienced more complications after surgery than did "cold reactors." Although these complications were relatively minor, they did result in a longer average hospital stay and in more medication.

Those patients who had both high life-event stress and high reactivity used three times more medication after surgery than any other group.

The researchers also cited other studies suggesting that immune function and risk of postoperative infection also are affected by stress. And one Ohio State study suggests that perhaps reduction of stress can enhance immune function. Relaxation training three times a week for a month improved immune function among nursing home residents, compared with a control group who received only social contact or no intervention.

The authors of the VA study suggest it might be worthwhile for surgeons to do all they can to allay patients' presurgical anxiety and fears, even in routine surgery such as hernia repair. This view is certainly consistent with the American College of Surgeons, who some years ago recognized that the emotional state of the patient was an important consideration when they concluded that an optimistic octogenarian was a better surgical risk than a pessimistic younger patient.

sent out by the heart (stroke volume), elevates body temperature, and speeds up respiration. At the same time, noradrenaline works with adrenaline in circulating free fatty acids, while also raising blood pressure and constricting certain blood vessels in the body.

The Endocrine System

Simultaneously, a part of the **endocrine** (or hormone) **system** is turned on to work in tandem with the sympathetic nervous system. When the cerebral cortex detects a threat, it sends a message through the reticular activating system to the hypothalamus. A tiny organ at the base of the brain, the hypothalamus controls the body's response to threat.

One of the ways it does so is by activating the sympathetic nervous system, which we have just described. The second is by sending a chemical message through a small network of blood vessels to the **pituitary gland,** which is located nearby. The pituitary in turn sends two chemicals into the bloodstream. One, **thyrotropic hormone** (TTH), is designed to activate the **thyroid gland** when it reaches that destination. The thyroid, in turn, secretes **thy-**

Outline of Key Players in the Stress Response

The Nervous System
Central Nervous System
    Brain
        Cerebral Cortex
        Limbic System
        Visceral System
        Reticular Activating System
    Spinal Cord
Peripheral Nervous System
    Somatic Network
    Autonomic Nervous System
        Sympathetic Nervous System
        Parasympathetic Nervous System
The Endocrine System
    Pituitary Gland
    Adrenal Gland
        Cortex
        Medulla
    Thyroid Gland

---

roxine into the bloodstream. Thyroxine increases the rate at which the body consumes fuel. During the stress response, thyroxine speeds up metabolism in tissues and cells. Thyroxine also seems to make the body more sensitive and responsive to adrenaline.

The pituitary gland at the same time secretes **adrenocorticotropic hormone (ACTH),** which stimulates the outer part of the adrenal gland, the adrenal cortex. It is interesting to note that as production of TTH and ACTH increases, production of sex hormones decreases. This probably accounts for the loss of interest in sex during stressful periods.

The adrenal cortex, in turn, secretes another important hormone, **glucocorticoids,** which stimulate the liver to produce more blood sugar. More fats and proteins also are released into the blood for more energy. Release of too much protein for energy can reduce protein normally available for construction of white blood cells and other antibodies, thereby weakening the body's immune system over the long run. Release of too much fat can promote atherosclerosis, the buildup of plaque in arteries of the brain and heart.

Mineral corticoids, primarily *aldosterone,* are the other products of the adrenal cortex. This hormone, in turn, helps to dissipate heat and water generated by increased metabolism, as well as to retain water and rise blood pressure and blood salinity through retention of sodium (salt). It also is a vital link in the body's mobilization of the immune response to fight infection.

The sympathetic nervous system and the endocrine system are at the core of the stress response. But three other systems are involved, activated through these two systems. These are the cardiovascular, immune, and muscular-skeletal systems.

The Cardiovascular System

As members of the Brazilian and French soccer teams entered the final moments before their 1998 World Cup championship game in Paris, it is likely their cardiovascular systems were in a zone of high arousal. This arousal, if not too great, turned into positive stress, helping to prepare them for peak performance.

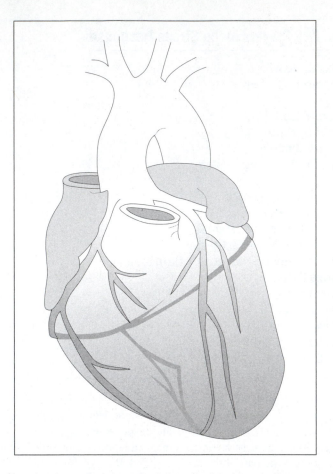

The heart is only about the size of a large fist but is actually a complex, intricate organ. It is at once a pump (the myocardium), a network of plumbing (coronary arteries and valves), an electrical system, and a sac (the pericardium). This complex system adapts in a host of ways to stressful situations calling for readiness for physical action.

In response to an "alert" message from the hypothalamus, the pituitary gland releases a number of hormones, some of which were just described. Others include **oxytocin** and **vasopressin,** which combine to constrict blood-vessel walls. Vasopressin also increases blood volume through action of the kidneys. Simultaneously, more sodium is retained in the blood. As a result of these combined, blood pressure increases. In order to pump more blood out to the body, the rate of heartbeat increases, as does output per beat, in response to electrical and hormonal messages originating in the brain.

In the box "Emotions and Heartbeats" on page 90, you can read about recent detailed studies of the ways emotions influence heart rhythm and other aspects of cardiovascular functioning. This is representative of a growing number of studies on the heart as a source of energy and even emotion (McCraty et al., 1995; Russek & Schwartz, 1996; Thompson, 1997; Watkins, 1997). What we have described are positive, helpful changes in the cardiovascular system. But in some persons changes can be harmful, even with deadly consequences. In Chapter 7, you will read more about ways stress can contribute to cardiovascular disorders.

The Immune System

The **immune system** is the body's surveillance system, guarding against allergens, infection, cancer, viruses, and bacteria. This protection occurs through two immunologic reactions. The first, *humoral immunity,* is mediated by B lymphocytes. When stimulated by antigens, B lymphocytes differentiate into several cells that produce antibodies that in turn flow through the bloodstream to the needed site. The second reaction is *cell immunity,* a slower-acting process. When T lymphocytes receive the message from the thymus gland that a threatening invader is present, they secrete chemicals that kill unwanted cells and aid in *phagocytosis,* a process through which invading cells are ingested.

A number of other cells and elements of the bloodstream, which we need not explain here, also are involved in the immune response, including monocytes, natural killer cells, mast cells, polymorphonuclear leukocytes, macrophages, and interferon (Borysenko, 1987; Borysenko & Borysenko, 1983; Jemmott & Locke, 1984; Kiecolt-Glaser & Glaser, 1988; Pelletier, 1994; Pelletier & Herzing, 1988; Taylor, 1986).

Immunocompetence refers to the body's ability to defend against a microbial invader. Taylor has noted that immunocompetence occurs through a number of complementary processes.

> Measures of immunological functioning are manifold and include the ability of lymphocytes to kill invading cells (lymphocyte cytotoxicity), the ability of lymphocytes to reproduce when stimulated artificially by a chemical (mitogen), the ability of the lymphocytes to produce antibodies, the ratio of suppressor and helper T cells, the ability of the white cells to ingest foreign particles (phagocytotic activity), and others. (1986, 197)

A considerable and growing body of research shows that stress can suppress the immune response, thereby increasing chances of immune-related illness (Borysenko & Borysenko, 1983; Dantzer and Kelley, 1989; Jemmott & Locke, 1984; Kiecolt-Glaser & Glaser, 1988; Leclere & Weryha, 1989; Pelletier & Herzing, 1988; Rogers, Dubey, & Reich, 1979.) Animal research conclusively demonstrates that experimentally manipulated stressors can reduce immunological functioning and increase susceptibility to disorders influenced by the immune system. Animal studies have shown, for example, that lymphocytes are suppressed by exposure to loud noise (Monjan & Collector, 1977), infant-mother separation (Laudenslager, Reite, & Harbeck, 1982), separation from peers (Reite, Harbeck, & Hoffman, 1981), and electric shock (Keller et al., 1981).

Studies of human populations under stress also are revealing. Infectious diseases have been shown to increase among children when their families are exposed to stressful events (Hinkle, 1974). Stressful events among adults have been linked to immune-related disorders such as the common cold, trench mouth, herpes recurrences, and mononucleosis (Jemmott & Locke, 1984). Levy (1989) found an association between stressful life events and natural killer (NK) cells. The lower the NK count, the more the sick days and the greater the illness. Apollo and Skylab astronauts were shown to have immunological deficiencies following their return to earth (Kimzey, 1975; Leach & Rambaut, 1974). Men and women in unhappy marriages have been shown to have weakened immune systems (Kiecolt-Glaser & Glaser, 1988). A recent study showed that among newlyweds, all of whom reported high marital satisfaction, those who displayed more negative and hostile behavior over a 24-hour period also showed lowering of their immune functions during this period (Kiecolt-Glaser et al., 1993).

Naturally occurring severe stressors also have been shown to depress immune strength. These include loss of spouse (Bartrop et al., 1977; Schleifer et al., 1979), marital separation among women (*American Health,* 1986), recovery from heart attacks (*Psychology Today,* 1986), flight training among young Italian Air Force pilots (Biselli et al., 1993), first-time parachuting (Schedlowski et al., 1993), and student examinations (Jemmott & Locke, 1984). In a recent study by Norman (1989), for example, undergraduate students' IgA levels (an indicator of immune response in the saliva) were measured one month

Emotions and Heartbeats

IHM (Institute of HeartMath) researchers measure the effects of different mental and emotional states on the heart's electrical system (ECG), brain waves (EEG), blood pressure, respiration, and muscle tension. In addition, we are correlating these physiological measurements with biochemical changes in the immune and hormonal systems. Individuals from many walks of life—students, housewives, laborers, office workers, as well as individuals skilled in mental and emotional self-management—have been tested in our laboratory. When participants experienced feelings of sincere love, care or appreciation, a corresponding coherence pattern appeared in the frequency spectrum of their ECG (electrocardiogram).

To gather this information, ECG data is analyzed through a process called Fourier Transforms to determine the frequency content of the ECG. Due to the increasing levels of stress in society today, most people's ECG frequency spectrum is scattered and incoherent, but it can become dramatically ordered and coherent when a person experiences deep feelings such as love, care, or appreciation. In contrast, individuals experiencing negative emotions such as anger, fear, worry, or frustration show incoherent patterns in their ECG frequency spectrum.

The time intervals between heartbeats are always changing. Heart rate variability (HRV) is a measurement of these beat-to-beat changes in heart rate. These changes are influenced by almost any stimulus the brain and mind process, such as emotions, thoughts, sound light, etc. Therefore, HRV can be used as an indicator of mental/emotional state changes. Analysis of HRV is used to measure the balance between the sympathetic nervous system, which speeds up the heart, and the parasympathetic nervous system, which slows down the heart. When the nervous system is functioning in balance and harmony, it "entrains" and creates HRV patterns similar to the bottom graph. Entrainment occurs when two or more oscillating systems phase-lock and work at maximum efficiency.

IHM research has shown that as people transform their negative mental/emotional states to positive states, their HRV can become more ordered, resulting in more harmony and efficiency in the cardiovascular system.

before a regularly scheduled examination week. They were retested during the exam week. Sure enough, the IgA count was lower during exam time than one month before. And the higher the test-related anxiety, the lower the IgA. Perhaps this explains why so many students "catch" colds and flu during exam time.

Emotions also have been linked with immunocompetence. For example, depression has been shown to suppress lymphocyte and T cell activity (Kronfol et al., 1983; Nerozzi et al., 1989; Schleifer et al., 1989; Targum et al., 1989).

On the other hand, laughter induced by a humorous video has been shown to result in proliferation of lymphocytes and natural killer-cell activity (Berk, 1989). Epinephrine levels decreased even before the videotapes were shown, suggesting that even the anticipation of a good time can help reduce stress level and enhance immunocompetence. Berk states, "The effect of anticipation of the event becomes as real for the individual as the

Figure 4-5

Heart Rate Variability Patterns

The heart rate variability pattern of frustration (top) is characterized by its random, jerky pattern. Deep sincere feeling states like appreciation (bottom) can result in ordered HRV patterns, generally associated with efficient cardiovascular function.

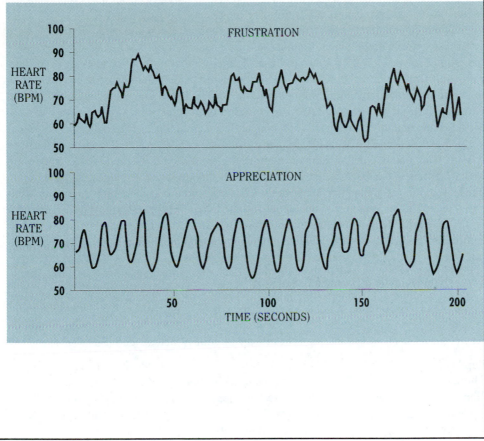
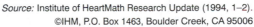

Source: Institute of HeartMath Research Update (1994, 1–2).
©IHM, P.O. Box 1463, Boulder Creek, CA 95006

event itself." He points out that nervous or uncomfortable laughter that does not necessarily reflect good feelings may not have the same effect.

How does stress depress immunocompetence? This question is still under investigation. Suspicion is strong among experts that the catecholamines (epinephrine and norepinephrine) and corticosteroids stimulated during the stress response may have anti-inflammatory and immunosuppressive effects. Stress might also suppress endorphins.

Although mediating pathways are not entirely clear at this point, evidence mounts that stress can sometimes suppress the immune system, heightening chances of stress-induced physical disorders. Psychoneuroimmunology is a new hybrid, interdisciplinary field of scientific study of these complex mind-body linkages (for reviews of research in this field, see, for example, Booth, 1996; Borysenko & Borysenko, 1983; Lloyd, 1996; and Pelletier & Herzing, 1988).

The Muscular-Skeletal System

Another system allowing us to function as human animals (and higher-level beings) is the integrated network of bones and muscles known as the **muscular-skeletal system.** This system enables us to stand, sit, walk, run—to do everything we do with our bodies.

Our muscles are always aroused to some degree, even when sleeping. When preparing for action, we activate muscles throughout our bodies, including skeletal muscles, which control movement and posture. When feeling threatened or challenged, these muscles prepare for action—and take action in response to messages from the cerebral cortex, as when running from danger or lifting something very heavy off a child.

However, positive, helpful responses of the muscles can and often do give way to several stress-related problems. One of these is chronic muscle tension, sometimes called **bracing** (Brown, 1977), when arousal is no longer temporary but becomes chronic. This can result from a state of constant vigilance, causing back pain, tension headaches, neck or shoulder pain, or even lingering pain in the arm or hand. These muscles can become chronically tight and can even be in spasm. Sometimes the joints get involved as well. Muscles tug at tendons, ligaments, and bones. Bones and joints can go out of proper alignment. Posture—even one's appearance to others—can be affected. Tics, involuntary spasms, can also occur. The temporomandibular joint (TMJ), connecting the upper and lower jawbones, can become tense or malaligned, creating severe pain in the face, neck, head, and even throughout the upper body. The most common source of TMJ pain is bruxism—clenching or grinding of the teeth (Tasner, 1986). Fortunately, the **TMJ syndrome** is treatable with dentally prescribed mouth splints, as well as through relaxation training. Entire disciplines of massage and body carriage have been developed to assist in correcting this and other stress-induced muscular-skeletal problems.

Readiness for Physical Action

Through activation of the systems just described, beginning with the sympathetic nervous system and endocrine systems, the body is prepared for direct, decisive, physical action. Key observable or measurable signs of this preparedness include the following:

Pupils dilate	Skin cools	Metabolism speeds up
Throat tightens	Brain waves become shorter	Cholesterol remains in
Neck, upper back, and	Blood pressure rises	bloodstream longer
shoulders tighten	Blood shifts from	Arteries and capillaries
Breathing quickens and	abdomen to limbs	constrict
becomes shallow	More glucose enters the	
Heart pumps faster	bloodstream	
Muscles and legs become	More white blood cells	
taut, especially in front	enter the bloodstream	

As Pelletier notes (1977), many of these internal changes have entered our common language.

Trembling with fear	Clammy hands	A knot in my stomach
A lump in my throat	Chills ran up and down my	A racing heart
Cold feet	spine	Butterflies inside

Part of effective stress management is learning to monitor and recognize these and other warning signs of distress, especially when they become chronic.

Through these intricate pathways, then, the body is prepared for direct, decisive, physical action. In an extremely threatening situation, this is the maxi fight-or-flight

Channelling the stress response toward positive stress is vital to peak performance.

response. In smaller ways, these changes occur constantly, resulting in chronic excitation of the mini stress response.

When physical action occurs, this readiness—this pent-up energy—is released. At one time in human history, such physical activity was constant, not necessarily at the moment of arousal, but certainly through the day as people worked, moved about, and played. In the past, too, more stress triggers were physical threats in which a physical stress response was appropriate.

However, three important changes have occurred. First, the faster pace of life in this century has increased the number of stressors we face. Second, most stressors today are psychological and social, rather than physical. Third, we have become more sedentary, resulting in less release of energy buildup. Hence, an increase occurs in the *need* for physical action to release energy and tension at the very time physical action no longer is included as a natural part of most of our daily lives. Thus, we find the buildup of **bound energy** and the rise of mental and physical tension. Stress-related disturbances and diseases often result.

On the other hand, the stress response can be useful, aiding us in responding to emergencies, in reaching higher levels of performance, in meeting deadlines, and more. Without the stress response, positive stress would be unavailable.

The Role of Behavior

At the beginning of this chapter, we emphasized that body, mind, and behavior are all interconnected. Yet thus far we have said little about the **role of behavior.** What part does it play? As we have defined stress, behavior is not part of the stress response itself. Yet it is closely related in four ways:

1.   Mental and physical arousal often are expressed in behavior.
2.   Behavior such as exercise and self-disclosure, for example, can help protect against out-of- control stress responses.
3.   Behavior is used to cope or interact with stress triggers.
4.   Behavior is used to react to distress, either constructively or destructively.

Thoughts and feelings also are related to the stress response because emotional and intellectual stress are closely interrelated with physical stress. The interplay of these forms of stress will be discussed in more detail later. Here, it is sufficient to recognize that thoughts and feelings may either trigger or reflect physical stress. However, thoughts and feelings do not exist apart from physical stress. This is important because altering the physical basis of stress through relaxation or exercise can alter troubling thoughts and feelings.

Stress and Adaptation

The General Adaptation Syndrome

Hans Selye (1974) many years ago identified a universal pattern of physical stress known as the **general adaptation syndrome (GAS),** which helps us understand how the body handles stress over time and how physical stress sometimes gives way to distress. The GAS also is useful in explaining the role of adaptation in managing stress effectively.

Selye maintains we go through three phases as we seek to handle stress, whatever the specific stressor and location in the body: alarm reaction, sustained resistance, and exhaustion.

These phases, shown in Figure 4-6, can be seen most easily in the body's reaction to physical trauma, such as fire, cold, or an accident. But Selye suggested that the same sequence is likely as you react to personal and social situations in daily life, such as a verbal attack, prolonged isolation, or chronic overload. The next box (on page 96) shows how the body responds during each stage of the GAS.

During the **alarm reaction** the body is immediately prepared for direct, decisive physical action (the fight-or-flight response), largely through instantaneous activation of the sympathetic nervous system, sometimes before the person is even aware of the stressor. Large amounts of glucose and oxygen are supplied to organs most active in warding off danger, such as the heart, the brain, and the skeletal muscles. The curving line in Figure 4-6 falls below normal stress level because the body often is temporarily set back as it fights to restore internal balance.

Figure 4-6

The General Adaptation Syndrome

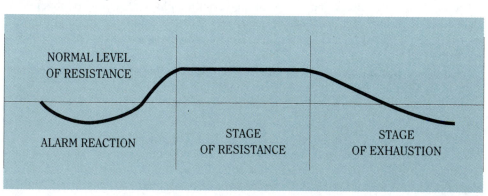

NORMAL LEVEL
OF RESISTANCE

ALARM REACTION   STAGE
                        OF RESISTANCE

STAGE
OF EXHAUSTION

Source: Selye (1974, 27)

As the body mobilizes additional resources, largely through arousal of the stress hormones, the **stage of resistance** ensues. The body and mind cope with the difficulty in a sustained way, usually quite effectively. If the stressor is too intense for too long, however, the body's adaptive reserves begin to become depleted, at which time the **stage of exhaustion** begins. At this stage, wear and tear is progressive. Stress becomes distress, and illness is likely. The type of illness will be determined by particular weaknesses in the individual's organ systems.

As noted, Selye demonstrated with laboratory rats that this sequence of adaptation occurs irrespective of the specific stressor, such as electric shock, cold, forced muscular work, drugs, or injections. He suggested the same is true of humans. This discovery and Selye's resulting general adaptation syndrome have important implications for understanding how humans adapt to stress.

How Humans Adapt to Stress

A remarkable feature of human beings is the ability to adapt—both to changing external circumstances and to internal stress levels. As you move from one place to another, change jobs, meet and lose friends, or confront challenges in the classroom or on the athletic field, you may experience intense stress. Sometimes you wonder if you will make it. Yet you do. And you will again—because you adapt to stressors and to stress. You get used to new situations.

Some years ago, selected inmates from Oregon State Prison participated in Project Newgate, a college education program. They attended classes inside the prison until a few months before parole or discharge. Their last several months as prisoners were spent at a halfway house at the University of Oregon campus. From the prison to the campus, the increase in stimulation level was enormous. Sometimes inmates found themselves overwhelmed by sounds, sights, choices, competition, dates, and the availability of alcohol and drugs. A few inmate-students were so overwhelmed that they broke down, broke a rule, or simply asked to be returned to the "joint." Yet most adapted. Their zone of positive stress shifted upward. They learned to live with the higher stimulation of campus life. Their stress levels went down.

In track and field, swimming, and other sports, coaches deliberately control their athletes' adaptation to stress. The usual training program calls for practicing at a certain speed and distance for a designated period of time. During the first few days at a certain level of output, performance goes down while fatigue increases. After a few days, the athlete adapts to the new level of effort. The workouts, initially so demanding, become relatively easy within two or three weeks. In a systematic fashion, still more speed and distance are added until limits are reached. In this incremental manner, the athlete progresses to the point where maximum possible performance is attained.

Performance limits may be set by mental barriers, by effort, or by breakdown in muscles, joints, or tendons. The athlete must adapt carefully to increasing levels of stress, while remaining just below the point of distress—that fine edge beyond which one goes into injury, physical fatigue, or mental exhaustion.

You also have this capability to adapt, to adjust to different stresses as you take on new challenges. **Adaptation to stress** is important to achieve higher levels of self-fulfillment in the various facets of your life. Loehr (1993) calls this "toughness training for life."

An important word of caution is needed, however. We sometimes delude ourselves into believing we are adapting within our zone of positive stress. We become *comfortable* with a highly demanding job, fast pace of life, or troubled marriage, for example. We assume we are adjusting within our own tolerance limits and that our health will not be adversely affected. Often, however, this apparent adjustment is not successful adaptation at

> See Application Exercise 4-1 to write about personal experiences with two types of adaptation to stress.

Organismic Responses to Stressors According to the GAS Stages

Stage 1: Alarm Reaction
Physiologic response
Enlargement of adrenal cortex
Enlargement of the lymphatic system
Increase in hormone levels, such as epinephrine, leading to high physiological arousal
Behavioral response
Increased sensitivity to changes in stressor intensity
Increased susceptibility to illness
If Stage 1 is prolonged, the organism moves into Stage 2.

Stage 2: Resistance
Physiologic response
Shrinkage of adrenal cortex
Lymph nodes return to normal size
High hormone levels continue
The parasympathetic branch of the autonomic system attempts to counteract the high arousal
Behavioral response
Sensitivity to stress is increased
Individual attempts to endure the stressor and resist further debilitating effects
If the organism continues to be exposed to intense stress, hormonal depletion may ensue, leading to Stage 3.

Stage 3: Exhaustion
Physiologic response
Lymphatic structures become enlarged or dysfunctional, or both.
Hormone levels are further increased or maintained at high levels.
Adaptive hormones are depleted.
Behavioral response
Resistance to stressors (including the original one) is reduced.
The individual often becomes depressed.
The individual becomes physically ill and may die if the severe stress continues.

Source: Kaplan, Sallis, & Patterson (1993, 107)

all. Rather, we continue quite unaware for a lengthy period in Selye's stage of resistance without returning to our optimum stress level.

In time, our bodies give way in one form or another, depending on the individual. It may be chronic colds, hypertension, a skin disorder, migraines, or even a sudden heart attack. All reflect wear and tear as we enter the stage of physical exhaustion.

Selye maintains that our deep adaptive reserves are limited and can be used up. Disharmony exacts a toll in the long run. Premature aging is the ultimate result.

In brief, adaptation to stress does not mean simply becoming comfortable with a stressor or set of stressors. True adaptation means adjustment of your spirit and your body to those circumstances within the limits of your unique zone of positive stress. What is comfortable may not be healthy over the long run.

THE RELAXATION RESPONSE AND HOMEOSTASIS

The human organism, like other animals, possesses a strong and persistent drive toward equilibrium or **homeostasis.** Through the parasympathetic nervous system, the body is able to return itself to a more normal level of arousal.

As the pioneer in study of the relaxation response, Herbert Benson has noted it was Hess during the 1930s and 1940s who found that by stimulating specific brain tissues of laboratory animals, it was possible to create a response opposite to the stress response. He called this "a protective mechanism against overstress" (Benson, 1993). Benson said, "This response was characterized by a state of tranquility, relaxed muscles, and decreased blood pressure and breathing rate" (1993).

In his widely acclaimed book, *The Relaxation Response,* Benson points out it makes imminent sense that such a response should exist as a countervailing influence to the stress response.

> If the fight-or-flight response resides within animals and humans, is there an innate physiologic response that is dramatically different? The answer is yes. Each of us possesses a natural and innate protective mechanism against "overstress," which allows us to turn off harmful bodily effects, to counter the effects of the fight-or-flight response. This response against "overstress" brings on bodily changes that decrease heart rate, lower metabolism, decrease the rate of breathing, and bring the body back into what is probably a healthier balance. That is the Relaxation Response. (1975, 18)

More recently, Benson and Stuart noted:

> The relaxation response is an inborn set of physiological changes that offset those of the fight-or-flight response. These changes are coordinated: they occur together in an integrated fashion. (1992)

Compare the changes of the **relaxation response** to those of the **fight-or-flight response:**

	Physiology of the Fight-or-Flight Response	Physiology of the Relaxation Response
Metabolism	Increases	Decreases
Heart Rate	Increases	Decreases
Blood Pressure	Increases	Decreases
Breathing Rate	Increases	Decreases
Muscle Tension	Increases	Decreases

The stress response and the relaxation response are both natural, involuntary responses. Both also can be induced through deliberate effort. This is another illustration of how the mind can play either harmful or helpful roles in human experience.

Figure 4-7

Metabolism During Sleep and the Relaxation Response

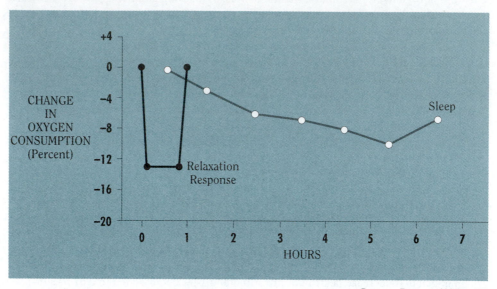

Source: Benson (1975, 65)

*The relaxation response
is quieting of mind and
body.*

As shown in Figure 4-7, Benson's research suggests deeper rest may occur during deliberately induced deep relaxation than during sleep, as measured by decreases in oxygen use.

In short, activity needs to be alternated with rest, arousal with relaxation, excitation with quiet. Research shows that 15 to 20 minutes set aside once or twice each day for **deep relaxation,** which takes bodily processes into a deeper quiet than the normal equilibrium level of daily living, can prove effective for both coping with distress already present and for preventing stress buildup from occurring in the first place. Later chapters will present a number of techniques for releasing the relaxation response.

It is important here to note that popular notions of relaxation may be quite inaccurate. A nonwork activity may be pleasant but not necessarily relaxing in the sense that physical and mental quieting occur. In fact, the exact opposite may ensue. The familiar coffee break may elevate the stress response through the stimulating effect of caffeine. A round of golf may arouse competitive urges, rather than quiet the hypothalamus, the pituitary gland, the adrenal cortex, and the sympathetic nervous system. The same may happen with a do-it-yourself home project. The activity may be beneficial by being a diversion but may not be *relaxing*. Certainly, it does not produce deep relaxation, so vital to counteracting chronic arousal of the stress response. In short, diversion and recreation may not be true relaxation.

See Application Exercise 4-2 for a simple technique for eliciting the relaxation response.

The stress response, which we examined in some detail earlier in the chapter, is a positive resource in the right amounts and at the right times. As Blair Justice states, "Our attitudes . . . toward the very subject of stress can influence our reactions when we are in trying situations. Our physiological responses will be considerably less intense if we see stress as an inevitable part of life and a challenge rather than something that is awful and must be avoided" (1987, 60). In the next chapter, we will examine a variety of symptoms that develop when stress is no longer helpful but instead turns into distress.

See Application Exercise 4-3 for assistance in explaining the stress response and the relaxation response to someone you know.

References

American Health (1986). Women's health: More sniffles in splitsville, 96, 98.

Asterita, M. F. (1985). *The physiology of stress.* New York: Human Sciences Press.

Bartrop, R. W., Lockhurst, E., Lazarus, L., Kiloh, L. G., & Penny, R. (1977). Depressed lymphocyte function after bereavement. *Lancet, 1,* 834–836.

Benson, H. (1975). *The relaxation response.* New York: William Morrow.

Benson, H. (1993). The relaxation response, in Goleman, D., & Gurin, J., *Mind/body medicine.* Yonkers: Consumer Reports Books, 233–257.

Benson, H., & Stuart, E. M. (1992). *The wellness book.* New York: Birch Lane Press.

Berk, L. (1989). Laughter and immunity. *Advances, 6,* 5.

Biselli, R., et al. (1993). Influence of stress on lymphocyte subset distribution—a flow cytometric study in young student pilots. *Aviation Space and Environmental Medicine, 64,* 116–120.

Booth, R. (1996). Contrary to Lloyd, the animating idea of psychoneuroimmunology has *not* lost its heuristic value. *Advances, 12,* 12–16.

Borysenko, J. (1987). *Minding the body, mending the mind.* New York: Bantam Books.

Borysenko, J., & Borysenko, M. (1983). On psychoneuroimmunology: How the mind influences health and disease . . . and how to make the influence beneficial. *Executive Health, 19,* 1–7.

Brown, B. (1977). *New mind, new body.* New York: Harper & Row.

Cousins, N. (1979). *Anatomy of an illness.* New York: W. W. Norton.

Cousins, N. (1989). Belief becomes biology. *Advances, 6:3,* 20–29.

Dantzer, R., & Kelley, K. W. (1989). Stress and immunity: An integrated view of relationships between the brain and the immune system. *Life Sciences, 44,* 1995–2008.

Dienstfrey, H. (1991). *Where the mind meets the body.* New York: HarperCollins.

Dossey, L. (1991). *Meaning and medicine.* New York: Bantam.

Eliot, R. S. (1994). *From stress to strength.* New York: Bantam Books.

Foss, L. (1996). Advancing psychosocial health education: A review of the Pew-Fetzer Report. *Advances, 12,* 43–50.

Girdano, D. A., & Everly, G. S., Jr. (1986). *Controlling stress and tension: A holistic approach* (2nd ed.). Englewood Cliffs: Prentice-Hall.

Hinkle, L. E., Jr. (1974). The effects of exposure to culture change, social change and changes in interpersonal relationships to health. In B. S. Dohrenwend & B. P. Dohrenwend (Eds.), *Stressful life events: Their nature and effects.* New York: John Wiley and Sons, 192–204.

Institute of HeartMath (1994). *Newsletter of the Institute of HeartMath.* Boulder Creek, CA.

Jemmott, J. B., III, & Locke, S. E. (1984). Psychological factors, immunologic mediation, and human susceptibility to infectious diseases: How much do we know? *Psychological Bulletin, 95,* 78–108.

Justice, B. (1987). *Who gets sick: Thinking and health.* Houston: Peak Press.

Kaplan, R. M., Sallis, J. F., & Patterson, T. L. (1993). *Health and human behavior.* New York: McGraw-Hill.

Keller, S. R., Weiss, J. M., Schleifer, S. J., Miller, N. E., & Stein, M. (1981). Suppression of immunity by stress: Effect of a graded series of stressors on lymphocyte stimulation in the rat. *Science, 213,* 1397–1400.

Kiecolt-Glaser, J. K., & Glaser, R. (1988). Psychological influences on immunity. *American Psychologist, 43,* 892–898.

Kiecolt-Glaser, J. K., et al. (1993). Negative behavior during marital conflict is associated with immunological down-regulation. *Psychosomatic Medicine, 55,* 395–409.

Kimzey, S. L. (1975). The effects of extended spaceflight on hematologic and immunologic systems. *Journal of the American Medical Women's Association, 30,* 218–232.

Kronfol, Z., Silva, J., Greden, J., Dembinski, S., Gardner, R., & Carroll, B. (1983). Impaired lymphocyte function in depressive illness. *Life Sciences, 33,* 241–247.

Laudenslager, M. L., Reite, M., & Harbeck, R. J. (1982). Suppressed immune response in infant monkeys associated with maternal separation. *Behavior and Neural Biology, 36,* 568–570.

Leach, C. S., & Rambaut, P. C. (1974). Biochemical responses of the Skylab crewmen. *Proceedings of the Skylab Life Sciences Symposium, 2,* 427–454.

Leclere, J., & Weryha, G. (1989). Stress and auto-immune endocrine diseases. *Hormone Research, 31,* 90–93.

Levy, S. M. (1989). Age, stress, and immunity. *Advances, 6,* 7.

Linn, B. S., Linn, M. W., & Klimas, N. G. (1988). Effects of stress on surgical outcome. *Psychosomatic Medicine, 50,* 230–244.

Lloyd, R. (1996).New directions in psychoneuroimmunology: A critique. *Advances, 12,* 5–12.

Loehr, J. E. (1993). *Toughness training for life.* New York: Penguin Books.

Lovallo, W. R. (1997). *Stress and health: Biological and psychological foundations.* Thousand Oaks: Sage Publications.

Lynch, J. J. (1985). *The language of the heart.* New York: McGraw-Hill.

Maslow, A. (1962). *Toward a psychology of being.* New York: Van Nostrand.

McCraty, R., Tiller, W.A., & Atkinson, M. (1995). Head-heart entrainment: A preliminary survey. In: *Integrating the science and art of energy medicine.* Boulder. CO: ISSSEEM.

Monjan, A., & Collector, M. I. (1977). Stress-induced modulation of the immune response. Science, 196, 307–308.

Muller, J. E., et al. (1987). Circadian variation in the frequency of sudden death. *Circulation, 75,* 131.

Murchie, G. (1978). The seven mysteries of life. Boston: Houghton Mifflin.

Neimark, J. (1997). ImPERTinent ideas. *Psychology Today, 30,* 43–45, 72–74.

Nerozzi, D., Santoni, A., Bersani, G., Magnini, A., Bressan, A., Pasini, A., Antonozzi, I., & Frajese, G. (1989). Reduced natural killer cell activity in major depression: Neuroendocrine implications. *Psychoneuroendocrinology, 14,* 295–301.

Norman, J. (1989). Stress and the immune system. Paper presented at Annual Meetings of Pacific Division of American Association for the Advancement of Science, Chico, CA.

Pelletier, K. R. (1977). *Mind as healer, mind as slayer.* New York: Dell.

Pelletier, K. R. (1994). *Sound mind, sound body.* New York: Simon & Schuster.

Pelletier, K. R., & Herzing, D. L. (1988). Psychoneuroimmunology: Toward a mind/body model. *Advances, 5,* 27–56.

Pert, C. (1997). *Molecules of emotion.* New York: Scribner.

Phillips, D. P., & King, E. W. (1988). Death takes a holiday: Mortality surrounding major social occasions. *Lancet, 2:8613,* 728–732.

Phillips, D. P. (1990). Postponement of death until symbolically meaningful occasions. *Journal of the American Medical Association, 263,* 1947–1951.

Psychology Today (1986). Putting the heart in cardiac care, *18,* 18.

Rabkin, S. W., et al. (1980). Chronobiology of cardiac sudden death in men. *Journal of the American Medical Association, 244:12,* 1357–1358.

Rahe, R. H. (1988). Acute versus chronic psychological reactions to combat. *Military Medicine, 153,* 365–372.

Reite, M., Harbeck, R., & Hoffman, A. (1981). Altered cellular immune response following peer separation. *Life Sciences, 29,* 1133–1136.

Rogers, M. P., Dubey, D., & Reich, P. (1979). The influence of the psyche and the brain on immunity and disease susceptibility: A critical review. *Psychosomatic Research, 7,* 520–526.

Russek, L. G., & Schwartz, G. E. (1996). Energy cardiology: A dynamical energy systems approach for integrating conventional and alternative medicine. *Advances, 13,* 4–23.

Schedlowski, M., et al. (1993). Changes of natural killer cells during acute psychological stress. *Journal of Clinical Immunology, 13,* 119–126.

Schleifer, S. J., Keller, S. E., Bond, R. N., Cohen, J., & Stein, M. (1989). Major depressive disorder and immunity: Role of age, sex, severity and hospitalization. *Archives of General Psychiatry, 46,* 81–87.

Schleifer, S. J., Keller, S. E., McKegney, F. P., & Stein, M. (1979). The influence of stress and other psychosocial factors on human immunity. Paper presented at the American Psychosomatic Society Annual Meetings, Dallas.

Selye, H. (1974). *Stress without distress.* Philadelphia: Lippincott.

Targum, S. D., Marshall, L. E., Fischman, P., & Martin, D. (1989). Lymphocyte subpopulations in depressed elderly women. *Biological Psychiatry, 26,* 581–589.

Tasner, M. (1986). TMJ. *Medical self-care,* Nov.–Dec., 47–50.

Taylor, S. E. (1986). *Health psychology.* New York: Random House.

Thompson, B. (1997). Change of heart. *Natural Health.* Sep./Oct., 97–101, 155–157.

Watkins, A. D. (1997). Medicine and the heart's energy. *Advances, 13,* 70–74.

Application Exercise 4-1

Adaptation to Stress

You read in this chapter that adaptation to stress has two meanings. First, you raise your threshold of distress as your mind and body become accustomed to a given level of arousal or exertion. This is illustrated by the training effect during athletic training. As your body experiences progressively more cardiovascular or muscular demands, your body comes back ready to do that much plus more. The same holds in your life more generally as you become accustomed to a new job, a challenging relationship at work, or a level of academic challenge. At a higher level of effort, your distress diminishes. Second, you learn to adapt to distress. Although the pain or discomfort remains, you learn to live with it, as in a period of loss, extreme financial hardship, or a period of intense and temporary overload.

1. With this in mind, write brief essays describing for yourself each type of adaptation to stress, either past or present.

2. What are the circumstances?

3. What are your mental, physical, and behavioral symptoms of distress as you enter the experience?

4. Do the symptoms diminish as you adapt? Or do you simply become accustomed to the distress? Explain.

Application Exercise 4-2

Breathing Away Tension

As a step toward learning to elicit the relaxation response, try this simple exercise. Practice it once each day for the next week. Be aware of your mind and body quieting during this simple response.

1. Sit or lie in a comfortable position with hands open and legs uncrossed.
2. Be aware of the weight of your entire body on the floor, bed, couch, or chair. Your muscles need not help support your body at all.
3. Softly close your eyes.
4. Focus attention on your nostrils and "see" the air entering each side. Follow its path down into your lungs, "watch" it swirling around, and "observe" it moving back up and out.
5. As it leaves, tell yourself it is carrying away tension, pain, and disease, if present.
6. Continue for three to eight minutes.

Application Exercise 4-3

Explaining the Stress Response and the Relaxation Response

Find a friend, family member, or acquaintance who knows nothing about the stress response or the relaxation response. Better yet, try this with an 8-year-old. See if you can explain the following to him or her:

1. The physiology of the stress response
2. The role of interpretation (self-talk) in the stress response
3. The fight-or-flight response
4. The part played by the pituitary, thyroid, and adrenal glands in the stress response
5. The importance of the parasympathetic and sympathetic nervous systems
6. The contribution of catecholamines to the stress response
7. The physiology of the relaxation response
8. How mind, body, and behavior interact during the stress response and the relaxation response

Which explanations came easily? Which showed you need to deepen your understanding?

Stress is like spice—in the right proportion it enhances the flavor of a dish. Too little produces a bland, dull meal; too much may choke you.

—DONALD TUBESING

How the Stress Experience Varies

Contrasting Stress Zones

Sue had been accustomed to a fast pace of life since childhood. She thrived on challenge and productivity. Difficult work situations seldom threatened her. Rather, she attacked them with vigor and optimism. She did not seek out overload, yet her life seemed full most of the time. In short, she had high stress tolerance. She seldom missed work because of illness. She was productive and quite satisfied with her work and family life.

Fred was awed by Sue's apparent endless ability to tolerate challenge without showing signs of wear and tear. Fred by nature was more slow-going and required more time per work task. He tended to become flustered and ineffective when work piled up. He deliberately let others take on difficult confrontations with clients because he disliked the tension. Fred had considerably lower stress tolerance than Sue and became emotionally and intellectually overloaded at a point where Sue thrived.

In Chapter 1, you read about one important variation in the stress experience: stress (arousal) can be experienced as neutral, positive, or negative (distress). We emphasized that the nature and extent of symptoms are influenced not so much by environmental circumstances themselves as by the person's perception and assessment of these circumstances. Let us assume, for example, that two college students are given an assignment to make a public presentation about their term project to the class. Student one takes this on as an exhilarating challenge—as positive stress. Student two sees this as a terrible threat—a source of potential humiliation. Clearly, the assignment itself does not cause the distress in student two. His distress is produced by his own interpretation of the stressor. In this chapter we will look at other ways individual experiences with stress can vary.

DISTRESS FROM OVERLOAD AND UNDERLOAD

Stressors can be few or numerous with respect to a given time period. Similarly, stress can occur from understimulation or overstimulation, with "under" and "over" varying with the person. Hans Selye (1974) developed a chart, known as the "experience continuum," that illustrates stress shading into distress at either high or low extremes of stimulation. In slightly modified form, the **experience continuum** is shown in Figure 5-1.

This chart shows that the amount of stress can increase or turn into distress at either extreme, overstimulation or understimulation. But even in the middle range of stimulation, the experience line does not touch bottom, since the only time one reaches the point of no stress is death. At all other times, some amount of arousal is experienced.

Let us examine stress and distress at the two extremes of stimulation. A number of laboratory experiments on "sensory deprivation," the extreme of **underload,** show that most people soon begin to experience disorientation, anxiety, depression, or other discomforts when deprived of light, touch, sound, and smell (Goldberger, 1982). One journalist who volunteered for such a study in order to write a story acted confident and pleased immediately after leaving the tank. But toward the end of his interview with the scientist in charge, he said, "I honestly believe if you put a person in there, just kept him and fed him by vein, he would just flat die." He never wrote the story (Tanner, 1976).

In real life, **deprivational stress** arises from many circumstances. For example, understimulation and boredom are common among assembly-line workers. Unfortunately,

Figure 5-1

The Experience Continuum

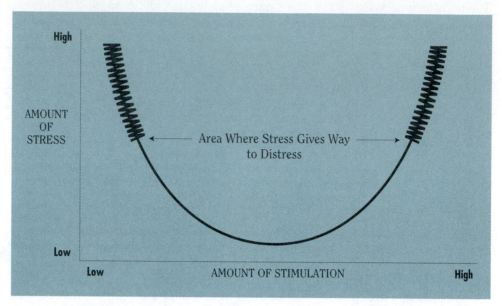

the elderly too often are plagued with sensory deprivation as a result of withdrawal from previous roles and social supports. At the same time, senses of hearing and vision sometimes are dulled. Physical abilities diminish (too often as a result of inactivity, rather than true aging). Human touch is often totally lacking. Prisoners-of-war have been known to break down after only a few days of total isolation. Children living without touch or other forms of attention and affection suffer in physical and emotional development.

Too little stimulation—**sensory deprivation**—can create serious mental and physical difficulties. A less extreme form of understimulation is boredom. You probably have experienced the heaviness of mind or body, the feeling of depression, or the growing tension that sometimes accompanies too much stillness, too little to do.

Curiously, recent years have witnessed commercialization of sensory reduction in the form of "flotation tanks." These are enclosed environments in which the individual floats with a blindfold, with or without music in the background, in highly salinated water. Though I know of no studies, anecdotal reports suggest this can be a soothing, renewing experience. Of course, the fact that this is a short-term, temporary, freely chosen situation—and that money has been paid—may contribute to the positive quality of the experience and distinguish this from sensory deprivation in real-life circumstances.

See Application Exercise 5-1 for an assessment of your recent underload and overload distressors and distress symptoms.

Also on the positive side, we know that residents of nursing homes can escape the stultifying understimulation common in such settings by simply being given the opportunity to care for a houseplant. Even this minimal contact can impart a sense of control and purpose that seems to infuse meaning and connection into nursing home residents' lives.

At the opposite extreme are studies of people on the battlefield, in the workplace, or in school who are **overloaded.** The results are familiar—the person may be tense, anxious, fired up, hostile, upset, short-tempered, confused, or unable to sleep. As in understimulation, too much stimulation generates an intricate network of changes in body, mind, and behavior. A vicious cycle sometimes starts, in which a series of damaging reactions feed on one another. The chances of high blood pressure and heart attack increase markedly with chronic overload.

We are familiar with periods of time when we simply have more to do than time available. When this is temporary, we adapt fairly easily. However, when it is chronic, the result can be burnout and breakdown. Ivancevich and Matteson drew this analogy between an electrical system and an overloaded worker:

> An electrical system that is unable to handle all of the electricity introduced to it is overloaded. In most instances a fuse blows or a circuit breaker is tripped, stopping the input and preventing damage to the system. When an individual is unable to handle all the work input, that person may become overloaded. Unfortunately, unlike the electrical system, people do not have an automatic safety device, and the overload condition can lead to physical, mental, and job performance problems. (1980, 113)

Overload can take two forms: **quantitative** (too much to do in the time available) or **qualitative** (impossibly demanding expectations). In either case, the key is not external reality but how the person appraises or interprets the reality.

ANTICIPATORY, CURRENT, AND RESIDUAL STRESS

Anticipatory Stress

Mind and body prepare in advance for change, crisis, or challenge. Examples of this type of **anticipatory stress** are numerous: tension before a test, "butterflies" before a race, apprehension about a parent's response to your breaking a rule, fear of an impending hurricane, dread of forced retirement.

Anticipatory stress is arousal stimulated by an expected stressor.

A common form of anticipatory stress for college students is test anxiety. Over the years, my observations of students lead me to believe that five key factors contribute to test anxiety. Figure 5-2 is a list of these five, together with steps for preventing each one.

Figure 5-2

Causes and Prevention of Test Anxiety

Causes	Prevention
1. Indequate preparation	1. Pacing and planning
2. Negative self-talk	2. Using realistic and positive self-talk
3. Negative mental images	3. Using mental rehearsal
4. Physical tension	4. Practicing daily deep relaxation and using Six-Second Quieting Response
5. Inadequate exercise, nutrition, and sleep	5. Maintaining a wellness lifestyle, especially during exam weeks

This formulation is consistent with studies (Crouse, Doffenbacher, & Frost, 1985; Lent, Lopez, & Romano, 1983) showing that test anxiety can indeed be reduced.

Psychologist Richard Lazarus points out that "Having a warning of an upcoming harm or benefit is a powerful adaptational tool, especially in humans, who are able to think in terms of past, present, and future, and to engage in *anticipatory coping*" (his italics; 1991, 106). In other words, anticipatory stress can be positive stress, useful in moderate amounts by preparing your body and mind for events that are about to happen. Such stress increases sharpness and motivation. I recently experienced this as I approached Colorado River rapids in the Grand Canyon in my hardshell kayak—rapids that sometimes can be heard for at least a half-mile upstream. You no doubt have felt it in preparation for an exam, speech, date, or job interview.

Although anticipatory stress can be positive, it can also turn into distress. We are all familiar with too much arousal before a speech, an introduction to someone important, an appearance on radio or television, or an exam. When anticipatory stress becomes distress, it interferes with performance, relationships, or other aspects of life in the present. This sometimes accompanies chronic overload as a person gives more attention to what *might happen* than to what *is happening*. It also affects people who lack confidence or choose to escape from involvement in the present.

Current Stress

Current stress is arousal during an experience.

Examples of **current stress** are plentiful: the body's extreme alarm during an auto accident, mental alertness in the midst of a debate, the surge of energy in the final 100 meters of a running or bike race, the excitement during a first-time conversation with an attractive person of the opposite sex. Current stress, if harnessed effectively, is vital for optimal performance. Too much (or too little) can lead to debilitating distress.

Residual Stress

Residual stress is arousal after an experience has passed.

During **residual stress,** the body remains in a state of arousal after the event has passed. Again, it may be positive or negative stress. Nearly everyone experiences alarm for some time after a near-collision on the highway. Athletes may have difficulty sleeping the night after a victory. Overstimulation, whether pleasant or unpleasant, can have the same effect.

During the spring of 1990, the *San Francisco Chronicle* ran a large story under the banner "The earthquake isn't over yet: Psychological scars still linger months after Loma Prieta." This story was about the lingering effects of the October 17, 1989, Bay area earthquake.

- A pastor whose church slipped off its foundation regularly feels as if she is listing to the right.
- A counselor who lost nothing in particular is terrified of crossing the Bay Bridge, riding in elevators and entering brick buildings.
- A retired schoolteacher who survived nearly every kind of natural disaster without fear now can't shake her earthquake worries.

This is "afterstress." Seven months after the October 17 quake, after much of the rubble has been cleared, the homes and the broken bridge patched and the pancaked freeway demolished, the psychological scars linger. (Minton, 1990)

In a report on the emotional aftereffects of fires, Whiting (1990) notes that residual stress often merges into anticipatory stress as victims experience both mourning and fear. Other studies have documented residual distress among police officers involved in shooting accidents, especially within the first three days but continuing on for about three weeks

The devastation and lingering effects of an earthquake can cause many victims to experience residual stress.

(Loo, 1986); firefighters exposed to a dangerous chemical for whom psychological symptoms persisted even after 22 months (Markowitz, 1989); and hurricane victims for whom symptoms continued for up to an average of 16 months (Krause, 1987). I know of no studies on the psychological aftereffects of the Chernobyl tragedy, but they must be considerable. Residual distress also has been reported among disaster rescue and cleanup workers, rape victims (Rose, 1989), children directly exposed to a sniper attack on an elementary school (Nader, 1989), survivors of the New York City World Trade Center bombing— who have had to relive their terror by returning to the same scene every day on the way to work in one of the twin towers (Difede, 1993), children surviving the terrible massacres in Algeria (Ganley, 1997), and, of course, soldiers experiencing shell shock after World War II and posttraumatic stress disorder (PTSD) after Vietnam.

For many Vietnam veterans, the effects of PTSD have lingered on for many years. In a study (Elias, 1997) comparing 332 Army soldiers diagnosed with PTSD with 1,067 other Army men who served in Vietnam, those with PTSD had:

- More than double the rate of infectious and nervous system diseases such as hepatitis and tuberculosis.
- Nearly twice the risk of getting muscle and skeletal diseases. Among them: hypertension and fibromyalgia.
- A 62 percent higher rate of circulatory ailments, such as strokes, hypertension and coronaries (Elias, A7).

One expert believes that combat even alters the brain. According to Lawrence Kolb, a Veterans Administration psychiatrist, "Excessive and prolonged sensitizing stimulation" may lead to changes in the synapses (1988). Another expert (Yehuda, 1997) suggests that some people may be biologically vulnerable to PTSD due to lower than normal levels of cortisol in their blood.

The Write Thing

In their discussion of traumatic experiences, Sobel and Ornstein underscore the value of writing to externalize emotions. They note:

> It's hard work to inhibit deep feelings. Over time, the cumulative stress undermines physiological defenses. Confiding or writing forces us to translate feelings into words and helps sort them out. It helps us understand and assimilate the traumatic event, and eventually put it behind us. We feel a sense of release and control, and the harmful effects of inhibition are reduced. (Sobel and Ornstein, 1994, 5)

For support, the authors summarize a study by Pennebaker (1990), in which a sample of people who wrote about traumatic experiences, especially painful, buried feelings from the past, reported fewer distress symptoms, fewer days off work and visits to their doctor, improved moods, and a more positive outlook. Sobel and Ornstein then offer these guidelines for writing to clear emotions, whether from residual distress or any other painful experience.

> Try the "write thing" when anything is bothering you—when you find yourself thinking or dreaming too much about an experience; when you avoid thinking about something because it is too upsetting; when there's something you would like to tell others, but can't for fear of embarrassment or punishment.

Here are some guidelines for writing as a mental medicine technique:

- Explore not just the facts, but your *very deepest feelings* and *why* you feel the way you do. Be sure to explore any negative emotions such as sadness, hurt, hate, anger, fear, guilt, and resentment.

Mardi Horowitz, another expert in the field, estimates that 25 to 30 percent of people who survive car accidents, major burglaries, or other traumas experience symptoms of posttraumatic stress (Butler, 1987). In my home state of California, millions of residents recently have faced huge earthquakes, forest fires, and floods, sorely testing the coping skills of a large segment of this state's population. College students too can suffer PTSD, as reflected in the depression experienced by southern Florida students after Hurricane Andrew (Pickens, 1995).

Entertainer Ben Vereen lost his 16-year-old daughter in a tragic auto accident. He describes his lingering grief: "It devastated me. It still does. You keep hearing the voice that tells you your daughter is dead. I wanted it to stop" (Carter, 1990, 4). Yet he has moved on, painfully but steadily.

"Now when I have a problem and find myself feeling anxious," he added, "a voice inside me says, 'This too will pass.' When I'm going through trauma, the voice says, 'You've suffered greater loss. This is nothing. Get up. Get on.'"

As Carter states, "And so he has. Ben Vereen is back, performing his one-man show across the country, dazzling audiences with his enthusiasm and style and heart" (1990, 5).

"God endowed me with a wonderful gift, which I had not awakened to," he [Vereen] said. "My work, my art, what I do. I haven't even begun to fulfill that commitment that God made to me, and I made to Him or Her. I'm really looking forward to the next chapter of my life with great expectations" (Carter, 1990, 5).

- Set a specific schedule, for example 15 minutes a day for four consecutive days, or one day a week for four weeks.
- Write in a place where you won't be interrupted or easily distracted.
- Don't plan to share your writings—that could inhibit your honest expression. Keep your writings, or destroy them, as you wish.
- Write continuously without worrying about grammar, spelling, or sentence structure. Don't worry about organization or coherence. If clarity and coherence come later, so much the better. If you run out of things to say or reach a mental block, just repeat what you have already written.
- If you find the writing awkward at first, try to keep going. It gets easier. If you are truly uncomfortable writing, try talking into a tape recorder about your deepest thoughts and feelings for 15 minutes.
- If you are coping with death, divorce, rape, or other major trauma, don't expect to feel better instantly. But you will most likely develop a better understanding of your thoughts and feelings and have a clearer perspective on your life.
- You may feel sad or depressed when your deepest feelings begin to surface. This usually dissipates within an hour or two, or a day or two at most. The overwhelming majority of people report feelings of relief, happiness, and contentment soon after writing for several consecutive days.
- Don't use writing as a substitute for action or as a way of avoiding things. In most instances writing will help you clarify what actions you need to take. (6)

SOURCE: Sobel & Ornstein (1994, 5–6)

As Ben Vereen illustrates, and as he demonstrated again later on after a serious accident involving himself, a significant challenge in managing stress is to develop ways of returning the body and mind to normal levels of stress—sooner, rather than later—after challenges, crises, and changes. If normalcy is not regained relatively quickly, the individual is likely to experience some type of distress. Based on a review of scientific studies, Sobel and Ornstein (1994) have suggested several self-help guidelines for surviving traumatic experiences:

- Feel your feelings.
- Don't do it alone.
- Look for the positive.
- Write down your feelings.
- Tell your story to others.

ZONES OF STRESS

Each of us possesses a distinctive **zone of positive stress.** A vital part of managing stress is to learn the range and limits of that zone. We must learn to recognize warning signs near its edges and to live within that zone most of the time.

A zone of positive stress is the tolerance range of stress within which the person is healthy, productive, and satisfied.

Figure 5-3

Range of Stress Tolerance

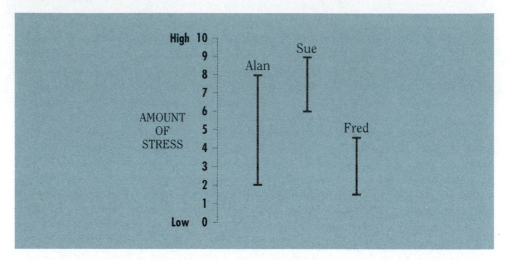

We can visualize the zone of positive stress better by studying Figure 5-3. The scale on the left represents an objective **range of stress tolerance,** which might be measured by physical indicators such as blood pressure, heart rate, muscle tension, or brain waves, or by indicators of emotional anxiety.

Three illustrative cases are shown in this figure. Alan, with a zone of positive stress from 8 to 2, is the most adaptable of the three, because he is comfortable, productive, and healthy at either a fast or slow pace, with high or low arousal. His well-being is more in-dependent of his environment than the other two, in that he thrives within a wider range of stimulation and personal stress.

Sue's zone is narrower at a relatively high level. She is what Selye (1974) calls a **"racehorse,"** a person with intrinsically high energy. She is bored and even experiences a bit of distress at point 4 or 5 on the scale, which is Alan's midrange. Sue generates a high activity level at home and work to keep her stress level high when her outside environ-ment does not do it for her. She is a **"sensation seeker"** (Ogylvie, 1973; Zuckerman, 1979), and perhaps even what one psychologist calls a **Type T**—a thrill seeker (Farley, 1986; Leo, 1990). A particularly destructive manifestation of the Type T person is the compulsive gambler (Gwinne, 1997.)

Fred is what Selye (1974) would call a **"turtle,"** a low-energy person with a narrow zone near the lower end of the scale. As noted earlier, he quite wisely avoids challenge and unfamiliar situations. He is somewhat of a plodder, yet he is dependable and effective in his work.

A common source of job stress is a misfit between the demands of the job and the zone of positive stress of the worker. A key challenge for managers and supervisors is to achieve an optimal job-personality fit among employees. Another is to fit employees to-gether with relatively compatible tolerance zones whenever possible.

Another common problem is incompatible zones of positive stress between marriage partners. Let us hope that Sue, the racehorse, does not fall in love with and marry Fred, the turtle. Such a marriage would be destined for difficulty from the start because of the quite different paces of life.

Crowing Corky: Pet or Distressor?

STOKE, England (AP)—As dawn breaks over rural Devon, Corky belts out the cock-a-doodle-doo that bankrupted his owner.

Not that the rooster is anything to crow about. It's the emotions he brings out in people.

This cock has stirred a flap of sleepless nights, frayed nerves, a ruined career, months of courtroom brawling between neighbors and a partially finished book.

"It's just like World War III," said Margery Johns, who last week decided that Corky, aged 5, should be allowed to retire with his hens despite a court order that limits the amount of noise he is allowed to make in sleepy Stoke.

Her irate neighbor, John Ritchings, complains Corky's calls kept him awake and agitated for four years. He won the most recent lawsuit, so Mrs. Johns risks being jailed for contempt.

Mrs. Johns, who cleans hotel rooms, is unable to pay $45,000 in legal fees and recently declared herself bankrupt. But she calls Corky's right to crow a worthy cause.

Ritchings says another court date is inevitable. He calls Corky's crowing "a recognized form of torture" that kept him out of work for five years.

Corky appeared in fine spirits, strutting confidently among five hens.

Despite receiving insurance payments of $33,000, Ritchings says the battle has left him with psychological trauma similar to that suffered by Gulf veterans.

Source: Associated Press (1994)

Zones of positive stress are determined and shaped by a variety of influences: physical energy levels, background, personality, choice, and demands of the home, work, or school situation.

Everyone's zone is changeable to some degree, of course. The decision to leave a life of relative leisure in order to return to law school brings with it a choice to raise the upper limit of one's zone. Entering a demanding new job also may require living with a higher stress level than before. Similarly, getting married or having a baby results in the need for greater tolerance than before. Each person has limits of adaptability. A great deal of ill health and unhappiness results from efforts to push one's limits too far—at either the upper or lower end of the scale.

As we have emphasized, mental and physical distress can result from either too little or too much stress. Each person, then, possesses three zones—a zone of positive stress, a zone of overload distress, and a zone of underload distress. Symptoms of the two types of distress may be similar or different—for example, emotional anxiety, insomnia, or irritability.

Thus far, we have used one dimension (zero to ten) to describe the zone of positive stress. In order to enhance the usefulness of this model for understanding common stress difficulties, we will add a horizontal dimension that includes **zones of distress.**

A relatively distress-free day is presented in Figure 5-4. Note that stress level fluctuates throughout the day. In reality, of course, blood pressure, brain waves, and other physiological processes vary throughout the day in much finer degrees than shown here. Larger swings, however, are shown. This individual stayed within her zone of positive stress most of the time, exceeding her upper limit only briefly. This is a desirable stress pattern.

Figure 5-4

Zones of Stress

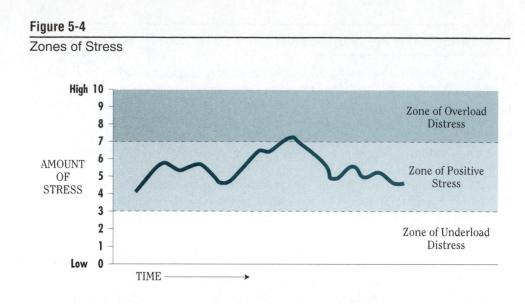

EIGHT COMMON STRESS DIFFICULTIES

Figure 5-5 shows the same tolerance limits (between three and seven) that appeared in Figure 5-4. Here, however, are eight **common stress difficulties.** Each illustrates actual cases I have seen in the Enloe Hospital Stress and Health Center. No individual, in reality, would experience all eight in the same day—or even the same year. For graphic simplicity, I have drawn together a composite of separate persons and time periods into a single chart. **Baseline stress level** refers to the hour-after-hour tension level when the individual is neither pressed nor experiencing deep relaxation. The following stress difficulties are illustrated in Figure 5-5.

1. **Baseline stress level too low** Following retirement by her and her husband, Mildred was perpetually bored, with no personal goals, little social contact, and little meaning in her life. She had difficulty sleeping at night yet was listless and devoid of energy. As Mildred stagnated, her baseline stress level was too low.

2. **Baseline stress level too high** José, an ambitious college junior, felt overwhelmed much of the time. He constantly was driven by the need to excel, to serve on various campus committees, and to show his best side to classmates and friends. He not only studied hard most nights but also spent several hours each week helping friends with study problems, as well as attending a variety of organizational meetings. He had a robust dating life and was a do-it-yourselfer at his apartment, frequently offering to fix his roommates' cars and appliances. He had been a perfectionist since childhood, driven ever upward toward some illusory standard with little satisfaction along the way. José suffered from gastritis, insomnia, and frequent colds. Clearly, his baseline stress level was too high.

3. **Hair-trigger stress reaction** John, an insurance agent whose baseline stress level was too high, had virtually no tolerance for the noise or flippancy of his 11-year-old son. In earlier years, they often had joked and played together. Now, however, the slightest disturbance or demand on John after work produced an outburst of put-downs and discounts toward the boy. John often was defensive with his wife, coworkers, and friends. He displayed a **hair-trigger stress reaction.**

Figure 5-5

Common Stress Difficulties

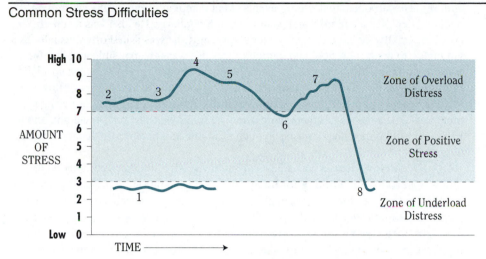

4. **Peak arousal too high** Sharon, a 38-year-old mother of four teenagers, decided last year to return to college after a 19-year layoff. Understandably, her baseline stress level was too high much of the time, and she, too, was often overreactive to high demands or deviations. In addition, she sometimes experienced debilitating test anxiety. She knew some anxiety helped her to prepare, but lately this arousal had gotten out of hand, resulting in serious mental blocks during tests. She also sometimes had angry outbursts at home, far out of proportion to the situation. Both the test anxiety and the displays of anger were instances where **peak arousal** was too high.

5. **Recovery too slow** Julie, a teacher and mother of three, had been quite involved during recent months with the marriage breakup of her best friends, who lived nearby. She became the primary listener for both the man and the woman, which often put her in a considerable bind, since she had to be careful what she said to whom. This involvement began to interfere with her own family life, especially as her concentration and attentiveness diminished at home. She found it difficult to put her friends' problems out of her mind as she tried to find possible solutions to suggest. Her sleep was often disturbed. In short, her **stress recovery** from emotions and complex events was too slow.

6. **Recovery not low enough** Alberta, a 58-year-old bank manager, was hardly able to tolerate the thought that four years stood between her and retirement. The volume of her work was not only overwhelming, but also meaningless. During a series of stress consultations, she became aware that she had no effective means of releasing tensions or bringing her mental and physical stress level down to a more tolerable level in the evenings. Not only was her baseline stress level too high and her recovery too slow, but also her recovery was not low enough. Although she had not exercised since her teens, she began a moderate program of walking and jogging after work, which got her out of the office earlier and helped her release built-up physical tension from the day, thereby bringing her emotional tension down to a reasonable level for the evening.

7. **Stress build-up** Willie was a pleasant, kind, responsive, overweight elementary teacher of age 41 who not only kept his family of seven in bread, butter,

See Application Exercise 5-2 for a personal assessment of the eight stress difficulties—and what you plan to do about it.

and shoes on a meager salary but also gave a great deal of time to the activities of his children. He carpooled to scouting events, went camping often, built a swimming pool and deck for his family, and went to church regularly. He also was a superb cook, especially for large banquets. Not surprisingly, he was asked often, usually as a volunteer, to cook for school and church events. He was a responsible and helpful teacher who took his job seriously. Thus, he was an easy target to organize special events or to take on difficult committee assignments. After several years of this, Willie became aware of a severe **stress build-up.** His easygoing manner became more tense, he snapped at others more often, he felt joyless, he put on weight, and he had recurrent bouts with psoriasis, an uncomfortable and potentially dangerous skin disorder.

8. **Recovery too low** George was a 23-year-old university student who decided to return to school after working for three years as a gas-station attendant. He studied hard to compensate for his limited abilities and his three-year absence from book learning. At midterm and final exam time, he would cram very hard, often long into the night, then resume studying in the morning. He would be emotionally up during these periods but then would take a depressive nose dive after exams were over. It sometimes took three to four weeks for him to recover his usual emotional level. In short, he experienced too low a recovery period. He was not seriously manic-depressive, but his pattern resembled manic-depression in its basic form.

These eight common stress difficulties can occur in combination or independently. When baseline stress level is too high, several other difficulties tend to follow: hair-trigger stress reaction, too high peak stress, too low recovery, recovery not low enough and too slow, and stress build-up. These stress difficulties manifest themselves physically, emotionally, intellectually, and in behavior. The eight illustrations underscore the fact that effective stress management does not rest on a single, simple solution but on an integrated lifestyle approach involving control of time, release of physical tension, relaxation skills, altered relationships, and more.

SIX WAYS OF RELATING TO STRESS

People vary in how they relate to stress. Recognizing that no one is ever totally one or the other, we can distinguish among the following types of persons and their approaches to stress. Consider how each "stress style" relates to wellness as well.

Stress-Seeking or Stress-Avoiding?

Stress-seekers thrive on challenge, risk, and sensation.

Stress-avoiders thrive on security and familiarity, avoiding challenge, sensation, and risk.

Distress-Seeking or Distress-Avoiding?

Distress-seekers thrive on misery, illness, crisis, and martyrdom. They are often addicted to this pattern since childhood.

Distress-avoiders thrive on health, contentment, involvement. They do all they can to avoid and reduce distress.

Distress-Provoking or Distress-Reducing?

Distress-provokers thrive intentionally or unintentionally on creating misery, disharmony, illness, or upset for others.

Distress-reducers thrive on doing everything possible to promote health, happiness, and growth in those whose lives they touch.

See Application Exercise 5-3 for an assessment of how much each of the six stress styles applies to you—and what you plan to do about it.

These patterns of thought and action often are set in motion during childhood through the **life script,** one's blueprint for living developed through early internalized messages from significant others and early decisions in response to these messages. The pattern is perpetuated through a powerful internal drive of habit known as the **repetition compulsion. In** the next chapter, we examine the stress response and the relaxation response, both of which can be influenced by both the life script and its driving force, the repetition compulsion.

References

Associated Press, *Chico Enterprise-Record,* August 22, 1994, 6C.

Butler, K. (1987). Survivors of sudden tragedies face rage, tears. *San Francisco Chronicle,* November 11, B3.

Carter, C. (1990). What a father learned from grief. *Parade Magazine,* July 29, 4–5.

Crouse, R. H., Doffenbacker, J. L., & Frost, G. A. (1985). Desensitization for students with different sources and experiences of test anxiety. *Journal of College Student Personnel, 28,* 315–318.

Difede, J. (1993). Twin-tower terror. *Psychology Today, 26,* 11.

Elias, M. (1997). War stress linked to serious ills. *Sacramento Bee,* December 1, A7.

Farley, F. (1986). The big T in personality. *Psychology Today, 20,* 44–52.

Ganley, E. (1997). Child survivors of massacre live double trauma. *Chico Enterprise-Record,* November 3, 5C.

Goldberger, L. (1982). Sensory deprivation and overload. In L. Goldberger & S. Breznitz (Eds.), *Handbook on stress: Theoretical and clinical aspects.* New York: Free Press, 410–418.

Gwinne, S. C. (1997). How casinos hook you. *Time,* November 17, 68–69.

Ivancevich, J. M., & Matteson, M. T. (1980). *Stress and work: A managerial perspective.* Glenview: Scott.

Kolb, L. (1988). Combat trauma may alter brain. *Brain/Mind Bulletin, 13,* 2.

Krause, N. (1987). Exploring the impact of a natural disaster on the health and psychological well-being of older adults. *Journal of Human Stress, 13,* 61–69.

Lazarus, R. S. (1991). *Emotions and adaptation.* New York: Oxford University Press.

Lent, R. W., Lopez, F. G., & Romano, J. L. (1983). A program for reducing test anxiety with academically underprepared students. *Journal of College Student Personnel, 24,* 265–266.

Leo, J. (1990). Looking for a life of thrills. *Time, 125,* 92–93.

Loo, R. (1986). Post-shooting Stress Reactions Among Police Officers. *Journal of Human Stress, 12,* 27.

Markowitz, J. S. (1989). Long-term psychological distress among chemically exposed fire fighters. *Behavioral Medicine, 15,* 75–83.

Minton, T. (1990). The earthquake isn't over yet: Psychological scars still linger seven months after Loma Prieta. *San Francisco Chronicle,* May 25, B3.

Nader, K. (1989). Stress persists after sniper's attack on school. *Family Practice News, 19,* 33.

Ogylvie, B. S. (1973). The stimulus addicts. *The Physician and Sports Medicine, 1,* 61–65.

Pennebaker, J. S. (1990). *Opening up: The healing power in confiding in others.* New York: Avon Books.

Pickens, J., Field, T., Prodromis, M., Palaez-Nogueras, M, & Hossain, Z. (1995). Post-traumatic stress, depression and social support among college students after Hurricane Andrew. *Journal of College Student Development, 36,* 152–161.

Rose, D. S. (1989). Post-traumatic stress disorder said to affect most rape victims. *Family Practice News, 19,* 52.

Selye, H. (1974). *Stress without distress.* Philadelphia: Lippincott.

Sobel, D., & Ornstein, R. (1994). Surviving traumatic experiences. *Mental Medicine, III,* 7.

Tanner, O. (1976). *Stress.* New York: Time-Life.

Yehuda, R. (1997). Predisposed to PTSD? *Psychology Today, 30,* 9.

Whiting, S. (1990). Waiting for the fire: Survivors live in fear of the next one. *San Francisco Chronicle,* August 1, B3.

Zuckerman, M. (1979). *Sensation seeking: Beyond the optimal level of arousal.* Hillsdale, NJ: Lawrence Erlbaum Associates.

Application Exercise 5-1

Situations and Symptoms of Underload and Overload

Try to recall recent situations in which you experienced distress symptoms from underload and overload. In the spaces below, briefly describe the situations and the symptoms. The two lists need not correspond.

Underload Situations	Underload Distress Symptoms
1.	1.
2.	2.
3.	3.

Overload Situations	Overload Distress Symptoms
1.	1.
2.	2.
3.	3.

Application Exercise 5-2

Monitoring Your Stress Difficulties

You read in the discussion of eight common stress difficulties that problems arise from too much or too little arousal, which can be easily understood and applied to yourself within the framework of "zone of positive stress." In order to know your stress pattern more completely, and as an additional basis for targeting your stress management efforts, complete the following exercise.

1. Indicate by checking the appropriate blank how often you have experienced each of the following stress difficulties during the *past three months*.

	Occurred			
	Almost Constantly	Several Times	Once or Twice	Did Not Occur
Too-High Baseline Stress Level	_____	_____	_____	_____
Too-Low Baseline Stress Level	_____	_____	_____	_____
Hair-Trigger Stress Reaction	_____	_____	_____	_____
Too-High Peak Arousal	_____	_____	_____	_____
Too-Slow Recovery	_____	_____	_____	_____
Recovery Not Low Enough	_____	_____	_____	_____
Stress Build-Up	_____	_____	_____	_____
Recovery Too Low	_____	_____	_____	_____

2. Write a brief description of what symptoms you had during those times you experienced a stress difficulty almost constantly or several times.
3. Now go back and underline stress difficulties that you have encountered during the past week.
4. What have you learned?
5. Specifically, what do you need to do to prevent this (these) from recurring so often in the future? When will you start?
6. What do you need to do *now* to remedy the item(s) you underlined for this week? Do it.

Application Exercise 5-3

Personal Assessment of Six Stress Styles

1. To what degree does each of the labels in the section "Six Ways of Relating to Stress" apply to you? How would you rank yourself on each of the six, using these categories?

	Applies to Me		
	A Great Deal	Somewhat	Very Little
STRESS-SEEKING	_____	_____	_____
STRESS-AVOIDING	_____	_____	_____
DISTRESS-SEEKING	_____	_____	_____
DISTRESS-AVOIDING	_____	_____	_____
DISTRESS-PROVOKING	_____	_____	_____
DISTRESS-REDUCING	_____	_____	_____

2. If needed, what steps might you take during the next six months to create a more positive profile?

To ward off disease or recover health, men [and women] as a rule find it easier to depend on healers than to attempt the more difficult task of living wisely.

—RENE DUBOS

Distress Symptoms: Monitoring Early Warning Signs

CAUTION: OVERCONCERN WITH SYMPTOMS

EMOTIONAL DISTRESS SYMPTOMS

>ANXIETY
>DEPRESSION
>ANGER
>FEAR
>SADNESS
>FRUSTRATION
>GUILT

SHAME
MISLABELING EMOTIONAL DIFFICULTIES
A SAMPLING OF COMMON EMOTIONAL DISTRESS
   SYMPTOMS

COGNITIVE DISTRESS SYMPTOMS

BEHAVIORAL DISTRESS SYMPTOMS

>DIRECT SYMPTOMS
>INDIRECT SYMPTOMS

PHYSICAL DISTRESS SYMPTOMS

THE DISTRESS OF LOSS

Alice Loren was a 76-year-old grandmother who had lived alone since her husband of 52 years died. She had been a faithful, devoted wife who looked after her husband, children, home, and garden with great care and pride throughout her life. She had never been sickly, although her general condition had weakened somewhat in recent years. After her husband's death, she took a serious nose dive, emotionally and physically. She seemed lost, lonely, and unable to find meaning. Last month she died of a stroke.

As traumatic as the death of a long-time spouse may be, most surviving mates do not experience such a severe downturn in health and spirit. This suggests that more effective ways of adapting to such crises must exist. Yet the fact remains that the death rate is very high for surviving spouses during the year after a mate's death.

In previous chapters, we saw that stress in moderate amounts can be pleasant, stimulating, and even helpful for meeting challenges and emergencies. Positive stress can help you to reach your potentials. But distress from either overstress or understress must be avoided whenever possible. Otherwise, wellness is impeded, health can be impaired, quality of life suffers.

Occasional distress is unavoidable. For example, two or more people who relate through time will have disagreements. The physical environment is largely uncontrollable. Financial problems are bound to arise for most people. Illness and deaths of loved ones are inevitable. Pushing your limits is sometimes painful. But, in general, the less the distress the better.

In this chapter we will point out some of the ways distress begins to manifest itself through early warning signs or **distress symptoms.**

CAUTION: OVERCONCERN WITH SYMPTOMS

Carried to the extreme, the following information about stress symptoms could readily be misunderstood and misused. I do not advocate narcissism, "blissing out," disengagement, or hypochondriasis. Rather, I advocate continued awareness of what you are experiencing inwardly as you focus your energies and activities outward. Learning to self-monitor and regulate your life accordingly is intended to help you stay healthy, satisfied, and productive while engaged with the world around you.

This point is reinforced negatively by the fact that "neurotic" individuals, as well as many drug-oriented youth, often are so preoccupied with themselves that they find it extremely difficult to see beyond their own eyelashes, much less engage constructively with people or issues around them. For many who begin our stress health-management programs this is true. Certainly, I do not want to reinforce such inward fixation.

As noted in Chapter 1, research shows that "good stress managers" are highly committed to and involved in activities in the world around them. They engage in life rather than hang back on the fringes of it. This is the opposite of alienation and narcissistic preoccupation with subjective symptoms and signs of stress.

What I suggest, then, is an inward-outward balance with appropriate concern about the self in order to progress toward the self-in-action. The following discussion is intended to sharpen your perception of stress signals and to help you understand how to use them as a basis for continually regulating your daily activities and personal care. In this way, I hope, you will be better able to realize your potentials while contributing to the world around you.

EMOTIONAL DISTRESS SYMPTOMS

Soldiers react to the extreme stressors of battle in a variety of ways. Some are relatively calm and confident. Most react at some time with emotional distress of one type or another. Similar reactions occur among refugees and among victims of natural disasters. Toffler has pointed out that different types of people show striking parallels in their reactions to overstimulation.

> First, we find the same evidence of confusion, disorientation, or distortion of reality. Second, there are the same signs of fatigue, anxiety, tenseness or extreme irritability. Third, in all cases there appears to be a point of no return—a point at which apathy and emotional withdrawal set in. In short, the available evidence suggests that over-stimulation may lead to bizarre and anti-adaptive behavior. (1971, 348)

The stressors facing soldiers, refugees, and victims of disaster are much more intense than those generally faced in daily life. Yet each time you move, change jobs, go away to college, or in some other way drastically alter your daily patterns of living, you run the risk of becoming emotionally upset—depressed, angry, fearful. When you live so fast you experience the chronic overload of microstressors, mild emotional stress (nervousness or tension) may give way to severe depression, anxiety, or disorientation. Similar results may accompany a chaotic life with little routine. Awareness of these emotions is healthy. Denying them can damage health. Yet one study (Ketterer, 1998) shows that up to 40 percent of men deny their negative emotions. Emotional and physical distress often feed on one another, as illustrated by the all-too-common tragedy described in the opening vignette.

Let us examine more closely eight of the most common distress emotions: anxiety, depression, anger, fear, sadness, frustration, guilt, and shame.

Anxiety

Anxiety in moderate amounts is a normal part of living. In sports, optimal performance is achieved when precontest anxiety is in the middle range, neither too high nor too low. The same is true of occupational or academic performance.

Anxiety can become a stress problem in two ways. One is when arousal before or during a critical event is debilitating or otherwise interferes with performance. Earlier, we referred to this stress difficulty as too-high peak arousal. Difficulty in speaking before a group, disoriented thinking because of panic during a test, profuse sweating during an uncomfortable conversation, and the intense fear before a job interview—all are examples of out-of-control situational anxiety. Some experts believe that panic attacks in such situations have unknown chemical or other biological origins, rather than cognitive or emotional causes, and that in these cases medical treatment may be needed.

Shaking off Bad Moods

Most of us spend about three days of every 10 trying to shake off bad moods, according to a University of Michigan study.

Source: Psychology Today (1994, 22).

Symptoms of Generalized Anxiety Disorder

KEY FEATURE: Unrealistic or excessive anxiety and worry (apprehensive expectations) about two or more life circumstances

MOTOR TENSION
- Trembling, twitching, or feeling shaky
- Muscle tension, aches, or soreness
- Restlessness
- Easily fatigued

AUTONOMIC HYPERACTIVITY
- Shortness of breath or smothering sensations
- Palpitations or tachycardia
- Sweating or cold, clammy hands
- Dry mouth
- Dizziness or lightheadedness
- Nausea, diarrhea, or other abdominal distress
- Flushes or chills
- Frequent urination
- Trouble swallowing or lump in throat

VIGILANCE AND SCANNING
- Feeling "keyed up" or on edge
- Exaggerated startle response
- Difficulty concentrating or mind going blank due to anxiety
- Trouble falling asleep or staying asleep
- Irritability

Source: American Psychiatric Association (1987, 252)

The second type of anxiety problem is **chronic anxiety,** sometimes referred to as **anxiety neurosis.** As Mason notes, "A person suffering from anxiety neurosis may exhibit certain physical symptoms: palpitations, chest pain, cold and sweaty extremities, band-like pressure around the head, constriction of the throat, fatigue, lack of appetite, vomiting, and diarrhea" (1980, 140). Thus, anxiety is not just an emotional state, it is intellectual, physical, and behavioral as well.

Depression

Depression, the second primary stress emotion, also is multifaceted, as reflected in the following list of symptoms.

- **Emotional:** a dull, tired, empty, sad, numb feeling with little or no pleasure from ordinarily enjoyable activities and people
- **Behavioral:** irritability, excessive complaining about small annoyances or minor problems, impaired memory, inability to concentrate, difficulty making decisions, loss of sexual desires, inability to get going in the morning, slowed-down reaction time, crying or screaming, excessive guilt feelings
- **Physical:** loss of appetite, weight loss, constipation, insomnia or restless sleep, impotence, headache, dizziness, indigestion, and abnormal heart rate (Cohen, 1977, 13)

Specific combinations of symptoms vary from one person to the next. All sufferers tend to have the following in common: reduced energy level, withdrawal from interac-

---

The Karoshi Plague

Tokyo: The Ministry of Health has identified **karoshi** as the second leading cause of death in Japan.

Officially defined as the fatal mix of apoplexy, high blood pressure, and stress, karoshi strikes primarily middle managers in their forties and fifties who are characterized as being **morestu sha-in** (fanatical workers) and *yoi kigyo senshi* (good corporate soldiers).

Source: Eliot (1994, 13)

---

tions with others, gloomy and dark affect, self-criticism, and a sense of helplessness (Klein & Wender, 1988). Recent research suggests that depression-induced suicide may involve a marked lowering of serotonin, an important neurotransmitter in the brain (Associated Press, 1996).

Greenberg and colleagues (1993) have estimated that depression, the "common cold" of emotional disorders, costs our society nearly $44 billion per year through expenses related to treatment, work life lost to suicide, and decreased worker productivity. Considerable evidence supports the negative influences of depression on health. Recently, for example, researchers found depression to be associated with faster progression of HIV (Patterson et al., 1996). Women are twice more likely than men to be clinically depressed and four times more likely to suffer from seasonal affective disorder or the "winter blues" (Japenga, 1998).

Like anxiety, depression is a common and expected reaction to events that temporarily seem overwhelming or negative in other ways (Goode, 1990). Short-run bouts are little to be concerned about. But depression that lasts for weeks or months is cause for concern and may require positive, aggressive steps. One woman who suffers from periodic bouts states: "When I have a depressive episode, it feels like I'm all alone in a big black hole" (Levinson, 1994, 7E). Major depression affects 2.5 million men and 5 million women at any one time in the United States (Tollefson, 1990).

Sometimes depression has chemical origins (Dalack & Roose, 1990). Other times it is a temporary result of a traumatic loss, such as the death of a spouse. Sometimes depression results from accumulated fatigue, and in still other instances it can accompany a pro-

---

Frustration Causes Aggression?

During the 1950s and 1960s, aggression was considered the response to the frustration or thwarting of a goal commitment, with anger being viewed as the motivator (drive) of aggression. It was mainly aggression rather than anger that was studied in those days. One of the problems with this outlook is that the frustration of a goal may be followed by *any* negative emotion, such as anxiety, guilt, shame, sadness, envy, or jealousy. To the extent that there is a possibility of *future harm,* which translates to threat, a likely result is anxiety; when negative conditions are *irrevocable* (entailing helplessness) and without the assignment of blame, a likely result is sadness; and when there has been harm or loss to ourselves and *others are not victimized,* a likely result is envy or resentment toward the ones who remain unscathed or have benefited.

Source: Lazarus (1991, 218)

found sense of disharmony with work and marriage. A recent study (Choi et al., 1997) found that among adolescents smoking was a strong predictor of the onset of depression. In Chapter 9, you will read that a pessimistic approach to explaining both good and bad events also heightens risk of depression.

Whatever the origins of depression, the negative effects on quality of life, relationships, and performance can be severe. A recent study, for example, reported that the greater the depression among college students, the lower the grade point average (Haines, Norris, & Kashy, 1996). These authors note (1996, 524), "individuals with depressive symptoms have a limited amount of attention span and sustained attention that they are able to use, and once these resources are depleted, cognitive deficits may be observed."

Six of 10 Americans who are depressed do not receive appropriate treatment for three reasons (Smith, 1997). First, they blame self for their symptoms and do not seek help. Second, they don't seek help because the very symptoms for which help is needed are too disabling. Third, their symptoms are misdiagnosed or mistreated.

Fortunately, depression usually passes. Psychiatry professor Davis Kupfer emphasizes that depression is treatable: Up to 70 percent of depressed people regain normal function with medication, therapy, or both (Levinson, 1994). While medications may help in the short-run, lifestyle modification may be called for. As we shall see, running and other types of aerobic exercise have been shown to be very effective in reducing depression, partly by helping to overcome the helplessness so often inherent in depression. In other instances, cognitive therapy focusing on correcting distorted patterns of thinking can also help.

Anger

Anger, the third distress emotion, may be apparent as mild irritation, hostility, or intense aggressiveness. Often, anger results from blaming others. As Parrino states:

> The angered individual is intent on placing blame and leveling punishment for some misgiving. The angry self-dialogue often includes statements such as "You should not have done that to me." "It is your fault, and you should be punished." "If it weren't for you, I wouldn't be in this situation." "I'll get you for that." (1979, 24)

Anger is a secondary emotion in the sense that it always is preceded by other emotions, thoughts, actions, or circumstances. Eliot (1994, 143) has identified several common ones:

Perfectionism	Circuit overload	Denial
Unassertiveness	Loss of control	Depression

Some of the other emotions for which anger is a cover-up or response include:

Frustration	Feeling rejected or lonely	Hurt, or anticipated hurt
Fear	Defensiveness	
Self-doubt	Guilt	

A relatively new expression of anger is "road rage." According to the head of the National Highway Traffic Safety Administration, "We estimate that about one-third of these crashes and about two-thirds of the resulting fatalities [up to 28,000 deaths] can be attributed to behavior associated with aggressive driving" (Associated Press, 1997, 7B). He said, "Aggressive drivers were more likely to speed, tailgate, fail to yield, weave in and out of traffic, pass on the right, make improper lane changes, run stop signs and lights, make hand and facial gestures, scream, honk, and flash their lights." According to one study, "violent aggressive driving" increased 51 percent between 1990 and 1996 (Associated Press, 1997).

Molly Ivins (1997, B6), a social commentator, believes a "valuable national resource" is wasted when people direct their anger energy toward "things that (a) don't matter at all or (b) matter so little that they might as well not exist." It's far better, she argues, to save your anger energy for political, social, or personal issues that truly matter. Later you will read that such "positive anger" can be constructive for personal and social change.

Anger brings with it physical arousal much like anxiety. When unexpressed and unresolved, it can lead to clear damage in tissues and organs. A study by University of Michigan researchers reported that blood pressure was highest among people who resolved anger by repressing it, next highest among those who explode with it, and lowest among those who discuss it (Harburg et al., 1973). The challenge is to look behind the immediate anger at the patterns of interpretation that produce anger in the first place. When we discuss anger in Chapter 14, you will note three key questions about managing anger:

1. How can I prevent anger in the first place?
2. How can I catch it in progress?
3. How can I handle it constructively, once present?

Fear

Fear, the fourth distress emotion, involves a mild to severe feeling of apprehension about some perceived threat. Fear may be residual (consequence of something that already has happened), current (an immediate physical threat), or anticipatory (something believed likely to happen).

Fear is based on conscious or unconscious appraisal of a threat. This appraisal may or may not be based on reality. Someone once said that the letters in the word *fear* stand for "faulty evaluation of actual reality," which often is true, especially among phobic, paranoid, or other persons lacking in confidence. Fear can elicit a very powerful and immediate stress response.

OUR BIGGEST FEARS

In June 1997, *USA Weekend* magazine commissioned a random-sample telephone survey of 1,009 adults from around the country about their fears (De Becker, 1997). Here are the top 10 fears found in the survey, published in August. In every category blacks are more fearful than whites.
Percentage saying they are "afraid" or "very afraid" of the following:

Being in a car accident	54%	Getting Alzheimer's	35%
Having cancer	53%	Pesticides in food	34%
Inadequate social security	50%	Being a victim of individual violence	33%
Not enough money for retirement	49%	Inability to pay current debts	32%
Food poisoning from meat	36%	Exposure to foreign viruses	30%

Sadness

Sadness, the fifth primary distress emotion, is the dreary, dark feeling associated with a real, imagined, or anticipated loss. This loss may be a thing, achievement, expectation, illusion, limb, or whatever. The result is a gap in internal reality. Physical consequences can include, for example, insomnia, chest pain, upset stomach, fatigue, or loss of appetite. Behavior may become withdrawn. Thought processes may become fuzzy and characterized by loss of concentration.

Frustration

Frustration, the sixth primary distress emotion, is the sense of irritation, anger, or outrage at being blocked from something you want to have or do. It is familiar to everyone, since part of living with others is to compromise, giving up bits and pieces of what you would like for yourself. The key issue is your reactivity to frustration. Very disturbed or deranged persons are hyperreactive, often becoming violent when they do not get what they want. Handling frustration calmly is a continuing challenge, especially when you are blocked from something you very much want. High internal reactivity without expression is perhaps the most dangerous of all to health because it can result in chronic excitation of the stress response. Essential (unexplained) hypertension often is the result of this pattern.

Guilt

Guilt is a common type of emotional distress. Although I have no supporting data, my anecdotal observations from years of teaching and conducting workshops have led me to hypothesize that women suffer from guilt more than men.

Guilt is regret and self-reproach over the belief that one has done (or will do) something wrong or inadequately. It results from the perception of falling short of expectations from the self or others. Causing guilt are such self-talk statements as "should have," "would have," and "could have." Lazarus (1991, 240) maintains guilt arises when persons perceive they have "transgressed a moral imperative."

Often—perhaps usually—guilt is unwarranted self-criticism. Too often, it lingers on and on as the person ruminates, regrets, and self-punishes.

Yet sometimes guilt is entirely rational, reasonable, and justified, as when one has hurt someone else, blundered badly on the job, or made a poorly informed decision about family finances. Still, the challenge is to turn that guilt as soon as possible into positive learning for the future. In that way, temporary distress can turn into constructive steps forward.

Shame

A negative emotion that has received a good deal of attention recently among psychologists and therapists is **shame**—feeling disgraced or humiliated, especially in the eyes of someone considered to be important. As Lazarus (1991) notes, shame is based, first, on an internalized image of what others expect, and, second, on the perception that one has fallen short in others' eyes. Shame can be debilitating and threatening to health.

Whereas the action impulse with guilt is to make amends, atone, or even to seek punishment, the action tendency with shame is to hide or avoid others in order to minimize the perceived damage to one's image with others (Lazarus, 1991). This assertion is supported by a study showing that when volunteer research subjects are asked to wait for a stressor, which was to engage in socially embarrassing acts, they preferred to be alone (Sarnoff & Zimbardo, 1961), whereas another study showed that subjects preferred to wait with others when awaiting a stressor likely to generate anxiety (Schachter, 1959).

Positive Emotions and Health

In his excellent book, *Sound Mind, Sound Body,* psychologist Kenneth Pelletier argues persuasively for

> the inclusion of the positive emotions in any comprehensive model of health. According to Norman Cousins, these include "the positive forces"—love, hope, faith, will to live, determination, purpose, festivity, laughter—which are powerful antagonists of depression and help to create an environment that makes medical care more effective.

Source: Pelletier (1994, 68)

Extreme effects of shame are illustrated by instances of sudden death among primitive people when they believe they have violated a strong taboo (Dossey, 1991). Less extreme effects occur every day among people who believe they are publicly devalued or humiliated because of something they have done.

Mislabeling Emotional Difficulties

Mental illness is a term often applied to stress-related emotional difficulties. Application of this label, however, sometimes leads to feelings of hopelessness and helplessness. The "mentally ill" often are stigmatized by neighbors and friends. Emotional strains sometimes are better understood and handled if they are seen for what they are—acute stress, too much stress for too long, or a harmful reaction to stress—rather than as mental illness. This term is better reserved for serious psychological disorders, many of which have a strong genetic or biochemical component and usually are treatable with a combination of medications and psychotherapy.

Nervous breakdown is another term often mistakenly applied to stress-related emotional and behavioral difficulties. A nervous breakdown has nothing to do with a breakdown of nerves or the nervous system. Usually it refers to a feeling of helplessness, loss of control, or confusion in a temporary crisis. People who feel they are about to break down or lose control may need the help of family, clergy, or mental health specialists in getting through a crisis. But their sense of helplessness usually passes as the stressful circumstances are overcome.

A Sampling of Common Emotional Distress Symptoms

People differ, of course, with respect to the point at which mild emotional stress gives way to harmful distress.

Let us look now at a sampling of **emotional distress symptoms.** Recognizing the following emotional symptoms requires no great skill or insight. Understanding them as messages about stress does require greater attentiveness and awareness. Do they reflect positive, temporary arousal associated with an intense but positively challenging situation? Or do they reflect more troublesome, ongoing distress? What can you learn from the following list of symptoms?

Depressed feelings: blue, down, helpless, gloomy
Emotional ups and downs
Strong urge to cry

Strong urge to "run away from it all"
Strong urge to hurt someone

Feelings of being emotionally unstable
Feelings of joylessness
Feelings of anxiety

Feelings of being "fed up"	Fear that others are "out to get me"	More impatience than usual
Feelings of sadness	Difficulty falling asleep	Struggling to get up to "face another day"
Fear of the future	Difficulty sleeping through the night	Feeling that things are out of control
Fear of others' disapproval	Decreased interest in sex	Feelings of hopelessness
Fear of failing		

These signals may be temporary messages from your mind and body that arousal has been too high (or too low) for too long. Distress may be present or on the way. Positive steps to regulate inputs or your responses to them may be required.

COGNITIVE DISTRESS SYMPTOMS

Stressful situations sometimes produce a lack of concentration, poor memory, fuzzy or illogical thinking, or confusion. Students who have not paced themselves properly often find their heads "jammed up" in the middle of final exam week—they are unable to think clearly or remember very well. Young people who feel caught between pressures from their parents and those from their friends or between the tugs of one divorced parent and the other often find they cannot concentrate in class, complete assignments on time, or perform well on tests. These are examples of intellectual distress from overload—too many stressors in too short a time.

At the other extreme, assembly-line workers often become bored, dull, and intellectually stifled after many years on the job. This also happens to isolated retirees, to housewives, and to students who find school unchallenging. Such people also are victims of intellectual distress—from understimulation rather than from overload.

Which of these **cognitive distress symptoms** have you experienced lately?

Fuzzy, foggy thinking	Difficulty organizing thoughts	Inward preoccupation, interfering with listening
Forgetfulness	Inability to concentrate	Nightmares
Mental block	Bizarre, disjointed thoughts	

Disturbed thinking is closely intertwined with emotions, especially with emotions of fear, anxiety, depression, and anger. Disturbed thinking also may be associated with a distressed body. Observing your thought processes sometimes can cue you about other distress warning signals that otherwise might not be noticed.

For many people, signs of distress are more apparent behaviorally than emotionally or cognitively. Let us examine behavioral distress.

BEHAVIORAL DISTRESS SYMPTOMS

Direct Symptoms

The following is a list of direct **behavioral distress symptoms.** They usually are direct reflections of internal tension.

Compulsive, spur-of-the-moment actions	Stuttering or stumbling in speech	Verbal attack on someone
Talking faster than usual	Grinding teeth	Difficulty staying with one activity very long
Easily startled	Difficulty sitting still	

Significant interpersonal conflict

Short-tempered

Withdrawn

Crying spells

Lashing out at something or someone

Indirect Symptoms

The following are indirect symptoms. These are indirect in that they reflect increased use of specific actions to release the physical and mental pain of distress. In other words, if these increase in frequency, they may reflect an increased level of distress to which they are a response.

Increased smoking

Increased alcohol consumption

Increased use of prescribed medications to reduce tension

Use of sleep as an escape

Use of television as an escape

Increased use of over-the-counter aids for sleeping or relaxing

Use of illegal drugs

Increased consumption of coffee, tea, colas, or chocolate (caffeine)

Seeing medical doctor for tension-related health problem

Irrational spending sprees

PHYSICAL DISTRESS SYMPTOMS

How you move and hold your body conveys a great deal about your internal tension. The following is a list of **physical distress symptoms.**

- Toe jiggling and foot tapping often reflect impatience and irritability.
- Tight, hunched shoulders, which can become chronically sore, can signal anxiety, fear, or embarrassment.
- Tightly folded arms may signal disapproval, anger, apprehension, or the desire to be left alone.
- Tightly crossed or coiled legs can convey several messages: wanting to be left alone, anxiety, fearful anticipation.
- Sagging, sloping shoulders and back can reflect fatigue, temporary or cumulative, or feeling burdened (or simply not knowing how to stand straight).
- Nail biting often conveys worry, tension, anxiety—and low self-esteem.
- A jutting jaw often shows apprehension and tension.
- Clenched hands or taut fingers reflect anxiety, usually of a current or anticipatory kind.
- Furrows and frowns in the forehead are another sign of worry, fatigue, or depression.

These are illustrations of a more extensive list of physical stress signals that also includes the following. The specific meaning and importance of these signals can best be determined by the person experiencing them. All have been described to me by participants in my stress-management workshops, groups, and classes in recent years.

Trembling or nervous twitch

Dryness of mouth or throat

General fatigue or heaviness

Pounding of heart

Diarrhea

Constipation

Frequent need to urinate

Upset stomach

Neck pain

Back pain	Loss of appetite	Heart palpitations
Dizzy spells	Increase of appetite	Tension throughout the
Decreased interest in sex	Chest pain	body

Sometimes these occur in clusters, at other times singly. In many instances, they are only minor irritants, but sometimes they interfere with behavior and performance.

A fascinating form of physical distress is "**network nerves,**" a phenomenon experienced by people who appear on television talk shows. Network nerves can include panic, stomach distress, flushed skin, tightness of the larynx, poor circulation, fast pulse, even vomiting. Psychologists sometimes help performers overcome their intense fear of on-camera blundering by suggesting pleasant, relaxing images they can call forth before their appearance.

See Application Exercises 6-1 through 6-3 for personal assessments with the 50-Item Distress Symptom Scale.

Minor physical distress symptoms, when cumulative, do not remain minor. They often turn into full-blown stress illnesses. Whether or not this progression occurs is tied to the effectiveness of the coping process. Part of this process is whether one reacts to early warning signs with constructive or destructive responses.

Exercises at the end of this chapter provide a range of opportunities to assess and monitor your own distress symptoms.

In Chapter 7 we will examine a number of stress-related illnesses—the all-too-frequent result of escalating once-minor distress symptoms.

References

American Psychiatric Association (1987). *DMS-III R.* Washington, D.C.

Associated Press. (1996). Brain chemistry linked to suicide. *Chico Enterprise-Record,* November 24, 1B.

Associated Press. (1997). More deaths blamed on aggressive driving. *Chico Enterprise-Record,* July 20.

Choi, W. S., Patten, C. A., Gillin, J. C., Kaplan, R. M, & Pierce, J. P. (1997). Cigarette smoking predicts development of depressive symptoms among U.S. adolescents, *Annals of Behavioral Medicine, 19,* 342–350.

Cohen, J. (1977) Depression: The sickness of the 70's. *San Francisco Chronicle,* April 13.

Dalack, G. W., & Roose, S. P. (1990). Perspectives on the relationship between cardio-vascular disease and affective disorder. *The Journal of Clinical Psychiatry, 51 Supplement.*

De Becker, G. (1997). Conquering what scares us. *USA Weekend ,* August 22–24, 4–6.

Dossey, L. (1991). *Meaning & medicine.* New York: Bantam Books.

Eliot, R. S. (1994) *From stress to strength.* New York: Bantam.

Goode, E. (1990). Beating depression. *U.S. News & World Report,* March 5, 48–56.

Greenberg, P. E., et al. (1993). The economic burden of depression in 1990. *Journal of Clinical Psychiatry, 54,* 405–418.

Haines, M. E., Norris, M. P., & Kashy, D. A. (1996). The effects of depressed mood on academic performance in college students. *Journal of College Student Development, 37,* 518–526.

Harburg, E., Erfurt, J., & Chape, C. (1973). Socioecological stress areas and black-white blood pressure: Detroit. *Journal of Chronic Diseases, 26,* 595–611.

Ivins, M. (1997). A nation of wasted anger. *Sacramento Bee,* May 7, B6.

Japenga, A. (1998). Depression: Are men hiding? *USA Weekend.* January 2–4, 20.

Ketterer, M. (1998). The danger of denial. *Psychology Today , 31,* 14.

Klein, D. F., & Wender, P. H. (1988). *Do you have a depressive illness?* New York: New American Library.

Lazarus, R. S. (1991). *Emotions and adaptation.* New York: Oxford University Press.

Levinson, A. (1994). America's hangup with mental illness lingers. *Chico Enterprise-Record,* September 4, 7E.

Mason, J. L. (1980). *Guide to stress reduction.* Culver City, CA: Peace.

Parrino, J. J. (1979). *From panic to power: The positive use of stress.* New York: John Wiley.

Patterson, T. L., Shaw, W. S., Semple, S. J., Cherner, M., McCutchan, J. A., Atkinson, J. H., Grant, I., & Nannis, E. (1996). Relationship of psychosocial factors in HIV disease progression. *Annals of Behavioral Medicine, 18,* 30–39.

Pelletier, K. R. (1994). *Sound mind, sound body.* New York: Simon & Schuster.

Psychology Today (1994). Bad moods: Strategies for smiles, *27,* 22.

Rifkin, A. (1990). Solving panic disorder problems. *Postgraduate Medicine, 88,* 133–138.

Sarnoff, I., & Zimbardo, P. (1961). Anxiety, fear and social affiliation. *Journal of Abnormal and Social Psychology, 62,* 356–363.

Schachter, S. (1959). *The psychology of affiliation.* Stanford: Stanford University Press.

Smith, A. (1997). Depressed? *Healthy Bites,* December, 7.

Toffler, A. (1971). *Future shock.* New York: Bantam Books.

Tollefson, G. D. (1990). Recognition and treatment of major depression. *American Family Physician, 42 Supplement,* 59S–69S.

Application Exercise 6-1

Distress Symptom Scale

Complete the following inventory of your current distress signals. While some of these items may reflect positive stress (for example, talking faster than usual or difficulty falling asleep), the scale as a whole is intended to measure distress. It correlates highly with a number of other stress-related scales, suggesting that it is a valid measure of distress symptoms. The most important thing for you is that it will give you a fairly vivid picture of what you are experiencing in mind, body, and behavior. When you are finished, add your score, using the numbers given at the top of the scale.

Indicate which of these occurred during the past two weeks. Use numbers as follows:

__0__ Did not occur   __5__ Occurred several times
__1__ Occurred once or twice   __10__ Occurred almost constantly

_____ Irritability
_____ Depressed feelings
_____ Dryness of mouth or throat from tension
_____ Impulsive, spur-of-the-moment actions
_____ Emotional ups-and-downs
_____ Strong urge to cry
_____ Strong urge to "run away from it all"
_____ Strong urge to hurt someone
_____ Fuzzy, foggy thinking
_____ Talking faster than usual
_____ General fatigue or heaviness
_____ Feelings of being "overwhelmed by it all"
_____ Feelings of being emotionally unstable
_____ Feelings of joylessness
_____ Feelings of anxiety
_____ Emotional tension
_____ Easily startled
_____ Hostility
_____ Trembling or nervous twitch
_____ Stuttering or stumbling in speech
_____ Inability to concentrate
_____ Difficulty organizing thoughts
_____ Difficulty sleeping through the night
_____ More impatience than usual
_____ Grinding teeth

_____ Difficulty sitting still
_____ Nightmares
_____ Diarrhea
_____ Verbal attack on someone
_____ Mental block
_____ Frequent need to urinate
_____ Upset stomach
_____ Headache
_____ Neck pain
_____ Pain in back
_____ Loss of appetite
_____ Decreased interest in sex
_____ Increased appetite
_____ Forgetful
_____ Chest pain
_____ Significant interpersonal conflict
_____ Struggling to get up to "face another day"
_____ Feeling things are "out of control"
_____ Feelings of hopelessness
_____ Difficulty staying with one activity very long
_____ Short-tempered
_____ Withdrawn
_____ Difficulty falling asleep
_____ Slow recovery from a stressful event
_____ Pounding of heart from tension

Application Exercise 6-2

Questions about Your Distress Symptom Score

1. Add your score on the Distress Symptom Scale. Your score
2. In which of these three categories does your score fall?
   High Distress Symptoms   50 or higher
   Medium Distress Symptoms 20–49
   Low Distress Symptoms   0–19

3. Is your score higher than you would like? Explain.

4. What do you see that is new or surprising?

5. Underline the two or three items most troublesome to you during periods of overload and underload.

6. What can you learn about your zone of positive stress from the items you underlined?

7. How do you suppose your mate, a close friend, or a working partner would rate you in the scale? Ask him or her.

Application Exercise 6-3

Comparing Your Distress Symptom Score

Compare your score with the following groups who have taken the same scale. What can you learn?

Group	Number of Respondents	Median Score	Percentage With Scores Higher Than 100
Participants in weight loss clinic	26	36	15%
Employees of county housing authority	15	74	33%
Mothers of nursery-school children	70	52	16%
Dental support staff	71	35	8%
Dentists	41	19	5%
Special-education teachers	54	50	17%
Elementary school teachers	15	40	20%
Physicians	24	37	0%
College students (first week of classes)	282	65	8%
Small-town newspaper editors	48	41	8%
Certified public accountants (nontax season)	52	34	5%
Certified public accountants (tax season)	52	45	19%
Realtors	29	22	7%
Pharmacists	40	27.5	10%
Members of secretarial organization	78	40	11%
College custodians	54	20	4%
College department secretaries	26	9	8%
City Managers	225	14	6%

When health is absent, wisdom cannot reveal itself, art cannot become manifest, strength cannot be exerted, wealth becomes useless, and reason is powerless.

—HEROPHILUS, 300 B.C.

When It Eats Away At You: Distress-Related Illnesses

In this chapter we will discuss how minor distress symptoms turn into stress-induced illnesses. But first we will step back and put individual-level illnesses in a larger social and historical context.

CAUSES OF DEATH IN AMERICA

As we approach the turn of the century, we confront quite different challenges in seeking to control disease and death than our ancestors who opened the century. Then, the leading **causes of death** were **infectious diseases** such as pneumonia, influenza, and tuberculosis. Now, the leading causes of death are **lifestyle diseases** or **diseases of civilization.**

Figure 7-1 presents the 10 leading causes of death in 1996. While genetics, chance, and germs (bacteria and viruses) play key roles in several, lifestyle also is a contributing cause in every single one. To put it simply, your chances of dying in any given year are influenced by such choices as whether and how much you smoke cigarettes, drink alcohol, engage in intravenous drug use and unsafe sex, drive without seat belts, eat high-fat foods, and lead a sedentary and nonactive life.

Here is an illustrative study that makes the point. McGinnis and Foege recently pointed out that the 10 leading causes of death as shown in Figure 7-1 are based on "the primary pathophysiological conditions identified at the time of death, as opposed to their

Figure 7-1

Causes of Death in the United States, 1996

	Percent of Total
Heart disease	32
Cancer	23
Stroke	7
Pulmonary diseases	5
Accidents	4
Pneumonia and influenza	4
Diabetes	3
Other infectious and parasitic diseases	2
Suicide	1
Liver diseases	1
Other	_18_
	100%

Source: Bureau of the Census (1998, 100)

root causes" (1993, 2207). In an effort to trace "root causes," McGinnis and Foege report that in 1990, approximately 2.148 million people died in the United States and that about half of these deaths could be attributed to the following factors:

Tobacco	400,000 deaths
Diet and Activity Patterns	300,000 deaths
Alcohol	100,000 deaths
Microbial Agents	90,000 deaths
Toxic Agents	60,000 deaths
Firearms	35,000 deaths
Sexual Behavior	30,000 deaths
Motor Vehicles	25,000 deaths
Illicit Use of Drugs	20,000 deaths

Looking ahead, the same authors conclude:

> Change can occur. In recent years, trends have been salutary on several dimensions, e.g., reductions in tobacco use, saturated fat consumption, and motor vehicle fatalities. The discouraging trends with respect to the effects of sexual behavior, firearms, and illicit use of drugs need not be inexorable. If the nation is to achieve its full potential for better health, public policy must focus directly and actively on those factors that represent the root determinants of death and disability. (1993, 2211)

What about the role of stress in disease and mortality as we approach the end of the century? While it is difficult to trace all the possible linkages, we can reasonably identify a series of plausible **mediating pathways** between stress and specific causes of death, as shown in Figure 7-2.

To the degree these linkages are valid, it becomes clear that as more and more people come to understand and manage stress effectively, positive results should reduce stress-related illnesses and extend life. Of course, countertrends will continue in some instances, as the stressors of modern life grow in frequency and intensity.

Still, we have reason to be hopeful. As Robert Eliot states, "We now know that often we can teach rather than treat. Nobody ever told me that in medical school" (1994, 19). Simply put, we can do more to prevent illness and at the same time find ways to improve and expand treatment, which brings us to the topic of health-care reform.

Still Unpopular

Dying is not popular. It has never caught on. That's understandable; it's bad for the complexion. It also upsets your daily routine and leaves you with too much time on your hands.

Source: George Burns (Bortz, 1991, 284)

Figure 7-2

Mediating Pathways to Stress-Related Deaths

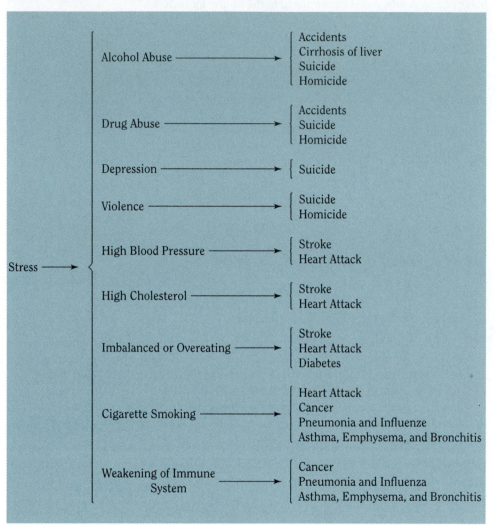

STRESS, WELLNESS, AND HEALTH CARE REFORM

Unless we change our course, the country will go bankrupt in a few years due to rising medical-care costs. We have now passed $1 billion in annual medical-care expenses, and costs continue to grow at a rate higher than that of inflation. Politicians and the public are increasingly aware that change is needed.

Accordingly, we have embarked on a great national debate on what is called "health care reform" but what more accurately is "medical care reform." As I have followed the debate, it has become clear that this is not about health care but about treatment of illnesses. It is not about health reform at all but about reforming the "sick-care industry."

The political and public debate has been about three key questions, all of which represent a **supply-side approach to health-care reform** or to treatment services:

1. How can we extend medical treatment services to more Americans, including the nearly 40 million who are without medical insurance?

2. How will we pay for these added costs?
3. How can medical care costs be controlled and contained?

Note that none of these questions relate to the health status of Americans but only to treatment once people are sick. Little attention has been given in the public debate to how we can reduce demand for medical services in the first place. (See the box "Upstream/Downstream: A Contemporary Fable" for an allegory about treatment and prevention.) If we were to engage in a true **demand-side approach to health-care reform** we would ask such questions as these:

1. How can we develop social policies and programs that will generate more positive, health-enhancing lifestyle choices among more Americans?
2. How can we reduce demand for medical care services in the first place?
3. How can we pay for programs of health promotion/disease prevention?

James Fries of the Stanford University School of Medicine recently pointed out that if utilization demand in all U.S. medical care plans could be reduced by 20 percent, we could

---

Upstream/Downstream: A Contemporary Fable

Here is a story about prevention versus treatment, wellness versus medicine.

It was many years ago that villagers in Downstream recall spotting the first body in the river. Some old-timers remember how spartan were the facilities and procedures for managing that sort of thing. Sometimes, they say, it would take hours to pull 10 people from the river, and even then only a few would survive.

Though the number of victims in the river has increased greatly in recent years, the good folks of Downstream have responded admirably to the challenge. Their rescue system is clearly second to none: most people discovered in the swirling waters are reached within 20 minutes—many in less than 10. Only a small number drown each day before help arrives—a big improvement from the way it used to be.

Talk to the people of Downstream and they'll speak with pride about the new hospital by the edge of the waters, the flotilla of rescue boats ready for service at a moment's notice, the comprehensive health plans for coordinating all the manpower involved, and the large number of highly trained and dedicated swimmers always ready to risk their lives to save victims from the raging currents. Sure it costs a lot but, say the Downstreamers, what else can decent people do except to provide whatever is necessary when human lives are at stake.

Ah, a few people in Downstream have raised the question now and again, but most folks show little interest in what's happening Upstream. It seems there's so much to do to help those in the river that nobody's got time to check how all those bodies are getting there in the first place. That's the way things are, sometimes.

Source: Ardell (1979, 189). Donald Ardell publishes the Ardell Wellness Report. *A free sample copy can be obtained by sending a SASE to Ardell Wellness Report, 345 Bayshore Blvd. #414, Tampa, FL 33606.*

A Reaction to "Upstream/Downstream"

Below is one of my student's reactions to "Upstream/Downstream," as expressed in a brief paper.

I see a great correlation between the story and society today. It is definitely true to the times. So many people lead reckless or unhealthy lives and face the consequences. Fortunately, some of the people are "pulled out of the river" and get a second chance. My sister-in-law's father, Jerry, had a heart attack a couple years ago. He did not lead a healthy lifestyle. He ate whatever he wanted, worked long hours, and had a lot of stress in his life. They operated on him and surgery was a success.

Today Jerry's lifestyle has totally changed. He walks daily, eats much healthier foods, and has retired. He enjoys life much more now. He and his wife have recently moved to a new home and are, in a way, starting a new life. Jerry was very lucky. He did not do the right things from the start, but he was given a second chance and is making the most of his life in a healthy way.

Some people are not as fortunate as Jerry was. Heart disease is the number one killer in the United States today. People just don't seem to care about their health until something bad happens. More and more kids are smoking these days, eating junk food, and doing little, if any at all, exercise. Our culture today needs a better outlook on life and its value.

Hopefully Americans will wake up to their bad habits and live healthier lifestyles. This would do so much good for individuals as well as the country as a whole with our current health care problems. The more people take care of themselves, the less burden there would be on our hospitals. We need to deal with our health "upstream" before problems arise "downstream."

save up to $180 billion per year in this country. Herbert Benson notes that a truly effective health care system must be seen like a three-legged stool: surgery, medicines, and self-care.

See Application Exercise 7-1 to give your personal reactions to "upstream/downstream."

In short, we need to think about prevention as well as treatment as we seek new approaches in "health care reform." Prevention begins with the individual. An important part of prevention is handling stress effectively.

As we move back to the individual level, it is important to remember that distress makes itself known first through minor symptoms. It is important to be aware of these signals in mind, body, and behavior—and then to respond constructively to them—before they turn into a major stress-induced illness. Stated differently, recognizing distress signals at an early stage is a vital first step in preventing moderate, useful stress from turning into harmful, destructive distress. Before examining several types of distress signals, let us turn to a note of caution.

STRESS-RELATED DISORDERS

The term **psychosomatic illness** is popularly misused to refer to an illness that has no organic origin but is "all in your head." To be sure, disease states often are imagined rather than real, as any practicing physician can attest. This may be why placebo pills are effective about one-third of the time.

Psychosomatic illness properly refers to sickness in which the mind plays a causative part. Illnesses usually do not have one single origin but, rather, result from the convergence of a number of factors: deficient nutrition, fatigue, exposure to germs, weakened immunity, and more. Through emotional and cognitive distress, the mind sometimes contributes to illness in four ways:

1. Long-term wear and tear from excessive stress makes the body more *susceptible* to breakdown, such as peptic ulcers, colitis, cancer, migraines, or high blood pressure.
2. An acute episode of intense emotional stress can directly *precipitate* physical ailments, such as heart attacks, tension headaches, or muscle spasms in the back.
3. High stress, chronic or acute, can *aggravate* an existing illness, such as angina, diabetes, arthritis, or hypertension.
4. Stress can *alter health habits,* such as alcohol consumption, exercise, sleep, or adherence to prescribed medications, thereby raising chances of illness.

The box "Hypotheses About Stress and Illness" describes one expert's summary of hypotheses about pathways between stress and pathology of organs and tissues.

As we noted in Chapter 1, experts on stress and health estimate that between 50 and 80 percent of all illnesses are stress related in one of these ways. This is not to say that all such illnesses are unreal or imagined. But stress often helps to induce or aggravate them. More effective management of stress may be one of the best means of reducing the soaring costs of health care (or, more accurately, illness care) in this country.

Let us examine several prevalent **stress-related illnesses** in more detail.

Cardiovascular Disorders

In Chapter 4, we noted that arousal of the cardiovascular system is integrally tied to the stress response. When the human animal is faced with true physical threats, this arousal is useful, even essential. Now most of our stressors are not physical threats, but our cardiovascular system still responds as though they were. Consequently, we are faced with increased risk of a number of stress-induced **cardiovascular disorders,** the first of which is high blood pressure.

High Blood Pressure

Hypertension, or **high blood pressure,** is among the most lethal, widespread, and baffling ailments of our time (Weinberger, 1990). More than 1 in 4 Americans suffers from it, with blacks exceeding whites by 50 to 100 percent (Galton, 1973; Pelletier, 1973). High blood pressure alone accounts for thousands of deaths per year, but if its indirect mortal impact through long-range effects on strokes, heart attacks, and kidney ailments are taken into account, it is a contributing factor in millions of deaths. The absence of subjectively detectable symptoms makes hypertension especially insidious and dangerous. Thus, hypertension is known as "the silent killer."

Robert Eliot describes high blood pressure and its link with stress as follows:

To help illustrate how blood pressure can become elevated, think of your cardiovascular system as a garden hose in which water pressure may be increased in one of three ways:

1. by opening the faucet and increasing the flow
2. by restricting the flow with a nozzle or a clamp
3. by a combination of the first two methods

Hypotheses About Stress and Illness

Below are hypotheses about how the experience of stress sometimes leads to pathology of tissues and organs.

1. The acute body response itself may cause damage, particularly if an already compromised organ is involved.
2. The acute response may cause transient insult to a tissue, but repeated occurrence of the stress may cause permanent tissue damage.
3. The acute physiological reaction can become chronic if it becomes conditioned to a benign stimulus resembling the stressor. Such a benign stimulus may be a more regular part of the individual's environment and provoke an unnecessary coping response.
4. A coping strategy may be used successfully but the physiological component is not terminated when the challenge is mastered. A reverberating circuit is established, which puts unusual strain on the body.
5. A minor stress provocation releases an inappropriately severe physiological response. Modulation is lacking that grades the body's reaction according to the nature of the threat. When all stresses are responded to as major assaults, abnormal physiological reactions are possible.
6. A physiological response appropriate and adequate to cope with a given threat may result in damage to some other aspect of the body through inhibiting a benign but vital body process or stimulating an irritating one.
7. Coping strategies can misfire when the behavioral component is inhibited but the physiological aspect is expressed (fight behavior inhibited but not its physiological component). The physiological aspects of a blocked action can be continuously repeated since no appropriate cutoff or signal is received (Zegans, 1982).

Source: This summary of Zegans's work appears in Genest and Genest, 1987, 98.

The open faucet is a metaphor for what can happen when the heart pumps too much blood through the system. Medically, the amount pumped is called the *cardiac output.* The second metaphor illustrates the kind of pressure resulting when blood vessels become clamped down. Medically, this constriction results in elevated *total systemic resistance.* Like the pressure in a garden hose, blood pressure also can increase because of a combination of both processes.

Stress can cause all three increases; and whether you're talking about water in a hose, or blood in your body, too much pressure will tax the system—weakening or even rupturing the pipes, while also putting an unhealthy strain on the pump. (1994, 14)

Blood pressure is measured with two numbers, *systolic* and *diastolic.* **Systolic blood pressure,** the numerator and larger number, refers to millimeters of mercury raised on a scale at the moment of contraction of the heart. **Diastolic blood pressure,** the denomina-

Psychoneuroimmunology: New Frontiers in Mind-Body Studies

In commenting about the new field called **psychoneuroimmunology** in the study of role of the mind and stress in illness, Kenneth Pelletier recently wrote:

Psychoneuroimmunology research opens a window onto the complex psychological and behavioral factors that influence the onset and course of stress and immune-related diseases. Correlations between high levels of stress and myriad health problems have been found, including cardiovascular disease, high blood pressure, headaches, back pain, ulcers, anxiety, insomnia, sexual problems, chronic fatigue syndrome, depression, increased accident rates, alcohol and drug abuse, suicide, increased susceptibility to infectious disease, autoimmune disorders (such as lupus), and even the common cold. This new research is a growing testament to the mind-body connection between health and disease.

Source: Pelletier (1994, 104).

tor and smaller number, refers to the millimeters of mercury raised on a scale at the moment between beats, when the ventricles (pumps) of the heart are refilling with blood and less pressure is exerted against blood vessel walls.

Blood pressure tends to rise with age. Most medical authorities, however, agree that in younger and middle-aged people, repeated readings above 140/90 warrant careful monitoring. Repeated readings higher than 150/95 often are treated with medications.

CAUSES OF HYPERTENSION   While glandular and other disorders contribute to hypertension in some cases, most cases are considered to be "essential hypertension"—of unexplained origin. A medical textbook states that "a specific cause for the increase in peripheral resistance which is responsible for the elevated arterial pressure cannot be defined in approximately 90 percent of patients with hypertension disease" (Isselbacher, 1981, 86).

We do know that high salt consumption contributes to high blood pressure in a small percentage of the population who are salt sensitive by genetic disposition. So can lack of exercise, obesity, and certain glandular disorders.

Herbert Benson and other experts (Benson, 1975; Benson, Cotch, & Crasswell, 1978) contend that a substantial proportion of essential hypertension may result from prolonged, unreleased chronic excitation of the stress response. Conditions of modern life expose us to greater risks of hypertension. Benson begins by quoting Ostfeld and Shekelle (1967):

"There has been an appreciable increase in uncertainty of human relations as man has gone from the relatively primitive and more rural to the urban and industrial. Contemporary man, in much of the world, is faced every day with people and with situations about which there is uncertainty of outcome, wherein appropriate behavior is not prescribed and validated by tradition, where the possibility of bodily or psychological harm exists, where running or fighting is inappropriate, and where mental vigilance is called for." The elevation of blood pressure will depend upon the extent to which the individual is exposed to accelerated environmental change and uncertainty, and on his innate and acquired abilities to adapt. (1975, 45)

Numerous studies lend credibility to this position that hypertension at least in part results from social stressors (Mustacchi, 1990). For example, hypertension is a major problem for black Americans, which may be due less to genetic disposition than to the greater life stresses of blacks. A study of blacks residing in middle-class neighborhoods showed that they had a rate of hypertension only about one-half that of blacks residing in ghetto environments for whom crime, unstable neighborhoods, pollution, and overcrowding are likely to create much more daily tension (Harburg et al., 1970).

Another study shows that air traffic controllers have a rate of hypertension about five times greater than comparable work groups, probably because of the intensely demanding pressures in the air traffic towers (Greenberg & Valletutti, 1980). Cottington (1986) found that men with high job stress who suppress their anger are more likely to experience hypertension than high-job-stress men who do not suppress their anger. At the same time, other studies show that both exercise and meditation are sometimes effective in reducing blood pressure (Benson, 1975, 1984; Johnsgärd, 1989; Thomas et al., 1981).

LABILE HYPERTENSION   Recently, medical researchers have given attention to a pattern called **labile** (unstable) **hypertension.** Some persons appear to have resting blood pressure in the normal range, yet their blood pressure shoots up to very high levels when they are emotionally aroused (Caudillo et al., 1993; Fredrikson and Matthews, 1990; Manuck, Kasprowisz, & Muldoon, 1990; Pickering & Gernin, 1990).

One form of this pattern is "white coat hypertension"—high blood pressure seems to appear only in the presence of a doctor or a nurse but never at home. It is interesting to note a recent study showing that patients with white coat hypertension, when compared with those with chronic, persistent hypertension, reported higher levels of happiness during the day, greater optimism while at work, and more excitement at home. Those with persistent hypertension scored higher on measures of sadness and boredom (Thyrum et al., 1994). Curiously, Eliot (1989) reports that about 17 percent of family physicians also manifest labile hypertension.

Another pattern is the "hot reactor"—blood pressure soaring in response to emotional upset, especially from anger (Eliot & Breo, 1984). Since studies suggest that the chances of eventual chronic hypertension are greater later in life among such hot reactors, it is vital for young hot reactors to learn ways to control it. In Chapter 4, we cited Lynch's research showing that blood pressure tends to rise each time a person talks. He also found that hypertensives usually have greater elevations during talking than normotensives (1985). Lynch raises the fascinating question of whether the chronic elevation of blood pressure might be the result of years of minor hot reactions during millions of communications over many years. Learning early to keep one's body as calm as possible during conversation might be especially vital, then, among persons disposed by family history toward hypertension. We will explore the hot reaction as a cardiovascular disorder in its own right in a later section.

In short, hypertension is a severe health hazard resulting in part from the stresses of late twentieth-century existence, especially for certain population groups. In the long run, understanding and minimizing stress may be a more potent means of containing this epidemic than even the most effective medications. Meanwhile, treatment programs using exercise, diet modifications, and relaxation training have been shown to be effective in many cases in treating this dangerous disorder.

Coronary Artery Disease

The coronary arteries wrap around the heart to furnish the heart muscle with newly oxygenated blood. If these arteries are partially blocked, insufficient blood supply reaches the heart. When the continuous flow of blood through the arteries is cut off, death to heart tissue results. This is a heart attack or myocardial infarction.

DEVELOPMENT OF CORONARY ARTERY DISEASE   Beginning early in life (Wissler, 1990) and continuing into adulthood, the inner lining of some individuals' coronary arteries develop tiny streaks of fat and **cholesterol.** Research continues into precisely how this occurs biochemically and why people differ in the number and severity of such lesions. What is known is that in some persons, especially in Western nations, this process continues on for some years until larger deposits develop. These partial blockages are called **atherosclerosis.**

The deposits (**coronary plaque**) not only increase in size, but also they sometimes develop tiny breaks and tears. Fortunately, the body is equipped to repair these minor internal injuries, just as it can repair a minor external trauma. Through a complex series of messages from the brain, blood clots and scar tissues emerge. New cells develop, and the tiny wound is repaired. But as this happens, the size of the passageway through the coronary artery is narrowed slightly. The scar tissue continues to build up on new lesions along the coronary arteries or in old scar tissue.

Scars continue both in number and size, partly because of continued clotting and partly because fatlike substances get stuck in tiny openings in the scar tissue. After a time, the scar tissue contains many of these fatty substances.

The most dangerous of these is cholesterol, a waxlike chemical that is vital for building cells throughout the body, for constructing hormones, and for other purposes. When too much cholesterol travels in the bloodstream, it tends to attach itself to the walls of the arteries. This is especially true if the bloodstream has a high percentage of **low density lipoproteins (LDL),** which "deliver" the cholesterol throughout the body, and a low percentage of **high density lipoproteins (HDL),** which "discard" cholesterol to the liver. LDLs, then, are the "bad guys" in the cholesterol family, HDLs the "good guys."

More lesions, more clotting and scarring, more closure, less blood flow, more lesions—on and on the cycle goes. Finally, a blood clot may break away, blocking the line at a narrowed spot. Or arteries narrowed from high blood pressure may completely close off blood flow, and the rhythmic pumping of the heart may go awry (**arrhythmia**) and stop altogether. The part of the heart deprived of blood soon dies and nearby cells are severely weakened. The heart can no longer pump blood to the lungs or throughout the body. If enough heart muscle dies from lack of oxygen, the result is death.

The term **coronary artery disease** refers to the partial closing of one or more coronary arteries. A **heart attack** or **myocardial infarction** occurs when a coronary blockage causes a complete cessation of blood to an area of the heart. The result is death of heart tissue (myocardium).

You read at the beginning of this chapter that coronary heart disease is by far the leading cause of death in this country. Over half of all deaths of middle-aged men are caused by coronary disease (Green & Shellenberg, 1991). One of four of the people who die from heart disease is under age 65 (American Heart Association, 1985). On the positive side, the rate of heart attacks and death from heart disease has dropped steadily for the past 25 years.

RISK FACTORS   The emergence of heart attacks as a major cause of death in this century has stimulated scientists to devote substantial time and energy to studying causes. While much remains to be learned, a number of fairly definite **risk factors for heart disease** have been identified (Kannel, 1990). These include:

Age	Elevated blood pressure	Low aerobic fitness
Being male, before age 50	Elevated cholesterol	Obesity
Family history	A high ratio of total cho-	Diabetes
Cigarette smoking	lesterol to HDL	Coronary-prone behavior

Note that all these risk factors except for family history are related to lifestyle and choice. Even diabetes is influenced, of course, by diet and exercise—and sometimes emotions. Fortunately, risk factors can be changed—even in entire communities, as reported by Farquhar and colleagues (1990). Evidence has even been reported that the combination of exercise, very low fat diet, social support, and meditation can *reverse* coronary plaque buildup (Ornish, 1990).

The last on this risk-factor list is "coronary-prone behavior." This is a catchall category, including the most well-known factor, Type A behavior, but also including hostility, depression, and the hot reaction. A recent review of literature concludes that depression is indeed a risk factor for coronary heart disease but that the studies on this factor have almost all been done on men, even though women suffer from depression twice more often than men (Dimsdale, 1993). Considerable evidence suggests that psychosocial factors influence heart health among women as well as men (Elliott, 1995; Krantz, et al., 1996).

The physiological linkages to coronary-prone behavior are still being studied. Pelletier has summarized what we now know about how stress contributes to heart disease as follows:

1. Direct injury to the arterial wall caused by turbulence in the blood and repeated or sustained increases in heart rate;
2. Disruption of the brain's control over heart rate, which can cause a fibrillation leading to sudden death;
3. Toxic effects on the arteries from the stress hormones catecholamines and corticoids;
4. Possible indirect influences of these and other stress hormones to increase platelet aggregation or clotting, which in turn could block arteries and/or increase levels of fats in the blood;
5. Release of hormones that induce a vasospasm or sudden constriction of coronary arteries, especially those that have been blocked by plaques;
6. A newly discovered direct influence of these hormones on thrombosis, or the sudden rupture of sites of injury in the arteries. (1994, 85)

Redford Williams and others have explored the physiological pathways through which hostility contributes to heart disease. Proof that hostility is a partial cause of coronary artery disease specifically rests on research findings showing that hostility precedes coronary artery disease in time and on identification of physiological pathways between the hostility and coronary artery disease. Research on these physiological linkages is yet in an early stage. Yet Williams maintains enough is known to tentatively identify two interrelated processes (Williams, 1989).

First, hostile individuals (like Type A persons more generally) have been found to be physiologically more reactive to challenge than nonhostile persons. Stated differently, they are more likely to display heightened "emergency branch" (that is, sympathetic nervous system and endocrine) reactions under pressure, as in a timed mathematics quiz in a laboratory. This physiological volatility may damage coronary arteries directly through the impact of adrenaline and noradrenaline on the inner walls of the arteries. And, indirectly, it may do harm through repeated episodes of blood pressure and cholesterol elevation. Still further, the greater emotional and cognitive vigilance of hostile persons tends to be associated with heightened testosterone secretions. We know that testosterone tends to decrease high density lipoproteins, the "good kind" that carries cholesterol away from deposits on arteries to the liver for discharge. This may also help explain why hostility does damage to the coronary arteries.

Second, hostile individuals have been found by Suarez and Williams (1989) to display a weaker "braking" action of their parasympathetic nervous system—that is, their "calming branch." Thus, they not only overreact in their bodies, but they also stay aroused for a longer time.

Pilots and Cholesterol

Some of the most interesting data regarding stress and cholesterol involves navy pilots. As consultant to the war colleges of the National Defense University, I have observed differences in the cholesterol levels of three types of pilots, all of whom regularly eat the same active-duty diet. Transport pilots (incidentally, the oldest members of the study) had the lowest levels, land-based fighter pilots had the next highest levels, and pilots assigned to aircraft carriers registered the highest levels of blood cholesterol. The results are hardly surprising, Carrier pilots must land an aircraft (while it's still going 130 miles per hour) on a bobbing, four-acre airfield, with the hope that a hook will catch a big steel wire on the plane's underbelly. Faced with these daily challenges, the brain perceives danger, triggers release of high-energy fats for a nonphysical struggle. Again, moment-to-moment control over outcome is the basic issue.

Source: Eliot (1994, 41)

These combined effects of heightened arousal in the emergency branch of the autonomic system and a weaker braking effect of the calming branch may help explain not only the harmful effects of hostility on the coronary arteries and the heart but also on the body more generally.

The "Hot Reaction"

We noted earlier that some individuals tend to evoke very strong physiological responses to perceived threat. These individuals experience what Robert Eliot refers to as the **hot reaction.** These hot reactors experience what researchers more formally call excess "cardiovascular reactivity"—a topic of research to which entire issues of professional journals have been devoted. Sufficient danger to health and well-being occurs—independent of other risk factors—to qualify the hot reaction as a stress-related disorder in its own right.

In brief, the hot reaction is the tendency of the body to generate a cardiovascular response that is out of proportion to the nature of the threat. As Eliot puts it, "For Hot Reactors, the alarm reaction triggers a bigger bang for their catecholamine bucks. Instead of a nudge, they get a shove. Instead of a firecracker, they get a bomb" (1994, 27). During both the alarm and vigilance stages of the stress response (corresponding to Selyes's alarm and resistance stages of the general adaptation syndrome), the sympathetic nervous and endocrine systems fire quickly and very powerfully to prepare the body to defend itself by fighting or fleeing. Usually, however, the situation does not require such a strong response. Eliot states, "These walking time bombs burn a dollar's worth of energy for a dime's worth of trouble" (1994, 15). A recent study (Jiang et al., 1996) confirms Eliot's statement among post-heart attack patients: The stronger the cardiovascular reactivity during mental stress, the greater the incidence of recurrent heart attacks.

As we noted earlier, studies reported by Redford Williams (1989, 1993) and others suggest that another physiological characteristic of hot reactors may be a weaker braking response caused by a sluggish parasympathetic nervous system. Not only does it appear that hot reactors physiologically react more quickly and powerfully to perceived stressors, but they also quiet down more slowly.

Several additional observations from Eliot about hot reactors are important to note. These are based on more than 11,000 subjects with whom Eliot, a cardiologist, and his associates have worked.

Possible Effects of the Hot Reaction

Eliot maintains there are 10 possible effects of the hot-reaction pattern:

1. Permanent high blood pressure
2. Damaged blood vessel linings
3. Atherosclerosis
4. Accelerated blood clotting
5. Ruptured heart muscle fibers (contraction band lesions)
6. Heart rhythm disturbances
7. Kidney and heart failure
8. Heart attack
9. Stroke
10. Sudden death

Source: Eliot (1994, 18)

Of those apparently healthy subjects tested (using noninvasive measures of cardiovascular reactivity), one in five was found to be a hot reactor.

- Most hot reactors experience this hyperreactivity in response to microstressors such as missing a green light, standing in a grocery line, or running out of dental floss.
- Hot reactors are often cool (even Type Bs) on the outside.
- For many hot reactors, perceived loss of control is a major matter, even seen by the person as a personal defeat. Eliot nicknamed this form of stress the FUD factor—Fear, Uncertainty, and Doubt.
- Physical fitness does not guarantee protection against the hot reaction.
- During the past 20 years, women show signs of catching up with men in prevalence of the hot reaction—at the same time heart disease has become the number one killer among women in the U.S. (1994, 14).

For the past several years, Eliot and his associates have conducted an intensive program aimed at teaching people to control their hot reactions. Many of their techniques are the same as those presented in this textbook. Although Eliot probably is right that physical fitness is no guarantee against the hot reaction, a recent study by Boutcher and Nugent (1993) showing less heart-rate arousal during and after repeated exposure to a controlled psychological stressor among physically fit subjects suggests that fitness may at least decrease chances of hyperreactivity in response to stressful events. A recent study by Gerin and colleagues (1995) found that social support significantly reduced cardiovascular reactivity among a sample of 26 females participating a laboratory study. Another study (Vögele et al., 1997) found that among men, anger suppression was associated with a tendency toward elevated cardiovascular reactivity, especially when combined with initial hypertension. We will explore physical fitness, social support, and anger prevention as distress-protective factors in a later chapters.

Sudden Death

Robert Eliot also made a startling discovery during his service as a cardiovascular consultant to the U.S. space program in 1967: "Young aerospace workers, some as young as twenty-nine, were dropping dead of heart attacks at an alarming rate" (Eliot & Breo, 1984,

15). Though showing no unusual coronary risk-factor patterns, these employees did experience dangerous levels of emotional stress.

> What I found instead were anxiety and depression and a universal, pervasive feeling of hopelessness and helplessness. Cape Canaveral families led the nation in drinking, drug-taking, divorce, and sudden heart attacks. The space workers were a whole population suffering from the acute stress of knowing that at any moment they could lose their work income, status, and identity as skilled professionals.

> At the lab, I analyzed autopsies of workers who had dropped dead without warning. What I found suggested that adrenaline and other stress chemicals had spewed into their bodies with such strength that they had literally ruptured the muscle fibers of their hearts. It appeared that the brain had the power to trigger heart-stopping emotional reactions to stress. (1984, 15)

A recent study found that Type A men were significantly more likely to experience *ischemic heart disease* (shortage of oxygen to the heart muscle, a condition that carries a high risk of sudden death) than Type Bs (Perini et al., 1993).

George Engel (1971) has investigated the circumstances surrounding the unexplained sudden deaths of a large number of persons. Most were healthy at the time of their demise. Engel discovered four categories of stressful life events that precipitated **sudden death.**

> The most common (135 deaths) was an exceptionally traumatic disruption of a close human relationship or the anniversary of the loss of a loved one. The second category (103 deaths) involved situations of danger, struggle, or attack. Loss of status, self-esteem, or valued possessions, as well as disappointment, failure, defeat, or humiliation, accounted for the third group of deaths (21 in all). And the fourth category (16 deaths) consisted of people who died suddenly at moments of triumph, public recognition, reunion, or "happy ending." Fifty-seven deaths in the first category were immediately preceded by the collapse or death—often abrupt—of a loved one. Some survivors were reported to have cried out that they could not go on without the deceased. Many were in the midst of some frantic activity—attempting to revive the loved one, get help, or rush the person to the hospital—when they, too, collapsed and died.

> One common denominator emerges from the medical literature and the 275 press reports on sudden death. For the most part, the victims are confronted with events which are impossible to ignore, either because of their abrupt, unexpected, or dramatic quality or because of their intensity, irreversibility, or persistence. The individual experiences overwhelming excitation.

> Implicit, also, is the idea that he no longer has, or no longer believes that he has, mastery or control over the situation or himself, or fears that he may lose what control he has. (1977, 118)

The following story by L. J. Paul illustrates the point.

> A 45-year-old man found himself in a totally unbearable situation and felt forced to move to another town. But just as he was ready to make the move, difficulties developed in the other town that made the move impossible. In an anguished quandary, he, nonetheless, boarded the train for the new locale. Halfway to his destination, he got out to pace the platform at a station stop. When the conductor called, "All aboard," he felt he could neither go on nor return home; he dropped dead on the spot. He was traveling with a friend, a professional person, with

whom he shared his awful dilemma. Necropsy showed myocardial infarction [heart attack] as the cause of death. (1966)

Engel suggests these sudden deaths often can be explained by "derangement of cardiac rhythm" (arrhythmia) in response either to overwhelming discharge of catecholamines or to breakdown from rapid shifts between excitatory and withdrawal responses. Homeostatic balance within the organism is lost. Engel cites several additional specific cases, including the following:

- A dramatic example is the death of the 27-year-old army captain who had commanded the ceremonial troops at the funeral of President Kennedy. He died 10 days after the President of a "cardiac irregularity and acute congestion," according to the newspaper report of the medical findings.
- A 39-year-old pair of twins who had been inseparable died within a week of each other; no cause of death was mentioned.
- A 64-year-old woman who was said never to have recovered from the death of her son in an auto accident 14 years earlier died 4 days after her husband was murdered in a holdup. (1971, 774)

While such incidents are rare, they illustrate the intricate mind-body connection and the extremes to which this linkage can go awry. A recent study further illustrates this point but with another emotional factor, depression (*Psychology Today,* 1994). The study shows that depressed heart patients are much more likely to experience ventricular tachycardia (VT), a rhythm disturbance that carries a high risk of sudden death. Another study showed that heart attack survivors suffering from depression had three to four times the risk of dying within six months compared with nondepressed survivors (Frasure-Smith et al., 1993). Since about 1 in 5 heart patients suffers from depression during and after their heart crisis, depression needs to be addressed along with the physical condition of the heart itself.

Immune System Disorders

In Chapter 4, you read about the relationship of the immune system to the stress response. You read about a number of studies strongly suggesting that either chronic or acute distress can weaken the immune system to the point where various illnesses become more likely. As we turn to **immune system disorders,** a recent study further illustrates the point.

As reported in the prestigious *New England Journal of Medicine,* psychologist Sheldon Cohen and his colleagues (1991) conducted an ingenious study in which they injected volunteers with a measured dose of five different cold viruses or with a placebo. Not surprisingly, some came down with colds, some did not. In the first well-controlled demonstration that stress can raise risk of infection, the investigators found that the greater the amount of stress during the past year among volunteers, the greater the incident of catching the cold virus and, among those who did, the greater the chances of developing actual cold symptoms. This study is entirely consistent with my anecdotal observations that students tend to come down with colds disproportionately around exam time, the period when they are likely to be most tired and stressed. On the positive side, studies suggest that personal journal writing and relaxation training can strengthen the immune system of students (Kiecolt-Glaser & Glaser, 1993) and others (Van Rood et al., 1993).

Experts suspect that stress may play a part in a host of immune-related disorders, including a form of herpes (Glaser & Kiecolt-Glaser, 1997) and mononucleosis (Kasl et al., 1979). For a comprehensive review of studies on stress and immunity, see Ursin (1995). We will briefly examine two immune-related disorders, rheumatoid arthritis and cancer.

Scientific Foundations of PNI

As mentioned earlier, psychoneuroimmunology is an emerging hybrid discipline bringing together publications and scholars dealing with the interconnections among the mind, the immune system, and the nervous system. Robert Ader, a pioneer in this field and co-editor of its major journal, *Brain, Behavior, and Immunity,* recently summarized the scientific foundations of psychoneuroimmunology as follows. These points are quoted from another major recent publication, *Mind-Body Medicine.*

- Nerve endings have been found in the tissues of the immune system.
- Changes in the central nervous system (the brain and spinal cord) alter immune responses, and triggering an immune response alters central nervous system activity.
- Changes in hormone and neurotransmitter levels alter immune responses, and vice versa.
- Lymphocytes can produce hormones and neurotransmitters.
- Activated lymphocytes—cells actively involved in an immune response—produce substances that can be perceived by the central nervous system.
- Psychosocial factors may alter the susceptibility to, or the progression of, autoimmune disease, infectious disease, and cancer.
- Immunologic reactivity may be influenced by "stress."
- Immunologic reactivity can be influenced by hypnosis.
- Immunologic reactivity can be modified by classical conditioning.
- Psychoactive drugs and drugs of abuse influence immune function.

Source: Goleman & Gurin (1993, 58)

Rheumatoid Arthritis

About 1 in 5 of all Americans under age 65 and half of all Americans over age 65 have some kind of painful condition of joints, muscles, or bones that requires medical attention (Pincus, 1993). In fact, arthritis—inflammation of the joints—is the most common chronic health problem in this country, resulting in an excess of $50 billion in lost wages each year.

The minor aches and pains most of us experience from time to time are usually fleeting and disappear in a short time without treatment. **Rheumatoid arthritis,** a more serious chronic condition, usually starts during young adulthood or middle age, continues into old age, and affects women three times more often than men (Pelletier, 1977), resulting in total disability for more than 60 percent of people who have had the disease for 10 or more years.

This illness manifests itself through swelling and soreness in joints throughout the body. Stress often appears to play a part in the course of this illness and perhaps in its inception. Like ulcerative colitis and perhaps cancer, rheumatoid arthritis is a disease of the immune system. Specifically, it is an autoimmune illness in which antibodies become directed against the body's own cells, thereby inflicting tissue damage. Usually, the immune system has little difficulty distinguishing the self from nonself. For reasons not entirely understood, this discriminating ability breaks down in rheumatoid arthritic patients, resulting

Rheumatoid Arthritis and Family Crisis

A 48-year-old woman had developed rheumatoid arthritis soon after marrying at age 18 while pregnant. The swelling and pain had plagued her off and on ever since. Three years prior to her entering our hospital-based, 12-week stress control program, her husband had left her after a bitter series of feuds in which she felt discounted and unloved. For several months after the split, she was almost totally bedridden with pain and swelling. Gradually, she made her way back to independence and strength, though she was still very vulnerable and emotionally unstable. During and after our work together, she enrolled in a community college, began to swim daily, and practiced deep relaxation. Her symptoms subsided in harmony with the increase in her physical fitness, confidence, and optimistic outlook toward the future.

in chronic joint inflammation, usually in the shoulders, elbows, hips, wrists, fingers, knees, ankles, and feet. Ultimately, cells of the synovial joint multiply at an abnormally faster rate, contributing to the swelling and finally filling up the joint space itself and eroding the cartilage and bone ends. Enzymes are produced that attack and eat away over time at the cartilage on joint surfaces that is essential for easy motion. Scar tissue may form, resulting in deformation and pain.

Rheumatoid arthritis, like other illness, has varied causes. For example, heredity seems sometimes to play a part through a blood protein called the "rheumatoid factor," which is found in about half of rheumatoid arthritics. The factor increases susceptibility but does not always cause rheumatoid arthritis.

Research has not yet produced definitive conclusions as to why rheumatoid arthritis develops when it does in specific people. However, certain personality traits have been associated in many cases. According to Mason:

> The following are typical: shy, inhibited, masochistic, self-sacrificing, anxious, depressed, resentful, and repressed anger. People who possess these characteristics along with the rheumatoid factor are the most likely to be candidates for this disease; people who have a healthy psychological balance and risk factor rarely suffer from this disease. (1980, 128)

My experience working with a handful of rheumatoid arthritic patients is consistent with references by a number of writers to a common pattern: Emotional tension significantly worsens the symptoms.

The case of the 48-year-old woman described in the box is consistent with studies showing that emotional distress, especially depression and anxiety, are sometimes tied to the exacerbation of this illness (Backus & Dudley, 1977; Crawford, 1981; Katz & Yelin, 1993; Weiner, 1977). A study by Flor and Turk (1988) found that the belief systems and interpretation patterns had considerable impact on pain and disability among a sample of rheumatoid arthritis patients. Another study has shown that the greater the helplessness among rheumatoid arthritis sufferers, the greater the pain and the greater their day-to-day functional impairment (Callahan, Brooks, & Pincus, 1988). On a more positive note, another study of 900 people with this ailment found that the higher the score on a sense-of-coherence measure, the lesser the difficulties with daily living and the better the overall health (Pincus, 1993). Still another study revealed that a class designed to increase self-efficacy—confidence in one's ability to carry out specific tasks—among rheumatoid arthritis patients did in fact increase task-specific confidence and that this enabled them to better deal with the disease (Pincus, 1993).

Like other stress-induced or stress-aggravated illnesses, rheumatoid arthritis often can be contained, if not diminished, through an integrated program of stress management.

Cancer

A hazard in discussing stress and **cancer** is that readers with cancer might conclude that they induced their own illness in a direct cause-effect fashion. Cancer is not that simple. No one knows for sure why cancer appears when and where it does. A number of factors can contribute: diet, carcinogens in the environment, viruses, the immune system, and others. While stress and personality probably do not cause cancer in a straightforward way, they may well play a part. Therefore, it is important to understand how they sometimes interrelate.

Everyone's body conducts its own continuous surveillance for outside invaders and internal imperfections, including cell mutations. Cell mutations, unpredictable changes in hereditary material, usually are recognized immediately and the deviant cell is quickly destroyed before it can multiply and turn into a wayward, uncontrolled tumor. But in rare instances, the mutant cells escape destruction, gradually multiply, and become a runaway tumor, sometimes consuming normal tissue and organs as they grow. If not stopped, the tumor can cause death as it impedes normal functioning of key body parts. In other instances, cancer can metastasize and break away to take up residence and multiply at another location in the body. This process of growth and metastasis can occur within a few weeks or over many years. Tragically, many cancers are not diagnosed and treated with radiation, chemotherapy, or surgery until it is too late.

THE ROLE OF STRESS IN CANCER   Stress sometimes contributes to cancer by weakening the body's immune system. McQuade and Aikman have stated:

> Stress helps to cause cancer because it depresses the immune system, the body's only real means of defending itself against malignant cells. It does this through the action of the adrenal cortex hormones, which partly affect t-lymphocytes. Searching out foreign antigens in the body is one of the tasks of the t-lymphocytes, and significantly they measure at low levels in the tissues of most cancer patients. (1974, 76)

Other studies have shown the number of t-cells to be lower in mice that have been exposed to stressful experiences (Riley, 1975). Though subject to criticism (Feist & Brannon, 1988; Fox, 1978), other studies have found an association between cancer and previous clustering of multiple life changes (Graham et al., 1971; Horne & Picard, 1979). A study by Shaffer and others (1987) found a 16-times-greater incidence of cancer over a 30-year period among 972 physicians who had been tested as "loners," likely to suppress emotion when in medical school. Other studies on the stress-cancer linkage were cited in the previous chapter. An illustrative recent study by Cooper and Fragher (1993) found risk of cancer to be greater among women with certain types of coping strategies and personality patterns but especially among those who, following major life events, were unable to externalize their emotions and obtain appropriate assistance from counselors or others.

EMOTIONAL FACTORS IN CANCER   What kinds of emotional patterns or experiences have been linked with increased risk of cancer? No simple answers exist, since mind-body interplay here is quite complex and varied. Several studies, however, are suggestive (Holland & Lewis, 1993). In a well-known study of 455 cancer patients, LeShan found four common elements:

1. A childhood marked by loneliness, guilt and self-condemnation, usually because of painful, troubled relations with parents and siblings. Often this is accentuated by specific events such as divorce or the death of a parent or sibling.
2. During late adolescence or early adulthood, the individual perceived a chance to come out of this deep loneliness by developing a "safe" relationship—usually with a spouse, child, or career. Feelings of isolation and loneliness greatly diminished though never completely disappeared. A great deal of emotional investment was poured into this new linkage, which lasted anywhere from 1 to over 40 years.
3. Then the safe world collapsed—retirement, death of spouse, children leaving home, divorce. On the surface, the person "adjusted," going about daily business as usual. But underneath, despair and hopelessness had returned. "Nothing gave them real satisfaction. It seemed to them as though the thing they had expected and feared all their lives—utter isolation and rejection—was now their eternal doom. . . ."
4. Helplessness and hopelessness followed. Meaning and zest went out of life. Energy declined. The fantasy from childhood that something was basically wrong with them returned. At some time between 6 and 18 months later, the cancer appeared. (1966, 482)

This scenario does not lead inevitably to cancer. Rather, LeShan's work suggests an increased risk, given such a sequence of events.

A study of experimental mice by Vernon Riley (1975) of the Fred Hutchinson Research Center in Seattle also is suggestive. Laboratory mice born to mothers with a known mammary-tumor virus were exposed to a variety of environmental stressors, including isolation and severe crowding. Mice demonstrated that mammary tumor occurrences in these already vulnerable offspring increased up to 90 percent under stress but remained at 7 percent in a protected, stress-free environment. A generalization from experimental mice to humans cannot be made without extreme caution, yet this study is consistent with the position that stress may play a part in cancer. In *Getting Well Again,* Simonton, Matthews-Simonton, and Creighton (1978) cite other important studies.

Schmale and Iker (1966) noted a tendency among their female cancer patients to have given up, to have fallen into a sense of hopeless frustration in dealing with an unresolvable conflict. Their study revealed that this conflict often seemed to occur about 6 months before the diagnosis of cancer.

Schmale and Iker then studied a sample of women who were presently cancer-free but who were determined to be a high biological risk for cancer of the cervix. After obtaining these women's scores on a psychological measure of "helplessness-prone personality," they predicted which ones would develop cancer. They were accurate 74 percent of the time. The authors did not claim that this proves that feelings of helplessness cause cancer. Rather, they suggested that a helpless orientation may have been a contributing factor, along with others.

In another study, this one lasting 15 years, W. A. Greene (1966) investigated the previous personal and social experiences of patients who contracted leukemia and lymphoma. He found unusually frequent incidents of loss, of a death or threat of death of a mother or, for men, a "mother figure," such as a wife. For men, other significant losses or threatened losses included job termination and career termination through retirement. For women, major losses included menopause or change of residence.

A focus of considerable controversy in this field is the potential influence on cancer of the cancer-prone behavior pattern: "a constellation of behavioral proclivities, attitudes, emotional tendencies, and concomitant physiological reaction patterns which includes self-sacrifice, extreme 'niceness,' passive coping, appeasement, and nonexpression of emotions—especially anger and other 'negative' feelings. This constellation has been associated with cancer risk and progression, although statistically the link is stronger and more conspicuous with regard to disease progression or recovery" (Temoshok & Dreher, 1994). The authors of a leading book on this topic note that just as the "pathological core of Type A behavior is hostility, the core factor associated with cancer progression seems to be the nonexpression of emotion. This assertion is supported by a long-term study of graduates of the Johns Hopkins School of Medicine showing that the greater the tendency to bottle up emotions, the greater the incidence of fatal cancers of all types" (Thomas, 1976). Yet Dossey (1991, 83), in commenting on this study, notes that "keeping this inside" is a way to get ahead in medical school. What is valued and rewarded by medical professors is machismo—the "I can take it" attitude.

A good deal of controversy exists among medical scientists about the relationship between depression and cancer. While animal studies have been reported suggesting depression may increase cancer risk, this is still an open question (Holland & Lewis, 1993). Anxiety has been shown to be harmful to the immune systems of breast cancer patients, increasing their future risk of recurrence (Recer, 1998).

The linkage between stress and cancer is complex and not entirely understood. Controversy and disagreement remains (Blaney, 1985; Cooper, 1984a; Cooper, 1984b; Levy, 1985). For a particularly strong critique from a humanistic and literary viewpoint, see Sontag (1990). It is safe to assert that the likelihood is considerable that stresses of certain types can, in some instances, increase chances of cancer. On the positive side, evidence was recently presented that group therapy can prolong survival time for breast cancer patients (Spiegel, 1990) and for patients with malignant melanoma (Fawzy et al., 1993). Several writers have developed detailed counseling approaches for assisting cancer patients with the stressful aspects of having the disease (Goodare, 1994; Rowland, 1994). Dreher (1996, 1997) maintains that early results of studies of psychosocial intervention with cancer patients warrant the same kind of broad-based clinical applications of these techniques as resulted similarly positive intervention studies with chemotherapy. He notes, however, that mainline medicine holds considerably greater skepticism toward psychosocial intervention studies than toward more traditional medical interventions.

Headache Disorders

If you ever have had one—or worse yet, have had recurrent or chronic ones—you know that headaches are no laughing matter. The extent to which people with chronic headaches indeed suffer is underscored by a recent study of 208 chronic-headache patients who sought assistance from a headache clinic. Using a questionnaire measure of quality of life, Solomon and colleagues (1993) found that headache patients had significantly worse mental health and worse physical, social, and role functioning than did patients with chronic diseases such as arthritis and diabetes. Their quality of life was comparable to patients with recent heart attacks or congestive heart failure. This study suggests that chronic **headache disorders** cause even more impairment of function than was previously thought.

Ever since observing as a child my father's tension-induced, debilitating headaches and later experiencing my own, I have sought to understand their origins, meaning, and physiological dynamics. More important, I have sought ways to not only control but also prevent them. Fortunately, I seldom have headaches anymore, owing to personal use of many of the whole-person, lifestyle-oriented practices presented in this book.

Let us now focus on the two main categories of stress-related headaches: migraines and tension headaches. Other types of headaches not discussed here include cluster headaches, sinus headaches, and temporal arteritis headaches (National Headache Foundation, 1994).

Migraine Headaches

Migraine headache is a painful condition associated with alternating constriction and dilation of cerebral arteries that supply blood to the brain (Blanchard & Andrasik, 1985; Kunkel, 1990a). During the first stage (prodrome), arteries constrict. Subjective signs of the prodrome include dizziness, flushness, visual static, and a familiar sense of uneasiness. Little or no pain may be felt at this stage. The second stage is the intense, usually one-sided pain associated with dilation of the arteries. Migraines can be devastating, often leading to nausea and to complete temporary incapacitation. Women suffer from them more often than men. Migraines occur most often between the ages of 16 and 35 and tend to decline by age 50.

A curious feature of migraines is that they do not usually occur simultaneously with intense stress, but afterward. Sundays and vacations are notorious migraine days, as if internal permission finally can be given to let down.

Migraines resemble heart attacks in that both are vascular problems. In many respects, the migraine sufferer also resembles the coronary-prone individual. Both tend to have perfectionist tendencies, for example. But whereas coronary-prone individuals are more likely to be aggressive, controlling, and hostile as they struggle to control their environment, the so-called migraine personality is more likely to be characterized by self-sacrifice, compliance, and inability to delegate.

Research on migraine patients many years ago by Harold Wolff (1950), still considered definitive by many experts, suggests that the typical migraine sufferer is basically insecure. As McQuade and Aikman have stated:

> What he really wants is to be loved, but he will settle for being admired, or simply approved of: anything to still his gnawing sense of worthlessness. It is for this reason that he drives himself so hard, selflessly taking on thankless chores, burdening himself with ever-increasing responsibilities, conscious, rigid, somewhat fanatical. It is not surprising, then, that when leisure finally does catch up with him, he cracks. (1974, 41)

The conversation-vascular system linkage discovered has relevance for migraines, as noted by Lynch.

> As I have already noted, the abnormalities of the circulatory system in the hypertensive patient and the disordered vascular responsiveness of the typical migraine patient can both be viewed as hidden or internal blushing. That is, just as the ordinary blush denotes an alteration in blood flow—triggered by human interaction—to a particular vascular bed, so too the circulatory changes observed in migraine and hypertensive patients also are triggered by human dialogue.(1985, 209)

Another consistent behavior pattern often preceding onset of the migraine is withdrawing emotional energy from another person. Emotion is blocked from flowing outward. Anger and resentment are contained—turned inward where they boil and fester. At this point, the patient often will report a cold, clammy feeling in feet and hands, sometimes contributing to sleep-onset insomnia.

A study at the Johns Hopkins School of Medicine asked 324 people, half of whom had frequent migraines, to complete a questionnaire (Brandt et al., 1990). The migraine group was 2.5 times more likely to be anxious, depressed, or tense than the control group. Of course, it could be that the migraines caused the emotional distress, rather than the other way around. Yet, most experts agree that emotional distress probably does help cause migraines.

> ## Headache Facts
>
> Here are a few facts about headaches from the National Headache Foundation.
>
> - More than 45 million Americans get chronic, recurring headaches.
> - Of these, 16–18 million suffer from migraines.
> - About 90 percent of all headaches are tension headaches.
> - It is estimated that industry loses $50 billion per year due to absenteeism and medical expenses caused by headaches.
> - Migraine sufferers lose more than 157 million workdays each year.
> - More than $4 billion are spent annually on over-the-counter pain relievers for headache.
> - 70 percent of all migraine sufferers are women.
> - Migraine headaches can be hereditary. If both parents have them, there is a 75 percent chance their children will have them; if only one parent is a migraine sufferer, there is a 50 percent chance. If even a distant relative has migraines, a 20 percent chance exists that any offspring will be prone to migraine headaches.

Source: National Headache Foundation (1994)

Experts continue to search for medical and behavioral methods of preventing and treating migraines. Several types of medications sometimes are prescribed, with mixed results.

Through meditation, autogenic relaxation, or biofeedback, the individual often can learn to arrest progression of the migraine at the point of the prodrome by learning to divert blood to the extremities and away from the head area. One study shows that biofeedback can be effective in reducing the frequency and severity of migraines (Lisspers et al., 1992). Another stress specialist reports that "85 percent of migraine patients I work with respond positively to stress reduction practices." He also reports:

> The people who do not get better usually are not practicing consistently because for their own reasons, they are not quite ready to give up their migraines and discover a headache-free existence. I strongly recommend that migraine sufferers study the secondary gains they get from migraines and evaluate their lives to determine what needs are not being met appropriately. (Mason, 1980, 118)

Tension Headaches

Tension headaches differ from migraines in that pain comes from tense muscles rather than from constricting and dilating of blood vessels (Kunkel, 1990b). As Holroyd, Appel, and Andrasik (1983) point out, however, it is not always easy to distinguish between the two types of headaches.

Tension headaches tend to appear in late afternoon and evenings for many persons, corresponding to their general fatigue level. One study found tensions tend to be more associated with minor hassles of daily life than with major life events (Howarth, 1965).

Tension headaches are part of a more general category of body discomforts from partially constricted or tense muscles. As a result of aroused emotions, muscles around the head tighten and do not let go (Gannon et al., 1987). For others, the target muscles for tension are in the neck and shoulder areas or the lower back.

A study found a significant correlation between frequency of headaches and depression (Chung & Kraybill, 1990). In fact, 3 of 4 persons with headaches recurring almost every day had a significantly elevated level of depression. The authors, writing in a medical journal, concluded, "Headache is an important marker for depression in the primary care setting. It can be inferred from this study that the clinician may need to focus more on treating the entity of depression than on treating just the symptom of headache." Of course, the causal direction could also be reversed: Perhaps depression is a response to chronic headaches, rather than the other way around. In any event, this study suggests they tend to be associated.

In all these cases, relaxation techniques usually can help. For example, I frequently have students in my classes tell me they come to class with a headache but that it disappears during or after a deep relaxation exercise. Regular exercise, consistent sleep, healthy nutrition, and daily deep relaxation can help prevent tension headaches in the first place. So can the use of self-talk methods to prevent emotional volatility and worry. Finally, a study found that high scores on a Headache Self-Efficacy Scale were associated with less depression, anxiety, and physical symptoms, and with less use of passive coping strategies (Martin et al., 1993). This study suggests that the belief that you can control events and experiences leading up to a headache can in fact reduce the frequency and severity of headaches.

Gastrointestinal Disorders

Among the most common stress-related maladies are **peptic ulcers** in the stomach or the duodenum, the upper part of the small intestine (Sanowski, 1990a; Weinstock & Clouse, 1987; Young et al., 1987). Ulcers can result from excessive gastric secretion in the stomach. Ultimately, a lesion or open sore develops, causing pain and sometimes bleeding.

Evidence (Whitehead, 1993) strongly suggests that a bacterium, *Helicobacter pylori,* is the dominant cause of peptic ulcers, although stress can play a part, sometimes as an independent cause, other times in aggravating bacterium-caused peptic ulcers. Duodenal ulcers, which are similar to gastric ulcers in the stomach except that lesions occur in the small intestine just beyond the stomach, usually take longer to heal because of the constant flow of food and gastric juices through that area. Experts believe that stress plays a greater role in the development and exacerbation of duodenal than stomach ulcer disease (Whitehead & Schuster, 1985). In both cases, "host factors" such as stress may be decisive in determining who does and does not develop ulcers, given the presence of the ulcer-causing bacterium (Melmed & Gelpin, 1996).

Clear evidence points to an elevation of digestive acids from the stress response (Cassileth & Drossman, 1993; Feist & Brannon, 1988; Folkenberg, 1989; Tennant, 1988; Weiner, 1977). This was observed directly for a number of years by Stewart Wolf in a patient who was forced to live with an opening in his stomach because of an unusual injury in his esophagus (Wolf, 1965). Wolf found that whenever his patient became more emotional, greater amounts of stomach acids were secreted.

Selye, who began his research on ulcers in rats more than 45 years ago, has summarized the link between stress ulcers as follows:

> The gastro-intestinal tract is particularly sensitive to general stress. Loss of appetite is one of the first symptoms in the great "syndrome of just being sick," and this may be accompanied by vomiting, diarrhea, or constipation. Signs of irritation and upset of the digestive organs may occur in any type of emotional stress. This is well known not only in soldiers who experience it during the tense excitation of battle, but even to students who pace the floor before my door awaiting their turn in oral examinations. (1976, 259)

Ulcer-prone people usually are driven "go-getters" who strive very hard in pursuit of ever- receding career goals. Underlying hostility often is present but seldom is expressed. An even stronger unconscious urge to be accepted and loved similarly is repressed. Men with ulcers have a high incidence of unhappy marriage. Curiously, one study found that wives with rheumatoid arthritis often have husbands with peptic ulcers. Such women tend to possess strong drives to achieve public recognition and esteem, something the traditional husband cannot accept or understand. The husband is driven by his own success need yet also craves emotional support, something the wife does not offer because of her resentment. "So the wife's bones and the husband's digestive tract ache to a common beat" (Tanner, 1976, 49).

Other studies on both animals and humans suggest that controllability of stressors influences chances of ulcers. Feist and Brannon point out:

> Ulcers are most likely when the animal anticipates painful stimuli but is helpless to do anything to avoid it, when it is not warned prior to pain and thus has not time to prepare, or when it must make decisions and remain constantly vigilant. If these findings can be generalized to the human situation, then it would appear that jobs with strongly distasteful elements that cannot be avoided, those with unexpected nuisances and exasperations, and those which require tough decisions with little real control are the ones most likely to lead to the development of ulcers.(1988, 129)

Smith and others (Smith et al., 1978) indeed found that those with lower- and middle-level jobs, where employees are harassed by the public, by supervisors, or by subordinates, were found to have ulcers more often than upper-level managers.

Whitehead has noted that the effects of stress on the gastrointestinal (GI) tract varies from person to person. One study he reports, for example, found that "In those who suffered mostly from constipation, food moved through the small intestine more slowly when the patients were under stress; in diarrhea-predominant IBS [irritable bowel syndrome] patients under stress, food moved more rapidly. Other researchers have found the same kind of variability" (1993, 166).

Whitehead also points out that "You don't need to have a chronic disorder to experience gastrointestinal discomfort under stress" (1993, 167). He cites one study at the University of North Carolina in which two-thirds of healthy people reported that stress caused an "altered bowel pattern—usually diarrhea." Half said stress has caused them abdominal pain. The box "Common GI Reactions to Everyday Trouble" presents Whitehead's description of several GI problems sometimes precipitated by "everyday troubles." For an excellent review of research literature on the role of psychosocial factors in gastrointestinal disorders, see Cassileth and Drossman (1993).

Physical exercise, controlling pace of life, containing the drive to prove oneself, deep relaxation, and support from a warm, accepting partner—all are likely to help reduce emotional pressures toward **GI disorders.** Conventional medical treatment may also be needed, especially in the case of ulcers (Rogers, 1990; Sanowski, 1990b).

Insomnia

Among self-observable signs of stress, Selye lists "insomnia, which is usually a consequence of being keyed-up." He also notes, "muscular activity or mental work which leads to a definite solution prepares you for rest and sleep, but intellectual efforts which set up self-maintaining tensions keep you awake" (1976, 175).

Difficulty sleeping takes two forms: inability to fall asleep (onset insomnia) and inability to sleep through the night. Onset insomnia usually results from being keyed-up or

---

Common GI Reactions to Everyday Trouble

Heartburn

This common problem results when acid from the stomach leaks up into the esophagus, a problem called *acid reflux.* You are more likely to have this problem if you overeat—which many people do under stress—because the excess food puts extra pressure on the esophageal sphincter, the valve that separates the two organs. Alcohol and nicotine also relax this sphincter, so more acid gets through if you deal with stress by smoking or drinking.

Indigestion (Dyspepsia)

Overeating may also lead to this problem, characterized by pain, a bloated feeling, and nausea. If stress causes you to gulp down your meals—swallow air along with your food—you increase the amount of gas in the GI tract, which can lead to belching, bloating, flatus, and abdominal discomfort. About one-quarter of all adults say they suffer frequently from bloating and repeated belching.

Stomach Pain

Pain that occurs on an empty stomach, and is not caused by an ulcer, may be worsened when stress increases the flow of stomach acid. Again, smoking and drinking make the problem worse: nicotine increases acid flow, and alcohol can inflame stomach tissues.

Functional Disorders of the Esophagus

A strong feeling of a "lump in the throat"—technically called the *globus symptom*—is a reaction of the esophagus almost always precipitated by strong emotion and more common in anxious people. Chest pain that begins in the esophagus also seems to be more common in people who are anxious or depressed.

Functional Dyspepsia

Troubling 20 to 30 percent of adults, this is characterized by recurrent upper abdominal pain or discomfort—often associated with bloating, nausea, or vomiting—in people who do not have peptic ulcer disease or cancer. Abnormal movement of food through the stomach or small intestine seems to cause the symptoms in some patients. Some studies suggest that patients with functional dyspepsia experience more stress and have more anxiety and depression than the general population, although not every study has found this.

Functional Anorectal Pain

About 9 percent of adults experience fleeting sharp pains in the anal canal or rectum, usually only a few times a year. More seriously, about 7 percent experience a dull and aching rectal pain, associated with muscle tenderness, which lasts for several minutes to days. Both conditions are believed to be linked to chronic muscle tension or spasm as well as to stress and anxiety, although not enough research has been done to be certain of this.

Source: Whitehead (1993, 168)

excessively aroused throughout the day and especially during the evening. The mind fails to quiet itself, and the body stays aroused. Even though physical fatigue may be very great, continuing excitation of the stress response makes quieting of brain waves into the delta zone, which is needed for sleep, difficult or impossible.

Either type of **insomnia** can result from excessive residual or anticipatory stress—inability to leave events, thoughts, and feelings from the previous day or mental preoccupation with events anticipated for the next day. In either case, the challenge is to control the mind, which in turn can exert control over bodily tension.

Occasional Insomnia

It is important to accept occasional insomnia without too much concern. A "high" from an intimate encounter, worry over something left unsaid or undone the previous day, excitement or worry about a challenge the next day—all will result in occasional sleeplessness, even for the healthy, well-balanced person. Missing part or even all of a night's sleep will have little effect on one's performance. When I was a collegiate middle-distance runner, one of my best-ever performances came after not sleeping at all the previous night.

Some people find it useful to get up during a sleepless night to read, write, study, think, or work on some other project. This is one way to turn a potential problem—lack of sleep—into an opportunity. I view these nights as "gifts of time."

See Application Exercise Exercise 7-2 for an assessment of the stress-insomnia linkage.

Chronic Insomnia

Quite a different matter is chronic insomnia, which can contribute to wear and tear and to stress buildup over days and weeks. Unfortunately, loss of sleep, worry, and tension often reinforce each other in a frustrating cycle, as shown in Figure 7-3.

Sometimes, this problem has purely physical origins (Moore, Clay, & Williams, 1990). When physical causes are not involved, the key questions with chronic insomnia are as follows: Where is the disharmony creating chronic off-balance tension or arousal? What needs to be done to resolve it? Meanwhile, a number of steps can be taken to facilitate sleep: regular exercise, daily deep relaxation, deliberate steps to taper off activity during the evening, avoiding caffeine late in the day, and the practice of specific relaxation techniques just before and after going to bed. Such techniques are discussed in more detail in Chapter 13.

See Application Exercise 7-3 to explore the possible role of stress in your own recent illnesses.

We have reviewed how stress can contribute to cardiovascular disorders, immune system disorders, gastrointestinal disorders, and insomnia. All result from some direct or

Figure 7-3

Sleep and Stress

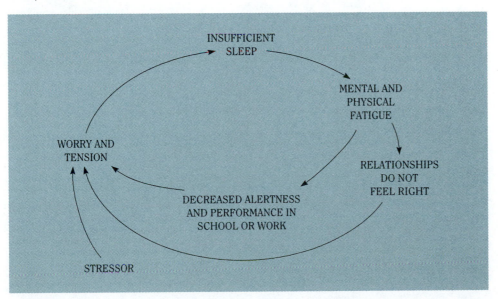

indirect difficulty with the stress response—a part of human experience so useful yet potentially so harmful. Other illnesses shown to be linked with stress as either a contributing cause or an aggravating influence include back pain, certain dental disorders, asthma, allergies, panic attacks, premenstrual syndrome, skin disorders such as psoriasis, hyperthyroidism, premature births, and even certain eye disorders.

In this chapter, we have examined in some detail the role of distress in a number of disorders. In order to gain still more understanding of these linkages, we turn in the next chapter to common distress-prone personality patterns.

References

American Heart Association (1985). *Heart facts.* Dallas.

Ardell, D. B. (1979). *High level wellness: An alternative to doctors, drugs, and disease.* New York: Bantam Books. Also see revised edition (1986). Berkeley: Ten Speed Press.

Backus, F. I., & Dudley, D. L. (1977). Observations of psychosocial factors and their relationship to organic disease. In Z. J. Lipowski, D. R. Lipsitt, & P. C. Whybrow (Eds.), *Psychosomatic medicine: Current trends and clinical applications.* New York: Oxford University Press, 13–26.

Benson, H. (1975). *The relaxation response.* New York: William Morrow.

Benson, H. (1984). *Beyond the relaxation response.* New York: Times Books.

Benson, H., Cotch, J. B., & Crasswell, K. D. (1978). Stress and hypertension: Interrelations and management. *Cardiovascular Clinics, 9,* 113–124.

Blanchard, E. B., & Andrasik, F. (1985). *Management of chronic headaches: A psychological approach.* New York: Pergamon Press.

Blaney, P. H. (1985). Psychological considerations in cancer. In N. Schneiderman & J. T. Tapp (Eds.), *Behavioral medicine: The biopsychosocial approach,* 533–563.

Bortz, W. M. (1991). *We live too short and die too long.* New York: Bantam Books.

Boutcher, S. H., & Nugent, F. W. (1993). Cardiac response of trained and untrained males to a repeated psychological stressor. *Behavioral Medicine, 19,* 21–27.

Brandt, J., Celentano, D., Stewart, W., Linet, M., & Folstern, M. F. (1990). Personality and emotional disorder in a community sample of migraine headache sufferers. *American Journal of Psychiatry, 147,* 303–308.

Bureau of the Census (1998). *Statistical Abstract of the United States: 1998.* Washington DC: Bureau of the Census, 100.

Callahan, L. F., Brooks, R. H., & Pincus, T. (1988). Further analysis of learned helplessness in rheumatoid arthritis using a "Rheumatoid Attitudes Index." *Journal of Rheumatology, 15,* 418–426.

Cassileth, B. R., & Drossman, D. A. (1993). Psychosocial factors in gastrointestinal illness. *Psychotherapy and Psychosomatics, 59,* 131–143.

Caudillo, C., et al., (1993). Psychophysiological reactivity and cardiac end-organ changes in white coat hypertension. *Hypertension, 21,* 836–844.

Chung, M. K., & Kraybill, D. E. (1990). Headache: A marker of depression. *The Journal of Family Practice, 31,* 360–364.

Cohen, S., Tyrell, D. A. J., & Smith, A. P. (1991). Psychological stress and susceptibility to the common cold, *New England Journal of Medicine, 325,* 606–612.

Cooper, C. L. (Ed.; 1984a). *Psychosocial stress and cancer.* Chichester, England: Wiley.

Cooper, C. L. (1984b). The social-psychological precursors to cancer. *Journal of Human Stress, 10,* 4–11.

Cooper, C. L., & Fragher, E. B. (1993). Psychological stress and breast cancer: The interrelationship between stress events, coping strategies, and personality. *Psychosomatic Medicine, 23,* 653–662.

Cottington, E. M. (1986). Job stress and suppressed anger lead to hypertension. *Family Practice News, 16,* 43.

Crawford, J. S. (1981). The role of rehabilitative medicine. In D. A. Gordon (Ed.), *Rheumatoid arthritis.* New York: Medical Examination Publishing, 301–318.

Dimsdale, J. E. (1993). Coronary heart disease in women: Personality and stress-induced biological responses, *Annals of Behavioral Medicine, 15,* 119–123.

Dreher, H. (1996). Can hypnosis rotate a breech baby before birth?" *Advances, 12,* 46–50.

Dreher, H. (1997). The scientific and moral imperative for broad-based psychosocial interventions for cancer. *Advances, 13,* 38–49.

Dossey, L. (1991). *Meaning & medicine.* New York: Bantam Books.

Eliot, R. S. (1989). Labile HT is found in about 17% of FPs; Prevalence appears to vary by specialty. *Family Practice News, 19,* 3.

Eliot, R. S. (1994). *From stress to strength.* New York: Bantam Books.

Eliot, R. S., & Breo, D. L. (1984). *Is it worth dying for?* New York: Bantam Books.

Elliott, S. J. (1995). Psychosocial stress, women and heart health: A critical review. *Social Science and Medicine, 40,* 105–115.

Engel, G. L. (1971). Sudden and rapid death during psychological stress. *Annals of Internal Medicine, 74,* 771–782.

Engel, G. L. (1977) Emotional stress and sudden death, *Psychology Today, 11,* 115–121.

Evans, T. (1987). Exercise self-tests. *The Stanford Health & Exercise Handbook.* Stanford, CA: Stanford Alumni Association.

Farquhar, J. W., Fortmann, S. P., Flora, J. A., Taylor, C. B., Haskell, W. L., Williams, P. T., Maccoby, N, & Wood, P. D. (1990). Effects of communitywide education on cardiovascular disease risk factors: The Stanford Five-City Project. *Journal of the American Medical Association, 264,* 359–365.

Fawzy, F. I., et al. (1993). Malignant melanoma: Effects of an early structured psychiatric intervention, coping, and affective state on recurrence and survival 6 years later. *Archives of General Psychiatry, 50-9,* 676–689.

Feist, J., & Brannon, L. (1988). *Health psychology: An introduction to behavior and health.* Belmont, CA: Wadsworth Publishing Company.

Flor, H., & Turk, D. C. (1988). Chronic back pain and rheumatoid arthritis: Predicting pain and disability from cognitive variables. *Journal of Behavioral Medicine, 11,* 251–266.

Folkenberg, J. (1989). Ulcers and stress: The missing link? *Psychology Today, 23,* 24–25.

Fox, B. H. (1978). Premorbid psychosocial factors as related to cancer incidence. *Journal of Behavioral Medicine, 1,* 45–133.

Frasure-Smith, N., Lesperance, F., & Talajic, M. (1993). Depression following myocardial infarction: Impact on 6-month survival. *Journal of the American Medical Association, 270,* 1819–1825.

Fredrikson, M., & Matthews, K. A. (1990). Cardiovascular responses to behavioral stress and hypertension: A meta-analytic review. *Annals of Behavioral Medicine, 12,* 30–39.

Galton, L. (1973). *The silent disease.* New York: Signet.

Gannon, L. R., Haynes, S. N., Cuevas, J., & Chavez, R. (1987). Psychophysiological correlates of induced headaches. *Journal of Behavioral Medicine, 10,* 411–423.

Genest, M., & Genest, S. (1987). *Psychology and health.* Champaign: Research Press.

Gerin, W., Milner, D., Chawala, S., & Pickering, T. G. (1995) Social support as a moderator of cardiovascular reactivity in women: A test of the direct effects and buffering hypotheses. *Psychosomatic Medicine, 57,* 16–22.

Glaser, R., & Kiecolt-Glaser, J. K. (1997). Chronic stress modulates the virus-specific immune response to latent herpes simplex virus type 1. *Annals of Behavioral Medicine, 19,* 78–82.

Goodare, H. (1994). Counseling people with cancer: Questions and possibilities. *Advances, 10,* 4–26.

Graham, S., Snell, L. M., Graham, J. B., & Ford, L. (1971). Social trauma in the epidemiology of cancer of the cervix. *Journal of Chronic Diseases, 24,* 711–725.

Green, J., & Shellenberger, R. (1991). *The dynamics of health and wellness: A biopsychosocial approach.* Fort Worth: Holt, Rinehart and Winston.

Greenberg, S. F., & Valletutti, P. J. (1980). *Stress and the helping professions.* Baltimore: Brooks.

Greene, W. A. (1966). The psychosocial setting of the development of leukemia and lymphoma. *Annals of the New York Academy of Sciences, 125,* 794–801.

Harburg, E., Schull, W. J., & Erfurt, J. C. (1970). A family set method for estimating heredity and stress: A pilot study of blood pressure among Negroes in high and low stress areas. *Journal of Chronic Diseases, 23,* 69–81.

Holland, J. C., & Lewis, S. (1993). Emotions and cancer: What do we really know? In D. Goleman & J. Gurin (Eds.), *Mind-body medicine.* Yonkers: Consumer Reports Books, 85–110.

Holroyd, K. A., Appel, M. A., & Andrasik, F. (1983). A cognitive-behavioral approach to psychophysiological disorders. In D. Meichenbaum & M. E. Jaremko (Eds.), *Stress reduction and prevention.* New York: Plenum Press, 230–241.

Horne, R. L., & Picard, R. S. (1979). Psychosocial risk factors for lung cancer. *Psychosomatic Medicine, 41,* 503–514.

Howarth, E. (1965). Headache, personality and stress. *British Journal of Psychiatry, 111,* 1193–1197.

Isselbacher, K. (1981). *Principles of internal medicine.* New York: McGraw.

Jian, W., Babyak, M., Krantz, D. S., Waugh, R. A., Coleman, R. E., Hanson, M. M. Frid, D. J., McNulty, S., Morris, J. J., O'Connor, C. M, & Blumenthal, J. A. (1996). Mental stress-induced myocardial ischemia and cardiac events. *Journal of the American Medical Association, 275,* 651–656.

Johnsgård, K. (1989). *The exercise prescription for depression and anxiety.* New York: Plenum.

Kannel, W. B. (1990). CHD risk factors: A Framingham study update. *Hospital Practice, 25,* 119–130.

Kasl, S. V., Evans, A. S., & Niederman, J. S. (1979). Psychosocial risk factors in the developpment of infectious mononucleosis. *Psychosomatic Medicine, 41,* 445–466.

Katz, P. P., & Yelin, E. H. (1993). Prevalence and correlates of depressive symptoms among persons with rheumatoid arthritis, *Journal of Rheumatology, 20,* 790–796.

Kiecolt-Glaser, J. K., & Glaser, R. (1993). Mind and immunity. In D. Goleman & J. Gurin (Eds.), *Mind-body medicine.* Yonkers: Consumer Reports Books, 39–61.

Krantz, D. S., Kop, W. J., Santiago, H. T., & Gottdiener, J. S. (1996). Mental stress as a trigger of myocardial ischemia and infarction. *Cardiology Clinician, 14,* 271–287.

Kunkel, R. S. (1990a). Office management of benign headache syndromes: I. Migraine headache. *Modern Medicine, 58,* 50–58.

Kunkel, R. S. (1990b). Office management of benign headache syndromes: III. Tension-type headache. *Modern Medicine, 58,* 2–74.

LeShan, L. (1966). An emotional life-history pattern associated with neoplastic disease. *Annals of the New York Academy of Sciences, 125,* 780–793.

Levy, S. M. (1985). *Behavior and cancer.* San Francisco: Jossey-Bass Publishers.

Lisspers, J., Ost, L. G., & Skagerberg, B. (1992). Clinical effects of biofeedback treatment in migraine: The relation to achieved self-control and pretreatment predictors. *Scandinavian Journal of Behaviour Therapy, 21,* 171–190.

Lynch, J. J. (1985). *The language of the heart.* New York: McGraw-Hill.

Manuck, S. B., Kasprowisz, A. L., & Muldoon, M. F. (1990). Behaviorally-evoked cardiovascular reactivity and hypertension: Conceptual issues and potential associations. *Annals of Behavioral Medicine, 12,* 17–29.

Martin, N. J., Holroyd, K. A., & Rokicki, L. A. (1993). The headache self-efficacy scale: Adaptation to recurrent headaches, *Headache, 33,* 244–248.

Mason, J. L. (1980). *Guide to stress reduction.* Culver City, CA: Peace.

McGinnis, J. M., & Foege, W. H. (1993). Actual causes of death in the United States. *Journal of the American Medical Association, 270,* 2207–2212.

McQuade, W., & Aikman, A. (1974). *Stress.* New York: Bantam Books.

Melmed, R.N., & Gelpin, Y. (1966). Duodenal ulcer: The helicobacterization of a psycho-somatic disease? *Isreali Journal of Medical Science, 32,* 211–216.

Moore, C., Clay, H., & Williams, R. L. (1990). Sleep disorders: Practical management. *Hospital Medicine, 26,* 96–104.

Mustacchi, P. (1990). Stress and hypertension. *Western Journal of Medicine, 153,* 180–185.

National Headache Foundation (1994). *National Headache Foundation Fact Sheet.*

Ogylvie, B. S. (1973). The stimulus addicts. *The Physician and Sports Medicine, 1,* 61–65.

Ornish, D. (1990). *Dr. Dean Ornish's program for reversing heart disease.* New York: Random House.

Ostfeld, A. M. & Shekelle, R. B. (1967). Psychological variables and blood pressure. In J. Stamler, R. Stamler, & T. N. Pullman (Eds.), *The epidemiology of hypertension.* New York: Grune and Stratton, 321–331.

Paul, L. J. (1966). Sudden death at impasse. *Psychological Forum,* I, 88–89.

Pelletier, K. R. (1973). *Holistic medicine: From stress to optimum health.* New York: Delacourte Press.

Pelletier, K. R. (1977). *Mind as healer, mind as slayer.* New York: Dell.

Pelletier, K. R. (1994). *Sound mind, sound body.* New York: Simon & Schuster.

Perini, C., et al. (1993). Ischemic ECG changes are found more often in asymptomatic men with a coronary prone behavior pattern. *Journal of Psychosomatic Research, 37,* 355–360.

Phillips, P. (1990). Bacterium-ulcer link clinched. *World Medical News, 31,* 17.

Pickering, T. G., & Gernin, W. (1990). Cardiovascular reactivity in the laboratory and the role of behavioral factors in hypertension: A critical review. *Annals of Behavioral Medicine, 12,* 3–16.

Pincus, T. (1993). Arthritis and theumatic diseases: What doctors can learn from their patients. In D. Goleman & J. Gurin (Eds.), *Mind-body medicine.* Yonkers: Consumer Reports Books, 177–192.

Psychology Today (1994). The death of the blues, *27,* 10.

Recer, P. (1998). Anxiety may harm breast cancer patients, *Sacramento Bee,* January 7, A7.

Riley, V. (1975). Mouse mammary tumors: Alterations of incidence as apparent function of stress. *Science, 189,* 465–467.

Rogers, A. I. (1990). Medical treatment and prevention of peptic ulcers. *Postgraduate Medicine, 88,* 57–60.

Rowland, J. (1994). Psychosocial counseling in cancer: In pursuit of the perfect paradigm. *Advances, 10,* 19–26.

Sanowski, R. A. (1990a). Peptic ulcer disease: Update on its etiology and diagnosis. *Modern Medicine, 58,* 46–47.

Sanowski, R. A. (1990b). The changing spectrum of therapy for active peptic ulcer disease. *Modern Medicine, 58,* 50–51.

Schmale, A. H., & Iker, H. (1966). The psychological setting of uterine cervical cancer. *Annals of the New York Academy of Sciences, 125,* 807–813.

Selye, H. (1974). *Stress without distress.* Philadelphia: Lippincott.

Selye, H. (1976). *The stress of life* (rev. ed.). New York: McGraw-Hill.

Shaffer, J. W., Graves, P. L., Swank, R. T., & Pearson, T. A. (1987). *Journal of Behavioral Medicine, 10,* 441–448.

Simonton, O. C., Matthews-Simonton, S., & Creighton, J. L. (1978). *Getting well again.* New York: Bantam Books.

Smith, M., Colligan, M., Horning, R. W., & Harrel, J. (1978). *Occupational comparison of stress-related disease incidence.* Cincinnati: Cincinnati National Institute for Occupational Safety and Health.

Solomon, G. D., Skobieranda, F. G., & Gragg, L. A. (1993). Quality of life and well-being of headache patients: Measurement by the medical outcomes study instrument, *Headache, 33,* 351–358.

Sontag, S. (1990). *Illness as metaphor and AIDS and its metaphors.* New York: Doubleday.

Spiegel, D. (1990). Group therapy said to prolong breast cancer survival: *Family Practice News, 20,* 9.

Suarez, E. C., & Williams, R. (1989). Situ- ational determinants of cardiovascular and emotional reactivity in high and low hostile men. *Psychosomatic Medicine, 51,* 404–418.

Tanner, O. (1976). *Stress.* New York: Time-Life Books.

Tennant, C. (1988). Psychosocial causes of duodenal ulcer. *Australian and New Zealand Journal of Psychiatry, 22,* 195–201.

Temoshok, L. R., & Dreher, H. (1994). Disconnects in understanding *The type C connection. Advances, 10,* 64–72.

Thomas, C. (1976). Precursors of premature disease and death: The predictive potential of habits and family attitudes. *Annals of Internal Medicine, 85,* 653–658.

Thomas, G. S., Lee, P. R., Franks, P., & Paffenbarger, R. S., Jr. (1981). *Exercise and health: The evidence and the implications.* Cambridge, MA: Oelgeschlager, Gunn & Hain.

Thyrum, E. T., Blumenthal, J. A., & Siegel, W. (1994). Positive mood ratings distinguish white coat from persistent hypertension, presented at the Society for Behavioral Medicine.

Ursin, H. (1991). Stress, distress, and immunity. *Annals of the New York Academy of Sciences, 41,* 204–211.

Van Rood, Y. R., et al. (1993). The effects of stress and relaxation on the *in vitro* immune response in man: A meta-analytic study. *Journal of Behavioral Medicine, 16,* 163–181.

Vögele, C., Jarvis, A., & Cheeseman, K. (1997). Anger suppression, reactivity, and hypertension risk: Gender makes a difference. *Annals of Behavioral Medicine, 19,* 61–69.

Weinberger, M. H. (1990). Advances in hypertension in the 1980s. *Practical Cardiology, 16,* 58–65.

Weiner, H. M. (1977). *The psychobiology of human illness.* New York: Elsevier.

Weinstock, L. B., & Clouse, R. E. (1987). A focused overview of gastrointestinal physiology. *Annals of Behavioral Medicine, 9,* 3–6.

Whitehead, W. E. (1993). Gut feelings: Stress and GI tract. In D. Goleman & J. Gurin (Eds.), *Mind-body medicine.* Yonkers: Consumer Reports Books.

Whitehead, W. E., & Schuster, M. M. (1985). *Gastrointestinal disorders: Behavioral and physiological basis for treatment.* New York: Academic Press.

Williams, R. (1989). *The trusting heart: Great news about type A behavior.* New York: New Times Books/Random House.

Williams, R., & Williams, V. (1993). *Anger kills.* New York: HarperCollins.

Wissler, R. W. (1990). Autopsy findings in large study confirm that CHD starts early. *Family Practice News, 20,* 7.

Wolf, S. (1965). *The stomach.* New York: Oxford.

Wolff, H. G. (1950). Life stress and cardiovascular disorders. *Circulation, I,* 187–203.

Young, L. D., Richter, J. E., Bradley, L. A., & Anderson, K. O. (1987). Disorders of the upper gastrointestinal system: An overview. *Annals of Behavioral Medicine, 9,* 7–12.

Zegans, L. S. (1982). Stress and the development of somatic disorders. In L. Goldberger & S. Breznitz (Eds.), *Handbook of stress: Theoretical and clinical aspects.* New York: Free Press, 134–152.

Application Exercise 7-1

Your Personal Reactions to "Upstream/Downstream"

1. What exactly is meant by Upstream and Downstream?

2. What implications does this metaphor hold for your own life? For your community? For state and national policymakers?

3. What other metaphors can you create having to do with stress, distress, positive stress, prevention, healthy lifestyles, and/or the role of thinking in distress?

Application Exercise 7-2

Insomnia and Stress

Either during recent or coming weeks, be aware of episodes of insomnia. Write about them as follows.

1. Was the insomnia of the sleep-onset or interrupted-sleep type, or both? Describe what happened—or did not.

2. What was your emotional and physical condition that evening? Were you bothered, preoccupied, or upset? About what? Were you keyed up for other reasons?

3. What events that evening, day, or week preceded and might have contributed to your insomnia?

4. Looking back, how might you have prevented the insomnia? How might you minimize it in the future?

Application Exercise 7-3

Personal Examples of Stress-Related Illnesses

Think back to an instance of personal illness.

1. To what extent do you suspect stress might have contributed to this illness, if at all?

2. If you think stress did contribute to this illness, which of the four intervening linkages between stress and illness discussed in this chapter do you think were at work?

3. Looking back, what early warning signs (distress symptoms) did you or might you have detected before the onset of the illness itself?

4. Looking back, what might you have done, if anything, in advance to deal with stress differently in order to prevent this illness? Explain.

PART III

Distress-Prone and
Distress-Related Influences

CHAPTER 8

Before I had my heart attack, I didn't have any friends. When I played poker, I played to win from the bastards.

—JESSE LAIR

Distress-Prone Personality Patterns: Type A Behavior and Hostility

INTRODUCTION: DISTRESS-PRONE AND DISTRESS-RESISTANT INFLUENCES

A Student Faces Cancer

As a high school sophomore, I was diagnosed as having cancer, a word I had always thought synonymous with death. Until I had cancer, I never understood what it was like. Hell, I felt fine! I then decided, "If I don't feel sick, then I'm not going to be sick." The tumor was removed, and I fought the adversity. I would not let it stop me.

I was a three-sport athlete in high school and the doctors told me I would never play a contact sport such as football or basketball again, my two favorites. I took my doctor's advice. That's right, I took it and used it as a motivator! Six months later I played in the Oakland Coliseum for the North Coast Section 3A Championship, and even though we lost, when I look back now, I feel it was one of the biggest victories of my life.

My parents were devastated. All my friends were shook up, and rightfully so. This could have been a very traumatic situation. I didn't let that happen. I took what most thought to be a terrible stroke of fate and turned it to my favor. To this day, I am still playing football. I feel as if that experience has helped me, as a person as well as a player.

I have a six-inch circular scar on my back most would consider a burden. I think of it as a way to meet women at the beach!

It's all in the interpretation.

The story in the box from one of my students graphically describes the reaction of an obviously resilient, strong individual to a life-threatening experience, an experience that might send another person into a depressive, self-pitying downward spiral. This young man displayed a distress-resistant personality.

Contrast the scenario in the first box with the true story in the next box. This unfortunate woman displayed an all-too-common distress-prone personality style—the helplessness-hopelessness that researchers have determined to be not only erosive of quality of life but a threat to health.

The next four chapters are about distress-prone and distress-resistant influences, both within the person and in the environment. This chapter and Chapters 9 and 10 focus on internal influences—distress-prone and distress-resistant personality patterns. We then turn attention in Chapter 11 to conditions in the environment that are distress-producing and distress-resisting.

Personality is a person's enduring set of habits of thinking, feeling, and acting. Personality is the "style" we carry through time.

Our first order of business is to clarify the term **personality.** Personality is a person's enduring set of habits of thinking, feeling, and acting. Personality is the "style" we carry through time. Personality is formed through a combination of "nature" and "nurture." We know that both genetics and social learning play a part in the formation of personality. We need not concern ourselves here with trying to establish the precise balance between the two, since scholars who study this issue are still searching for answers themselves.

It is reasonable to assume that total personality is relatively stable. Yet specific parts of personality certainly are malleable and open to change. Illustrations include reducing aggressiveness, becoming a better listener, becoming more tolerant and forgiving, developing more realistic expectations of the self and others, and reducing the tendency to react to challenge with depression or overreactions. Many experts believe behavior is more changeable than attitudes or beliefs, though this is open to debate.

> ## Utter Hopelessness
>
> A 45-year-old woman undergoing psychoanalysis . . . had a growing belief that death was the only possible solution for an intolerable situation. She felt a hopeless inability to resolve the problems of an unhappy marriage that she believed would destroy her, and she felt too old and too afraid of being alone to break away to start a life anew. She collapsed an hour after what she interpreted as a rejection by her analyst and within several minutes after a rejection by her husband. This had been preceded by the deaths within 7 months of both parents and a disappointing visit to her only daughter. Rushed to a hospital, she was pulseless and [died] . . . in ventricular fibrillation.

Source: Coolidge

Individuals vary along a continuum of distress-proneness or distress-resistance. We will draw on a number of theories from the personality and stress fields to better understand these tendencies, beginning with several (from among many more) **distress-prone personality patterns.** We begin in this chapter with Type A behavior and hostility.

Distress-prone personality pattern is the person's enduring habits of thinking, feeling, and acting that contribute to personal distress.

THE TYPE A PERSONALITY PATTERN

Every now and then, a concept from the behavioral sciences so captures the public's attention that it enters into mass consciousness and becomes part of our common parlance. **Type A behavior** is one such term.

The Type A pattern has been one of the most intensely studied topics in the stress field. This section is intended to deepen your understanding of Type A behavior and to clear up several popular misconceptions, including the mistaken notion that Type A behavior is all bad. We will describe the historical antecedents of this concept, what Type A behavior is, its measurement, its effects on health and well-being, and how and why it has these effects. We then will examine the one component of Type A behavior, hostility, that is most toxic. The review of research literature presented here should be understood as touching on highlights related to these two fields, rather than as a comprehensive review. This is necessitated by the truly voluminous amount of research that has been conducted in recent years.

Early Studies of Emotions and the Heart

The idea that emotions affect the heart is hardly new. Redford Williams notes that "Over the centuries, two Roman emperors, a Catholic pope, and a king of Spain have been reported to have died suddenly while in the throes of acute emotional distress" (1989, 18). As early as the 17th century, some physicians spoke of the link between emotions and heart problems. For example, William Harvey, one of the founders of modern physiology and medicine, wrote in 1628 that "Every affection of the mind that is attended with either pain or pleasure, hope or fear, is the cause of an agitation whose influence extends to the heart" (Williams, 1989, 19). In 1868, a German doctor, T. von Deusch (1868), described the person prone to heart attacks as often speaking in a loud voice and working through the night.

While a professor of medicine at Oxford University, Sir William Osler (1892) contributed some of the most significant early ideas about mind-body connections. As Williams points out, Osler specifically wrote important insights about the role of emotions in heart disease. Osler described the typical heart patient as "not the delicate, neurotic person . . . but the robust, the vigorous in mind and body, the keen and ambitious man, the indicator of whose engine is always at 'full speed ahead'" (cited in Williams, 1989, 19). Osler saw coronary heart disease as caused by "the high pressure at which men live and the habit of working the machine to its maximum capacity" (Williams, 1989, 19).

More recently, Menninger and Menninger (1936) wrote about heart patients' frequent tendency toward an aggressive personality. Dunbar (1943), another pioneer of psychosomatic (mind-body) medicine, went a step further, believing heart patients possessed a coronary-prone personality. Dunbar's sample was based on unstructured interviews with only 22 patients, certainly too small a sample on which to base sound scientific conclusions (Storement, 1951; Weiss et al., 1957). Since these observations were based on patients already diagnosed with heart disease, nothing was proven. Still needed were studies of the development of coronary disease in individuals who exhibited some or all of these emotional tendencies but who at the outset of the study were free of the disease (Roskies, 1987).

In the 1950s, Friedman and Rosenman led a team of medical scientists investigating the role of cholesterol and other risk factors in the development of coronary artery disease. After finding that as many as half of all heart attacks could not be explained by "conventional risk factors" (e.g., family history, cigarette smoking, high blood pressure, elevated cholesterol), they began to suspect that emotions or personality should be studied. Not only were they influenced by the early hunches of Harvey, von Deusch, Osler, the Menningers, and others, but also they were influenced by a couple of leads of their own. One was the casual observation by an upholstering company that the front edges of the waiting room seats in Friedman and Rosenman's clinic seemed to be unusually worn down. The workers wondered what kind of patients came here—people who would be so impatient and on edge that they would wear down the front edge of the seats (Friedman & Ulmer, 1984).

The other lead came from what Friedman has described as the "first bona fide research effort in this field," a study of 40 volunteer public accountants.

> The blood cholesterol of these accountants and also the speed at which their blood clotted in January, 1957, was completely normal and remained so when they were studied biweekly for the remainder of January and through February and March. During these same months the accountants did not alter either their eating or exercise habits. During the first two weeks of April, however, as the tax-filing deadline approached and our subjects were desperately striving to finish their clients' tax forms and get them signed and in the mail, their average blood cholesterol level rose abruptly and their blood began clotting at a dangerously accelerated rate. In May and June, with no further deadlines to face, the blood cholesterol and clotting times of these men returned to normal levels. For the first time in medical history, a clear-cut demonstration of the power of the mind alone to alter man's blood cholesterol and clotting time had been achieved.(Friedman & Ulmer, 1984, 6)

When this finding was reported at the annual scientific meetings of the American Heart Association, it was met with dead silence (Friedman, Rosenman, & Carroll, 1958). Scientific experts in the audience were highly skeptical that anything other than diet could affect cholesterol level in the bloodstream.

When Friedman and Rosenman applied for government agency funding to conduct a broader study of the effect of "emotional stress" on coronary heart disease, they were twice turned down. After inquiring what had gone wrong, they were advised informally to avoid the term "emotion" in their grant application in order not to offend psychiatrists

Emotions and the Heart in Everyday Language

A few years ago, a friend and fellow Chicoan, Ruth Hornaday, began to experience symptoms of heart valve disease. Open-heart surgery eventually corrected the problem, but along the way she inquired deeply into the interplay of emotions and the heart, a subject that interested her for both personal and professional reasons, as a heart patient and a psychotherapist.

In the course of her studies, she was struck by the multitude of linkages in our common language between emotions and the heart. Here is the list she constructed from various sources and passed along to me one day during a morning walk at our Enloe Hospital Cardiac Rehabilitation Program.

Heartaches and sorrows

Heartaches and suffering

Heartburn

Softhearted

Hardened his (her) heart

Lighthearted

Weakhearted

Chickenhearted

Understanding heart (responds)

Lonely heart

Stingy hearted

Cracked heart

Sick at heart

Heart of stone

Heart pounding like a (trip) hammer

Bent heartstrings

Pain in my heart

Take heart

Lose heart

Corner of my heart

Warmed my heart

Warmed the cockles of my heart

Eat your heart out

The heart of the matter

Heart fund

"A merry heart doeth good like a medicine" (Bible)

Cut to the heart (negative feeling of hurt)

Openhearted and open heart surgery

Cross my heart and hope to die

Downhearted

Fainthearted

Heavyhearted

Hardhearted

Bighearted

Bleeding heart

Falsehearted

Brokenhearted

Aching heart

Tenderhearted

Blackhearted

Heartsick and weary

Heart like a stone

Disheartened

Heart fluttering

Plucked the strings of my heart

Played on heart strings

On the strings of my heart

Pure in heart (see God)

Change of heart

Bottom of my heart

Learned by heart

Eat "hearty"— "hearty" appetite

Right to the heart of . . .

Heart association

Touched my heart

Like a knife in my heart (betrayal)

Heart is closed off

who reviewed the applications—and who apparently believed that cardiologists could not possibly be equipped to study emotional matters. Said a government employee, "I believe you fellows are describing a behavior pattern, something you've actually witnessed. Why don't you just label it Type A behavior pattern?" (Friedman & Ulmer, 1984, 6). They did, they were funded, and a new term entered the American lexicon.

Before summarizing the results of this research, it is important to describe the nature of Type A behavior. For more detail on the conceptual and research literature, see the anthology edited by Strube (1990) and especially its review article by Rosenman (1990).

What Is Type A Behavior?

The Type A personality pattern is characterized by a never-ending struggle to accomplish, produce ("hard-driving"), and get more things done than time permits ("hurry sickness") and by a generalized orientation of impatience, irritability, and anger-expression ("free-floating hostility").

Friedman and Rosenman, who conducted the pioneering early studies on the subject, maintain that about three of every four individuals living in cities are probably Type A. They point out that some of the elements of Type A, notably hard-driving and hurry sickness, are valued and rewarded in the competitive work environment in this country.

In their informative book, *Treating Type A Behavior and Your Heart,* Friedman and Ulmer (1984) discuss the components of Type A behavior and their relationships to **pathophysiological processes** (for a summary, see Figure 8-1). Let us examine several of these key components.

Insecurity of Status

Why do Type A persons engage in their incessant struggle? The key reason is that they typically suffer from a hidden lack of self-esteem that in turn results in **insecurity of status.** Thus, they feel compelled to compare themselves with others. They usually come out looking deficient in their own eyes. A fascinating by-product of this perceived deficiency is greater tendency to self-referencing in conversation (Fontana et al., 1990), part of an ongoing struggle to protect or enhance self-esteem.

Self-esteem is a product of the gap between self-expectations and personal achievement. Type A's usually hold such unrealistically high expectations of themselves and are so self-critical that they feel chronically driven to do more and get more—with never a let-up.

Time Urgency (Hurry Sickness)

Type A behavior is a common antecedent to perpetual overload. Out of her or his insecurity and low self-esteem comes the Type A's struggle with time. Most often this means, very simply, taking on more obligations or commitments than time available—and then taking on still more.

The person swirling in this maelstrom feels driven, yet overwhelmed. The only way out seems to be to accelerate, to speed up. Friedman and Ulmer point out:

Figure 8-1

The Nature of Type A Behavior and Its Outcomes

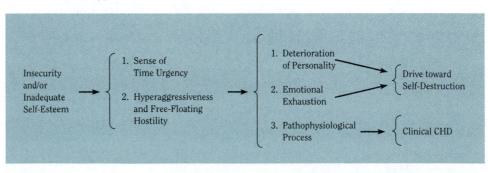

Source: Friedman & Ulmer (1984, 70)

To keep up with his overload of projects, the Type A is forced to accelerate the rate at which he thinks, plans, and executes almost all his daily functions. Thus he increases not only his own rate of speech but also forces others to speak more quickly to him; attempts to read and write faster; to walk and eat faster; to drive his car as fast and as cleverly as he can without actually violating traffic regulations (or getting caught at it). Even his minor activities will be accelerated. For example, the male Type A may seek to shave faster by discarding soap, brush, and blade for the most efficient electric razor he can find. One Type A physician friend of ours has already bought ten different electric razors, in a search for the one that shaves fastest. And we know of three Type A's who use two electric razors so that they can save time by shaving both sides of the face simultaneously! (1984, 37)

One notable aspect of **time urgency** or **hurry sickness** is "polyphasic thinking and behavior"—thinking and doing more than one thing at a time. Not satisfied with accomplishing enough every minute of the day, the Type A person tries to get still more done by doing (or thinking about) more than one thing at a time. Commonly, this takes the form of thinking about something else while "listening" during a conversation. While on the telephone, he or she might read the paper, write a check, prepare dinner, or check the mail, all made easier by portable phones. He might read the paper and eat breakfast—while shaving. Or read the morning paper while driving to work.

Hyperaggressiveness

To possess a high-achievement orientation means to strive for high goals. **Hyperaggressiveness** goes beyond that to include a desire to dominate, with little regard for the feelings or rights of others (Friedman & Ulmer, 1984). As author Jess Lair once stated, "Before I had my heart attack, I didn't have any friends. When I played poker, I played to win from the bastards" (Friedman & Ulmer, 1984, 33).

This pattern often develops very early, sometimes manifesting itself in the play and social habits of small children. Low self-esteem and status insecurity usually accompany this characteristic even at an early age.

As Type A's become frustrated in their incessant struggles, their self-esteem is further damaged—and they struggle even more, typically causing still more aggressiveness.

Free-Floating Hostility

"Free-floating hostility is a permanently indwelling anger that shows itself with ever-greater frequency in response to increasingly trivial happenings" (Friedman & Ulmer, 1984, 34). The person with this pattern is perpetually agitated. In their earlier book, Friedman and Rosenman referred to this tendency as **AIAI (Anger, Irritation, Aggravation, Impatience).**

The Type A person generally sees the darker side of other people, displaying suspiciousness and distrust. Free-floating hostility is always present and ready to be triggered by whatever the Type A person judges to be wrong. This may be almost anything in the environment—too-loud stereos, slow store clerks, laughter of children, the neighbor who has not mowed his grass for three weeks, a coworker who displays idiosyncratic habits,

---

When It's All Over

And when all the clocks and calendars have stopped their counting for you, what then has your life added up to?

Source: Friedman & Ulmer (1974, 274)

government regulations, welfare mothers who should be working, police who are not tough enough in enforcing traffic laws, the idiot driver in the next freeway lane, and more. Friedman and Ulmer report:

> One of our Type A patients, for example, having stopped for a red light, lit a cigarette just as the signal turned green. The female motorist behind him honked several times. Reacting, he slowly got out of his car, sneeringly smiled at her and then sauntered to the front of his car, opened the engine hood, and pretended to look for some mechanical breakdown. "I think the bitch got the message," he later remarked to a friend. (1984, 34)

Later in this chapter, we will examine hostility, the most dangerous component of the Type A pattern in more detail.

The Drive Toward Self-Destruction

Less obvious, especially to the Type A person himself or herself, is the **drive toward self-destruction.** This was not apparent to Friedman and Rosenman when they wrote *Type A Behavior and Your Heart* in 1974. Subsequently, it has become more clear. To illustrate this point, Friedman and Ulmer quote Henry Kissinger's comment about Richard Nixon: "It was hard to avoid the impression that Nixon, who thrived on crisis, also craved disasters" (1984, 41). A close friend told Peter Sellers's son after Sellers's death, "Your father was always searching for a bloody heart attack as if it were a letter he knew had been posted and hadn't arrived" (Friedman & Ulmer, 1984, 41).

Type A's usually feel the crush of their pressured lifestyle and know they cannot sustain it indefinitely. Thus, they unconsciously pursue some avenue of escape, some way out. Friedman and Ulmer quote these heart attack patients as they lay in their respective intensive care units.

See Application Exercises 8-1 and 8-2 for a self-administered survey on Type A behavior and your reactions to your score.

> "I'm glad it finally came. I just couldn't seem to find any other way to get out from under all the junky stuff loading me down."
>
> "It may seem strange to you, but I knew I was going to get this attack and I sort of looked forward to it."
>
> "I wouldn't ever admit this, not even to my wife, but I knew this was coming and so I wanted to get it over with, one way or the other. And frankly, I didn't care a damn which way it came out just as long as I didn't have to have someone wheeling me around the rest of my life." (1984, 41)

Other Type A Qualities

The components discussed so far are the core elements of Type A behavior. Others include:

- A tendency to use numbers a great deal when thinking and talking
- Failure to use imagery, metaphors, and similes
- Love of competition
- Intense concentration and alertness
- Perfectionism

Type A Behavior and the Social Environment

It is important to note that Type A behavior can remain latent or can become overtly manifest, depending on the social situation. If a person with Type A tendencies lives and works in a culture, subculture, or setting that is relatively easygoing with a preponderance of Type B people, the Type A person may never display many of his Type A qualities. The same person in a rapid-paced, frenetic setting is much more likely to show her or his Type A personality.

This fact is consistent, of course, with the transactional, coping theory of stress of Lazarus and Folkman (1984) noted in Chapter 1, since from the point of view of this theory, stress is the result of the interplay between the situation and the self.

Gender and Type A Behavior

It is important to realize that Type A behavior characterizes women as well as men in our society (Lawler et al., 1990; Thoreson & Low, 1990). To be sure, most of the Type A qualities we have described seem to fit more readily into a male perspective and style of life. Yet, as Friedman and Ulmer (1984, Chapter 5) have noted, a dramatic rise in Type A behavior among women has occurred since the 1970s as more women have entered workplaces dominated by Type A men and a Type A atmosphere. More recently, Bedeian, Mossholder, and Touliatos (1990) found that men and women respond differently to similar work-related challenges. For example, hours worked and role conflict tend to be associated with Type A behavior among men but not women. On the other hand, Greenglass (1990) found that university faculty women tended to be much more Type A than Type B and that the greater the Type A behavior, the greater the conflict of their work roles with family roles, mostly because Type A women worked longer hours.

Research investigators have found a four-times-higher incidence of coronary heart disease among Type A employed women than Type B employed women (Haynes, 1984). Yet for reasons not well understood, women are more likely to develop angina pectoris (chest pain from inadequate flow of blood through the coronary arteries to the heart muscle) as their first sign of blocked arteries than men, for whom myocardial infarction (heart attack) is usually the first sign. Perhaps women simply recognize and acknowledge the early warning sign of anginal chest pain earlier than do men.

Effects of Type A Behavior

Type A behavior inherently is neither good nor bad. Rather, it is to be judged by its consequences. Like most things in life, it has mixed effects—some positive, some negative.

Most research on the effects of Type A behavior have focused on coronary artery disease, heart attacks, and cardiac-related mortality. Later, we will examine this research literature. Before doing so, however, let us examine the effects of Type A behavior on quality of life.

Quality of Life

While there may be positive benefits of some elements of Type A behavior (e.g., being hard-driving helps one get ahead and complete tasks—including those that may be socially beneficial), my research indicates that, on balance, the effects are more negative than positive.

Participants in my 10-session community class, Reducing Perfectionism, Irritability, and Hurry Sickness, complete before and after the class the Personal Stress Assessment, a questionnaire measuring various aspects of stress, health, and quality of life. Included is the Pace of Life Index, a 20-item measure of Type A behavior.

When we compare several of these quality-of-life measures among those who are Type A and Type B (top and bottom quartiles on the Pace of Life Index), we find that Type A's come out significantly less positively on every single variable. When compared with Type B's, Type A's display the following:

More distress symptoms	Less health satisfaction	Lower self-esteem
Less internal control	Less job satisfaction	Less energy and vitality
More depression	Less home satisfaction	More anxious reactivity
More emotional tension	Less happiness	More irritability and anger
Less life satisfaction	Less fun and playfulness	More time-related stress

One Day in the Life of Mr. A and Mr. B

Potential Stressors	Mr. A: (Stressed, ineffective responses)	Mr. B: (Relaxed, effective responses)
1. 7 a.m. Alarm clock did not go off. Overslept.	**Action** Rushed through shaving, dressing. Left without any breakfast.	**Action** Called colleague to say he would be 30 minutes late. Got ready for work and breakfasted as usual.
	Thoughts I can't be late. This is going to foul up my whole day.	**Thoughts** This is not a big problem. I can manage to make up the 30 minutes later on.
	Results Left home in a hurried state.	**Results** Left home in a relaxed state.
2. 8 a.m. Traffic jam caused by slow driver in fast lane.	**Action** Honked horn, gripped steering wheel hard; tried to pass and later tried to speed.	**Action** Waited for traffic jam to end. Relaxed and listened to the radio while waiting; later drove at his normal rate.
	Thoughts Why can't that jerk move into the slow lane? This infuriates me.	**Thoughts** I'm not going to let this upset me because there is nothing I can do about it.
	Results Blood pressure and pulse rate rose. Arrived at work hurried and harried.	**Results** Remained calm and relaxed. Arrived at work fresh and alert.
3. 10 a.m. Angry associate blew up over a staffing problem.	**Action** Was officially polite but nonverbal behavior signaled impatience and anger.	**Action** Relaxed while listening attentively and mentally rehearsed how to handle this encounter. Remained calm in demeanor.
	Thoughts This guy is a prima donna. I can't tolerate outbursts	**Thoughts** Beneath all his anger he does have a point. I

Potential Stressors	Mr. A: (Stressed, ineffective responses)	Mr. B: (Relaxed, effective responses)
	Thoughts like these; I'll never get my work done.	**Thoughts** can take care of this problem now before it gets more serious.
	Results Associate stormed out unsatisfied. Mr. A. was too aggravated to take care of important business on his agenda.	**Results** Associate's temper was calmed. He thanked Mr. B. for hearing him out. Mr. B. was glad that he was able to take care of the problem.
4. Noon. Behind.	**Action** Ate lunch in office while working. Could not find needed materials in files. Made telephone calls but parties were out.	**Action** Went for a 20-minute walk in park. Ate lunch in park.
	Thoughts I'll never get out from under all this work. I'm going to plow through this if I have to work through dinner.	**Thoughts** A break in routine refreshes me. I work better when I allow myself intervals to relax.
	Results Made mistakes in work because of exasperation.	**Results** Returned refreshed. Proceeded with work rapidly and with fresh insight.
5. 11 p.m. Bedtime	**Action** Couldn't get to sleep. Had insomnia for two hours.	**Action** Fell asleep rapidly.
	Thoughts Why don't I accomplish more? I am a disappointment to myself and my family.	**Thoughts** This has been a good day. I'm glad I was able to head off several potential problems.
	Results Awoke exhausted and depressed.	**Results** Awoke refreshed and happy.

Figure 8-2

Mean Distress-Symptom Score by Type A Behavior

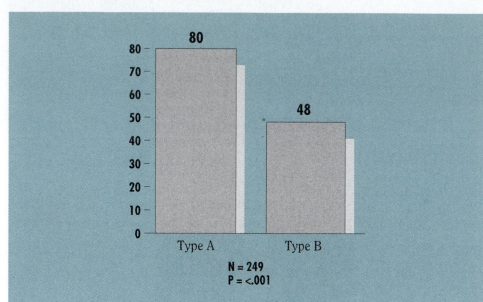

MEASURES: *Distress Symptoms:* 50-Item Distress Symptom Scale
          Type A Behavior: 20-Item Pace of Life Index

FINDING: Type A respondents scored significantly higher than Type B respondents in distress
         symptoms

These findings are consistent with personal reports from many of my students from both community and campus classes, illustrated by Figure 8-2, which shows that among my undergraduate Human Stress students, Type A behavior is associated with higher average distress-symptom scores. They often report that life seems like a constant struggle. They feel perpetually overwhelmed, pressed, frustrated, and unhappy. Relationships usually are rocky and a source of added frustration.

One study also found a higher incidence of upper respiratory infections among Type A students compared with Type B's (Stout & Bloom, 1982). Another found a higher incidence of migraine headaches (Woods et al., 1984). The same researcher, as well as others, have found a wide range of more frequent symptoms and illnesses among Type A's (Offutt & Lacroix, 1988; Suls & Sanders, 1988; Woods & Burns, 1984).

Recent studies by Bryant and Yarnold (1990) reported that Type A college students report *more positive* scores of subjective well-being and emotional state. These findings, discrepant with mine, might result from different measures or samples. Alternatively, they might suggest that Type A's begin with more emotional vigor and positiveness early in adulthood but that this subjective "advantage" disappears over the years, since my sample's average age was early 40s.

To be sure, positive elements of Type A behavior may exist, as suggested earlier—drive, ambition, dedication, high personal standards. Unfortunately, these potential positive ingredients often are accompanied with the negative and harmful elements of hostility, chronic time urgency, struggle, hyperaggressiveness, and irritability.

Heart Disease and Other Causes of Death

We noted earlier that physicians as long ago as the 17th century suspected that emotions affected the heart. It was not until the 1960s that the first scientific investigators, Friedman and Rosenman, began systematically to examine the effect of Type A behavior on coronary artery disease and heart attacks.

Coronary artery disease (CAD), the number-one cause of death in this country, is the progressive buildup of plaque on the inside of the coronary arteries that supply blood to the heart muscle. Medical scientists have long known that a number of risk factors increase chances of CAD, as you read in Chapter 7.

Friedman and Rosenman concluded after several years of research that in combination these risk factors account for less than half of all heart attacks in this country. We noted earlier in the chapter that they suspected back in the 1950s that emotions or personality might help explain much of the remaining incidents of heart attack.

In the early 1960s Friedman and Rosenman created a longitudinal, prospective research design to study the impact of Type A behavior among previously heart-healthy subjects. The results of this Western Collaborative Group Study made headlines everywhere (Friedman & Rosenman, 1971). Over the 8.5 years of the study, Type A subjects were twice more likely to suffer from coronary disease, to have heart attacks, and to die from heart attacks than Type B's. This effect held up even after Type A and Type B subjects were equated on such potential confounding factors as smoking, elevated blood pressure, and high blood pressure.

This and other early studies prompted two panels of scientific experts to conclude that Type A behavior indeed is a risk factor for heart disease, that it exerts an effect independent of other risk factors, and that it is equal in impact to high blood pressure, elevated cholesterol, and cigarette smoking (Review Panel, 1981).

Subsequent studies documented that not only could Type A behavior predict the rise of coronary artery disease and heart attacks but also the degree of coronary disease (e.g., number of blocked arteries and percentage of blockage in given coronary arteries; Blumenthal et al., 1978; Frank et al., 1978; Sundin, et al., 1995; and Zyzanski et al., 1976).

Experts continue to speculate as to why Type A behavior has these harmful cardiovascular effects. Possible mediating pathways include increased insulin and adrenaline secretion of Type A's, greater blood-pressure volatility, increased tendency to secrete more cholesterol and platelets when under pressure, and greater difficulty in removing cholesterol from the bloodstream (Abbott & Sutherland, 1990; Friedman & Rosenman, 1974; Friedman & Ulmer, 1984; Rosenman, 1990).

As noted at the beginning of the chapter, Type A behavior entered into the common language of most Americans as a result of these studies and the publicity that ensued. Spouses and friends hastened to warn Type A's to slow down and simmer down—mostly to slow down. Wisely so, since the costs appeared to be high, both for quality and length of life.

Yet the full scientific story had not yet been written about Type A behavior. For, by the mid-1980s, a series of new studies, most notably the Aspirin Myocardial Infarction Study (Shekelle et al., 1985) and the Multiple Risk Factor Intervention Trial (MRFIT; Case et al., 1985) reported no association at all between Type A behavior and coronary artery disease, heart attacks, or heart attack-induced deaths. (For a review of these and other studies with negative findings, see Haynes & Matthews, 1988; Matthews & Haynes, 1986; Rosenman, 1990.) To some extent, these negative findings might have resulted from measurement problems (Haynes & Matthews, 1988; Rosenman, 1990).

Yet, as Williams (1989) has noted, euphoria turned to uncertainty among behavioral medicine and cardiology researchers in this field. As Joel Dimsdale stated in a 1988 *New England Journal of Medicine* editorial:

> It is important to acknowledge that *something* is going on in terms of the relation between personality and heart disease. However, the nature of that influence is far more complex than is conveyed by the simple assertion that Type A behavior is a risk factor for coronary heart disease. (1988, 110)

Then clarity and renewed optimism began to return, for scientists turned to a new question. Might one or more components of Type A behavior be harmful to the heart, even if the syndrome as a whole might not be? After a series of studies in which the negative effects of the various Type A elements were separated out, attention focused on one key component: *hostility,* to which we will soon turn as a second distress-prone personality style. Before doing so, it is important to note that several studies show that Type A behavior can be changed, even among older heart-attack victims.

Can Type A Behavior Be Changed?

It is one thing to recognize Type A behavior in the self and others. But can it be changed? A number of studies strongly suggest that indeed it can. Here is evidence to consider.

The most important research on reducing Type A behavior has been conducted by Friedman and associates, who studied more than 1,000 post-heart-attack patients in California (Friedman et al., 1984; 1986). These investigators were interested in two questions. First, can Type A behavior be changed? Second, if it can be changed, will doing so reduce the risk of a second heart attack? Nearly 80 percent of an experimental group who completed monthly behavior-change groups over a 3.5 year period did show measurable reductions in Type A behavior. And those in the behavior-change groups reduced their incidence of repeat heart attacks by one-half, compared with two control groups. Friedman and associates note that this is a more significant reduction in the occurrence of repeat attacks than any medication ever studied and is even greater than bypass surgery.

But does reducing Type A behavior depend on having experienced such a life-threatening event as a heart attack? Can it be changed among those who have not been face-to-face with death? A more recent study, again by Friedman and colleagues, strongly suggests that reducing Type A behavior can be accomplished among adult men who have not suffered a myocardial infarction (Gill et al., 1985). This time, the investigators sought the cooperation of the U.S. Army War College. Half of a group of healthy, middle-aged career officers who volunteered for the study were assigned to a control group and received no special attention or instruction. The other half participated in classes over a 9-month period aimed at reducing Type A behavior. Again, a significantly higher percentage of those in the experimental group decreased their Type A patterns. Of interest is that their colleagues reported no adverse effects on the subjects' work performances—allaying the apprehension that to reduce Type A qualities would endanger one's chances of a successful career.

The third study is one I have been conducting for several years at the Enloe Hospital Stress and Health Center. Several hundred community residents have taken my class aimed at reducing Type A behavior. Called Reducing Perfectionism and Hurry Sickness, this class meets in groups of 10–15 persons (61 percent have been women; the average age is 42) every other week for 10 sessions. Individual relaxation training sessions are optional. A blend of behavior and attitude-change methods is used to reduce Type A behavior. These include heightened awareness of Type A behavior and of the physiology of stress in general, brief and deep relaxation techniques, time management methods, steps for redefining situations so they become less irritating, methods of handling anger more effectively, and more.

At the outset and again at the end of the class, participants complete a questionnaire containing a series of stress-related scales. Unfortunately, we have no control group, so findings must be viewed with caution.

As shown in Figure 8-3, several positive findings have emerged among persons who have completed the class and filled out both pre- and post-measures. First, Type A behavior did appear to change, using three measures: the Pace of Life Index, the Framingham Type A Scale (a well-known 10-item measure), and the Pace of Life Rating Scale, which is completed before and after by someone who knows the participant.

Figure 8-3

Average Before-After Scores for Participants in a Five-Month Class on Reducing Type A Behavior

Measure	Before	After	Direction of Change*
Pace of Life Index	42	34	+
Pace of Life Rating Scale (Completed by another)	40	34	+
Framingham Type A Scale	28	22	+
Distress Symptom Scale	93	35	+
Irritability Quotient	52	41	+
Internal Control**	56	71	+
Emotional Tension	71	49	+
Depression	47	33	+
Life Satisfaction	56	69	+
Health Satisfaction	53	67	+
Job Satisfaction	59	68	+
Home Satisfaction	62	73	+
Health Optimism	68	75	+
Life Optimism	68	76	+
Happiness	60	73	+
Fun and Playfulness	46	62	+
Self-Esteem	58	74	+
Vitality and Energy	53	67	+
Anxious Reactivity	24	20	+
Wellness Behavior Test	2.50	2.86	+
Time Stress Questionnaire	128	86	+

*All differences are significant at <.001 except for Time Stress Questionaire, which is significant at .01.

**Internal control through vitality and energy are from the author's Quality of Life Index. All of these scores are given after being multiplied times 10. N = 429

Second, stress level seemed to decline markedly, based on responses to the Distress Symptom Scale. Third, health habits seemed to improve, based on responses to the Wellness Behavior Test. Fourth, participants seemed to become less easily irritated and angered, based on responses to a 25-item Irritability Quotient. Fifth, quality of life seemed to improve in a number of other respects among most participants—for example, a sense of being in control of things; less depression; less emotional tension; happiness; satisfaction with job, home, and life in general; higher self-esteem; vitality and energy; and fun and playfulness. Sixth, participants seemed to experience less stress associated with time, based on responses to the Time Stress Questionnaire, described in Chapter 16.

Consistent with my own study is a recent report by Möller and Botha (1996) that a rational-emotive therapy program as brief as 9 weeks succeeded in reducing Type A behavior, especially its time urgency component. These improvements were maintained at followup 10 weeks later and were accompanied by self-reports of significant positive changes in Type A behavior.

In short, Type A behavior does appear to be amenable to change. It is not locked into our thinking, feeling, and acting forever. Reducing it does appear to improve the quality of life. Perhaps it can also improve the length of life. For a comprehensive review of studies on alteration of Type A behavior, see Roskies (1990).

TIPS FOR MANAGING TYPE A BEHAVIOR

Many of the guidelines and techniques presented in Part IV of this book can be directly applied to preventing and reducing Type A behavior, especially the harmful parts of the pattern. These include stress-management methods related to time management, self-talk related to self-esteem and anger, deep relaxation, on-the-spot tension reducers, and health buffers such as exercise. Here are a few additional tips for managing Type A behavior, drawn from Friedman and Rosenman (1974, Chapter 15).

1. **Review your successes.** You will find that your successes are not caused by Type A behavior but occur in spite of it. Impatience, hostility, and hyperaggressiveness do not contribute to success but detract from it. Friedman and Rosenman note that they never met anyone who failed because they failed to do a job too slowly or too well. But they have met many who failed because they rushed too fast.

2. **Believe in your ability to change.** Type A behavior is learned. Therefore, it can be changed.

3. **Enter into a thorough self-appraisal.** This often is difficult for the entrenched Type A, who typically is set in her or his ways and thoroughly believes in the virtuousness of present commitments and patterns of conduct. Become aware, especially, of patterns of negative self-talk that produce insecurity, time urgency, or hostility. The box on page 193 contains Friedman and Rosenman's suggestions for such a self-appraisal.

4. **Retrieve your total personality.** Reactivate your right brain—the part that relates to literature, art, music, and appreciation of beauty in the environment. These are the sorts of interests that tend to bore hard-driving, impatient Type A's. Take time to take in the beauty around you each hour of the day. Surround yourself with symbols of beauty and tranquility.

5. **Make gestures toward myth, ritual, and tradition.** Friedman and Rosenman note that:

Friedman and Rosenman's Guidelines for a Thorough Self-Appraisal

1. In a meaningful self-appraisal, you must first attempt to determine just how intelligent, how percipient, and how creative you have been in your job.

2. You must examine your sense of humor to determine how it has served you. Is it chiefly a repository for jokes and anecdotes? Or does it function—as it should—to help you perceive your own occasionally ludicrous aspects?

3. You must assess your capacity for flexibility, for change of pace, and for rapid adaptability to change.

4. You must look at your leadership qualities and determine their worth.

5. You must examine all the activities that now absorb your intellectual, emotional, and spiritual interests. How many of these activities have to do with your concern with art, litera ture, music, drama, philosophy, history, science, and the wonders of the natural world that envelop you?

6. You must seek out and assess the intensity of your free-floating hostilities. As you do so, don't allow either rational ization or sophistry to blind you to their possible presence.

7. You must try to estimate the ease with which you can re ceive and give loyalty and affection.

8. You must attempt to determine the amount of sheer courage you possess. And if in this assay you detect some very large yellow splotches of frank fear in your personality, don't over look them. Treasure them, just as you will treasure the steel-gray masses of frank courage you are likely to find there, too.

9. You must dare to examine critically your ethical and moral principles. How honest have I been in my life, how often and under what circumstances have I cheated, lied, and borne false witness against my neighbor? are questions you must not fail to present to yourself. And painful as it may be in the beginning, stubbornly persist in providing yourself with true answers.

10. Finally, you must not be afraid to ask, and to persist in asking yourself over and over, until you have answered the question: What apart from the eternal clutter of my every day living should be the essence of my life?

Source: Friedman & Rosenman (1974, 218)

Perhaps our Western Society will prove to have acted in a supremely wise fashion when it began to replace them (myth, ritual, and tradition) with mechaniza-tion, automation, and total bureaucratic social security. Except for one thing: this is the first time in the experience of man on earth that a large group of individu-als is attempting to live in so absolute a spiritual void. (1974, 225)

Find routines with family and friends that you repeat regularly. Place high value on long-term friendships. Nurture and cultivate them. Find means of "centering," looking inward for guidance if that is your spiritual bent. Or pray to whatever higher power gives you strength.

Certain components of Type A behavior clearly have advantages: strong drive, achievement orientation, attention to detail. Similarly, elements of Type B are desirable: patience, empathy, ability to listen, calm under pressure, flowing more easily with time.

In their stimulating and helpful book, *The C Zone: Peak Performance Under Pressure,* Kriegel and Kriegel (1984) propose a third option that combines the best elements of Type A and Type B, plus other qualities, into a model of attitude and behavior for thriving under pressure.

HOSTILITY

The Nature of Hostility

Hostility is cynicism toward others' motives and values, easily and frequently aroused anger, and a tendency to express that anger toward others.

A leader in research on **hostility** has been Redford Williams of Duke University. Williams and his wife, Virginia, describe the nature and effects of hostility as follows:

> We're speaking here not about the anger that drives people to shoot, stab, or otherwise wreak havoc on their fellow humans. We mean instead the everyday sort of anger, annoyance, and irritation that courses through the minds and bodies of many perfectly normal people.
>
> • If your immediate impulse when faced with everyday delays or frustrations— elevators that don't immediately arrive at your floor, slow-moving supermarket lines, dawdling drivers, rude teenagers, broken vending machines—is to blame somebody;
> • If this blaming quickly sparks your ire toward the offender;
> • If your ire often manifests itself in aggressive action;
>
> then, for you, getting angry is like taking a small dose of some slow-acting poison—arsenic, for example—every day of your life. And the result is often the same: Not tomorrow, perhaps, or even the day after, but sooner than most of us would wish, your hostility is more likely to harm your health than will be the case for your friend whose personality is not tinged by the tendencies to cynicism, anger, and aggression just described." (1993, xiii)

The Williamses maintain that about 1 in 5 Americans suffers from levels of hostility sufficient to be threatening to health.

At the end of this chapter is a hostility self-assessment questionnaire that you might want to complete later. Meanwhile, in order to get some sense of the types of situations that hostile people often find intolerable, resulting in easily and frequently aroused upset, consider how you would typically react to each of the following five events:

• Your car is stuck in the mud or snow.
• You have hung up your clothes, but someone knocks them to the floor and fails to pick them up.
• Your car is stalled at a traffic light, and the guy behind you keeps blowing his horn.
• You have had a busy day, and someone you live with starts to complain about how you forgot to do something you agreed to.
• You need to get somewhere in a hurry, but the car in front of you is going 25 mph in a 40 mph zone, and you cannot pass.

Source: Friedman & Ulmer (1984, 274)

Key Question

Ask yourself why you are so much more aware of the irritating qualities of other persons than their good qualities.

Hostile people approach these types of situations with an orientation of **cynicism,** tending to see the dark side of other people's motives and intentions. They are quickly angered by things that nonhostile people hardly bat an eye at. And hostile individuals have no hesitation to let others know how upset they are.

This triad seems to be not only dysfunctional for emotional life and relationships but dangerous to your health:

- a cynical attitude,
- frequently aroused anger feelings, and
- a tendency to display anger overtly.

Measuring Hostility and Its Effects

Hostility is usually measured with questionnaires. The most widely used is one in which Cook and Medley (1954) regrouped 50 questions from the Minnesota Multiphasic Personality Inventory (MMPI) for a number of years. Using this scale or an abbreviated version of it as their measure of hostility, a series of investigators found a definite association between hostility, on the one hand, and coronary artery disease, heart attacks, and all-cause mortality, on the other hand. Here is a sampling of those studies (Smith & Pope, 1990; Swan, Carmelli, & Rosenman, 1990):

- Williams and colleagues (1980) found that the higher the hostility score among 424 Duke heart patients, the greater the likelihood of having one or more blocked coronary arteries.
- Shekelle and colleagues (1983) reported higher mortality from heart disease, cancer, and all other causes among 1,877 middle-aged men (employees of Western Electric) who had scored high on the Cook-Medley measure 20 years before.
- University of North Carolina researchers found a 7-times higher mortality rate by age 50 from all causes among a group of physicians who had scored high on the MMPI hostility scale 25 years before when compared with those who had scored low on that same scale (Barefoot, Dahlstrom, & Williams, 1983).
- Using a new 27-item combination of hostility items from the Cook-Medley scale, Barefoot et al. (1988) found that over a 20-year period the death rate (all causes) among 118 lawyers was 4 times higher among high- than low-hostility individuals.
- Williams and Siegler (1990) found that college students who scored high on a hostility scale in the 1960s were significantly more likely 20 years later to have elevated total cholesterol and lowered levels of HDL, the good kind of cholesterol.
- Mittleman and associates (1995) recently found that among 1,623 post-heart attack patients an anger episode increased chances of a heart attack within two hours by 2.3 times.
- Julkunen and colleagues (1994) found that chances of 2-year progression of carotid atherosclerosis increased 2-fold even after controlling for other risk factors among a sample of 119 Finnish men who scored high on measures of cynical distrust and anger-control.

• Helmers and Krantz (1996) found that defensive hostility, a subset of hostility, was associated with higher blood pressure among a sample of 33 men, thereby increasing their risk of coronary artery disease.

According to Williams and Williams, a few studies show no harmful effects of hostility on health, but most have been clear—the greater the hostility, the worse the health outcomes.

Other studies have also shown that hostility has harmful psychological and interpersonal effects as well. For example, one study by Timothy Smith (1988) of the University of Utah found that the greater the hostility, the more the hassles and negative life events. Davis Mace reported similar effects of hostility on marriages (1982). According to the Williamses:

> . . . failure to deal effectively with anger destroys intimacy by resulting in too many to too few disagreements.
>
> Arguments between spouses can become bitter because the individuals know each other well enough to attack in ways that hurt the most. Each partner feels frustrated, hurt, and even angrier. Arguments escalate, with eventual attacks not only on how the spaghetti will be prepared but also on one spouse's character as well as the other spouse's relatives. (1993, 40)

We know from other studies that being socially connected is healthy, being (or feeling) isolated is unhealthy. Hostility may have its harmful effects on health partly through the isolation it creates with resulting heightened stress and worse health habits than otherwise would be true. The impact of hostility on distress is illustrated in Figure 8-4, which shows among students in my Human Stress class that the higher the hostility, measured by Redford Williams's 9-item hostility scale, the higher the distress-symptom score.

Nature and Nurture in the Development of Hostility

You have read that the most dangerous component of Type A behavior for the development of coronary artery disease is hostility. Williams (1989) points out that propensity toward hostility probably develops as a combined result of heredity, especially the tendency toward hyperactivity, and environment. After detailed analysis, Carmelli, Swan, and Rosenman (1990) suggested that about one-quarter of hostility is inherited, the rest the result of environment.

In an argument consistent with the interactional, dynamic, coping perspective toward stress (Lazarus & Folkman, 1984), Williams notes that a parent who tends to hyperreact physically, emotionally, and behaviorally to common daily events is more likely to engender unfriendly responses from others, including his or her own children, than a parent who reacts more evenly and moderately. This occurs in very subtle ways through facial expression, body language, and tone of voice.

When this type of interaction occurs thousands of times over the course of the child's early life, he or she is likely to see the world as an unfriendly, hostile, even dangerous, place. Then if the child in turn has inherited a tendency toward quick and strong physical and emotional responses (accompanied with relatively few endorphins that would make interactions more pleasant), he or she is likely to behave in ways that turn the world into what he or she has expected, since others around the child feel the same apprehension, distrustfulness, and hostility that the child picked up from the parent.

See Application Exercise 8-3 to consider child-rearing practices that develop and deter hostility.

For example, the child squirms and cries a lot when held; wears facial expressions of disgust, tension, apprehension, or anger; and is not very outgoing. In turn, adults are likely to be less kind and to withdraw from the child, confirming his or her assessment that the

Figure 8-4

Mean Distress-Symptom Score by Hostility

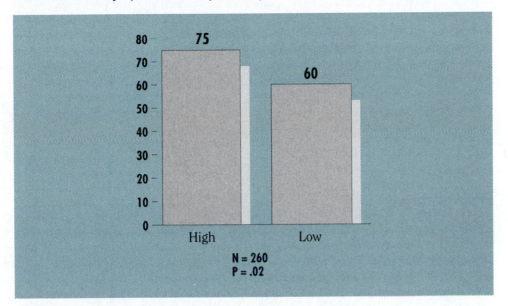

MEASURES: *Hostility:* 9-Item Scale developed by Redford Williams (Williams & Williams, 1993)
    Distress Symptoms: 50-Item Distress Symptom Scale

FINDING: High-hostility respondents scored significantly higher in distress symptoms than low-
    hostility respondents.

world is unfriendly, unpredictable, and hostile, justifying again social-distancing behavior, hostility, and even overt anger. The cycle mounts.

Although nature (heredity) no doubt plays a role in development of hostility, social learning plays an even greater part, probably in interaction with biological tendencies. Since hostility is learned, it can be prevented and even unlearned. These coping methods are presented in a practical, readable guide in the Williamses' book, *Anger Kills* (1983). We will discuss approaches to managing anger in more detail in Chapter 14.

We now turn to several other distress-prone personality patterns, including perfectionism, which is viewed by some experts as a component of both Type A behavior and hostility.

References

Abbott, J., & Sutherland, C. (1990). Cognitive, cardiovascular and haematological responses of Type A and Type B individuals prior to and following examinations. *Journal of Social Behavior and Personality, 5 (Special Issue),* 343–368.

Barefoot, J. C., Dahlstrom, W. G., & Williams, R. B. (1983). Hostility, CHD incidence, and total mortality: A 25-year follow-up study of 255 physicians. *Psychosomatic Medicine, 45,* 59–63.

Barefoot, J. C., Dodge, K. A., Peterson, B. L., Dahlstrom, W. G., & Williams, R. B. (1988). Predicting mortality from scores on the Cook-Medley Scale: A follow-up study for 118 lawyers. *Psychosomatic Medicine, 51,* 46–57.

Bedeian, A. G., Mossholder, K. W., & Touliatos, J. (1990). Type A status and selected work experiences among male and female accountants. *Journal of Social Behavior and Personality, 5 (Special Issue),* 291–305.

Blumenthal, J. A., Williams, R. S., King, Y., Schanberg, S. M., & Thompson, L. (1978). Type A behavior pattern and coronary atherosclerosis. *Circulation, 58,* 634–639.

Bryant, F. B., & Yarnold, P. R. (1990). The impact of Type A behavior on subjective life quality: Bad for the heart, good for the soul? *Journal of Social Behavior and Personality, 5 (Special Issue),* 369–404.

Carmelli, D., Swan, G. E., & Rosenman, R. H. (1990). The heritability of the Cook and Medley hostility scale revisited. *Journal of Social Behavior and Personality, 5 (Special Issue),* 107–116.

Case, R. B., Heller, S. S., Case, N. B., & Moss, A. J. (1985). Type A behavior and survival after acute myocardial infarction. *The New England Journal of Medicine, 312,* 634–639.

Cook, W., & Medley, D. (1954). Proposed hostility and pharasaic-virtue scales for the MMPI. *Journal of Applied Psychology, 38,* 414–418.

Coolidge, J. C. (1969). Unexpected death in a patient who wished to die. *Journal of the American Psychoanalytical Association, 17,* 771–782.

Dimsdale, J. E. (1988). A perspective on Type A behavior and coronary disease (editorial). *The New England Journal of Medicine, 318,* 110–112.

Dunbar, H. F. (1943). *Psychosomatic diagnosis.* New York: Paul B. Hoeber, Inc.

Fontana, A. F., Rosenberg, R. L., Burg, M. M., Kerns, R. D., & Colonese, K. L. (1990). Type A behavior and self-referencing: Interactive risk factors? *Journal of Social Behavior and Personality, 5 (Special Issue),* 215–232.

Frank, K. A., Heller, S. S., Kornfield, D. S., Sporn, A. A., & Weiss, M. B. (1978). Type A behavior pattern and coronary angiographic findings. *Journal of the American Medical Association, 240,* 761–763.

Friedman, M., & Rosenman, R. H. (1974). *Type A behavior and your heart.* New York: Fawcett.

Friedman, M., Rosenman, R. H., & Carroll, V. (1958). Changes in the serum cholesterol and blood clotting time in men subjected to cyclic variation of occupational stress. *Circulation, 17,* 852–861.

Friedman, M., & Ulmer, D. (1984). *Treating Type A behavior and your heart.* New York: Knopf.

Gallup Poll (1994). Between city survey on hostility.

Greenglass, E. R. (1990). Type A behavior, career aspirations, and role conflict in professional women. *Journal of Social Behavior and Personality, 5 (Special Issue),* 307–322.

Haynes, S. G. (1984). Type A behavior, employment status, and coronary heart disease in women. *Behavioral Medicine Update, 6,* 11–15.

Haynes, S. G., & Matthews, K. A. (1988). Review and methodological critique of recent studies of Type A behavior and cardiovascular disease. *Annals of Behavioral Medicine, 10,* 47–59.

Helmers, K. F., & Krantz, D. S. (1996). Defensive hostility, gender and cardiovascular levels and responses to stress. *Annals of Behavioral Medicine, 18,* 246–254.

Julkunen, J., Salonen, R., Kaplan, G. A., Chesney, M.A., Salonen, J.T. (1994). Hostility and the progression of carotid atherosclerosis. *Psychosomatic Medicine, 56,* 519–525.

Kriegel, R., & Kriegel, M. (1984). *The C zone: Peak performance under pressure.* Garden City, NY: Anchor Press.

Lawler, K. A., Schmied, L. A., Armstead, C. A., & Lacy, J. E. (1990). Type A behavior, desire for control, and cardiovascular reactivity in young adult women. *Journal of Social Behavior and Personality, 5 (Special Issue),* 135–158.

Lazarus, R. S., & Folkman, S. (1984). *Stress, appraisal, and coping.* New York: Springer Publishing Company.

Mace, D. (1982). *Love and anger in marriage.* Grand Rapids: Zondervan.

Matthews, K. A., & Haynes, S. G. (1985). Type A behavior pattern and coronary risk: Update and critical evaluation. *American Journal of Epidemiology, 123,* 23–96.

Menninger, K. A., & Menninger, W. C. (1936). Psychoanalytic observations in cardiac disorders. *American Heart Journal, 11,* 10.

Mittleman, M. A., Maclure, M., Sherwood, J. B., Mulry, R. P., Tofler, G. H., Jacobs, S. C., Friedman, R., Benson, H., & Muller, J. E. (1995). *Circulation, 92,* 720–725.

Möller, A. T., & Botha, H. C. (1996). Effects of a group rational-emotive behavior therapy program on the Type A behavior pattern. *Psychological Bulletin, 78,* 947–959.

Offutt, C., & Lacroix, J. M. (1988). Type A behavior pattern and symptom reports: A prospective investigation. *Journal of Behavioral Medicine, 11,* 227–237.

Osler, W. (1892). *Lectures on angina pectoris and allied states.* New York: Appleton.

Review Panel on Coronary-Prone Behavior and Coronary Heart Disease (1981). Coronary-prone behavior and coronary heart disease: A critical review. *Circulation, 63,* 1199–1215.

Rosenman, R. H. (1986). Current and past history of Type A behavior pattern. In T. H. Schmidt, T. M. Dembroski, & G. Blumchen (Eds.), *Biological and psychological factors in cardiovascular disease.* Heidelberg: Springer-Verlag, 15–40.

Rosenman, R. H. (1990). Type A behavior pattern: A personal overview. *Journal of Social Behavior and Personality, 5 (Special Issue),* 1–24.

Roskies, E. (1987). *Stress management for the healthy Type A: Theory and practice.* New York: The Guilford Press.

Roskies, E. (1990). Type A intervention: Where do we go from here? *Journal of Social Behavior and Personality, 5 (Special Issue),* 419–438.

Shekelle, R. B., Gale, M., Ostfeld, A. M., & Paul, O. (1983). Hostility, risk of coronary disease, and mortality. *Psychosomatic Medicine, 45,* 219–228.

Shekelle, R. B., Hulley, S., Neaton, J., Billings, J., Borhani, N., Gerace, T., Jacobs, D., Lasser, N., Mittlemark, M., & Stamler, J. (1985). The MRFIT behavioral pattern study: II. Type A behavior pattern and incidence of coronary heart disease. *American Journal of Epidemiology, 122,* 559–570.

Smith, T. W., & Pope, M. K. (1990). Cynical hostility as a health risk: Current status and future directions. *Journal of Social Behavior and Personality, 5 (Special Issue),* 77–88.

Smith, T. W., Pope, M. K., Sanders, J. D., Allred, K. D., & O'Keefe, J. (1988). Cynical hostility at home and work: Psychosocial vulnerability across domains. *Journal of Research in Personality,* December, 524–548.

Storement, C. T. (1951). Personality and heart disease. *Psychosomatic Medicine, 13,* 304–313.

Stout, C. W., & Bloom, L. J. (1982). Type A behavior and upper respiratory infections. *Journal of Human Stress, 8,* 4–7.

Strube, M. J. (1990). *Type A behavior.* Corte Madera, CA: Select Press.

Suls, J., & Sanders, G. S. (1988). Type A behavior as a general risk factor for physical disorder. *Journal of Behavioral Medicine, 11,* 201–226.

Sundin, O., Ohman, A., Palm, T., & Strom, G. (1995). Cardiovascular reactivity, Type A behavior, and coronary heart disease: Comparisons between myocardial infarction patients and controls during laboratory-induced stress. *Psychophysiology, 32,* 28–35.

Swan, G. E., Carmelli, D., & Rosenman, R. H. (1990). Cook and Medley hostility and the Type A behavior pattern: Psychological correlates of two coronary-prone behaviors. *Journal of Social Behavior and Personality, 5 (Special Issue),* 89–106.

Taylor, S. E. (1986). *Health Psychology.* New York: Random House.

Thoreson, C. E., & Low, K. G. (1990). Women and the Type A pattern: Review and commentary. *Journal of Social Behavior and Personality, 5 (Special Issue),* 117–133.

von Deusch, T. (1868). *Lehrbuch der Herzkrankheiten.* Leipzig: Verlag von Wilhelm Engelman.

Weiss, E., Dlin, B., Rollin, H. R., Fischer, H. K., & Bepler, C. R. (1957). Emotional factors in coronary occlusion. *Archives of Internal Medicine, 99,* 628–641.

Williams, R. B. (1989). *The trusting heart: Great news about Type A behavior.* New York: Times Books.

Williams, R. B., Haney, T. L., Lee, K. L., Kong, Y., Blumenthal, J., & Whalen, R. (1980). Type A behavior, hostility, and coronary atherosclerosis. *Psychosomatic Medicine, 42,* 539–549.

Williams, R. B., & Siegler, I. (1990). Hostility tied to heart trouble. Paper presented at annual scientific meetings of American Heart Association, Dallas, November.

Williams, R. B., & Williams, V. (1993). *Anger kills.* New York: HarperCollins.

Woods, P. J., & Burns, J. (1984). Type A behavior and illness in general. *Journal of Behavioral Medicine, 7,* 411–415.

Woods, P. J., Morgan, B. T., Day, B. W., Jefferson, T., & Harris, C. (1984). Findings on a relationship between Type A behavior and headaches. *Journal of Behavioral Medicine, 7,* 277–286.

Zyzanski, S. J., Jenkins, C. D., Ryan, T. J., Flessas, A., & Everist, M. (1976). Psychological correlates of coronary angiographic findings. *Archives of Internal Medicine, 136,* 1234–1237.

Application Exercise 8-1

Pace of Life Index

Indicate how often each of the following applies to you in daily life. After you have checked the appropriate column, total your score using the number that appears above each column.

		3 Always or Usually	2 Sometimes	1 Seldom or Never
1.	Do you find yourself rushing your speech?	_____	_____	_____
2.	Do you hurry other people's speech by interrupting them with "umha, umhm" or by completing their sentences for them?	_____	_____	_____
3.	Do you hate to wait in line?	_____	_____	_____
4.	Do you seem to be short of time to get everything done?	_____	_____	_____
5.	Do you detest wasting time?	_____	_____	_____
6.	Do you eat fast?	_____	_____	_____
7.	Do you drive over the speed limit?	_____	_____	_____
8.	Do you try to do more than one thing at a time?	_____	_____	_____
9.	Do you become impatient if others do something too slowly?	_____	_____	_____
10.	Do you seem to have little time to relax and enjoy the time of day?	_____	_____	_____
11.	Do you find yourself overcommitted?	_____	_____	_____
12.	Do you jiggle your knees or tap your fingers?	_____	_____	_____
13.	Do you think about other things during conversations?	_____	_____	_____
14.	Do you walk fast?	_____	_____	_____
15.	Do you hate dawdling after a meal?	_____	_____	_____
16.	Do you become irritable if kept waiting?	_____	_____	_____
17.	Do you detest losing in sports and games?	_____	_____	_____
18.	Do you find yourself with clenched fists or tight neck or jaw muscles?	_____	_____	_____
19.	Does your concentration sometimes wander while you think about what's coming up later?	_____	_____	_____
20.	Are you a competitive person?	_____	_____	_____

Total Score _____

Application Exercise 8-2

Questions About Pace of Life Index

Here are categories for assessing your score on the Pace of Life Index:

45–60	High Type A behavior
35–44	Medium Type A behavior
20–34	Low Type A behavior

1. Is your score higher than you wish? Explain.

2. During the next two days, focus on reducing Type A behavior by modifying two or three specific things on which you scored "always" or "usually." Record your experiences here.

3. Ask your mate or friend to rate you on this scale. Then ask for suggestions about modifying your Type A tendencies.

Application Exercise 8-3

Raising a Hostile or Nonhostile Child

1. Based on your reading about hostility in this chapter, what kind of child-rearing steps would you take to create a hostile child? Be specific about parenting for hostility—setting an example, use of rewards and punishments, repeated messages you would convey, and so on.

2. Now write about what kind of child-rearing steps you would take to minimize hostility in a child. Again, be specific.

CHAPTER **9**

Bernard was right. The microbe is nothing, the terrain is everything.

—LOUIS PASTEUR ON HIS DEATHBED, 1895

OTHER DISTRESS-PRONE PERSONALITY PATTERNS

Learning and Unlearning Helplessness

Below is an example of how learned helplessness can be taught to children by parents and how it can be unlearned. This was written by a woman who had returned to college in her 40s and sought to understand family influences on her development.

> For myself, I found I would be criticized by my mother whether I did something correctly and nicely or if I did something unpleasant. Criticism would come my way even in the presence of strangers who were paying me compliments. My mother would have to negate any positive input that would come my way. This kind of ongoing, negative environment left me with a psychology of "why bother trying." If I did anything well it would not be appreciated anyway.
>
> I recall one incident, while listening to a barrage of criticism, I said to my mother, "Well, Mom, there must be something I do well, I couldn't be doing everything wrong." She answered, quite seriously, "I'm sorry, S, but there is nothing you do right, nothing."
>
> Intellectually, I did not accept this, but emotionally I was crushed. I am certain that a little more of me gave up hope of ever being loved by mother. It did not, however, stop me from trying. . . .
>
> It has been a long, painful struggle for me to learn that I could indeed set myself a goal and then go about reaching that goal. Each time I was able to reach a goal I had set for myself, I gained a little more confidence in my ability to set and reach a new goal. This learning is still occurring in my life, and I seem to take two steps ahead and one step back.

Source: Berger (1990)

In this chapter, we continue to explore distress-prone personality patterns, beginning with perfectionism, which is closely related to the Type A pattern discussed in Chapter 8.

PERFECTIONISM

Life is never easy and seldom enjoyable for a **perfectionist** (Burns, 1980a; Burns, 1980b; Burns, 1989; Grieger & Boyd, 1980; McKay, Davis, & Fanning, 1981; Pacht, 1984). Nothing is wrong, of course, with high standards. Genuine pleasure comes from healthy pursuit of excellence. As a University of Pennsylvania psychologist states, "Without concern for quality, life would seem shallow and true accomplishment would be rare" (Burns, 1980b, 34).

Perfectionism refers to impossibly demanding expectations toward others (external perfectionism), the self (internal perfectionism), or both.

Types of Perfectionists

External perfectionists constantly find fault with others, who seldom seem to match their standards of conduct. They believe they know what is right and how things should be done. Almost always a gap exists between their standards and others' behavior. Consequently, they are plagued by frustration and hostility.

Internal perfectionists put unrelenting and excessively demanding expectations on themselves. Burns makes an important distinction between those who seek personal improvement through striving for realistic standards and true perfectionists.

> The perfectionists I am talking about are those whose standards are high beyond reach or reason, people who strain compulsively and unremittingly toward impossible goals and who measure their own worth entirely in terms of productivity and accomplishment. For these people, the drive to excel can only be self-defeating.
>
> Evidence is mounting that the price this kind of perfectionism pays for the habit includes not only decreased productivity, but also impaired health, poor self-control, troubled personal relationships, and low self-esteem. The perfectionist also appears to be vulnerable to a number of potentially serious mood disorders, including depression, performance anxiety, test anxiety, social anxiety, writer's block, and obsessive-compulsive illness. (1980b, 34)

Internal perfectionism has been found to have these negative outcomes for college students as well. As Arthur and Hayward (1997, 622) recently noted, most studies "have linked perfectionism with a variety of negative outcomes such as procrastination, underachievement, feelings of guilt and failure, indecisiveness, and low self-esteem. Perfectionism has also been associated with more serious outcomes including depression, eating disorders, and alcoholism."

Characteristics of Perfectionists

Perfectionists suffer under their burden of unrealistic pressures because of several beliefs, including the following:

- I must be perfect in anything I attempt.
- I should not make mistakes. Neither should others.
- I try so hard to do the right thing that I deserve exemptions from life's pains and frustrations.
  - There is always a right way that things should be done.
  - If I do something wrong, I have totally blown it.
  - When others do not do what they should, they are rotten human beings.
  - I must be perfect, or I am a failure.

See Application Exercise 9-1 to assess the fit between the "perfectionism pitfalls" and your own experience.

Perfectionists usually engage in all-or-nothing thinking, seeing things as all black or all white (Butler, 1981). For a student perfectionist, a B is a catastrophe. Perfectionists fear mistakes and tend to overreact to them. They are also perpetually at odds with others around them who "in their shades of grayness" seldom meet their standards. Perfectionists overgeneralize, fearing that a single negative performance will start a downward drive toward inevitable failure: "I never do anything right." Self-punishment, rather than self-reward, prevails with predictably depressing effects. Figure 9-1 shows how perfectionism affects the distress-symptom score.

Perfectionists are beset and preoccupied with "shoulds" in relation to both the self and others. They harangue themselves with some of these "shoulds":

- I should be the epitome of generosity, consideration, dignity, courage, unselfishness.
- I should be the perfect lover, friend, parent, teacher, student, spouse.
- I should be able to endure any hardship with equanimity.

Perfection Pitfalls

Besides putting many of us under enormous pressure, the perfectionist's creed can propel us into self-defeating behaviors that far outweigh the rewards of avoiding errors. Here are some examples of those behaviors.

- **Procrastination.** Many perfectionists chronically have trouble getting their work done or even getting started. They tend to procrastinate because all tasks loom large when they have to be done flawlessly.
- **Overdoing it.** A trait related to the need to be flawless is the need to be *thorough.* Bowing to this pressure when preparing a presentation or written report, the perfectionist will include far more information than necessary. She can't draw the line between what is and isn't important and can't risk leaving anything out for fear someone will think she wasn't fully informed.
- **Hoarding.** Some perfectionists have trouble discarding things. They are crippled by the fear that they will throw away something they may need later and by their inability to prioritize.
- **Defensiveness.** Perfectionists will go to great lengths to avoid making a mistake. Should an error be absolutely undeniable, they may still have trouble calmly acknowledging it. Often they will become defensive, tossing off so many *but's, howevers,* and other qualifications that their listeners can barely hear the admission within the verbal thicket.
- **Pickiness.** Not only does the perfectionist have high expectations of herself, she tends to be upset over the flaws in *other* people or things. While most people would prefer an ideal spouse to an imperfect one, they generally accept that much of life is imperfect, and they don't invest too much time or energy in fretting over minor flaws in their mate. If you're a critical perfectionist, however, you're a true expert at finding fault, and you can't help feeling upset over the shortcomings you find in your partner, children, friends, coworkers—anyone who crosses your path.

Source: Mallinger & De Wyze (1992, 76)

- I should be able to find a quick solution to every problem.
- I should never feel hurt; I should always be happy and serene.
- I should always be spontaneous and at the same time I should always control my feelings.
- I should never feel certain emotions, such as anger or jealousy.
- I should love my children equally.
- I should never make mistakes.
- My emotions should be constant—once I feel love I should always feel love.
- I should be totally self-reliant.
- I should assert myself and at the same time I should never hurt anybody else.
- I should never get tired or sick.
- I should always be at peak efficiency.(McKay, Davis, & Fanning, 1981, 24)

Figure 9-1

Mean Distress-Symptom Score by Perfectionism

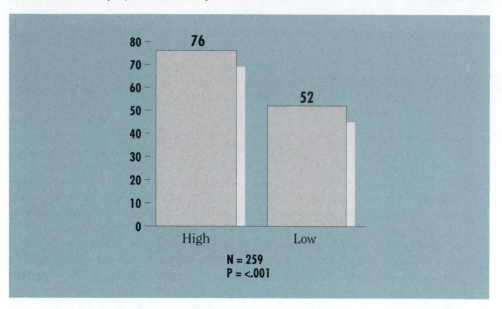

MEASURES: *Distress symptoms:* 50-Item Distress Symptom Scale
            Perfectionism: 20-Item Perfectionism Scale

FINDING: Respondents who scored high in perfectionism scored significantly higher in distress
         symptoms.

One study found that perfectionistic insurance salespersons sold less insurance than those not so perfectionistic (Burns, 1980b). This illustrates that perfectionism can block productivity and creativity. Another study (Ashby et al., 1995) of college students found that adult children of alcoholics were more likely to score high in perfectionism and to report experiencing more procrastination, higher levels of anxiety, and greater difficulties with relationships.

Mallinger and De Wyze note that two major fears produce perfectionism:

- You're afraid people won't like you.
- You're afraid of being embarrassed. (1992, 76)

Perfectionists also fear self-disclosure because of their fear of appearing foolish or inadequate. They are greatly concerned with maintaining an outward image of doing everything "right." Not surprisingly, perfectionists usually are lonely and isolated. Because of their vulnerability to rejection and disapproval, they tend to react defensively to harmless and even helpful criticism. They keep their distance, missing out on the warmth that would provide the very assurance and comfort they so badly want and need.

See Application Exercises 9-2 and 9-3 for a self-assessment survey on perfectionism.

In summary, perfectionists exhibit the following tendencies:

1. Plagued by "shoulds" and "should haves"

2. Self-critical and self-punishing, rather than self-rewarding (internal perfectionists)

3. Hypercritical of others (external perfectionists)

Perfectionism and Achievement: Two Philosophies

One might ask, is not internal perfectionism vital for personal, academic, and professional success? Doesn't setting exceedingly high standards motivate one to strive higher? It is my position that perfectionism (impossibly demanding expectations) is counterproductive rather than helpful for success. Consider the following contrasting philosophies of achievement.

Perfectionism Philosophy
- I *must* do it perfectly.
- If I do not do it perfectly, I deserve to *punish* myself.
- Since I did not do it perfectly, I certainly *must* do it perfectly next time.

Wellness Philosophy
- I will strive to do my best.
- I will accept what I have done—for now.
- I will learn from that effort to seek to improve next time.

---

4. Overgeneralize from single events

5. Use all-or-nothing thinking

6. Guarded and protective of image

7. Plagued by frustration, guilt, or both

8. Hostile (especially external perfectionists)

9. Less productive, less creative

10. Unhappy

In Chapter 14, you will read about constructive self-talk steps for minimizing perfectionism.

PROCRASTINATION

Several of the distress-prone patterns we have examined are time-related. A pattern that overlaps with several others but is worth addressing in its own right is procrastination. It is inevitable that we will put things off. We must, in fact, since we cannot do all things at once. **Procrastination** means putting off those things we know we need to do—and doing this repeatedly. For some people, the problem is in getting started; for others, with finishing a task.

As Burka and Yuen (1983) state, procrastination becomes troublesome in two ways. One is when delaying creates external problems such as not paying a bill on time or failing to hand in a paper on its due date. The second is internal, when the procrastinator feels guilt, regret, or even self-condemnation or despair.

Sometimes, people use procrastination as a way of perpetuating a life script of feeling bad and not succeeding. Burka and Yuen (1983) note that as children continually search for coping strategies that work for them, procrastination sometimes emerges. First, as a child you might have found that you could take the easy road and avoid responsibility by procrastinating—with no real consequences. Second, procrastination in the form of not

Procrastination is to put off doing something until a future time because it is perceived as being too onerous, unpleasant, or unappealing.

handing in homework on time or cleaning up your room might have been a means of quiet rebellion. Third, you might have found that one way to distract yourself from challenges or potential threats—tests, speeches, or social situations—was to keep busy with other things. Fourth, if you were bored and not challenged at school, you might have procrastinated in order to get the adrenaline zing from preparing at the last minute.

Whatever the process of becoming a procrastinator, one usually has developed a set of reinforcing beliefs that Burka and Yuen refer to as The Procrastinator's Code:

- I must be perfect.
- Everything I do should go easily and without effort.
- It's safer to do nothing than to take a risk and fail.
- I should have no limitations.
- If it's not done right, it's not worth doing at all.
- I must avoid being challenged.
- If I succeed, someone will get hurt.
- If I do well this time, I must *always* do well.
- Following someone else's rules means I'm giving in and I'm not in control.
- I can't afford to let go of anything or anyone.
- If I expose my real self, people won't like me.
- There is a right answer, and I'll wait until I find it. (1983, 16)

Procrastination, which is entirely the result of self-talk, most often arises from fear—fear of failure, fear of success, fear of pain, and fear of closeness or intimacy. Of course, it can also result simply from habituation to comfort and lack of effort—otherwise known as laziness. At the end of this chapter, you will be given the opportunity to complete a procrastination self-assessment. In Chapter 16 you will read a number of guidelines for avoiding procrastination.

THE TYPE E WOMAN

Harriet Braiker, a clinical psychologist, believes the Type A pattern does not accurately capture the distress-producing experiences of most contemporary women. In response, she has developed the concept **Type E** (1986).

Braiker explains the Type E pattern as follows:

The Type E woman thinks and acts according to one dominating and pervasive principle: EVERYTHING FOR EVERYBODY.

Success for achievement-oriented women today is defined as achievement in both realms: career and personal. But the success formula is a calculus that often yields enormous frustration and exhaustion. There seems to be only one way for women to play the game and win: be Everything to Everybody. Many working women adapt to the enigmatic problems of trying to "have it all" by pushing themselves to *do* "it" all themselves, and to excel in all their roles, often at tremendous cost to their physical and emotional health.

Bombarded with daily life stress, working women are swelling the epidemiological ranks of ulcer cases, drug and alcohol abuse, depression, sexual dysfunction, and a score of stress-induced physical ailments, including backache, headache, allergies, and recurrent viral infections and flu.

They suffer in legion numbers in various degrees from what stress specialist Barbara B. Brown calls "states of unwellness"—those in-between states in which one is not sick enough to have a real diagnosis, but where stress incu-

A Type E Woman's Day

Here is how one of my female students describes the Type E pattern and its relation to her future.

The sun is rising as she pulls herself out of bed and into the shower. After a quick shower, she wakes her husband and then proceeds to wake, bathe, and dress the children. While getting the children ready and trying to fix a well-balanced breakfast, she is also preparing herself for the day in the office. After a quick breakfast, she kisses her husband 'bye as he rushes off to work, and she piles the kids into the car to take them to day care and elementary school. Along the way she stops to pick up the rest of the kids for the car pool. After depositing the children at their appropriate locations, she then heads off to work herself. Getting onto the freeway, both her beeper and cell phone simultaneously sound. She answers both while she continues on her way to work. As she arrives at work, she is bombarded with meetings, phone calls, appointments, and deadlines. Five o'clock is approaching and she is hurriedly finishing up last-minute details and emergencies, since she was left in charge while her boss is on vacation. She rushes to pick up the children from day care and mentally plans the dinner menu. When she gets home, there is a battery of phone calls that she effectively maneuvers as she prepares dinner. These phone calls range from PTA meetings, dental appointments, Mommy and Me club, piano lessons, friend calling with an invitation for Friday night, and the vet calling to say that the family dog is in need of her shots. Dinner is finished, and the nightly routine is just beginning. She spends some quality family time with her husband and children just before she works out and then starts doing the dishes, laundry, and general house cleaning. The night is silent as she checks one final time on her sleeping children and climbs into bed with her husband.

She is a woman of the nineties. Her name is not important, because she is your daughter, friend, mother, or even yourself. She wants to do everything, and do it well. She wants to accomplish all that she undertakes, and she undertakes a lot. She juggles a career, family, and other activities in her already busy life. She is exhausted by the end of the day, but she gets up every morning and replays her daily duties once again. Tomorrow she promises herself that she will accomplish more.

I believe that the Type E woman will become more prominent in society as Generation X becomes a larger part of society's work force. I feel the pressures of the Type E woman, and I have not yet entered the workforce.

bates and serious stress illnesses, such as heart attacks, strokes, and ulcers, insidiously breed.

Of course, many women seem able to accomplish truly dazzling feats. In spite of heavy workloads, they manage a host of other commitments to family, personal relationships, community and other organizations—for a while. But

---

Reducing Type E Behavior and Beliefs

Harriett Braiker proposes several exercises for reducing Type E beliefs and behavior. Here is a summary of those exercises:

1. Redefine role requirements.
2. Prioritize your activities in rank order.
3. Create and rehearse "No" scripts.
4. Develop a pleasurable activities schedule.
5. Brainstorm and problem-solve with friends to find practical, personal solutions.
6. Use guided imagery and deep relaxation for desensitization.
7. Practice stress inoculation with role-playing and script rehearsal.
8. Use constructive self-talk.
9. Take mental mini-vacations.
10. Correct faulty time allocations with time-management analysis.

Source: Braiker (1986, Chapter 10)

---

behind the dazzle, behind the multifaceted competence and ostensible strength, you can almost hear the stress bombs ticking away.

Too often, the high-achieving woman is the proverbial candle burning at both ends. What's worse, she has unwittingly baited a trap with her own competence: she is the victim of her own success. Paradoxically, the more she demonstrates that she *can* do, the more others demand of her. She indeed proves that she can do it all, and her admiring fans—at home and at work—scream for more. Her driving achievement needs force her to stretch her resources even thinner until she gets caught in a self-perpetuating *dis*-stress cycle.

At some point, her complicated life may begin to backfire, and everything that she has worked so hard to attain and maintain may appear threatened. The stress takes its toll on her physical health—in short, on her life. Recognition of her own limitations may further threaten her self-esteem and heighten feelings of inadequacy. She may fight back by trying to do even more, but it won't work; it can't work. (1986, 5)

It is not difficult to see how chronic overload emerges from the Type E pattern. Braiker points out that the Type E pattern is both social and psychological in origins. The complex roles of working women result in excessive, incompatible demands—this is the external or social source. But partly in response to these demands, many women develop a series of what Braiker calls "erroneous expectations." It is this internal, psychological source that is the immediate source of the Type E pattern.

According to Braiker, 10 common erroneous expectations or beliefs form the cognitive basis of the stressful behaviors and feelings of Type E women:

1. I have to do things perfectly.
2. I should be able to accomplish more in a day.
3. I should be able to do everything without feeling stressed or tired.
4. I have to please others by doing what they ask me to do.
5. I have to prove myself to everyone.
6. "Having it all" should make me happy.

7. I can't be happy until "I have it all."
8. I can't relax until I finish what I have to do.
9. If I can make people need me because of everything I do for them, they'll value me.
10. I should be everything to everybody.(Braiker, 1986, 151)

Braiker provides two Type E scales. One measures Type E behaviors, the other Type E beliefs. Braiker also proposes several exercises for reducing Type E beliefs and behavior, along with a three-week plan for carrying them out. These are summarized in the box.

THE WORRIER

In *Not to Worry,* Mary and Robert Goulding describe worriers in this way:

> Worriers are really nice people. They are the kind of people who pay their taxes, vote in all elections, and put their garbage into secured garbage cans that dogs cannot pry open. They don't carry knives. They try hard to do what is right. Their children are clean and, if they too are worriers, tend to be polite and well-mannered.
>
> Worriers are creative. They can take any small stimulus and weave it into an elaborate fiction. One bounced check can grow into an entire bankruptcy scenario, and one poor report card can become a fantasized failure of epic proportions.
>
> Worriers are more intelligent than average, which can be seen by their quick ability to move from the concrete to the abstract and back, within seconds.
>
> Worriers are sufferers. When people worry, they leave the here-and-now in order to create unpleasant, imaginary stories. During a wonderful meal at a fancy restaurant, they imagine a burglar breaking into their home and stealing everything. During the peaceful moments of the late afternoon before the children have returned from play, they write imaginary horror stories of child abduction. During sex, they think about contraceptive failure.
>
> Worriers are caring people. They will tell you, "If I didn't love you so much, I wouldn't worry about you."
>
> In fact, worriers are exactly the sort of people everyone wants for neighbors, as long as they don't corner you to talk about their worries. The worst fault worriers have is that they tend to be boring. Listening to their worries is about as fascinating as listening to a recital of bowel problems. (1989, 13)

Goulding and Goulding point out a number of messages parents give their children as ways of teaching them to *worry*.

> "What if . . ."
> "You never know when lightning will strike!"
> "Someday you won't be so lucky!"
> "Watch out!"
> "Be careful!"
> "Troubles come in threes!"
> "When you're a mother, you'll know what it is to worry!"
> "If you feel so good, something bad is sure to happen!"
> "A person can't help worrying about . . ."
> "The time to worry is when everything seems to be going right."
> "I worry myself sick about you kids."
> "This job is one big worry."
> "Troubles come when you're not looking."
> "It's crazy not to worry about . . ."

Worry is concern taken to overconcern, usually including excessive rumination.

"You kids be quiet. Your father is worried about something."

"If you don't worry, you must not care."

"It's the things you don't worry about that happen."

"Just when you think everything is going well, all hell breaks loose."

"If you expect the worst, you'll never be disappointed." (1989, 29)

Goulding and Goulding note that families weave their own "worry myths" of beliefs out of self-talk such as those given. These myths include the following:

- Worrying keeps your worries from coming true. Other people make you worry.
- Events make you worry.
- If you care, you worry.
- If you love, you worry.
- If you are sensitive, you worry.
- If you are intelligent, you worry.
- If you are human, you worry. (1989, 30)

Like so many stress-prone personality patterns, the most fruitful approach to modifying the pattern is the cognitive approach—learning to correct distorted, negative thinking (1997a, 1997b). Chapter 14 describes skills and exercises for this purpose.

LEARNED HELPLESSNESS/LEARNED PESSIMISM

Another distress-prone personality pattern is learned helplessness/learned pessimism. We noted in Chapter 1 that distress develops when individuals perceive demands from the environment as exceeding their coping resources. Seligman (1975, 1979) has developed a theory that helps us understand how some individuals get to the point of feeling overwhelmed by environmental demands.

We all experience trying unsuccessfully to make an event happen: calling someone for a date and being turned down, applying for a job and never getting that call for an interview, trying to get an idea across to a professor who never seems to get the point of what you are saying. Most people go on with only minor disappointment.

Learned helplessness is a tendency to give up prematurely.

Sometimes these uncontrollable events become chronic occurrences. Research shows that both animals in the laboratory and humans in society can develop **learned helplessness** in response. In other words, people sometimes learn to become helpless when faced with repeated uncontrollable events.

In one experiment with students, for example, Hirito and Seligman (1975) assigned subjects to one of three groups. Group one was exposed to loud noise that could be terminated by pushing a button. Group two received loud noise but had no control over its termination. Group three received no noise. In the second session, all three groups were exposed to loud noise that, unknown to them, could easily be stopped by pushing the button. The "controllable" and "no noise" group quickly discovered how to stop the noise and did so. By contrast, the "uncontrollable noise" group failed to discover how to stop the noise and instead passively endured it. They had "learned"—quite incorrectly—that the noise was uncontrollable.

Seligman and his colleagues (Maier & Seligman, 1976) concluded from this and many other studies that learned helplessness takes on three dimensions: motivational, cognitive, and emotional. The result is earlier entry into the "stage of exhaustion," described by Selye in the general adaptation syndrome.

This theory of learned helplessness has generated a great deal of interest. Yet it has been criticized on a number of grounds, including its failure to take into account individual differences as well as the duration of helplessness (Taylor, 1986). Thus, Seligman and his colleagues reformulated the model to take into greater account individual explanations of negative events (Abramson, Garber, & Seligman, 1980).

According to this revised model, three dimensions of cognitive interpretation become important for explaining and predicting the depth, pervasiveness, and duration of helplessness or what Seligman now calls "learned pessimism" (Seligman, 1990).

According to Seligman, **learned pessimism**—a distress-prone personality pattern—is a particular style of interpreting good and bad events. Let's assume as a bad event that you are passed over for a job you applied for and very much wanted. Three dimensions of interpretation become important. First is **personalization**—*internal or external cause.* When the individual experiences negative events (e.g., not getting a job very much wanted), does he or she attribute the cause internally ("If only I had tried harder") or externally ("I did my best; they must have wanted different skills than mine")?

The second dimension is **permanence**—*permanent or temporary.* Permanent attributions assume it will always be this way ("I'll never get a job that amounts to anything"). A temporary attribution is to see this event as a minor and short-lived glitch in personal growth and success ("I know I will get a good job; it will just take patience and perseverance").

The third is **pervasiveness**—*universal or specific.* This refers to the extent to which the interpretation is limited to one sphere of life ("I have lots of other things going well in my life right now") or many ("This is one more part of my life where things don't go my way").

Curiously, learned pessimism leads to the opposite interpretation for good events. A high grade on a test, for example, would be seen as external, temporary, and specific. See the box that includes a summary of these contrasting styles of interpretation with learned pessimism and **learned optimism.**

Learned pessimism is the tendency to interpret bad events as personally caused, part of a permanent pattern, and pervasive into all parts of one's life; and the tendency to interpret positive events as caused by luck or external forces, temporary, and limited to this one instance.

Explanatory Styles in Learned Pessimism and Learned Optimism

Pessimistic Explanatory Style in Response to Bad Events

Internal: "It's me."
Permanent: "It's going to last forever."
Universal: "It's going to undermine everything I do."

Optimistic Explanatory Style in Response to Bad Events

External: "It's circumstances, at least in part."
Temporary: "It's temporary; it won't last."
Specific: "My misfortune is limited to this one event."

Pessimistic Explanatory Style in Response to Good Events

External: "It's circumstances, not me."
Temporary: "It's temporary; it won't last."
Specific: "My good fortune is limited to this one event."

Optimistic Explanatory Style in Response to Good Events

Internal: "It's me."
Permanent: "It's going to last forever."
Universal: "It's going to affect everything I do."

Taylor gives an example of how the learned helplessness model might fit the situation of coping with a romantic relationship in which one person is continually disappointed. Here is how someone who tends toward internal, permanent, and pervasive interpretations might react.

> Every time you think a problem is solved, it arises again or a new one takes its place. Eventually, you will lose interest in the relationship, think about it less, and make few efforts to keep it afloat. With repeated unsuccessful efforts, you may conclude that internal, stable, global factors are responsible. Consequently, you may give up trying in the expectation that future relationships will be as disappointing as those in the past. (Taylor, 1986, 229)

Learned pessimism also helps explain why uncontrollable events are more distressing than controllable ones. When events are interpreted as uncontrollable and unmodifiable, the person is more likely to conclude that no personal effort can possibly make any difference anyway. Thus, one's perceived inner sources to cope soon are overwhelmed by perceived demands of the environment. Subjective feelings of distress follow—and so do physical and behavioral consequences (Taylor, 1986), such as ill health, lower achievement, and lower performance under pressure.

Seligman has summarized recent findings on the effects of learned pessimism as follows:

- Pessimism promotes depression.
- Pessimism produces inertia rather than activity in the face of setbacks.
- Pessimism feels bad subjectively—blue, down, worried, anxious.
- Pessimism is self-fulfilling.
- Pessimists don't persist in the face of challenges, and therefore fail more frequently—even when success is attainable.
- Pessimism is associated with poor physical health.
- Pessimists are defeated when they try for high office.
- Even when pessimists are right and things turn out badly, they feel worse. Their explanatory style now converts the predicted setback into a disaster, a disaster into a catastrophe. (1990, 113)

The learned helplessness/learned pessimism theory, then, sheds further light on the complex interplay of individual and environment in the emergence of distress and the person's coping response. It is clear that both personal and situational factors must be acknowledged. Since attributional styles are learned, it stands to reason that educational and therapeutic programs can succeed in teaching learned optimism.

THE ADDICTION-PRONE PATTERN

My initial plan for this section included the heading "The Addictive Personality." But after reading more, I concluded that heading would be inappropriate, since there is no consensus among experts that such a personality exists at all.

As Joann Rodgers wrote, "The news . . . is that brain, mind, and behavior specialists are rethinking the whole notion of addiction" (1994). Rather than addiction-proneness rising out of a particular type of personality, it is most useful to see this tendency as the result of the interplay of personality style, brain biology, and social influences. Rather than speak of the addiction-prone personality, it is probably more accurate to focus on the **addiction-prone** pattern or process. Let us look further.

The addiction-prone pattern is an enduring, compulsive need for a substance or behavior.

Modeling Learned Pessimism

Listen in as Sylvia reacts to a bad event in the presence of her 8-year-old daughter Marjorie. The scene begins as they get into a car at a shopping-center parking lot. As you listen, try to discern Sylvia's explanatory style.

MARJORIE: Mommy, there's a dent on my side of the car.

SYLVIA: Damn, Bob will kill me.

MARJORIE: Daddy told you to always park his new car far away from the other cars.

SYLVIA: Damn, things like this always happen to me. I'm so lazy, I just want to carry groceries a few feet, not a hundred yards. I'm so stupid.

Sylvia is saying some pretty disheartening things about herself, and Marjorie is listening very carefully. It is not only the content that is disheartening but also the form. In content, Marjorie hears that Sylvia is in big trouble and that she is stupid, lazy, and chronically unlucky. Bad enough. But the form of what Sylvia says is even worse.

Marjorie can hear that a bad event is being explained. Sylvia gives Marjorie (quite inadvertently) four explanations.

1. *"Things like this always happen to me."* That explanation is permanent; Sylvia uses "always." Pervasive, too: "Things like this" not "car dents"; Sylvia does not qualify the misfortune or set any boundaries for the troubles that always happen to her. And personal "They happen to me," not to everyone. Sylvia singles herself out as a victim.

2. *"I'm so lazy."* Laziness, as Sylvia has cast it, is a permanent character trait. (Contrast Sylvia's explanation with this one: "I was feeling lazy.") Laziness hurts in many circumstances and thus is pervasive. And Sylvia has personalized it.

3. *"I want to carry groceries a few feet"*—personal, permanent (not "I wanted"), but not particularly pervasive since it is just about physical labor.

4. *"I'm so stupid"*—permanent, pervasive, personal.

You weren't the only one who analyzed what Sylvia was saying. Marjorie did, too. Marjorie has heard her mother explain a crisis by giving four highly pessimistic causes. She has heard her mother's view that bad events are permanent, pervasive, and her own fault. Marjorie is learning that this is the way the world is.

Every day Marjorie hears her mother make permanent, pervasive, and personal analysis of the untoward events that happen around the house. Marjorie is in the process of learning from the most influential person in her life that bad events are going to last, are going to hurt everything, and are appropriately blamed on the person to whom they happen. Marjorie is forming a theory of the world in which bad events have permanent, pervasive, and personal causes.

Source: Seligman (1990, 127)

We know that the United States is more addiction-prone than any other industrialized nation. According to experts, we top the Western world (and probably the world as a whole) in a whole range of addictions: alcohol, drugs, gambling, eating, spending, and more. We no longer are number one in tobacco addiction, but we are right up there in addiction to love and sex—and perhaps to excessive, self-indulgent exercise. A recent target of addiction is the Internet (Cotera, 1998). As Dobson (1998, 6D) notes, "Internet abuse has created millions of on-line addicts who suffer withdrawal symptoms when they switch off their computer and have anxiety and panic attacks if they have no e-mail. They suffer cyber shakes and screen sickness and are more likely to have terminal love or virtual affairs with strangers than talk to their partners—the cyberwidows." A recent book (Young, 1998) gives advice for breaking this new addiction.

The very nature of the human brain is such that everyone carries the potential to become addicted to something. In fact, we all engage in behaviors that can become addicting. As G. Alan Marlatt, director of Addictive Behaviors Research Center at the University of Washington, notes, "Everyone engages in addictive behaviors to some extent because such things as eating, drinking, and sex are essential to survival and highly reinforcing. We get immediate gratification from them and find them very hard to give up indeed" (Rodgers, 1994, 34). States another expert, Steven Childers, "The inescapable fact is that nature gave us the ability to become hooked because the brain has clearly evolved a reward system, just as it has a pain center" (Rodgers, 1994, 34).

So why do some persons become addicted to one substance or activity or another and others do not?

As Rodgers (1994) notes, if you ask others about causes of addiction, you will get a wide range of answers, depending on whom you ask:

- Some will tell you addictions result from moral weakness or influence of the devil.
- Others will tell you most addictions are simply crimes by antisocial people who will not take responsibility for their actions.
- For still others, addictions result from the drive of some people to self-destruct, usually the result of very low self-esteem.
- For the teetotaler and some politicians, it is a self-control issue.
- Many psychiatrists and psychologists will tell you it's a matter of personality traits, temperament, or "character."
- Social-learning theorists will point to conditioned responses and to intended or unintended reinforcement of inappropriate behavior.
- Biologists see addictions growing from genetic or biochemical roots.
- Anthropologists and sociologists look for origins in the culture, especially the culture of poverty, while educators point to ignorance.
- The physician and others see addictions as diseases, much like diabetes, cancer, or asthma.
- The social critic will blame our materialistic, gratification-oriented society.
- Dan Quayle blames the breakdown of family values.

Truth probably resides in a combination of these explanations. Experts generally agree with the following characteristics of addictions that trouble society. Note that these points constitute more a process than a set of singular causes or personality-proneness. Some of these points are adapted from Rodgers (1994, 38).

- Some individuals probably are more susceptible to addictions than others purely for biochemical or genetic reasons. This may be especially true of addiction to alcohol.

- Some persons are probably more susceptible to addictions than others for psychological reasons: because of the degree of psychological pain in their lives, their low frustration tolerance (with resulting tendency to "numb out"), their need to be accepted, their low internal control, their risk or thrill-seeking tendencies, or their orientation to immediate gratification.
- The substance or activity initially causes feelings of pleasure.
- Chances of addiction resulting are influenced by access, opportunities, and incentives in the social environment. If you are surrounded by others who use drugs or binge drink, your chances of becoming addicted are heightened.
- After repeated use, the body develops a physical tolerance to the substance or activity, so ever-larger doses are needed for the same amount of pleasure.
- Stopping results in painful withdrawal.
- Psychological dependence develops, which becomes independent of the physical dependence.
- The growing addiction causes physiological and chemical alterations in the brain—changes that in turn influence behavior toward continuing the addiction.
- Addictions cause a series of personal and social problems that add to the person's difficulties relating to the world. These problems may relate to money, family life, school or work performance, crime, violence, or other issues. They may develop directly from obsession with the substance (stealing for money to get the fix) or behavior or may be an indirect result of its use or actions (being late to work, missing classes, or beating up one's girlfriend or spouse).
- People often get additional kicks—sometimes another kind of "high"—out of withdrawing, going straight, flirting with the addiction again, avoiding detection, and getting caught (with all the sympathy—or uproar—that follows).

This sequence of tendencies and events can be applied to most addictions, whether to substances such as alcohol or tobacco or to behaviors like bulimia, gambling, spending, extreme sexual promiscuity, or extremes of aerobic exercise. The process outlined here is consistent with the framework toward stress outlined in Chapter 1—it is an interactional coping process through time between the person and his or her environment.

Stress can be both the cause and effect of addictions. Finding alternative approaches to coping with the pains of life often are needed. So are alternative, less personally—and socially—destructive ways of fulfilling our natural need for pleasure. Methods and skills in this textbook may help.

People with addiction problems usually are not alone. Rather, they are linked with others in their daily lives—and receive intentional or unintentional support from those others, who become codependents.

THE CODEPENDENCY PATTERN

Just as it is more accurate to refer to an addictive pattern than to an addictive personality, it is more useful to see codependency as a pattern than a personality.

Codependency is a term that arose in the 1980s out of efforts to understand alcoholics and alcoholism. Originally, alcohol treatment programs focused solely on the alcoholic as a separate and presumably isolated individual. It became increasingly clear to therapists and counselors that others in the family needed also to be brought into the treatment process. It became even more clear that others in the family suffered from their own addiction—a complementary addiction with the unintended effect of reinforcing or "enabling" the alcoholic.

Codependency is an addiction to other people and their problems.

The **codependency pattern** usually includes 1) subtly inducing the primary addict to become dependent on the codependent; 2) simultaneously trying to "change" or correct the addict and actually facilitating the addiction; and 3) self-validating the codependent's worth through these "helping" efforts. Many experts consider codependency to be just as much a disease as other forms of addictions, requiring equally potent and specific treatment strategies. Codependency does have in common with other illnesses that it is harmful, progressive, consuming, chronic, and out-of-control (Schaef, 1986). Although criticized as too inclusive a pattern to be useful (Katz & Lieu, 1991), this model no doubt has some validity—at least enough validity to be useful in understanding the stress dynamic in many individuals and families.

Melodie Beattie, author of a best-selling book (1987) on this topic, has presented a series of characteristics of the codependent, some of which are summarized here. In combination, they give a fairly comprehensive picture of the codependent personality pattern and process. Because codependents are most often women, I will refer to them as "she."

Caretaking

- She tends to be attracted to needy people, to feel responsible for others' well-being, feelings, wants, and needs, and to feel compelled to help the needy person (usually an addict of one type or another) solve the problem, whether this means fixing feelings, giving advice (even if unwanted), or ignoring one's own needs or desires.
- She tends to say yes when she really wants to say no, with the result that she feels overwhelmed, trapped, doing more than her share, and doing things others could very well do themselves.
- She tends to feel bored, empty, or worthless unless there is a crisis to solve or someone to help.

Low Self-Worth

- She usually comes from a troubled or dysfunctional family where repression of feelings and of expression is customary.
- She blames herself for everything and puts herself down for how she thinks, feels, or behaves.
- She feels she is not quite good enough, takes things personally, and yet fends off compliments or praise.
- Repression
- She represses her own thoughts and feelings out of fear and guilt.
- She feels she cannot express who she really is.
- To others, she appears controlled and rigid.

Obsession

- She worries about small things and feels overly anxious about other people and their problems.
- She focuses most of her energy fixing other people's problems, often interrupting or abandoning her own routines to give energy to others.
- She seldom finds satisfactory answers to problems yet continually checks up on how others are faring.

Controlling

- She most likely has lived through traumatic events herself, leading to sorrow and disappointment, resulting in a compulsive need to keep things under control now.
- She tries to control people and events through guilt, coercion, threats, manipulation, helplessness—or whatever else will work.
- She still feels controlled—and resentful about it.

Denial

- She denies her fear of loss of control.
- Even though she obsesses and worries, she may deny that things are as bad as they are, especially if her partner is alcoholic or abusive.
- She believes lies and lies to herself.

Dependency

- Feeling quite unhappy and discontent, she looks for happiness outside herself, most often in the form of desperately seeking love and approval.
- She feels very threatened by the loss of anything or anyone she thinks provides her happiness.
- She looks to relationships as the source of all her good feelings.

Poor Communication

- She does not say what she means or mean what she says—and in fact may not even know what she means.
- To get what she wants or to be taken seriously, she blames, threatens, coerces, begs, bribes, and lies.
- She avoids talking about her own opinions, feelings, or problems and believes others do not take her seriously.

Weak Boundaries

- She gradually increases her tolerance until she tolerates and does things she never thought she would.
- She keeps letting herself get hurt by others.
- She says she will not tolerate certain actions by others—but she does.

Lack of Trust

- As time passes, she does not trust others—or herself.
- Yet she continues to trust unworthy people, reinforcing further her belief that people cannot be trusted.
- She feels that God has abandoned her and begins to lose her faith.

Anger

- She lives with people who are very scared, hurt, and angry—and more and more she feels those things herself.

- She is afraid both of her own anger and the anger of others, especially of her partner if he is abusive or alcoholic.
- Because she is afraid of her own anger and represses it for periods of time, she cries a lot, overeats, often gets sick, and does nasty things to get even—or she periodically explodes.

Sex Problems

- She has sex when she does not want to and when she would much rather be held, comforted, and nurtured.
- She has difficulty asking her partner for what she wants in bed and often feels sexual revulsion.
- She loses interest in sex and has imaginary or real extramarital affairs.

Other

- Over time, she becomes a martyr, sacrificing her own happiness yet finding it difficult to feel close to other people.
- She has difficulty having fun or feeling spontaneous yet sometimes laughs when she feels like crying.
- Over time, she becomes depressed, withdrawn, and lethargic—and may become suicidal or may herself become addicted to alcohol or other drugs.

Unfortunately, this pattern and process is quite common, especially among partners of alcoholics or drug addicts. It is estimated that more than 80 million people in this country are chemically dependent or in a relationship with someone who is. Thus the addiction or codependent processes may affect as many as one-fourth of all Americans. The coping approaches and skills presented in this textbook represent constructive alternatives.

DISTRESS-SEEKING: THE COMMON THREAD AMONG DISTRESS-PRONE PERSONALITY PATTERNS

In Chapter 5, you read about distress-seekers—people who thrive on misery, crisis, illness, and even martyrdom. After reading this chapter, it should be apparent that many of the distress-prone personality patterns we have described are in fact **distress-seeking** patterns. For a host of varying reasons, people become accustomed—perhaps even addicted—to feeling tense, unhappy, depressed, in crisis, threatened, put upon, anxious, on edge, in trouble, sick, or on the verge of collapse.

Some people go through periods of getting more than their fair share of bad breaks or find themselves through no fault of their own in terrible circumstances. To support the point, one needs only consider the urban poor in this country, where the death rate of young males approaches that of many Third World nations and where 11-year-old girls think about what to wear at her own funeral because they assume they will die an early violent death; troublesome elementary school children who were born drug-addicted; or today's Rwandans, Haitians, Bosnians, Somalians, and Kosovars. For these people, we would be falling into the trap of **blaming the victim** if we attribute their distress entirely to themselves, ignoring overwhelming influences from the social environment.

Yet a great many people whose life circumstances are nowhere nearly as dire (like most reading this book) find themselves in distress because of habitual reliance on destructive coping styles through which they repeatedly re-create their own misery. I see this pattern among many college students for whom life is a continuous crisis, largely of their own making. Prosecutors, probation officers, and mental health workers see people repeatedly who seem to be addicted to riding the edge, getting tied into destructive relationships, and coping with temporary adversity by overreacting or reacting by making things worse.

Although the environment has helped bring them to where they are, Type A's ultimately create their time struggles and troubled relationships out of their insecurity and compulsive drives. People with a "hostile heart" become alienated and isolated through their cynicism, hair-trigger irritability, and anger explosions. Pessimists confirm their negative images of themselves and the surrounding world through their interpretations of both good and bad events. Type E women create their own overload through their "must please" coping styles. Perfectionists and worriers generate their own frustrations, guilt, and paralysis. The addiction-prone person and the codependent ultimately make their own choices to perpetuate their destructive habits. The same applies to procrastinators. This book is intended to facilitate the rewriting of these destructive life scripts and to aid you in moving toward more constructive patterns of wellness and coping.

We now turn to a review of key distress-resistant personality patterns. These patterns represent positive alternatives to the distress-prone personality patterns reviewed here and in the previous chapter.

References

Abrahamson, L. Y., Garber, J., & Seligman, M. E. P. (1980). Learned helplessness in humans: An attributional analysis. In J. Garber & M. E. P. Seligman (Eds.), *Human helplessness: Theory and applications.* New York: Academic Press, 78–92.

Arthur, N., & Hayward, L. (1997). The relationship between perfectionism, standards for academic achievement, and emotional distress in postsecondary students. *Journal of College Student Development, 38,* 622–632.

Ashby, J. S., Mangine, J. D., & Slaney, R. B. (1995). An investigation of perfectionism in a university sample of adult children of alcoholics. *Journal of College Student Development, 36,* 452–456.

Braiker, H. (1986). *The Type E Woman.* New York: Dodd, Mead.

Beattie, M. (1987). *Codependent no more.* San Francisco: HarperCollins.

Burka, J. B., & Yuen, L. M. (1983). *Procrastination: Why you do it, what to do about it.* Reading, MA: Addison, Wesley.

Burns, D. D. (1980a). *Feeling good: The new mood therapy.* New York: Signet.

Burns, D. D. (1980b). The perfectionist's script for self-defeat. *Psychology Today, 14,* 34–38.

Burns, D. D. (1989). *The feeling good handbook.* New York: Plume.

Butler, P. E. (1981). *Talking to yourself: Learning the language of self-support.* New York: Harper & Row.

Cotera, C. (1998). Trapped in the web. *Psychology Today, 31,* 66–72.

Dobson, R. (1998). Hooked on the Internet: A life-wrecking addiction. *Chico Enterprise-Record,* February 22, 6D.

Goulding, M., & Goulding, R. (1989). *Not to worry.* New York: William Morrow.

Grieger, R., & Boyd, J. (1980). *Rational-emotive therapy: A skills-based approach.* New York: Van Nostrand Reinhold Company.

Hallowell, E. M. (1997a). Why worry? *Psychology Today, 30,* 34–40, 66–71.

Hallowell, E. M. (1997b). *Worry.* New York: Pantheon Books.

Katz, S., & Lieu, A. (1991). *The codependency conspiracy.* New York: Warner Books.

Knaus, W. J., & Hendricks, C. (1986). *The illusion trap: How to achieve a happier life.* New York: World Almanac Publications.

Maier, S. F., & Seligman, M. E. P. (1976). Learned helplessness: Theory and evidence. *Journal of Experimental Psychology: General, 195,* 3–46.

Mallinger, A. E., & De Wyze, J. (1992). The perfectionist trap. *New Woman,* July, 75–77.

McKay, M., Davis, M., & Fanning, P. (1981). *Thoughts & feelings: The art of cognitive stress intervention.* Oakland: New Harbinger Publications.

Pacht, A. R. (1984). Reflections on perfectionism. *American Psychologist, 39,* 386–390.

Rodgers, J. E. (1994). Addiction—A whole new view. *Psychology Today, 27,* 32–38, 72–79.

Schaef, A. W. (1986). *Co-dependence: Misunderstood—mistreated.* San Francisco: HarperCollins.

Seligman, M. E. P. (1975). *Helplessness: On depression, development, and death.* San Francisco: W. H. Freeman.

Seligman, M. E. P. (1979). *Helplessness.* San Francisco: W. H. Freeman.

Seligman, M. E. P. (1990). *Learned optimism: The skills to overcome life's obstacles.* New York: Pocket Books.

Taylor, S. E. (1986). *Health psychology.* New York: Random House.

Young, K. S. (1998). *Caught in the Net: How to recognize the signs of Internet and a sure-fire strategy for recovery.* New York: John Wiley & Sons.

Application Exercise 9-1

Examining Your "Perfectionism Pitfalls and Philosophies of Achievement"

1. Which of the "Perfectionism Pitfalls" fit you? Explain.

2. How do these affect you? Others?

Now consider the "Perfectionism" and "Wellness" philosophies of achievement.

1. Which most closely fits your own outlook? Explain.

2. What do you think are the results of each philosophy for you and others?

3. Which philosophy will you strive toward in the future? Explain.

Application Exercise 9-2

Assessing Your Own Perfectionism

Do you sometimes: Yes   No

1. Take life too seriously?
2. Feel intense, uptight, and defensive?   _____   _____
3. Hate to admit when you are wrong?   _____   _____
4. Feel overwhelmed with responsibilities?   _____   _____
5. Worry about making a mistake?   _____   _____
6. Fail to organize your affairs effectively?   _____   _____
7. Get impatient with people?   _____   _____
8. Believe that people should follow the rules?   _____   _____
9. Feel anxious when things get out of order?   _____   _____
10. Think you are nobody unless successful?   _____   _____
11. Get impatient when things get out of order?   _____   _____
12. Easily find fault with others?   _____   _____
13. Go from one extreme to another?   _____   _____
14. Refuse to accept limitations?   _____   _____
15. Feel aggravated by your lover's physical imperfections? _____   _____
16. Have trouble making decisions?   _____   _____
17. Feel upset because you are wasting your potential?   _____   _____
18. Think you are better than most other people?   _____   _____
19. Feel an urgent need to stay in control?   _____   _____
20. Worry about giving the wrong impression?   _____   _____

SCORING: YES = 1 NO = 0   YOUR SCORE: _____

Source: Knaus & Hendricks (1986, 108)

Application Exercise 9-3

A Closer Look at Your Perfectionism

Compare your perfectionism score to the following distribution of scores among 259 of my students who recently completed the Perfectionism Scale. The higher the score, the greater the perfectionism, with the potential range of scores between 0 and 20.

Mean and Median: 10

Score	% of Respondents
0–5	11
5–10	41
11–13	39
14–20	9
	100%

1. How satisfied are you with your score? Explain.

2. Do you tend to be an internal perfectionist, external perfectionist, or both? Explain.

3. How does your perfectionism affect you? Others?

By perseverance, the snail reached the ark.
—CHARLES SPURGEON

Distress-Resistant Personality Patterns

Hardiness and Loss

Bill B. is the kind of person who has an immediate reassuring effect on those around him. At 55 years of age, he has a twinkle in his eye and an easy, relaxed manner. He seems to have all the time in the world as he asks the interviewer what the research is about and how it is done. All the details seem to interest him. . . .

When he begins describing his work at the phone company, the curiosity he has for what he does know shades over into zest for the familiar. He embellishes his descriptions all the while making his role in planning commercial telephone services come alive. Although he has a clear sense of the importance of broader social issues concerning his work, and certainly feels that his role requires innovative planning, it is the moment-to-moment activities of the day that intrigue him the most. He claims to learn fairly continuously, even then the task appears at first to be routine. . . .

Bill's wife died seven years ago in an accident while they were on vacation. He can still evoke the pain and shock of that unfortunate event. Her death depressed him for more than a year, though he showed few signs of guilt. He missed her more than he felt guilty. By the time of her death, their two children were grown, with spouses and children of their own. One of these families lives in the same city, but the other is out of state.

Since his wife's death, Bill has lived alone. Although this was difficult at first, he has long since developed a satisfying routine. When he wants company, he invites friends for a meal he enjoys cooking or visits his children and grandchildren. Often, however, he spends time alone, reading or building furniture. Though he hasn't ruled out remarriage, he doesn't feel any pressing need for a spouse. He enjoys satisfying social interactions yet is not bored when alone. Even when he relaxes, he finds much in himself and the passing scene that is of interest. (Maddi & Kobasa, 1984, 10–11)

For everyone, life is hard. For many, it is downright tough. Most reading this book are afflicted with a host of minor daily hassles, and some face major challenges—money, career, relationships, unexpected disasters, graduation uncertainties. But it is all quite relative. If you are a youngster growing up in an inner city, your problems are quite different than those just listed, and most are not minor at all—poor schools, unstable families, drugs, crime, violence, and inadequate housing. Worse, consider the daily stressors facing children (and adults) in such places as Rwanda, Haiti, Bosnia, Cuba, and Somalia.

Many people suffer immeasurably in their mental and physical health and their human spirits in response to such adversity. Yet many do not fold, give up, and cave in. Most humans possess amazing resilience and distress-resistance. Victor Frankl's book, *Man's Search for Meaning* (1959) on survivors of World War II concentration camps, is a classic illustration of such resilience.

In this chapter, we will examine several personality syndromes that help provide distress-resistance, beginning with the Type B personality pattern. This is an important chapter that we will refer back to frequently in Part IV of the book as we focus on specific stress-management methods.

THE TYPE B PATTERN

We noted in Chapter 8 that the image of the Type A individual has become well-known throughout this society as the term *Type A* has taken hold in our language: a person who is hurried, hassled, driven, irritable, quick-tempered. Much less attention has been given either by scholars or by popular writers to the **Type B** person.

The image we sometimes associate with Type B's is lack of ambition and dullness. Friedman and Ulmer point out that this image of the Type B individual is quite inaccurate.

Type B is a personality pattern of thinking, feeling, and acting marked by the relative absence of Type A qualities.

> It is important to us that no one get the idea that all Type B's lead sane but dull lives or that their main excitement in life comes from changing the brand of cereal they eat at breakfast, the route they drive to work, or the television programs they view in the evening. Actually . . . many Type B's live magnificent lives, lives in which their capacity to appreciate beauty, affection, and creative novelty offers them the chance to experience a myriad wonderful events—the first flowering of a cattleya orchid they have been nurturing, their grandchild stutter-mumbling his first sentence, the shy smile of thanks of an old lady on the street, granted because they took the time to notice her existence by smiling at her. Some Type A men *talk* with more spice and zing, but Type B's often *do* far more satisfying things. (1984, 71)

Type B behavior is the absence of any of the qualities we have described for Type A. This definition is important because of a tendency of researchers to use Type A qualities as the definers of personalities. For instance, Friedman prefers to label as Type A anyone who displays even one of the Type A qualities, even though such a person would be a mild Type A (Friedman & Ulmer, 1984). The more of these qualities a person possesses, the more Type A she or he is. Thus, Type A ranges from very mild to very severe.

Let us examine Type B behavior.

Absence of Time Urgency

Friedman and Ulmer (1984) point out that Type B's are distinguished by being on "gracious terms with time," that is, by the **absence of time urgency.** They seldom experience time urgency. They are responsible and diligent in relation to time, but they seem able to move through their day without the Type A's "overtones of frenzy and rage." One Type B quoted Jonathan Swift in explaining his attitude toward time: "Whoever is out of patience is out of possession of his soul." Type B's take "the long view" toward their activities, being more concerned with the calendar than the minute and second hands of their watch. Type B's feel sufficiently secure not to feel compelled to approach every task from the point of view of a deadline.

Type B's find it easier to delegate, since they are more likely to accept others', including subordinates', divergent ways of doing things. By contrast, Type A's usually delegate with reluctance, trepidation, and impatience, sure that tasks will not be completed to their high standard.

Friedman and Ulmer (1984, 74) noted the contrast between Lyndon Johnson, a flaming Type A with constant impatience, a monumental temper, and a critical attitude toward most around him, and Harry Truman. Truman no doubt would have agreed with Thoreau's statement, "Nothing can be more useful to a man than a determination not to be hurried." His cousin remarked, "There was no sense of frantic urgency, no burning need to hurry; Harry was always a deliberate man."

Type B's usually take time for contemplation. They value each moment and are less compulsively preoccupied with the future than Type A's. They take time to appreciate themselves, as well as those they care about. Type A's seldom "have time."

Absence of Free-Floating Hostility

Unlike Type A's, Type B's need not control everyone and everything in their environments. Because of their greater personal security, they find it reasonable to tolerate diversity in the thinking and actions of those around them. Consequently, Type B's are much less often frustrated by the flow of daily events and are characterized by **absence of free-floating hostility.**

Friedman and Ulmer tell this humorous story about the contrast between Type A's and Type B's in toleration.

> In recent years, we have run into a curious illustration of the way Type A men, in marked contrast to Type B's, are likely to take the silliest things seriously. More than half of them seem to be prepared to argue heatedly about the manner in which a toilet paper roll is placed in its receptacle: so that the paper unrolls over the top, or comes out underneath. It may be hard to believe, but we have witnessed grown men very nearly come to blows over this issue. The medieval churchmen who fought over how many angels can dance on the head of a pin must have been Type A's. (1984, 76)

The blunders of other drivers make a Type B more cautious, whereas a Type A becomes irritated, angered, and even outraged. Because Type B's are able to overlook small mistakes by others, their family life is marked by less tension and displays of AIAI, or anger, irritability, aggravation, and impatience.

Perhaps most importantly, Type B's are more able to practice empathy—to put themselves in the shoes of the other, to see events through her or his eyes. They seldom sermonize to their spouses or children and seldom find it necessary to resort to corporal punishment. They find it much easier than Type A's to express affection.

Why the relative absence of hostility in Type B's? Again, the answer is their higher self-esteem and sense of personal security.

A Sense of Self-Esteem

Friedman and Ulmer maintain that the most important difference between Type A's and Type B's is that Type B's possess adequate rather than deficient **self-esteem.** Type B's, having usually received a greater abundance of unconditional love and affection, grow up believing they are worthwhile human beings—irrespective of their achievements. Consequently, they find no need to develop the burning drive to win approval through unending achievements.

This does not mean Type B's are unmotivated to succeed or that they do not work hard. But Type B's are more likely to feel at peace with themselves whether or not they are accomplishing something. And their self-expectations are "in healthy balance with their perceived capabilities" (Friedman & Ulmer, 1984, 78).

A man well over 90 years of age told a friend his secret to a long, happy life: "My mother told me to always do the best I could and be satisfied with the result. I've tried to do just that" (Friedman & Ulmer, 1984, 78).

As Type B's give and receive love and affection from those close to them, their self-esteem is further enhanced.

Type B's as Leaders

It is a myth that one must be Type A to succeed in America. Type A's who make it to the top generally do so despite many of their Type A qualities, not because of them. Are aggravation, impatience, anger, or irritability assets in any profession? It is doubtful.

Figure 10-1

The Presence of Type A and Type B Behavior in 106 National Leaders

Types of Leaders	Total Number	Type A Behavior	Type B Behavior
1) University Presidents	11	6 (55%)	5 (45%)
2) Bank Presidents	5	3 (60%)	2 (40%)
3) Corporation Chairpersons	30	21 (70%)	9 (30%)
4) Generals, Admirals	11	6 (55%)	5 (45%)
5) Archbishops, Bishops, Rabbis	4	2 (50%)	2 (50%)
6) Journalists, Publishers	22	16 (73%)	6 (27%)
7) Nobel Laureates	11	6 (55%)	5 (45%)
8) Congressmen, Senators	7	3 (43%)	4 (57%)
9) Federal Judges	5	2 (40%)	3 (60%)
Total:	106	65 (62%)	41 (39%)

Source: Friedman & Ulmer (1984, 81)

Friedman and Ulmer present data (see Figure 10-1) suggesting that many Type B's make it to the top of their professions.

THE TRUSTING HEART

You read in Chapter 8 that "the hostile heart" consists of three main ingredients:

1. Cynicism, which is a basic mistrust of the motives, intentions, and values of others
2. Readily and frequently aroused feelings of anger
3. A tendency to display those angry feelings in overt language or behavior

You also read that the hostile heart is dangerous for health—even for length of life.

Redford and Virginia Williams have made an important contribution to the stress field by identifying, describing, and providing guidance for modifying the hostile heart (Williams, 1989; Williams & Williams, 1993). They also have contributed by describing "the trusting heart." Redford Williams's following description elaborates on this definition as follows:

> The trusting heart believes in the basic goodness of humankind, that most people will be fair and kind in relationships with others. Having such beliefs, the trusting heart is slow to anger. Not seeking out evil in others, not expecting the worst of them the trusting heart expects mainly good from others and, more often than not, finds it. As a result, the trusting heart spends little time feeling resentful, irritable, and angry.

The trusting heart is a personality pattern including belief in the basic goodness of humans and that most people will be fair and kind in their relationships. Not expecting the worst in others, persons with the trusting-heart personality pattern spend little time feeling irritable, resentful, or angry, treating others instead with consideration, tolerance, and kindness.

From this it follows that the trusting heart treats others well, with consideration and kindness; the trusting heart almost never wishes or visits harm upon others. Just as our research has shown that the hostile heart is at risk of premature death and disease, it also can reassure us that the trusting heart appears protected against these outcomes.

This . . . is the best news of all. (1989, 71)

Just as the hostile heart breeds social isolation, the **trusting heart** engenders social integration and social support. As in so many other circumstances, the self-fulfilling prophecy takes over. If your perspective is a cynical and angry one, you probably will generate troubled relationships. If you are more trusting, you probably will reap what you sow in a positive way.

In the previous chapter, you read that the higher the hostility, the higher the distress-symptom scores among students in my university-level Human Stress class. The converse, of course, is that the less hostile, the less the distress. These respondents also completed a 3-item trust measure. For example, they were asked, "Generally speaking, would you say that most people can be trusted or that you can't be too careful in dealing with people?" Figure 10-2 shows that those scoring high in trust also reported significantly lower distress-symptom scores.

The Williams's support for the concept of the trusting heart is consistent with a central ethic of all the world's religions, illustrated as follows by Redford Williams:

- **Christianity** . . . and as you wish that men would do to you, do so to them.
- **Judaism** You shall not take vengeance or bear any grudge against the sons of your own people, but you shall love your neighbor as yourself.
- **Buddhism** When men speak evil of ye, thus may ye train yourselves: "Our heart shall be unwavering, no evil word will we send forth, but compassionate of other's welfare will we abide, of kindly heart without resentment" . . . we will suffuse the

Figure 10-2

Mean Distress-Symptom Score by Trust Score

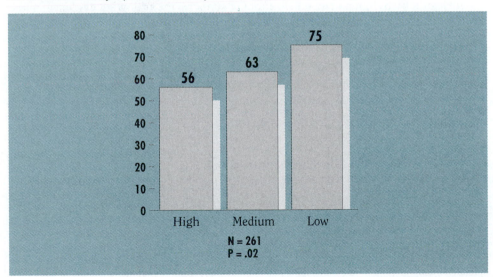

MEASURES: *Distress Symptoms:* 50-Item Distress Symptom Scale
       Trust: 3-Item Trust Scale
FINDING: Respondents high in trust scored significantly lower in distress symptoms than those who were low in trust.

> whole world with loving thoughts, far-reaching, wide-spreading, boundless, free from hate, free from ill-will. . . .

- **Confucianism** The Master said, The gentleman calls attention to the good points in others; he does not call attention to their defects. The small man does just the reverse of this.

- **Taoism** The aspect of Taoism that is most relevant to the trusting heart is the emphasis Taoism places on doing away with the distinction between the self and the world. Knowing that all beings are one, the Taoist pursues the ideal of *wu-wei*, a form of action in which there is no act, yet nothing is left undone. Since all beings and everything are fundamentally one, there is no need to oppose others. (1989)

The trusting heart, then, is likely to lead to relationships and circumstances that are less distress-producing. And when adversity does come one's way, it is certainly more advantageous to meet it with a trusting heart than a hostile heart.

LEARNED OPTIMISM

See Application Exercise 10-1 for a guide in personalizing the tips in the box for reducing hostility.

You read in the previous chapter that learned pessimism, emerging from a particular style of interpreting good and bad events, leads down the path toward helplessness; depression; adverse mental and physical health; decreased effectiveness in school, work and sports; and even to less effective teams and organizations (Seligman, 1991).

Conversely, we know that optimism is health—and distress—protective. I am not talking here about Pollyannish thinking, wherein everything is sweetness and roses when it obviously is not. I refer to a basic belief in the viability of the future, in the likelihood that things will turn out well.

Learned optimism is a pattern of thinking in which good events are explained by factors that are internal, permanent, and pervasive, while bad events are explained by factors that are external, temporary, and limited in scope.

Seligman has provided important insights into the nature and effects of learned optimism. Since we reviewed the details of what he termed "**explanatory style**" relative to good and bad events in the previous chapter, we need not go into great detail here.

Research by Seligman and others strongly supports the following evidence on the positive effects of health and well-being from learned optimism:

- Optimists respond to adversity with internal control.
- Optimists become depressed less often.
- Optimists are more likely to succeed in school, work, and sports.
- Optimists maintain better health habits.
- Optimists have a stronger immune system.
- Optimists are healthier.
- Optimists win elections more often.
- Optimists may live longer than pessimists.

In short, learned optimism is an important personality style yielding not only a more satisfying life but a life with less likelihood of distress as a result of either the hassles of daily living or major life events.

Students in my Human Stress class completed a single-item measure of optimism, as well as the Distress Symptom Scale. As shown in Figure 10-3, those high in optimism showed significantly lower distress-symptom scores. While this measure of optimism does not assess the three dimensions of learned optimism (personalization, permanence, pervasiveness), it nevertheless supports the notion that optimistic thinking as a general tendency influences chances of distress.

Tips for Reducing Hostility

In their excellent book, *Anger Kills,* Williams and Williams present 17 strategies for "controlling the hostility that can harm your health."

1. Reason with yourself.
2. Stop hostile thoughts, feelings, and urges.
3. Distract yourself.
4. Meditate.
5. Avoid overstimulation.
6. Assert yourself.
7. Care for a pet.
8. Listen.
9. Practice trusting others.
10. Take on community service.
11. Increase empathy.
12. Be tolerant.
13. Forgive.
14. Have a confidant.
15. Laugh at yourself.
16. Become more religious.
17. Pretend today is your last.

Source: Williams & Williams (1993, Part III)

Figure10-3

Mean Distress-Symptom Score by Optimism

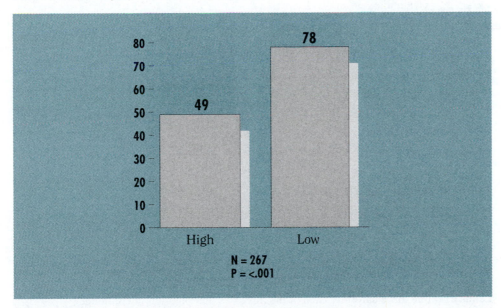

MEASURES: *Distress Symptoms:* 50-Item Distress Symptom Scale
      Optimism: Question 12 from Quality of Life Assessment in Chapter 1

FINDING: Those who scored high in optimism scored significantly lower in distress symptoms, compared with those who scored low in optimism.

HARDINESS

A quarter-century of research demonstrates that the more the clustering of stressful life events, the greater the risk of illness. In recent years, researchers have addressed a corollary question: Given the presence of potentially stressful events, who stays well? Who is distress-resistant?

Maddi and Kobasa (1984) developed several reservations about the clustering-of-life-events research and conclusions based on it. First, they noted that even though findings consistently were reported showing a correlation between life-event scores and illness, the correlations usually were not very strong (Kobasa, 1979). Second, they questioned the recommendations that emerged from the early studies on life events—that change ought to be avoided or at least minimized. "Popular accounts of the research often advise people simply to avoid stressful life events if they want to stay healthy" (Maddi & Kobasa, 1984, 22). They question whether such advice is realistic or even desirable. Third, they observed that these studies tend to ignore individual differences in perceptions of stressful events and responses to them. "By these omissions, stress researchers appear to be saying that individuals' perceptions and coping responses do not matter. We are all poor victims of our environments and the changes they impose on us; when stressful life events mount, we are all at risk" (1984, 23).

In response to these concerns, Maddi and Kobasa initiated a different type of study on clustering of life events: Who stays well and why, given lots of personal change? During the next several years, they and others identified a pattern they called **hardiness** that clearly set apart those who succeeded in surviving change without illness. Many of their subjects, in fact, seemed to thrive under conditions of rapid and clustered change.

Hardiness is a personality style showing a liking of challenge, a strong sense of commitment, and a strong sense of control.

Characteristics of Hardiness

Thus, hardiness has come to be known by its three *C*'s:

See Application Exercise 10-2 for a self-assessment on hardiness.

1. Challenge
2. Commitment
3. Control

People high in hardiness display several qualities. They:

1. Work hard because they enjoy it, rather than because they feel compelled or driven
2. React optimistically and take positive action
3. Experience events as stressful, but also as:

- Interesting
- Important
- Influenceable
- Of potential value for personal growth

By contrast, those low in hardiness see stressful events as:

- Terrible
- Outside their influence
- Disruptive to their security

Let us examine more carefully each of the three *C*'s. People high in **challenge:**

- Consider it natural for things to change
- Anticipate change as a useful stimulus for creativity
- Thrive under conditions of challenge, difficulty, and adversity

- Turn change and difficulty into opportunity and challenge
- Rise to the occasion

People high in **commitment:**

- Find it easy to be contented in whatever they are doing
- Do what they love and love what they do
- Rarely are at a loss for things to do
- Make a maximum effort
- Do so zestfully

People high in **control:**

- Believe they can influence events and their reactions to events
- Reflect on how to turn difficult situations into opportunities
- Have a strong sense of initiative
- Are slow to give up on a challenge

Effects of Hardiness: Illustrative Research Evidence

Studies by Kobasa, Maddi, and Kahn (1982), as well as many others, clearly show that hardiness offers protection against distress and illness in the face of clustered change. Figure 10-4, for example, shows that among 259 executives, having a high life-events score increased severity of illness with or without hardiness. But the presence of hardiness resulted in lower illness severity risk among both those with low stressful-events scores (415 versus 529) and high stressful-events scores (513 versus 1061). The impact of hardiness was greatest among those with high stressful-events scores.

See Application Exercise 10-3, which explores how to develop hardiness in children.

Figure 10-5 shows that hardiness is also associated with lower distress symptoms in a study of my students. The same study revealed that the higher the hardiness:

- The higher the happiness
- The lower the depression
- The higher the self-esteem
- The higher the sense of energy and vitality
- The higher the optimism
- The more positive the self-reported health
- The higher the sense of meaning and direction

Figure 10-4

Average Severity of Illness for Groups Defined by Hardiness and Stressful-Events Scores

		Hardiness	
		High	Low
STRESSFUL EVENTS	**HIGH**	514	1,061
	LOW	415	529

Source: Kobasa, Maddi, & Kahn (1982)

Figure 10-5

Mean Distress-Symptom Score by Hardiness

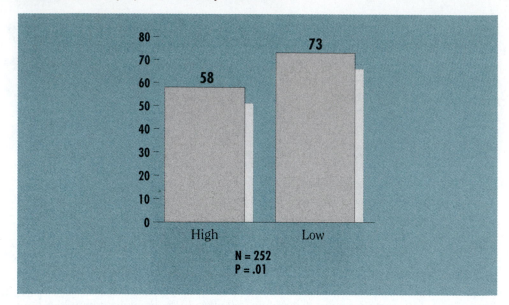

MEASURES: *Distress Symptoms:* 50-Item Distress Symptom Scale
Hardiness: 12-Item Hardiness Scale developed by Kobasa (1984)

FINDING: Those high in hardiness scored significantly lower in distress symptoms than those low in hardiness.

- The fewer the days of school missed due to illness
- The higher the total wellness score
- The higher the total quality of life

The key point here is that hardiness is a valuable antidote to distress from too much change in too short a time. In short, hardiness is a personality style that tends to lead to distress resistance. In Chapter 14, we will explore self-talk techniques for strengthening hardiness.

SENSE OF COHERENCE

A quarter-century ago, Aaron Antonovsky, an Israeli medical sociologist, was impressed by a striking observation: Nearly one-third of female Israeli concentration camp survivors in one of his studies were found to be in reasonably good emotional health. While this proportion was significantly lower in a control group of women who had not experienced concentration camps, Antonovsky was impacted by the fact that the number was as large as it was. "To have gone through the most unimaginable horror of the camp, followed by years of being a displaced person, and then to have reestablished one's life in a country which witnessed three wars . . . and still be in reasonable health" left a lasting impression (1987, xi).

This experience stimulated Antonovsky to consciously pursue a career formulating and testing "the salutogenic model." Whereas a "pathological orientation seeks to explain why people get sick, why they enter a given disease category, a salutogenic orientation (which focuses on the origins of health) poses a radically different question: Why are people located toward the positive end of the health ease/dis-ease continuum, or why do they move toward this end, whatever their location at any given time?" (1987, xii)

Thus, Antonovsky has devoted nearly three decades to the study of who stays well, even in the face of severe adversity. His investigations and thought led him to develop the concept "sense of coherence," which he defines as follows:

> The **sense of coherence** is a global orientation that expresses the extent to which one has a pervasive, enduring though dynamic feeling of confidence that (1) the stimuli deriving from one's internal and external environments in the course of living are structured, predictable, and explicable; (2) the resources are available to one to meet the demands posed by the stimuli; and (3) these demands are challenges, worthy of investment and engagement. (1987, 19)

Three core components make up the sense of coherence.

1. **Comprehensibility** The extent to which one perceives the external stimuli as making sense—as information that is ordered, consistent, structured, and clear (as opposed to seeming chaotic, random, accidental, or inexplicable).
2. **Manageability** The degree to which one perceives resources are available within oneself or the immediate surroundings to meet the demands posed by the stimuli.
3. **Meaningfulness** The extent to which one feels life's demands are worthy of commitment and engagement and that challenges are welcomed rather than dreaded because they are worthwhile investing energy into.

Antonovsky has developed a highly refined questionnaire measuring these three core components of sense of coherence. Several hundred studies using this measure have been conducted around the world, most of which document that sense of coherence indeed heightens chances of distress-resistance and of good mental and physical health. Figure 10-6 shows that among my students a brief measure of sense of coherence is inversely associated with distress symptoms. In another recent study of health social workers, those

Figure 10-6

Mean Distress-Symptom Score by Sense of Coherence

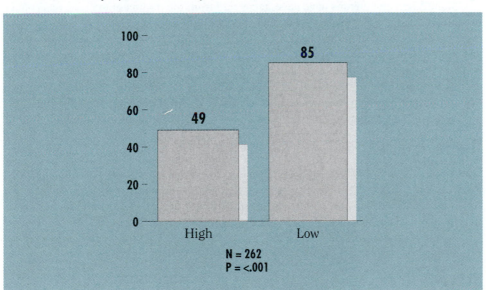

N = 262
P = <.001

MEASURES: *Distress Symptoms:* 50-Item Distress Symptom Scale
  Sense of Coherence: 13-Item Sense of Coherence Scale, developed by Antonovsky
  (1987)

FINDING: Those with high sense-of-coherence scores scored significantly lower in distress symptoms.

with a strong sense of coherence were found to experience significantly less burnout than those with a weak sense of coherence. (Gilbar, 1998)

Antonovsky (1994) has encouraged viewing sense of coherence in a social context, since it is not a personal quality developed in isolation. Rather, it is a personal perspective developed through social learning and reinforcing by social circumstances. Thus, Antonovsky encourages attending to such social factors as family background, ethnicity, social class, workplace, region, national culture, and other social circumstances in seeking to understand why some persons develop a strong sense of coherence and become distress-resistant, while others do not. It follows that, in seeking to promote health and well-being, the focus must be on social environments as well as on the individual.

In short, sense of coherence is the personal belief (developed in part through social influences) that life's demands make sense and are worth responding to and that one has the resources available to cope with those demands. The greater the presence of the sense of coherence, the greater the distress resistance.

THE SURVIVOR PERSONALITY

Psychologist Al Siebert for years has been fascinated by why some people survive a major event such as serious illness or injury, while others suffer (Siebert, 1983; Siebert, 1993; Walker, 1988; Walter & Siebert, 2000). He observes that some individuals rise to the occasion and are better for the experience, while others wither, are weakened, or become embittered by adversity.

People with survivor personalities are those who: have survived a major crisis or challenge; surmounted the crisis through personal effort; emerged from the experience with previously unknown strengths and abilities; and afterwards find value in the experience.
—Siebert, 1993

Siebert points to several examples of the **survivor personality.** During the Nazi era, millions experienced horrible torture in concentration camps. Some victims were able to protect themselves by retreating to a reserve of inner strength. If they avoided the gas chambers, many of these individuals emerged stronger, not weaker, and went on to live long, healthy, and productive lives.

Some Vietnam veterans have never recovered from the trauma of the war; others have been able to put the memories to rest and get on with their lives.

Physicians marvel at the fact that two patients of similar age, socioeconomic status, and disease state can respond quite differently to treatment. One recovers and resumes a normal life; the other withers and dies.

In the same way, students respond quite differently to the heavy pressures of college. Why do some thrive and others become overwhelmed, discouraged, ill, and dispirited?

After studying hundreds of "survivors," Siebert discovered several patterns.

Biphasic Traits

Siebert observed that survivors display counterbalanced, seemingly paradoxical traits. They are playful and serious, trusting and cautious, intuitive and logical, impulsive and stable, gentle and strong, easygoing and strong-willed, childlike and mature. These **biphasic traits** might seem at first glance to make for unpredictability, even schizoid tendencies. But Siebert believes they serve an important positive function: allowing the individual to respond with versatility under a wide range of demanding circumstances.

Serendipity

Survivors have **serendipity,** a knack for responding with insight and wisdom under the pressure of an accident or other misfortune. They do not waste time moaning and groaning but instead look ahead at how best to solve the problem. Instead of asking, "Why did this terrible event happen to me?" they look ahead and ask, "Now that this has happened to me, what am I going to do about it? How can I turn this around?"

They are able to respond to events that would be highly distressing for others by turning them into a possible challenge, from negative stress into positive stress. Their ability to find seemingly fortuitous answers and solutions works for them in remaining level-headed and centered during adversity.

Synergy

Survivors produce **synergy**—making things go well for themselves and others. Their inner "life force" seems to take them in directions that work out, even under enormous pressure and hardship. They care so deeply about the well-being of others that they are unusually flexible and adaptive, with little ego investment in a given solution and willingness to learn and listen. They leave whatever world they pass through better than they found it. Siebert notes that survivors are "foul-weather friends."

Self-Actualization

Survivors seek **self-actualization.** They enjoy taking reasonable risks. They challenge themselves and welcome the unknown. Like those studied by Maslow, these people are curious and self-motivating. They become better and smarter as they grow older. Able to adapt easily to change, they have no fear of looking foolish. They focus more on discovery than safety, security, or looking good.

Creativity

Survivors are less judgmental than others. They are not as quick to label something good or bad, right or wrong. They accept others' fallibilities. Most of all, they are inventive in finding solutions to problems and adversities. This **creativity** results from not being limited by fear of ridicule. They think spontaneously as the need arises. Their solutions are often a surprise to others.

Intuition

Survivors can sense subtle, even subliminal, cues and clues. With unusual **intuition,** they are sensitive to feelings and nuances and consider them valuable sources of information. Siebert believes this extraordinary sensitivity and perceptiveness sometimes even borders on extrasensory perception (ESP). He states, "My guess is that people who are fully functioning as humans achieve harmony with some unknown energies in the universe" (Walker, 1988, 15).

Humor

The trait most often found in survivors, according to Siebert, is **humor.** The survivor personality is able to laugh at what has happened and to find something amusing even in the midst of difficult events. Siebert noted that even hardened Korean War combat veterans, with whom he served in the 1950s, were able to respond to their own mistakes with humor. Rather than feel threatened or deeply disappointed, they were able to take difficulty with good humor and lightheartedness.

Competence Under Pressure

According to Siebert, the survivor personality displays **competence under pressure.** Trying circumstances are transformed into positive challenges because the person:

- Can sit back and let things run themselves
- Expends much less energy than people who are struggling
- Has chunks of optional time for being curious about the early signs of new developments
- Can spot early indications of potential trouble and take action to prevent it
- Can work on future happenings so, when they occur, things fall into place easily
- Can put high-quality time and energy into emergency developments without having other basic matters interrupted
- Responds to an emergency or crisis with an attitude reflective of both expecting and needing things to work out well (1983, 21).

Finally, Siebert notes that:

The really competent, synergistic people in every sphere of human activity are those individuals who have gone beyond their teachers. They have learned what no one can teach them. Competence results from self-motivated, self-managed learning. People who follow instructions on how to function successfully are never as skillful as people who are self-motivated learners. (1983, 21)

THE TYPE C PATTERN

A useful theory of thriving under pressure, whether such pressure be difficult, ongoing circumstances, such as the Great Depression, or a specific event, such as an athletic contest or a job interview, is the **Type C** pattern. The Type C pattern draws some of the best attributes from the Type A and Type B patterns and adds new elements to form a cluster of ingredients for meeting challenge head-on with success and vitality. The originators of this concept, Robert and Marilyn Kriegel, note:

Type C behavior is a performance model for us all. Everyone . . . can perform as a Type C. Whether you're directing a multi-billion-dollar corporation or managing a small office, selling or speaking, running a machine or running for election, marketing or manufacturing, teaching or training, researching or reporting, out looking for a first job or wanting to change careers—WHATEVER YOU DO, YOU CAN DO IT AS A TYPE C. (1990, xvi)

The Type C pattern is peak performance under pressure.

The Type C model is based on the Type C experience—where everything seems to flow naturally at a very high level of performance. Barbara Boxer, a U.S. senator from California, states, "It's like being on a roll. I feel confident and enthusiastic and everything seems to work. I am able to accomplish a great deal with a minimum of effort. My energy keeps building and gets transferred to whomever I am working with" (Kriegel & Kriegel, 1990, 1).

An award-winning reporter describes his Type C episodes this way: "Sometimes when I'm rushing to meet a deadline, I become so involved in what I am doing that I am unaware of anything going on around me. I get calm and everything becomes easy. It's unbelievable. I've done my best work at these times" (Kriegel & Kriegel, 1990, 2).

Type C episodes are marked by several qualities, experienced by most people at one time or another (Kriegel & Kriegel, 1984, 2).

Transcendent You go beyond your usual level to new heights of personal performance.

Effortless Your performance flows easily, without special effort or struggle.

Positive You are optimistic and confident, thoroughly enjoying what you are doing.

Figure 10-7

The Performance Zone Diagram

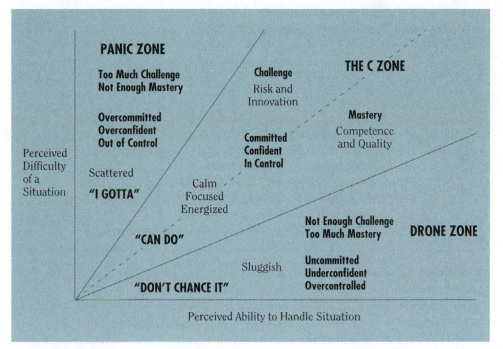

Source: Kriegel & Kriegel (1984, 20)

Spontaneous Thought and action are naturally unified. Choices come easily.

Focused Your concentration is complete. You are fully engaged with the process. You are totally involved and fully connected.

Vital You feel unusually alive and energetic. You feel total joy in what you are doing and accomplishing.

The "C" in this model stands for three *C*'s in the Type C pattern: **challenge, confidence,** and **control.** These are the characteristics most often reported by people asked to describe their Type C experiences.

Based on countless workshops and consultations, as well as interviews with more than 400 business executives, the Type C concept closely resembles the three *C*'s of hardiness. Curiously, however, Kriegel and Kriegel never cite the work of Maddi and Kobasa, even though scientific publications on hardiness had appeared several years before. Despite this flaw, the Type C model does merit attention as a tool for better understanding how to thrive under pressure.

According to Kriegel and Kriegel, the Performance Zone Diagram, shown in Figure 10-7, can be useful in assessing the balance between your perceived difficulty of a challenge and your perceived ability to handle that challenge. Peak performance occurs in the C Zone, either slightly to the right or left of the dashed line.

SELF-ESTEEM

Self-esteem leads to appreciation of your own worth and importance. Out of self-esteem flow caring for self, caring for others, and translation of this caring into action (California Task Force, 1990).

Self-esteem is self-acceptance and confidence in one's abilities to cope with life's demands.

Self-Talk and Self-Worth

Here are several interrelated points about self-talk and self-worth. Do you agree or disagree? How does each apply to you?

1. I create my own inner reality.
2. I deserve to create feelings of self-worth because I am a unique human being.
3. My self-worth can be (even if it is not now) positive, steady, and independent of social position, accomplishments, others' opinions, and my own fallibilities.
4. Because my own self-worth can exist unconditionally, it need be neither proven nor protected.
5. Self-created distress associated with perfectionism, hurry sickness, anger, and anxiety often results from unnecessary struggles to prove or protect my self-worth.
6. I accept responsibility for my own sense of self-worth.

Self-esteem begins in childhood, of course, as a result of early messages and early decisions in relation to significant others. High self-esteem is reinforced and sustained by supportive and loving self-talk. Low self-esteem is perpetuated by negative, self-deprecating self-talk. Self-esteem rests on self-appraisal. Dimensions and standards for such self-appraisal vary, of course, by the individual.

Another way of thinking of self-esteem is to see it as the result of the size of the gap between one's self-standards and perceived "performance" relative to that standard. As shown in Figure 10-8, persons with high self-esteem tend to experience less distress.

It helps to have had unconditionally loving parents and to have been surrounded by siblings, an extended family, a peer group, and a community that continually gave reassuring, loving messages. It also helps to have had lots of success experiences growing up.

But given that many of us did not enjoy these early beginnings, how can self-esteem be raised (Branden, 1992)? The most direct way is to learn to reprogram your thinking about yourself. In Chapter 14, you will read about a number of ways to strengthen self-esteem. The key is reprogramming your self-talk.

THE SELF-ACTUALIZED PERSON

Self-actualization is the full use and exploitation of talent, capacities, potentialities, personalities, etc. Such people seem to be fulfilling themselves and doing the best they are capable of.
—Maslow, 1954

A classic study of high-level mental health was carried out by Abraham Maslow. Conducted rather informally over a long period of years, Maslow's investigations began while he was still a young Ph.D. in New York City. He noted with curiosity two older professors who seemed to be different from others, to be truly outstanding human beings. After watching them for some time, he discovered they shared certain distinguishable qualities. He then decided to broaden his observations to include others around him—friends, students, and present and past public figures (Goble, 1970).

After a time, Maslow put into writing his discoveries (1954; 1959; 1962; 1965; 1966; 1971). Self-actualization is the state of highest possible functioning, usually reached only in later years and only by a small percentage of people. He described self-actualization as being "fully human," including "the full use and exploitation of talent, capacities, potentialities, personalities, etc. Such people seem to be fulfilling themselves and doing the best that they are capable of doing" (1954).

Figure 10-8

Mean Distress-Symptom Score by Self-Esteem

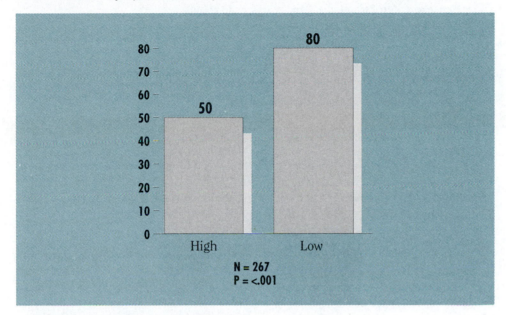

MEASURES: *Distress Symptoms:* 50-Item Distress Symptom Scale
              Self-Esteem: Single question from Quality of Life Assessment in student manual

FINDING: Respondents who scored high in self-esteem reported significantly lower distress-symptom scores.

Maslow included a number of qualities in his description of the self-actualized person (Goble, 1970, Chapter 3). It is useful to understand thriving under pressure in the context of this cluster of high-level qualities of model human beings.

- Ability to see reality as it is, rather than as they wish it to be
- Perception and understanding undistorted by desires, anxieties, fears, hopes, and false optimism or pessimism ("desireless awareness")
- Ability to see people for what they are and to see through the fakery
- Ability to be decisive in decision-making
- Clear sense of what is right and just
- Sense of humility, combined with willingness to listen to others and to learn
- Dedication to some work, mission, or value larger than themselves
- Ability and commitment to work very hard, yet experiencing a blurring of work and play
- High creativity, along with spontaneity, willingness to make mistakes, openness, and flexibility
- Uninhibited and hence expressive, natural, and simple
- Ability to ignore criticism, ridicule, and cultural constraints, with resulting "psychological freedom"
- More concerned with the task or outcome than with building image or ego—"self-transcendent"
- Relative absence of inner conflict. "He is not at war with himself; his personality is integrated" (Goble, 1970, 29).

- Pleasure at seeing pleasure in others
- Confidence and self-respect; absence of severe self-condemnation
- Sense of control over events and reactions to events
- Ability to thrive alone or with others
- Tolerance of others' shortcomings
- Ability to develop long-lasting, stable, supportive intimate relationships and friendships
- Ability to maintain composure under pressure

This last quality—composure under pressure—emerges naturally from a context of confidence.

> These healthy individuals are not often threatened by the external situation as they have great confidence in their ability to handle whatever confronts them. They are almost uniformly unthreatened by the unknown and the mysterious. In fact, they are usually attracted to the unknown.(Goble, 1970, 35)

We must keep in mind again Maslow's observation that this cluster of "fully human" qualities is attained only by a relatively few individuals. Certainly, they represent high ideals. Yet it is important not to discount or criticize yourself because you are "not there yet." Remember Maslow's contention that those few who are so fortunate usually reach this level only after age 60.

We have examined a number of personality patterns that previous studies have demonstrated help build resistance to distress, even during periods of trial and difficulty. From these syndromes—clusters of attitudes, beliefs, and approaches to adversity—emerge several separate qualities as especially vital in distress resistance:

- Self-esteem, self liking, self-acceptance, self-worth
- Internal control and sense of efficacy
- Sense of meaning, direction, purpose
- Resilience, flexibility, adaptability
- Optimism
- Humor
- Frustration tolerance
- Interpreting adversity as challenge
- Openness to giving and receiving social support

These are consistent with David Myers's observations from his own and others' studies of the factors that seem to contribute to happiness (1992).

In the next chapter, we turn to a discussion of distress-prone and distress-preventing social influences.

References

Antonovsky, A. (1979). *Health, stress and coping: New perspectives on mental and physical well-being.* San Francisco: Jossey-Bass.

Antonovsky, A. (1987). *Unraveling the mystery of health: How people manage stress and stay well.* San Francisco: Jossey-Bass.

Antonovsky, A. (1994). A sociological critique of the "Well-Being" Movement. *Advances, 10*(3), 6–12, 39–44.

Branden, N. (1992). *The power of self- esteem.* Deerfield, FL: Health Communications, Inc.

California Task Force (1990). *Toward a state of esteem: The final report of the California Task Force to promote self-esteem and personal and social responsibility.* Sacramento: California State Department of Education.

Gilbar, O. (1998). Relationship between burnout and sense of coherence in health social workers. *Social Work in Health Care, 26:3,* 39–49.

Goble, F. G. (1970). *The third force: The psychology of Abraham Maslow.* New York: Pocket Books.

Frankl, V. E. (1959). *Man's search for meaning.* New York: Washington Square Press.

Friedman, M., & Ulmer, D. (1984). *Treating Type A behavior and your heart.* New York: Knopf.

Kobasa, S. C. (1979). Stressful life events, personality and health: An inquiry into hardiness. *Journal of Personality and Social Psychology, 37,* 1–11.

Kobasa, S. C., Maddi, S. R., & Kahn, S. (1982). Hardiness and health: A prospective study. *Journal of Personality and Social Psychology, 42,* 168–177.

Kriegel, R., & Kriegel, M. (1984). *The C zone: Peak performance under pressure.* New York: Anchor Press/Doubleday.

Maddi, S. R., & Kobasa, C. S. (1984). *The hardy executive: Health under stress.* Homewood, IL: Dow Jones-Irwin.

Maslow, A. H. (1954). *Motivation and personality.* New York: Harper & Row.

Maslow, A. H. (1959). *New knowledge in human values.* New York: Harper & Row.

Maslow, A. H. (1962). *Toward a psychology of being.* New York: Van Nostrand.

Maslow, A. H. (1965). *Eupsychian management.* Homewood, IL: Irwin-Dorsey.

Maslow, A. H. (1966). *The psychology of science.* New York: Harper & Row.

Maslow, A. H. (1971). *Toward the farther reaches of human nature.* New York: Viking.

Myers, D. G. (1992). *The pursuit of happiness.* New York: Avon Books.

Seligman, M. E. P. (1970). *Learned optimism: The skills to overcome life's obstacles.* New York: Pocket Books.

Siebert, A. (1983). The survivor personality, *Association for Humanistic Psychology Newsletter,* 19–22.

Siebert, A. (1993). *The survivor personality.* Portland, OR: Practical Psychology Press.

Walker, M. (1988). The survivor syndrome, *The Courier Journal Magazine,* 14–15.

Walter, T., Siebert, A., & Smith, L. (2000). *Student success: How to succeed in college and still have time for your friends.* (8th ed.). Fort Worth: Harcourt Brace & Company.

Williams, R. B. (1989). *The trusting heart: Great news about Type A behavior.* New York: Times Books.

Williams, R. B., & Williams, V. (1993). *Anger kills.* New York: HarperCollins.

Application Exercise 10-1

Applying Tips for Reducing Hostility

1. List below those tips for reducing hostility from Williams and Williams that you think would be most beneficial for you.

2. What concrete differences will occur as you apply these changes?

3. Specifically, what will you do to apply the tips you listed above? When?

Application Exercise 10-2

Self-Assessment of Hardiness

How do you measure up on the three qualities of hardiness? Rate yourself below.

	Applies a Great Deal to Me	Applies Somewhat to Me	Applies Very Little to Me
Challenge	_____	_____	_____
Commitment	_____	_____	_____
Control	_____	_____	_____

Give examples below of circumstances in which you have experienced each of these qualities during recent periods of clustered change or particular difficulty.

The following person I know is a model of hardiness for me and for these reasons:

Application Exercise 10-3

Exploring How to Develop Hardiness in Children

How might parents develop a strong sense of hardiness in their children? What messages might they repeatedly send? What kind of example would they set? What opportunities would they create? How might they use rewards and punishment?

Truly to understand optimal health, we must consider the many ways in which individuals are linked—with their spouses, families, and friends, as well as with their emotional and physical environments.

—KENNETH R. PELLETIER

Distress-Promoting and Distress-Preventing Social Influences

Why are some people more distressed than others? Part of the answer, as we have seen in the previous three chapters, lies within individuals—their characteristics, habits, and outlooks. Less often recognized in the stress field is another important part of the answer: social circumstances and social experiences.

Social environments—families, peer groups, living units in college, work organizations and work groups, neighborhoods, communities, and society—can be distress-producing or distress-preventing (Hobfoll 1998; Schafer, 1998). In this chapter we examine both types, beginning with **distress-promoting social influences.**

LINKING PERSONAL DISTRESS AND SOCIAL INFLUENCES: THE SOCIOLOGICAL IMAGINATION

Consider the two instances of personal distress in the box.

Social Roots of Personal Problems

- Imagine a man who left his inner-city high school at the first opportunity, without a degree and without basic skills; who spent years unemployed or underemployed; who finally got a factory job he managed to hold onto long enough to make a down payment on a house and to start a family; who was among the first laid off when the product his factory produced could not compete with similar items made where labor costs are lower; and whose unemployment compensation has run out.
- Imagine a woman who married young because she was pregnant; who had two more unplanned children in quick succession; who took a boring and unpleasant job at minimum wage because her husband could not support the family; whose husband says she trapped him into marriage, is embarrassed that she has a job, and gives her little help with the children and housework; who cannot always find someone to look after the children, cannot afford day care, and cannot afford to miss work; whose boss gave her a bad report for being absent or late too often; and who has just learned she is pregnant again.

Source: Mirowsky & Ross (1989, 3)

Not surprisingly, these two people show symptoms of mental and physical distress. In this sense, their problems are very personal. Yet their problems are also social in two important ways.

First, they are not alone in their symptoms. Rather, their difficulties are *shared and patterned*—not randomly but, to a considerable extent, according to social circumstances. People with similar social circumstances (e.g., undereducated, unemployed, married young, multiple children at a young age) quite predictably share many of the same distress symptoms and personal problems.

Second, these personal problems are partly *caused by* social influences that go well beyond the immediate life circumstances of these two unfortunate individuals. Both live in a society that allocates rewards and opportunities differentially and that teaches people to value themselves and to value others by social ranking and material success. Both live in a society where not everyone is assured work, child care, transitional support, a

The sociological imagination is the ability to understand that personal experiences are socially patterned and are partly caused by larger social forces. It is the ability to place individuals in a social context, to look for outside as well as inside causal influences.

family-friendly employer, or health care. Both live with an economy marked by ups and downs, an economy that especially impacts poor people when it is down. **Sociological imagination** gives them the ability to place themselves in a social context and to look for outside as well as inside causal influences.

When applied to the field of stress, the sociological imagination is vital to both understanding and coping. We need to know that no man or woman is an island, that we need to *improve social conditions* causing distress at the same time we seek to *constructively adapt* to them. We will address this issue again in the textbook's final chapter.

This chapter explores some of the main ways social circumstances and experiences help cause distress. A word of caution is needed here about internal and external causes of distress. If we take either cause to the extreme, we get into trouble. On the one hand, if we attribute personal distress entirely to internal causes, we fall into the trap of **blaming the victim** for circumstances not of her or his own making that would cause distress for most reasonable people. This applies, for example, to people who live in areas hard hit by poverty, unemployment, discrimination, crime, or environmental pollution. On the other hand, if we attribute personal distress entirely to external factors, we fall into **blaming the system**. Here the risk is avoidance of responsibility for how we personally handle life's adversities. Such avoidance of responsibility sometimes leads to an unproductive victim mentality. Blaming the victim is likely to emerge from "radical individualism," while blaming the system is likely to emerge from "radical social determinism."

What we need is a blend of inside and outside perspectives. To be sure, certain social influences and experiences carry a high probability of distress. As Antonovsky (1994), Dreher (1995), and Schafer (1998) have noted, mind/body researchers have largely ignored the influences of social factors. Still, the presence/absence, degree and type of distress are determined by how the individual responds to the circumstances—his or her coping style, beliefs and self-talk, health habits, communication style, and more.

Having made these general points about personal problems and social influences, we now turn to three conditions in the larger society that sometimes cause distress in our society: accelerating social change, economic inequality, and distress-producing conditions in the workplace.

Accelerating Social Change

In my opinion, the most incisive book on social change in America—and the Western world—was written three decades ago by Alvin Toffler. For good reason, *Future Shock* was the number-one best seller for many months and has sold millions of copies since. The validity of Toffler's social analysis of **future shock** and the probable accuracy of his predictions remain. Here is an excerpt from the book's first chapter:

We may define future shock as the distress, both physical and psychological, that arises from an overload of the human organism's physical adaptive systems and its decision-making processes. Put more simply, future shock is the human response to overstimulation.
—Toffler, 1970, 326

> Western society for the past 300 years has been caught up in a fire storm of change. This storm, far from abating, now appears to be gathering force. Change sweeps through the highly industrialized countries with waves of ever accelerating speed and unprecedented impact. It spawns in its wake all sorts of curious social flora—from psychedelic churches and "free universities" to science cities in the Arctic and wife-swap clubs in California.
>
> It breeds odd personalities, too: children who at twelve are no longer childlike; adults who at fifty are children of twelve. There are rich men who playact poverty, computer programmers who turn on with LSD. There are anarchists who, beneath their dirty denim shirts, are outrageous conformists, and conformists who, beneath their button-down collars, are outrageous anarchists. There are married priests and atheist ministers and Jewish Zen Buddhists. (1970, 9)

Toffler makes a strong case that accelerating social change is not just an abstract macro-social trend. Rather, it reaches into each of our lives.

For the acceleration of change does not merely buffet industries or nations. It is a concrete force that reaches deep into our personal lives, compels us to act out new roles, and confronts us with the danger of a new and powerfully upsetting psychological disease. This new disease can be called "future shock...." (1970, 9)

Accelerating change reaches into every sector of society and therefore into every part of our lives: family, religion, education, business, agriculture, travel, politics and government, the arts, science, transportation, neighborhoods, crime and law enforcement, health and medical care, leisure, friendships, and more. All are marked by constant **social change** and **personal change,** change that accelerates with each passing decade.

Social Change Impacts the Person: Future Shock

One reason for the increase in the pace of social change is rapid **population growth** around the world. The world's population is expected to double in about 47 years at its present growth rate. In many countries, population will double in only 25 years. Already we number nearly 6 billion people. An increase, of course, will mean more mouths to feed, more bodies to clothe, more houses to build, more goods and services to be produced, and more crowding.

A second reason for the faster rate of change is **technology**—the increasing use of sophisticated mechanical and electronic devices to solve problems and produce goods. Our reliance on science, combined with the need for more goods and services and the need to keep ahead of competition, leads manufacturers to constantly produce new goods and devices. What used to take weeks, months, or even years now can be accomplished in seconds. Yet technology exists not only in factories and computer centers but also has rippled outward to affect entire communities. One look at a modern kitchen, compared with one in your grandparents' time, should be enough to convince you of the broad impact of technology.

As Toffler points out, if we think of technology as the great engine of change, then knowledge is the fuel on which that engine runs. The fantastic speed-up in the generation of **new knowledge** is the third factor responsible for the faster rate of social change. The computer is partly responsible for this increase in knowledge, especially in the sciences. The number of new scientific books and articles is staggering—and still growing. A chemistry professor comments that he could pass few college examinations these days because so much has been discovered in recent years. Another professor notes that more than half of all knowledge has been developed in his own brief lifetime.

C. P. Snow, the novelist and scientist, has remarked that "until this century, social change was so slow that it would go unnoticed in one person's lifetime. That is no longer so. The rate of change has increased so much that our imaginations cannot keep up" (Toffler, 1970, 22). Signs of this speed-up are all around us—faster transportation, consumer fads, whole new skylines in big cities and the disappearance of old ones, new shopping centers, people moving from one place to another, and a higher divorce rate.

Accelerating social change since the turn of the century has brought with it four major trends that bear on personal stress.

1. From rural living to urban living
2. From stationary to mobile
3. From self-sufficient to consuming
4. From physically active to sedentary

As these social changes have occurred—and continue—a speed-up in personal change also takes place. One way of understanding how social change affects the person is to

Social change refers to change in the world outside the person, illustrated by population growth, economic recession, increasing immigration, rising crime rate, development of the information highway, end of the Cold War, and the breakup of the Balkans.

Personal change, partly a consequence of social change, refers to changes in the individual's life, such as moving, changing jobs, divorcing, getting older, and becoming more assertive.

think of daily life as consisting of situations, each of which is made up of five simple elements.

1.   Things
2.   Places
3.   Persons
4.   Organizations
5.   Ideas

Each of these elements is more temporary than before, speeding up the "**flow of situations**" (Toffler, 1970, 33). *Things* are more and more transient. If you are like most people, you buy things, then discard them more quickly than your parents did. Consequently, you make and break emotional ties with things more often than people did 25 to 50 years ago. Each time you do, you must adjust.

Advertising is a prime reason for this faster turnover of things. We think we need new products partly because we are told that we do. Another reason is we move more often and cannot take all our possessions with us. Still another is we think we need to "keep up with the Joneses." If your friends or neighbors have a snowmobile, a new car, a swimming pool, or new skis, you may believe you need them too. So you adopt a "throw-away mentality." You come to expect more temporary connections with such things as clothing, cars, houses, toys, art, and furniture.

With *places* too, we make and break ties more often. Think about place of residence, for example. Many Europeans are the 9th, 10th, or 15th generation in their communities. Many visit their nearby churchyard cemetery every Sunday to pay respects to their ancestors—and to reinforce their linkages with the past. In contrast, 1 of every 5 persons in the United States—nearly 60 million—moves each year. Place loses much of its emotional meaning as we come and go.

Our changing relationship with place also is affected on a daily basis. In times past, home and work were close together. Shop and farm were next to living quarters. But with the development of the large factory and the large store, people went away from home to work. Now the daily commute to work may take up to an hour or two each way. One college professor traveled every Wednesday from Northern California to Salt Lake City to complete his graduate studies—returning in time for his full load of teaching duties the next day. A minister traveled from Phoenix to Chicago for studies every Tuesday, then returned to Phoenix for pastoral duties on weekends. Place is more fleeting than ever before.

People also are less permanent in your life than they were for your parents and grandparents. Because you move more often (and if you do not, your neighbors do), you must make and break relationships more often. In the college dormitory, for example, very close friendships develop during a school year. For many students, these relationships are the most meaningful of their lives. Yet the year ends, and the entire dorm social system for that year disappears. Some friendships remain steadfast, but most disappear. Each time you make and break ties, an adjustment must be made. Stress—and sometimes distress— results. And many people wonder why they should get involved, since they, their neighbors, or their friends probably will be leaving soon.

The *organizations* in which you work, play, worship, and study also flow through your experience more rapidly. This occurs in two ways. One is that organizations appear and disappear more often. The other is that organizations change more quickly. Whereas organizations once tended to be rigid bureaucracies, resistant to change, many now are much more fluid. More and more workers—and students—must adjust more often and more quickly to shifting organizational environments. As a result, many people sink roots less deeply into their organizations and groups, just as they hesitate to get too attached to their neighborhoods and friends.

Finally, *ideas* and *information* come and go more quickly, requiring increasingly rapid turnover of images in your mind. The English language is changing constantly, as illustrated by the change in ethnic terms from "Negro" to "Black" to "African American" and by the rapid appearance and disappearance of such words as "teach-in," "sit-in," "hassle," "psychedelic," "fast-back," "wash-and-wear." Toffler points out that if William Shakespeare were alive today, he would be virtually illiterate because so many English words are new. Faster change also occurs in intellectual fads, best-selling books, and trends in art and music. Referring to the rapid pace at which we must change our conception of reality and our mental images of the world, Toffler raises the question: "How fast and how continuously can the individual revise his inner images before he smashes up against these limits?" (1970, 180). No one knows for sure. But we may be approaching those limits.

In his more recent book, *The Third Wave,* Toffler points out that confusion and ambiguity are other realities we face in this era of rapid change.

> A powerful tide is surging across much of the world today, creating a new, often bizarre, environment in which to work, play, marry, raise children, or retire. In this bewildering context, businessmen swim against highly erratic economic currents; politicians see their ratings bob wildly up and down; universities, hospitals, and other institutions battle desperately against inflation. Value systems splinter and crash, while the lifeboats of family, church, and state are hurled madly about. (1980, 2)

In this rapidly changing and confusing world, more and faster adjustments are needed. More stress sets in. One way of looking at this is to think of the individual as a channel through which a multitude of experiences flow—as diagrammed in Figure 11-1.

As you enter the next century, you must process more experiences than just a few decades ago. In short, you must face a greater number, variety, and intensity of stressors than people did in earlier times. While you can and do adjust to this faster tempo, the chance of distress is greater. Not only do individuals risk illness, intellectual and emotional distress, or behavioral difficulties, but also our entire society may be showing symptoms of too rapid change (Toffler, 1970, 2).

> The malaise, mass neurosis, irrationality, and free-floating violence already apparent in contemporary life are merely a foretaste of what may be ahead unless we come to understand and treat this illness . . . unless man quickly learns to control the rate of change in his personal affairs as well as society at large, we are doomed to massive adaptational breakdown. (Toffler, 1970, 9)

Figure 11-1

Faster Flow of Experience

Figure 11-2

Social Change and Stress

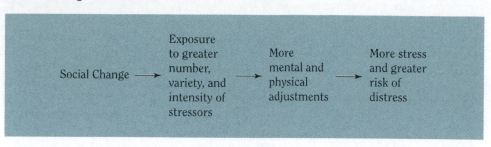

One way of illustrating how faster social change causes stress and distress is shown in Figure 11-2.

A recent study by Levine and others (1989) reported that pace of life can be studied not only at the individual level but at a community and regional level as well. They reported that when pace of life is measured by aggregate averages of walking speed, talking speed, work speed, and concern with clock time, strong correlations are found between a U.S. city's or region's pace of life and mortality from coronary heart disease. This may partly result from unhealthy habits (for example, more smoking) in faster-paced areas. Whatever the reason, pace of life can affect stress and health.

How does accelerating social change lead to personal distress? We will discuss six ways.

How Social Change Contributes to Personal Distress: Selected Links

OVERCHOICE   As Toffler points out, an important by-product of rapid change is a vast increase in options:

> Ironically, the people of the future may suffer not from an absence of choice, but from a paralyzing surfeit of it. They may turn out to be victims of that peculiarly super-industrial dilemma; choice. (1970, 264)

Many social critics have attacked the creeping standardization of modern life, believing we are all being pressured toward fewer choices—toward acting, thinking, and feeling the same. Their protest is symbolized by the computer, which they see as a tool for making everyone alike. But they probably are wrong. The real problem seems to be too much choice, too many options. Many Americans feel overwhelmed by the choices they must make: what to do, how to live, what to believe, what to buy, where to move, how to look, what to wear. **Overchoice** adds to stress and distress, since every option is a stressor.

One aspect of overchoice is the tremendous increase in the *variety of consumer goods*. Some people feel uncomfortable in the supermarket; they are numbed by so many options on the shelves. Toffler points out that two economic factors account for this trend toward diversification of goods.

> . . . first, consumers have more money to lavish on their specialized wants; second, and even more important, as technology becomes more sophisticated, the cost of introducing declines.
>
> This is the point that our social critics—most of whom are technologically naive—fail to understand: it is only primitive technology that imposes standardization. Automation, in contrast, frees the path to endless, blinding, mind-numbing diversity. (1970, 266)

Depression and Social Change

Martin Seligman (1988) pointed out an astounding fact: The rate of depression has risen roughly tenfold over the last two generations. He went on to raise the pressing question, "Why have we become more depressed?"

Seligman notes that in less-developed countries, depression is almost nonexistent. When depression does occur in China, which is only occasionally, its symptoms tend to be physical rather than psychological. While manic depression, which tends to have physiological origins, was found to be almost the same (1–2 percent) among residents of Baltimore and the Amish, the rate of unipolar depression (depression without mania) among the Amish is about one-fifth to one-tenth that of Baltimore residents.

These findings suggest that something about our society and our way of life, not just about individual depressives, explains the rise in depression in this country.

Seligman suggests two main causes. First, we have moved toward individual explanations for events, especially bad events. For a variety of cultural and economic reasons, this has become the "age of the individual." We expect individual happiness, ease, and comfort. If an individual falters, we see it as his or her problem—a lack of effort, character, or personal gumption.

Second, we have become loosened from older attachments to the larger society. Vietnam, Watergate, assassinations, and political scandal have combined to cause questioning of the value of relying on larger institutions. This has happened at the very time extended family, neighborhood, and church are fading as significant attachments for the individual.

The result of these two trends is predictable, according to Seligman: When the person goes through troubling or unsettled times, what can she or he rely on for support? Mostly the self. And the self is, at best, a precarious anchorage on which to lean. Widespread depression results as the individual, in relative isolation from external supports, blames the self and does his or her best to draw on inner resources, often to find little there.

Seligman contends that to slow the rising tide of depression, we need to reach a better balance between individual and collectivity, between self and society.

"There is a final possibility, a more hopeful one: We can retain our belief in the importance of the individual but scale down our preoccupation with comfort and discomfort and make a renewed commitment to the common good. A balance between individualism, with its perilous freedoms, and commitment to the common good should lower depression and make life more meaningful. In this age of choice, this choice, surely, is ours." (1988, 55)

In Chapter 18, we will return to issues of transcending our own problems by focusing more on the common good.

Automobiles are a good example: The number of options can be staggering. In Toffler's words:

Thus the beautiful and spectacular Mustang is promoted by Ford as the "one you design yourself," because as critic Reyner Banham explains, "there isn't a dung-regular Mustang anymore, just a stockpile of options to meld in combinations of

3 (bodies) x 4 (engines) x 3 (transmissions) x 4 (basic sets of high performance engine modifications)—1 (rock-bottom six-cylinder car to which these modifications don't apply) x 2 (Shelby Grand Roaring and Racing setups applying to only one body shell and not all engines/transmission combinations)." This does not even take into account the possible variations in color, upholstery and optional equipment. (1970, 268–269)

The same kind of diversification—and overchoice—has taken place in movies, magazines, television sets, soaps, houses, clothing, arts, and illegal drugs.

The material goods of the future will be many things, but they will not be standardized. We are, in fact, racing toward "overchoice"—the point at which the advantages of diversity and individualization are cancelled by the complexity of the buyer's decision-making process. (Toffler, 1970, 269)

Another aspect of overchoice is the increase in *lifestyle* options. Should you live in the country or in the city? If in the country, should you live in the mountains, on the coast, in the forest, or in the desert? What size city? What type of house—two-story, ranch-style, modular, suburban cardboard, or corner duplex? And with whom should you spend your time—drug users, hot-rodders, Jesus converts, Zen Buddhists, vegetarians, meditators, executives, scientists, gays, or athletes? To consider all possible options—or even a few of them—is to be bombarded by choices. The mind boggles. Subcultures are everywhere. Which to join? None? Try a few, one at a time? Which ones? Why?

Meanwhile, what happens to you? Are you still there? Or are you simply whatever you are *doing*, whichever group you are with, wherever you live this year, this month, this week? This is the third aspect of overchoice: more frequent *identity crises,* especially among young people. Identity crisis refers to uncertainty—and sometimes intense anxiety—over these questions: Who am I? What kind of a person am I? do I want to be? can I not be? can I be? In a stable, slow-moving society such questions do not arise. A person's position in life, beliefs, and identity are given. The choices are few. In our society, at least for many of us, the choices are too many.

The level of personality disorder, neurosis, and just plain psychological distress in our society suggests that it is already difficult for many individuals to create a sensible, integrated, and reasonably stable personal style. Yet there is every evidence that the thrust toward social diversity, paralleling that of the level of goods and culture, is just beginning. We face a tempting and terrifying extension of freedom. (Toffler, 1970, 269)

In the face of overchoice, you must be centered and self-directed in order to retain your sanity, dignity, and self-control. Otherwise, you risk being overwhelmed by too many options.

OVERLOAD IN PACE OF DAILY LIFE   Consider this: Experts estimate that the average American is exposed to 65,000 more stimuli *per day* than our ancestors a mere 100 years ago (Ferguson, 1980). This means we live a much faster daily **pace of life.**

Pace of life is the number, variety, and intensity of stressors, per day, week, or year.

It is likely that the average American can be described by the faster pace we have depicted. We process more situations; we cram more into an hour, a day, a week. If you live at a faster pace, you probably experience the following.

- A greater number of stressors
- A greater variety of stressors
- A higher proportion of new, unfamiliar stressors
- A greater number of intense stressors

MARGINLESS LIVING

The conditions of modern-day living devour margin. If you are homeless, we direct you to a shelter. If you penniless, we offer you food stamps. If you are breathless, we connect the oxygen. But if you are marginless, we give you yet one more thing to do.

Marginless is being thirty minutes late to the doctor's office because you were twenty minutes late getting out of the hairdresser's because you were ten minutes late dropping the children off at school because the car ran out of gas two blocks from the gas station—and you forgot your purse.

Margin, on the other hand, is having breath left at the top of the staircase, money left at the end of the month, and sanity left at the end of adolescence.

Marginless is the baby crying and the phone ringing at the same time; margin is Grandma taking the baby for an afternoon.

Marginless is being asked to carry a load five pounds heavier than you can lift; margin is a friend to carry half the burden.

Marginless is not having to finish the book you're reading on stress; margin is having the time to read it twice.

Marginless is fatigue; margin is energy.

Marginless is red ink; margin is black ink.

Marginless is hurry; margin is calm.

Marginless is anxiety; margin is security.

Marginless is culture; margin is counterculture.

Marginless is reality; margin is remedy.

Marginless is the disease of the 1990s.

Margin is its cure (Swensen, 1992).

- Faster movement from one stressor to the next, with frequent overlap
- More demands for adaptation or adjustment
- A greater amount or intensity of stress
- Higher chances of distress because of the greater amount and intensity of stress

Faster and slower paces of life theoretically are measurable, assuming separate actions could be recorded, counted, and weighted in terms of the stressfulness to the person. In that sense, pace of life is quantifiable in the abstract. Practically, of course, this is virtually impossible. However, it is worth noting that, analytically, a faster pace of life may or may not breed distress. It depends entirely on the upper limit of the individual's zone of positive stress. "Racehorses" thrive on a pace that would overwhelm a "turtle." Often, however, Type A persons and others delude themselves into believing they are racehorses by nature. At the onset of physical breakdown, such as a heart attack, persistent dizziness, or chronic trembling, they begin for the first time to realize they have overestimated their tolerance for a fast pace. An important point of this textbook is that effective health buffers probably can increase our tolerance of a fast pace, thereby increasing the amount of potential productivity and the number of other experiences we can encounter with less hazards to our health and emotional life.

See Application Exercise 11-1 to personalize the ideas of lead-time and afterburn.

How Overload Leads to Distress   Associated with any activity are two necessary time periods: **lead time** and **afterburn**. Consider, for example, a student facing an examination in history, an especially important one because she needs a *B* to qualify for a scholarship to college. Lead time is the period of emotional and intellectual preparation she needs the day before and on the morning of the examination. Afterburn is the time needed after the exam to think about how she did, to feel it, to talk to her friends, to set it to rest. If she has neither enough time to prepare nor enough time afterward to "come down"—to relieve the pressures of the exam—she will feel slightly off-balance, a bit tense. No single instance is terribly significant. But ignoring the need for adequate lead-in and afterburn time thousands of times during a lifetime can create an enormous buildup of many small tensions and stresses.

Swensen (1992) maintains we become chronically overloaded because we leave too little margin in our lives. (See "Marginless Living" box on p. 259 for more on this. His notion of margin is similar to my idea of lead-time and afterburn time. According to Swensen, leaving too little margin results in a host of types of overload including activity overload, change overload, choice overload, hurry overload, information, people overload, and possession overload.

A fast pace of life, especially for someone who needs quite a bit of lead-in and afterburn time, can be a significant source of tension, stress, and distress. Various ailments—colds, asthma, chest pains, high blood pressure, and sore back—often result if too many activities are crammed into too short a span of time, leaving inadequate margins.

TRANSITIONS

"Who are you?" said the Caterpillar. . . .

"I—I hardly know, Sir, just at present," Alice replied rather shyly, "at least I know who I was when I got up this morning, but I think I must have been changed several times since then."

Alice's Adventures in Wonderland (Carroll, 1960)

Another stressor related to change and time is **transition.** In a fast-paced society, you no doubt experience less permanence than your parents or grandparents did. You make and break ties to the world around you more often. You more frequently change how you live and what you do. Each change requires a transition. Each transition requires an adjustment. Stress always results; distress sometimes follows. In her excellent book *Overwhelmed: Coping With Life's Ups and Downs* (1989), Nancy Schlossberg presents a summary of types of transitions.

Schlossberg points out that a particular transition can affect the individual in a number of ways, some positive and some negative.

It can change your roles—you have a baby, and suddenly you have become a parent; you change jobs, and you take on a whole new set of responsibilities.

It can change your relationships—being a parent puts you in touch with new people, as does a new job. Both experiences may also transform your existing relationships.

It can change your routines—a new baby alters living and sleeping habits; a new job may require a shift in schedule and in commuting patterns.

It can also affect your assumptions about yourself and the world—a new father discovers he is more protective and responsible than he thought he would be; a person in a new secretarial position may discover personal strengths and weaknesses that went unrecognized in the old clerk-typist job.

Three types of transitions stand out as especially significant for many people.

Geographic mobility—moving from one community or neighborhood to another—is a type of transition experienced by millions of Americans each year. When a family moves, each member must pass through a host of transitions—from familiar to unfamiliar places, from one set of friends to another, from one school or work setting to another, and from old routines to new ones. Research has shown that the stresses of moving are especially painful for children between the ages of 2 and 4 and for teenagers, for whom the trauma of leaving their home towns and their friends may be extreme. Research also has shown that a variety of illnesses, including coronary heart disease, occur more frequently among uprooted adults.

Role transition also can create substantial stress. Promotions, demotions, marriage, divorce, remarriage, becoming a parent, a job transfer, or becoming a high school or college student cause stress and sometimes distress. A distress reaction is especially likely under certain conditions: if the transition is from a high- to a low-stimulation environment (or vice versa); if the transition is involuntary; or if several role transitions occur simultaneously. When a person's new role requires behavior that falls outside his or her comfort zone, the chances of distress will be heightened.

A **lifestyle change** also can be highly stressful, yet thousands of Americans undergo changes in lifestyle each year. Part of the problem with such transitions is the in-between space—the void, the search, the uncertainty, the absence of anchorage. Severe stress symptoms are common during such transitions. Yet they do not always show up in the short run. A 19-year-old youth once described his experiences of the previous four years as follows: In the ninth grade, he was into athletics. Finding that world unsatisfying, he took up with a motorcycle gang in the tenth grade. The following summer, he became involved with heavy drug use. A year later, his senior year, he was "rescued" from that lifestyle by the "Jesus people." In a discussion group that included a 75-year-old woman who had lived on the same ranch for 50 years, he later commented: "It took me a whole month to get over that one." He showed few immediate signs of stress or distress in this case, yet one wonders about the outcome over the long run.

A serious loss is a wrenching transition. The death of a family member is almost always traumatic. So are the loss of a home through fire, separation and divorce, termination of a professional career, involuntary retirement, theft of a valued personal possession, disappearance of a family pet, and loss of an arm. In each case, one must "say goodbye" and adjust to life without the lost object or person. Whatever the loss, people pass through remarkably similar steps of mourning.

Horowitz (1976) points out that individual differences affect the order of entry into phases, how much time is spent in each phase, and the signs of stress or distress that occur in each phase. But, in general, people tend to follow this pattern. Let us focus, for example, on the loss of a spouse.

Outcry is an almost automatic emotional response that may take varied forms—weeping, screaming, panic, or fainting. For example, a woman told that her husband has just died in an accident may cry out in anguish, "No, no, it can't be true!"

Denial refers to a numbing avoidance of the reality of the loss. For example, relatives of the widow just described might come to help out and provide comfort. Since they are less deeply affected by the loss, they may already have entered the intrusive phase. For example, they are likely to think of the deceased constantly, to cry, and to express intense sadness. The widow, in contrast, may be numb and busy with planning and "entertaining," giving the appearance of strength. But she only appears to be "doing very well."

Intrusion, which follows denial or outcry, is a preoccupation with the lost person through dreams, recurrent reminders of past events, and even visual images of the deceased. This phase may not begin until after the relatives have left. Weeks or months later, "she might begin to oscillate between periods of denial and numbing episodes in which she experiences waves of searching grief, ideas about the emptiness of her life, and even an hallucinatory sense of the 'presence' of her lost husband" (Horowitz, 1976, 52). *Working through* is gradually coming to terms with the reality of the loss and adjusting to life without the person. In most cases involving the death of a family member, this requires six months to one year of emotional adjustment, decisions and planning, and changing of daily routines.

Completion is reached when the person is able to get on with a new stage of life without denial or serious intrusion of the loss.

People always have had to cope with the expected and the unexpected. Even for our ancient ancestors, the uncertainties of climate, food supplies, and relations with neighboring tribes made life a continuing process of adaptation. In contemporary times, change is inherent in the life cycle itself. One writer refers to these predictable life-cycle events as **marker events.** Marker events begin early. The 5-year-old entering kindergarten experiences a dramatic confrontation with the unfamiliar—new faces, new routines, new expectations, and new challenges. To some extent, this is repeated every time a student enters the next level of school. The move from high school to college can be especially stressful because of the need for greater self-reliance, increased financial concerns, keener competition, and new social demands. Marriage is another stressful "passage," pleasurable as it may be. Having children, especially if several are closely spaced, creates stress on each parent and on the marriage. So does the child-rearing process and, later on, the departure of children from the home. Retirement is a difficult and sometimes lethal adjustment. Death of a spouse is the last major change for many people.

Throughout the life cycle, a number of intense personal adjustments must be made, regardless of the pace of social change. But rapid social change and a faster pace of life bring a number of additional life changes. These are relatively new in human history, at least on such a mass scale. Among the most important of these are divorce, remarriage, and geographic mobility.

Schlossberg contends four potential **resources**—four S's—are vital **for managing change:**

1.   Your overall *Situation*
2.   Your *Self*
3.   Your *Supports*
4.   Your *Strategies* for coping

CLUSTERING OF LIFE EVENTS   In the preceding section, we focused on stressful, single life transitions. Emphasis here is on the high risk to health, life satisfaction, and productivity of the accumulation of too many life changes in too short a time.

Carolyn, described in the box, is but one illustration of a common pattern among highly stressed patients referred to the Center by physicians: too much change in too short a time. Her experience is consistent with a growing number of studies showing that the greater the **clustering of life events,** the greater the chances of becoming ill.

Clustering and Distress: Research Evidence. One study, for example, examined the illness rates of 2,500 sailors at sea for 6 months (Rahe, 1968). Just before embarking, the sailors were given a long checklist of life changes to determine how many they had experienced the previous year. These ranged from apparently insignificant changes in daily habits to dramatic, wrenching changes.

The questionnaire went on to probe such issues as the number of times he moved to a new home. Had he been in trouble with the law over traffic violations or other minor infractions? Had he spent a lot of time away from his wife as the result of job-related travel or marital difficulties? Had he changed jobs? Won awards or promotions? Had his living conditions changed as a consequence of

Effects of Too Much Change

When referred to the Enloe Hospital Stress and Health Center by her physician, Carolyn, 55 years old, suffered from diarrhea, insomnia, hemorrhoids, hypertension, and swings between severe anxiety and depression. The symptoms had appeared within a few short months quite unexpectedly to Carolyn, who had been emotionally stable and free of illness throughout most of her adult life. An interview and paper-pencil test revealed a clustering of the following events in her life during the preceding nine months.

She retired after 32 years of elementary-school teaching.
Her husband sold his hardware business and retired.
They decided to move to a retirement community in another part of the state.
They sold their home.
They left their neighborhood, church, and extended family.
They bought a new home.
They adapted to a new climate.
They developed a new friendship group and entered a new church.
They readjusted their marriage to both being at home.
They adjusted to a 50 percent reduction in income.
She deliberately lost 50 pounds, which seemed a good idea at this transition time.
She and her new doctor decided it was time to stop hormone treatments prescribed earlier for menopause.
Their only daughter filed for divorce.
Their 15-year-old cat died.

Clearly, this woman faced an enormous number of virtually simultaneous adjustments in mind, body, and behavior. She was overwhelmed. Her body and spirit began to break. She felt near a "nervous breakdown."

Fortunately, greater awareness of why she was experiencing these difficulties, together with proper temporary medications, daily deep relaxation, and daily brisk walking, brought her out of this intense period of worry and frustration. This program, combined with medical treatment, helped to restore her health and emotions to a normal level after a few brief months.

---

home remodeling or the deterioration of his neighborhood? Had his wife started or stopped working? Had he taken out a loan or mortgage? How many times had he taken a vacation? Was there any major change in his relations with his parents as the result of death, divorce, marriage, etc.? (Toffler, 1970, 331)

The questionnaire did not ask whether the sailor thought the change was pleasant or unpleasant or good or bad but simply whether or not it had happened. Results showed that "life-change scores" for the previous year were correlated with illness rates while at sea. The greater the number of life changes, the greater the chances that illness would occur. Furthermore, the more significant or serious the changes, the more serious the illness was likely to be.

This study is illustrative of hundreds during the past two decades consistently showing that the greater the clustering of life events, the greater the harmful impact on health, emotions, and quality of life. These studies have been conducted across all age groups and

Figure 11-3

Distress-Symptom Score by Life-Change Score

	Distress-Symptom Score				
Life-Change Score	High	Medium	Low	Total	(N)
High	53%	42%	6%	101%	(36)
Medium	32	27	41	100	(34)
Low	14	31	55	100	(29)
				P = < .001 N = 99	

in such diverse countries as the United States, England, Wales, El Salvador, Malaysia, Japan, France, Belgium, Denmark, Sweden, Norway, and Peru (Rice, 1987, 157). A fascinating recent study in Beirut found that the greater the number of violence-related events an individual had encountered, the greater the incidence of cardiac problems.

Like adults their own age and older, college students are likely to be negatively affected mentally and physically by a clustering of life changes. One study found that students with high life-change scores experienced greater number and severity of illnesses during the following semester (Marx, Garrity, & Bowers, 1975).

College athletes are not immune from these effects, as first reported in a study of the impact of life changes on football injuries among University of Washington football players. As shown in Figure 11-3, I found a similar pattern among football and soccer players at California State University, Chico: The more numerous the life changes during the year preceding the season, the greater the number and severity of injuries (Schafer & McKenna, 1981). We found a similar pattern in the study of 572 adult runners: The higher the life-change score, the greater the number of injuries, the more days missed running, the more often the runners sought medical attention for an injury, and the more often they got sick for reasons other than running injuries (Schafer & McKenna, 1985).

Many studies now have documented the contribution of individual life changes to physical and psychological distress (Dohrenwend, 1986; Dohrenwend & Dohrenwend, 1974; Dohrenwend & Dohrenwend, 1981). While technical and scientific questions still remain about some of these studies, the overall pattern of findings is clear: The greater the number, clustering, and intensity of life changes, the greater the chances of illness, injury, or psychological problems. A recent study even shows that clustering of life events contributes to kidney stones (Associated Press, 1997). Two scientists have summarized findings on the association of clustering of life events and personal well-being as follows:

> In both retrospective and prospective investigations, modest but statistically significant relationships have been found between mounting life change and the occurrence or onset of sudden cardiac death, myocardial infarctions, accidents, athletic injuries, tuberculosis, leukemia, multiple sclerosis, diabetes, and the entire gamut of minor medical complaints. High scores on checklists of life events have also been repeatedly associated with psychiatric symptoms and disorders, and such scores have been found to differ between psychiatric and other samples. (Rabkin & Struening, 1976, 1014)

Three final points need to be made about the life events–stress connection. First, clustering of life events is more likely to lead to distress to the extent those events are unpredictable, involuntary (uncontrolled), and negative. Second, events experienced by one person as quite negative may not be seen that way at all by the next. An example is the death of a spouse. If the death is sudden and unexpected to an otherwise healthy person, it will of course be subjectively experienced as a negative event. If, on the other hand, the death occurred after a lingering, painful illness, the death might well be seen as a gift to all concerned. Third, it follows that no direct causal link between clustering of life events and distress or illness has been found. A series of factors potentially intervene—the very factors on which Part IV of this book focuses. These factors include:

- Coping style—constructive or destructive
- Beliefs, self-talk, and meaning—especially hardiness
- Health buffers—exercise, nutrition, sleep habits, and healthy pleasures
- Social support

Let us look briefly at several strategies for minimizing distress from clustered change.
Minimizing Distress From Clustered Change. Mental and physical illness is not inevitable, by any means, during or after clustering of life changes. But the chances do increase. The question becomes, What can I do to protect myself, to minimize chances of distress from clustered change?

Consider the following advice from Holmes and Holmes in a booklet published by Blue Cross, a health insurance company with a great deal at stake in minimizing illness.

It all sounds pretty grim. But there may be ways in which you can soften the blow. Change is not entirely random. You have a large amount of personal control over whether and when to marry, go to college, move or have a family. You may have little control over whether to get divorced, change jobs, take out a loan or retire. But you may have a pretty good idea of when these events might take place.

So the future is not a complete blank. You can predict it to a certain degree. And to this degree, you can order your life by managing the change that is a vital part of living. You can weigh the benefits of change against its costs, pace the timing of the inevitable changes and regulate the occurrence of voluntary change to try to keep your yearly life-change score out of the danger zone.

If you are considering your third job change in two years, you might stay for a while and consider a more long-lasting alternative. Or if divorce is imminent, you might avoid the temptation to plan to remarry right away and give yourself time to sort out the implications of all the changes that divorce brings with it. If you are approaching 65, a gradual rather than sudden transition from full-time work and responsibility could help reduce the feeling of uselessness that often accompanies retirement. (1974, 75)

See Application Exercise 11-2 to personalize the suggestions for minimizing distress from clustering of life events.

Here are six useful strategies for dealing with clustering of life events.

1. Insofar as possible, minimize the clustering of life events.
2. Anticipate the likely additive effects on stress of a life change you are considering—before deciding.
3. Maintain effective health buffers to be prepared for unavoidable clustering of life changes.
4. Manage your self-talk during periods of clustered change in order to keep events in perspective.

5.   Cope constructively rather than destructively with any distress that does result from clustering of life changes.
6.   When experiencing change, control those parts of your life that are controllable.

DAILY HASSLES   You may recall that Lazarus (Lazarus & Folkman, 1984) views stress as a transactional, interpretive coping process. Distress is the result of an individual's appraisal of an event or situation as personally important and as exceeding her or his resources for effectively coping with it. It is not surprising, then, that Lazarus and his colleagues at the Berkeley Stress and Coping Project would focus on small events as potentially stressful for some individuals. Thus, they decided to study micro-events—**daily hassles**—as the person moves through time (DeLongis et al., 1982; Lazarus & Folkman, 1984). At the same time, they studied the effects of **daily uplifts.**

A sample of 100 middle-aged people were asked to check how often 117 different hassles and 135 daily uplifts had occurred during the past month and how severe or pleasant the hassle or uplift was. Thus, two scales resulted: a Hassle Scale and an Uplift Scale. Figure 11-4 lists the frequency with which leading items were checked.

Others previously had suggested that these familiar, seemingly minor daily events often are taken for granted because they seem so innocuous compared with major life events, yet they can have harmful effects on the individual. Earlier writers sometimes referred to these as "common annoyances."

Lazarus and Folkman (1984) point out that life events and daily hassles tend to supplement each other in the sense that a major change, such as divorce or job change, sets in motion a whole series of minor adjustments. A man who just left his wife and family, for example, may need for the first time to confront paying bills, taking care of his laundry, fixing his lunch, cleaning his new apartment, and shopping for groceries (Oppenheimer, 1987). Thus, one might expect a positive correlation between clustering of life events and daily hassle scores.

Yet Lazarus and Folkman (1984) note that only a modest association has been found between these two measures. This means that, while clustering of life events partly explains the occurrence of daily hassles, hassles most often occur independently of major life events.

Which experience, clustering of life events or daily hassles, are most likely to produce distress? In summarizing several years of research, Lazarus and Folkman note:

> Our research findings have shown, in a regression-based comparison of life events and daily hassles, that hassles are far superior to life events in predicting psychological and somatic symptoms. Hassles accounted for almost all the outcome variance attributable to life events, whereas life events had little or no impact on health outcomes independent of daily hassles. (1984, 311)

In other words, it seems to be the accumulation of small rather than large negative events that wears the individual down mentally and physically. Interestingly, uplift scores added little predictive power for distress beyond that of hassles scores alone, although respondents tended to check uplifts more often than hassles. Wolf and others (1989) also found that hassles correlated more strongly with mood over a nine-year period than did life events. Burks and Martin (1985) reported a similar result, using their own measure of "everyday problems."

These findings point again to the role of interpretation in understanding and predicting individual distress. Whether something is a hassle depends entirely on the person's self-talk about that event. If, for example, a person tends to awfulize, negativize, or catastrophize, he or she is much more likely to see daily events as hassles.

Yet in an increasingly fast-paced, changing world marked by overchoice, overload, transitions, and clustering of life events, chances increase that events indeed will be experienced as hassles by many.

Figure 11-4

Ten Most Frequent Hassles and Uplifts

Item	Percentage of Times Checked
Hassles	
1. Concerns about weight	52.4%
2. Health of a family member	48.1
3. Rising prices of common goods	43.7
4. Home maintenance	42.8
5. Too many things to do	38.6
6. Misplacing or losing things	38.1
7. Yard work or outside home maintenance	38.1
8. Property, investment, or taxes	37.6
9. Crime	37.1
10. Physical appearance	35.9
Uplifts	
1. Relating well with your spouse or lover	76.3%
2. Relating well with friends	74.4
3. Completing a task	73.3
4. Feeling healthy	72.7
5. Getting enough sleep	69.7
6. Eating out	68.4
7. Meeting your responsibilities	68.1
8. Visiting, phoning, or writing someone	67.7
9. Spending time with family	66.7
10. Home (inside) pleasing to you	65.5

Source: Kanner et al. (1981, 61)

LOSS OF COMMUNITY AND SOCIAL ATTACHMENT   A century ago, the early sociologist Emile Durkheim (1896) conducted pioneer research demonstrating that the degree of integration of social systems—social connectedness and clarity of shared expectations—was a key influence on rates of suicide. This research set in motion a line of social research, continuing to this day, which examines community and individuals' relationships to it as sources of distress.

Urbanization and industrialization have produced a host of positive benefits for quality of life, health, and well-being over the past century and a half. More recently, the information age has enabled people and organizations to reach previously unforeseen levels of speed, access, and knowledge. Yet costs have been serious, especially in the last part of this century. These costs are **loss of community** and **loss of social attachment** among large numbers of Americans.

A number of indicators point to this reality, including the rising divorce rate, the high rate of geographic mobility (about one in five move every year) and job change, the rise in the rate of single-parent households and nonmarried householders, and the increased use of contract and temporary employees. As a result, more people are detached from one another and from large social units such as community organizations, neighborhoods, interest groups, churches, and political groups.

At the same time, a decline of shared core values and expectations of appropriate behavior (social norms) is apparent. This includes concern for the well-being of others and for the common good, respect for others' property and safety, assisting those in need, respecting ethnic and racial diversity, and valuing the sacred.

At the individual level, this has resulted in a likely rise in five types of alienation, each of which in turn heightens distress (Seeman, 1983). **Alienation** takes these forms:

- **Powerlessness**: The belief that one has little influence over events, which occur mainly as a result of luck, chance, fate, or others' decisions. As Mirowsky and Ross note, "the belief that 'There is really no way I can solve some of the problems I have,' or that 'I have little control over the things that happen to me' increases distress over time, whereas the belief that 'I can do just about anything I really set my mind to,' or that 'What happens to me in the future mostly depends on me' decreases distress over time" (1989, 134).

- **Self-estrangement:** The sense of being separated from the fruits of one's labor; "the sense of being separate from that part of one's thoughts, actions, and experiences given over to the control of others; of work being foreign to oneself rather than an expression of oneself" (Mirowsky & Ross, 138).

- **Isolation:** The sense of being detached from social connections; "the sense of not having anyone who is someone to you and not being someone to anyone" (Mirowsky & Ross, 1989). This can take the form of quantitative isolation (number of ties) or qualitative isolation (depth and meaning of ties).

- **Meaninglessness:** The sense that life has little meaning or purpose; a lack of clarity of where one wants to go and how to get there; lack of a sense of significance and value in one's existence. As Mirowsky and Ross note, "a world that cannot be understood also cannot be controlled. . . . Thus, a sense of meaninglessness implies a sense of powerlessness, which increases distress" (1989, 145).

- **Normlessness:** The belief that socially unapproved behaviors are necessary and justified to achieve one's goals (Seeman, 1959). With normlessness, individuals believe they are warranted in stealing, burglarizing, and cheating to get ahead. In addition, many feel justified in rejecting traditional community values, such as family, home ownership, and making money through a legitimate job, preferring

Figure 11-5

Five Types of Subjective Alienation, Each Scored from Low (–) to High (+)

Alienation	
(–) ———————————————————————— (+)	
Control	Powerlessness
Commitment	Self-Estrangement
Support	Isolation
Meaning	Meaninglessness
Normality	Normlessness

Source: Mirowsky & Ross (1989, 122)

instead to seek elementary pleasures in sex, drugs, and thrills (Mirowsky & Ross, 1989, 146). "The essence of normlessness, as broadly defined, is the rejection of the community as a source of behavioral standards." As Etzioni, founder of the communitarian movement, notes, growing numbers place more emphasis on individual rights than on obligation and responsibility to the community. While short-term pleasure might occur, long-term distress often follows—for others as well as the self.

These five forms of alienation and their opposites are described in Figure 11-5. It is reasonable to trace all sorts of contemporary markers of distress to loss of community, loss of social attachment, and growth of alienation: for example, a rising rate of depression; youth violence; increasing drug use among teenagers; low voter turnout, especially among the young; disregard for the property and well-being of others; and sexual exploitation.

It follows that in seeking to prevent distress, we need to strengthen community and social attachments; at the same time, we need to focus on tempering individuals' personal responses to these alienating conditions.

Social Inequality

We live in a society of rankings—by income, occupation, education, wealth, power, prestige, material possession, gender, race and ethnicity, opportunity, age, attractiveness, and more. That is, we live in a stratified society. Some rankings have special significance because they influence many aspects of our lives. Examples are occupation, income, and race.

Social Class and Economic Uncertainty

Evidence abounds that the more prestigious the occupation and the higher the income, the lower the distress. Mirowsky and Ross estimate, based on their studies, that at the extreme of distress, socioeconomic status makes a great deal of difference.

> If we split society into two halves socioeconomically, better and worse, the worse half of society has 83.8% of all severe distress. The advantaged half has only 16.2%. Stated another way, the odds of being severely distressed are 5.9 times greater in the worse half than in the better half. (1989, 17)

Social status has its impact on distress for several reasons. First is the process of selection. Higher-ranking professional, technical, and managerial occupations are likely to recruit people who have more self-confidence, better health habits, and more effective coping skills. Second, higher-ranking occupations are likely to pose fewer major life problems. While work and life are indeed challenging for these people, their problems are likely to bring less chaos and to be less threatening to personal and family life than the problems faced by lower-ranking individuals. Third, people of higher social rank have more financial and social resources to cope with problems. They can afford a marriage counselor, a financial adviser, a special mentor for their children in need. So, the higher the social standing, the fewer the significant problems and the better the internal and external resources for coping with them. These factors also may help explain the consistent finding that the higher the socioeconomic status, the better the health (Adler et al., 1994; Pincus & Callahan, 1995).

Economic uncertainty, independent of social rank, brings its own demands. Evidence is clear that unemployment heightens risk of distress because of the anxiety, financial crunch, and stigma from being out of work. Though supportive data is only anecdotal, it is also reasonable to predict that the growing trend toward utilizing contract and temporary employees will bring additional distress to individuals and families because of uncertainty and instability.

An earlier study reported to the congressional Joint Economic Committee (Brenner, 1979) showed that seven indicators of social stress (all reflections of a high rate of personal distress) were statistically related to unemployment in the United States: homicide, suicide, deaths from cardiovascular disease and kidney disease, deaths from cirrhosis of the liver, total deaths, number of people sent to jail, and admissions to mental hospitals. This study suggests that the stressors of economic uncertainty affect not only those who are poverty-stricken but also anyone faced with the threat of not being able to make ends meet. Catalano (1994) reported that people who had been laid off within the past year were six times more likely to report violent behavior than those who were not laid off.

Williams (1995, 24) has summarized the health-related influences of socioeconomic factors in this way: "Indeed, . . . low socioeconomic status is *itself a contributor to and determinant of the development of psychoisocial characteristics that lead, via biobehavioral processes, to ill health*" (his italics). Clearly, socioeconomic well-being influences personal well-being. For this reasons, contends Dreher (1995), "Socioeconomic policy may very well be health policy."

Race and Ethnicity

In the United States, ethnic and racial minorities are disproportionately disadvantaged. African Americans, Latinos, and Native Americans all experience lower average socioeconomic rank than Caucasian Americans. Each minority group also ranks higher in various indicators of distress—in part because of their lower average social-class standing. For example, Native Americans have higher levels of alcoholism than any other group, while African Americans have higher levels of psychological distress—even at the same level of social class (Kessler & Neighbors, 1986). As Mirowsky and Ross note, "Perceptions of blocked goals are especially likely to make a person feel helpless, powerless, and unable to control life" (1989, 95). Greater distress may also result from being the target of daily stereotyping and discrimination, even beyond the effect of lower socioeconomic status.

Gender

Although research findings are not unanimous, women most often have been found to experience more distress than men (see, for example, Aikin, 1993; Cohen & Williamson, 1988; Jick & Mitz, 1985; Weissman & Klerman, 1985). In using my 50-item Distress

Symptom Scale in workshops and classes during the past 15 years, I have found this same pattern dozens of times, sometimes at a level of statistical significance, sometimes not.

Freud contended that women by nature are meant to be housewives and mothers and are sure to be unhappy and distressed when they work outside the home. Talcott Parsons, a renowned social theorist of the 1950s and 1960s, argued that "society and the people in it function most smoothly when women specialize in the loving, nurturing family realm and men specialize in the competitive, acquisitive job-holding realm" (Mirowsky & Ross, 1989, 86). But it does not turn out this way at all. Contrary to the armchair theorists, employed women consistently score lower than unemployed women, not higher, on measures of distress—especially when husbands contribute to child care and housework (Gove & Tudor, 1973; Kessler & McRae, 1982; Mirowsky & Ross, 1989; Ross, Mirowsky, & Ulbrich, 1983).

Explanations for this gender difference favoring men over women in terms of distress are complex and still being studied. It may be, for example, that women are more honest in their responses to questionnaires and interviews; that they are more in touch with distress symptoms; that they experience more distressors (because their roles are more complex and demanding) and therefore more distress in their daily lives; that female socialization generates more guilt, frustration, and self-doubt; or that women use less-effective coping skills.

Thus far, we have discussed two major categories of social distressors: those associated with social change and with social inequality. We now turn to distress-prone conditions in the workplace.

Distress-Prone Conditions in the Workplace

Organizational Conditions

Most of us spend a large portion of our lives at work, usually in some type of organizational setting. That organizational environment can vary from wellness-enhancing to distress-producing. Pfifferling and Eckel (1982, 264) have identified a number of work conditions carrying a high risk of employee distress and burnout. According to the authors, presence of three or more of these conditions qualifies an organization as burnout-prone. This is one of many formulations. For an excellent collection of articles and reviews of research on job stress, see Perrewé (1991).

1. Continuously high stress levels
2. A norm of constantly giving to others
3. Discouragement of hierarchical staff interaction
4. Expectations of extra effort with minimal rewards
5. No reinforcement for suggestions on improving morale
6. Repetitive work activities
7. Minimal additional resources available for extra-effort tasks
8. Lack of encouragement for professional self-care
9. Discouragement of mutual participation in decision making
10. Evangelistic leadership styles
11. Policy changes unrelated to problem priority
12. Policy changes too frequent to be evaluated
13. Rigid role typing for workers
14. A belief that playfulness is unprofessional
15. Pervasive "isms" (ageism, sexism, nepotism, and so on)
16. Emphasis on past successes
17. Constant shifting of ground rules for policy

18.   Minimal emphasis on positive feedback
19.   Minimal emphasis on comfort of environment

Later in this chapter, we will discuss steps employers and supervisors can take to minimize these distress-producing conditions. Meanwhile, we look at one more set of social influences increasing the risk of distress, this time at the role level rather than the society or the organization.

Role-Related Distressors

Attention thus far in this chapter has been given to distress-prone features of the societal and other environments surrounding the individual. Next we turn to the micro-level of analysis, that is, to characteristics of social roles that increase chances of personal distress. By social role, I mean clusters of expectations associated with a social position such as student, parent, friend, employee, supervisor, neighbor, sibling, or team member. Research evidence abounds that role-related difficulties are major sources of tension, anxiety, depression, irritability, and distress-related illness. Here we examine several such **role-related distressors.** In order to focus the discussion, we will concentrate largely on the workplace.

ROLE CONFLICT   **Role conflict** refers to incongruent expectations associated with social roles. It comes in two forms. One is within-role conflicts, in which role partners associated with a single position send incompatible expectations. For example, a school superintendent is expected by teachers to raise salaries, but taxpayers expect him to keep taxes down. Another example is a waitress expected by management to serve more tables but expected by customers at a specific table to give prompt and courteous service.

The second form of role conflict is incompatible expectations associated with two or more roles. A common illustration is mother-employee. Here a direct conflict in what others expect often arises. Meeting the expectations associated with one role results in falling short of the expectations sent by partners of the second role.

Periodic role conflicts of these types are, of course, unavoidable in all jobs. But when they are a chronic condition of work, stress and health can suffer. Early researchers on this, for example, found that the greater the presence of role conflicts, the less the job satisfaction, especially when conflicting messages are received from persons in authority (Kahn et al., 1964). Other studies have linked role conflicts with heart disease, high blood pressure, elevated cholesterol, and obesity (Cassel, 1974; Warr & Parry, 1982). Ivancevich and Matteson have summarized these studies by stating:

> Thus, as a stressor, role conflict undermines job satisfaction (with all the negative outcomes so frequently found to be associated with that) and is associated with physiological changes that have both personal and organizational costs. Other difficulties, such as decreased quality of decisions made and reduction of creativity, are very likely to result from the tension and anxiety associated with conflict. (1980, 111)

While role conflicts sometimes cannot be avoided in jobs with multiple role partners, managers need to be sensitive to creating conditions with as few conflicts as possible. Individual workers need to feel confident about bringing supervisors' attention to avoidable role conflicts; they should be reasonable and clear when giving directions or expectations to their role partners, as well. And, as with other role difficulties, the more a person practices the stress-management methods described in this book, the less role conflict is likely to have harmful effects on morale, productivity, and health.

ROLE AMBIGUITY   Rose, a new secretary at a weight-control clinic, is quite confused about what her job priorities should be. This confusion is partly the result of the newness of the clinic itself and partly the result of an unclear definition of her duties by her supervisor. Understandably, Rose is more anxious and uncertain than she expected to be in this new job. Her sleep has been affected, and she is more irritable at home than before she took the job.

Rose is suffering the effects of **role ambiguity**—lack of clarity about the work role. Lack of certainty about role priorities, about the balance of duties, and about how to do specific tasks are unavoidable, of course, when one is new to a job, when the job itself is new or redefined, or when the organizational policies or procedures are in a state of flux. However, when role ambiguity is a long-term condition of work, a number of adverse consequences are likely, according to research studies (Matteson & Ivancevich, 1987).

- Job dissatisfaction
- Job-related tension
- Lower self-confidence
- Elevated blood pressure
- Depression
- Anxiety
- Less work motivation
- Feelings of resentment

No organization can be structured to avoid role ambiguity entirely. Nor can individual workers ever hope to avoid it completely, whether they are self-employed or work for others, lower-level workers, or professionals. However, managers need to do everything possible to define work responsibilities clearly, to keep policies and procedures updated, and to maintain clear communication channels. The individual needs to be assertive in seeking clarification when needed.

ROLE OVERLOAD We are all familiar with periods of time when we simply have more to do than time available. When this is a temporary condition, we seem to be able to adapt fairly easily. However, when the condition becomes chronic, the result can be burnout and breakdown. As Ivancevich and Matteson have stated:

> An electrical system that is unable to handle all of the electricity introduced to it is overloaded. In most instances a fuse blows or a circuit breaker is tripped, stopping the input and preventing damage to the system. When an individual is unable to handle all the work input, that person may become overloaded. Unfortunately, unlike the electrical system, people do not have an automatic safety device, and the overload condition can lead to physical, mental, and job performance problems. (1980, 113)

Role overload can take two forms: quantitative (too much to do in time available) and qualitative (impossibly demanding expectations by supervisors). Either type, when chronic, can lead to stress and health difficulties. Overload among tax accountants around April 15, for example, has been found to lead to elevated cholesterol in the blood (Friedman, Rosenman, & Carroll, 1958). Other negative outcomes reported by researchers include increased risk of heart attacks, low job satisfaction, escapist drinking behavior, high absenteeism, low confidence, high accident rates on the job, and high tobacco consumption (French & Caplan, 1973).

Occasional overload is probably unavoidable. Overload as a chronic condition can be avoided through wise role definitions, proper assessment of human resources needed to carry out a given workload, and establishing a good fit between individual capabilities and needs of the job (Maslach & Lieter, 1997b). Learning to cope effectively with temporary

Erosion of the Soul: Three Dimensions of Burnout

In terms of personal functioning, burnout can cause such physical problems as headaches, gastrointestinal illness, high blood pressure, muscle tension, and chronic fatigue. Burnout may lead to mental distress in the form of anxiety, depression, and sleep disturbances. To try to cope with the stress, some people increase use of alcohol and drugs. If they bring burnout home, their exhaustion and negative feelings begin to affect relationships with family and friends.

Burnout can have a deadly impact even beyond its erosion of the soul. It can be detrimental to your health, your ability to cope, and your personal lifestyle. It can lead to a serious deterioration in your job performance. And these costs are not just yours alone—they are felt by everyone who is affected by you, both on the job and at home.

Let's assume that you are working in a situation of chronic imbalance in which the job demands more than you can give and provides less than you need. You feel overworked, undervalued, and no longer in control of the job you do. What might happen if you begin to burn out? Actually three things happen: you become chronically exhausted, cynical and detached from your work, and you feel increasingly ineffective on the job.

Let's take a closer look at each of the three dimensions of burnout.

EXHAUSTION

When people feel exhaustion, they feel overextended, both emotionally and physically. They feel drained, used up, and unable to unwind and recover. When they awake in the morning, they are just as tired as when they went to bed. They lack the energy to face another project or another person. Exhaustion is the first reaction to the stress of job demands or major change.

CYNICISM

When people feel cynical, they take a cold, distant attitude toward work and the people on the job. They minimize their involvement at work and even to give up their ideals. In a way, cynicism is an attempt to protect oneself from exhaustion and disappointment. People feel it may be safer to be indifferent, especially when the future is uncertain, or to assume things won't work out rather than get their hopes up. But being so negative can seriously damage a person's well-being and capacity ro work effectively.

INEFFECTIVENESS

When people feel ineffective, they feel a growing sense of inadequacy. Every new project seems overwhelming. The world seems overwhelming. The world seems to conspire against each of their attempts to make progress, and what little they do accomplish may seem trivial. They lose confidence in their ability to make a difference. And as they lose confidence in themselves, others lose confidence in them.

Source: Maslach & Leiter, 1997a, 5.

overload and to be assertive enough, individually or collectively, to minimize chronic overload when working for others can be useful steps for minimizing distress from role overload. Finally, role overload often is self-created. We need to be sensitive to our limits of time and energy in order to avoid chronic overload when we can.

ROLE UNDERLOAD   This occurs when the occupant experiences too little to do or insufficient variety on the job. This is especially true of repetitive jobs, such as assembly-line work (Brief, Schuler, & Van Sell, 1980). Like role overload, underload can occur from time to time in most jobs. We usually adapt to these conditions with little difficulty. When understimulation is an ongoing experience, demoralization, anxiety, depression, and physical symptoms of distress become common. One study found that executives at the high and low end of a stress scale had more medical problems, suggesting a curvilinear association between stimulation and health (McLean, 1979). This study "seems to demonstrate that those who are bored or understimulated and those who feel highly pressured represent the two ends of a continuum, each with a significantly elevated number of symptoms" (McLean, 1979).

Role underload more often results from too little variety in work tasks (qualitative underload) than from too little to do (quantitative underload). The challenge facing managers, then, is to structure work so it has sufficient variability over the long run. The individual employee needs to seek out a job with sufficient variety and quantity for her or his needs, to structure the job's pace and variety for one's tastes insofar as possible, and to tolerate temporary underload—perhaps even welcome it.

HIGH ROLE EXPECTATIONS—LOW CONTROL   Among the most risky conditions of all for worker distress is a role that has heavy responsibilities and high expectations combined with little opportunity to control how the job is carried out or the conditions of work (Cooper & Payne, 1978; Winslow, 1997). A good example is the position of secretary, say, in a lawyer's office. She (have you ever seen a male legal secretary?) is likely to be besieged with time deadlines, heavy time demands from her boss, unhappy clients over the phone, and the need for precision in filling out forms and in typing documents. Yet she is likely to have little to say about the physical conditions of work, about interruptions, about the workload, or about the format of reports and forms she must complete. A recent study shows that low sense of job control was associated with elevated blood epinephrine levels among men, perhaps helping account for the linkage sometimes found between job distress and cardiovascular disease among men (Pollard, 1996).

Another example is the hospital technician whose work must be very carefully executed because a life and certainly the patient's comfort may depend on it. Expectations of superiors, the public, and the patients are high. Yet technicians in the X-ray department, the surgery room, the cardiology laboratory, or the respiratory department are likely to have little to say about their pace of work, about the demeanor of physicians, or about the layout of the hospital facility in which they work. The result for occupants of such positions often is a high incidence of distress symptoms.

Managers can minimize such symptoms by giving employees as much opportunity as possible to determine the manner and pace with which tasks are carried out. Decentralized decision making with maximum involvement by work groups can help, as we saw earlier. As with other role stressors, the individual is challenged here to be assertive in requesting as much leeway as possible in controlling conditions of work. Maintaining good mental and physical coping habits is vital for handling effectively the distress that sometimes does occur from these conditions.

DIFFICULT ROLE RELATIONSHIPS   Difficult role partners may be supervisors, coworkers, or those served by the role occupant: patients, students, customers, or clients, for example. The potential for distress is especially likely among those at boundary-spanning points in the organization; that is, where members of the organization deal with others outside the organization. Illustrations include teachers, customer service representatives, nurses, ministers, and lawyers (Bramson, 1981).

See Application Exercise 11-3 to personalize the various types of role difficulties.

The degree to which distress in fact occurs depends on the skill of the role occupant in handling difficult role partners, especially those who are angry. Here are several suggestions for handling an angry person at work.

1. Be attentive. Use effective listening, as described in Chapter 17.
2. Avoid allowing your self-esteem to be threatened. Be thick-skinned, using positive self-talk.
3. Allow the angry person time to vent.
4. See her or his anger as a problem to be solved, rather than as something to return with anger.
5. Use the "grain of truth" approach. Try to acknowledge even a small degree of truth in what the person is saying.
6. Show empathy. This itself often will defuse the other's anger.
7. If needed, be assertive. There comes a point where it is okay to tell the angry person that enough is enough—to stop dumping on you. This can be done assertively, without hostility or aggressiveness, as described in Chapter 17.

Even the most tactful and patient individuals have their off-days, of course. Effective managers ensure that their employees are adequately trained in listening skills, in handling angry persons, and in problem-solving for difficult persons served by the organization. The effective employee makes certain that she or he continues to update and refine these vital job skills.

CAREER INSECURITY AND INOPPORTUNITY   This role-related stressor has to do with those features of a person's career development affecting her or his perceptions of present and future options. These features may become sources of concern, anxiety, frustration, or loss of motivation (Ivancevich & Matteson, 1980).

One of these factors is job insecurity. Another is lack of opportunity for job advancement. Erikson and his associates found that job satisfaction was greatest among individuals whose promotion matched or exceeded their hopes (Erickson, Pugh, & Gunderson, 1972). As advancement rates fell behind expectations, job satisfaction decreased. Blau found a number of stress-related consequences, including reductions in work output, high accident rates, alcoholism and/or drug abuse, worsening interpersonal relations on the job, and increased resentment and resistance to supervision (1978).

Such career problems may be inherent in certain job settings and job categories. Further, they may be partly caused by nonwork factors in the private lives of employees, such as a midlife crisis, faltering career commitment, or self-doubt.

Yet it is incumbent on the sensitive manager to be alert to evidence of such conditions. For the individual worker, this is an example of using personal distress signals as a sign of disharmony between inside ideals and outside reality—which can lead either to further distress or to constructive steps to alter or advance one's career direction.

OTHER COMMON ROLE-RELATED DISTRESSORS IN THE WORKPLACE   Those stressors listed thus far are hardly exhaustive. Other common ones, which in fact may be primary in given situations, include:

- Lack of appreciation by supervisors
- Low public image
- Low wages
- Conflict of work with childrearing
- Underuse of abilities
- Irritating habits of co-workers
- Having to act contrary to personal ethics

Distress-Preventing Social Influences

Thus far in this chapter we have focused on distress-prone social influences with emphasis on the total society and the workplace. Just as social environments can generate distress, so, too, can they minimize it, enhancing wellness instead. In this section, we briefly examine some of these positive social conditions.

Wellness-Enhancing, Distress-Preventing Social Policies: Illustrations

Here are illustrations of social policies whose likely effects are to contribute to health and well-being and to minimizing distress for families and individuals:

- Creation of accessible, affordable, high-quality child care
- Creation of maximum job opportunities—for youth as well as adults
- Reduction of tobacco addiction through elimination of the tobacco subsidy, increase of cigarette taxes, and increases in antismoking campaigns
- Creation of affordable, universally accessible medical services
- Inclusion of health education and alternative treatments in health insurance coverage
- Expansion of seat belt and helmet laws
- Improvements in food labeling
- Creation of biking, walking, and running paths
- Improvements in health education
- Creation of policies to minimize violence in the media
- Creation of policies and programs to minimize sexual and racial harrassment
- Equalization of educational opportunities at all levels
- Support and encouragement of community-based health-promotion programs
- Funding for expanded counseling services for families and individuals

These are mere examples from a potentially much longer list of distress-preventing social policies that can be imagined. Such policies are needed at all levels: national, state, and local. We next turn to a brief sampling of what organizations can do to create distress-preventing social environments in the workplace.

Conditions in the Workplace to Minimize Distress

Shapiro (1982) maintains that burnout is not the result of either the person or the organization alone but of the interaction between the two. He contends that supervisors can follow several constructive practices to minimize burnout potential.

- Leadership that provides support, structure, and information
- Communication that is timely, appropriate, and accurate
- An environment that is planned, efficient, and orderly
- Workers who participate meaningfully in decision making
- Support and nurturing from supervisory staff
- Encouragement of employee creativity and innovation
- Peer friendship and support networks

Especially important to minimizing burnout potential is anticipatory socialization of new employees (preparation for potential burnout traps and how to avoid them). Kramer

(1974) reports a program of anticipatory socialization that significantly reduces the reality shock for new nurses, thereby lessening chances of burnout.

Effective managers and supervisors push not only for maximum short-run productivity; they know that healthy and satisfied workers are also vital for the long-term benefit of all concerned—managers, workers, and clients. They know that positive job stress needs to be sought (Cartwright & Cooper, 1997).

Here are several ways managers and supervisors can move toward achieving this ideal.

1. They can make the organization a sufficiently appealing place to work so satisfaction is high and turnover is low.
2. They can ensure that role expectations are as clear and congruent as possible in order to minimize role conflicts and role ambiguity.
3. They can manage the work process so it is appropriately varied and is chronically neither overloaded nor underloaded.
4. They can strike a good balance between continuity and change in the organization. While self-renewing change is vital for keeping up with shifting conditions outside the organization, such change must not occur at a pace so fast it produces wide spread distress among employees.
5. Managers and supervisors can provide continuing support and encouragement to their employees. They can ensure that each employee feels needed and appreciated. Similarly, they can encourage the formation of cohesive, supportive work groups among co-workers.
6. To the degree possible, every person can be given maximum flexibility to work at the pace and manner that will ensure maximum long-term health, satisfaction, and self-expression—as well as short-term productivity.
7. They can provide meaningful opportunities for ongoing involvement by all employees in decisions affecting them.
8. They can be attentive to stress levels within the organization—and to work conditions that might contribute to unnecessary distress.
9. They can provide supportive stress-management services for employees in distress. Such services, ranging from fitness programs to counseling services, can be provided within the organization, or referral networks can be established.
10. Managers and supervisors can provide opportunities for all workers—themselves included—to learn more about stress and distress, especially related to work.

Cultures of Wellness

When occasionally working with public school students, I am struck by the great variations I hear in their stories about family life. Some families have little stability, schedule, discipline, order, or predictability. Residents of the household come and go, abuse of women and children is rampant, drugs and cigarettes are abundant, the television is always on, foods are high-fat and irregularly served. Other families stand in sharp contrast, with stability, lots of support, positive health habits, and close linkages with the surrounding community (Schafer, 1998).

Similarly, I have been impressed in recent years with variations in the health-enhancing or health-detracting environment of worksites I have visited. In some offices and plants, doughnuts and candy are served daily, smoking is common (outside the back door, if not allowed inside), the handful who exercise during off hours are chided, and there is no evidence that supervisors give a whit about good health habits for themselves or others. In other workplaces, I observe keen interest among workers and supervisors in matters of health, with people actively supporting each others' positive health choices and sharing stories about recent bike trips or running adventures.

These observations—combined with my sociological background—have led me to see the importance of environmental influences on people's decisions about wellness. In short, I have come increasingly to recognize the importance of **cultures of wellness**—those features of a group or organization that encourage, reward, and support wellness choices.

In contrast, a **culture of worseness** is made up of those features of the social environment that discourage healthy choices and that encourage, reward, and support unhealthy, unwholesome choices. Like individual wellness and worseness, cultures are best seen along a **wellness/worseness continuum,** from cultures of high-level wellness at one extreme to cultures of low-level worseness at the other.

Every group or organization carries a culture of wellness/worseness. Thus, cultures of wellness exist in one degree or another in peer and friendship groups, families, workgroups and worksites, schools, campuses, campus organizations, neighborhoods, apartments and apartment complexes, communities, regions, and nations.

As Willis Harmon recently stated, it makes little sense to ignore the social context, especially if it is thoroughly incompatible with health enhancement. As an example, he writes as follows about children growing up in a poor urban area.

> . . . in normal development, favorable experiences from childhood on slowly build up a salutogenic [healthy] personality orientation. But people growing up in a poor urban area may not experience such a salutogenic milieu. There the environment is likely to be characterized by: broken and single-parent homes, individuals and families without homes, drug peddling and crime in the streets, no opportunity for joyous interaction with nature, frequent contact with industrial poisons, low cultural integration, a general feeling of powerlessness to change anything, a siege mentality in the schools, and little incentive to learn because of the pervasive belief that the economy won't provide opportunities for these people anyway. (Harmon, 1994, 22)

Moving from the community to the organizational level, Judd Allen and his late father, Robert Allen (1987), developed a useful framework for understanding, assessing, and promoting cultures of wellness in the workplace. Included are three components: a sense of community, a shared vision, and a positive culture. To the degree these ingredients of a culture of wellness are present, individuals will be more productive, satisfied, and healthy, according to the Allens. More recently, Winston and colleagues (1997) have developed a measurable framework for characterizing the climates of college student organizations.

Of course, groups and organizations like schools, campuses, or worksites do not themselves exist in isolation. Rather, they are imbedded in larger social, political, economic, and cultural systems. The likelihood of a culture of wellness emerging and thriving in a specific setting in turn is influenced by forces from those larger environments.

These observations lead us to the model of wellness presented in Figure 11-6. At the center of the wheel is "Self-Responsibility." Ultimately, we each are responsible for our choices related to health and well-being, whatever the surrounding micro-environment or macro-environment. Surrounding this core are the seven dimensions of wellness as presented earlier.

The next ring in the wheel is cultures of wellness. Whatever the specific setting (school, campus, neighborhood, worksite), cultures of wellness include the following, as shown in Figure 11-6.

Figure 11-6

A Multilevel Model of Wellness

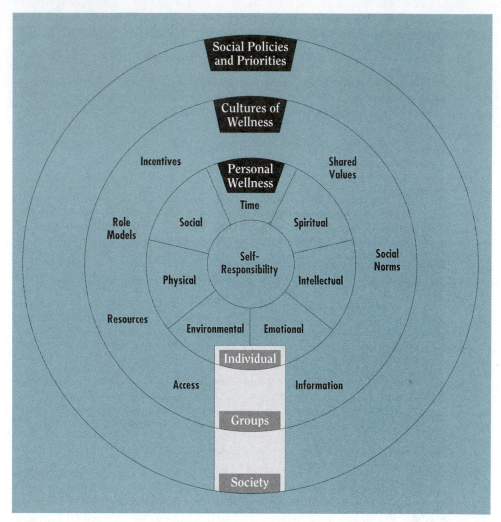

Wellness = Living at one's highest potential as a whole person and promoting the same for others.

Cultures of Wellness = Features of the social environment that encourage, reward, and support wellness choices. Cultures of wellness exist in peer groups, families, worksites, schools, neighborhoods, and communities.

PEOPLE WHO MODEL WELLNESS LIFESTYLE

Peers	Teachers	Neighbors
Siblings	Supervisors	
Parents	Coworkers	

SHARED VALUES AND SOCIAL NORMS THAT ENCOURAGE, REWARD, AND SUPPORT WELLNESS CHOICES

- Values refer to what is considered in the group or organization to be valuable, worthwhile, or important.

- Norms refer to shared expectations about do's and don'ts, about acceptable and unacceptable behavior.

INFORMATION, RESOURCES, AND INCENTIVES IN SUPPORT OF WELLNESS CHOICES   Information might include reading materials related to health or healthy relationships.

Resources might include the presence of adequate recreational or fitness facilities in a community, school, or worksite and adequate money or transportation enabling a child to participate in a community program.

Incentives refer to tangible rewards for healthy choices. Examples include recognition of a group in an elementary school for riding their bikes or walking/running a certain number of miles in a month; a weight-loss contest in a workplace; a fraternity or sorority giving special recognition to a member for completing a recent marathon.

MAXIMUM AND EQUAL ACCESS TO SUCH INFORMATION, RESOURCES, AND INCENTIVES   Equal access might include availability of locker rooms to all workers in a plant, not just to management.

Maximum access might include wide availability of intramural programs on a campus and open display and distribution of health-enhancing information in a school, campus, or worksite.

Just as individuals are influenced by outside influences, so are groups and organizations in any specific setting shaped, facilitated, or limited by societal policies and priorities. Thus, the outer ring of Figure 11-6 refers to societal policies and priorities. Some examples contribute to wellness, others to worseness.

- Health care insurance payments for health education
- Federal subsidies for tobacco growers
- State or federal tax incentives for employers to offer employee wellness programs
- A shift in the national school-lunch program toward foods lower in fat and higher in complex carbohydrates
- A voter-created fund in California for a massive antismoking media campaign
- National emphasis on what some believe to be "radical individualism," contributing to widespread cynicism toward government and low commitment to the common good at the community level

In sum, this is a highly useful wellness framework because it directs attention not just to the individual but also to social environments influencing the individual. This is consistent with recent approaches to health promotion and disease prevention. As Wallace and Winkleby (1987, 928) wrote, "If there is an overriding purpose of prevention, it is to create a social and physical environment that promotes the establishment and maintenance of good health behaviors and discourages health damaging choices." In a leading book on health promotion, Green and Krueter (1991, 4) state, "Health promotion is the combination of education and environmental supports for actions and conditions of living conducive to health."

This person-environment approach also is consistent with the approach to stress management presented in the first chapter of this book—an approach including ways the person is influenced by the surrounding social world and the need for the individual to do what he or she can to better conditions in that larger environment, whether at the micro or macro level.

This wellness approach emphasizing both individual and social forces influencing the individual has provided the basis for the burgeoning healthy community movement in this country and Europe. An illustration is Healthy Chico Kids 2000, a comprehensive health promotion campaign that is a collaborative initiative of The Pacific Wellness Institute at California State University, Chico, and the Chico community.

In this chapter, we have reviewed a number of social influences toward distress as well as distress-prevention. We have suggested a number of steps you and others can take to promote wellness-enhancing, distress-preventing social environments. In Part IV, we turn back to the individual level of stress management.

By way of transition, it is worth noting that, after reviewing a vast research literature and reporting their own studies on social causes of psychological distress, Mirowsky and Ross (1989) identify several steps individuals can take to prevent their own distress, given the named social causes of personal distress. They can:

1. Develop **instrumentalism**—the belief you make things happen and get things done, that outcomes depend on your own choices and actions.
2. Develop **flexibility**—the ability to imagine complex or multiple solutions to problems and the many sides to an issue.
3. Become *educated*—not only because of what you will learn but because the very process of learning develops flexibility, instrumentalism, confidence, self-assurance, and the ability to communicate and to cope with adversity.
4. Get a *good job*—not only one that pays well but also one that includes some measure of autonomy and minimal conflict between work and family.
5. Maintain *supportive relationships*—relationships that involve caring for someone and being cared for and that are balanced and fair.

Being educated, having a good job, and maintaining supportive relationships are likely to promote instrumentalism and flexibility, while these two qualities will help one get educated, get a good job, and maintain supportive relationships. Thus, one can create a positively reinforcing cycle. We now turn to practical ways of managing stress to keep these and other positive cycles going in your life.

References

Adler, N. E., Boyce, T., Chesney, M. A., Cohen, S., Folkman, S., Kahn, R. L., & Syme, S. L. (1994). Socioeconomic status and health: The challenge of the gradient. *American Psychologist, 49*(1), 15–24.

Aikin, K. K. (1993). Perceived stress and life satisfaction: Gender differences and life situation correlates for women. Unpublished master's thesis, California State University, Chico.

Allen, R. F., & Allen, J. (1987). A sense of community, a shared vision and a positive culture: Core enabling factors in successful culture based health promotion. *American Journal of Health Promotion, 1,* 40–47.

Antonovsky, A. (1994). A sociological critique of the "well-being" movement. *Advances.* 10, 6–12.

Associated Press. (1997). Study finds link between stress and kidney stones. *Chico Enterprise-Record*, November 23, 5D.

Blau, B. (1978) Understanding mid-career stress. *Management Review, 67,* 57–62.

Brenner, H. (1970). Mortality and the national economy. *Lancet, 2,* 568–573.

Brief, A. P., Schuler, R. S., & Van Sell, M. (1980). *Managing job stress.* Boston: Little, Brown.

Burks, N., & Martin, B. (1985). Everyday problems and life change events. *Journal of Human Stress, 11,* 27–35.

Carroll, L. (1960). *Alice's adventures in wonderland.* New York: Signet Books.

Cartwright. S., & Cooper, C. L. (1997). *Managing workplace stress.* Thousands Oaks, CA: Sage Publications.

Cassel, J. (1974). Psychosocial processes and stress: Theoretical formulation. *International Journal of Health Services, 4,* 471–484.

Catalano, R. (1994). Study: Layoffs can make people violent. *Chico Enterprise-Record,* August 17, 6B.

Cohen, S., & Williamson, G. M. (1988). Perceived stress in a probability sample of the United States. In S. Spacepan & S. Oscamp (Eds.), *The social psychology of health.* Thousand Oaks, CA: Sage, 31–67.

Cooper, C. L., & Payne, R. (Eds.; 1978). *Stress at work.* New York: John Wiley and Sons.

Delongis, A., Coyne, J. C., Dakof, G., Folkman, S., & Lazarus, R. S. (1982). Relationship of daily hassles, uplifts, and major life events to health status. *Health Psychology, I,* 119–136.

Dohrenwend, B. P. (1986). Note on a program of research on alternative social psychological models of relationships between life stress and psychopathology. In M. H. Appley & R. Trumbull (Eds.), *The dynamics of stress: Physiological, psychological, and social perspectives.* New York: Plenum Press, 283–294.

Dohrenwend, B. S., & Dohrenwend, B. P. (Eds.; 1974). *Stressful life events: Their nature and effects.* New York: John Wiley and Sons.

Dohrenwend, B. S., & Dohrenwend, B. P. (Eds.; 1981). *Stressful life events and their contexts.* New York: Prodist.

Dreher, H. (1995). The social perspective in mind-body studies: Missing in action? *Advances, 11,* 39–54.

Durkheim, E. (1893). *The division of labor* (trans. George Simpson, 1966). Glencoe, IL: Free Press.

Erickson, J., Pugh, W. M., & Gunderson, E. K. (1972). Status incongruency as a predictor of job satisfaction and life stress. *Journal of Applied Psychology, 56,* 523–525.

Friedman, M. R., Rosenman, R. H., & Carroll, V. (1958). Changes in serum cholesterol and blood-clotting time in men subjected to cyclic variation in occupational stress. *Circulation, 17,* 852–861.

Gove, W. R., & Tudor, J. F. (1973). Adult sex roles and mental illness. *American Journal of Sociology, 78,* 812–835.

Green, L. W., & Krueter, M. W. (1991). *Health promotion planning: An educational and environmental approach.* Mountain View, CA: Mayfield Publishing.

Harmon, W. W. (1994). A different sort of inner work: A response to Antonovsky's challenge. *Advances, 10,* 2126.

Hobfoll, S.E. (1998). *Stress, culture, and community.* New York: Plenum.

Holmes, T. H., & Holmes, T. S. (1974). How stress can make us ill. *Stress.* Chicago: Blue Cross.

Holmes, T. H., & Rahe, R. H. (1967). The social readjustment rating scale. *Journal of Psychosomatic Research, 11,* 213.

Horowitz, M. J. (1976). *Stress response syndromes.* New York: Jason Aronson.

Ivancevich, J. M., & Matteson, M. T. (1980). *Stress and work: A managerial perspective.* Glenview: Scott.

Jick, I. T., & Mitz, L. F. (1985). Sex differences in work stress. *Academy of Management Review, 10*(3), 408420.

Justice, B. (1994). Critical life events and the onset of illness. *Comprehensive Therapy, 29, 232–238.*

Kahn, R. L., Wolfe, D. M., Quinn, R. P., Snoek, J. D., & Rosenthal, R. A. (1964). *Organizational stress.* New York: John Wiley and Sons.

Kanner, A. D., Coyne, J. S., Schaefer, C., & Lazarus, R. S. (1981). Comparison of two modes of stress measurement: Daily hassles and uplifts versus major life events. *Journal of Behavioral Medicine, 4,* 1–39.

Kessler, R. C., & McRae, J. A. (1982). *American Sociological Review, 47,* 216–227.

Kessler, R. C., & Neighbors, H. W. (1986). A new perspective on the relationship among race, social class, and psychological distress. *Journal of Health and Social Behavior, 27,* 107–115.

Kramer, M. (1974). *Reality shock: Why nurses leave nursing.* St. Louis: Mosby Press.

Lazarus, R. S., & Folkman, S. (1984). *Stress, appraisal, and coping.* New York: Springer Publishing.

Maslach, C., & Leiter, M. (1997a). Erosion of the soul: Three dimensions of burnout. *Mind & Body Health Newsletter, VI,* 5.

Maslach, C., & Leiter, M. (1997b). *The truth about burnout: How organizations cause personal stress and what to do about it.* San Francisco: Jossey-Bass.

Matteson, M. T., & Ivancevich, J. M. (1987). *Controlling work stress.* San Francisco: Jossey-Bass.

McLean, A. A. (1979). *Work stress.* Reading: Addison-Wesley.

Mirowsky, J., & Ross, C. E. (1989). *Social causes of psychological distress.* New York: Aldine de Gruyter.

Oppenheimer, K. (1987). The impact of daily stressors on women's adjustment to marital separation. *The Journal of Family Practice, 24,* 507–511.

Perrewé, P. L. (Ed., 1991). *Handbook on Job Stress.* Corte Madera, CA: Select Press.

Pfifferling, J. H., & Eckel, F. M. (1982). Beyond burnout: Obstacles and prospects. In W. S. Paine (Ed.), *Job stress and burnout.* Beverly Hills, CA: Sage.

Pincus, T., & Callahan, L. F. (1995). What explains the association between socioeconomic status and health: Primarily medical access or mind-body variables? *Advances, 11,* 4–36.

Pollard, T. M., Ungpakorn, G., Harrison, G. A., & Parkes, K. R. (1996). Epinephrine and cortisol responses at work: A test of the models of Frankenhaeuser and Karasek. *Annals of Behavioral Medicine, 18,* 229–237.

Rabkin, J. G., & Struening, E. L. (1976). Life events, stress and illness. *Science, 194,* 1013–1020.

Rahe, R. H. (1968). Life-change measurement as a precipitator of illness. *Proceedings of the Royal Society of Medicine, 61,* 1124–1126.

Rice, P. L. (1987). *Stress and health: Principles and practice for coping and wellness.* Monterey, CA: Brooks/Cole.

Ross, C. E., Mirowsky, J., & Ulbrich, P. (1983). Distress and the traditional female role: A comparison of Mexicans and Anglos. *American Journal of Sociology, 89,* 670–683.

Schafer, W. (1998). Introducing social factors into the mind/body and wellness fields. *Advances in Mind/Body Medicine, 14,* 43-51.

Schafer, W. E., & McKenna, J. F. (1981). Life change, stress and injury: A study of male college athletes. Unpublished paper.

Schafer, W. E., & McKenna, J. F. (1985). Life changes, stress, injuries, and illness among adult runners. *Stress Medicine, I,* 237–244.

Schlossberg, N. K. (1989). *Overwhelmed: Coping with life's ups and downs.* Lexington, MA: Lexington Books.

Seeman, M. (1959). On the meaning of alienation. *American Sociological Review, 24,* 783–791.

Seeman, M. (1983). Alienation motifs in contemporary theorizing: The hidden continuity of classic themes. *Social Psychology Quarterly, 46,* 171–184.

Seligman, M. E. P. (1988). Boomer blues. *Psychology Today, 21,* 50–55.

Shapiro, C. H. (1982). Creative supervision: An underutilized antidote. In W. S. Paine (Ed.), *Job stress and burnout.* Beverly Hills, CA: Sage, 280–291.

Swensen, R. A. (1992). *Margin.* Colorado Springs: NavPress.

Toffler, A. (1970). *Future shock.* New York: Bantam.

Wallace, L., & Winkleby, M. (1987). Primary prevention: A new look at basic concepts. *Social Science and Medicine, 25,* 923–930.

Warr, P., & Parry, G. (1982). Paid employment and women's psychological well-being. *Psychological Bulletin, 91,* 498-516.

Weissman, M. M., & Klerman, G. L. (1985). Gender and depression. *Trends in Neuroscience, 8,* 416–420.

Williams, R. B. (1995). Conditions of low socioeconomic status increase the likelihood of the biological bases underlying psychosocial factors that contribute to ill health. *Advances, 11,* 24–29.

Winslow, R. (1997). Lack of control over job is seen as heart risk. *Wall Street Journal,* July 25, 5.

Winston, R. B., Jr., Bledsoe, T., Goldstein, A. R., Wisbey, M. E., Street, J. L., Brown, S. R., Goyen, K. D., Rounds, L. E. (1997). Describing the climate of student organizations: The student organization environment scales. *Journal of College Student Development, 38,* 417–428.

Wolf, T. M., Elston, R. C., & Kissling, A. R. (1989). Relationship of hassles, uplifts, and life events to psychological well-being of freshmen medical students. *Behavioral Medicine, 15,* 37–45.

Application Exercise 11-1

Lead Time and Afterburn Time

1. Discuss several instances of lead time in your own life—when you have had enough and too little. Also discuss the effects on your own distress.

2. Discuss several instances of afterburn time in your own life—when you have had enough and too little. Also discuss the effects on your own distress.

Application Exercise 11-2

Applying Strategies for Handling Clustering of Life Events

Read carefully the six strategies for handling clustering of life events.

1. Looking back over recent periods of clustering of events in your life, which of these strategies have you used? Be specific.

2. Which strategies might you strengthen as you deal with future clustering of life events?

3. What specific steps will you take to apply one or more of these strategies?

Application Exercise 11-3

Examples of Role Difficulties

Before completing this exercise, be sure you understand the various types of role difficulties. Give one or more examples, preferably from personal experience, of each type of role difficulty.

1. Role conflict:

2. Role ambiguity:

3. Role overload:

4. Role underload:

5. High role expectations—low control:

6. Difficult role relationships:

PART IV

Managing Stress:
Strategies and Methods

Life is not the way it's supposed to be. It's the way it is. The way you cope with it is what makes the difference.

—VIRGINIA SATIR

Your Coping Response

After a long and distinguished career as a family therapist and writer, Virginia Satir died of cancer in 1989. In her obituary in the *Los Angeles Times,* she was quoted as saying:

> I think if I have one message, one thing before I die that most of the world would know, it would be that the event does not determine how to respond to the event. That is a purely personal matter. The way in which we respond will direct and influence the event more than the event itself. (1989, 24)

Satir was correct. Life is tough. The world in which we live is imperfect. The Garden of Eden disappeared some time back in Genesis. The very facts of social and personal change inevitably produce pressures, strains, and challenges. So does the life cycle, as we move through phases and transitions. Economic uncertainties and international tensions will continue.

In discussing "how to learn lessons from life experiences," Walter and Siebert (1990) cite the old saying that "Good mariners are not created by calm seas." They note that during times of severe adversity, some people survive remarkably well.

> During the Depression in the 1930's, some people went against the tide and refused to be swept away by mass despair. Even though thousands were destitute, some people found ways to be happy and to enjoy being alive. Using their imaginations and inner resources, they maintained a positive direction for themselves and their families during hard times. (1990, 162)

This chapter is about how we cope with ever-present stressors—not only to survive but also to thrive, to reach our uppermost potentials. We will explore the coping process, coping styles, coping options, reactions to temporary distress, and tips for thriving under pressure. This chapter serves as a framework for a variety of stress management techniques that follow.

UNDERSTANDING THE COPING PROCESS

Both of the students described in the box on page 293 faced multiple stressors. Both responded in patterned ways. They engaged in a continuous process of coping, each reflecting her own coping style.

What Is Coping?

Lazarus and Folkman define **coping** as:

> . . . constantly changing cognitive and behavioral efforts to manage specific external and/or internal demands that are appraised as taxing or exceeding the resources of the person. (1984, 141)

In other words, your coping response is what you think and do as you deal with demands. Notice that this definition calls attention to a process through time. It is also specific to the circumstance. Thus, your coping response is constantly shifting and changing as you react and adapt to the situation or persons with which you are dealing. Coping is not what you should, would, or could do. It is what you in fact do as you react to particular conditions and demands. Coping, then, is an *ongoing, dynamic, interactional process.* Your repeated pattern of coping becomes your **coping style.** Sally's and Maria's coping styles contrasted clearly.

Coping Styles

- Maria came to the university from a working-class family fully supported by her mother. Her father, an alcoholic, had left when Maria was 2 years old and had not been heard from in years. She, her three brothers, and one sister were proud of their home and their strong support for each other. As a college junior, she worked 20 hours a week waiting tables. She delegated her time carefully and still managed to nurture several close friendships. She drank an occasional beer but no more. She did not do drugs. During final exams, she was confident she would do well, having kept up with her studies all semester. She seemed to thrive under this kind of pressure. Clearly, she coped actively and constructively.

- Sally's coping style contrasted sharply. Attending the same university, she came from a home where life was relatively easy and predictable. Her parents, both prominent professionals in a small valley town, had provided all the money and support Sally needed to be among the "in" crowd in high school and, later, in her college sorority. Yet Sally felt overwhelmed with college most of the time. She had a habit of procrastinating on her term papers and preparation for exams. Several sorority sisters resented her "mopiness" and her tendency to come off as helpless, put upon, and passive. She drank heavily on weekends and sometimes even during the week. The next morning, she always felt terrible—hung over and guilty. But the pattern continued. She caught the flu twice last semester and felt TATT—Tired All The Time. Sally's coping style clearly was maladaptive.

Stages of Coping

According to Lazarus and Folkman (1984), you go through three **stages of coping** with a difficult situation (such as three exams, two papers, a speech, and an important date—all within two days). First, you engage in **primary appraisal** of the stressor (or cluster of stressors, as in this example). Here you decide, given your knowledge of yourself and the situation, whether you are potentially threatened or are in jeopardy. In other words, is this worth being concerned about? If the situation is judged to be irrelevant or trivial, the coping process ends. If the circumstance is meaningful and potentially threatening, the stress-coping process continues. In the example just cited, most students would regard this circumstance as meaningful and potentially threatening.

Next, you engage in **secondary appraisal**—you assess your resources for dealing with the stressor. As Holroyd and Lazarus note, this assessment is influenced by "previous experiences in similar situations, generalized beliefs about the self and the environment, and the availability of personal (e.g., physical strength or problem-solving skills) and environmental (e.g., social support or money) resources" (1982, 23). Following our example, you would ask, "Given that I want to succeed in school, given my past experiences and my knowledge of myself, and given my options right now, what will I do to get through this?" Important to this secondary appraisal is an assessment of how much control you have over the situation. The less the perceived control, the more threatening the situation will be and the greater the probability of mental and physical distress.

The third phase is *coping*. You take whatever actions seem appropriate. This response might involve action or a cognitive adjustment—redefining the situation through self-talk—or both. Whether your coping response is helpful and constructive is, of course, another matter (Frese, 1986; Krohne, 1986; Laux, 1986). For example, in facing the college pressures noted earlier, you might decide to organize your next two days very precisely, to avoid distractions, to moderately exercise and eat well, to make up your mind that the best way to get through this temporary crunch is to dig in and work very hard—and to see it all as a manageable challenge.

Coping Resources

Lazarus and Folkman (1984, 159) note that a wide variety of personal and environmental **coping resources** are potentially available as you appraise your options. Antonovsky (1979, 1987) refers to these as **generalized resistance resources.** Included are these examples, all of which are discussed elsewhere in the book:

1. Exercise
2. Situational self-talk skills
3. Positive beliefs

   • Sense of coherence (Stressors are seen as comprehensible, manageable, and meaningful.)
   • Hardiness (sense of challenge, commitment, control)
   • Optimism

4. Problem-solving skills
5. Communication skills
6. Social support
7. Material resources
8. Community services

Constraints Against Using Coping Resources

Of course, internal and environmental **coping constraints** act against using these resources. These include, for example:

   • Guilt
   • Unexpressed anger
   • Hostility
   • Fear
   • Lack of confidence
   • Perceived social prohibitions
   • Unwillingness to seek or accept assistance from others
   • Social norms emphasizing self-sufficiency
   • Lack of financial resources
   • Absence of health care or counseling services
   • Lack of available child-care programs
   • Time

Some of these constraints can be easily overcome through awareness and choice. Others, such as lack of health care, child-care programs, or finances, are not so simple. Thus, some people have a much harder time than others coping with adversity—for both personal and external reasons.

Deliberate Versus Scripted Coping Responses

Are your reactions to stressful events, including your own temporary distress, deliberate or scripted? If you react with little awareness or deliberate choice, you probably behave with **scripted coping responses.** Many people cope in the same ways as their parents without realizing it, handling stressful events much like they did as children. Others respond with thoughtfulness and intention—with **deliberate coping responses.**

Unless you become aware of your coping style, you may be seriously limited by your **life script**—a blueprint for thinking, feeling, and acting that usually emerges from adolescence as a result of repeated early messages and early decisions (James & Jongeward, 1971; Steiner, 1974). As an actor follows a stage script, people most often spend their lives blindly living out their own life script. Included in the script are directives related to:

> See Application Exercise 12-1 to explore your scripted and deliberate coping responses.

- How to be masculine or feminine
- How to get love and attention
- How to feel good about yourself
- How to feel about others
- How to spend time
- Whether to and how to succeed or fail
- How to cope with stressful events

Maturity and independence include freedom from one's life script, especially if it keeps one bound to old, destructive, maladaptive patterns.

COPING OPTIONS

Literally hundreds of **coping options** are available to the individual dealing with specific stressful events and circumstances. It is useful to examine coping categories several experts have identified.

Adaptive Versus Maladaptive Coping

Coping can be **adaptive,** helping the individual deal effectively with stressful events and minimizing distress. Or it can be **maladaptive,** resulting in unnecessary distress for the self or others. Positive coping outcomes depend on having a range of options available and on accurate linkage of options with the situation.

Adaptive coping options, especially when part of a broader positive coping style (cluster of coping habits) contribute to wellness—good health, productivity, life satisfaction, and personal growth. Maladaptive coping options erode wellness. Let us now explore a range of coping options.

Emotion Focus Versus Problem-Solving Focus

Several writers (Folkman, Schaefer, & Lazarus, 1979; Pearlin & Schooler, 1978) have identified two broad coping options:

1. **Emotion-focused coping,** in which the focus is dealing with your own fear, anger, or guilt as you react to the situation.
2. **Problem-focused coping,** in which the focus is attempting to deal constructively with the stressor or circumstance itself. In the example of a crunch of exams, papers,

Figure 12-1

Target and Outcome of Coping

Outcome of Coping	Target of Coping	
	Stressor	Self
Adaptive	Put communication problem on agenda for next meeting.	Share frustrations with friend.
Maladaptive	Blow up at boss.	Drink away frustrations.

a speech, and a date, this option would include deciding how to organize time and energy during the next two days.

Both these options can be adaptive or maladaptive, of course. Figure 12-1 shows the possibilities. A study (Santiago-Revera, 1995) of college students found that interpreting stressful events as challenges rather than threats led to more problem-focused coping. For a review of other studies on the effectiveness of emotion-focused and problem-focused coping, see Auerbach and Gramling (1998, 30).

Five Coping Strategies

Cohen and Lazarus (1979) propose five optional strategies in confronting a stressful event. Let's take the example of airport noise (Taylor, 1986, 202).

Example of Emotion-Focused Coping

This last weekend, I was studying for my exam on Monday, and an incident came up. My roommate came home with three or four other friends from the bars, and they decided they were going to watch TV, and so they did. The only problem was I was trying to study, and they were being extremely noisy. My roommate and his friends were being very inconsiderate about the noise they were making, and it was pissing me off. I had to turn to a coping device in order to keep my cool.

I chose the Emotion-Focused coping method. I am a very hot-tempered person, and something can set me off really quickly, especially this incident with my roommate and his friends. I dealt with my own anger as the problem occurred. I used a method of self-talk, and I was telling myself that I'm in college, it's his house also, and I shouldn't have waited until the last moment to study. I saw it as partly my fault because I could have gone to the library and studied. Instead, I procrastinated and tried to study at my house on a weekend night in Chico. This was not a good choice.

I felt by having a coping device was like having a trump card in my corner. It helped me get through the problem, and I talked to my roommate about the incident the following day. The coping method probably saved me some from blowing up and possibly getting in a fight.

---

1. **Information-seeking** What is the noise level at different neighborhood locations throughout the day?
2. **Direct action** Circulate petitions among neighbors.
3. **Inhibition of action** Control the urge to shoot down the next noisy airplane.
4. **Intrapsychic efforts** Use self-talk to tolerate the noise.
5. **Turning to others** Share frustrations with neighbors, working together to circulate petitions and to confront officials.

See Application Exercise 12-2 to write about the five coping strategies.

The COPE Scale

The COPE Scale (Carver et al., 1989) was developed to measure a range of ways people handle stressful events. Below are the 14 coping styles measured by the scale, together with illustrative questions for each quoted from Kleinke (1998, 7).

- Active coping

  "I take additional action to try to get rid of the problem." "I concentrate my efforts on doing something about it." "I do what has to be done, one step at a time."

- Planning

  "I try to come up with a strategy about what to do." "I make a plan of action." "I think hard about what steps to take."

- Suppression of competing activities

  "I put aside other activities so I can concentrate on this." "I focus on dealing with this problem and, if necessary, let other things slide a little." "I keep myself from getting distracted by other thoughts or activities."

- Restraint coping

  "I force myself to wait for the right time to do something." "I hold off doing anything about it until the situation permits." "I make sure not to make matters worse by acting too soon."

- Seeking social support for instrumental reasons

  "I ask people who have had similar experiences what they did." "I try to get advice from someone about what to do." "I talk to someone to find out more about the situation."

- Seeking social support for emotional reasons

  "I talk to someone about how I feel." "I try to get emotional support from friends or relatives." "I discuss my feelings with someone."

- Positive reinterpretation and growth

  "I look for something good in what is happening." "I try to see it in a different light, to make it seem more positive." "I learn something from the experience."

- Acceptance

  "I learn to live with it." "I accept that this has happened and that it can't be changed." "I get used to the idea that it happened."

- Turning to religion

  "I seek God's help. "I put my trust in God." "I try to find comfort in my religion."

- Focus on and venting emotion

  "I get upset and let my emotions out." "I let my feelings out." "I feel a lot of emotional distress, and I find myself expressing those feelings a lot."

- Denial

  "I refuse to believe that it has happened." "I pretend that it hasn't really happened." "I act as though it hasn't happened."

- Behavioral disengagement

  "I give up the attempt to get what I want." "I just give up trying to reach my goal." "I admit to myself that I can't deal with it and quit trying."

- Mental disengagement

  "I turn to work or other substitute activities to take my mind off things." "I go to movies or watch TV so that I think about it less."

- Alcohol and/or other drugs

  "I use alcohol or drugs to make myself feel better." "I try to lose myself for a while by drinking alcohol or taking drugs." "I use alcohol or drugs to help me get through."

Transformational Versus Regressive Coping

Maddi and Kobasa (1984) maintain that hardiness is likely to lead to **transformational coping**—taking constructive action to change the stressor. This coping option emerges from a sense of internal control, a sense of challenge, and a sense of commitment. Fundamentally, it is based on optimism. This was Maria's approach (described in the Coping Styles box on page 293).

Regressive coping is thinking pessimistically and avoiding the stressor. This was Sally's way (also described in box).

Schafer Coping Model

Having explored various coping approaches, let us now examine a range of options for dealing with stressful situations and your reactions to them, keeping in mind that this is a complex, dynamic, interactional process.

Assuming an event is perceived to be important and sufficiently taxing of your resources to need a response, what are your adaptive options? The following possibilities in the **Schafer coping model** constitute the three A's of adaptive coping. Of course, another option of the maladaptive variety is a fourth A: awfulize about the stressor. But let's stay on the positive side by examining the following options. Each of these steps is discussed in detail in later chapters.

Alter the Stressor

Is the stressor controllable, changeable, or influenceable? Can I take action by myself? Is group action possible and desirable? What are the likely gains and costs for myself and others? This action might include the following:

- Seeking to change a specific situation
- Changing a physical stressor
- Pacing myself and my stressors better
- Spacing my life changes better
- Increasing challenges in my life (if the problem is boredom)
- Organizing time better
- Asking someone to alter his or her behavior

Adapt to the Stressor

Is it best to accept the stressor, finding ways to prevent or lower my distress? These might include:

1. **Manage self-talk**
   Alter irrational beliefs.
   Control situational self-talk.
   Take it less seriously.
   Turn the "threat" into an opportunity.
   See this person or event as temporarily bearable.
   Be okay no matter what.

2. **Control physical stress response**
   Breathing methods
   Muscle relaxation methods
   Mental methods

3. **Manage actions**
   Use effective listening.
   Be assertive.
   Be self-disclosing.
   Use an appropriate communication style.
   Take action that will get all those involved what they want.

4. **Maintain health buffers**
   Exercise
   Nutrition
   Sleep
   Healthy pleasures

5. **Use available coping resources**
   Social support
   Money
   Community or campus services
   Beliefs or faith

6. **Avoid maladaptive reactions to distress**
   Alcohol or drug abuse
   Smoking
   Overeating
   Dumping on or abusing others
   Escapism
   Spending sprees
   Blaming others

Avoid the Stressor

Is it best for me to avoid or withdraw from this stressor? What would be the gains and costs? Have all other options been exhausted?

A briefer and simpler approach brings together many key stress management methods into a single framework, easy to recall with the initials **AAAABBCC.** These are coping options. Consider which fits your challenges best. The first is easiest, of course, and therefore followed by many. Do not stay stuck there.

1. Awfulize about the stressor
2. Alter the stressor
3. Avoid or withdraw from the stressor
4. Accept the stressor, by
5. Breathing away tension
6. Building health buffers

Coping and the Stress Response

The first time Joe gave a class presentation during his first semester in college, he trembled beforehand, sweated, stumbled several times over simple words and phrases, and developed a temporary mental block in the middle of his speech. Afterward, he felt extremely depressed, resolving never to get up before a group again.

Six weeks later, after working with a stress counselor, it was his turn to give another speech. This time he practiced his deep relaxation technique two hours beforehand, practiced his speech before the mirror one hour beforehand, and accepted the modest tension build-up during the hour before the talk as natural. Immediately before his turn arrived, he did a deep-breathing exercise, relaxed his muscles, took his time, and presented a flawless speech with composure. Afterward, he gave himself several internal pats on the back for doing so well—and for mastering his fear of speaking.

7. Changing your interpretation
8. Communicating differently

For an excellent review of research on the outcomes of different coping options under different conditions, see Auerback and Gramling (1998).

The Role of Emotions in Coping: Primary or Secondary?

Read Joe's story in the following box, Coping and the Stress Response. His challenge was to control his stress response in such a way that his speech would be effective the second time around. In short, he needed to learn to control his stress response so his behavior could be up to potential.

In this situation and others like it, emotions, thoughts, and behavior are interwoven in a complex web. The parts can be separated only for purposes of discussion and analysis. In reality, they occur together.

Yet, which do we focus on in the immediate stress situation like Joe's class presentation? A key assumption in this textbook is that although emotions, thinking, body, and behavior are interwoven and inseparable, we use key targets.

- Controlling interpretation of the stressor
- Controlling the physical stress response
- Controlling the behavior or coping response

This leaves out emotions. This does not mean that emotions are unimportant or to be denied. To the contrary, I believe them to be a valuable, central part of human experience, during stress and all other parts of life. But emotions occur and change largely in response to what we think, do, and experience in our bodies. While we will give attention to feelings in this chapter, we assume they can best be controlled or altered by regulating what we think and do and by regulating our bodies.

This view is consistent with Lazarus, who emphasizes the role of mental and behavioral coping in determining emotions. "You will note that this analysis reverses the usual wisdom that coping always follows emotion (or is caused by it) and suggests that coping can precede and even influence its form and intensity" (1975, 553).

Parrino expresses a similar view within his holistic "human response system" framework.

In the human response system model, emotions do not precipitate problems. Rather problems or maladaptive responses lead to emotional upset and disturbance. Human responses such as disordered thinking habits can precipitate anger in frustrating situations. A nervous system that is easily aroused by threatening life events can produce a state of chronic anxiety and tension. Behavioral habits such as procrastination can induce deep states of depression. In summary, habits of living are seen as the instigators of emotional reactions. (1979)

Of course, through a loop-back effect, emotions in turn affect physical arousal, thinking, and behavior. But in terms of a stress control strategy, it is best in stressful situations to approach emotions indirectly through one of these other channels, rather than directly. In fact, this probably is the only way.

EXTINGUISHING MALADAPTIVE REACTIONS TO DISTRESS

Part of the coping is reacting to one's own temporary distress. Handling distress maladaptively means trying to reduce it in ways that make it worse for the self or others. Many times what seems constructive in the short run (getting high on drugs or buzzed on alcohol) turns out to be destructive in the long run.

A great proportion of stress problems seen by physicians, therapists, and stress consultants are not from reactions to original stressors but are outcomes of coping behavior that makes things worse rather than better.

Just as one must identify and change destructive ways of coping with stressors, so must we recognize our maladaptive reactions to our own distress. Let us now examine some of these maladaptive reactions to distress, what effects they have, and how they can be reduced or extinguished. In each case, the key to stopping is substituting constructive alternatives.

Alcohol Abuse

According to the American Psychiatric Association's official manual on psychiatric disorders (1987), two alcohol disorders exist. The first is alcohol abuse, distinguished by repeated use of alcohol in physically hazardous situations or continued use in the face of knowledge that doing so worsens a personal problem. The second, more serious disorder is **alcohol dependence.** Here, all the symptoms of alcohol abuse occur, plus the inability to control the drinking. *Tolerance* often occurs at this stage—increasing amounts of alcohol are needed to achieve the desired effect. *Withdrawal* usually is present, in which shakiness, malaise, or behavioral disturbance accompany stopping or reducing consumption.

National per-capita alcohol consumption has increased during the past three decades, rising 33 percent since 1964 (Prokop et al., 1991). According to the National Center for Health Statistics (1989), about 8 percent of the adult American population drinks heavily—1 ounce or more of pure alcohol per day. The rate of heavy drinking is nearly 5 times greater for males than females. Approximately one tenth of the U.S. population consumes about half of the alcoholic beverages sold in this country.

Alcohol consumption is higher among younger age groups, especially males, than often thought. For example, national surveys of the young in 1985 revealed that 34 percent of males and 28 percent of females between ages 12 and 17 had used alcohol during the past month. Fully 78 percent of men and 64 percent of women between 18 and 25 reported use during the past month (National Center for Health Statistics, 1989).

College Student Drinking

CHICAGO (AP)—Nearly half of U.S. college students are binge drinkers who make life miserable for much of the other half, according to a survey.

"Students on campuses where there's a lot of binge drinking are affected in a number of ways—including physical assault, sexual harassment, property damage and interrupted sleep or study time," said Henry Wechsler, director of the Alcohol Studies Program at Harvard School of Public Health.

His team surveyed 17,592 students on 140 campuses nationwide last year. Findings appear in Wednesday's *Journal of the American Medical Association.*

Forty-four percent reported binging on alcohol, defined as downing five drinks in a row for men or four in a row for women on at least one occasion in the two weeks before the survey. Nineteen percent of all students were frequent bingers, defined as those who have had at least three binges during the period.

Binge drinkers were seven times as likely to have unprotected sex as a non-binge drinker, 10 times as likely to drive after drinking and 11 times as likely to fall behind in school, the survey found.

At about one-third of the schools, more than 50 percent of students were bingers. At another third, fewer than 35 percent were bingers.

At the big drinking schools, sober students were twice as likely as those at the lowest-level schools to be insulted or humiliated; to be pushed, hit or assaulted; and to experience unwanted sexual advances from drinking students.

They were also about 2½ times as likely to sustain property damage; to end up taking care of a drunken student; and to have their study or sleep interrupted because of classmates' drinking, the survey revealed.

Wechsler said sober students should "be encouraged to speak up and not to tolerate the impairment to the quality of their colleges."

Katharine C. Lyall, president of University of Wisconsin System, agreed. "We have a host of orientation programs and counseling programs that are directed at the binge drinkers, but quite frankly they've not been very successful," said Lyall, who chaired the advisory board for the Harvard study.

Jeffrey Merrill, vice president of the Center on Addiction and Substance Abuse at Columbia University in New York, said the study "provides a tremendous amount of evidence about the need to rethink this whole problem on college campuses."

Source: Paulsen (1994, 46)

A 1989 Gallup Poll found that among those who drink, 35 percent answered "yes" when asked, "Do you sometimes drink more than you should?" This response was given by 42 percent of the males who drink, compared with 26 percent of female drinkers. The age group with the highest percent responding "yes" was 18–29 years (Gallup Poll, 1990).

Costs of alcohol abuse are extremely high in this country: premature death from liver disease, fatal auto accidents associated with drunk driving, lost productivity and absenteeism, spousal and child abuse, crime, incarceration, medical treatment, and more.

Driving under the influence of alcohol can produce unwanted residual distress.

Combined costs from these and other consequences of alcohol abuse are estimated to total more than $100 billion each year (Green & Shellenberger, 1991).

Alcohol advertisements add to the problem by helping reinforce the beliefs, now translated into widely shared social norms, that by drinking you will be transformed into someone better than you are—and that you "deserve a drink." One of my students wrote:

> Alcohol ads tell us that alcohol will make us sexier, more creative, more power-ful, and will help us to buffer the punches of a cruel world. They tell us we have a right to drink—we worked for it; we deserve it.

> We deserve to Partyyyy! After a long week of dealing with professional egos (at school or work), irate customers, demanding mates, George Bush with his finger on the trigger, a hole in the ozone, we deserve a cold one, or two—and we don't need to feel guilty about it. We can handle it. We know when to stop. We know what our limits are. And if we want to start the weekend early on Thursday or Wednesday, that's okay too. We're Americans, we have rights, so pour us up an-other one!

Clearly, advertising and social norms create a climate in which alcohol becomes a convenient means of dulling anxiety and depression. Moreover, a recent study reveals that even modest viewing of music videos on TV resulted in substantial exposure to glamoriz-ing depictions of alcohol and tobacco use and that such use is often coupled with sexuality (DuRant et al., 1997). Students must be aware that alcohol and drug abuse can harm their educational process—as well as their health. Certainly, alcohol and drugs are destructive approaches to "feel better" in times of pressure.

A commonly accepted guideline is slight or moderate consumption (no more than a single drink daily) for healthy people without central nervous system, liver, cardiovascu-lar, or gastrointestinal disorders. Any more than this should never be used as a means of coping with tension, upset, or distress.

A key problem, of course, is that in many subcultures heavy use of alcohol is sup-ported as acceptable coping behavior—social norms that receive strong support from al-cohol advertisements. Closely related is the social norm equating "a good time" or "party-ing" with heavy drinking. A persistent danger is that many individuals, especially those with a family history of alcoholism, probably inherit a genetic predisposition to become addicted to alcohol. What begins as "good times" in youth too often transforms in later years into severe alcoholism.

A recent and promising approach to reducing binge drinking among college students is to wage information campaigns to decrease the number of students who believe binge drinking is the norm (Haines & Spear, 1996). The researchers state, "Display ads appeared weekly in the campus newspaper; flyers highlighting the actual drinking norms on cam-pus were distributed; and pamplets were put in high student traffic areas." The result over five years was a significant drop in the both the perception and actual amount of binge drinking.

Smoking

The bottom line is that smoking will increase chances of dying prematurely from heart at-tack, lung cancer, emphysema or bronchitis, pneumonia, or stroke. Roglieri (1980, 81) es-timates the odds of death from each of these causes increased as shown in Figure 12-2, compared with nonsmokers. Still, the percentage of first-year college students who smoke reached the highest level in many years during 1997, with 16 percent reporting they smoke frequently, up from only 9 percent in 1987 (Hayward, 1998).

Figure 12-2

Increases in Mortality Risk

	1–1½ Packs per Day	2 Packs or More Per Day
HEART ATTACK	80 percent	220 percent
LUNG CANCER	480 percent	500 percent
BRONCHITIS/EMPHYSEMA	70 percent	210 percent
PNEUMONIA	300 percent	300 percent
STROKE	50 percent	50 percent

Source: Roglieri (1980, 81)

The idea that smoking reduces stress is a cruel illusion. Smoking decreases energy level for coping with daily hassles. By coating the lungs with tar and nicotine, by surrounding red cells with carbon monoxide, by making it more difficult for them to transport oxygen, and by accelerating heart rate, smoking means less ability to take in, circulate, and use oxygen—hence a greater struggle to do the same as a nonsmoker can do more easily, other things being equal.

Smokers may feel a lessening of tension from drawing that first smoke after a 20- to 40-minute break from smoking. But ironically, this is a slight reduction of tension caused by a mini-withdrawal crisis from going 20 to 40 minutes without a cigarette. The cigarette

---

Health Benefits of Smoking Cessation

Here are major conclusions of a report from the U.S. surgeon general on stopping smoking.

1. Smoking cessation has major and immediate health benefits for persons of all ages and provides benefits for persons with and without smoking-related disease.
2. Former smokers live longer than continuing smokers.
3. Smoking cessation decreases the risk for lung and other cancers, heart attack, stroke, and chronic lung disease.
4. Women who stop smoking before pregnancy or during the first three to four months of pregnancy reduce their risk for having a low-birth-weight infant to that of women who never smoked.
5. The health benefits of smoking cessation substantially exceed any risks from the average five-pound weight gain or any adverse psychological effects that may follow quitting.

Source: Surgeon General of the United States (1990)

A Nation of Drug Users

"Americans represent only 2 percent of the world population, but consume 60 percent of the world's illicit drugs," says Dr. Arnold Washton, an expert on addiction.

"If that is not an indictment of our culture, I don't know what is."

Washton is coauthor of a new study that provides some clues to a question rarely touched in the debate over the war on drugs: Why do Americans use more drugs than anyone else?

Experts say U.S. per-capita consumption of illicit drugs is the world's highest. In addition, millions abuse prescription drugs from tranquilizers to sleeping pills. Alcohol and tobacco, usually excluded from the drug debate, account for 450,000 deaths a year.

"We are not only talking about cocaine or crack," Washton said. "We are now seeing high school kids who are getting high from typewriter correction fluid. We are becoming a nation of compulsive drug users, a chemical people."

The reason is rooted in a society driven by obsessions with perfection, performance, possessions, money, and power, according to the study, titled *Willpower's Not Enough.* At the same time, the support traditionally provided by the extended family or community is breaking down. In this environment, the study says, people are vulnerable to the temptation of "mood changers."

Addictions in the United States go beyond drugs, according to Washton. No other country has as many compulsive overeaters (estimated at 40 million to 60 million) or gamblers (12 million).

"It is a form of collective insanity to believe that if all illicit drugs were somehow removed from this country, we would become a society of non-compulsive, life-embracing people," said Washton, director of the Washton Institute on Addictions in New York and founder of the first national cocaine hot line.

The fact that so many other types of compulsive behavior are springing up testifies to the fallacy of that belief.

Source: Debussman (1990)

relieves tension caused by the very addiction to smoking. Smoking not only shortens life, decreases coping ability through less energy, and creates tension, but it also decreases life chances and causes immediate discomfort for those who must inhale secondary smoke. It is expensive and a poor example for children. Smoking is a maladaptive response of the worst kind to distress.

The American Cancer Society, the American Lung Association, the Seventh Day Adventist Church, and other groups now conduct very effective smoking cessation programs. Recent evidence suggests that stopping cold turkey may be the most effective way. Social support from others helps make the struggle easier.

Drugs

Prescribed medications sometimes are temporarily useful and appropriate in reducing stress, as we will explain later in this chapter. Unfortunately, the "pill for every ill" approach is widely embedded in the popular mind and in medical practice.

Drugs and the Gospel of Materialism

The following letter appeared in the *Chico Enterprise-Record*. The author, Albert Mitchell (1989), clearly believes the solution to the U.S. drug problem must go deeper than Red Ribbon Day or "Just Saying No." *What do you think?*

Dear Editor—

Who is kidding who? This nation has a drug abuse problem for the simple reason that American society has been, for the most part, spiritually dead for years. There is an emptiness that millions seek to assuage by indulging in booze, pills, crack, uppers, downers, heroin, whatever.

The most gigantic communications juggernaut the world has ever seen—television, radio, motion pictures, the press, billboards—are at work incessantly preaching the gospel of materialism to the corporate consumer cattle we have become.

Never has a nation been so ravaged by venality, by greed. Anyone with sufficient money can have a go at raping society if it is thought a buck can be made doing so. In the process we have created vast fear, vast suspicion, vast loneliness, vast emptiness of spirit.

"Just say no," we say to the kids, or "Let's all wear a red ribbon to show we're against all that stuff." This simplistic prattle goes on while other Americans go about coughing up over two hundred billion dollars a year to pay off drug suppliers around the world. Why do they do so? Because there is a spiritual vacuum.

We have created a society that is lawless, greedy, self-indulgent, with a devil-take-the-hindmost attitude toward the weak, the poor, the elderly. The fault lies not with Colombia, or the poppy fields of Peru or Thailand. The fault lies with a society whose great god is money. A society where greed tramples on whatever lies in its path.

We reap the whirlwind, and it is of our own making. Until we do something about reordering our rapacious society there will be drugs, drugs, and more drugs.

—Albert Mitchell

Three groups of psychoactive substances are widely used to relieve tension.

1. **Depressants:** tranquilizers, barbiturates, and alcohol, for example
2. **Stimulants:** caffeine, cocaine, and amphetamines, for example
3. **Distortants:** LSD, mescaline, and marijuana, for example

In the short run, all these may relieve distress by one means or another. However, in the long run, they lose their effectiveness because of increased tolerance to the drug, because the stress triggers remain the same, because the person's ability to cope with the stressors remains undeveloped, or some combination of these reasons. The diminished capacity to cope through drug-induced numbness or psychological distortion may increase tension later. Psychological or physical dependency becomes worse, and tension increases in the long run. A surge of dopamine may be the mechanism through which addition occurs (Nash, 1997).

Yet illegal drug use continues to mount. So does reliance by patients on prescribed stress-related medications. Valium alone is consumed to the tune of 3.2 billion pills per year in the United States—a $25 million business in itself. Except for short-run, special situations, medications are a nonproductive, ineffective substitute for long-term relief of distress, although as psychologist Allen Kanter states, "We're a consumer-oriented society, so the idea of using drugs to solve problems is completely consistent with the way that we approach much of life" (Gabrels, 1997, 1). Alternatives suggested in this book are far better.

Here is a sound principle to follow: Do not take anything to feel better emotionally, except after careful consideration with your physician. In this respect, Virshup states, "I raised three teenagers who were exposed to the drug scene, yet survived and thrived. I like to think that advice I gave them was of some help. I suggested: don't use anything in order to feel better when you are feeling bad" (1987, 169).

Overeating

Curiously, calorie consumption per person in the United States has decreased since 1900, yet the percentage of the population at least 20 percent overweight has increased dramatically. This has been caused largely by decreasing physical activity throughout the population, as we have suburbanized, industrialized, mechanized, and "automobilized." An increased percentage of fat in our diets has contributed to a lesser extent. So, too, no doubt, has been the tendency to eat in response to stress—especially when food is high in sugar or fat.

Eating to "relieve" tension is learned often in childhood. Mother feeds the child at any sign of distress. As a consequence, the child may never learn to distinguish between hunger and emotions such as fear, anxiety, and anger. Any state of arousal is experienced as hunger. In other cases, the child learns by parental example that a quick way to deal with tension is to stuff it, hide it, and not let it out by overeating.

I have found that about half of those I ask in workshops about appetite during stress report an increase, the other half a decrease. For many, it depends on the type of stress: overeating (often through hurried stuffing) during anger, irritation, or rush but losing appetite during worry or apprehension, or vice versa.

Overeating is a maladaptive response to distress for several reasons.

1. It often evokes guilt.
2. The stress emotion remains.
3. It ignores the distress-producing situation.
4. It adds weight. More weight means less energy. More weight often erodes self-liking.

Finding suitable substitutes for eating binges or chronic overeating in response to stress is vital. Regular aerobic exercise is perhaps the best alternative of all, because it will reduce inches and pounds at the same time that it helps relieve physical and emotional tension.

Escapism

In coping with original stressors, escapism through television, flight, drugs, books, or fantasy can be highly destructive. The stress response is likely to remain elevated, the distress emotion denied, and the stress triggers unchanged. While temporary, intelligently used withdrawal may be constructive, escapism as a habit is potentially dangerous, both for the self and others.

Spending Sprees

Often part of a manic-type response to tension, this can be devastating in its consequences. Like escapism, careless spending is actually a form of evasion of true stress emotions and the original situation.

Physical and Verbal Abuse

Too often, personal distress does not remain personal. Rather, it is transferred to others in the form of physical and verbal abuse. Tragically, we seem to take out our frustrations on those closest to us—especially our spouses, lovers, and children. Recent studies show a surprisingly high percentage of college students are involved in abusive love relationships. Most homicides are inflicted on friends or family members. Wife beating and child abuse are among the most destructive of all reactions to our own distress.

Blaming Others

By blaming others, one can temporarily escape responsibility both for being distressed and for doing anything about it.

Overworking

Another form of deflection is overworking. Digging in harder sometimes is a way to reduce distress. Often, however, it is a temporary palliative, ultimately multiplying problems for health, frame of mind, and family.

Denial

The subculture of masculinity is especially prone to teach boys and men: "keep moving," "if you don't think about it, it will go away," "be tough," "boys don't cry," and, above all, "look strong." Temporary denial may be useful for seeing a difficult event or period through, but not when it is extended for very long. The result for both men and women who use this response to stress for extended periods is internal wear and tear until relationships and performances are seriously affected, emotional disturbances become extreme, or the body breaks.

Magnification

"Making a mountain out of a molehill" can directly add to a stress buildup already started by other stressors. In essence, the stress response itself becomes a new stressor. This is a common maladaptive reaction to stress that needs to be extinguished. One approach is to ask: What is the worst possible outcome of this situation? Usually, you will find you could live even with that outcome.

Martyrdom

Unfortunately, many people are habituated to distress—so addicted that they go out of their way to find it. This happens not out of deliberate choice, but because misery and pain are so familiar the person seems to need his or her daily dose. The repetition compulsion overpowers the drive toward growth.

Self-created distress is perpetuated by rackets or games (Berne, 1964). **Rackets** are what people produce inside their heads to keep themselves miserable—angry, anxious, or afraid. **Games** refer to interpersonal exchanges people use to make themselves or others feel bad. A "kick-me" game player handles distress by encouraging others to make him or her feel useless or incompetent. A "stupid" player blunders again and again in order to be constantly reminded by others how inept or dependent he or she is.

Strange as it may seem, many people who have a history of distress go to great lengths to cope with their distress by creating more of it—thereby playing out their life script as a loser. This often is the tragic story of the alcoholic, the heroin addict, the habitual criminal, or the psychotic. Changing this pattern requires enormous courage, awareness, and support. Most of all, it requires overcoming the immense inertia of the repetition compulsion.

Except when very stressful circumstances cannot be changed or when temporary distress is self-chosen for a good reason (like preparing for a concert performance), the approach of simply living with distress is unacceptable to people who seek good health and self-development. A better way usually exists.

Lethal Effects of Maladaptive Responses to Distress

These, then, are illustrative maladaptive responses to distress. Focusing on death, the ultimate distressful side effect of maladaptive coping responses, Roglieri (1980) estimates that through the effects of overeating, depression (which he takes to be a type of coping rather than a distress symptom), smoking, heavy drinking, and high blood pressure about 5 or 6 of every 1,000 white men aged 40–45 will die an early death directly as a result of "mismanagement of stress." This does not include, of course, the contribution of the original stress itself to various causes of death, such as heart attacks or cancer. Roglieri argues that you are responding inappropriately to your distress if:

1. You light up a cigarette whenever challenged by a person, event, or situation.
2. You take a drink in response to, or in anticipation of, a stressful event.
3. You put your heart into your driving by speeding or driving aggressively.
4. You use food to calm yourself down.
5. You feel your heart beating rapidly or your heart pounding when frustrated (indicating high blood pressure).
6. You use sleeping pills or tranquilizers frequently.
7. You become depressed (loss of appetite, loss of sleep, and loss of libido).

Roglieri concludes, "Because prolonged dependence on these inappropriate mechanisms for dealing with stress leads to a lifestyle that increases your risk of premature death and disability, these habits have been referred to as 'slow motion suicide'" (1980, 202). Short of that, these and other maladaptive responses to distress lessen the quality of life for others, if not oneself.

STRENGTHENING ADAPTIVE REACTIONS TO DISTRESS

Medications

Most stress experts believe medications are overprescribed and overused. Yet there are four conditions when they may be called for.

1. **To reduce intense pain.** Certainly, medications are called for in cases of terminal cancer, postsurgery, accident trauma, intense headaches, and other intensely painful stress-induced pain.
2. **When a temporary crisis interferes with the ability to carry on with daily life.** A prescribed relaxant may help you to continue to function until the circumstances are resolved by lowering your anxiety level, raising your mood in times of depression, or helping you sleep.
3. **Chronic long-term disturbances.** Included, for example, are schizophrenia, hypertension, and manic depression.

4. **When life is threatened by elevated stress.** For example, if a heart patient has anxiety-induced arrhythmias that could cause cardiac arrest, tranquilizers certainly may be called for.

After reviewing available literature on sleeping patterns, the National Academy of Medicine Institute of Sciences concluded that rarely, if ever, should sleeping pills be prescribed for longer than 2 to 4 weeks (Roglieri, 1980). Similarly, other medications usually should be viewed as temporary treatment while attempts are made to find long-term coping and lifestyle buffer methods.

Solitude

When was the last time you were away by yourself, truly alone, for 24 hours? Forty-eight hours? A week? Ever? We are in almost constant contact with others—and need to be for emotional and practical reasons. Yet we also can benefit from being alone from time to time, perhaps routinely each year for a few days, perhaps occasionally to remove ourselves from stressful situations (Buchholz, 1998). As I write this, I am in a mountain cabin, truly alone, and I have been for many days. The experience is exhilarating—the opportunity to focus, rest, renew my spirit, appreciate the environment, and experience simplicity. For more on solitude in modern life, read Anne Morrow Lindberg's *Gifts From the Sea* (Lindberg, 1978). This is a beautiful, inspiring personal statement about the beauty of solitude.

Professional Assistance

This book is based on the principle of personal responsibility for one's health and stress control. In the past, far too much reliance has been placed on one or another professional: the doctor, the chiropractor, the minister, the psychologist, the marriage counselor, and the social worker. The techniques presented throughout this textbook can be learned and used at home, using your good judgment and willpower. Certain circumstances can be identified, however, when professional assistance definitely is called for.

- To learn more about specific stress control methods, such as aerobic exercise, meditation, massage, time management, and active listening
- To express frustrations, worries, plans, and the like to an objective trained listener
- To jointly solve a specific problem
- To trace under careful guidance the present or past roots of a specific emotional or practical problem in order to leave or solve it
- To receive a massage or other physical treatment
- To receive inspiration to do something on your own
- To receive group support for a lifestyle change

Hobbies

Favorite recreational activities— gardening, woodworking, golf, backpacking, photography, fishing, hunting, rock collecting, birdwatching, or watching professional basketball on television—can all help prevent or reduce distress in several ways.

- Diversion—getting away from the stressor
- Solitude
- Companionship

- Enhancement of self-worth
- Play
- Appreciation of the minor nature of your immediate problem within the larger picture

Exercise

In Chapter 13 you will read extensive evidence that exercise is a highly effective coping step—perhaps the most effective of any presented in this textbook. Consistent daily or near-daily aerobic exercise can serve as prevention of distress, a type of health buffer. When you are going through a difficult period—interpersonal conflict, adjustment to a new circumstance like a job or new college, depression, time pressure, even overload—exercise can help release physical tension, lift you out of an emotional pit, provide time to plan solutions, and more. By itself, of course, exercise will not solve problems. But it can certainly help bring forth the strength and creativity to approach those problems with zest and vitality.

Deep Relaxation

Meditation, yoga, self-hypnosis, and other methods for eliciting the relaxation response have been used for centuries to cope with the stressors of daily living. Like exercise, deep relaxation is best utilized as an everyday, routine part of living. As such, it becomes a natural part of one's repertoire of coping tools. Deep relaxation restores energy, yields creative solutions to problems, and creates mental and physical calm for facing difficult episodes. Deep relaxation is discussed in more detail in Chapter 15.

Play

George Sheehan, the runner/doctor/author, has stated that humanity is animal, child, scholar, and saint (Sheehan, 1978). Perhaps it would be more accurate to say it is *potentially* all of these. Too often, an imbalance is reached where the animal and the child are lost in the quest for money and status. Play is part of a good balance. Whether through active games, dance, running, Frisbee, cards, pranks, parties, or practical jokes, play can be enormously valuable in dealing with periods of distress—and in reducing chances of its occurrence in the first place.

Reflect on your answers to these questions: How much fun and playfulness are you having? How much time are you taking for your playful self? What would you most like to do during the next two weeks to lift your morale and provide a fun diversion? If you have fallen prey to the trap of all work/no play, see what specific steps you can take to bring a better balance back into your life.

During periods of overload, trauma, or depression, play seems far away. Yet it can be created, rediscovered. One of the gifts children give to adults is to stimulate us to play every now and then. Try it.

Prayer

For centuries, prayer has been used to cope with tension. Prayer perhaps can be effective. Repetition of a verse as a focus of meditation can be relaxing. In fact, the relaxation response can be produced just as during secular methods of meditation. The time away praying can lower activity level and anxiety. Prayer can increase hope and optimism. It can bring practical solutions. It can help tune in to one's "inner voice," which can be a source of enlightenment and direction. All these benefits can occur whatever one assumes about divine intervention—which may be the most important benefit of all.

Certainly, the belief in divine guidance and solace helps create a positive self-fulfilling prophecy. Unfortunately, the religious pathway sometimes leads to dependency and escape from personal responsibility for managing stress. Yet managing stress wisely through awareness of self-direction is entirely consistent with religious belief and practice. After all, God helps those who help themselves.

Intimacy

Unfortunately, marriage or courtship can be terribly destructive, adding to, rather than lessening, distress during difficult periods. Yet perhaps no more powerful antidote to weariness, tension, being upset, or depression exists than the authentic touching of two human spirits at the level of true intimacy. Something magical can happen that words fail to convey. Spirits rekindle, barriers come down, true emotion emerges from its submerged place, reassurance is given, and distress lessens.

The adaptive responses to temporary distress discussed in this section are a mere sampling of all the specific possibilities in our individual lives. Many other approaches are discussed in other chapters. Still other very useful techniques are not discussed in this textbook at all. The important thing is to view yourself as an experiment-of-one—find what works for you in responding constructively to temporary upset and tension.

A theme of this book is that managing stress is not a matter of simply surviving. It is worthwhile to achieve higher levels of well-being, which includes thriving under pressure. We now turn to "**coping-plus**"—approaches to thriving under pressure.

THRIVING UNDER PRESSURE

Pressure's the name of the game today. Not just the pressure to get ahead but the stress of trying to make it in a world where every time you look up the rules of the game have changed. There's good reason we feel pressured. The world around us is becoming more competitive and less predictable with each passing day. In the past forty years the human race has entered the atomic age, the space age and the computer age. (Kriegel & Kriegel, 1984, xiii)

In a rapidly changing, fast-paced, competitive world, **thriving under pressure** is vital for health, enjoyment, and success. Sometimes pressure is a specific event (a final exam or speech), other times an ongoing circumstance (senior year in college or adapting to single parenthood after a divorce). Here are other examples.

- The high school student striving for a respectable grade point average.
- The university sophomore (a music major) taking a chemistry final.
- The college athlete performing at a young age before thousands or even millions.
- The young professional seeking upward mobility in her corporation.
- The NBA star stepping to the free-throw line with the score tied in the final 20 seconds of the seventh game of the championship series.
- The single working mother with a family to care for at the same time her job exerts high demands.
- The business executive with hundreds of employees and stockholders depending on her decision-making abilities.

- The surgeon making vital decisions and moves under the operating-room spotlight and with a life depending on him.
- The public official whose every move is watched by the public and the press while he makes decisions affecting thousands of people and millions of dollars.

Thriving under pressure, then, is a challenge in many circumstances and at any age. *Stress Management for Wellness* means more than relaxing or escaping in order to avoid pressure. It means being all you can be. It means reaching higher and higher levels of well-being, performance, and fulfillment. In short, it means not only surviving but thriving, even under the most difficult circumstances. As a first step, we will examine a study of stress and health—of thriving under pressure—among local public officials.

Thriving Under Public Pressure

A colleague of mine, Barbara Gard, served for 12 years as a city council member in a northern California community. During that time, she was struck by the many local elected officials she met at statewide meetings who seemed to love their political service, despite its time demands and frequent public criticism. We decided to look into the matter further by conducting an informal survey of local elected officials at several conferences she attended (Schafer & Gard, 1986).

When asked "Do you enjoy your job as an elected official?," 90 percent of the 85 subjects responded "very much," and the other 10 percent said "somewhat." None responded "not very" or "not at all." It would appear, then, that the vast majority thrived on the pressures of this elected position.

We were also interested in how these people coped with the stress they did experience. A number of options were given, and they could write in their own responses as well. The most commonly used methods were these:

- Exercise
- Taking vacations
- Watching television
- Reading
- Participating in sports
- Watching movies

Written comments included:

"I believe in taking the job seriously but not personally."
"Through the years I've learned that all you can do is your best. As long as I have done my best, I don't worry."
"Interpersonal conflict with fellow council members—I love it."
"I rarely feel stress about anything."
"Keeping a balance in job council position and family is a never-ending struggle. With a large family still at home, I feel the diversity of my roles helps eliminate stress" (Schafer & Gard, 1986, 8).

This modest study suggests that respondents in our small sample of elected local officials genuinely enjoyed their public service and that they experienced relatively little distress despite the presence of a host of potential irritants. Moreover, they seemed to cope quite effectively with the little stress they did develop. They thrived under pressure.

After reading about the above study of city council members, several city managers—those persons hired by city councils to manage city government—requested "equal time."

They asserted that, although city council members might score low on measures of their own stress, they often are stress-givers—to city managers. They wondered how city managers might compare with city council members, as well as with other professions.

Our curiosity whetted, we decided to conduct a mailed survey of city managers in California to investigate how stress is experienced by members of this very challenging profession. Two hundred nineteen of the 404 city managers responded (Schafer & Gard, 1988a; 1988b). Comparison of our sample with a previous study suggested we had tapped a representative sample of California city managers. The average age was 46 years, 71 percent had graduate degrees, and 96 percent were male. The average time as a city manager was 10 years; the average time in their present position was 6 years.

One of our objectives was to identify the stressors causing these city managers the most distress during the past year. Figure 12-3 shows the 15 top-scoring stressors. It is clear that city managers found themselves the objects of frequent role conflict and role overload, with pressures to perform, lack of support, inadequate resources, weighty decisions, and more.

To our surprise, their average distress-symptom score was only 18—very low compared with most other occupations we had studied. Clearly, most city managers seemed to sustain very well the rigors of a very challenging job.

We went one step further. Among these high-functioning officials, who seemed especially to thrive? What were the characteristics, attitudes, and habits of those who scored especially low in distress symptoms?

To investigate these questions, we divided the sample into two groups: those who scored in the highest 75 percent on the Distress Symptom Scale and those who scored in the lowest 25 percent. We then compared key differences between the two groups.

Here are some of the key findings (Schafer & Gard, 1988b).

Low-stress city managers scored lower in Type A behavior, measured with the Framingham Type A Scale.

Figure 12-3

Ranking of Stressors Reported by Managers During Past Year

1. Having to tolerate council members who spend too much time on trivial matters and too little time on larger policy matters
2. Chronic overload
3. Pressures from individual council members
4. Too little funding to provide needed level and quality of services
5. Constant interruptions in work
6. Having to discipline or fire employees
7. Too few staff
8. Staff not sufficiently competent or responsive
9. Weight of responsibility for entire city government
10. (Tie) Lack of support from council
    Conflict between politics and professional management
12. Dealing with uninformed, unintelligent, or incompetent council members
13. Work intrudes into personal or family life (for example, after-hours calls, meetings)
14. Labor relations
15. Dealing with unethical or illegal requests from council members

Source: Schafer & Gard (1988a, 15)

Low-stress city managers scored higher in hardiness, measured with a 12-item hardiness scale (Kobasa, 1984).

Low-stress city managers reported better health and higher energy levels. Of course, good health can be seen as both cause and effect in relation to job stress. Stress drains energy and contributes to illness. Viewed differently, good health helps buffer against distress. Since our survey was cross-sectional (a single point in time), we cannot distinguish between cart and horse. For clues as to why low-stress city managers scored higher in health and energy, it is useful to note differences in their patterns of exercise.

Low-stress city managers were more likely to engage in some form of aerobic exercise, they exercised longer per session, and they exercised more times per week. Nearly 9 of 10 in the total sample reported regularly engaging in some form of exercise. Three of four participated in some form of aerobic fitness activity.

Low-stress city managers were set apart, not by their more frequent use of constructive coping methods, but by their less frequent use of negative ones. Specifically, low-stress city managers were less likely to do the following to help them cope with temporary distress, based on responses to a checklist of more and less constructive coping methods:

• Drink more wine, beer, or liquor than usual
• Just suffer through and endure the problem as best you can
• Become more careful and conscientious than usual—like checking and rechecking your work
• Allow yourself to become more irritable
• Treat or indulge yourself—like buying something you wanted
• Avoid other people, get away by yourself
• Work harder than usual—either at home or at your job
• Sleep more than usual
• Get in the car and drive

Caution is needed in drawing conclusions from these findings about the effectiveness of specific coping methods. Yet it does appear that low-stress city managers were less inclined toward escapism, withdrawal, and irritability, as well as toward less compulsiveness in work. No statistically significant differences appeared among constructive coping methods.

Low-stress city managers reported higher job satisfaction, more inclination to choose the same career again, and higher overall happiness scores.

The city manager profession is among the most challenging—and potentially stressful—of any in this country. Yet as a group this sample of city managers scored low in distress symptoms and high in job satisfaction. We have noted a number of attitudes and behavior patterns of those who scored especially low in distress symptoms. These are people who seem to thrive under pressure.

Beyond Survival: Lessons From a Vietnam POW

When a younger friend, neighbor, and kayaking buddy of mine introduced me to his father, who was visiting from Hawaii, I was struck the father's immediate impression of strength, confidence, ease, and depth. Later I asked what his father does for a living. He responded that Gerald Coffee, his father, was a full-time speaker. When I then asked, what kind of a speaker, he said his father was an inspirational speaker, appearing before all manner of corporate, professional, and community groups on the topic "Beyond Survival." His talk, David said, was based on the father's lessons from 7 years as a prisoner of war in Hanoi between 1966 and 1973. David was 3 when his father was shot down just off the North Vietnamese shore. David's brother was born soon after the imprisonment.

During coming months, I listened to an audiotape and watched a videotape of his dad's lecture, then read his amazing and inspiring book, *Beyond Survival: Building on The Hard Times—A POW's Inspiring Story (1990)*. In both spoken and written word, Capt. Coffee recounts the incredible trials—physical, mental, spiritual—he and his colleagues went through. They were tortured, threatened many times with death, given selective and inaccurate information from back home, separated from one another for long periods while in solitary confinement, forbidden to talk, given minimal and barely digestible food, and more. Through it all, Capt. Coffee and his fellow officers never lost hope or support for one another, made possible through an elaborate secret code that the guards were never able to break. Nor did they lose their humor.

Upon his return, Capt. Coffee resolved that his 7 years of confinement would not be wasted. Instead, he would look back, learn from the experience, and share with others not only how to survive adversity but how to go beyond survival. His message is best summarized in his own words, spoken at a church reception upon his return to his Florida home:

> Each and every day I felt your thoughts and your prayers and the faith that you were keeping in me. In fact, faith was really the key to my survival all those years. Faith in myself to simply pursue my duty to the best of my ability and ultimately return home with honor. Faith in my fellow man, starting with all of you here, knowing you would be looking out for my family, and faith in my comrades in those various cells and cell blocks in prison, men upon whom I depended and who in turn depended upon me, sometimes desperately. Faith in my country, its institutions and our national purpose and cause, especially the one in Southeast Asia all those years. And, of course, faith in my God—truly, as all of you know, the foundation for it all (Coffee, 1990, 278).

10 *C*'s for Thriving Under Pressure

From these city managers and other high-functioning persons, we learn that no single coping practice makes the difference. Rather, it is a combination of positive practices that enables us to thrive under chronic pressure. Most of these practices can be drawn together into a single framework we have termed "the 10 *C*'s for thriving under pressure" (Schafer & Gard, 1986). You will note that this formulation includes the components of hardiness, the Type C pattern, health buffers, coping styles, and more. Explanations for each of the 10 *C*'s as they appear in Figure 12-4 follow.

See Application Exercise 12-3 to assess your strengths and weaknesses among the 10 *C*'s of thriving under pressure.

Conditioning refers especially to regular exercise but also includes good nutritional and sleep habits.

Caring refers to participating in supportive, caring relationships with family, friends, and coworkers. It includes both giving and receiving.

When these two ingredients are present, then the four key *C*'s of this expanded version of hardiness (incorporating one from Type C behavior) become more likely.

Challenge is the ability to interpret difficulty and change as a positive challenge or opportunity.

Confidence is belief in your ability to master whatever difficulties and challenges come along.

Commitment is positive involvement in your activities and strong belief in your ideals—giving it your best shot.

Control is belief in your ability to influence events and your reactions to events.

Figure 12-4

The 10 *C*'s of Thriving Under Pressure

CONDITIONING   CHALLENGE   CALMNESS

CONFIDENCE   CREATIVITY

COMMITMENT   COPING   COMPETENCE

CARING   CONTROL

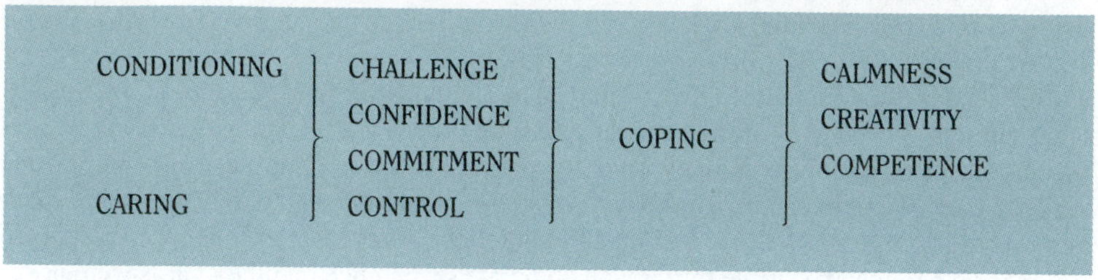

Given the presence of these four core ingredients of a "thriving perspective," another *C* becomes more likely.

Coping is your ability to respond constructively to challenging events and to your own temporary distress.

When one copes constructively, three other *C*'s follow.

Calmness is your ability to maintain a moderate level of physical and emotional arousal in the face of difficulty.

Creativity refers to the ability to generate innovative and situationally specific solutions to difficulties and dilemmas.

Competence is your ability to handle the demands of a job or task effectively.

While no research has been conducted on these 10 *C*'s for thriving under pressure, it is likely that their presence, especially in combination, will lead to thriving under the pressure of long-term stressors.

Thriving under chronic pressure also becomes easier to the degree that you move along the continuum of maturation toward the level Maslow called "self-actualization," as you read earlier. This does not happen overnight through the application of any specific technique, of course, but is the result of long-term personal growth and development. To the degree that such growth occurs, change and adversity come to be seen as two more challenges in the flow of experience—difficult but hardly overwhelming. The same holds for the gradual emergence of the Type C pattern in your own life.

You have seen in this chapter, then, that coping can be constructive or destructive, deliberate or scripted, inner-directed or outer-directed, focused on merely surviving or on reaching our higher potentials. Central to any effective coping style must be effective health buffers and positive or realistic self-talk, rational beliefs, and a sense of meaning and direction, topics to which we turn in Chapters 13 and 14.

References

American Psychiatric Association (1987). *Diagnostic and statistical manual of mental disorders, III-R.* Washington, DC.

Antonovsky, A. (1979). *Health, stress and coping: New perspectives on mental and physical well-being.* San Francisco: Jossey-Bass.

Antonovsky, A. (1987). *Unraveling the mystery of health: How people manage stress and stay well.* San Francisco: Jossey-Bass.

Associated Press (1994). Students' binge drinking harms others on campus, *Chico Enterprise-Record,* December 11, 6A.

Auerback, S. M., & Gramling, S. E. (1998). *Stress management: Psychological foundations. Upper* Saddle River, NJ: Prentice-Hall.

Berne, E. (1964). *Games people play.* New York: Grove Press.

Buchholz, E. (1998). The call of solitude. *Psychology Today, 31,* 50–54, 80–82.

Cohen, F., & Lazarus, R. S. (1979). Coping with the stresses of illness. In G. D. Stone, F. Cohen, & N. E. Adler (Eds.), *Health psychology: A handbook.* San Francisco: Jossey-Bass, 110–118.

Coffee, G. (1990). *Beyond survival: Building on the hard times—a POW's inspiring story.* Aiea, HI: Coffee Enterprises.

Debussman, B. (1990). A nation of drug users. *San Francisco Chronicle,* November 25, C1.

DuRant, R. H., Rome, E. S., Rich, M., Allred, E. Emans, S. J., & Woods, E. R. (1997). Tobacco and alcohol use behaviors portrayed in music videos: A content analysis. *American Journal of Public Health, 87,* 1131–1135).

Folkman, S., Schaefer, C., & Lazarus, R. S. (1979). Cognitive processes as mediators of stress and coping. In V. Hamilton & D. M. Warburton (Eds.). *Human stress and cognition: An information processing approach.* London: Wiley, 265–298.

Frese, M. (1986). Coping as a moderator and mediator between stress at work and psychosomatic complaints. In M. H. Appley & R. Trumbull (Eds.). *Dynamics of stress: Physiological, psychological, social perspectives.* New York: Plenum Press, 183–206.

Gabrels, S. T. (1997). Diets, drugs, and values. *Christian Science Monitor,* September 30, 1.

Gallup Organization (1990). A measure of worry. *Boston Globe,* April 16, 24.

Auerbach, S. M., & Gramling, S. E. (1998). *Stress management: Psychological foundations.* Upper Saddle River, NJ: Prentice-Hall.

Green, J., & Shellenberger, R. (1991). *The dynamics of health and wellness: A biopsychosocial approach.* Fort Worth: Holt, Rinehart and Winston.

Hayward, B. (1998). College freshmen show conservative side. *Sacramento Bee,* January 12, A4.

Holroyd, K. A., & Lazarus, R. S. (1982). Stress, coping, and somatic adaptation. In L. Goldberger & S. Breznetz (Eds.). *Handbook of stress: Theoretical and clinical aspects.* New York: Free Press, 21–35.

James, M., & Jongeward, D. (1971). *Born to win.* Reading, MA: Addison-Wesley.

Kleinke, C. L. (1998). *Coping with life challenges.* Pacific Grove, CA: Brooks/Cole.

Kriegel, R., & Kriegel, M. H. (1984). *The C zone: Peak performance under pressure.* Garden City, NY: Anchor Press.

Krohne, H. W. (1986). Coping with stress: Dispositions, strategies, and the problem of measurement. In M. H. Appley & R. Trumbull (Eds.). *Dynamics of stress: Physiological, psychological, and social perspectives.* New York: Plenum Press, 207-228.

Laux, L. (1986). A self-presentational view of coping with stress. In M. H. Appley & R. Trumbull (Eds.). *Dynamics of stress: Physiological, psychological, and social perspectives.* New York: Plenum Press, 233–254.

Lazarus, R. S., & Folkman, S. (1984). *Stress, appraisal and coping.* New York: Springer.

Lindberg, A. M. (1978). *Gifts from the sea.* Westminster: Random.

Los Angeles Times (1989). Obituaries, September 12, 24.

Maddi, S. R., & Kobasa, S. C. (1984). *The hardy executive: Health under stress.* Homewood, IL: Dow Jones-Irwin.

Mitchell, A. (1989). Drugs and the gospel of materialism. *Chico Enterprise-Record,* September 9, 4B.

Nash, J. M. (1997). Addicted. *Time,* May 5, 69–76.

National Center for Health Statistics. (1989). *Health, United States, 1988.* DHHS Publication No. PHS 89-1232. Washington, DC: U.S. Government Printing Office.

National Council on Alcoholism, 1992.

Parrino, J. J. (1979). *From panic to power: The positive use of stress.* New York: John Wiley.

Pearlin, L. I., & Schooler, C. (1978). The structure of coping. *Journal of Health and Social Behavior, 19,* 2–21.

Prokop, C. K., Bradley, L. A., Burish, T. G., Anderson, K. O., & Fox, J. E. (1991). *Health psychology: Clinical methods and research.* New York: MacMillan.

Roglieri, J. L. (1980). *Odds on your life.* New York: Seaview.

Santiago-Rivera, A. L., Bernstein, B. L., & Gard, T. L. (1995). The importance of achievement and the appraisal of stressful events as predictors of coping. *Journal of College Student Development, 36,* 374–383.

Schafer, W., & Gard, B. (1986). How elected officials handle the stress and pressure of public office . . . and thrive! *Western City, 62,* 7–10.

Schafer, W., & Gard, B. (1988a). Stress and California's city managers, *Western City, 64,* 13–15.

Schafer, W., & Gard, B. (1988b). Stress: How low-stress city managers differ from the rest, *Western City, 64,* 15–17.

Schneider, V. (1982). *Infant massage.* New York: Bantam.

Sheehan, G. (1978). *Running and being.* New York: Simon & Schuster.

Smith, C. A., Wallston, K. A., Dwyer, K A., & Dowdy, S. W. (1997). Beyond good and bad coping: A multidimensional examination of coping with pain in persons with rheumatoid arthritis. *Annals of Behavioral Medicine, 19,* 11–21.

Sperling, D. (1981). The myth of the natural athlete, *Success Magazine, 28,* 31.

Steiner, C. (1974). *Scripts people live.* New York: Grove Press.

Surgeon General (1990). *The health benefits of smoking cessation: A report of the Surgeon General.* Washington, DC: U.S. Government Printing Office.

Taylor, S. E. (1986). *Health psychology.* New York: Random House.

Virshup, B. (1987). *Do we have to know this for the exam?* New York: W. W. Norton

Walter, T., Siebert, A., & Smith, L. (2000). *Student success: How to succeed in college and still have time for your friends.* (8th ed.). Fort Worth: Harcourt Brace & Company.

Application Exercise 12-1

Scripted and Deliberate Influences on Your Coping Style

1. When I was growing up, messages I received about coping with stress *by watching my parents* included these do's and don'ts:

2. When I was growing up, messages about coping with stress I *heard from my parents* included these do's and don'ts:

3. Ways I am *still influenced* by these stress-coping messages include:

4. Ways I *have changed* my stress-coping habits include:

5. Ways I would still *like to improve* my stress-coping habits include:

Application Exercise 12-2

Five Coping Strategies

Assume you were asked to give advice to a fellow student, coworker, friend, or family member about options she or he might use to adaptively cope with a neighbor who repeatedly plays a stereo late at night at a volume level that disturbs her or his sleep. In the space below, list one or more specific possibilities you might suggest within each of the five coping strategies proposed by Cohen and Lazarus.

1. Information-seeking:

2. Direct action:

3. Inhibition of action:

4. Intrapsychic efforts:

5. Turning to others:

Application Exercise 12-3

Assessing Your Strengths and Weaknesses Among the 10 C's

1. My strengths among the 10 *C*'s include:

2. This is so because:

3. My weaknesses among the 10 *C*'s include:

4. This is so because:

CHAPTER 13

Give your body a message of love and value.

—VIRGINIA SATIR

Health Buffers: Exercise, Nutrition, Sleep, and Healthy Pleasures

Beauty on the Run

I had such a lovely run yesterday. I left home at 5:30 a.m. trying to race the sunrise to the top of my ridge two and one-half miles away (up). I run on a winding dirt road until the last two hundred feet or so. Then it is straight to the top. Just as I rounded the last bend and could see the top, the sun broke over the hills and across the valley. The sky was a brilliant redorange and pink with rays of sunlight streaking up through high rain clouds. Standing in the middle of the road on the horizon were a doe and buck (his antlers were in full velvet) staring at me. The deer silhouetted against the sky was incredible. At that point, even though I was running uphill, I lost all conscious feeling of my running. The sight before me and movement of my body simultaneously became one glorious experience. I ran another three miles on top of the ridges with the cool early morning air and the sun bathing me. It then suddenly began to softly rain large summer rain drops. Wow! I was home by 6:30. I had already experienced so much and my day was just beginning! Stress? What stress?

You have read throughout this textbook several theories of stress that emphasize factors intervening between stressors and stress. Cognitive theories emphasize perspective, self-talk, or interpretation, the focus of Chapter 14. Lazarus and others emphasize the individual's coping response in dealing with major events and especially with daily hassles (Lazarus & Folkman, 1984).

Of particular relevance here is the notion of "generalized resistance resources (GRRs)," which we noted in our review of sense-of-coherence theory (Antonovsky, 1979, 1987). GRRs help build stress resistance. They enable the individual to build up a protective reserve so when tough times come along, the person is ready to cope effectively.

In this chapter, you will read about four resistance resources that can help build protection against distress: aerobic exercise, good nutrition, adequate sleep, and healthy pleasures.

Aerobic Exercise

The Need for Physical Activity

Two health-related trends have marked the 20th century.

1. **Acceleration in pace of life.** This takes two forms: more personal changes in shorter periods of time and a faster daily tempo.
2. **Sedentary living.** At the turn of the century, most of our grandparents were physically active. They depended more on their bodies than on machines to move from place to place, to work, to maintain their households, to play. Experts estimate that in 1860 one-third of the American economy was human-powered. Today that figure is less than 1 percent.

How do these two historical trends affect stress and health? Increasing personal adjustments are required, year by year and day by day. Tension mounts, physically and mentally. Without sufficient release through physical activity, this tension turns into bound energy, pulling and tearing inside our bodies.

Stress-induced illnesses result. These can include migraine and tension headaches, ulcers, back pain, high blood pressure, and atherosclerosis. Emotional distress abounds, evidenced by irritability, joylessness, depression, chronic anxiety, and insomnia. Obesity reaches epidemic proportions. Destructive coping behavior is rampant—alcohol and drug abuse, smoking, violence, escapism, attraction to cults, and overeating. The United States leads the world in many forms of addictive behavior.

Social and technological change has deluded us into the false belief that inactivity is a normal way to live. But the fact is that exercising—if not during work, then during play—restores your body to its true optimum condition. Those who take time to exercise live as the body was intended—actively. Exercise prevents and reduces bound energy, thereby preventing and reducing distress. Even modest amounts of physical activity add to well-being—and to life expectancy. Paffenbarger estimates from his research that for every hour exercised, two hours of life expectancy are added (Blair, 1989; Paffenbarger et al., 1986).

You may not be able to control the pace of life and the rate of change around you. But you can control your readiness to cope with the stresses of modern life by becoming—and staying—physically active.

In one of his early, influential books on exercise, Kenneth Cooper uses the following conversation with a patient to underscore the central importance of cardiovascular fitness for health and vitality.

Doc, I don't need much endurance. I work at a desk all day, and I watch television at night. I don't exert myself any more than I have to, and I have no requirements for exerting myself. Who needs large reserves? Who needs endurance?

You do. Everyone does. Surely you know the usual symptoms caused by inactivity as well as I do. Yawning at your desk, that drowsy feeling all day, falling asleep after a heavy meal, fatigue from even mild exertions like climbing stairs, running for a bus, mowing the lawn or shoveling snow. You can become a social cripple, "too tired" to play with the kids, "too tired" to go out to dinner with your wife, "too tired" to do anything except sit at your desk or watch television, and maybe you're even getting tired of doing that. And the final clincher, "I guess I'm getting old." You're getting old all right, and a lot sooner than you should. (1977, 11)

For most who read this book, employment affords little chance for physical exercise. For full-time homemakers, housework requires lots of movement but little real exercise of any benefit for stress control or health. The answer is to set aside 30 to 60 minutes each day to exercise.

Not surprisingly, most people turn to other options when emotionally troubled. These include alcohol, food, cigarettes, prescription medicines, and street drugs. These may provide temporary relief, of course, but are hardly long-term solutions. Regular exercise is a far better approach that uses the body's natural resources and restores you to being fully human.

Exercise and Emotions: A Sampling of Scientific Evidence

As Johnsgård points out (1990), it has long been folk wisdom that exercise has a positive effect on mood. When children drive their parents to distraction from being cooped up too long, parents know enough to send them outside to play in order to "work off some steam." When friends or family are mired in the blues, we do all we can to "get them up and moving."

Such folk wisdom has received countless support in recent years from scientific studies. Here is a sampling.

- John Greist and associates at the University of Wisconsin conducted a pilot study comparing the effects of running therapy with two kinds of conventional individual

---

Physical Activity Is Normal

A kitten chasing a ball of yarn, a seal taking a morning plunge, a stallion romping in an open meadow—joyous physical expression is a fact of life for most animals. It is not, however, for most humans, who are often content to get by with the bare minimum of physical exertion.

Source: Eliot & Breo (1984, 134)

psychotherapy (Griest et al., 1978). Subjects were depressed students who came to the University Counseling Center for help. At the end of the treatment, all three groups showed similar reductions in depression. Running reduced depression more rapidly than the other types of treatment and had more lasting effects after several months of followup.

- Griest and colleagues (Griest et al., 1979) expanded their studies by taking in referrals from private psychiatrists in the local community. An 80 percent recovery rate was reported—and a majority of those few who did not show quick recovery never did begin to run. This success rate is much higher than for most studies of antidepressant medications.

- A study conducted by *Runner's World* magazine (1989) found that 82 percent of the nearly 700 respondents to a random survey of magazine readers reported that running had enhanced their energy level, 73 percent said it had helped their life control, and 69 percent said running had increased their optimism. Most reported that running exceeded their initial hopes in increasing mental fitness and relieving stress. Other perceived gains included improved diet, weight loss, and fewer colds.

- Aerobic exercise was shown in a study conducted through the Veterans Administration Medical Center in Salt Lake City to improve cognitive function in formerly sedentary elderly patients (Dustman, 1989). Specifically, after a four-month exercise program, participants improved in mental flexibility, reaction, and memory—mental skills likely to make coping with the stressors of living during the later years more constructive and effective.

- Fifty-five college students who reported a high number of recent negative life events participated in an experiment comparing physical exercise, relaxation training, and no treatment. While all reported improved health over the 11-week period of the study, the exercise group showed a greater drop in depressive symptoms (Roth & Holmes, 1987).

- McCann and Holmes (1984) conducted a similar study among 47 female undergraduate students who had been found through a psychological test to be mildly depressed. Like the Roth study, those assigned to an exercise group showed a greater decline in depression than either a relaxation or a no-treatment group.

- A telephone survey of 401 Illinois residents found a positive association between amount of exercise and psychological well-being, especially among low- and middle-income groups (Hayes & Ross, 1986).

- Wesley Sime of the University of Nebraska Stress Physiology Laboratory found that among 15 moderately depressed men and women ranging in age from 26 to 53, depression scores were significantly lower after 10 weeks, 6 months, and 21 months of exercise (Sime, 1987). Interestingly, Sime found that durability of positive change was dependent on continuation of exercise.

- A study at the University of London found that among 75 sedentary adults, those assigned to a moderate aerobic exercise group showed improvements in tension and anxiety, while no changes occurred in the high-intensity exercise or no-activity groups (Moses, 1989). The authors suggest that the high-intensity group perhaps experienced too much demand for this brief 10-week period.

- A great deal of research has been conducted on the influence of exercise on self-esteem. For example, Brown (1986) found a positive effect on self-concept after a 12-week program of exercise for both young and mature women. One reviewer points out that "self-esteem is more likely to be elevated when exercise is introduced to special populations" (Johnsgård, 1989, 200).

- Brown (1987) has been testing students for many years through his mental health courses at the University of Virginia. Studies of more than 5,000 men and women show that regular exercise is inversely associated with hostility.

- Berger and Owen (1983) found that exercise has an immediate or acute effect in reducing hostility among both conditioned and unconditioned swimmers.

- Morgan and Costill studied male world-class marathoners and college runners compared with normative college samples. They reported that runners' scores were much lower than college students in general on depression, fatigue, confusion, and tension but significantly higher in vigor (Ungerleider et al., 1989).

- A larger study of 348 nonelite male and female marathoners compared their Profile of Mood scores to those of 856 college students. Marathoners were significantly less tense, less fatigued, less depressed, less confused, and more vigorous than the male and female college students. No difference was found on the anger scale (Ungerleider et al., 1989).

- Another study of 464 nonelite female runners found that their moderate running program was at least as beneficial as the marathoners' heavier training regimen (Ungerleider et al, 1989).

- Many studies have demonstrated that adolescents, like adults, are vulnerable to stressful life events. A study of 220 adolescent girls showed that clustering of stressful life events had notable debilitating effects on the emotional and physical health of nonexercisers but that these negative effects were significantly less among girls who exercised frequently (Brown & Lawton, 1986).

- A recent study showed that even a six-week combined aerobic-anaerobic exercise regimen reduced the intensity of the stress response among college students (Morse, Walker, & Monroe, 1994).

- I have conducted a series of studies on exercise and stress among my undergraduate students. In Figure 13-1 are findings from a survey of 129 students, in which they were asked a number of quality-of-life questions. They also were asked how many times on the average they exercised the previous semester for at least 20 minutes. The average was the same for both males and females: 3.4 times per week. All but 12 reported averaging at least once per week. The results showed no significant differences in any of the quality-of-life measures between not exercising and exercising 1 to 3 times per week. But when those who exercised 0 to 3 times per week were compared to those who exercised 5 or more times per week, the pattern became clear: The greater the frequency of exercise, the better the quality of life, whatever the measure. More frequent exercisers reported fewer distress symptoms, less irritability, more internal control, less emotional tension and depression, more vitality and energy, higher self-esteem, more fun and playfulness, less loneliness, and more close friends.

Figure 13-1

Stress and Quality of Life by Frequency of Exercise

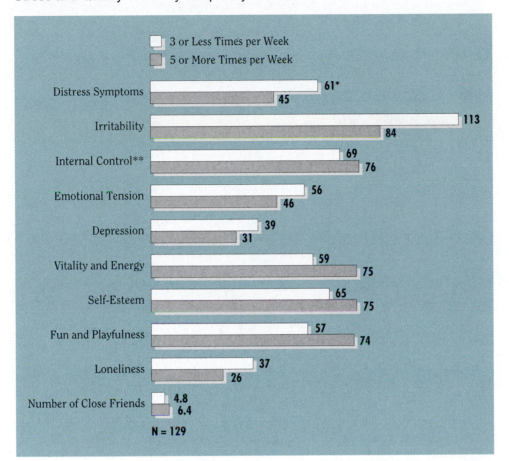

All associations are statistically significant at .04 or less, except for distress symptoms (p = .08).
External Control through Fun and Playfulness are from the Quality of Life Index (Schafer, 1996, 228) with scores multiplied by 10.

- Finally, more recent students in my Human Stress class who completed a series of measures on stress and health (N = 282) were asked the same question about frequency of exercise. As before, the average was 3.4 times per week. This time I divided respondents into those who exercised 0 to 2 times per week and 5 to 7 days. Most of the findings duplicated results from the smaller sample from several years earlier. In addition, frequent exercisers in this new sample showed significantly higher scores on a 13-item quality-of-life index on sense of coherence, optimism, happiness, self-reported health, and meaning and direction.

This is a mere sampling of studies showing positive effects of exercise on emotions. Of course, because my own studies, like many of the others, were cross-sectional, one-time surveys, we do not know causal direction. That is, more frequent exercise might be the effect rather than the cause of higher quality of life, better health, and lower distress. At a minimum, we can conclude that the data support the hypothesis that exercise helps control stress and adds to a positive quality of life. Countless anecdotes also could be cited. To illustrate, note the following from a letter to Johnsgård:

I started running and gave up smoking at age 33 when I began to take over responsibility for my health. I began walking and jogging around a golf course near my home long before the running craze hit us. I noticed that after I exercised, I always felt so much better. It left me with a warm afterglow. I was a very aggressive lacrosse player (even a dirty player), but I found that running left me calm and relaxed without any desire to hurt or even dominate. I just love gentle running. . . . (1989, 203)

What Is Aerobic Exercise?

Any form of exercise is better than none. A recent study shows, for example, that even minimal physical activity increases life expectancy (Blair et al., 1989). But the most effective type of activity in terms of stress control is **aerobic exercise.** Aerobic means, literally, "activity with oxygen."

Other forms of activity are **anaerobic exercise** (activity without oxygen), such as all-out sprinting or swimming underwater while holding the breath; *strengthening* exercises, such as weight-lifting and isometrics; and *stretching,* such as yoga and warm-ups before running. Aerobic exercise is any form of activity in which the heart rate is elevated substantially above resting level in response to sustained movement by large muscle groups and in which higher amounts of oxygen are used to produce energy. Examples of aerobic exercise include the following:

Running	Stationary bicycling	Rope skipping
Brisk walking	Cross-country skiing	Stair climbing
Swimming	Mini-trampolining	Brisk circuit training
Bicycling	Aerobic dancing	

How Much Aerobic Exercise Is Needed?

For minimum cardiovascular fitness, the following criteria need to be met, according to the American College of Sports Medicine (1990). You can recall these by remembering the acronym **FIT.**

1. **Frequency:** At least three times per week.
2. **Intensity:** Heart rate between 60 and 90 percent of maximum for entire exercise session. To estimate these percentages, subtract your age from 220, then multiply that figure times .60 and .90.
3. **Time:** At least 20 minutes per session.

My experience with stress-management clients and students leads me to recommend the following aerobic exercise guidelines for purposes of *effective stress control and high-level wellness*—beyond minimal cardiovascular fitness. This recommendation is consistent with findings reported here in Figure 13-1. It receives further support from a recent report, presented to the American Heart Association, that reduction of cardiovascular risk factors decreased with higher amounts of exercise (Associated Press, 1994). This recommendation also is consistent with the position of Paul Gibson, a leading expert on exercise physiology (McDonald, 1997).

1. **Frequency:** Five to seven days per week.
2. **Intensity:** Heart rate between 60 and 90 percent of estimated maximum.
3. **Time:** At least 30 to 40 minutes per session.

Evidence suggests that most Americans undertrain, even by the minimal criteria noted above. A recent report by the President's Council on Physical Fitness and Sport (1997) reveals that 71 percent of American adults are not regularly active or are inactive. At the same time, it is important to avoid overtraining both for reasons of injury prevention and general well-being. A recent study by Fry and associates (1993), for example, identified a number of results of deliberately induced overtraining among a small sample of males, including severe fatigue, immune system deficits, mood disturbance, various physical complaints, sleep difficulties, and reduced appetite. Physically handicapped people may have difficulty, of course, meeting either set of criteria. In many instances, exercise videos and books have been designed specifically to provide appropriate physical activities for these persons.

Physiological Changes With Aerobic Training

Three main changes will occur with aerobic exercise, all of which improve your overall energy level through more efficient use of oxygen. This is called the "**aerobic training effect**" (Clarke, 1975; Fahey, Insel, & Roth, 1994).

1. **Improvements in oxygen intake (respiration)**

   Strengthening of diaphragm muscle
   Greater lung flexibility and capacity

2. **Improvements in oxygen (circulation)**

   More output per heartbeat
   Slower heart rate at given exertion level
   More blood volume
   More red corpuscles
   Less blood stickiness
   Expansion in size of blood vessels and capillaries
   Opening of new capillary networks

3. **Improvements in oxygen use (metabolism)**

   More efficient extraction of oxygen from blood
   More efficient burning of oxygen within muscle cells
   More efficient discharge of carbon dioxide

How Aerobic Exercise Can Help Control Stress

Psychological and Physiological Pathways

Research continues on the mental and physiological pathways through which aerobic exercise helps control tension, anxiety, depression, and other stress symptoms. Here is a summary of what is known or considered by experts as likely explanations for the exercise-stress control linkages.

Psychological pathways related to tension control from exercising are likely to include the following.

- Release of pent-up emotions
- Creative problem-solving during the exercise session, resulting in more constructive coping the rest of the day
- Enhanced self-liking, self-acceptance, and self-esteem
- Heightened internal control
- Feeling of well-being and calm—"afterglow" from exercise

- Mood stabilization
- "Time away" benefit (not unique to exercise, of course)
- Decreased negative thinking and rumination

Physiological pathways through which exercise is thought to improve stress control involve a number of factors.

- Release of muscle tension
- Burning off of stress-induced adrenaline, which leaves the bloodstream and is consumed in the muscles
- Postexercise reduction of adrenaline production
- Postexercise quieting of the sympathetic nervous system (the part of the system that produces tension)
- Production of beta-endorphins, the body's own morphine-like painkiller and source of euphoria
- Lowered baseline tension level
- Faster recovery time from acute stress
- Body becomes familiar with and habituated to physiological arousal

For more on the physiological effects of exercise, see Johnsgård (1989). In short, a vital step in harnessing stress, preventing illness, and reaching higher levels of potential is to restore exercise into daily life. Doing so meets a basic need of the healthy human body—to be physically active.

Running—My Way

My particular aerobic exercise is running, although I do bike at times and lift weights at a modest level. As I write, I am celebrating my 50th year of running. Someone asked if I am addicted. "Perhaps," I answered. "Let's wait and see."

Benefits of Running

While other types of aerobic exercise can be equally beneficial and enjoyable, I do want to share a few thoughts about running as an approach to stress control.

As this chapter's opening vignette suggests, running can be immensely rewarding and surprisingly easy. People often associate running with pain and competition. Many athletes stop exercising after high school or college because of their memories of painful training or pressure from coaches to win. And fans who watch them never begin for the same reasons.

Recently, millions of Americans have discovered an entirely new way to run—for health, friendship, and the beauty of the body in motion. Some compete in low-key races, but competition is less important than the process of running. This type of running can be started at any age, regardless of ability. It can become a regular part of everyday life. And it can be continued into old age.

Running for the purposes of enjoyment and good health has several features. First, it is done as regularly as eating or sleeping. You do not feel guilty about taking time to eat or read the newspaper. Nor do runners feel guilty about taking 20 to 60 minutes each day or two to run. Rain or shine, good mood or bad, they run.

Second, running involves a minimum of strain or pain. Runners usually run at a pace at which they can carry on a reasonable conversation. They are willing to push into the "pain zone" once in a while, but not every day. For they know they can achieve substantial benefits by running fairly easily—and can enjoy it at that pace.

Third, runners can run alone or with others. They do not require the presence of others to get their regular run, but they often do "run socially." Sometimes, in fact, deep friendships develop "on the run."

Fourth, running is a long-term proposition. Continuing to exercise in this way over many years is more important than achieving short-range goals. Running, therefore, is approached with patience. Comments from runners interviewed by Glasser for his book on positive addictions include the following.

> When I am settled into my run I concentrate on running as much as possible but the mind wanders to thoughts of most anything. The state of mind is one of almost total complacency and privacy. Although you are in sight of people, cars, buses, school kids, dogs, etc., I feel a very privateness when I run. People may yell at me or a kid may bug me for a few hundred yards, but due to the nature of running (it is hard and physically demanding) you are pretty much left to yourself and no one can invade your runners' world because they physically are not able. If another runner enters or intrudes it is fine because he is running for the same reasons and for a lot of the same feelings.

> Running is extremely personal to each runner. Its importance shapes the lives of many people who enjoy running long distances. I can really never see myself quitting unless an accident should occur. It has been an integral part of my life for a number of years, and I am quite happy with myself and my life and I wouldn't trade places with anyone.

> I can describe two states of mind when I have settled into my run. Sometimes both will occur when I am settled into a run. Strangely enough these minds seem to be a function of the weather. Nice crisp days yeah, hot humid days, too. Novelty of the course, physical features of the course include whether the course is beautiful, easy to run, etc. The first mind state that I would describe is that of a rational cognitive nature and coincides with runs that are generally unsatisfactory in some way. The weather is hot, the dogs are harassing me, the course is becoming boring because I have been on it many times. The second mind state is [and here I believe he describes the PA (positive addiction) state quite clearly] not cognitive or rational, instead it is ego-transcending. I simply perceive as I run. I react instinctively to obstacles which suddenly appear. I float. I run like a deer. I feel good. I feel high. I don't think at all. My awareness is only the present. Even that cannot be called awareness. Brain chatter is gone. This mind set normally coincides with running along a cross-country course in autumn on a crisp day but definitely appears other times of the year as well. (1976, 108, 109, 113)

I have run for 50 years because through running I gain:

- A personal stability zone, a personal anchorage
- A daily mini-vacation
- Diversion from other concerns
- Enjoyment of the natural environment
- Joy, exhilaration
- Time for contemplation, thought, and planning
- Solitude when I run alone
- Friendship when I run with others
- Challenge
- Self-awareness of:

Physical processes within my body
How my mind and body interact
Performance under pressure

- Release of tension
- Physically
- Emotionally
- An enhanced self of inner control and mastery
- Increased energy
- Healthy weight
- Prevention of disease, deterioration, and decline.

Cautions About Running

A word of caution is needed when discussing running. Running carries its risks, the main one being injury to joints or muscles. A high percentage of habitual runners, especially those who diligently train for and participate in competitive road races, periodically experience injuries of sufficient seriousness to require complete rest for days, weeks, or months. Because of anatomical anomalies, some individuals are especially injury-prone. The most common injuries are to knees.

Many runners believe the sense of accomplishment from pushing their limits justifies this risk of injury. At the same time, it is wise to be cautious if your primary goal is to run for many years. Effective exercise need be quite moderate over the long run.

Are Other Physical Activities Beneficial?

Quality and perhaps even length of life can benefit from such activities as walking several blocks to work, climbing stairs rather than taking the elevator, doing yoga and other stretching exercises, and working vigorously on the job.

Other physical activities, such as gardening, fishing, hunting, softball, and golf clearly can have diversionary and recreational value. All these activities certainly can be beneficial in controlling tension and rejuvenating one's spirit. But aerobic exercise is the most beneficial of all for maintaining high-level wellness and managing stress. As noted earlier, this is simply returning the body to its normal state of existence. See Figure 13-2 for a comparison of some of the physiological strengths of nine types of exercise. For a chart including many more activities, see Fahey, Insel, & Roth (1994). Most desirable of all is a comprehensive program of physical fitness that promotes cardiovascular endurance, muscular flexibility, muscular strength, and appropriate body composition.

Brisk walking is an especially attractive and beneficial form of life-long aerobic exercise. If you suffer from chronic back pain or have chronic joint problems, running may not be for you. Walking can produce many of the same benefits as running, especially for older adults, while greatly reducing injury risk. More Americans walk than engage in any other type of fitness activity. As Rippe and associates have noted in the *Journal of the American Medical Association* (Rippe et al., 1988), there are a variety of positive mental and physical benefits from walking. Lamb (1981) has listed some of the key ones as follows:

- Walk to stay lean
- Walk to clean out your arteries
- Walk to lower your lower blood pressure
- Walk to control your blood sugar

Running: Her Personal Anchorage

A student—a mother in her 30s who had returned to college—recently submitted this brief "Application Assignment" in my Human Stress class.

Personal anchorages are referred to in this class as things, places, activities, people, and beliefs that hold us together, even when things around us may be dynamically changing.

Before taking this class, I had not realized the importance of running as a personal anchorage. What I now recognize is that the benefit of running is more than for health and fitness. It is always there for me, supporting, challenging, and encouraging me whether the chips are up or down.

Running is something I can do alone, with friends, on vacation, in most any weather, to meet new people, to let off steam, to start my day, to compete for time, to collect thoughts, and so on. Running is always there for me. It keeps me disciplined, builds self-esteem, and maintains vitality and energy.

One of the favorite things about running is the social support attained. I have run with a group of people for over four years. If we were not all runners looking for early morning partners, our paths may not have ever crossed. As it is, strong friendships have formed. We help one another when the waters are troubled and celebrate when achievements are made. Much of our socializing is preceded by exercise. In fact, we have our own personal half-marathon once a year followed by brunch and swim. We also enjoy training for such events as the Bidwell Classic Half-Marathon and Whiskeytown Relays.

Running is also something I share with my husband. Since we both have hectic schedules, we most always can share an hour of the day running together. As a result, much discussion and problem-solving can be accomplished. Furthermore, running keeps our marriage stable, moods and tempers are mellowed, and we enjoy a harmonious relationship—at least most of the time!

Running can also be productive. Running alone is an especially good time to collect and organize thoughts for upcoming tests, assignments, speeches, etc. In fact, much of the context of this paper was mentally organized while I was running!

Running has become second nature to me. No matter where I am or what the pressures are, running most always starts my day.

- Walk to condition your heart
- Walk to stimulate your bone marrow
- Walk to improve other physical functions (e.g., strengthen leg muscles, improve bowel function, strengthen bones)

A recent study (Perkins, 1998) of older adults shows that walking extended life expectancy, especially by reducing cancer rates. Commenting on this study, May Haan, director of the Center for Aging and Health at the University of California, Davis, said, "If I

Figure 13-2

Does Your Workout Make the Grade?

	Endurance	Flexibility	Upper-Body Strength	Lower-Body Strength	Fights Osteoporosis	Low Stress to Joints
Aerobic Dance	E	E	E	E	M	M
Cycling	E	P	P	E	P	E
In-Line Skating	E	P	P	E	P	E
Stair Climbing	E	P	P	E	M	M
Swimming	E	M	E	M	M	E
Rowing	E	M	E	E	M	E
Running	E	P	P	E	M	M
Weight Training	P	P	E	E	E	M
Walking	M	P	P	E	M	E

P = Poor   M = Moderate   E = Excellent

Source: *Running and Fitnews* (1994, 5)

had to choose one thing to tell everyone, it would be 'Exercise.' Even with moderate exercise like walking you can lose weight, improve muscle tone, and prevent osteoporosis and memory loss in older people. It's a great thing to do" (Perkins, 1998). Charles Holly, a physician from the same university, commented, "Probably fewer than 10 percent of the population exercises vigorously enough to increase cardiovascular fitness. And probably about 60 percent do less than required for health benefits. The key is to view exercise as 'adult play' and do 30 minutes or more most days of the week" (Perkins, 1998).

Self-Talk for Exercise

Nonexercisers use a variety of negative self-talk statements to continue their sedentary ways. If this is so for you, reprogram your thinking by writing these statements on a 3-by-5-inch card that you carry with you. Here are several optional self-talk statements. Pick one to begin with.

1. I love being in good shape.
2. I take care of myself and keep myself fit.
3. Regular exercise gives me energy, mental clarity, and emotional stability.
4. My daily exercise is my daily minivacation.
5. I like the positive effects that exercising creates in my life.
6. I am proud of how I look, feel, think, and live. Exercise helps me continue to become better and better.
7. I can MAKE TIME to exercise.

8. Exercising is my long-term commitment. Missing a day or two is no reason to stop altogether.
9. Some of the busiest and most important people in this country make time to exercise. So can I.
10. I love my body. Taking good care of it is very important to me.
11. Getting fit takes time. I am patient.

Tips for Getting Started—and Sticking With It

Here are 11 tips for getting started and sticking with an exercise program, whatever your personal preference.

1. **Find the types of exercise you like.** You will stay with it if it is fun. Be sure to include at least 20 minutes (preferably 30 or more) of some form of aerobic exercise at least three times a week (preferably five or more). Mix in different types of exercise if that suits you.
2. **Make a four-month commitment.** Decide that come hell or high water, you will stick with it.
3. **Make a weekly plan.** Before going to bed on Sunday night, for example, write down when you will work out the next week.
4. **Practice moderation, gradualism, and patience.** Your fitness buildup need not be painful. Start walking, rather than running, for instance. Add a few steps of running each week. This type of gradual buildup minimizes discouragement, fatigue, and injury.
5. **If it's helpful, exercise with a friend or group.** Knowing someone is waiting at 7 A.M. can make the difference. Companionship adds to the enjoyment. Of course, some prefer to experience this time in solitude. That is okay, too.
6. **If it's helpful, set goals.** Look forward to completing a three-mile fun run six months from now. Swim one mile by spring. Bicycle to the bridge 25 miles away within a month.
7. **Introduce variety.** This may mean changing the course where you walk, run, or bike. Or it may mean alternating types of exercise, within a given week or by season.
8. **Do it even when you do not feel like it.** The fatigue you feel at the end of the workday is more mental than physical. The moment you begin to dance, run, swim, or bike, you will forget you ever felt tired, and you will have more energy afterward.
9. **If you miss a session or two, do not quit altogether.** Be tolerant of your own imperfections. View a missed session or two as a mere wrinkle in your way to a lifetime of fitness.
10. **Be aware of negative self-talk about exercise.** Use thought-stopping. Change it to positive thinking.
11. **Start.**

> See Application Exercise 13-1 to plan to start—and stick with— an aerobic exercise program.

NUTRITION

A second vital health buffer is good nutrition. Just as regular aerobic exercise helps build stress resistance, so will sound nutrition practices.

The linkages between nutrition and stress are complex and numerous. Before setting forth practical nutritional guidelines for helping build stress resistance, let us examine some of the fascinating ways nutrition relates to stress, positively and negatively. This is a mere sampling.

Linkages Between Nutrition and Stress

The most basic place to start is with the fact that *sufficient calories are needed* to provide energy for coping with the stresses of life. The **TATT** feeling (Tired All The Time) so often reported by students, homemakers, laborers, and executives alike is sometimes the result of skipping meals, going on crash diets, or simply undereating in the press of daily life. The amount of calories needed varies by body size and activity.

More common among Americans is *overconsumption of calories,* which relates to stress in several ways. When caloric intake exceeds energy outgo, the obvious result is weight gain. Being overweight increases chances of cancer, diabetes, and heart disease, which, in turn, are obvious sources of stress. Being overweight is damaging to self-esteem, especially in our appearance-conscious culture. This problem is intensified when the overweight individual repeatedly tries without success to shed pounds. Excess weight decreases energy available for daily living and coping.

Irregular and inconsistent eating habits are a leading nutritional problem for many in modern life. Students allow the press of midterms to interfere with the regularity of meals. So do harried salespersons, full-time mothers, busy executives, and the urban poor struggling to make ends meet and coping with the dangers and tensions of daily life—and too often with barely enough money to make ends meet.

Too much or too little of specific food substances also relate to stress. Perhaps the most damaging is *excess fat* in most of our diets. Consuming less than 25 to 30 percent of all calories in the form of fat is ideal. Most Americans exceed this amount. This is one factor contributing to the high rates of death from cardiovascular diseases and cancer in this country, which was noted in Chapter 1. Especially damaging is our too-high proportion of saturated fats. Since fat concentrates calories more than do carbohydrates or protein, high fat consumption increases chances of obesity.

Excess cholesterol also heightens risk of heart disease, which in turn leads to untold fear, anxiety, disability, and grief. Later in this section, we will review ideal figures for fat, cholesterol, and other foods.

High amounts of refined sugar—sugar put back into foods such as soft drinks, ice cream, candy bars, and cakes—also can be a stress-related problem for several reasons. Refined sugar is "empty calories" in the sense that it includes no vitamins and minerals. It quickly adds up to caloric excess. And it can result in mood swings. Glucose in the bloodstream quickly rises with ingestion of high-sugar foods. Glucose just as quickly elicits secretion of insulin, which quickly brings energy and emotions down. So the sugar addict alternates between blood-sugar-related ups and downs.

Inadequate vitamins and minerals can contribute to loss of energy, irritability, insomnia, and anxiety. Vitamin B is used in the construction of adrenaline. While B-complex vitamins (thiamine, riboflavin, niacin, pantothenic acid, and pyrodoxine hydrochloride) can be safely consumed in unusually large amounts, experts increasingly agree that a well-balanced diet can provide daily needs, even during times of high stress. We will say more on this later.

High salt consumption, especially in salt-sensitive individuals, increases chances of high blood pressure. And the higher the blood pressure, the more reactive blood pressure will be during stressful episodes. Stated differently, hypertensives are more likely to have sharp increases of blood pressure when challenged by stressors.

Some evidence indicates that *stress interferes with absorption of calcium* in the intestine. At the same time, it can increase excretion of calcium, potassium, zinc, copper, and magnesium. This becomes especially significant in women who are disposed to osteoporosis, a condition of weak and brittle bones.

Excess alcohol consumption is another obvious stress-nutrition link. Excess alcohol intake brings with it many risks: high caloric intake, damage to the liver and the brain, danger in driving, addiction, malnutrition, emotional dependence, and impaired judgment. There is little evidence that modest consumption—a drink a day or so—does harm. The problem is some individuals seem genetically disposed toward easy addiction. And many resort to alcohol overuse, either chronically or episodically, as a way to "numb out" or to blindly conform to group pressure during stressful times.

Sympathomimetic agents—especially caffeine—stimulate the stress response through activation of the sympathetic nervous system. Not only do they increase baseline arousal level, but they also increase reactivity. These agents include coffee, cola, tea, chocolate, and, perhaps especially in some children, food coloring and preservatives. Tea also contains other sympathomimetic agents: theobromine and theophylline, which are thought to stimulate increases in metabolism and alertness. Like other foods, moderation is the key. More than the equivalent of two or three cups of coffee per day can increase risk of high blood pressure, heighten reactivity to stressful events, and contribute to insomnia.

This, then, is a sampling of nutrition-stress linkages. Next, we examine generally sound nutritional principles, with the key assumption that wise nutritional principles and practices are sound guidelines for stress control as well. Later, we will make several recommendations specifically related to stress.

A number of national entities have issued nutritional reports in recent years. Most display a high degree of agreement. As an example, we will briefly examine a 1988 report from the U.S. surgeon general.

America's Nutritional Habits

The Surgeon General's Report

Former U.S. Surgeon General C. Everett Koop will best be remembered for his reports and statements on smoking. But he also issued a significant report on diet and health in America (Surgeon General, 1989). This 712-page study was the first ever issued by a U.S. surgeon general and reflects the growing concern in health circles that dietary flaws represent a real threat to the health of Americans. Several basic and urgent recommendations comprised the core of this report:

1. Reduce fats, especially saturated fats such as butter and untrimmed red meat.
2. Reduce cholesterol consumption.
3. Increase consumption of fish, poultry, lean meats, and low-fat dairy products.
4. Reduce total calorie intake; balance caloric intake with energy expenditure.
5. Increase consumption of foods containing complex carbohydrates and fiber such as whole grains, cereals, leafy vegetables, dried beans and peas, and fruit.
6. Choose foods low in sodium, and minimize addition of table salt.
7. Consume no more than two alcoholic drinks per day and none during pregnancy.

Other recommendations included caution when purchasing products labeled "natural" or "organic." Koop noted that Americans spend far too much on unproven vitamin and mineral supplements and on fad diets.

Curiously, he said, this country suffers from twin problems: on the one hand, malnourishment among the poor, especially children; and, on the other hand, widespread overeating and obesity.

The recommendations in this report from the surgeon general are congruent with those from the American Heart Association, the American Cancer Society, and most other

---

Teen Overweight

Twenty-two percent of U.S. teens are overweight, up from 15 percent less than 30 years ago, a series of studies has shown. About 12 percent are so overweight that their health is in jeopardy. That figure has doubled in the past 10 years. . . .

Why have so many teens come to have weight problems?
- Extreme lack of exercise
- Long hours of watching TV and "grazing" on snacks
- Fewer family dinners together, where youngsters used to learn from parents about balanced meals and sensible portions
- More youngsters catching their own meals at fast-food restaurants, where "supersize" portions are all the rage.

Source: Cummins (1998)

---

leading groups and experts. Says Dr. Richard J. Havel, director of the Cardiovascular Research Institute at the University of California, San Francisco, and chairman of the National Research Council's Food and Nutrition Board, "There is now a broad consensus among people in all fields related to nutrition. There just is not a lot of conflict among the experts" (Petit, 1989).

How are Americans doing relative to these guidelines? Not very well, although some improvements are showing, according to Koop and others. When issuing his report, Koop noted that most of the leading causes of death in this country are diseases of "dietary excess and imbalance." Of the 2.1 million Americans who died during 1987, he said, 1.5 million were killed by diseases associated with poor diet. According to Dr. J. Michael McGinnis, Koop's deputy assistant secretary in charge of health promotion, "Five of the ten leading causes of death in the United States—coronary heart disease, certain types of cancer, stroke, diabetes mellitus, and atherosclerosis—are diseases in which diet plays a part" (Perlman, 1988).

The National Cancer Institute Report

The National Cancer Institute recently issued a report on daily eating habits of Americans as part of a long-term study of diet and health (Associated Press, 1988). In interviews with more than 11,000 people, researchers found, for example:

- On a typical day, 40 percent of Americans do not eat any fruit, and 20 percent consume no vegetables.

- More than 80 percent of those surveyed ate no high-fiber cereals or whole-grain breads. Overall, daily fiber intake averaged less than half the recommended amount.

- More than 4 of 10 reported eating at least one serving each day of lunch meat or bacon—foods high in salt and fat and usually cured with nitrates.

Gladys Block, a National Cancer Institute scientist and coauthor of the report, stated, "We really need to change the way we eat. I really believe that could make a difference in the amount of cancer we have." A more recent survey of eating habits of Californians found similar eating patterns and came to similar conclusions (Lowman, 1990).

The director of another national nutrition study by the National Research Council concludes that Americans need to cut protein consumption by 10 percent, overall fat by

---

The Stress Diet

BREAKFAST

½ grapefruit

1 slice whole-wheat toast

8 oz. skim milk

LUNCH

4 oz. lean broiled chicken breast

1 cup steamed zucchini

1 Oreo cookie

Herb tea

MIDAFTERNOON SNACK

Rest of the package of Oreos

1 quart Rocky Road ice cream

1 jar hot fudge

DINNER

2 loaves garlic bread

Large pepperoni and mushroom pizza

Large pitcher of beer

3 Milky Way candy bars

Entire frozen cheesecake eaten directly from the freezer

Source: Unknown.

20 percent, and saturated fat and salt by 25 percent. At the same time, they need to increase complex carbohydrates by 20 percent (Petit, 1989).

Nutritional Guidelines for Building Stress Resistance

Based on what we know about nutrition and health in general and about nutrition and stress in particular, three simple guidelines need to be followed to eat in ways that will ensure good health and maximum stress-resistance. These guidelines are entirely consistent with the **Food Guide Pyramid** (Figure 13-3), which is now the widely accepted framework for nutritional policy and practice in this country.

1. Eat a balanced, consistent diet with sufficient but not excessive calories, vitamins, and minerals.
2. Minimize the following in response to stress:
    Undereating
    Overeating
    Excess alcohol—no more than one or two drinks per day

Figure 13-3

The Food Guide Pyramid

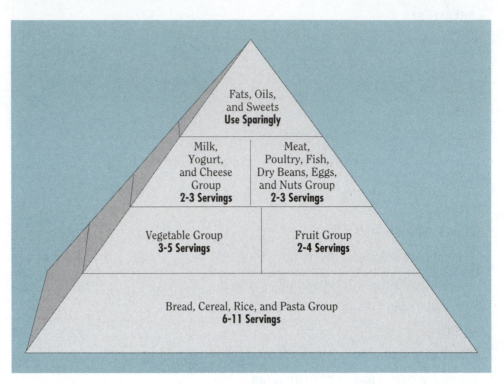

Daily Servings

Source: 1993 Pyramid Packet, Penn State Nutrition Center, 417 East Calder Way, University Park, PA 16801-5663; (814) 865-6323

"Sugar hits"
Excess caffeine—no more than the equivalent of a cup of coffee or two per day

3. Follow these simple principles:
    Low salt—less than 6 grams per day
    Low fat, especially saturated fat—less than 25 or 30 percent of calories through fat;
        less than 10 percent through saturated fat
    Low cholesterol—less than 300 milligrams per day
    Low refined sugars
    High complex carbohydrates—50 percent or more of total calories
    High fiber—20 to 30 grams per day
    Plenty of water—6 to 8 glasses per day

Controlling Dietary Habits

Reduce Fat in Your Diet

Evidence continues to mount that high-fat dietary habits heighten risk for coronary artery disease, cancer, and other illnesses. One study suggests that among teenagers the main source of saturated fat—the bad kind—is dairy products (Associated Press, 1989a). The Florida Department of Citrus and the Mazola Fat and Cholesterol Tip Service provided the following guidelines for reducing fat in your diet (Associated Press, 1989b):

1. Eat more fish, chicken, and turkey or nonmeat alternatives such as legumes or tofu.
2. Make sandwiches with lean meats or skinless poultry rather than with high-fat hamburgers, bologna, or yellow cheeses.
3. Select beef cuts that are trimmed of excess fat, with little marbling.
4. Remove skin from poultry before cooking.
5. Select low-fat dairy products. Use yogurt instead of sour cream, ice milk or sherbet rather than ice cream, and skim milk cheeses rather than regular cheeses.
6. Use margarine instead of butter.
7. Use only a small amount of oil in salad dressings and in frying or sauteing.
8. Eat more fruits, legumes, vegetables, oats, and oat bran.
9. When making selections from the salad bar, avoid high-fat items such as bacon bits, olives, and creamy dressings.
10. For a light dessert or snack, serve fresh fruits. Choose sorbet or nonfat frozen yogurt instead of creamy ice cream.
11. Read labels carefully. Limit foods high in saturated fats such as palm and coconut oils, lard, and animal shortenings.

Cholesterol and Stress

UNDERSTANDING CHOLESTEROL AND STRESS   Cholesterol has a bad reputation, of course, since it is the substance that helps clog coronary arteries, as you read in Chapter 7. But **cholesterol** has a positive side as well. In fact it is a vital element for the human body, used for construction of adrenaline, for repair of cell walls, and for other important functions. It is a waxy fat that originates from two sources: food intake (about 10 percent) and the liver (about 90 percent).

Cholesterol does not travel by itself but attaches to small protein substances called lipoproteins, as described earlier. These come in three forms: **very low density lipoprotein (VLDL), low density lipoprotein (LDL),** and **high density lipoprotein (HDL)** (Brand, 1988). HDL is known as the "good guy" of the cholesterol family because it is the type of lipoprotein that picks up cholesterol already deposited on the inside of coronary arteries and takes it away to the liver for discharge. The higher the HDL, the better.

LDL is the "bad guy" of cholesterols, in that it is the type of lipoprotein that carries cholesterol from the liver and intestines out to the body and deposits some of it along walls of the coronary arteries (Gotto, 1988).

Cholesterol in the bloodstream is influenced by a number of factors, one of which, though not widely recognized, is emotional stress. For example, studies show that cholesterol is elevated among students during exams, among night-shift workers, during unemployment, during flight training, during periods of high anxiety, and during tax season among public accountants (Friedman & Rosenman, 1959; van Doornen & Orlebeke, 1982).

LOWERING CHOLESTEROL   On the positive side, studies show that cholesterol can be controlled or reduced by regular practice of deep relaxation and aerobic exercise as well as by reduction of saturated fat and cholesterol in the diet. One might speculate that other stress-management methods such as modification of self-talk habits might have similar effects.

It is commonly assumed that cholesterol in the bloodstream is influenced by diet, mainly through cholesterol consumed in foods we eat. However, serum cholesterol also is influenced by fat in the diet. Specifically, the higher the proportion of fat intake that is saturated—mostly from animal sources such as meat and dairy products—the higher the cholesterol in your bloodstream. That, in fact, is the main reason it is so important to minimize dietary fat.

Fortunately, one study found that an occasional high-fat meal does not elevate choles-terol in your bloodstream if your routine dietary habit is low-fat (Denke, 1988). Stated Margo Denke in her presentation to the American Heart Association:

> As a doctor, I can't recommend high-fat meals, but these findings suggest that it is the overall consumption of saturated fat over time, rather than occasional high-fat meals, that have the most effect on the lipid profile. It means that when your best friend gets married and they put out a big buffet dinner . . . or when you have a board room lunch meeting and the sandwiches are brought in . . . you don't have to worry too much if you stick to the good diet most of the time.

Another study suggests that if a person follows a low-fat, high-fiber diet, then even an egg a day does not raise cholesterol levels in the blood. In the group studied, the major reduction in cholesterol occurred after the participants had changed to a low-fat diet (Edington, 1987).

Vitamins and Other Supplements

One expert estimates that 40 to 60 percent of Americans use dietary supplements such as vitamin pills, calcium powder, and high-fiber compounds or capsules (Petit, 1989). Yet their value for health or stress control (prevention or reduction) is open to debate (Meyeroff, 1990). On one hand, many experts contend that supplementary vitamins and minerals are not needed if one eats a balanced diet. For example, Dr. Arno Motulsky, a University of Washington professor of medicine and director of a nutrition and health study by the National Research Council, says, "Although supplements make some people think they feel better, the evidence that this helps prevent chronic disease is nonexistent. Having no evidence of scientific benefits, we don't recommend it" (Meyeroff, 1990).

Similarly, a coalition of health and consumer groups led by the American Dietetic Association has charged that the nation's $2.6 billion-per-year vitamin-supplement industry markets products most adults and children do not need to maintain good health and that can cause toxic reactions if overused (*Eugene Register-Guard,* 1987). The report asserts that "there are no demonstrated benefits" in the use of vitamin supplements by otherwise healthy men, women, and children. The American Medical Council on Scientific Affairs issued a report at nearly the same time reaching the same conclusion: "healthy adults, 18 years of age and older, receiving adequate diets should have no need for supplementary vitamins" (*Eugene Register-Guard,* 1987).

Exceptions to this general rule may be smokers, who perhaps need vitamin C supple-mentation; endurance athletes, who sometimes need additional zinc and other trace miner-als (although a wholesome diet usually is sufficient even for them); women who take in too little calcium in their diets to prevent osteoporosis; women who need iron supplemen-tation; pregnant women; and other special groups, including the very elderly. Supplemen-tation also may be needed, of course, for individuals who do not eat a balanced, consistent diet with plenty of vegetables and fruits. Many experts agree that in general, however, eat-ing a balanced diet rich in fruits and vegetables will yield sufficient vitamins and minerals to meet daily needs.

Other experts contend there is sufficient evidence now to recommend that everyone take vitamin and mineral supplements. Recommendations range from a multiple one-a-day to antioxidants such as vitamin C, vitamin E, and beta-carotene, which are thought to reduce risk of heart disease, perhaps through blocking some of the harmful effects of a fatty meal, and of free radicals (Cooper, 1994). The *University of California at Berkeley Wellness Letter* (1998a) recommends that a basic multivitamin/mineral supplement makes sense for older adults and that everyone should take doses of vitamin C and E beyond the recommended daily allowances.

What about the association between vitamin B and stress? Vitamin supplements, especially in the B group, are commonly advertised as helpful in combating stress. Some companies mention physical stress; others refer to mental stress, as well. Still others do not distinguish between the two, relying instead on "stress" to sell their products.

One leading company until recently based its promotion of a "stress vitamin" on a 1952 report of the National Academy of Sciences. Close examination of this report, however, shows that it recommends vitamin supplements only for people suffering from severe physical trauma such as major surgery, major fractures, and serious burns. Even in the case of physical stress, the report stated that "in minor illnesses or injury where the expected duration of the disease is less than 10 days and when the patient is essentially ambulatory and is eating his diet . . . a good diet will supply the recommended dietary allowances of all nutrients" (Schafer, 1987). Nutrition experts agree that, with rare exception, recovery from or prevention of physical stress associated with illness or injury seldom requires vitamin supplements, since needs seldom exceed recommended daily allowances.

What about emotional stress? No evidence exists that emotional stress increases our need for vitamin supplementation—or that vitamin supplements will prevent such stress. Again, a normal dietary regimen will provide all vitamins needed by most people. The chief of nutritional science at Lederle Laboratories, manufacturers of Stresstabs, acknowledged this fact in an interview in *Consumer Reports* magazine, when he stated that "people who eat a balanced diet do not need stress vitamins—or for that matter any vitamin supplement at all" (Schafer, 1987).

In New York state, one vitamin manufacturer was successfully prosecuted in 1986 for advertising that "stress resulting from work situations, physical activity, smoking and complications of everyday life can increase your need for certain vitamins."

In short, do not be misled by advertisements for "stress vitamins." Except in rare cases, you do not need them.

Eating Habits and Disorders

Eating Disorders

The message women constantly get from mass media in this country is "You are not quite right like you are. You had better do something about your . . . weight, eyes, hips, feet, skin, hair, scent, breast size, etc., etc." One result is overconcern with appearance, especially weight.

Since weight is associated with health risks and with aerobic fitness, we have good reason to try to minimize weight gain. Among many young people, especially women, this concern becomes an obsession, often resulting in the eating disorders of *anorexia nervosa* and *bulimia nervosa*. These disorders most often are the direct result of intense stress, and they in turn add immeasurably to human distress.

Anorexia nervosa remains a disorder mainly affecting young women, with onset usually between ages 12 and 25 (Giannini, Newman, & Gold, 1990). It includes refusal to maintain minimal normal body weight over time, intense fear of weight gain or looking fat, and distorted body image (e.g., feeling "fat," even when emaciated, and believing that one area of the body is "too fat," even when obviously underweight).

Anorexia afflicts between 2 and 5 percent of young women, with women of upper-middle socioeconomic status overrepresented. It carries a mortality rate of about 5 percent during the first two years, but, when untreated, it can carry a mortality risk of 20 percent.

Although more Americans die of anorexia than any other mental illness, insurance companies often refuse to pay for needed care (Fox, 1997).

According to one source, "A perfectionistic lifestyle, punctuated by one or more performance-related stresses, predisposes to anorexia nervosa" (Giannini, Newman, & Gold, 1990, 1170).

Bulimia nervosa, which has a prevalence of about 5 percent among adolescent females and less than 1 percent among adolescent males, most often takes the form of binge eating, accompanied by voluntary vomiting, use of laxatives, or use of diuretics to prevent weight gain. Vigorous exercise and distorted body image usually accompany it. According to the same source, those afflicted disproportionately come from families with a history of emotional instability and obesity.

A study in the mid-1980s found young girls dieting at an alarming rate, perhaps an indication of more eating disorders still ahead and certainly underscoring the obsessive concern about weight and appearance in our society (Associated Press, 1986). University of California, San Francisco, researchers surveyed 500 girls in grades 4 to 12 at San Francisco parochial schools about their attitudes and behavior related to body weight. Consider these findings.

- Thirty-one percent of the 9-year-olds said they were worried they were or would become fat.
- Almost half of the 9-year-olds and almost 80 percent of the 10- and 11-year-olds reported dieting to lose weight.
- The number of girls who reported binge eating increased steadily with age, and all of the 18-year-olds reported current episodes of vomiting, using laxatives, fasting, or taking diet pills.
- Although 58 percent of the sample said they considered themselves overweight, their actual height and weight showed that in reality only 17 percent were, an indication of the extent of distortion of body image among young females.

According to the study director, Laurel Mellin, "While eating disorders in adolescents have been studied before, the prevalence of these patterns in children had not been investigated. The results, which are both surprising and alarming, underscore the need for preventive education in the very early school years, possibly even pre-school."

Unfortunately, available data suggest a rise in eating disorders. The most common and difficult barrier to treatment is denial of the extent of the problem, with resulting resistance to change. Often a multidisciplinary focus is needed, including physician, counselor, dietitian, and support group. Willingness to change is vital to success. Learning to manage tension, anxiety, boredom or depression can help.

Is Nibbling Healthy?

A common debate among those struggling to lose weight is whether it is best to skip a meal a day, to eat three modest-sized meals, or to nibble all day long. This same issue is equally important, of course, to everyone.

Most dietitians agree on two key principles. First, skipping meals does more harm than good, for several reasons.

1. Resting metabolism slows down when the digestive system is inactive for long periods. Therefore, fewer calories are burned.
2. When a meal is skipped (and even more so if two are missed), the body believes it is entering a period of prolonged deprivation. In response, it is more likely to convert calories to fat to be stored for later survival.

Eating Disorders on Campus

The extent of eating disorders on U. S. college campuses is reflected in a recent cover story, "Wasting Away" by *People Weekly (*1999, 52) Here are excerpts from that article:

At first it seemed like a minor, if mystifying, problem: In the spring of 1996, plastic sandwich bags began disappearing by the hundreds from the kitchen of a sorority house at a large northeastern university. When the sorority's president investigated, she found a disturbing explanation: The bags, filled with vomit, were hidden in a basement bathroom. "I was shocked," says the president (who later learned that the building's pipes, eroded by gallons of stomach acid, would have to be replaced). "Yet in a way it made sense." Most of her 45 housemates, she recalls, worried about weight. "It was like a competition to see who could eat the least. At dinner they would say, 'All I had today was an apple,' or 'I haven't had anything.' It was surreal."

And, sadly, all too typical of scenes at colleges across the country. Since singer Karen Carpenter's death from complications of anorexia nervosa first jolted the nation into an awareness of the disease in 1983, the numbers of women seeking treatment for eating disorders has skyrocketed. Sufferers—5 to 10 million females and 1 million males—tend to be young (from 14 to 25), white, affluent, "perfectionistic, type A personalities," says Marcia Herrin, codirector of Dartmouth College's Eating Disorders Education, Prevention, and Treatment Program. It's a problem that is raging on college campuses. In a *People* poll done last fall of 500 coeds, the figures were alarming: More than half of the young women respondents said they knew at least two schoolmates with an eating disorder. In a second poll of 490 college health officials commissioned by *People,* 70 percent said the problem was "common" on their campuses. According to Seattle's Eating Disorders Awareness and Prevent Group (EDAP), an estimated 5 to 7 percent of American's 12 million undergraduates are afflicted with anorexia (a pathological fear of weight gain leading to extreme weight loss, bulimia (bingeing followed by purging) or binge eating (compulsive overeating). "College women are away from their families, and there's tremendous pressure to find their way in the world," says Jennifer Biely, EDAP's director "Food is one thing they can control."

The idolization of wispy models and actresses adds to the problem. "I can tell a girl that what matters is what's going on in her head and heart," says sociologist Tracy Mann, author of a 1997 study on campus prevention programs. "But when she turns on the TV, she sees what matters is how you look."

3. Skipping meals leads to low energy, which can negatively affect productivity, relationships, and emotional well-being.

Second, eating small meals combined with several snacks is better than eating three big meals a day. Again, here are several reasons.

1. For one thing, energy level is likely to be higher and more stable. This, in turn, will improve productivity, relationships, and emotional stability.
2. A higher proportion of calories you eat is likely to be burned rather than stored, resulting in better weight control.
3. You will feel never very hungry nor very full.
4. An unexpected benefit recently found by medical researchers is that both total cholesterol and low density lipoprotein cholesterol (the bad kind) are lower than if the same foods and the same amount of calories are consumed in three meals per day (Jenkins et al., 1989).

For someone trying to lose weight, here is a suggested plan for taking in 1,500 daily calories through three meals and three snacks (*Running and Fitnews,* 1990).

Breakfast	300 calories
Snack	200 calories
Lunch	300 calories
Snack	200 calories
Dinner	400 calories
Snack	100 calories

The authors suggest designing menus of this type for about a week at a time.

"Yo-Yo" Dieting

No one could question that obesity increases risk of distress, illness, and a shortened life span. Yet recent evidence suggests that cyclical or **"yo-yo" dieting** can sometimes do more harm than good.

Steen, Oppliger, and Brownell (1988) point out that weight cycling has the following effects:

*   Increases preferences for fatty foods
*   Lowers metabolism rate, making subsequent dieting even more difficult
*   Increases risk of cardiovascular disease

In a recent presentation to the American Dietetic Association, Brownell stated, "There is evidence that the more dieting one does, the harder it is to lose weight. This seems to be due to the body's adaptation to weight loss by lowering its energy requirements" (Higgins, 1988).

For example, Brownell's study of high school wrestlers found that some were cyclical dieters, others "noncyclers" (Brownell, 1988). The investigators discovered that the weight cyclers had a significantly lower resting metabolic rate and lower resting energy expenditure than did noncyclers.

See Application Exercise 13-2 for developing a plan to improve your nutritional habits.

Mormon Lifestyle and Life Expectancy

A study by a University of California, Los Angeles, epidemiologist credits the positive lifestyle habits of Mormons with their unusually low mortality rate and their high life expectancy (Enstrom, 1989).

Enstrom studied the health habits and death rates of about 5,000 Mormon men who had risen to the highest lay rank of their church, as well as similar data on their wives. Here are highlights of his findings:

- Middle-aged Mormon men who adhered to three key positive health habits—never smoking, getting regular exercise, and consistently sleeping seven to eight hours per night—had only 34 percent of the mortality rate from cancer and only 14 percent of the mortality rate from cardiovascular disease of middle-aged, white U.S. men. The overall mortality rate of these Mormon men was only 22 percent of the overall rate of middle-aged U.S. men.
- Middle-aged Mormon wives adhering to all three habits had mortality rates, compared with middle-aged, white women, of 55 percent (cancer-related death), 34 percent (cardiovascular-related death), and 47 percent (overall rate).
- Enstrom points out that positive characteristics of the Mormon lifestyle other than the three noted might also contribute to their longer life expectancy (85 years for a 25-year-old Mormon male, compared with 74 years for a comparable white non-Mormon): avoidance of caffeine, alcohol, and drugs; a low-fat, well-balanced diet; higher than average education; and a strong family life.

Concludes Enstrom, "If people want to minimize their mortality rate and maximize their longevity, this [maintaining positive lifestyle habits] is certainly one way of doing it. I'm not a Mormon, and I don't recommend that people have to become Mormons to do this" (Scott, 1989).

Preliminary results from a Swedish epidemiological study suggest that "a history of weight fluctuation is associated with a risk of heart disease" (Higgins, 1988). Other adverse results include elevated blood pressure (Blair, 1992; Sonne-Holm, 1989).

The implication appears to be that, while obesity has its costs, continually losing and regaining weight has even more. Most experts agree regular moderate exercise is the key to losing weight and keeping it off. Without exercise, the probabilities are very high that within a few months lost weight will return.

SLEEP

Stages of Sleep

The third health buffer that helps protect against distress is adequate sleep. Sleep is vital for rejuvenating the body and mind. Sleep deficiency, either in amount or quality, makes one more vulnerable to irritability, anxiety, depression, disturbed thinking, and physical disorders.

Sleep is an altered state of consciousness in which brain waves go through five stages: four stages of non-rapid-eye movement (NREM) and one stage of rapid-eye-movement sleep (REM). As you close your eyes and sink into deep quiet, your brain emits *alpha waves,* low-amplitude waves of about 8 to 13 cycles per minute (Rathus, 1990). This is the same brain-wave zone that can be learned through biofeedback and meditation. Entering Stage 1 sleep results in further slowing of the brain, into the zone of *theta waves,* with a frequency of about 6 to 8 cycles per second. The transition from alpha to theta waves may be accompanied by a *hypnogogic state,* in which you experience dreamlike images. Yet this is the lightest stage of sleep.

After a half hour or so of Stage 1 sleep, you experience a rather steep dive into Stages 2, 3, and 4. Here your brain emits *delta waves,* from about one-half to seven cycles per second. Stage 4, reached after less than an hour, is the deepest sleep, from which it is most difficult to be awakened. After perhaps half an hour in the depths of Stage 4, you begin a relatively rapid return upward through the stages into the stage of REM. During REM sleep, you experience relatively rapid, low-amplitude brain waves similar to those of Stage 1. During REM sleep, most intense dreaming occurs.

How Much Sleep Do You Need?

Most adults function best when getting about eight hours of sleep, but individual differences occur. For example, Albert Einstein typically slept 11 hours a night, and Calvin Coolidge slept 12 (Carlinsky, 1990). By contrast, shorter-period sleepers include Margaret Thatcher, Leonard Bernstein, Bryant Gumbel, David Stockman, Cloris Leachman, Jerry Falwell, and John Barrymore. The late Robert Maxwell, the British publishing baron, slept (grudgingly) only about four hours a night and was still going strong at nearly 70.

A Cornell University sleep researcher, James Maas, estimates that more than 100 million Americans—nearly every other adult and teenager—work and play with insufficient sleep (Kates, 1990). He suggests that our on-the-go lifestyle is turning the nation into "walking zombies." A more recent report states, "Eighty percent of us stumble around sleep-deprived. It can cost us our health—even our lives—and it costs the country billions" (Sullivan, 1998). Berman and colleagues, medical sleep researchers, point out that "Excessive daytime sleepiness and inappropriate sleep may constitute the most underrated health-risk factor in America today" (Berman, Nino-Murcia, & Roehrs, 1990). *Time* magazine noted in an article called "Drowsy America" that "millions of Americans are chronically sleep deprived, trying to get by on six hours or even less. In many households, cheating on sleep has become an unconscious and pernicious habit" (Toufexis, 1990, 79). Just how harmful sleep deprivation can be is illustrated by a recent Australian study in which 40 people were kept awake for 28 hours. Their hand-eye coordination suffered as much the next morning as being legally intoxicated. Driving under these conditions could be extremely hazardous (*University of California at Berkeley Wellness Letter,* 1998b).

Studies show that high school seniors average 6.1 hours per night—but need about 10 hours to function effectively. Close to one-third fall asleep in class at least once each week (Kates, 1990).

Insomnia and Sleep Deprivation

Insomnia can be caused by anything from calcium deficiency to breathing difficulties. According to one report, 90 percent of the time insomnia is caused by stress (*Chico Enterprise-Record,* 1985). It is estimated that one-third of all Americans have difficulty falling asleep on any given night, while half have an occasional episode of disturbed sleep. About 1 in 5 have prolonged bouts of insomnia. Twice as many women as men are affected.

Consequences of sleep disturbance and deprivation can be quite minor if short-term and temporary—for example, increased irritability, sensitivity to criticism, difficulty concentrating, memory problems, the blues, and increased physical and emotional tension. Most agree little harm is caused by a short night or two (Associated Press, 1997).

Prolonged sleep deprivation can evoke more serious results. Sometimes these difficulties are associated with night shifts or changes in shift work. The Three Mile Island disaster happened at 4 A.M., Chernobyl at 2 A.M., the Bhopal accident at midnight, and the Exxon Valdez disaster shortly after midnight. Flight-crew sleep deprivation and disturbed sleep rhythm may have played a part in several major commercial airline disasters studied, according to chronobiologists William Holley and William Price (Perrin, 1987). A study of college students found that sleep-deprived individuals performed significantly worse than nondeprived individuals on a cognitive task. (Pilcher & Walters, 1997) Yet the sleep-deprived students rated their concentration and effort higher and estimated their performance significantly higher. Not only does sleep deprivation hamper performance, it also appears that college students are not aware of the extent to which sleep deprivation negatively affects their ability to succeed at a cognitive task.

As we noted in Chapter 5, chronic sleep problems themselves can become major stressors as the individual frets about not getting enough sleep. Beyond that, emotional volatility is likely to increase, thought processes become less effective, performance suffers, and health is impaired. *Time* correctly points out:

> Perhaps the most insidious consequence of skimping on sleep is the irritability that increasingly pervades society. Weariness corrodes civility and erases humor, traits that ease the myriad daily frustrations, from standing in supermarket lines to refereeing the kids' squabbles. Without sufficient sleep, tempers flare faster and hotter at the slightest offense. (Toufexis, 1990, 80)

Most of us know the time we are most susceptible to colds and flu—when we are "run down" from too many short nights of sleep. William Dement, director of Stanford University's sleep center, states, "Most Americans no longer know what it feels like to be fully alert" (Toufexis, 1990, 79). The only country with greater sleep deprivation may be Japan.

Tips for Preventing and Coping with Insomnia

While medications can sometimes work to control insomnia, experts agree it is far more desirable to try lifestyle approaches first. Here are a number of suggestions made by sleep experts:

1. **Establish a regular sleep routine.** Although this sometimes is difficult because of the changing demands of school, job, community meetings, and family, it is important to seek to go to bed at a regular time. It is also useful to follow established habits during the 15 to 30 minutes before falling to sleep—reading a novel or a news magazine, watching the news, watering the plants, getting a massage.

2. **Use relaxation methods.** In Chapter 15, you will read about several techniques that sometimes work in sleep inducement: progressive relaxation (tense and relax muscles), autogenic relaxation (inducing warmth and heaviness in muscles), meditation, imagery, and producing alpha waves through biofeedback learning.

3. **Exercise regularly.** Some evidence shows that those who exercise regularly experience a deeper, more restful sleep (Sobel & Ornstein, 1997). It makes sense that daily release of emotional and physical tension will decrease chances of going to bed in a

pent-up state. Intense exercise shortly before bedtime, however, can leave the body in a state of residual arousal, making it harder to get to sleep.

4. **Minimize noise.** Using earplugs often can do wonders when outside noise cannot be avoided.

5. **Practice sleep-congruent nutritional habits.** For example, avoid alcohol before going to bed. While a drink may help you fall asleep faster, alcohol disturbs sleep later in the night. A light snack, including milk, sometimes can help. Avoid a heavy meal just before bedtime, since that will stimulate the body. Avoid caffeine in coffee, tea, soft drinks, or chocolate for several hours before sleep. Arousal effects of caffeine can occur at doses as low as 50 mg. Be aware that caffeine appears in popular soft drinks such as Coke, Pepsi, and Mountain Dew (30-65 mg), as well as in tea (150 mg) and coffee (29-176 mg).

6. **Stop smoking.** Nicotine, too, is a stimulant. Further, withdrawal symptoms occur during the night, often disturbing sleep.

7. **Get up if you cannot sleep.** New York clinical psychologist Roy Shapiro advises insomniacs to get out of bed for 15 to 60 minutes and occupy their minds with thoughts other than sleeping. He states, "The worst thing a person can do is to stay in bed. All you accomplish is to brood even more about your problems and count the time you are not sleeping. Reading and watching TV are activities that will absorb the mind without stimulating it too much. Then, when you're sleepy, go back to bed. If another 15 minutes pass by, and you can't get to sleep, get out of bed again" (Levine, 1990).

8. **Maintain realistic self-talk about sleep.** As noted, sleep deprivation itself can become a major stressor. Believing your day will certainly be ruined unless you get to sleep *now* only makes things worse. Rathus (1990, 179) has identified a number of beliefs that increase bedtime tension and realistic alternatives.

Exaggerated Belief	Alternative Belief
If I don't get to sleep, I'll feel wrecked tomorrow.	Not necessarily. If I'm tired, I can go to bed early tomorrow night.
It's unhealthy for me not to get more sleep.	Not necessarily. Some people do very well on only a few hours of sleep.
I'll wreck my sleeping schedule for the whole week if I don't get to sleep very soon.	Not at all. If I'm tired, I'll just go to bed a bit earlier. I'll get up about the same time with no problem.
If I don't get to sleep, I won't be able to concentrate on that big test/ conference tomorrow.	Possibly, but my fears may be exaggerated. I may as well relax or get up and do something enjoyable for a while.

In short, adequate sleep is important for good health and prevention of distress. Like regular exercise and sound nutritional practices, management of your sleep habits is important to a whole-person, lifestyle approach to stress management.

HEALTHY PLEASURES

David Sobel, physician and coauthor of two well-known books on stress and health, *The Healing Brain* (Ornstein & Sobel, 1986) and *Healthy Pleasures* (Ornstein & Sobel, 1989), was featured in an article about how stress experts handle their health (Castleman, 1990).

In addition to his usual work as regional director for Patient Education and Health Promotion for Northern California Kaiser-Permanente (a large health maintenance organization) and his laborious writing work, Sobel had faced a challenging series of events in his personal life during the 18 months prior to the interview about how he handles his own stress.

Among other things, a member of his family died unexpectedly, and he and his family had several rooms added to their San Jose home. During the renovations, they moved out for two months. "It's been quite a time. Very stressful. But that's life," Sobel said.

How does Sobel cope? Here is what he told the interviewer:

Frankly, I don't worry much about managing my stress. I don't use any specific techniques. I'm not opposed to formal stress-management programs or exercises; some people need them. But I'm not involved in any. I simply try to fill my life with activities I personally find pleasurable, things that help rejuvenate me.

Beyond health, family and friends, and having your basic needs met, it's not the big things in life that make the difference. It's the little pleasures you create for yourself: playing with your kids, phone calls to old friends, a hug, a compliment, gardening, having pets, gazing into an aquarium.

Whenever I get upset about something in my little corner of the world, I spin my globe. San Jose is a tiny dot. California is a little sliver. It's a big world out there, and each of us is just a microscopic part of it. (Castleman, 1990, 38, 39)

I agree with Sobel. Cultivating **healthy pleasures** can be an effective approach to coping with the stressors of everyday life, large and small. For me, this includes:

- A cleansing conversation with my wife about our work that day
- The beauty of my daily run, usually along rural trails
- The quiet morning and evening routine of feeding our farm animals
- Cleaning up llama dung on a sunny Sunday afternoon while listening to *Prairie Home Companion* on my Walkman
- Enjoying my dog lying quietly at my side for hours on end as I write
- Long-distance telephone conversations with my grown daughters
- Strolling in our pasture with my wife, cat, and dog on a sunny weekend morning
- Inserting my earplugs, going to my recliner chair, and sinking into deep relaxation in the midst of a busy afternoon at the office
- Reading the newspaper before a sparkling, warm fireplace on a nippy winter evening
- Relaxing in a hot tub under the stars at the end of the day
- Kayaking down a Class III or IV river in Northern California with my wife and friends

For me, these healthy pleasures are more than means of coping. They have become **personal anchors**, offering quiet stability in the midst of a hectic, rapidly changing world.

See Application Exercise 13-3 for a closer look at your actual and desired healthy pleasures.

Lessons From White-Water Kayaking

One of my wife's and my healthy pleasures is white-water kayaking, a sport I took up after age 50. Kayaking is both great fun and a rich source of learning about stress management. Here are some lessons I have learned.

- The river is like anything else—there to experience in any way I choose. The river can be a threat or a challenge, a bore or a place of beauty, a world of loneliness or a place to share, a place to be fully engaged with or a place for mind-wandering or detachment.
- Kayaking offers a chance to grow through pushing my limits. Staying within my comfort zone is safe. But sometimes pushing my limits by tackling progressively more difficult rivers takes me to new levels of skill and confidence. I believe this personal growth ripples outward into other parts of my life.
- Equally important is knowing my limits. It is foolhardy to venture into waters that are unknown or beyond my skill level.
- Kayaking is at once a solo and social activity. I am tucked alone in my shell with my paddle. Yet I would never go down a river alone or out of reach of a nearby partner, readily available if needed and vice versa. This illustrates the essential balance between individuality and interdependence.
- Like any other demanding skill, there is no shortcut to the mastery of kayaking. The only way is hard work, repetition and practice—time on the water.
- Having a plan is vital. If the rapid is new or potentially dangerous, I always scout it from the bank. If not, I know in advance the line I will follow through the rapid. Having a plan is key in most challenging circumstances.
- When approaching a rapid, it is vital to see that all is in place—helmet is snapped on, life jacket is zipped up, spray skirt is in place, nose plug is on. The same holds for any situation requiring peak performance, especially if the negative consequences of not being prepared are great.
- Peak performance depends upon intense focus and concentration when entering a demanding rapid. This holds, of course, in any circumstance demanding peak performance, whether it be public speaking, acting, decision-making, taking an exam, making an opening statement to the jury, a job interview, or whatever.
- I can think of no better opportunity to practice positive self-talk and visualization. If I am flooded with self-doubt and negative mental images, chances are far greater of flipping upside down than if I feel confident and see myself doing well.

Many of these personal healthy pleasures center on being outdoors. My rewards are consistent with studies now being reported on the restorative benefits of spending time outdoors. Kaplan and Kaplan (1989), for example, have found both mental and physical benefits of being in nature. Cimprich is investigating how seriously ill people get a mental boost from in-

- When moving through the rapid, success depends on simultaneously maintaining a short-term view (sharp focus on boulders and waves immediately ahead) and a long-range view (being aware of rocks, pour-over, and turns farther ahead). This is true in most demanding situations, although short-term and long-range often relate to time rather than space.
- Vital to successful kayaking is composure under pressure—for example, when moving down the smooth tongue to the first big wave or when upside down underwater preparing to roll back up after a flip amid turbulent waves.
- When entering an extreme challenge, I do not freeze. I keep doing what I normally do in less extreme circumstances.
- Success—indeed, survival—depends not only on how I do when things are going well but on how I react to an unexpected crisis—getting "trashed" in a big wave hole, stuck against a wall, or broached across two rocks.
- When waves are coming at me fast and furiously in the midst of a long rapid, it helps to "slow down" my perception, taking one wave at a time. This way, I can avoid feeling overwhelmed and out of control. This can help in other life crises as well.
- It is important to find the proper balance between skill and confidence. If I am overly confident, I can get into dangerous situations that are beyond my skill level. If I am overly timid, I don't realize my potential.
- Through kayaking, I have learned the importance of holding steady in a potentially threatening, unpredictable environment. If I overreact, I increase chances of losing my concentration, making a wrong move through boulders, or flipping over. This lesson applies in many settings.
- Boils and whirlpools like those I encountered on the Grand Canyon's Colorado River are like unexpected life stressors. I knew they were coming but not when or where. They usually surprised me. They could be a piece of cake or they could unexpectedly stop me dead still, suck my boat under, flip me, or shoot me 15 yards sideways. I learned to anticipate them and then to hold steady, responding as needed.
- I have learned a good deal from watching myself come back after a bad rapid or a bad day. I have learned the value of resilience, of putting difficult events behind me as quickly as possible, learning from them, and moving forward to new challenges.
- Finally, I have learned to be as open to beauty back in my everyday life as on the river. I have learned about opening my senses and to be fully present in the here and now.

teracting with nature. She states, "Coping with a life-threatening disease requires so much mental energy that it can result in fatigue. Gardening, taking a walk in the woods or even watching birds outside a window can help restore some of that energy" (Hair, 1997, 8F).

In the next chapter, we will examine tools for managing self-talk.

References

American College of Sports Medicine. (1990). *The recommended quantity and quality of exercise for developing and maintaining cardiorespiratory and muscular fitness in healthy adults.*

American Heart Association. (1993). *A healthy challenge: The national nutritional test.*

Antonovsky, A. (1979). *Health, stress and coping: New perspectives on mental and physical well-being.* San Francisco: Jossey-Bass.

Antonovsky, A. (1987). *Unraveling the mystery of health: How people manage stress and stay well.* San Francisco: Jossey-Bass.

Associated Press. (1986). Study shows alarming rate of young girls dieting. *Chico Enterprise-Record,* October 30, 3A.

Associated Press. (1988). Cancer group finds Americans eat all wrong. *San Francisco Chronicle,* March 14, A1.

Associated Press. (1989a). Milk biggest source of bad fat in kids. *Chico Enterprise-Record,* February 19, 8D.

Associated Press. (1989b). Easy, painless changes that can cut fat from your diet. *Chico Enterprise-Record,* September 5, 8B.

Associated Press. (1994). Stepping up activity boosts value of exercise, study finds. *Los Angeles Times,* November 17, A12.

Associated Press. (1997). Study finds sleeping patterns have dramatic effect on mood. *San Francisco Chronicle,* February 22, A9.

Berger, B. G., & Owen, D. R. (1983). Mood alteration with swimming—Swimmers really do "feel better." *Psychosomatic Medicine, 45,* 425–433.

Berman, T. E., Nino-Murcia, G., & Roehrs, T. (1990). Sleep disorders: Take them seriously. *Patient Care,* June 15, 85–104.

Blair, S. N. (1992). Long-term benefits and adverse effects of weight loss: Data from two prospective epidemiological studies. NIH Obesity Technology Conference.

Blair, S. N., Kohl, H. W., III, Paffenbarger, R. S., Jr., Clark, D. G., Cooper, K. H., & Gibbons, L. W. (1989). Physical fitness and all-cause mortality: A prospective study of healthy men and women. *Journal of the American Medical Association, 262,* 2395–2401.

Brand, D. (1988). Searching for life's elixir. *Time,* December 12, 62–66.

Brown, J. D., & Lawton, M. (1986). Stress and well-being in adolescence: The moderating role of physical exercise. *Journal of Human Stress, 12,* 125–131.

Brown, R. D. (1986). *Effects of a strength training program on strength, body composition, and self-concept of females.* Unpublished doctoral dissertation. Brigham Young University.

Brown, R. S. (1987). Exercise as an adjunct to the treatment of mental disorders. In W. P. Morgan, & S. E. Goldston (Eds.), *Exercise and mental health.* Washington, DC: Hemisphere, 131–137.

Carlinsky, D. (1990). Not everyone needs eight-hour slumber. *San Francisco Chronicle,* March 14, B1.

Castleman, M. (1990). How the stress experts deal with theirs. *Medical Self-Care, 57,* 35–40, 74.

Chico Enterprise-Record (1985). Insomnia: If it's stress-related, fighting can only make it worse, October 27, C4.

Clarke, D. H. (1975). *Exercise physiology.* Englewood Cliffs, NJ: Prentice-Hall.

Cooper, K. H. (1977). *The aerobics way.* New York: Evans.

Cooper, K. H. (1994). *Antioxydant revolution.* Nashville: Thomas Nelson Publishers.

Cummins, H. J. (1998). 20 percent of American teens are overweight. *Chico Enterprise-Record*, February 1, 6D.

Denke, M. A. (1988). Occasional high-fat meal may not cancel effect of prudent diet. *Family Practice News, 18,* 5.

Dienstbier, R. A. (1989). Arousal and physiological toughness: Implications for mental and physical health. *Psychological Review, 96,* 84–100.

Dustman, R. E. (1989). Aerobics fitness helps cognitive function in aged. *Family Practice News, 19,* 37.

Edington, J. (1987). Egg may not need to be restricted in low-fat diet. *Family Practice News, 17,* 6.

Eliot, R. S. & Breo, D. L. (1984). *Is it worth dying for?* New York: Bantam.

Enstrom, J. E. (1989). Health practices and cancer mortality among active California Mormons. *Journal of the National Cancer Institute, 6,* 1807–1814.

Eugene Register-Guard (1987). Vitamin overuse alleged, April 9, 3A.

Fahey, T. D., Insel, P. M., & Roth, W. T. (1994). *Fit and well: Core concepts and labs in physical fitness and wellness.* Mountain View, CA: Mayfield.

Fox, C. (1997). Starved out. *Life,* December, 78–88.

Friedman, M., Rosenman, R. H. (1959). Association of specific overt behavior pattern with blood and cardiovascular findings. *Journal of the American Medical Association, 169,* 1286–1296.

Fry, R. W., Grove, J. R., Morton, A. R., Zeroni, P. M., Gaudieri, S., & Keast, D. Psychological and immunological correlates of acute overtraining. *British Journal of Sports Medicine, 28,* 241–246.

Giannini, A. J., Newman, M., & Gold, M. (1990). Anorexia and bulimia. *American Family Physician, 41,* 1169–1176.

Glasser, W. (1976). *Positive addiction.* New York: Harper.

Gotto, A. M., Jr. (1988). Lipoprotein metabolism and the etiology of hyperlipidemia. *Hospital Practice: Symposium Supplement, 23,* 4–13.

Griest, J. H., Klein, M. H., Eischens, R. R., & Faris, J. T. (1978). Running out of depression. *The Physician and Sportsmedicine, 6,* 49–56.

Griest, J. H., Klein, M. H., Eischens, R. R., Faris, J. T., Gurman, A. S., & Morgan, J. P. (1979). Running as a treatment for depression. *Comprehensive Psychiatry, 20,* 41–54.

Hair, M. (1997). A boost from nature. *Detroit Free Press,* August 12, 7F–9F.

Hayes, D., & Ross, C. E. (1986). Body and mind: The effect of exercise, overweight, and physical health on psychological well-being. *Journal of Health and Social Behavior, 27,* 387–400.

Higgins, L. C. (1988). Cyclical dieting poses dangers. *Medical World News,* November 14, 25–26.

Jenkins, D. A. J., Theiss, M. S., Vuksan, V., Brighenti, F., Cumnae, S. C., Rao, V., Kenkins, A. L., Buckly, G., Patten, R., Singer, W., Corey, R., & Josse, R. G. (1989). Nibbling versus gorging: Metabolic advantages of increased meal frequency. *New England Journal of Medicine, 321,* 929–934.

Johnsgård, K. W. (1989). *The exercise prescription for depression and anxiety.* New York: Plenum Press.

Kaplan, R., & Kaplan, S. (1989). *The experience of nature.* New York: Cambridge University Press.

Kates, W. (1990). America is not getting enough sleep. *San Francisco Chronicle,* March 30, B3.

Lamb, L. E. (1981). Walking to health. *The Health Letter,* XVIII, 1–2.

Lazarus, R. S., & Folkman, S. (1984). *Stress, appraisal and coping.* New York: Springer.

Levine, D. (1990). Relief from insomnia via lifestyle favored. *Medical Tribune, 31,* 2.

Lowman, M. (1990). Californians have a ways to go toward a well-balanced diet. *Chico Enterprise-Record,* C1.

McCann, I. L., & Holmes, D. S. (1984). The influence of aerobic exercise on depression. *Journal of Personality and Social Psychology, 46,* 1142–1147.

McDonald, K. A. (1997). U. of California scientist takes issue with government guidelines for exercise. *The Chronicle of Higher Education,* October 10, A15–A16.

Meyeroff, W. J. (1990). Vitamin use debated. *Medical Tribune, 31,* 4.

Morse, A., Walker, R., & Monroe, D. (1994). The effect of exercise on a psychological measure of the stress response. *Wellness Perspectives, (11)*1, 39–46.

Moses, J. (1989). Light exercise may yield more mental benefit. *Family Practice News, 19,* 51.

Ornstein, R., & Sobel, D. (1986). *The healing brain.* New York: Touchstone.

Ornstein, R., & Sobel, D. (1989). *Healthy pleasures.* Reading, MA: Addison-Wesley.

Paffenbarger, R. S., Jr., Hyde, R. T., Wing, A. L., & Hsieh, C. (1986). Physical activity, all-cause mortality, and longevity of college alumni. *New England Journal of Medicine, 314,* 605–613.

People Weekly. (1999). Out of control. April 12, 52.

Perkins, K. D. (1998). Walk—you'll live longer, seniors told. *Sacramento Bee,* January 8, 1998, A1.

Perlman, D. (1988). Koop says bad diet kills 1 million a year in U.S. *San Francisco Chronicle,* July 28, A5.

Perrin, F. (1987). Is weariness in cockpit contributing to crashes? *Medical Tribune, 27,* 7–9.

Petit, C. (1989). A new report tells Americans how to eat. *San Francisco Chronicle,* March 2, A4.

Pilcher, J. J., & Walters, A. A. (1997). How sleep deprivation affects psychological variables related to college students' cognitive performance. *Journal of American College Health, 46,* 121–126.

President's Council on Physical Fitness and Sports (1997). Physical activity in American adults, *Healthy Bites,* September, 3.

Rathus, S. A. (1990). *Psychology* (4th ed.). Fort Worth: Holt, Rinehart and Winston.

Rippe, J. M., Ward, A., Porcari, J. P., & Freedman, P. S. (1988). Walking for health and fitness. *Journal of the American Medical Association, 259,* 2720–2723.

Roth, D. L., & Holmes, D. S. (1987). Influence of aerobic exercise training and relaxation training on physical and psychological health following stressful life events. *Psychosomatic Medicine, 49,* 355–365.

Runner's World (1989). Up with people, May, 49.

Running and Fitnews (1990). It's better to nibble than to gorge, April, 2.

Schafer, W. (1987). On stress vitamins. *Stress and Health Report, 5,* 1.

Schafer, W. (1996). *Stress management for wellness.* (3rd ed.). Fort Worth: Holt, Rinehart, & Winston.

Scott, J. (1989). Mormon ways shown to be healthy. *Sacramento Bee,* December 6, A5.

Sime, W. E. (1987). Exercise in the prevention and treatment of depression. In W. P. Morgan & S. E. Goldston (Eds.), *Exercise and mental health.* Washington, DC: Hemisphere, 145–152.

Sobel, D., & Ornstein, R. (1997). Exercise improves sleep. *Mind/Body Health Newsletter, VI,* 1–2.

Sonne-Holm, S., Sorensen, T. I., Jensen, G., & Schnohr, P. (1989). Independent effects of weight change and attained body weight on prevalence of arterial hypertension in obese and non-obese men. *British Medical Journal, 299(6702),* 767–770.

Steen, S. N., Oppliger, R. A., & Brownell, K. D. (1988). Metabolic effects of repeated weight loss and regain in adolescent wrestlers. *Journal of the American Medical Association, 260,* 47–50.

Sullivan, R. (1998). Like you, I haven't been sleeping well. *Life,* February, 56–66.

Surgeon General (1989). *The Surgeon General's report on nutrition and health.* Washington, DC: U.S. Government Printing Office.

Toufexis, A. (1990). Drowsy America. *Time Magazine,* December 17, 78–85.

Ungerleider, S., Porter, K., Golding, J., & Foster, J. (1989). Mental advantages for masters. *Running Times, 156,* 18–20.

University of California at Berkeley Wellness Letter. (1998). Do you need a multivitamin? February, 2.

van Doornen, L. J. P., & Orlebeke, K. F. (1982). Stress, personality and serum-cholesterol level. *Journal of Human Stress,* 24–29.

Application Exercise 13-1

Personal Exercise Planning

1. Do you now meet the minimal criteria of aerobic exercise described in the chapter (frequency, intensity, time)?

2. If not, what are the barriers now interfering—for example, time, habit, weather, cost, child care?

3. Which aerobic activity do you choose?

4. Where will you do it?

5. What time of week and day?

6. With whom?

7. What equipment and supplies will you need?

8. What barriers do you expect to interfere with continuing to exercise?

9. What specific steps will you take to overcome these barriers?

10. How long a commitment are you making, rain or shine, no matter what?

11. When will you start?

Application Exercise 13-2

Planning for Nutritional Improvement

Based on the readings in this chapter and elsewhere, what specific steps will you take to improve your nutritional habits?

Application Exercise 13-3

Assessing and Improving Healthy Pleasures

1. My current healthy pleasures include:

2. Healthy pleasures I would like to begin or to which I would like to devote more time include:

3. Specific steps I will take to build healthy pleasures into my life include:

Our life is what our thoughts make it.

—MARCUS AURELIUS

It's How You See It: Self-Talk, Beliefs, and Meaning

Matters of Interpretation

- Jason faced three midterms, two term papers, an oral report, and an accounting club meeting during the next three days. He determined the only way to get through this period successfully was to dig in, take it as a challenge, focus his energy, and organize his time carefully. Jonathan faced a similar circumstance. He reacted quite differently: He felt overwhelmed and depressed, saw this as one more instance of how unfair his professors were, and procrastinated by watching television for hours and allowing himself to be distracted by his roommates.

- Terri was a court clerk who was caught between a court administrator who gave her one set of orders and a judge who tried to pull her in other directions. She found this role conflict unpleasant, but she nevertheless found satisfaction in her work and did her best to clarify for her two role partners the bind she was in so they would better agree on their expectations of her. Laurie was another court clerk in much the same situation. Her response, however, was to feel angry most of the time and to fantasize about not having to work at all. Her work performance was below par.

- You are in a crowded elevator taking you to the sixth floor. As the elevator stops at floor three, you are jabbed from behind, then pushed as others get out. You feel slightly irritated. The same thing happens at floor four. You feel your aggravation rise as you tell yourself, "What the heck does that person think he's doing? Can't he see I can't move because it's so crowded in here? Why doesn't he just relax?" As a bit of a hot reactor, you turn around—only to discover that the person is blind and that what jabbed you was his cane. Immediately, your thoughts change: "This person is blind. Now I understand why he couldn't see what was going on. No big deal. But how chagrined I feel for getting so upset."

SELF-TALK AND STRESS

Understanding Self-Talk

These stories illustrate two simple points:

1. Your interpretation of stressors, not stressors themselves, cause distress. Thoughts cause feelings.
2. You can control your interpretation of stressors.

Soon after it began, stress theory departed from the simplistic notion that human stress is a direct response to external stimuli. Throughout the book, I have emphasized that stress, whether positive, neutral, or negative, is the result of a transactional, meaning-centered coping process. This view is not new, illustrated by the following quotations:

> EPICTETUS: "People are disturbed, not by events, but by their view of those events."

SHAKESPEARE: "There is nothing either good or bad but thinking makes it so."

DONNE: "The mind is its own place and it can make hell of heaven or heaven of hell."

TWAIN: "I have had a great many troubles in my life, and most never happened."

The assumption expressed in these statements—that *how we think matters most*—has profound implications. Most of all, it gives power back to persons to shape their own experiences. It is no longer those "stupid, irresponsible, threatening, or inconsiderate people" who cause upset. Rather, it is your self-talk about them. As you will read later in this chapter, interpretations emerge from beliefs, and beliefs emerge from your sense of meaning, value, and purpose. This entire realm is the realm of thinking or cognition—the realm of **self-talk.**

You talk to yourself 100 percent of the waking time. You constantly process thoughts—thoughts about what to do next, what you just did, what you feel at the moment, what others think of you, what your senses tell you, how to deal with an upcoming event, and on and on. Some refer to this as "stream of consciousness."

In *The Bonfires of the Vanities* (1987), author Tom Wolfe does a superb job of describing Sherman's stream of consciousness. For example, Sherman, who considered himself to be a Master of the Universe (he sold institutional bonds on Wall Street and paid monthly bills of $1.2 million to maintain his lifestyle), told his wife he was taking their dog, Marshall, for a walk outside their Park Avenue apartment. His real intention, of course, was to get out of the house to call his lover. His wife says, "Did you know it was raining?"

Still not looking up [Sherman responds]: "Yes, I know." Finally he managed to snap the leash on the animal's collar.

"You're certainly being nice to Marshall all of a sudden."

Wait a minute. Was this irony? Did she suspect something? He looked up. But the smile on her face was obviously genuine, altogether pleasant . . . a lovely smile, in fact . . . *Still a very good-looking woman, my wife* . . . with her fine features, her big clear blue eyes, her rich brown hair . . . *But she's forty years old!* No getting around it . . . Today *good-looking* . . . Tomorrow they'll be talking about what a *handsome* woman she is . . . Not her fault . . . *But not mine either!* (Wolfe, 1987, 11)

Self-talk, the term I prefer to apply to this kind of internal dialogue, is an ever-present part of life. The question is, how much is it under your control, and how much does it take on a life of its own, pushed along by the **repetition compulsion**—the force of habit? You can learn to manage your self-talk (Zastrow, 1993).

Self-talk not only occupies your mind and your time. *Self-talk influences emotions, mental pictures, physical states, and behavior.* In short, you are a product of what you think.

Of particular relevance for human stress is that *self-talk is self-fulfilling.* If you believe others are untrustworthy and selfish, that probably is what you will get. If you assume you are capable and up to the task at hand, you probably will be relatively anxiety-free and will succeed. If you blame yourself when events do not go your way, if you think it is always this way, and it is this way in most parts of your life, you probably will be easily depressed.

Most of all, *self-talk can be self-regulated,* although it is not easy. Changing self-talk habits often takes hard work and lots of patience.

The place of self-talk or interpretation in stress can be expressed in a simple chart.

STRESSOR ⟶ INTERPRETATION ⟶ RESPONSE

Neustress

Positive Stress

Distress

If Epictetus, Shakespeare, and Donne are correct, then blaming, feeling victimized, and pointing the finger all become wholly inappropriate. For the nature of your response to potentially stressful events is determined by your own thinking and not by the events themselves.

See Application Exercise 14-1 to identify personal uses of self-talk skills.

You might find yourself thinking, "But sometimes events in fact are awful and terrible. To think otherwise would be Pollyannish." I agree that events often are unpleasant and unwanted. Sometimes even terrible. Yet most often events are terrible only because they are seen that way. In order to gain a better understanding of the role of interpretation in stress and distress, let us look more closely.

Stressful Events, Self-Talk, and Stress

My reading, personal experience, and work with thousands of people experiencing unwanted distress have led me to the following conclusions about the part interpretation plays in stress and distress.

1. **Stressors are distressors only when they are interpreted as threatening.** Stressors may be interpreted as a threat to any one of several parts of your existence.

   To life and safety: "I could get shot by this guy robbing me."
   To basic needs: "Getting laid off my job will eliminate income for me and my family."
   To self-worth: "Her bad grades mean I am a failure as a parent."
   To image or reputation: "My coworkers in this meeting will think I am incompetent if I don't give an intelligent answer to this question."
   To acceptance or approval: "If I don't do things just right tonight, he will never ask me out again."
   To satisfaction and enjoyment: "I will be miserable for two weeks if I blow this project."
   To pain limit: "This is more than I can bear."

2. **Sometimes it is rational and realistic to interpret stressors as threatening and therefore to be temporarily distressed.** For example:

   Fear and physical tension at hearing about a landslide up the hill from your house
   Grief and pain at word of death of a loved one
   Concern, disappointment, and temporary insomnia at word of an unwanted job transfer
   Anger and readiness for action at an attack by a neighbor's dog on your child.

3. **Stressors often are unnecessarily and unrealistically interpreted as threatening, thereby causing unnecessary distress.** This is especially true of perceived threats to self-worth, image, acceptance, and satisfaction. As we shall see, alternative interpretations are possible.

4. **Stressors are unnecessarily interpreted as threatening when you:**
   Perceive yourself as helpless to control your reactions to stressful situations.
   "I can't do anything about my test anxiety."
   "I can't control my temper when she makes me angry."
   "My depression is out of my control."
   "I can't help feeling like a wallflower."
   "I can't cope."
   "I'm totally overwhelmed."
   "I will have a nervous breakdown if this happens."

   Perceive yourself as helpless to influence events or people in the surrounding environment.
   "There is nothing I can do about that neighbor kid's blaring stereo."
   "Vandalism is out of control in this neighborhood."
   "My boss is oppressive and insensitive, but I am just a little guy here and can't do anything about it."
   "There is no way the poor quality of teaching in this school can be changed."

   Perceive the environment as unrealistically dangerous.
   "I know those teachers are out to get me, pure and simple."
   "Those bright graduate students will make me look bad for sure."
   "All whites (or blacks) are a threat to me."

5. **Unnecessarily interpreting a specific stressor as threatening results from unreasonable beliefs.** A number of common unreasonable beliefs are held by specific participants in my stress-control program.
   "I must maintain an image of strength and invulnerability."
   "I must be sure to act so others will like me."
   "I must always please others."
   "If I don't say yes to this, I will never have the opportunity again."
   "Anything new is dangerous."
   "I must appear feminine at all times—to both men and women."
   "I must appear masculine at all times—to both men and women."
   "If I relax, disaster will strike."
   "If I relax, I will fall behind."
   "Spending time on exercise, relaxation, or fun is wasteful."
   "If I am really me, I will get hurt."
   "Taking one hour a day for me would be selfish."
   "If I don't do it, nobody else can or will."
   "I must always say 'yes' when asked to help."
   "My actions are the main cause of others' emotions."
   "Most people are out to get me."

6. **Faulty interpretations resulting in unnecessary distress can be prevented or altered in two ways.**
   Controlling self-talk as it occurs in the immediate situation
   Altering unreasonable beliefs out of which negative self-talk arises

Common Styles of Negative Self-Talk

Self-talk is an ever-present part of life. You continually appraise or assess stressors as to their nature and likely effects on your experience. In short, you think about them. We noted earlier that the content of this thinking affects the emotional, physical, and behavioral responses that follow.

Life is challenging, hard, and sometimes downright difficult. Yet people's thinking often makes events worse than they truly need be. Several common **styles of negative self-talk** can be identified that sometimes make individuals miserable—or miserable to be around. Which do you use more than you would like?

1. **Negativizing:** Filtering out positive aspects of a situation, while focusing only on negatives.

    DISTORTED SELF-TALK: This job is nothing but one headache after another.

    RATIONAL SELF-TALK: This job has many negative things about it, but then it has some positive ones, too. Like most things, it is a mixture of good and bad.

2. **Awfulizing:** Turning a difficult or unsatisfactory situation into something awful, terrible, and intolerable.

    DISTORTED SELF-TALK: Drivers in this town are the worst this side of the Rockies. I can't stand it.

    RATIONAL SELF-TALK: Many drivers around here make bad judgments and sometimes even bad mistakes. However, like me, they are Fallible Human Beings (FHBs) who sometimes make mistakes—a circumstance hardly worth getting very upset about.

3. **Catastrophizing:** Expecting that the worst almost certainly will happen.

    DISTORTED SELF-TALK: I absolutely know that if my husband goes through with his plan to fly to New York, his plane will crash.

    RATIONAL SELF-TALK: I wish my husband didn't have to fly to New York, but the chances of anything happening to him are so remote it is hardly worth worrying about.

4. **Overgeneralizing:** Generalizing from a single event or piece of information to all or most such things. (After a salesman's failure to sell a product to a prospective client.)

    DISTORTED SELF-TALK: This again shows that I am totally inept in relating to people.

    RATIONAL SELF-TALK: What can I learn from this situation to continue to improve my effectiveness as a salesman?

5. **Minimizing:** Diminishing the value or importance of something to less than it actually is. (Self-deprecating professor after having his article accepted for publication by a professional journal.)

    DISTORTED SELF-TALK: It was accepted, but it certainly is not the quality of writing I expected to be turning out at this point in my career.

    RATIONAL SELF-TALK: The article may not be the greatest contribution I will ever make, but it is something I can be satisfied with for now.

6. **Blaming:** Attributing responsibility for events, especially negative ones, to someone else, even when such responsibility rightfully belongs to the self.

    DISTORTED SELF-TALK: If only my mother had been more loving, then I could have been happy.

RATIONAL SELF-TALK: It would have been nice if my mother had loved me more. However, I am now responsible for my own happiness or unhappiness.

7. **Perfectionism:** Impossibly demanding standards toward the self, others, or both in many situations.

DISTORTED SELF-TALK: Other drivers should obey all traffic laws and always should drive according to the standards of common courtesy I believe in.

RATIONAL SELF-TALK: It would be desirable if other drivers obeyed all traffic laws and followed standards of common courtesy. However, many don't and won't—a fact of life hardly worth getting very upset about.

8. **Musterbation:** The demand that events must turn out as you want them to—otherwise, it inevitably will be very upsetting to you.

DISTORTED SELF-TALK: I must have constant approval and acceptance if life is to be worthwhile and if I am to be happy.

RATIONAL SELF-TALK: It would be nice to be approved and accepted most of the time. However, my happiness does not depend on it.

9. **Personalizing:** Believing that others' behavior or feelings are entirely caused by the self.

DISTORTED SELF-TALK: I know he is depressed because of what I implied in my remarks yesterday.

RATIONAL SELF-TALK: I will handle situations like yesterday better in the future. Meanwhile, I need not unduly fret about his response.

10. **Judging human worth:** Evaluating total worth of the self or others on the basis of traits or behavior.

DISTORTED SELF-TALK: I really muffed that situation yesterday. How terrible of me. This proves again what a Rotten Person (RP) I am.

RATIONAL SELF-TALK: I didn't handle that situation yesterday very well. What can I learn from it so I can do better next time?

11. **Control fallacy:** The belief that happiness depends on cajoling or coercing others to do what you think they should.

DISTORTED SELF-TALK: There is no way I can enjoy my work unless I can get my employees to work as hard and effectively as I believe they should.

RATIONAL SELF-TALK: I will continue to strive to upgrade the work of my employees. Meanwhile, I refuse to let my job satisfaction depend on them.

12. **Polarized thinking:** Things are black and white, right or wrong, good or bad. No middle ground exists.

DISTORTED SELF-TALK: Either I do perfectly on this test, or I am a failure.

RATIONAL SELF-TALK: I will do my best on this test—and then be satisfied with my performance this time around.

13. **Being right:** You are continually on trial to prove that your opinions and actions are correct. Being wrong is unthinkable. Therefore, you must go to any length to demonstrate your rightness.

DISTORTED SELF-TALK: I must be certain they *know* I know what I am talking about.

> RATIONAL SELF-TALK: I have no need here to prove myself, because my self-worth does not depend on what others think of me.

14. **Fallacy of fairness:** Feeling resentful because the world does not conform to your sense of what is fair.

> DISTORTED SELF-TALK: It is just not fair that those questions were on that exam. I have every reason to be upset.

> RATIONAL SELF-TALK: I don't agree that those questions were on the exam. However, they were—something I cannot change and need not get upset about.

15. **Shoulding:** Constant imposition of *shoulds* and *should haves* on the self, others, or both.

> DISTORTED SELF-TALK: I should have said that differently. I should never behave like that.

> RATIONAL SELF-TALK: I would like to have handled that situation more effectively. Next time I will do it differently.

16. **Magnifying:** Making more of an event than it actually is.

> DISTORTED SELF-TALK: This low grade is the worst thing that ever happened to me. It's horrible. What a Rotten Person I am!

> RATIONAL SELF-TALK: How unfortunate I didn't do well on this test. I genuinely blew it. Yet it's not the end of the world. Next time I certainly will study harder.

TURNING SELF-TALK INTO A POSITIVE FORCE

The 16 common styles of negative self-talk manifest themselves in two forms: **situational self-talk** and **long-term beliefs.** Therefore, transforming negative self-talk habits into positive or realistic self-talk habits can be accomplished by two categories of self-talk methods: methods for managing situational self-talk and methods for managing one's perspective—that is, one's cluster of beliefs that endure through time. We will now address strategies and techniques for managing situational self-talk and beliefs. Following that, we will focus on meaning of life, which represents the spiritual dimension of wellness. It is from our sense of meaning and purpose that specific beliefs and situational self-talk patterns arise.

Managing Situational Self-Talk

John, who is described in the box on page 370, learned in his stress class that any of four tools can be very effective in managing his situational interpretation whenever this repetitive episode with his wife arises.

The P and Q Method

When John finds himself reacting defensively in the situation described, he now quickly turns to the **P** (Pause) **and Q** (Question) **Method.** He tells himself to take a deep breath, hesitates before going further, and asks of himself:

- What is my self-talk here?
- How am I upsetting myself?
- Is this truly worth getting upset about?
- How can I interpret this situation so I will respond with reasonable feelings and actions?

Self-Talk and Defensiveness

John tended to react defensively each time his wife even hinted that he had done something wrong. He knew she usually did not intend to hurt his feelings, question his competence, or offend him. Yet he seemed to react automatically, with little apparent ability to control his flareups. He wanted very much to change this negative habit.

John soon discovered what he usually tells himself when his wife questions something he has just done: "I can't stand to be criticized. Being criticized is awful, intolerable, and I can't let her get away with this. That would diminish my worth and stature. I must and will defend myself here at all costs. If she wins, I lose." As he began to question his self-talk, it gradually began to change. For a similar technique known as "freeze frame," see Childre (1994).

John sometimes uses another method to manage his situational self-talk.

Instant Replay

This method sometimes works for John's defensiveness (Bedford, 1981). An alternative to the P and Q Method, it, too, can work for you when you find yourself reacting to a stressor in an undesirable fashion (depression, anxiety, irritability, or anger). **Instant replay** involves using three *C*'s:

1. Catch (recognize) the negative self-talk.
2. Challenge it.
3. Change it. Substitute realistic or positive self-talk.

The following are questions to ask in challenging negative self-talk:

1. **Factual or distorted?**

   - Is this self-talk based on *fact*—on objective reality?
   - What *evidence* indicates this self-talk is *true?*
   - Is this self-talk a *distortion* of reality? If so, what type of distortion am I creating?

2. **Moderate or extreme?**

   - Is my self-talk part of an unnecessarily *hot reaction?*
   - Can I get along just as well with a *cooler* reaction?
   - Is this self-talk an unnecessarily demanding *should* on myself or others?
   - Am I thinking in a *rigid* or *extreme* way?

3. **Helpful or harmful?**

   - Is this self-talk helpful or harmful for me? For others?
   - How does this self-talk affect:
   - My *emotional stability* or being *upset?* That of others?
   - My *physical state* and *health?* Those of others?
   - My *relationships* with others?
   - My *behavior?* Will this self-talk lead to helpful or harmful behavior for me and others?

Moderate, focused stress arousal through breathing methods, visualization, and positive self-talk can help dancers like her reach their highest possible levels of performance.

Realistic Self-Talk

Here are a number of **realistic self-talk** statements that can be helpful in reacting to potentially stressful situations—at the moment they occur.

1. This too shall pass, and my life will be better.
2. I am a worthy person.
3. I am doing the best I can, given my history and awareness.
4. Like everyone else, I am an **FHB (Fallible Human Being).**
5. What is, is.
6. Look how far I have progressed, and I am still moving forward.
7. No failures exist, only different degrees of success.
8. I am true to myself.
9. I feel okay—guilt-free—about being temporarily upset.
10. I know I am not helpless. I can and will take necessary actions to pull through this difficult event.
11. I remain engaged and involved, rather than pulling back and retreating from this difficult set of circumstances.
12. This is an opportunity rather than a threat—to learn something new, to change direction, or to try a new approach.
13. One step at a time.
14. I can remain calm with this difficult person.
15. I know I am okay no matter what happens.
16. He or she is responsible for his or her reaction to me.
17. This unpleasant situation will soon be over.
18. This unpleasant situation is merely unpleasant—hardly horrible.
19. I can bear anything for a while.
20. In the long run, does this really matter?
21. Is this truly worth getting upset about?
22. I really don't need to prove myself in this situation.
23. Don't overreact. React appropriately.
24. Don't sweat the small stuff. It's all small stuff (almost).

Stop, See It Differently (S.S.I.D.)

1. When aware of becoming upset, stop.
2. Take one or two deep cleansing breaths.
3. Re-experience a positive past feeling *from your heart* such as:

   - Self-acceptance
   - Love
   - Care
   - Compassion
   - Tolerance
   - Patience
   - Appreciation
   - Kindness

4. *From your heart,* create a different interpretation of the event.

Managing Stress-Related Beliefs

Whenever you respond to specific situational stressors, your self-talk is influenced by your long-term perspective—that is, by your ongoing beliefs. A belief is an enduring as-

Example of Re-Examining Self-Talk

Below is the report from one of my students about how she recently went about re-examining her self-talk.

1. The *activating event* that spurred the stressor was a very personal situation that occurred between my mother and myself. My family is not one for touching each other to show affection. But my mother and I have grown increasingly closer day by day. When it was time for me to leave for Chico after spending Christmas with her, I felt an urge to hug her—showing my love for her. Anyway, we both stood in the driveway, hesitant of what should come next. So we said our goodbyes verbally, and I drove off.

2. The *negative self-talk* with which I upset myself was negativizing, awfulizing, and blaming her to not show me affection when I was younger. To prove to her that I do not need her warmth and not to take a risk would be more negative self-talk.

3. The *unwanted consequences* I created for myself are the awaiting of another chance to show affection toward her, blaming her, blaming myself. I created our barrier to continue. I also made myself feel less of a loving creature of earth.

4. The *realistic self-talk statements* that would have led to more positive results are to be true to myself, engage, rather than pulling back from the situation, take this as an opportunity rather than a threat, believe that I will be okay no matter what happens. I feel the most important self-talk is to be true to myself because this turns out to be true to others.

5. The *desirable consequences* I would like to create in similar future situations are to be true to myself and to recognize that benefits outweigh the negative consequences. I will gain more self-confidence, friends, and happiness.

sumption that you carry along from day to day, week to week, year to year. Perspective refers to a cluster of beliefs.

Behind every specific instance of negative self-talk are unreasonable beliefs. Albert Ellis, founder of Rational-Emotive Therapy, refers to these as irrational beliefs (Ellis, 1957; 1962; 1969; 1973; Ellis & Harper, 1975). Just as with situational self-talk, a belief is irrational or unreasonable if it is

- Distorted rather than *factual*
- Extreme rather than *moderate*
- Harmful rather than *helpful*.

As Rathus states, "We carry them (irrational beliefs) with us; they are our personal doorways to distress. They can give rise to problems in themselves, and, when problems assault us from other sources, these beliefs can magnify their effect" (1990, 438). It becomes vital as a first step, then, to be aware of your beliefs that influence situational interpretations. It also is important to find means of changing them when necessary.

Rewriting Irrational Beliefs

The following are 20 common unreasonable or irrational beliefs that often lead to negative situational self-talk. The first step in **rewriting irrational beliefs** is to recognize them in your own daily thinking. The next step is to question them. The third is to change them.

1. Other people and outside events upset me.
2. I am thin-skinned by genetic nature—I was born that way.
3. I cannot control my thoughts and feelings.
4. I cannot change. I am too old, too set in my ways, and beyond hope.
5. It is imperative that I be accepted by others, especially by those who are important to me.
6. Most people are wicked and cannot be trusted.
7. If things do not go my way, it will be awful, terrible, or even catastrophic.
8. The only way to improve my stress is to shape up others around me who do such dumb things.
9. It is easier to avoid responsibilities and difficulties than to face them.
10. My early childhood experiences determine my emotions and behavior, and I can do little about it.
11. I deserve to be upset or depressed over my shortcomings.
12. I am fully justified in being aggravated over others' shortcomings, deficiencies, and blunders.
13. I should be thoroughly competent, adequate, and achieving in all respects.
14. The world should always be fair, justice should always triumph, and I am fully justified in feeling angry when these do not occur.
15. I feel like I should do perfectly in nearly anything I attempt.
16. Usually a problem has one solution. It is almost intolerable when this solution is not found or followed.
17. I have a clear idea how other people should be and what they should do most of the time.
18. Others should treat me kindly and considerately at all times.
19. I have a right to expect a relatively pain-free and trouble-free life.
20. When people around me are upset, it is usually because of something I have said or done.

Disputation

Ellis and colleagues (Grieger & Boyd, 1980; Whalen, DiGiuseppe, & Wessler, 1980) have developed a simple and effective technique for challenging and changing irrational beliefs. This technique, called **disputation,** includes several steps.

1. What symptoms of distress do I want to reduce or eliminate?
2. What stressor is associated with my distress?
3. What specific interpretation intervenes between the stressor and my distress symptoms?
4. What is the unreasonable belief causing me unnecessary distress that I want to change? Here is an illustration in the life of Carla Bunin, a young university professor.

    Carla frequently "freezes" and stumbles when talking in a department faculty meeting. She perceives the situation as threatening, because she believes the impression she leaves on colleagues will influence their votes for or against her tenure next year. Her fear of looking bad creates the very blundering she so much wants to avoid.

The unreasonable belief she wants to change is "If I don't say the proper intelligent things in the proper intelligent manner, they will think I am not a worthy professor and will vote against me next year."

5. What evidence shows that this belief is true?
Carla: "None really. Tenure votes are influenced much more by publication records and teaching evaluations than on impressions left in faculty meetings."
6. What evidence shows that this belief is false?
Carla: "I have never known or heard of anyone who failed to be granted tenure because of what he or she said or did not say in a faculty meeting. Besides, no one has ever given any sign that they think less of me because of what I say or don't say in these meetings."
7. What alternative reasonable beliefs can you substitute for this unreasonable one?
Carla: "It makes no difference whether any colleagues approve or agree with what I say in faculty meetings. If I just relax, be myself, and do the important parts of my job well, I will probably get tenure; even if I don't, I will survive."

This process of disputation can be applied alone or with someone else, such as a spouse, close friends, or a counselor, who can assist you to rethink your irrational beliefs and try to change them.

See Application Exercise 14-2 for a personal application of the disputation tool.

From Vicious Cycle to Vital Cycle

The key role of beliefs in human experience is illustrated in Figure 14-1, which shows how beliefs can set in motion a self-fulfilling prophecy.

Consider the following examples of how a negative belief can set in motion a **vicious cycle.**

BELIEF: I never come through in the clutch.

INTERPRETATION (of challenging exam): This is the one exam I know I will fail.

EMOTION: Fear, test anxiety

PHYSICAL REACTION: Headache, fatigue, upset stomach

Figure 14-1

Vicious Cycle or Vital Cycle?

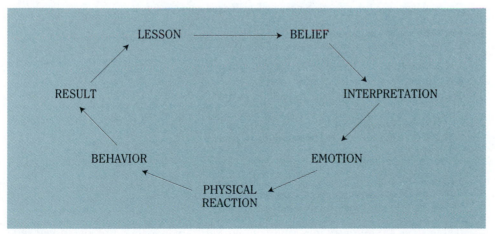

Source: Kriegel & Kriegel (1984)

BEHAVIOR: Procrastinates during three days before test. Unable to concentrate and lets mind wander during test.

RESULT: Does poorly on test

LESSON: See, I never come through in the clutch. This proves again that I'm a loser.

Suppose the same individual had begun with a contrasting assumption to initiate a **vital cycle.** "I am reasonably intelligent. I come through when I need to." The interpretation is likely to be "This test will be difficult, but I will take it on as a challenge." Emotions are likely to include appropriate anxiety that helps mobilize the person for study. The student may be a bit tense, which does no harm in moderate amounts. She or he prepares with confidence, although it takes a good deal of time and effort. The individual stays focused, directed, and confident during the test, convinced he or she will do reasonably well. The result? A reasonably good grade. The lesson? "See, this proves again that I thrive under pressure."

Reprogramming

Old, irrational beliefs will continue to provide the basis for situational interpretations—and for harmful distress—unless they are changed. As we have seen, doing so is not easy, although a number of methods are available for attempting this challenge.

Perhaps the most powerful tool I have used and taught is what I call simply **reprogramming.** Let us again consider the case of John, who reacts more defensively to his wife's suggestions than he wants. Underlying his situational interpretations were several assumptions or beliefs. For example:

- To be criticized is to be diminished.
- For others to criticize me is awful and intolerable.
- My worth as a human being depends on defending myself against any and all criticism.

Clearly, if John is to learn to respond more constructively, he needs to reprogram his thinking, including these enduring assumptions. Here is a simple self-talk statement that can counter the negative beliefs just noted:

- I respond to criticism with humor.

Several **criteria for effective new self-talk** are important:

1. **Personal**—Not general or abstract
2. **Positive**—To increase potency of the statement
3. **Present-tense**—As though you already are doing it
4. **Practical**—Achievable, doable
5. **Brief**—So it can be remembered and used

Note that the suggested alternative belief about responding to criticism with humor meets these criteria. So do the following beliefs:

1. I thrive on challenge.
2. I am calm and confident.
3. I am quietly self-assured.
4. I draw strength from my inner peace.

Three steps are followed in reprogramming self-talk, whether it be situational self-talk or long-term beliefs:

Step 1   Deliberately use new self-talk.
Step 2   Use repeatedly to gain familiarity.
Step 3   New self-talk then becomes natural.

Two principles need to be kept in mind in reprogramming self-talk.

1. Old self-talk habits will always resist change due to the repetition compulsion.
2. The strength of new self-talk depends on the amount of repetition.

An effective tool for the process of reprogramming is to write the desired new self-talk statement on a 3- by 5-inch card, carry it with you, or put in a conspicuous place, and review it many times each day. Soon the new statement will become so familiar it will seem to be a natural part of your thinking. Continue for two or three weeks for each statement. You will soon find your self-talk reprogrammed in those areas of your life you want to improve.

APPLICATIONS OF REPROGRAMMING

The method just described for reprogramming situational self-talk and beliefs can be applied to a number of specific problem areas. Examples from throughout this book include:

- Improving exercise habits
- Avoiding procrastination
- Reducing chronic hurry and hassle
- Reducing anger and hostility
- Turning anxiety into a positive force in performance situations like tests
- Building confidence
- Increasing social responsibility

Next you will read about how you can apply reprogramming to perfectionism, worry, hardiness, and self-esteem.

Perfectionism

In Chapter 9, you read about the potentially harmful influences of perfectionism on health and well-being. You may recall that **perfectionism** can be internal or external in its targets, since we defined this pattern as impossibly demanding expectations toward the self, others, or both.

Perfectionism can be reprogrammed, using the three-step process just described—deliberately using new self-talk statements, repetition and familiarity, and making new self-talk a natural part of one's thinking. Here are a series of self-talk statements that represent alternatives to perfectionistic thinking. If you are more perfectionistic than you wish, consider writing one of these on a 3- by 5-inch card, carrying it with you, memorizing it, and making it a normal part of your thinking.

1. I stop myself whenever I engage in all-or-nothing thinking. ("If I don't get an *A,* I will be a total failure.")
2. I stop myself whenever I overgeneralize from a single negative event. ("I'm always screwing up like this. I never seem to learn.")
3. I am a Fallible Human Being (FHB), doing my best most of the time.
4. Others are FHBs. It is unfair for me to expect them to be perfect—or to think and act like I think they should be.

5. I am becoming less critical and more accepting of others.
6. I reward myself for what I do, rather than punishing myself for what I do not do.
7. I set realistic goals and standards for myself.
8. I sometimes am satisfied with just getting the job done, even if it is not perfect.
9. I am conscious of how far I have come, rather than dwelling on how far I have to go.
10. I laugh at my own imperfections—and at my perfectionism.
11. I strive to do my best. I accept what I have done. I learn from my mistakes.

Knaus and Hendricks (1986) offer a number of useful suggestions for reducing and preventing perfectionism. Included is the advice to establish sensible standards. How do you know if a standard is sensible? Knaus and Hendricks (1986, 122) suggest it probably is sensible if you can answer yes to these questions:

1. Is your standard achievable, and does it allow you to challenge yourself, take risks, and feel good about trying?
2. Is your standard flexible? You cannot expect, for example, that you will perform as well when tired as when alert.
3. Can you modify your standard to accommodate changing circumstances?
4. Does your standard allow you to improve the quality of your life and feel pleased with yourself?
5. Does your standard incorporate the ideas of progressive improvement and human limitations?

Knaus and Hendricks suggest you apply these five guidelines to a perfectionistic standard like "I must be great or I'm nothing."

Worry

As noted in Chapter 9, **worry** is concern taken to overconcern. People often seem to think, "If I worry hard and long enough, I can prevent a bad thing from happening." Of course, worry does not make things better or prevent trouble at all. Rather, it interferes with clear thinking and can damage decision making, problem solving, and relationships. The following self-talk statements help to reprogram worry.

1. I am free of worry.
2. I concern myself only with those things I can do something about. I control my own thinking. I can stop worrying.
3. I am in tune with the positive.
4. I am confident, calm, and self-assured.
5. I think in a clear, decisive way.
6. I know things will work out okay. Worrying won't help at all.
7. I think thoughts that create health and well-being for myself and others.
8. I am an optimistic person.
9. I focus on only what is truly worth being concerned about.
10. I am in full control of events that are controllable.

Hardiness

A research finding from recent years with enormous implications is that stressful life events—even in clusters—need not be harmful to health and well-being. The key findings have been from studies on **hardiness,** the distress-resistant personality pattern we reviewed in Chapter 10 that includes three *C*'s: a liking of *challenge,* a strong sense of *commitment,* and a strong sense of *control.* Having been raised by hardy parents is probably the best assurance of being hardy oneself. But hardiness can be developed through reprogramming one's self-talk, using the same three-step process discussed earlier in this chapter. Here are self-talk statements for strengthening hardiness. You are invited to write one down on a 3-by 5-inch card, memorize and repeat it, then make it part of your natural thinking.

1. I thrive on challenge.
2. This is an opportunity, not a threat.
3. I come through when I need to.
4. I can do almost anything I set my mind to.
5. I am a special person.
6. I have confidence.
7. I like who I am—and I am getting better all the time.
8. I make things happen.
9. I have more talents and skills than even I have yet discovered.
10. I have lots of energy and vitality.
11. I am positive.
12. I am confident.
13. I thrive under pressure.
14. I am highly committed to . . .

Self-Esteem

Self-esteem, by which I mean self-liking or self-acceptance, is the result of positive self-talk about the self. As we noted in Chapter 10, self-esteem is a key personal quality adding to distress-resistance—as well as to chances of success, good health, and positive relationships.

It certainly helps the development of self-esteem to grow up with emotionally healthy parents who give an abundance of unconditional love and praise. But self-esteem, too, can be strengthened through reprogramming our self-talk.

Helmstetter (1986, 169) has proposed a number of self-talk statements for building self-esteem.

1. I really am very special. I like who I am, and I feel good about myself.
2. Although I always work to improve myself and I get better every day, I like who I am today. And tomorrow, when I'm even better, I'll like myself THEN, too.
3. It's true that there really is no one else like me in the entire world. There never was another me before, and there will never be another me again.
4. I am unique—from the top of my head to the bottom of my feet. In some ways, I may look and act and sound like some others—but I am not them. I am me.
5. I wanted to be somebody—and now I know I am. I would rather be me than anyone else in the world.
6. I like how I feel, and I like how I think, and I like how I do things. I approve of me, and I approve of who I am.
7. I have many beautiful qualities about me. I have talents and skills and abilities. I have talents that I don't even know about yet. And I am discovering new talents inside myself all the time.
8. I am positive. I am confident. I radiate good things. If you look closely, you can even see a glow around me.
9. I am full of life. I like life, and I'm glad to be alive. I am a very special person, living at a very special time.
10. I am intelligent. My mind is quick and alert and clever and fun. I think good thoughts, and my mind makes things work right for me.
11. I have a lot of energy and enthusiasm and vitality.

MANAGING ANGER

Positive and Negative Anger

It is vital at the outset to understand the distinction between positive anger and negative anger. It is my position that **negative anger** is a harmful and nearly always avoidable part of human experience. **Positive anger,** on the other hand, is a constructive, positive experience. Let us examine the difference between the two.

Negative anger involves the following steps.

1. I want something. "You must act like I think you should."
2. I am not getting it. "You are not meeting my expectations."
3. This frustrates me. "I'm boiling at what you just did."
4. This is intolerable. "I can't stand it."
5. You are to blame for my frustration. "You make me SO mad."
6. Therefore, you deserve to be punished. "I'll teach you not to do this to me again."

Positive anger, by contrast, begins the same but ends up at quite a different point.

1. I want something. "I sure like peace and quiet in my neighborhood."
2. I am not getting it. "Those neighbors' dogs bark and bark."
3. This frustrates me. "I sure have a terrible time getting to sleep with those dogs barking."
4. This is unacceptable. "This cannot go on."
5. I am motivated to do something to improve this situation. "I am going to call the neighbors and tell them something must be done to quiet down their dogs at night."
6. I will take constructive action to remedy the source of my frustration. "Hello, I need to talk with you about your dogs."

Notice that negative anger leads to hostility and aggressive impulses—and to distress within oneself. Positive anger leads to motivation to alter the situation in a positive way based on assertiveness.

This, of course, is how conditions of living improve. People become indignant and take action. The world around us becomes a better place—not just a source of frustration and upset.

Positive anger, then, is constructive and desirable from time to time. Negative anger is harmful and avoidable—and the source of a good deal of evil, if by evil we mean harm by humans toward each other.

A step toward understanding how to handle anger effectively is to recognize that it is often a **secondary emotion,** a cover-up for a prior, even stronger feeling that, for one reason or another, we keep hidden. It can cover up each of the following:

- Frustration
- Fear
- Self-doubt
- Feeling rejected and lonely
- Defensiveness
- Guilt
- Hurt

Negative anger usually arises in response to a perceived threat, frustration, or injustice. Perhaps the most difficult of all to allow into consciousness is anger from having been exposed, shown to be wrong, questioned, doubted. These are threats to personal worth. The greater the threat, the greater the potential anger. A key to dealing with negative anger as a cover-up emotion is to find out what the underlying emotion is, what is causing that feeling, and what can be done about it.

A number of constructive suggestions can be offered for dealing with anger in ways that minimize its unnecessary occurrence as a harmful experience, that acknowledge its existence, and that allow for expression in harmless yet fruitful ways.

Three Questions in Managing Anger

When most people think of managing anger, their first question usually is "Should I express it or hold it in?" Important as it is, this question needs to be set in a broader context of anger management.

Three key questions need to be addressed. You will note that our answers draw on suggestions and guidelines from previous chapters.

1. **How can I prevent negative anger?**

   - Enter each day with an attitude of patience, tolerance, and good humor.
   - Use these self-talk statements:

     Is this truly worth getting upset about?

     I remain calm with difficult people.

     I value diversity in others' opinions and behavior.

     I am okay no matter what.

   - Maintain good health buffers.

     Exercise   Nutrition   Sleep   Healthy Pleasure

   - Practice active listening.
   - Express feelings honestly and promptly.
   - When necessary, avoid distress-provokers.

2. **How can I catch negative anger in progress?**

   - Draw a long, deep breath.
   - Use Instant Replay or the P and Q Method for managing situational self-talk.

     Catch (recognize) negative self-talk

     Challenge it

     Change it

   - Pause and Question
   - Use thought-stopping and thought-switching.
   - Change actions from being upset to reasonable.
   - If appropriate, leave the scene momentarily.

3. **How can I handle negative anger constructively, once present?**

   - Reduce destructive responses.

     Anger in—repress

     Anger out—explode

     Poison darts

     Dumping on innocent bystanders

See Application Exercise 14-3 to write about steps you will take to better manage your anger.

- Use constructive options.

Discuss it with the person at whom you are angry.	Release it through exercise.	Take constructive action to remedy situation— turn negative anger into positive anger.
Discuss it with someone else.	Channel anger energy into constructive activity.	Express anger in harmless ways.
Dissolve it through self-talk.		

Other Anger Tips

1. When anger is present, ask: What am I really feeling? Am I truly frustrated at being wronged, blocked, or misunderstood? Or is anger a cover-up for another feeling hidden beneath? If so, what is that other emotion, and how can I deal with it directly and constructively?

2. Waste no time in dealing with anger within the limits of what is appropriate. The longer it boils away, the greater the potential for physical harm and boil-over later on.

3. Ask: Is my anger partly the result of being overloaded? As pointed out earlier, anger often will partly or totally subside when this awareness is brought to the surface.

4. Get to the root of your anger. What can be changed in the self, others, or the larger situation to reduce this anger and the chances that it will happen again?

5. In expressing anger to the target person, use "I" rather than "you" openers.

    "I am angry because dinner is late," rather than, "You are late again with dinner."

    "I am upset at your failure to do your household chores this week," rather than, "You failed again to fulfill your responsibilities."

    "I feel really discouraged by your forgetting my birthday," rather than, "Well, you blew it again this year."

    "You" messages set the stage for a defensive response from the listener. "I" messages lay the groundwork for understanding dialogue and for continuation of the conversation. This is a simple formula, but it can work wonders for the person who is angered, as well as for the person who is the target of anger.

6. Avoid collecting anger credits for your "slush fund" of bad feelings, tense body tissue, and righteous indignation. Far better that you deal with them one at a time, piece-by-piece, and immediately or soon after they arise. Otherwise, your bubble will explode or will eat away at your insides.

7. Express anger with forethought and good taste. Be rational about it. Does it really make good sense to explode at your 86-year-old father because of how he treated you when you were 10? Again, the key ethical questions are: What will the consequences be for others? And for myself? Is it moral to clear out my angry emotions in such a way that someone else clearly is hurt? Is there an alternative for reducing my anger while not inflicting harm on others? Obviously there is.

8. Avoid displaying anger at those closest to you who may be quite undeserving. A particularly common pattern is to transfer anger from the job to the family. Why? There are several reasons.

    They are available.

    They are safe to dump on (that is, relatively safe).

    They will not hurt us (not in the way a boss or customer can).

Their personalities might be receptive to this.

They will still love us.

They will not reject us.

They might understand us (if their emotional temperature is not too high).

Far better to handle anger at its source—at work—or at least to talk it out at home and then leave it, rather than to shoot it out at home through poisonous darts or to create volcanic explosions.

9. Use techniques of giving negative feedback and assertiveness, both discussed in Chapter 17, for expressing anger constructively and for getting what you want, but not at someone else's expense.

10. Be available to your coworkers, spouse, children, and friends to talk out their anger, using the techniques of active listening described in Chapter 17. Help enlighten them about some of these principles for handling anger in the future.

11. Pick the appropriate time and place to express anger.

12. Practice forgiveness. It is helpful for both relationships and your own health (Mc Cullough, 1997).

MEANING AND PURPOSE: THE SPIRITUAL DIMENSION OF WELLNESS

Throughout this book, we place strong emphasis on the role thinking plays on stress, health, and well-being. You have read about how negative situational self-talk and irrational beliefs can contribute to distress and maladaptive coping and how clear, reasonable thinking can buffer against distress. It is vital to understand that self-talk and beliefs do not occur in isolation but are integrally linked with a broader personal reality for each of us—our sense of meaning and direction.

Countless writers have emphasized the role of meaning in health and well-being. For example, Victor Frankl (1959) wrote of "man's search for meaning," drawing on his experiences and observations in Nazi concentration camps. More recently, in his book *Existential Psychology,* Yalom notes that "The human being seems to require meaning. To live without meaning, goals, values, or ideals seems to provoke . . . considerable distress" (1980). Donald Ardell expresses his opinion that "Life is without inherent meaning; to be optimally well, you must invest it with **meaning and purpose.** . . . The most fulfilling insights on meaning and purpose are discovered, not revealed. . . . The search for meaning and purpose never ends, until you do" (1994, 4). In his superb book, *Meaning and Medicine,* Dossey notes that "Meaning makes the problems of life bearable, and without it we cannot process or integrate them" (1991). Pelletier (1994) notes that a clear sense of meaning—mainly directed toward contributing to the common good—characterized all of the high-functioning people he investigated for his book, *Sound Mind, Sound Body.*

For support of the linkage between sense of meaning and direction, on the one hand, and distress, health, and happiness, on the other, see Figure 14-2. Among all the statistical findings from my study of my university students presented in this book, perhaps the strongest and most unequivocal are those summarized here. The stronger the sense of meaning and direction, the lower the distress-symptom score and the greater the proportion who report being very healthy and very happy.

The quest for meaning and purpose is the core of spiritual wellness. As Donald Tubesing (1994a; 1994b; 1994c) states in the box on page 385, we can be physically well but still incomplete in our total well-being unless we either possess a sense of meaning

Figure 14-2

Mean Distress-Symptom Score by Meaning and Purpose

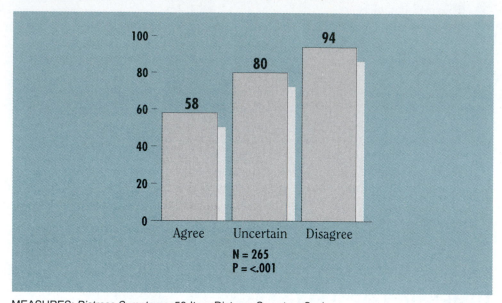

MEASURES: *Distress Symptoms:* 50-Item Distress Symptom Scale
    Meaning and Direction: "I have a pretty clear sense of meaning and direction in my life
    these days" (Agree, Uncertain, Disagree).
FINDING: Those who agree they have a clear sense of meaning and direction report significantly
    lower distress-symptom scores.

and purpose or, more importantly, engage in a quest for answers. As humans, we have a unique ability to ponder questions of purpose and our place in the scheme of things. Everyone grapples at some time with these issues. Some pass over them quickly and superficially; others spend a lifetime in the search—reading, thinking, discussing, writing, and praying. As Hawks notes in a recent review of literature on spiritual health, spirituality is not only an internal reality but is expressed outwardly as well. He states, "The themes of compassion, selflessness, integrity, honesty, and connectedness with others occur in most discussions of spirituality" (1994, 5).

Traditional world and tribal religions have been the source of meaning and purpose throughout most of human history. Whether you draw from one of these theological sources, from a naturalistic philosophy, or from your own formulations, the important thing is to search and gradually through time find or create answers—answers that usually evolve and change with the passing of years but that give clarity, direction, and purpose to each day and to your total journey.

The following are a number of methods used in the search for meaning and direction. Which ones do or might work best for you?

Reading	Writing	Being in nature
Talking with friends	Metaphors	Learning from action
Listening to spiritual guides	Praying	
	Solitude and contemplation	

In whatever way works for you, engage in the search. Parts of my own meaning and direction are expressed in Chapter 18, where I discuss egoistic altruism and balancing personal wellness with social commitment. Next, we turn to a chapter on relaxation methods.

The Quest for the Holy Grail: Quest-ions

The quest for true wellness does not end with physical well-being. We can be fit, have sharp minds and clear arteries, know how to deal with stress, relate effectively with others and have enough money to be secure—we can attain all of these worthwhile goals and still not be well. Why?

Because we cannot be truly healthy, well beings without a clear sense of purpose and direction. We need answers to the questions "Who am I?" "Where am I going?" "What is my purpose?" "Why am I here?" "What am I to do with my life?" We need answers to these spiritual questions. Life without attention to this spiritual depth soon becomes shallow and self-centered.

So, we search to see—to see meaning in our lives, to see a reason for being. King Arthur and his knights sought the Holy Grail year after year. Did they find what they sought? Probably not. Monte Python's parody of the search for the grail ends as a joke. The grail—that object of the spiritual search—is elusive. It's hard to find, tough to grab hold of and pin down.

The search for depth and understanding is universal. The quest is the key, not the grail itself. Like the Native American's traditional vision quest, our search is also a quest for true vision. Those who seek to see ultimately become the seers—the wise tribal leaders.

The search is essential for well-being.

Source: Tubesing (1994b, 6)

References

Ardell, D. B. (1994). Meaning and purpose in life! *Ardell Wellness Report, 36,* 4.

Bedford, S. (1981). *Stress and tiger juice.* Chico, CA: Scott Publications.

Childre, D. L. (1994). *Freeze frame.* Boulder Creek, CA: Planetary Publications.

Dossey, L. (1991). *Meaning and medicine.* New York: Bantam Books.

Ellis, A. (1957). *How to live with a "neurotic."* New York: Crown Publishers.

Ellis, A. (1962). *Reason and emotion in psychotherapy.* New York: Lyle Stuart.

Ellis, A. (1969). A cognitive approach to behavior therapy. *International Journal of Psychiatry, 8,* 896–900.

Ellis, A. (1973). *Humanistic psychotherapy: The rational-emotive approach.* New York: McGraw-Hill Paperbacks.

Ellis, A., & Harper, R. A. (1975). *A new guide to rational living.* Hollywood: Wilshire Book.

Frankl, V. E. (1959). *Man's search for meaning.* New York: Pocket Books.

Grieger, R., & Boyd, J. (1980). *Rational-emotive therapy: A skills-based approach.* New York: Van Nostrand Reinhold.

Hawks, S. (1994). Spiritual health: Definition and theory. *Wellness Perspectives, 10:*4, 3–13.

Helmstetter, S. (1986). *The self-talk solution.* New York: Pocket Books.

Knaus, W. J., & Hendricks, C. (1986). *The illusion trap: How to achieve a happier life.* New York: World Almanac Publications.

McCullough, M. (1997). *To forgive is human.* Chicago: InterVarsity Press.

Pelletier, K. R. (1994). *Sound mind, sound body.* New York: Simon & Schuster.

Rathus, S. A. (1991). *Psychology* (4th ed.). Fort Worth: Holt, Rinehart and Winston.

Tubesing, D. A. (1994a). What is spiritual wellness anyway? *Wellness Management, 10:*1, 6–7.

Tubesing, D. A. (1994b). The quest for the holy grail: Quest-ions. *Wellness Management, 10:*2, 6.

Tubesing, D. A. (1994c). The quest for the holy grail: Metaphors. *Wellness Management, 10:*3, 8–9.

Whalen, S. R., DiGiuseppe, R., & Wessler, R. L. (1980). *A practitioner's guide to rational-emotive therapy.* New York: Oxford University Press.

Wolfe, T. (1987). *The bonfire of the vanities.* New York: Farrar, Straus and Giroux.

Yalom, I. D. (1980). *Existential psychotherapy.* New York: Basic Books.

Zastrow, C. (1993). *You are what you think.* Chicago: Nelson-Hall Publishers.

Application Exercise 14-1

Identifying Personal Uses for Self-Talk Management

Self-talk can be used for a variety of personal issues and problems. Below is a partial list.

Preventing worry
Exercising
Listening
Assuming responsibility
Public speaking
Taking tests
Being self-directed
Building hardiness
Increasing self-esteem
Reducing self-criticism
Preventing anger and irritability
Giving constructive feedback
Avoiding procrastination
Organizing time
Reducing chronic hurry and hassle
Reducing chronic overload
Being criticized or attacked.
Meeting a challenge
Eating right
Making transitions
Stopping smoking
Acting with authority
Balancing work/family or community/family
Maintaining good posture
Staying calm under pressure
Pulling out of depression
Enjoying the present
Coping with unexpected emergencies
Reducing shyness
Reducing fear of disapproval
Avoiding working too hard
Avoiding overindulging
Increasing control over emotions
Avoiding taking work home (mentally)
Reducing perfectionism
Turning "musts" into "preferences"
Reducing "shoulding" toward self or others
Giving yourself credit
Building confidence

Check those items on the list to which you believe self-talk might be usefully applied. Then underline the three you want to begin to work on first.

Application Exercise 14-2

Personal Application of Disputation

Apply the disputation steps described in the chapter to a recent stressful event in your life. You can do this as a writing or discussion exercise.

1.   Distress symptoms?

2.   Stressor?

3.   Interpretation of the stressor?

4.   Unreasonable belief influencing the interpretation?

5.   Evidence this belief is true?

6.   Evidence this belief is false?

7.   Alternative beliefs?

Application Exercise 14-3

Steps for Managing Anger

1. In order to *prevent negative anger,* I will:

2. In order to *catch negative anger in progress,* I will:

3. In order to *handle anger constructively, once present,* I will:

Within you there is a stillness and a sanctuary to which you can retreat at any time and be yourself.

—HERMAN HESSE

Quieting the Mind and Body: Relaxation Methods

A College Student Learns Deep Relaxation

As I look at what we covered in the course so far, I can think of one skill that we have been introduced to that has helped me immensely. The skill is deep relaxation. When I came to Chico I was going through a rough time of increased stress. Because of some events that have happened in my life during the last couple of years, my ability to cope with the increased level of stress has been severely weakened. As a result of the high levels of distress, I was suffering from upset stomach and insomnia. In general, my health was not good. One factor that made things worse in my opinion was the fact that I wasn't exercising like I used to.

I have during the past couple years been able to sense when a distressor is beginning to affect me. Until I learned relaxation breathing in class, my only recourse was to try to avoid the distressor. Sometimes this action worked, sometimes it did not. Once the distressor got to me, it could take up to a week before I had control of my stomach again.

Once I learned relaxation breathing I had another option. When I started feeling my stomach tighten up in stressful situations, I have been able to settle things down with the breathing. I have been able to prevent the stomach discomfort before it gets out of hand. Since learning the skill I am using both options to give myself a buffer. When I am facing a distressor, I avoid it and do relaxation breathing. I have since not had any problems with my stomach nor with my sleep patterns. I have begun to eat better and have been consistently exercising. I feel better about my overall health. To go along with my better habits, I have been setting aside time outside of class to practice deep relaxation.

Relaxation has played a very important part in the turn around in my life. It has helped me get control of my body again. I once thought I was invincible and could make my body do anything. I now know I was wrong. However with the help of a very useful stress management technique, I have been able to stretch myself further than I have been able to in the last couple of years.

THE RELAXATION RESPONSE:
ANTIDOTE TO DISTRESS

The body possesses the natural ability to arouse and prepare for action; it also has a built-in ability to relax. Through the parasympathetic nervous system and quieting of the endocrine system, this ability is the body's natural tendency, on its own, to restore homeostasis. As you also read, this *relaxation response* creates physiological responses directly opposite to the stress response.

Unfortunately, our fast-paced lifestyle often keeps the stress response activated so continuously that the body and mind stay aroused at an excessively high level for days, weeks, or even years, without release or recovery. The result is wear and tear, breakdown, and stress illnesses such as those reviewed in Chapter 7.

The good news is that research during the past decades has conclusively shown that the mind is able to add to the body's natural tendency toward recovery by deliberately producing the relaxation response at will—even at a level well below baseline (Benson,

Figure 15-1

Two Approaches to Tension Control

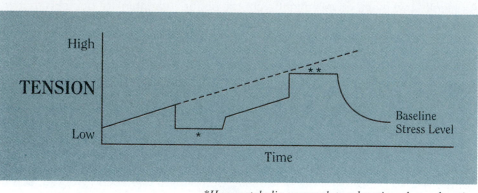

*Hypometabolic approach to relaxation: deep relaxation
**Hypermetabolic approach to relaxation: aerobic exercise

1993; Pelletier, 1993). Studies also show that when *deep relaxation* is produced once or twice a day for 10 to 20 minutes over periods of weeks or months, a host of positive benefits occur—benefits that combine for stress control and health enhancement (Antoni, 1993; Benson & Stuart, 1992; Kabat-Zinn, 1993). In this chapter, you will read about a range of specific methods for eliciting the relaxation response. All have in common the active role of the mind in releasing relaxation in the body.

Hypermetabolic and Hypometabolic Approaches to Stress Control

Aerobic exercise and deep relaxation are opposite approaches to controlling stress and tension. Running, swimming, and other aerobic activities temporarily elevate metabolism—indeed the entire physical system—in order to meet the demands for more energy output voluntarily placed on it by the person exercising. Deep relaxation, on the other hand, temporarily quiets metabolism and all the physical processes associated with it.

With both activities, the mind and body both return to a level below the starting point in terms of subjectively felt tension and even objectively measurable body activity. With aerobic exercise, it takes longer for the body to reach that postexercise level of deeper quiet, perhaps even several hours after an intense workout, as the body cools down.

As shown in Figure 15-1, a common pattern is for baseline stress level to begin low in the morning, then to rise as the day progresses, finally falling off with two martinis, television, or sleep in the evening. Another harmful pattern is for baseline stress level to begin at an elevated point as soon as the person awakens, then to stay up all day, never returning even at night.

As shown by the solid line, aerobic exercise and deep relaxation are complementary approaches to keeping baseline stress level down so it seldom leaves the person's zone of positive stress. Note that in both cases, the postsession level of stress is lower than beforehand. It makes eminent good sense, then, to practice both nearly every day, preferably with several hours separating the two.

Remember, they both are preparation for activity and stress, as well as recovery from tension already accumulated. Therefore, they are best done every day, whether you feel you need them or not. Their effects are cumulative over weeks, months, and years in keeping tension under control.

Words of Caution, Realism, and Individuality

For most people substantial benefits are to be gained from practicing one or more relaxation methods. At the same time, it is important to remember that no relaxation methods or disciplines are total, immediate panaceas for any mental or physical condition associated with distress. This is important to recognize at the outset of this chapter, so expectations are realistic.

Similarly, no consistent research findings indicate a given relaxation method will work best in allaying a given stress-related symptom or disorder. To my knowledge, no studies prove that practicing this or that technique is the absolute best way to reduce headaches, stomach tension, backaches, or irritability, although Auerbach and Gramling (1998) have recently reviewed studies showing differential effects of various relaxation techniques on various parts of the body.

Moreover, each person is unique in preferences and style. What is appealing and effective for one person may be ineffective and unappealing to the next. I like to meditate and have done so almost daily for nearly two decades. You might find that yoga touches something profound inside and is just the thing for you. The late cardiologist-runner-writer George Sheehan noted that you need to see yourself as an *experiment-of-one*—exploring, testing, integrating what works, and tossing out what does not.

Finally, if you have a lingering physical ailment or emotional condition, one or more of these relaxation techniques might well work, but consult an appropriate professional in the medical or psychological field if the condition is a serious threat to your well-being. The relaxation methods described here can sometimes head off serious disorders, but they should not be seen as substitutes for appropriate professional treatment, when needed.

We now examine the more common relaxation techniques. As you read, keep in mind that some of these can be used as **on-the-spot tension reducers,** others as means of eliciting *deep relaxation.*

RELAXATION METHODS

Breathing Techniques

Like sunrise and sunset, sleep and activity, summer and winter, pumping and recovery of the heart, breathing is one of the basic rhythms of life. Breath is vital to life itself. Without it, we die.

Pace and depth of breathing are part of both the stress response and the relaxation response. You are familiar with what happens to your breathing when you are frightened by an unexpected noise, the sudden appearance of a threatening dog, or a near miss at an open intersection: Your breathing quickens and becomes more shallow as your heart rate soars. This response has a good reason, of course: Faster breathing brings in more oxygen to enable the body to respond at a higher level of arousal to the perceived impending threat. Likewise, the heart rate speeds up by as many as one beat per second during physical exercise to supply more oxygen to working muscles. Conversely, your breathing slows and deepens as you relax, since muscles, tissues, and organs require less oxygen in this state of *hypometabolism.*

But breathing is not just on the receiving end of arousal and relaxation. It can also help initiate stress and quieting. If your lungs speed up, that, in turn, stimulates the rest of the body to accelerate. Conversely, if your lungs slow down, you will feel a calming effect throughout your system. Thus, breathing can be not only an active partner in the relaxation response but also a powerful *means* of creating quiet.

Diaphragmatic breathing, in which you draw long, very deep breaths through accentuation of the action of the diaphragm muscle is an especially powerful tool of relaxation, as any person knows who has taken Lamaze training. Diaphragmatic breathing may have a generalized calming effect throughout the body, in part through interrupting the normal vibrations to the body from the beating heart through the aorta. As breathing pauses, interruptions of the normal rhythm of these vibrations occurs, causing a systemwide slowdown (Bentov, 1988). Whatever the physiological pathways, it is clear that deliberately created deep, slow breathing quiets the body. This provides the basis for a number of specific **breathing techniques,** illustrated by the following (Antoni, 1993).

Diaphragmatic Breath

Begin by pushing your stomach out, then draw a long deep breath, keeping your rib cage and collarbone as still as possible. Exhale as long and slowly as possible. The key to this type of breathing is to use your diaphragm muscle to draw in as much air as possible. Relaxation occurs during the slow exhalation.

6-Second Quieting Response (QR)

This simple technique, a variation of diaphragmatic breathing, is one I teach at the outset of my campus and community classes. Users find the **6-second quieting response** surprisingly effective as a brief minirelaxation response. Do it many times a day, beginning once at the top of each hour. This will help you begin to use it routinely, whether or not you face a challenge or adversity. Draw on it especially when needing an on-the-spot tension reliever—entering a classroom for a test, at the beginning of a job interview, when dealing with a crisis in the intensive care unit, or when coping as a nurse without a difficult physician or patient.

See Application Exercise 15-1 to begin using the 6-second quieting response.

1. First push your stomach out, then draw a long, deep breath.
2. Hold for 2 or 3 seconds.
3. Exhale with a long breath, slowly and completely.
4. As you exhale, let your jaw and shoulders drop.
5. Feel the relaxation flow from your neck and shoulders down your arms to your fingertips.

This can be done with eyes opened or closed, with others or alone. It is unlikely anyone will ever detect you are doing anything unusual. This method is especially effective in correcting shallow breathing and releasing tension in your neck and shoulders.

Breathing Countdown

The **breathing countdown,** another breathing method, combines elements of meditation. It is simple and effective when used for a periodic three-minute break or when used routinely for deep relaxation.

1. Close your eyes in a sitting or supine position.
2. Take one deep breath, hunching your shoulders and holding your breath for several seconds.
3. Breathe out slowly and completely, allowing your shoulders and arms to become limp.
4. Resume normal breathing.
5. On your first out-breath, silently say "10." On the next out-breath, silently say "9." On the next out-breath, silently say "8" and on down to "1."
6. When you reach "1," you can repeat "1" over and over, count back to "10," or let your mind wander.

7. Continue for 3 to 20 minutes.
8. Slowly open your eyes, and resume normal activities.

Focus Attention on Breathing

This simple technique can help your mind and body in tense situations. It is very simple. Without trying to change anything, simply allow your mind to be fully aware for several moments of your breathing. Dwell on the rise and fall of your chest, the cooler air coming in, and the warmer air passing out. Be aware of whether your breaths are shallow or deep, quick or slow, or comfortable or uncomfortable. Dwell on the passage of air in and out of your right nostril for a few breaths, then your left. Simply allow this attentiveness to settle you, to quiet distracting or racing thoughts. It is important to accept what you observe, to simply be with it. Do not concern yourself with trying to change it.

Breathing Slowly for Calming Effect

Another technique, very effective for many people before a difficult speech, interview, physical performance, or athletic performance, is to deliberately breathe calmly and slowly, thinking of this slow breathing as soothing and calming your entire body. Leaving your breath out longer than normal can be especially helpful.

Breathing Away Tension

1. Sit or lie in a comfortable position with hands open and legs uncrossed.
2. Be aware of the weight of your entire body on the floor, bed, couch, or chair. Your muscles need not help support your body at all.
3. Softly close your eyes.
4. Focus attention on your nostrils, and "see" the air entering each side. Follow its path down into your lungs, "watch" it swirling around, and "observe" it moving back up and out.
5. As it leaves, tell yourself it is carrying away tension, pain, and disease, if present.
6. Continue for one to five minutes.

Remember, the better your physical fitness, the better your ability will be to extract and process large amounts of oxygen during exercises such as these throughout the day.

Meditation Techniques

The term **meditation** is often associated with religions, gurus, or mystics. Although it may sometimes be linked to some of these, in reality it is simply a technique of quieting mind and body.

To be sure, meditation has been around for a long time in both the East and West. Seaward points out that the roots of meditation have been traced to Asia as far back as the sixth century B.C., when "several individuals traveling separate paths to enlightenment took refuge and solace in contemplative and reflective thought" (1994, 267). Out of this search several philosophies gradually attracted followers, giving rise to the major Eastern religions of Hinduism, Buddhism, Taoism, and Confucianism. Meditation, or quiet self-reflection, came to be integrated into the common practice of these religions as a means of cleansing or purifying the soul.

Similarly, meditation has been central to Islam, Judaism, Christianity, and to most forms of worship of Native Americans. Meditation within all these traditions have one thing in common: turning inward for relaxation, contemplation, enlightenment—or simply for stillness.

So, while a variety of beliefs and related practices may be associated with meditation, depending on the social and ideological context, I use the term in a neutral, nontheological way to refer to a specific type of relaxation method. Meditation can be done within the tradition of a major religion, but it can also be done as a purely secular activity. Unfortunately (from my point of view), some of the more restrictive branches of Christianity are opposed to this practice for fear that being silent and turning inward will put people in touch with the devil inside. Many of these same people believe that meditation takes the place of prayer and leads to independence from an outside or higher power. In my view, the practice of meditation need not be a threat to any belief system. It is simply a way of relaxing.

Meditation is the practice of sitting or reclining comfortably and quietly with eyes closed for 10 to 20 minutes once or twice a day and using a repeated mental focus to quiet the mind, thereby quieting the body.

See Application Exercise 15-2 for a plan to begin to meditate or to use one of the other deep relaxation techniques.

It is important to distinguish meditation from contemplation. Contemplation refers to thinking about the meaning of something—contemplating the meaning of an event yesterday, considering a theological idea, or dwelling on a poem and its application to your life. Meditation is first and foremost a method of quieting by using a repeated internal focus to turn down normal thought processes. It does not involve thinking. Rather, it involves focus on an internal stimulus "with complete indifference, expecting nothing, desiring nothing" (Smith, 1985, 183). Examples of a stimulus are a silent sound or mantra: "ieem," "ohm," "hmmm," "maroom," "varoom," or "aroom." I sometimes simply hum silently. Other mental focal points might be your breathing, a sacred word, a short prayer, a line of music, a silent chant. I sometimes teach my students to repeat "I am" with each in-breath and "relaxed" with each out-breath.

Types of Meditation

Mindful meditation, taught and written about by Kabat-Zinn (1991, 1993) and others (Carrington, 1984; Roth, 1997), means to simply listen to internal thoughts and body processes—to be mindful of what you are experiencing at each moment in the meditative state. **Transcendental meditation (TM)** involves sitting with eyes closed twice a day and going into a meditative state (and metabolic quiet) by repeating a mantra—a sound without meaning from Sanskrit. **Zen meditation** calls for focusing on breathing. The **Benson Meditation Method** (Benson, 1975, 1994), an "Americanization" of TM based on years of research on the physiology of meditation in his Harvard Medical School laboratories, is simple: repetition of the word "one" or, more recently, of any word or phrase associated with one's faith or beliefs. In the latter instance, Benson calls this the "faith factor," believing that power is added when one combines the quieting effect of meditation with the power of one's beliefs. **Open meditation** differs from the other techniques in that one allows the mind to wander and drift, allowing in whatever comes and focusing on the image, sensation, or thought as it passes through.

Benefits of Meditation

Since 1970, thousands of careful studies have been conducted on various forms of deep relaxation, especially transcendental meditation, the Benson Meditation Method (sometimes called the Relaxation Response), and mindfulness meditation. They show a number of specific benefits, including the following (Alexander et al., 1996; Aron & Aron, 1986; Benson, 1975; Ferguson & Gowan, 1975; Frew, 1977; Smith, 1986).

- Increased measured intelligence
- Increased recall, both long-term and short-term
- Better "mental health" (decreased anxiety, depression, aggression, and irritability and increased self-esteem and emotional stability)
- Greater perceived self-actualization or realization of potential

- Better academic performance in high school and college
- Improved job performance
- Improved job satisfaction
- Improved athletic performance
- Better mind-body coordination
- Increased perceptual awareness
- Normalization of blood pressure
- Relief from insomnia
- Normalization of weight
- Reduced drug abuse
- Decreased chronic pain

Glasser, who maintains that meditation is a **positive addiction** similar to running, comments about the subjective benefits from transcendental meditation:

> Subjectively, almost everyone remarks that he or she feels "less tense, less worried." Most mention that they had previously experienced some kind of tension, some degree of strain. Students even speak of the "anxiety I felt about school and my future" but "now," said one man, "I feel a certain easiness, everything is smoother." "The main benefit of meditation for me," said another, "is the almost total reduction of serious worry." That means worry in the sense of nonproductive, nervous disruption. I can still be deeply concerned about important matters.
>
> One man stated that "for the first time since I can remember, I can relax, without drugs or drink." A girl wrote, "Before I began the transcendental meditation program, I used drugs, methedrine and narcotics. The effects of the drugs were that I was incredibly tense. Physically, my shoulders were up so high that one could barely see my neck." She said that, immediately after receiving instruction in the TM technique, "my shoulders had dropped, all the tension in my face was gone so that my whole facial structure had changed, and most important to me, I was completely at ease. My tension didn't come back." (1976, 32)

Advocates of TM maintain that the positive effects of meditation result not only from physiological processes but also from coming into greater harmony with one's inner nature. Later in this chapter, this is referred to as **"centering"** or tuning into one's "inner light." Whatever the term, increasing evidence shows that meditation and other forms of deep relaxation foster realization of higher potentials—and help to reduce stress.

Two further benefits of meditation have been reported in the past decade, both of which bear notice, even if the findings are more suggestive than definitive. One is an influential study by Ornish (1992) showing that coronary artery disease can be reversed when consistent meditation is combined with a very low-fat diet, exercise, and social support. Since all these factors occurred simultaneously, it is impossible at this point to know the extent to which meditation exerted an independent impact.

The second is a series of studies suggesting that when a critical mass of people gather together to practice an advanced form of transcendental meditation, positive changes occur in the social well-being of the surrounding environment. For example, studies have shown that when a certain number of meditators meditate together in a city for a month, reductions occur in expected numbers of crimes, heart attacks, suicides, and accidents (Aron & Aron, 1986). The theory is that internal harmony created by meditation reverberates outward to create harmony in the environment. Though skepticism abounds about these studies, further investigation certainly is warranted.

How to Meditate

All the meditation methods described share several simple ingredients:

- Quiet place
- Comfortable position
- Eyes closed
- Accepting, noncritical attitude
- Repeated mental focus
- When aware of mind wandering, gently return to mental focus

As you begin to meditate, you will note a tendency for your mind to wander. This is quite all right. In fact, it is part of the meditation process. It is important not to *concentrate* on the stimulus—concentration is something different altogether. Meditation means to allow your mind to wander, as it surely will. Gently return to the focus as you become aware your mind is wandering.

Smith describes the process in this way.

Thus, meditation is not so much a focusing exercise as a returning exercise, a way of coming home. In fact, all you need to know in the way of instruction for meditation is this:

CALMLY ATTEND TO A SIMPLE STIMULUS
AFTER EACH DISTRACTION CALMLY RETURN YOUR ATTENTION.

By patiently doing this, again and again and again, the mind is very gradually conditioned to attend for longer and longer periods of time. It is important to emphasize this return of attention should be patient, easy, and gentle—not forced or strained. The goal is not to keep your mind vigilantly glued on the focal task, as if you were playing baseball or a video game. Instead, as calmly and restfully as possible, ease your attention back to the task. Let your mind wander. Every time your mind drifts from the task, you have another opportunity to calmly return your attention. It is only through such opportunities to return that you gradually condition your mind to attend to the focus. It is through distraction and diversion that the experience of meditation deepens and embraces more and more of the world. (1986, 184)

Another meditation expert, Patricia Carrington, describes the focus aspect of meditation in this way.

When meditating, never force thoughts out of your mind. All kinds of thoughts may drift through your mind while you are meditating. Treat these thoughts just as you would treat clouds drifting across the sky. You don't push the clouds away—but you don't hold onto them either. You just watch them come and go. It's the same with thoughts during meditation, you just watch them, and then when it feels comfortable to do so, go back. (1978, 25)

Visualization Techniques

Visualization, also called mental imagery, guided daydreaming, or "**movies of the mind,**" is another technique that reduces rational mental activity and endues deep quiet (Brye, 1978; Green & Shellenberger, 1991; Samuels & Samuels, 1975). This is a method of imagining yourself in some very pleasant place, usually a natural setting, where you take yourself or someone guides you either in person or by audiotape. The technique usually is used to induce deep relaxation, although it also can be used as an on-the-spot tension reliever, for mental rehearsal, or to harness the mind toward healing. Several examples of visualization for relaxation follow.

A Private Place

Here is a visualization exercise I often use in my classes, modified from Ryan and Travis (1981, 43).

Imagine yourself in your own bedroom. Be aware of a new door that was not there before. Get up, approach the door, put your hand on the doorknob, turn the knob, and pass through the door into a completely new room. As you enter the room, be aware of the windows. Approach each window, and take a look out. Be aware of the varied scenes outside. Create whatever scene you wish—one window might look onto the mountains, another onto the ocean, the third onto a waterfall. Bring your attention back into the room. Notice the walls—texture, colors. As you notice the floor, create whatever surface you wish—carpet, wood, throw rugs, whatever. Now furnish the room—bookcases, plants, lamps, furniture. Among the furniture, create a couch, chair, or large pillow on which you now recline or sit comfortably, totally relaxed. If you wish to create background music, please do so. And now, for the next 10 to 20 minutes, be in this private place, feeling completely at ease and relaxed. Enjoy it.

When you feel ready, imagine getting up, then stretch, return to the door, open the door, and return to your room.

Now bring your attention back to the present, and resume your daily routine.

Remember, this is your very own, very special private place to which you can return at any time for rest, renewal, and inspiration.

The Beach

Become comfortable in a reclining or sitting position, preferably in a quiet place. Begin by completing the 6-second quieting response. Visualize the following, allowing your mind to roam free in its own way. If you find it useful, you might dictate the following instruction onto an audiotape, then play it back as you begin to relax. Feel free to modify as you wish.

Imagine you are on vacation. No cares, no worries. You feel completely free from your usual daily pressures and hassles. You are walking along the water's edge on a quiet, barely inhabited, warm ocean beach. You are in your bathing suit, either alone or with someone close to you, whichever you prefer. As you stroll, you feel the coolness of the damp sand under your feet. You hear the gentle rolling of the waves. Under one arm is a rolled-up towel. You turn away from the water onto soft, white, warm sand. You pick a spot where you can be alone and still. You put down your rolled towel as a pillow. You lie down on the soft, pleasantly warm sand. You feel the warmth of the sand on your back, the backs of your legs, the backs of your arms. You note the deep blue of the late morning sky. It is completely clear, except for one wispy cloud near the horizon over the water. You feel the gentle warmth of the sun on your skin, the pleasant warmth of the sand beneath. You feel utterly relaxed and still. For the next several minutes, continue to experience this place, allowing your mind to wander as it wishes. Enjoy this very pleasant sensation of stillness, warmth and quiet. . . .

And now, imagine getting up, gathering up your towel, and walking back to the water's edge. Again, you experience the cool, damp sand underfoot. You continue on along the beach, feeling alert, refreshed, peaceful, and renewed. You give yourself credit for this positive experience.

Bring your attention back to the present. Draw a deep breath. Resume your normal activities.

During meditation, a repeated mental focus is used to quiet the mind, thereby quieting the body. The result is heightened energy and greater calm.

Mountain Meadow

Imagine you are walking alone or with someone along a mountain path covered with pine needles. You hear the whisper of wind through the trees as you walk. A few birds chirp. The sky is deep blue at this altitude. In the middle of this afternoon, the sun is warm and soothing.

As you walk, you break out through the trees into a rich, green meadow with a small lake at one side. You walk toward the lake, which is perfectly calm, with water like glass. No wind is blowing here at all. The grass is short and dry. You decide to stay awhile. You sit, then lie down on a towel you happen to have along. You feel the warm sun on your face and arms. You are at complete peace. You are enormously grateful for this quiet spot. You allow your mind to take in all the aromas and soothing sounds from this incredible place. You stay; you drift; you refresh.

When you are ready, imagine getting up and resuming your walk, feeling fully refreshed and renewed.

Mental Rehearsal

Each evening before drifting off to sleep, imagine a difficult and challenging upcoming event—a test, a speech, an interview, or a confrontation with someone. Use any of the relaxation methods described in this chapter to take your mind and body into a state of deep quiet. Then visualize yourself first approaching, then moving through this situation with confidence, assurance, and competence.

Mental Rehearsal

Here is a technique for practicing mental rehearsal and for applying it in specific demanding situations. Included are two stages.

Stage 1 Mental Rehearsal
Complete these steps many, many times during the weeks, days, and hours leading up to the event in question. You can do this during deep relaxation; while walking, exercising, or driving; or just as you are falling to sleep.

1. Develop a clear mental picture of a demanding forthcoming event. Create as much imaginary detail as possible—place, persons, and events.
2. Create a clear, detailed image of how you want to handle this situation. Experience yourself as calm, confident, and effective.
3. While imagining this positive, successful response to the situation, use a *cue—form your thumb and forefinger into a circle.* Whenever creating the mental rehearsal, use this cue, so, in your mind, the cue comes to be linked to the image.

Stage 2 Application

1. Enter the situation.
2. As you do, use the cue. This will bring to your mind your oft-rehearsed positive response and the positive feelings associated with it.
3. In turn, chances will be enhanced that this desired response—and desired outcome—will occur.

Repeat this **mental rehearsal** for several days—even weeks—before the challenging event. Then repeat it several times the day of the event. See the box on page 401 for a more detailed technique of mental rehearsal.

Hypnosis and Self-Hypnosis

Hypnosis is an old and effective method of producing deep relaxation (Green & Shellenberger, 1991). Hypnosis is a condition of deep mental and physical quiet, induced by the hypnotic suggestion of a trained person who uses key words and images to elicit the desired internal change. He or she then gives posthypnotic suggestions, which, acting through the subconscious, can greatly reduce fears, phobias, smoking, overeating, anxiety, and other problems. When deep relaxation is suggested, the physiological changes associated with the relaxation response can be induced. Hypnosis should be attempted only under the guidance of a trained and experienced hypnosis practitioner.

As Morse and Furst have noted, different degrees of depth occur during hypnosis.

Some individuals can only achieve a light trance. In a light trance, a person often feels relaxed, both mentally and physically, but he is completely aware of his surroundings. In a medium trance, an individual is often able to take a mental "trip" and achieve an even deeper state of relaxation. A deep trance is called the somnambulist stage. In this stage, a person can generally realize the more distinctive phenomena of hypnosis, which include the following:

1. Hand levitation; a hand or an arm rises, apparently of its own free will.
2. Eyelid catalepsy—an inability to open the eyes.
3. Limb rigidity; an arm or a leg locks in a straightened position.
4. Automatic writing; a hand appears to write of its own free will.
5. Automatic movement; a hand or a leg moves continuously.
6. Dream induction; vivid dreams occur easily.
7. Dissociation—an ability to feel either as if one is in two places at the same time or that one can separate the mental from the physical state.
8. Hallucination—to be able to see, smell, hear, or feel objects that are not present (known as positive hallucination) or not to see, smell, hear, or feel objects that are present (known as negative hallucination).
9. Age regression and progression; the former is the ability to go back in time, while the latter is the belief that one can go ahead into the future.
10. Amnesia—to be able to forget that which has occurred during the hypnotic state.
11. Posthypnotic suggestibility—to act out, at a later time, a suggestion given by the hypnotist.
12. Analgesia—the ability not to perceive pain (perhaps, more appropriately, an exam ple of a negative hallucination) (1979, 245).

Experts estimate that about 70 percent of humanity can enter a medium hypnotic trance, while 20 percent seem capable of entering a deep trance.

Hypnosis can be useful in several ways in managing stress. For instance, it can help remove internal barriers and resistances, such as unfinished emotional trauma from the past. Second, it can help build "immunity" against harmful effects of specific future stressful events. Third, through suggestion, it can help the individual achieve deep relaxation at a later time.

Self-hypnosis is most commonly used to induce deep relaxation, rather than for medical or dental reasons. Usually, self-hypnosis is learned from a trained hypnotist, al-

Harnessing the Mind Toward Peak Performance

In a workshop for competitive roller skaters (figure, dance, and speed), I presented an integrated plan for preparing for competition. It met with remarkable success with several competitors. This sequence can be adapted to almost any type of challenging performance situation.

1. Know why you are training and competing; be sure it is for the right reasons.
2. Do not be an extreme perfectionist. Set realistic, personal goals.
3. Do not gunnysack your feelings. "Unfinished business" can interfere with concentration and block energy.
4. Be totally prepared through thorough practice.
5. Avoid these traps: fear of failure and fear of success.
6. Learn to use visualization—"positive mental movies."
7. During the day of competition, be unhurried, uncluttered, soothed, and focused.
8. Perform well for you, not for your impression on friends, teammates, coaches, and parents.
9. Stop negative thoughts and feelings. Substitute positive feelings and images through positive mental movies and key confidence-building words.
10. Be aware of body and emotional signals of your own best "activation level."
11. Let yourself do it, rather than make yourself do it. Concentrate; do not bear down. Be totally absorbed.
12. Do not be distracted, discouraged, or stopped by an error in performance.
13. Use the following steps in preparing for competition.
    a. The night before competition, do deep relaxation, with a positive mental movie of your performance.
    b. Two to 5 hours before the event, repeat deep relaxation.
    c. On the site, use deep breathing and key relaxing words to control physical tension. Then create a brief, positive, relaxed mental movie of your performance.
    d. Now let your mind become totally absorbed in your performance. Create "a cocoon of concentration"—not bearing down but becoming "one" with your movement and your partner, if present.
    e. Let your body take off and do its job.
14. After finishing, stroke yourself for what you *did* do well.
15. Remember the keys: practice, positive mental movies, and concentration.

though it can be self-taught. The point is to induce deep quiet through self-suggestion, much like meditation, autogenic relaxation, progressive muscle relaxation, or visualization (Parrini, 1979).

Biofeedback

A good deal of research has been conducted in recent years on **biofeedback**—the use of various detectors to give feedback to the user about her or his physiological arousal at a given moment, thereby aiding the individual in learning to lower arousal (Green & Shellenberger, 1991).

The point of biofeedback training is to discover how relaxation feels and then to learn to induce the feedback indicator downward through conscious focus of the mind (Green & Green, 1977). This usually is done with a therapist, stress consultant, or technician in a comfortable chair in an office or other clinical setting, although sometimes simple devices are used by the individual at home or work. The individual then learns to elicit the same state of relaxation in the absence of the detective device. Biofeedback can be used to create on-the-spot arousal, as well as deep relaxation (Brown, 1977) (Basjmajian, 1988).

A variety of biofeedback techniques have been developed to make visible otherwise invisible internal processes (Budzynski & Stoyva, 1984). **Electromyographic feedback (EMG)** detects muscle contraction through electrodes affixed to the skin surrounding a specific muscle in order to detect small electrical discharges that accompany muscle contraction. Like other types of biofeedback, the feedback may be in the form of a sound, a dial, or a graph. Occasionally, more exotic feedback is used: music, lights, or even an electric train. The greater the muscle contraction, the higher the tone, light, dial, or graph. As the individual relaxes, muscle tension drops, and so does the feedback. This information is used by the person to induce still more quieting. EMG biofeedback is often used to help the individual learn how to relax a tight forehead, neck, lower back—or the body generally (Schwartz & Schwartz, 1993).

As early as 1928 (Rice, 1992) Hans Berger discovered that the very small electrical discharges from the brain can be amplified and recorded. Thus, the **electroencephalograph (EEG)** was developed. This sensing device is attached to specific locations on the head and attuned to detect alpha, beta, theta, or delta waves. Alpha waves are associated with the deep quiet of meditation or falling off to sleep. EEG biofeedback is sometimes used for general relaxation training but more often to assist the individual in reducing or preventing headaches or for improving attentiveness or concentration.

Another form of biofeedback measures **skin temperature.** Usually, some type of finger thermometer is used. As tension mounts, skin temperature in the hands and feet falls. This is the result of constriction of capillaries, a process that shunts blood back to main muscles to be available during the stress response. Remember, your body cannot distinguish between physical threats and other stressors, so it assumes you are in physical danger, whatever the stressful situation. On the other hand, elicitation of the relaxation response brings more blood into the hands and feet, raising their skin temperature (Haynes et al., 1975).

Even beginners usually are able to raise their skin temperature several degrees when skin temperature monitoring is combined with other relaxation techniques. More advanced practitioners sometimes are able even to control temperature to the extent of raising the temperature in one ear lobe while lowering it in the other.

Skin temperature biofeedback sometimes is used to reduce migraine headaches, as well as to treat Raynaud's disease, a problem of constricted blood vessels in the hand, producing extreme cold and pain. This type of biofeedback also is used for general relaxation training.

The **galvanic skin response (GSR)** measures the skin's resistance to electrical conductance across its surface. The greater the relaxation, the greater the resistance—for reasons not entirely understood by experts. The most likely explanation is that with increased tension sweating is increased. This rise in moisture in turn conducts electricity more quickly. Whatever the physiological process involved, the GSR can be useful for general relaxation—as well as for demonstrations to groups, for which I use the device in my classes and workshops.

Cardiovascular activity measures comprise another type of biofeedback. Whether measuring heart rate, arrhythmias, or blood pressure, this practice can be useful, especially with people who have cardiovascular problems. Of course, monitoring heart rate is a simple practice anyone can constructively use to observe in a gross way one's physiological arousal.

Two key questions are debated by relaxation experts about biofeedback. First, does biofeedback yield benefits beyond those of other relaxation techniques, such as meditation, autogenic relaxation, or progressive muscle relaxation? Probably not. Biofeedback may enhance learning or enable it to occur more quickly, but probably nothing is unique about biofeedback-aided elicitation of the relaxation response, with one notable exception. Biofeedback may be useful for relaxing specific muscles or specific processes such as blood vessels in the hands or forehead.

Second, can relaxation training in the biofeedback clinic be readily transferred to the individual's ongoing life? Again, perhaps, and probably with no greater effectiveness than with other relaxation methods.

In sum, biofeedback has been demonstrated to be a useful aid in assisting individuals to learn how to relax—generally and in specific body locations. It is best seen as an adjunct to other relaxation methods, rather than as a method standing alone. For some, it may provide the type of feedback and structure that aids learning. For others, learning other techniques of deep relaxation and on-the-spot tension reduction can be accomplished just as well without biofeedback.

Muscle Relaxation Techniques

Autogenic Relaxation

This technique was first introduced by the German psychiatrist Johannes Schultz in 1932 and continues to have high popularity in Europe (Schultz & Luthe, 1959). Like meditation, **autogenic** ("self-produced") **relaxation** depends on a relaxed body state (sitting with or without back support or reclining) and a passive, accepting attitude. While this technique takes on several variations, it usually is practiced by focusing self-suggestions of warmth and heaviness in specific muscle groups throughout the body. To do it to completion, one needs to devote 30 to 60 minutes to the technique. Limited positive results can be experienced in as few as 5 minutes.

Norris and Fahrion (1984) have summarized a number of conditions for which autogenics have been employed, including anxiety, phobic disorders, and hysteria. They have also presented research findings showing positive results. Many other studies have produced similar positive results for clients suffering from everything from tension headaches to hypertension, smoking addiction, epilepsy, sexual dysfunction, and alcoholism.

While healthy skepticism is warranted in evaluating this technique, like the others described here, there does appear to be convincing evidence that autogenics can sometimes work to elicit the relaxation response with positive results for health and coping (Rice, 1992). Try the technique in the Autogenic Relaxation box for yourself.

Progressive Muscle Relaxation (PMR)

First written about by Edmund Jacobson (1929), **progressive muscle relaxation (PMR)** has come to be widely practiced and studied with consistent positive results (Greenberg, 1993). This technique is especially useful when people find themselves "bracing," as

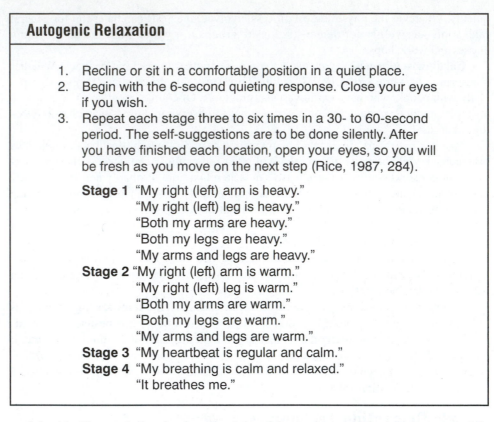

Autogenic Relaxation

1. Recline or sit in a comfortable position in a quiet place.
2. Begin with the 6-second quieting response. Close your eyes if you wish.
3. Repeat each stage three to six times in a 30- to 60-second period. The self-suggestions are to be done silently. After you have finished each location, open your eyes, so you will be fresh as you move on the next step (Rice, 1987, 284).

Stage 1 "My right (left) arm is heavy."
"My right (left) leg is heavy."
"Both my arms are heavy."
"Both my legs are heavy."
"My arms and legs are heavy."
Stage 2 "My right (left) arm is warm."
"My right (left) leg is warm."
"Both my arms are warm."
"Both my legs are warm."
"My arms and legs are warm."
Stage 3 "My heartbeat is regular and calm."
Stage 4 "My breathing is calm and relaxed."
"It breathes me."

explained in Chapter 3. Bracing is maintaining tightness in a specific muscle group while writing, studying, driving, or talking. If you frequently find yourself with tight neck and shoulders, abdominal muscles, or forehead, you may find this technique especially useful.

Very simply, PMR calls for alternately tensing and relaxing specific muscles throughout the body for 10 seconds or so. In more technical language, it involves switching between eliciting the sympathetic and the parasympathetic nervous systems—the emergency and calming branches of the autonomic nervous system. PMR can be practiced for a few moments or up to 30 minutes or longer.

Benefits, which have been demonstrated with as little as three-times-daily practice for only 5 minutes at a time (Curtis & Detert, 1981), occur in both physiological and psychological ways. Physically, for example, studies have shown positive outcomes for tension and migraine headaches (Blanchard & Epstein, 1978; Cox et al., 1975; Haynes et al., 1975; Mitchell & Mitchell, 1971; Otis et al., 1974), backaches (Belar & Cohen, 1979), muscular problems (Rice, 1992), gastrointestinal disorders, and cardiovascular problems (Brown, 1977). Psychologically, PMR has been shown to have positive benefits for self-concepts, depression, anxiety, sleep disorders, alcoholism, drug abuse—and even batting averages. As Greenberg notes (1993), every relaxation technique has the potential to produce anxiety because of the stillness involved. Because this is an active technique, it is especially advisable for those prone to anxiety in response to stillness.

The following is a simple exercise for trying out PMR. Try it, and if it works for you, generalize it to other parts of your body.

1. Find a quiet place where you can recline or sit comfortably.
2. Begin with the 6-second quieting response.

3. Squeeze each of the following, hold for 10 seconds, then release and draw a deep breath.

    When finished at one location, move on to another.

    • Right fist
    • Right forearm
    • Right upper arm
    • Left fist
    • Left forearm
    • Left upper arm
    • Shoulders and neck
    • Head and face

    If you wish, move to your feet and legs, then to your abdomen.

4. As you proceed, be aware of the contrast between tension and calm. Be aware of the pleasant sensation of relaxation. Most of all, be aware of your power to produce deep quiet.

Other Muscle Relaxation Techniques

Here is a sampling of other relaxation methods whose major focus is relaxing muscles throughout the body.

See Application Exercise 15-3 to assess the personal appeal of these relaxation methods for you.

STRETCHING   Notice how a cat often enjoys a full-body stretch and yawn after eating or before settling down. Try it, especially before a challenging event. Reach as high as possible with both hands. Then spread your feet and reach over your head with one straight arm while sliding the other down your opposite leg. Put both arms behind you, hands clasped. Pull down and back strenuously, opening up your chest and shoulders. Then yawn if you feel like it, with both arms falling easily to your sides.

TRUNK ROTATION   Large trunk rotations provide an excellent warm-up and relaxation method. Extend both arms straight out to the side. Slowly and gently rotate from the waist, first right, then left. Repeat several times with your hands resting on your hips. Be gentle, avoiding quick or strenuous movements. Never push beyond a point of mild tightness.

JOGGING IN PLACE   With your arms gently hanging at your side, slowly run in place for 1 to 3 minutes. Your feet need hardly leave the ground. You can release muscle tension, while mildly oxygenating your brain and the rest of your body.

FLOPPY DOLL   Stand with feet set apart to provide good stability. Allow your arms to dangle at your side. Then rotate your upper trunk back and forth with your arms and hands swinging gently and effortlessly along. Allow your entire upper body to relax as you slowly rotate back and forth. Repeat several times with a brief breather in-between.

SWIMMER'S SHAKEOUT   You will see competitive swimmers do this exercise during the few moments before the starting gun. Allow both arms to hang very loosely at your side. Beginning with your hands, rotate each arm from fingertips to shoulder. At the same time, let them swing gently from front to back. This will be relaxing only if you let your arms hang loosely, rather than raise them outward to the side. Notice how this relaxes your shoulders, as well as your arms.

ISOMETRIC ARM RELIEVER   Pull or push for a few seconds with each hand against a desk, a doorway, or another immovable object. Relax for a few seconds. Repeat several times. Notice the release of muscle tension during each rest interval.

LEG LOOSENER   Many women make it a habit to hold their legs tightly together, even when alone. Similarly, men often keep their legs quite tight, especially when pushed for time or in an intense situation. This commonly is reflected in foot jiggling or knee bobbing. Deliberately allow your leg muscles to let go. Let your thighs fall apart a little. Keep your ankles relaxed.

HEAD ROLL   Gently rotate your head from side to side and from front to back. Repeat in the opposite direction. Continue a number of times. It is very important to do this exercise slowly and gently in order to avoid muscle strain.

SELF-MASSAGE   Use your fingertips or your cupped hands to massage your facial muscles. This can also be done to your neck, shoulders, arms, or hands. You will find this to be surprisingly restful and tension-reducing.

SITTING STRETCH   Extend one leg forward and upward from a sitting position and hold for a few seconds. Then release and let it fall. Repeat with the other leg. This also can be done with shoulders and arms. For example, reach your hands behind your chair, clasp, then stretch backward. You will find your shoulders, arms, and chest relaxing, ready to return to a lower tension level than before.

BRISK 5-MINUTE WALK   The next time you have already accumulated physical tension or are about to enter a potentially distressful situation, take a brisk 5-minute walk. This can release muscle tension, allow greater oxygenation in your brain and body, and allow for mental diversion or positive affirmations. It can be amazingly effective.

Other Techniques

Music

In a 1991 survey study cited by Seaward (1994), 3 of 4 respondents reported that listening to music was their most commonly used relaxation method. This confirmed what most us can attest to personally—music can be soothing to the mind, body, and soul.

Music can have a variety of effects: arousal, warmth, sexuality, and playfulness. Music can create a sense of structure; it can rekindle nostalgic memories. It can stir you to action, add to your fear, make you angry or mournful, stimulate religious sentiments, lower tensions, slow you down, and keep you awake. Clearly, music can do many things, mentally and physically. People differ widely in musical tastes, and each person varies from time to time. Thoughtfully chosen music can indeed be restful, relaxing, and renewing. Find which kind works for you for specific occasions. Try to disregard what your particular social group thinks you should like. Listen to your own body and spirit for what works for you.

Yoga

The term **yoga** is from Sanskrit: union of mind, body, and soul (Seaward, 1994). With a history dating back at least to the sixth century B.C. in the Hindu tradition, yoga first entered this country in 1893. Since then it has gone through a number of phases. Its practice has increased substantially in recent years, as it became popularized in outpatient hospital programs, corporate health-promotion programs, commercial health clubs, and mind/body clinics.

Perhaps the most popular branch, hatha yoga, emphasizes uniting mind, body, and spirit through action, emotion, and intelligence (Seaward, 1994). Specifically, hatha yoga involves combining the arts of breathing, conscious stretching, and balance in a rigorous discipline that, for effectiveness, needs to be maintained over months and years. Central to yoga are a series of "asanas" or stretching positions that are entered, maintained, and exited smoothly, slowly, and gracefully with an attitude of focus, quiet, and spiritual depth.

Scientific evidence on the effects of yoga is scant, though occasional studies do show positive psychological benefits (Birkel, 1991). Certainly, there is an abundance of anecdotal testimony about the gains from regular practice of yoga. If you are interested in exploring this approach to stress control, classes probably are offered in your area.

T'ai Chi Ch'uan

This ancient discipline originating from China has been called the "softest of the martial arts" (Seaward, 1994, 339), bringing the mind and body into unity with the *chi* or life force in the natural world around us. While the practice of any form of martial art may seem by nature incompatible with relaxation, **t'ai chi ch'uan** is in fact widely acclaimed as a powerful tool for centering, for holding steady and calm under pressure, and for flowing *with* rather than *against* external threat and resistance.

In brief, t'ai chi involves a period of focused, very slow, measured, progressive simulation of defensive martial arts postures. It is graceful and fluid, contributing to calm, steadiness, and flexibility. It is practiced daily by millions in China and the Far East and has become increasingly popular in the United States among both the young and the elderly. As with yoga, the mental aspect of the discipline is as central as the physical.

As with yoga, scientific investigation is just now beginning, but t'ai chi's long history and widespread practice in the East suggests it can have profound value in the quest for health, well-being, and steadiness under life's pressures. Like yoga, classes probably are offered by a health club, martial arts center, or college in your area.

Massage

Massage can be beneficial in response to tension in a number of ways, as Jane Madders explains:

> Massage helps muscles relax. Physiological massage stimulates the flow of blood and improves the muscle tone. It assists in a clearing away of waste products, reduces muscle tension, and its assorted pain. It does far more than this, however. During massage, there is a subtle calming down of the whole body, a reduction of anxiety, a feeling of trust develops enabling the receiver to feel rather than to think. It offers recuperative rest from the turbulence of stress. (1979, 2)

More recently, Eisner (1997, 64) makes a strong case, based on a review of research studies, for the value of massage in promoting emotional and physical well-being. She notes, "Body work on deep tissues and massages of varying depths and pressure are a valuable and mostly underappreciated technique. They are particularly valuable when personal difficulties are not amenable to verbal strategies or when psychological resistance occurs."

Learning to offer massage to one's partner is a true gift. Receiving massage is to receive a noble gift of love.

Massage for infants can promote bonding, as well as relieve tension in the child. Our Enloe Hospital Stress and Health Center now conducts training programs for new parents in how to massage infants carefully and effectively. Vimala Schneider, author of *Infant Massage* (1982), trained our instructor, Audrey Downes, in the same methods she is teaching other parents and instructors across the country. For further information about infant massage, including training programs for parents and instructors, write to: Infant Massage Programs, N.T. Enloe Memorial Hospital, Chico, CA 95926.

A number of massage techniques for adults are available from professionals in most medium-sized and larger cities: chiropractic, acupressure, Rolfing, reflexology, Touch for Health, and more. Taking a class or receiving individual treatments can be most useful, both for immediate stress reduction and to learn techniques for use at home.

Combining Deep-Relaxation Methods

You are invited to try this brief technique, which combines meditation (repeated mental focus), autogenic relaxation (warmth and heaviness in hands), and visualization (imagining your hands in warm water or in the warm sun). This text was written by the relaxation expert, Jonathan Smith (1985).

"Let both of your hands fall to your sides. Let them become as relaxed as possible. Give yourself a while to settle into a position that feels very comfortable. Let your breathing be calm and even. Now, focus your attention on your hands. Simply repeat to yourself the phrase, My hands are warm and heavy. Let those words go over and over like an echo. There is nothing for you to try to do. Do not try to force your hands to feel warm and heavy. Simply let the words go over and over in your mind, like the words of a simple song or nursery rhyme. You might want to imagine your hands in warm water or in the warm sun" (1).

To purchase the deep relaxation audiotape, *Sojourn,* with original music, as well as oral instructions by Dr. Schafer much like those above, write for information to:

Walt Schafer, Ph.D.
Department of Sociology and Social Work
California State University, Chico
Chico, CA 95929-0470

Hydrotherapy

An approach to relaxation many find very effective is as primitive as imaginable: warm water. Whether in the form of a hot bath, a hot shower, or the more contemporary form of a hot tub or flotation tank, **hydrotherapy** can be a most effective relaxation method, especially at the end of a hard day of work. While formal research on the stress-reduction benefits of this approach are limited at best, anecdotal reports are endless, including from this writer.

Humor

The ability to infuse **humor** into everyday life is invaluable for health and happiness. Research evidence supports what folk wisdom has long held: chuckling at situations and the self is healthy (Dixon, 1980; Long, 1987; Martin & Lefcourt, 1983; Nezu, Nezu, & Blissett, 1988). Humor at the expense of others is something else altogether, of course (Blumenfeld & Alpern, 1986). But mirthful laughter, funniness, and joking in a playful spirit can enhance mental and physical well-being—and sometimes can even heal (Cousins, 1981; Graham, 1990; Ornstein & Sobel, 1989; Sobel & Ornstein, 1996; Wellingham-Jones, 1989). Studies suggest that humor may promote health partly through bolstering the immune system (Berk, 1989; Dillon, Minchoff, & Baker, 1985).

An example of humor in the direst of circumstances comes from the book *Beyond Surival* (1990), in which Gerald Coffee recounts his experiences as a 7-year POW in Hanio during the Vietnam War (see Chapter 12 for other lessons from Captain Coffee). He states:

> I decided one day to compose a poem about food to entertain Howie and Nels [other POWs in adjacent cells]. We had received bread a couple of times in lieu of the usual rice. It usually came in a small roll about six inches long, and it was

apparent that wherever they kept the flour for this bread—somewhere in the dungeonlike kitchens of Hao Lo—there were plenty of bugs and weevils and roaches and flies. But at least, I reasoned, they were protein supplements. Anyway, the next time we received bread, I was immediately inspired to compose my poem after taking the first bite:

> Little Weevil in my bread
> I think I just bit off your head.
> I see the place where you have bled
> The dough around it is all red.
> But that's okay, for now instead
> I know for sure you're really dead.
> I wonder if your name was Fred.

Well, when I passed it to Nels the next day [via an elaborate, secret tapping code devised by the POWs], he got so tickled after the first two lines, he was bangin' and scratchin' and scrapin' his laugh on the wall to me, and then I started laughin' and I never did get the rest of the poem to him. I allowed later as to how after those first two lines, things did sort of go downhill (Coffee, 1990, 191).

You have read here a mere sampling of some of the main methods of relaxation. A host of written sources are available for more detail and for broader coverage. See, for example, Carrington (1978, 1984); Charlesworth and Nathan (1982); Czimbal & Zadikov (1992); Davis, Eshelman, and McKay (1982); Hanson (1986); LeShan (1974); Schwartz (1982); and Smith (1985, 1986).

MAKING RELAXATION PART OF YOUR LIFE

We noted at the beginning of this chapter that two broad categories of relaxation can be identified: on-the-spot tension reducers and deep relaxation. Many of the techniques we have explored can be adapted to either category.

But the real challenge is not so much mastering the techniques themselves—with practice, most come rather easily—but rather building their use into one's daily life with regularity and consistency. Just as with aerobic exercise, the effect is cumulative. Thus, it is important for maximum effect that you practice one or more of these techniques daily over a period of months and years. If you do, you will surely benefit.

References

Alexander, C. N., Schneider, R. H., Staggers, F., Sheppart, W., Clayborne, B. M., Rainforth, M., Salerno, J., Kondwani, K., Smith, S. Walton, K. G., & Egan B. (1996). Trial of stress reduction for hypertension in older African-Americans. II. Sex and risk subgroup analysis. *Hypertension, 28,* 228–237.

Antoni, M. H. (1993). Stress management: Strategies that work. In D. Goleman, & J. Gurin, *Mind/body medicine.* Yonkers: Consumer Reports Books, 385–397.

Aron, E., & Aron, A. (1986). *The Maharishi effect.* Walpole, NH: Stillpoint.

Auerback, S. M., & Gramling, S. E. (1998). *Stress management: Psychological foundations.* Upper Saddle River, NJ: Prentice-Hall.

Basmajian, J. V. (Ed.). (1989). *Biofeedback: Principles and practice for clinicians* (3rd ed.). Baltimore: Williams and Wilkins.

Belar, C. D., & Cohen, J. L. (1979). The use of EMG feedback and progressive relaxation in the treatment of a woman with chronic back pain. *Biofeedback and Self-Regulation, 4,* 345–353.

Benson, H. (1975). *The relaxation response.* New York: Morrow.

Benson, H. (1993). The relaxation response. In D. Goleman, & J. Gurin, *Mind/body medicine.* Yonkers: Consumer Reports Books, 233–258.

Benson, H., & Stuart, E. M. (1992). *The wellness book.* New York: Birch Lane Books.

Bentov, I. (1988). *Stalking the wild pendulum: On the mechanics of consciousness.* Rochester, VT: Destiny Books.

Berk, L. (1989). Laughter and immunity. *Advances, 6,* 5.

Birkel, D. (1991). *Hatha yoga.* Dubuque: Eddie Bowers.

Blanchard, E. D., & Epstein, L. H. (1978). *A biofeedback primer.* Reading, MA: Addison-Wesley.

Blumenfeld, E., & Alpern, L. (1986). *The smile connection.* Englewood Cliffs, NJ: Prentice-Hall.

Brown, B. (1977). *New mind, new body.* New York: Harper & Row.

Brye, A. (1978). *Visualization: Directing the movies of your mind.* New York: Barnes and Noble.

Budzinski, T. H., & Stoyva, J. M. (1984). Biofeedback methods in the treatment of anxiety and stress. In R. L. Woolfolk & P. M. Lehrer (Eds.), *Principles and practice of stress management.* New York: Guilford Press.

Carrington, P. (1978). *Freedom in meditation.* New York: Anchor.

Carrington, P. (1984). Modern forms of meditation. In R. L. Woolfolk & P. M. Lehrer (Eds.), *Principles and practice of stress management.* New York: Guilford Press.

Charlesworth, E. A., & Nathan, R. G. (1982). *Stress management: A comprehensive guide to wellness.* New York: Ballantine.

Coffee, G. (1990). *Beyond survival: Building on the hard times—a POW's inspiring story.* Aiea, HI: Coffee Enterprises.

Cousins, N. (1981). *Anatomy of an illness as perceived by the patient: Reflections on healing and regeneration.* New York: Bantam.

Cox, D. J., et al. (1975). Differential effectiveness of electromyographic feedback, verbal relaxation instructions, and medication placebo with tension headaches. *Journal of Consulting and Clinical Psychology, 43,* 892–898.

Curtis, J. D., & Detert, R. A. (1981). *How to relax: A holistic approach to stress management.* Palo Alto, CA: Mayfield.

Czimbal, B., & Zadikov, M. (1992). *Stress Survival Kit: 52 Stress Management Tolls.* Portland, OR: Open Book Publishers.

Davis, M., Eshelman, E. R., & McKay, M. (1982). *The relaxation & stress reduction workbook* (2nd ed.). Oakland, CA: New Harbinger Publications.

Dillon, K. M., Minchoff, B., & Baker, K. H. (1985). Positive emotional states and enhancement of the immune system. *International Journal of Psychiatry in Medicine, 15,* 13–17.

Dixon, N. F. (1980). Humor: A cognitive alternative to stress? In I. G. Sarason & C. D. Spielberger (Eds.), *Stress and anxiety* (vol. 7). Washington, DC: Hemisphere.

Ferguson, P. C., & Gowan, J. C. (1975). Psychological findings on transcendental meditation. *Scientific Research on the Transcendental Meditation Program.* Switzerland: MERU.

Eisner, B. (1997). Body work and psychological healing. *Advances, 13,* 64–66.

Frew, D. R. (1977). *Management of stress: Using TM at work.* Chicago: Nelson.

Glasser, W. (1976). *Positive addiction.* New York: Harper.

Graham, B. (1990). The healing power of humor. *Mind/Body/Health Digest, 4,* 1–2.

Green, E., & Green, A. (1977). *Beyond biofeedback.* New York: W. W. Norton.

Green, J., & Shellenberger, R. (1991). *The dynamics of health and wellness: A biopsychosocial approach.* Fort Worth: Holt, Rinehart and Winston.

Greenberg, J. S. (1993). *Comprehensive stress management* (4th ed.). Dubuque: Brown and Benchmark.

Hanson, P. G. (1986). *The joy of stress: How to make stress work for you.* Kansas City: Andrews and McMeel.

Hatch, J. P., Fisher, J. G., & Rugh, J. D. (1987). *Biofeedback: Studies in clinical efficacy.* New York: Plenum Press.

Haynes, S. N., et al. (1975). Electromyographic biofeedback and relaxation instructions in the treatment of muscle contraction headaches. *Behavior Therapy, 6,* 672–678.

Jacobson, E. (1929). *Progressive relaxation.* Chicago: University of Chicago Press.

Kabat-Zinn, J. (1991). *Full catastrophe living.* New York: Delacorte.

Kabat-Zinn, J. (1993). Mindfulness meditation: Health benefits of an ancient Buddhist practice. In D. Goleman & J. Gurin, *Mind/Body Medicine.* Yonkers: Consumer Reports Books, 259–276.

Kabat-Zinn, J., Lipworth, A., & Burney, R. (1985). The clinical use of awareness meditation in the self-regulation of pain. *Journal of Behavioral Medicine, 8,* 163–190.

Lazarus, R. S. (1975). A cognitive-oriented psychologist looks at biofeedback. *American Psychologist, 30,* 553–561.

LeShan, L. (1974). *How to meditate.* New York: Bantam.

Long, P. (1987). Laugh and be well? *Psychology Today, 21,* 28–29.

Martin, R. A., & Lefcourt, H. M. (1983). Sense of humor as a moderator of the relation between stressors and moods. *Journal of Personality and Social Psychology, 45,* 1313–1324.

Mitchell, K. R., & Mitchell, D. M. (1971). Migraine: An exploratory treatment application of programmed behavior therapy techniques. *Journal of Psychosomatic Medicine, 15,* 137–157.

Nezu, A. M., Nezu, C. M., & Blissett, S. E. (1988). Sense of humor as a moderator of the relation between stressful events and psychological distress: A prospective analysis. *Journal of Personality and Social Psychology, 54,* 520–525.

Norris, P. A., & Fahrion, S. L. (1984). Autogenic biofeedback in psychophysiological therapy and stress management. In R. L. Woolfolk & P. M. Lehrer, (Eds.), *Principles and practice of stress management.* New York: Guilford Press, 220–254.

Ornish, D. (1992). *Dr. Dean Ornish's program for reversing coronary heart disease without drugs or surgery.* New York: Ballantine Books.

Ornstein, R., & Sobel, D. (1989). *Healthy pleasures.* Reading, MA: Addison-Wesley.

Otis, L., et al. (1974). Voluntary control of tension headaches. Paper presented at the Biofeedback Research Society Meeting, Colorado Springs.

Parrino, J. J. (1979). *From panic to power: The positive use of stress.* New York: John Wiley.

Pelletier, K. R. (1993). What is mind/body medicine? In D. Goleman, & J. Gurin, *Mind/body medicine.* Yonkers: Consumer Reports Books, 19–38.

Rice, P. L. (1992). *Stress and health: Principles and practice for coping and wellness* (2nd ed.). Monterey, CA: Brooks/Cole.

Roth, B. (1997). Mindfulness-based stress reduction in the inner city. *Advances, 13,* 50–58.

Samuels, M., & Samuels, N. (1975). *Seeing with the mind's eye: The history, techniques and uses of visualization.* New York: Random House.

Schneider, V. (1982). *Infant massage.* New York: Bantam.

Schultz, J., & Luthe, W. (1959). *Autogenic training.* New York: Grune & Stratton.

Schwartz, J. (1982). *Letting go of stress.* New York: Pinnacle Books.

Schwartz, M. S., et al. (1987). *Biofeedback: A practitioner's guide.* New York: Guilford Press.

Schwartz, M. S., & Schwartz, N. M. (1993). Biofeedback: Using the body's signals. In D. Goleman & J. Gurin, *Mind/body medicine.* Yonkers: Consumer Reports Books, 301–314.

Seaward, B. L. (1994). *Managing stress.* Boston: Jones and Bartlett.

Smith, J. C. (1985). *Research dynamics: Nine world approaches to self-relaxation.* Champaign, IL: Research Press.

Smith, J. C. (1986). *Meditation: A sensible guide to a timeless discipline.* Champaign, IL: Research Press.

Sobel, D. S., & Ornstein, R. (1996). *The healthy mind/healthy body handbook.* New York: Patient Education Media.

Wellingham-Jones, P. (1989). *Successful women.* Tehama, CA: PWL.

Application Exercise 15-1

Beginning to Use the 6-Second Quieting Response

1. Beginning on a day you designate in advance, use the 6-second quieting response (QR) at the top of each hour. Carry a copy of this sheet with you, and record what you are doing and what you experience each time you do the QR.

Time   Activity   Comments About QR Experience

2. For the next week, use the QR once each hour, plus whenever else it might prove helpful. Write your reactions to these experiences below.

Application Exercise 15-2

Plan for Deep Relaxation

1. Do you now regularly practice a deep relaxation method? If so, which type? With what effects? If not, proceed to the rest of this exercise.

2. To which type of deep relaxation are you most attracted?

3. When will you start?

4. What steps will you take to learn a deep relaxation technique (through reading, an audiotape, a videotape, a class or workshop, or individual instruction, for example)?

5. When and where will you practice deep relaxation each day?

6. What difficulties do you expect to encounter?

7. How will you overcome each of these difficulties? For example, what will you do 6 months from now when you become so busy you "just don't have time" to practice deep relaxation every day?

Application Exercise 15-3

Personal Appeal of Various Relaxation Methods

1. After reading this chapter, which *on-the-spot tension reducer* most appeals to you? Why?

2. After practicing different types of *on-the-spot tension reducers* for two or three weeks, which type do you prefer? Why?

3. After reading this chapter, which *deep relaxation* technique most appeals to you? Why?

4. After practicing different types of *deep relaxation* for 2 or 3 weeks, which type do you prefer? Why?

CHAPTER 16

Folks used to be willing to wait patiently for a slow-moving coach, but now they kick like the dickens if they miss one revolution of a revolving door.

—ED WYNN

Pacing and Balance: Managing Time

TIME, STRESS, AND HEALTH: A UNIVERSAL CHALLENGE

Time is a universal feature of life. In his autobiography, Nelson Mandela writes that on arriving at South Africa's isolated Robben Island prison in 1964, having been sentenced to life without possibility of parole, "One of the first things I did was to make a calendar on the wall of my cell. Losing a sense of time is an easy way to lose one's grip and even one's sanity" (Mandela, 1994). Time is always with us. The question is what we do with it.

You have said or heard it many times:

- "I don't have time."
- "I need 25 hours in a day."
- "There's just not enough time."
- "I am so disorganized."
- "I'm the world's worst procrastinator."

These familiar lines reflect a common concern we all share: how to manage time. Wherever and whenever we live, we must deal with time. We do so in many ways:

- Filling time
- Making time
- Organizing time
- Using time
- Saving time
- Passing time
- And more

For some people, time is a friend: It brings challenge, pleasure, and satisfaction. For others, time is an enemy, bringing anxiety, boredom, or confusion. For some, there is too little time; for others, too much.

The Cultural Relativity of Time

Our notions of time are culturally influenced. In the U.S. Virgin Islands, where two of my sisters lived for many years, time is approached quite differently than "on the mainland." If you arrive at a dinner party within an hour or so of the appointed time, that is quite acceptable. For many on the island of St. Croix, the concepts of punctuality and hurry are entirely foreign. Similarly, in rural Kenya, where I visited my daughter, a Peace Corps volunteer, the main mode of transportation is walking. Patience and endurance, rather than quickness and efficiency, are virtues. In this country, by contrast, we are brought up to value punctuality, productivity, and efficiency.

Variation in the **cultural relativity of time** is illustrated by a study reported by Levine and Wolff (1985) of time tolerance among college students in Brazil and the United States. When asked what they would consider "late" arrival for a lunch appointment with a friend, Brazilian students averaged more than 33 minutes. U.S. students averaged 19 minutes. Brazilian students allowed an average of 54 minutes before they would consider someone "early" for such an appointment, while U.S. students would allow an average of 24 minutes.

International differences are also illustrated by national rankings in the accuracy of public clocks, walking speed, and post-office speed in selling stamps, as shown in Figure 16-1.

Figure 16-1

Pace of Life in Six Countries

	Accuracy of Bank Clocks	Walking Speed	Post-Office Speed
JAPAN	1	1	1
UNITED STATES	2	3	2
ENGLAND	4	2	3
ITALY	5	4	6
TAIWAN	3	5	4
INDONESIA	6	6	5

Numbers (1 = top value) indicate the comparative rank of each country for each indicator of pace.

Source: Levine & Wolff (1985

Levine and Wolff note that even within the United States, standards of time and punctuality vary from place to place according to the rhythm and rules of different regions and cities. "Seemingly simple words like 'now,' snapped out by an impatient New Yorker, and 'later,' said by a relaxed Californian, suggest a world of difference" (1985, 32).

Levine (Levine et al., 1989) also has studied the pace of life in 36 U.S. cities, using four measures: the speed at which people walk, work, and talk and their overall concern with the concept of time. The fastest-paced city was Boston, followed by New York, Buffalo, Columbus, and St. Louis. He also found a positive correlation between cities' pace and their rate of heart disease.

Two important implications flow from awareness of these cultural influences in our ideas about time. First, no absolute rights and wrongs about punctuality, productivity, pace, or anything else about time exist. These standards are culturally influenced. This fact, of course, is difficult for many residents of the United States to accept, especially those with rigid expectations of the self and others about punctuality, efficiency, and pace. Second, as modern communication increasingly puts people in contact across national and regional boundaries, it is important to be aware of cultural differences in time. This can prevent misunderstanding of others' intentions and behavior.

Within a given cultural context, how we organize, fill, and pace our time influence stress and how we deal with it. Wise **time management,** taking account of social context and personal preferences, is a vitally important ingredient in effective stress management.

Feeling Rushed: What It Can Do to You

A problem with time that seems almost endemic in this country is feeling rushed, harried, and hassled. As Duncan Campbell notes, "Americans have more timesaving devices and less time than any other group of people in the world" (Keyes, 1991, 89). Whether it is the high school or college student trying to juggle work, studies, and play; the working mother struggling to balance all the conflicting demands; or the commuting urban professional, a significant proportion of our population seems to feel pressed for time, even overwhelmed.

Americans in a Hurry—1830s

After touring the United States for two years in the 1830s, Michael Chevalier's main impression was how *active* our predecessors were. The Frenchman observed:

> If movement and the quick succession of sensations constitute life, here one lives a hundred-fold more than elsewhere; all here is circulation, motion, and boiling agitation. The American is devoured with a passion for movement, he cannot stay in one place; he must go and come, he must stretch his limbs and keep his muscles in play. When his feet are not in motion, his fingers must be in action; he must be whittling a piece of wood, cutting the back of his chair, or notching the edge of the table, or his jaws must be at work grinding tobacco. Whether it be that continual competition has given him the habit, or that he has an exaggerated estimate of the value of time, or that the unsettled state of everything around him keeps his nervous system in a state of perpetual agitation—he always has something to do, he is always in a terrible hurry.

Source: Chevalier, 1967, 270

Throughout this textbook, I have presented the findings of a survey among my 282 Human Stress students at California State University, Chico. Some of the most striking results relate to their responses to the question, "How often do you feel more rushed than you would like—Almost Always, Sometimes, Almost Never?" One-quarter responded "almost always," 70 percent "sometimes," and 5 percent "almost never." Most interesting, however, were differences among the three groups with distress, quality of life, and self-reported health. Four of the key findings are shown in Figures 16-2, 16-3, 16-4, and 16-5. The more often students felt rushed:

- The greater their distress symptoms
- The higher their irritability
- The greater their likelihood of feeling tired
- The greater the chances of their reporting their health to be only fair or poor

There were other significant findings as well. The more often the feeling of being rushed:

- The higher the hostility
- The greater the emotional tension
- The less the fun and playfulness these days
- The greater the perfectionism (probably the cause is the perfectionist's need to rush, of course)
- The lower the total quality-of-life score
- The lower the sense-of-coherence score—perhaps helping cause the rush
- The greater the depression

In short, the more you feel rushed, harried, and hassled, the greater your chances of feeling distressed, unwell, and troubled in your relationships. These findings are consistent with studies (Reimer, 1996; Robinson & Godbey, 1997). Clearly, managing time is vital to managing stress. Perhaps we would be well advised to heed the Spanish proverb, "Those who rush arrive first at the grave." We begin by examining common time difficulties.

Figure 16-2

Mean Distress-Symptom Score by How Often Feel Rushed

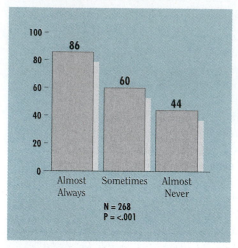

N = 268
P = <.001

Figure 16-3

Mean Irritability Score by How Often Feel Rushed

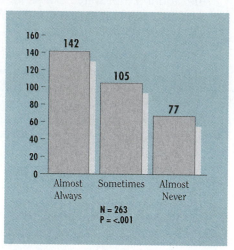

N = 263
P = <.001

Figure 16-4

Report "Often" Feel Tired by How Often Feel Rushed

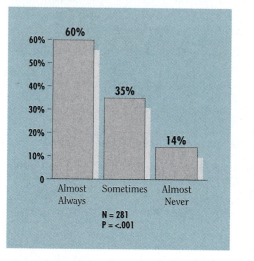

N = 281
P = <.001

Figure 16-5

Report Health To Be "Fair" or "Poor" by How Often Feel Rushed

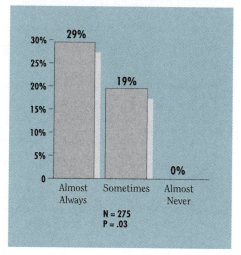

N = 275
P = .03

MEASURES: *Distress Symptoms:* 50-Item Distress Symptom Scale

Irritability: 49-Item Daily Hassle Index

Rushed: Single item: "How often do you feel rushed—almost always, sometimes, almost never?"

Health: Single item: "How would you describe your health these days—very good, good, fair, or poor?"

Tired: Single item: "How often do you feel more tired than you would like—almost always, sometimes, almost never?"

FINDINGS: The more often respondents reported feeling rushed, the greater their distress symptoms, irritability, and fatigue, and the worse their self-reported health.

Mismanaging Time: Common Patterns

Although I know of no systematic research on the subject, it is my impression from years of campus and community work that several common patterns of difficulty with time occur with considerable frequency, whatever the stage of life cycle, age, or social setting.

- Chronic overload
- Disorganization of time
- Procrastination
- Inadequate control over time
- Feeling trapped by unwanted obligations
- Spending too much time on low-priority activities
- Inadequate time for play, intimacy, friendship, and contemplation

Along the same lines, Rice (1992) has described the "seven deadly sins of time mismanagement" as follows:

1. Confusion: Where Am I Going?
2. Indecision: What Should I Do?
3. Diffusion: Mental and Physical Overload
4. Procrastination: That Will Keep for Another Day
5. Avoidance: Escape to Fantasyland
6. Interruptions
7. Perfectionism

See Application Exercise 16-1 for the time stress questionnaire, designed to identify your own time-related difficulties.

Whatever your own unique combination of time difficulties, two major sources of resistance to better time management are likely, as much as you might want it. First is the *repetition compulsion,* to which we referred in Chapter 1. By this, I mean the drive toward familiarity, the tendency to repeat what is familiar. Because a habit is comfortable, we tend to repeat it. We seek out repetitive patterns because they are comfortable in the short run, even if they are damaging to health, well-being, or relationships in the long run. Second, we often tend to repeat harmful habits of managing time because of the **lifestyle trap**—social roles, obligations, and commitments that are easy to get into, yet difficult to get out of, and that add up to too much to do in the time available. If you are a responsible person, which probably is true if you are reading this book, you have problems not only saying "no" but saying "no longer" if others depend on you. Getting out of lifestyle traps is possible but it takes gradualism, time, patience, and commitment to greater simplicity.

We can summarize our discussion thus far in this way:

- Time is a universal feature of life.
- Personal experiences with time are linked to rate of change and other aspects of the larger social environment.
- Our concepts about time are culturally relative.
- Time is central to many stress-related problems.
- Managing time effectively is vital to quality of life, health, and effective stress management.
- In seeking to improve our time-management habits, we need to be aware of and overcome the repetition compulsion and our unique lifestyle traps.

We now turn to time-management principles and methods.

MANAGING TIME: GUIDELINES AND TECHNIQUES

Following Seaward's (1999) lead, we will divide time-management principles and techniques into three categories:

1. Prioritizing

2. Scheduling

3. Implementing

Prioritizing

The first step in managing time more effectively is to be clear what is urgent to get done, what is rather important, and what can wait. Here are several methods for **prioritizing.**

Identifying Long-Term and Short-Term Goals

Students in my community and campus classes often get themselves into a time-management muddle because they lack clarity about where they are going and why. They are so taken with the helter-skelter of daily living that they have lost sight of what they consider to be important in their lives: where they hope to be in five years, one year, one month, one week, and tomorrow and why. The first step in prioritizing, then, is to clarify long-term and short-term goals.

Maintaining Balance

When time-related stressors become distressors, it usually is the result of an imbalance among the various sectors of our lives—for example, too little play, too much work; too much for self, too little for others; too much rush, too little solitude; too much output, too little recovery; and too much socializing outside the home, too little intimacy at home. **Maintaining balance** requires awareness of what is important to you. Here are some values in life I consider to be important and that I try to keep in balance. They are listed here in no particular order, since all are important.

See Application Exercise 16-2 for a checklist to assess the importance of these items plus others and for a plan to modify your time allocation, if needed.

Basic health	Family	Quality in what I do
Physical fitness—flexibility, endurance, strength	Friendships	Good communication at work
Enjoyment of each day	Experiencing beauty in everyday life	Free time
Play	Challenge and growth	Solitude and contemplation
Intimacy	Making a difference	

What are your values or broad priorities? To what extent are they in proper balance for you? What will you do about it? When?

The ABC Technique

Moving to a more concrete level of managing time, you might want to rank your tasks weekly or daily into:

A's Tasks that must get done—top-dog items

B's Tasks that are important but that can get done after the A's

C's Tasks you will get to sometime but not necessarily today or tomorrow

Using Asterisks in Your Daily Lists

I find it useful to designate tasks in my daily lists that have top priority for that day with asterisks—things that are urgent and top priority. I get to the other items when the designated ones are finished.

Americans Struggle With Time

Americans who struggle with time are not alone. A Gallup poll demonstrates just how pervasive constant time pressure is in American life (1990). Here are key findings from the nationwide survey.

- Nearly 8 of 10 Americans report that time moves too fast for them.

- More than half (54 percent) feel under pressure to "get everything done that you need to."

- The lower the age, the greater the struggle with time. For example, 68 percent of those 50 and older say they have enough time, compared with 44 percent of those younger than 50. Baby boomers with a college education struggle the most: Only 33 percent say they have enough time.

- The majority of Americans (54 percent) would prefer to work a four-day, 10-hour week, with only 37 percent preferring the conventional five-day, 8-hour day.

- Responses clearly suggest work has a negative impact on peoples' experiences with time. Monday is by far the least favorite day of the week. Friday, Saturday, and Sunday are most preferred. Least favorite hours of the day are 6 a.m. and 7 a.m.

- When given several choices, Americans say they wish they had more time for personal exercise and recreation (47 percent), hobbies (47 percent), reading (45 percent), family (41 percent), and thinking or meditating (30 percent).

Source: Gallup Poll (1990)

Scheduling

As Rice notes, "Scheduling is time allocation for prioritized responsibilities, or the skill of matching a specific task or responsibility with a designated time period in which to accomplish it" (1992, 237). In **scheduling** our time, it is important to exert internal control, lest you become a pawn to the pushes and pulls from outside pressures and action-opportunities. Yet, too rigid an approach can create more distress than it resolves. In fact, one of the qualities of Type A people that harms their health and their relationships is that they are too demanding, too inflexible. So what is needed is a good deal of internal control tempered with appropriate flexibility.

Time Blocking

This is a must to anyone with more to do than time available. **Time blocking** means to block out several hours on a given day for a category of activity—studying, letter writing, socializing, working, cooking, exercising, whatever. Within the block, you leave yourself room to maneuver and allocate your time as the time passes.

Detailed Scheduling of the Day

Sometimes called **time mapping,** this technique is to break each hour down into detailed segments and to assign a task to each segment. You might want to do this in 15-minute periods, for example. I find this useful on days when I have a great deal to do and know that I need to keep chipping away at tasks. This technique has a certain psychological advantage by freeing me up from anxiety about when I will get those papers read, that letter written, those telephone calls made, my daily run taken, my class preparation completed, and my deep relaxation worked in. You can use commercially created daily schedulers for this purpose, or you can create your own system.

Daily 3- by 5-inch-Card List

A method I have used for years is to make a daily 3- by 5-inch-card list each evening or early morning. Sometimes it will cover two or three days. My lists are divided into several categories (columns on my card): To Do (Office) To Do (Home) Town Tasks (shopping), Calls (to make or return). The list does not include routine tasks like my classes, runs, deep relaxation, office hours, or meals but, rather nonroutine tasks. As noted, I sometimes use asterisks to designate tasks I must get done that day. You may have your own system of listing tasks. If it works, keep it. If not, try the one I suggest here.

Be Realistic

A common trap of hurried, hassled people is that in their optimism, eagerness, and feelings of social commitment, they are prone to underestimating how long a task will take, so they end up overloading themselves again and again. They then feel pressed, frustrated, and put upon. Developing realistic schedules and to-do lists is vital. Take a few minutes to ask, Can I realistically get this done in the time I have allocated or have available?

Delegate Whenever Possible

In the big scheme of things, there always is more to do than time. Accordingly, we delegate to specialists. We do this constantly. Think about it. You do not investigate all the day's news. You delegate that to the television, radio, and newspaper journalists. You do not take a daily or even weekly trip to the dump; you probably pay someone to do that. You do not milk the cow; someone else does. And on and on throughout the sectors of our lives. To the extent that finances, family dynamics, and rules allow (no delegating term papers, please), delegate what you can. This is an important step for simplifying.

Implementing

One can develop a life plan, a set of priorities, and a schedule, but the real challenge lies in the **implementation.** In this phase of time management lurk the traps, diversions, and temptations that get us off-track, swamped, or buried in chaos. To avoid these problems, consider incorporating one or more of the following implementation techniques into your time-management plan.

Assign Time Goals

This sometimes is not realistic, but it usually can be done, whether the task takes hours, days, or weeks. Whether the task is writing a term paper, preparing a hospital reaccreditation report, developing the plan for a running race, writing a speech, or preparing a marketing strategy for a new product, setting time goals for the end product and for intermediate steps can be very helpful.

Avoid Procrastinating

Procrastination means to put off something you know you need to do or want to do. Some people have difficulty getting started. Others procrastinate finishing a task, preferring instead to be distracted or to open up a new task. Procrastination is always the result of self-talk. Be aware of what you tell yourself as you procrastinate. "Do-it-later" self-talk was discussed in Chapter 2, where we addressed the special challenges of college stress.

Break Large Tasks Into Smaller Ones

I find breaking large tasks down vital, whether applied to writing this textbook, directing footraces, planning a new course, or landscaping my yard. For many years, I directed races in my town, ranging from 5-kilometer races to marathons, some with as many as 2,500 participants. This I did as a volunteer activity on top of my normal campus and community workloads. Directing races is a complex endeavor involving scores of volun-

---

The Procrastinator's Code

In their helpful book, *Procrastination: Why You Do It, What To Do About It,* Burka and Yuen set forth the "procrastinator's code."

- I must be perfect.
- Everything I do should go easily and without effort.
- It's safer to do nothing than to take a risk and fail.
- I should have no limitations.
- If it's not done right, it's not worth doing at all.
- I must avoid being challenged.
- If I succeed, someone will get hurt.
- If I do well this time, I must *always* do well.
- Following someone else's rules means I'm giving in and I'm not in control.
- I can't afford to let go of anything or anyone.
- If I expose my real self, people won't like me.
- There is a right answer, and I'll wait until I find it.

Source: Burka & Yuen (1993, 16)

---

teers, thousands of dollars, and hundreds of tasks to be completed over a period of months, culminating with all the required people, supplies, equipment, and plans coming together on the race day. I often felt like I was a true systems engineer in this role. The only way I could possibly pull this off was to break the totality into small tasks.

Chip Away at Small Tasks, One by One

Continuing the same example, each year, with several months' lead time before each race, I developed a list of tasks in about 20 categories. From that I developed a time line, then weekly tasks, then daily lists. Directing each race was an enormous undertaking, yet it became simply a long list of small tasks, quite manageable when tackled one by one.

Focus Your Efforts

This is not always possible, of course, but focusing your efforts is a valuable guideline to follow when you can, whether the task is writing a term paper or performing manual labor. A personal example is focusing only on the completion of writing this textbook during a vacation from school. Only in this way can I focus without distraction or needing to turn to something else—something I find very difficult while school is in session.

Protect Your Time and Space

If you do not control your time and protect your personal space for work, others will control it. This may mean instructing others when you are available and when you do not want to be interrupted. It may mean closing your door, posting a sign on your door, taking the telephone off the hook, or letting your answering machine take calls.

Create a Pleasant Environment

Whether it is your den, office, apartment, or nurse station, the tone of your working environment can make a real difference in your sense of inspiration and satisfaction. I like plants, soft music, art and photographs, and pleasant lighting in my office at work and my study at home. You probably spend a whole lot of time where you work or study. Nurture that environment.

---

10 Techniques for Overcoming Procrastination

1. **"Knockout" Technique** The harder and more distasteful a task is, the more quickly it would better be done: so do it *immediately*.

2. **Small Sequential Steps** When you procrastinate on a task, break it down into smaller, manageable parts, and set yourself the goal of doing a small step by a specific dead line. Once you have finished one step, do the next one.

3. **5-Minute Plan** Take a task you have been procrastinating at, and work a minimum of 5 minutes on it. Once you have finished 5 minutes, then you can set yourself another 5 minutes and then another.

4. **"Work First" Approach** Identify the most difficult part of the task, and do it first.

5. **"Remember Forgetting" Technique** Whenever you re member a task you keep forgetting to do, do it—or at least some of it—*immediately*.

6. **"Swiss Cheese" Method** Do *anything at all* that is con nected to the task you want to accomplish. Gradually eat large chunks or holes in the task until it becomes easier to do.

7. **Self-Reward** Reward yourself with something pleasant when you have finished any difficult or onerous task.

8. **Self-Punishment** Penalize yourself by depriving yourself or forcing yourself to do something you do not like until you finish the task.

9. **Cost-Benefit Analysis** Make a list of all the good things that will happen if you stop procrastinating on an impor tant task, and review the list regularly. List all the miser able results of your procrastination, and review that list each night before bed.

10. **Stimulus Control** Make as many changes in your environ ment as necessary to remove distractions, ensure privacy, become neater, and have important materials on hand.

Source: Bernard & Wolfe (1993)

Schedule Personal Time

Even the busiest executives and public figures usually schedule into their day some time that is personal, whether that time be spent alone reading, snoozing, meditating, or with a loved one in nurturing, caring conversation. This time usually can be expected to pay rich dividends in heightened efficiency and productivity.

Make Time for Exercise and Deep Relaxation

Of particular value for the busy student, professional, parent, or politician is to make time each day for exercise and deep relaxation. Most of my students stop exercising during midterm and final exams because of the press of time. I tell them that even the busiest ex-

---

Risk Factors for Boredom

For some people, the problem is not overload but **boredom.** The dictionary defines boredom as "disinterest." You probably know the feeling of lethargy, detachment, and "ho humness." Four key **"risk factors" for boredom** exist. The more risk factors for boredom that are present for an extended period, the greater the chances of boredom.

- Insufficient challenge

- Too much isolation

- Too much routine

- Meaninglessness

---

ecutives and national leaders usually make time in the busiest of days for exercise and even brief moments of closing their eyes. They know this is a cost-effective use of their time. In addition to my normal midday run (my "daily mini-vacation"), I often will take my dog for an extra mile or two run in the early morning on those days when I know I will be especially busy or challenged. I know my mind will be clearer and my energy level higher this way.

Take Small Breaks

As I write this, I follow a routine of taking a 5- or 10-minute break at the top of each hour. This keeps me clear and focused and minimizes sluggishness and mind-wandering.

Screen Out

This may mean letting the phone ring unanswered, avoiding television, opening the mail later, throwing away junk mail, and even wearing ear plugs. In a broader sense, screening out may mean saying no to new opportunities if you are already overloaded.

Pace Yourself

Pacing has two meanings. First, it means to start early enough on a task (e.g., preparing for your first exam well in advance, or beginning your term paper soon after it is assigned, rather than two days before it is due). Second, it means moving through your day at a reasonable pace, without undue rush. Both of these become special challenges for people who have become virtually addicted to the buzz of being on the edge or in a chronic frenzy. Deliberate efforts to schedule tasks well in advance and to slow one's pace of talking, walking, and eating can help.

Reward Your Accomplishments

Do something that feels good, not only when you have completed the task but also for making significant progress: It's late at night; I've had a long and successful day of writing. Time to take a hot tub.

Other Time-Management Hints

Examine Your Irrational Beliefs About Time

You read in Chapter 14 that our behavior flows from beliefs—enduring assumptions about ourselves, events, and the world around us. In large part, these beliefs are the products of our culture. Beliefs are very much at the root of how we view and handle time.

Chronic time urgency is not just a result of external pressure. It is also a product of our beliefs about time. A key step for reducing chronic time urgency is to reexamine your beliefs or assumptions about time—and, where needed, to alter those that are irrational or unreasonable. The following are 11 common **irrational beliefs about time.** Which ones apply to you?

1. I must always be productive.
2. What matters most in life is getting ahead, being productive, or winning competitive struggles.
3. I cannot delegate because no one can meet my standards.
4. I will be able to enjoy myself only after catching up with all I have to do.
5. I must always get the most possible done in the least possible time.
6. I must usually hurry to get everything done.
7. If I spend time relaxing, resting, or exercising, I will certainly fall behind in more important things.
8. I cannot help but be upset or anxious when a task is incomplete.
9. I have no control over constant overload in my life.
10. There is no way I can be happy if I'm overloaded. I can't stand it.
11. I must be all things to all people.

Consider Your Strategies for Reducing Chronic Time Urgency

A potpourri of specific techniques to reduce chronic time urgency is presented in a later section. Here are eight broad options. Which one or ones seem most promising for you (other than the first)?

1. Continue your present pace—and stay distressed.
2. Continue your present pace but learn to live with it.

   - Self-talk
   - Relaxation methods
   - Health buffers

3. Cut back on your present activity level.
4. Say "no" to new opportunities if already overloaded.
5. Be more efficient.

   - Delegate.
   - Organize time better.
   - Waste less time.

6. Stop hurrying when not necessary.

See Application Exercise 16-3 for a plan to assess and use these options.

7. Periodically step back, contemplate, reestablish priorities, and reorganize your time.

8. Leave the particular role or environment.

Make Time for Healthy Pleasures

Fortunately, many truly pleasurable activities are also healthy in the sense that they are good for your bodies and spirits, as you read in Chapter 13. Since we often are so busy or stuck in our routines that healthy pleasures are few and far between, making time for healthy pleasures sometimes takes attentiveness. Be clear about what healthy pleasures you truly desire, then build them into your schedule. This often is the only way to make them happen (Ornstein and Sobel, 1989).

Consider These Miscellaneous Time-Management Tips

Here are a number of specific time-management tips. Check those you might benefit from using. Underline the two you plan to begin first. Then start.

1. If you are usually too busy, leave details to someone else whenever possible—the income tax return, fixing your car, or office details.
2. Move through your day slowly enough to experience beauty in your environment—on your way to school or work, for example.
3. Learn to live with unfinished tasks. Only a corpse is completely finished.
4. Leave enough time between activities so you minimize overlap.
5. Schedule only as many tasks each day as you can reasonably finish without pressure.
6. Leave time in your schedule for the unexpected.
7. Leave early enough so you need not rush to get where you are going, even if this means rising 20 minutes earlier in the morning.
8. Say "no" to new opportunities or responsibilities if they would overload or rush your day.
9. Take steps to "center": listen to your inner voice of wisdom.
10. Find a work environment that is not chronically high-pressured or harried. Avoid Type A organizations. If necessary, find another job.
11. Learn to slow your pace of talking, walking, and eating.
12. Find time each day to relax, meditate, and exercise.
13. Avoid doing more than one thing at a time.
14. Tell yourself at least once each day that failure seldom results from doing a job too slowly or too well. But failure often is caused by mistakes of judgment or from too much hurrying.
15. Ask yourself at least once each week: Apart from eternal distress and hurry, what is really important to me?
16. Measure success by quality, rather than by quantity.
17. "Screen out" whenever possible—even if this risks disapproval or missing something you may have thought important.
18. Surround yourself with symbols of tranquility—soft music, plants, and pleasant colors and lighting.
19. Use your noon hour for deep relaxation, exercise, or something else that will slow you down, lift your spirits, and restore energy.
20. Find time and space to be alone each day, other than at your desk or in your car.
21. Associate with Type B's or Type C's whenever possible.
22. Practice effective listening. Avoid interrupting out of impatience.
23. Catch your free-floating hostility in progress. Stop it. Take deliberate actions of graciousness and patience.
24. Ask whether something in fact must be done this hour or this day. Would catastrophe ensue if you could not squeeze it in?
25. Use waiting in line to observe people around you and to practice deep breathing techniques.
26. Whenever you find yourself jiggling your knees or tapping your fingers, immediately practice the 6-second quieting response.
27. Use realistic to-do lists to free your mind from preoccupation with all you have to do and to organize tasks. Prioritize items. Avoid self-reprisal if you do not finish the list.
28. Stop blaming others for falling short of your day-to-day accomplishment goals. Accept responsibility for trying to do too much in too short a time or for being poorly organized.

29.   Whenever you catch yourself about to race through a yellow light, immediately turn right and go around the block.

Simplify

A theme running through most of these specific time management tips is to simplify. Consider this by Jay Walljasper (1997, 42):

> Revving up . . . is often heralded as the answer to the problems caused by our overly busy lives. Swamped by the accelerating pace of work? Get a computer that's faster. Feel like your life is spinning out of control? Increase your efficiency by learning to read and write faster. No time to enjoy life? Purchase one of those handy products advertised on television that promise to help you cook faster, exercise faster, and even make money faster.
>
> Yet is seems that the faster we go, the farther we fall behind. Not only in the literal sense of not getting done what we set out to do, but at a deeper level too. . . .
>
> Speaking out against speed can get you lumped in with the Flat Earth Society as a hopelessly wrongheaded romantic who refuses to face the facts of modern life. Yet it's clear that more and more desperately want to slow down.

Increasing numbers of Americans are deciding to work part-time, cut down on consumption in order to get along with less income, and to move to smaller towns in order to simplify (Pooley, 1997). Time-use expert Juliet Schor, author of the 1992 best-selling book *The Overworked American,* says her research shows that "millions of Americans are beginning to live a different kind of life, in which they are trading money for time. I believe that this is one of the most important trends going on in America" (Walljasper, 43.) Kern (1996) proposes 14 ways toward "urban serenity" by simplifying your life.

Stephan Rechtschaffen (1996, 1997) refers to this radical shift in personal paradigm as "timeshifting." He argues we need to move from time management to time awareness as we simplify.

> Being consciously aware of rhythms, your own and those of the people around you, will allow you to shift the rhythms, and therefore shift time. But you must *slow down* in order to listen and feel. Understanding is impossible without serenity; serenity exists only when time moves slowly.
>
> Feeling rushed? Take a deep breath before you continue. In a fierce argument? Prescribe silence so you can both reflect on what you've been saying. Worried about the future? Come into the present moment.
>
> These are simple—even simplistic—suggestions, but they are the first steps toward becoming aware of ourselves *in the rhythmic flow of the present moment.* With this awareness, through the conscious focus on the present, we can regain the mastery of the speed and rhythm of our lives. (Rechtschaffen, 1996, 24)

In short, managing time for increased wellness may mean major steps to simplify rather than simply rearranging segments of time or becoming better organized within the context of perpetual overload and rush. Simplifying sometimes is necessary to gradually escape from one's lifestyle trap of too much to do in too little time. It's an alternative worth considering.

References

Bernard, M. E., & Wolfe, J. L. (1993). *The RET Resource Book for Practitioners.* New York: Institute for Rational-Emotive Therapy.

Burka, J. B., & Yuen, L. M. (1983). *Procrastination: Why you do it, what to do about it.* Reading, MA: Addison-Wesley.

Castleman, M. (1990). How the stress experts deal with theirs. *Medical Self-Care, 57,* 35–40, 74.

Chevalier, M. (1967). Society, manners, and politics in the United States. In J. W. Ward, (Ed.), *Letters on North America by Michael Chevalier.* Gloucester, MA: Peter Smith, 270.

Gallup Poll (1990). People feel time is running out. *San Francisco Chronicle,* November 5, 1990, B3.

Kern, D. (1996). Urban serentiy: 14 ways to simplify your life. *Wellness Management, 12,* 1, 5–6.

Keyes, R. (1991). *Timelock: How life got so hectic and what you can do about it.* New York: Ballantine Books.

Levine, R., & Wolff, E. (1985). Social time: The heartbeat of culture. *Psychology Today, 19,* 29–35.

Levine, R. V., Lynch, K., Miyake, A., & Lucia, M. (1989). The Type A city: Coronary heart disease and the pace of life. *Journal of Behavioral Medicine, 12,* 509–524.

Mandela, N. R. (1994) *Long walk to freedom: The autobiography of Nelson Mandela.* New York: Little, Brown, and Co. Excerpted in *Time* (1994), November 28, 52.

Ornstein, R., & Sobel, D. (1986). *The healing brain.* New York: Touchstone.

Ornstein, R., & Sobel, D. (1989). *Healthy pleasures.* Reading, MA: Addison-Wesley.

Pooley, E. (1997). The great escape. *Time,* December 8, 52–65.

Rechtschaffen, S. (1996). *Timeshifting: Creating more time to enjoy your life.* New York: Doubleday.

Rice, P. L. (1992). *Stress and health* (2nd ed.). Pacific Grove, CA: Brooks/Cole.

Robinson, J. P., & Godbey, G. (1997). *Time for life: The surprising ways Americans use their time.* State College: Penn State University Press.

Seaward, B. L. (1999). *Managing stress: Principles and strategies for health and well-being* (2nd. ed.). Boston: Jones and Bartlett.

Walljasper, J. (1997). The speed trap. *Utne Reader,* March–April, 41–46.

Application Exercise 16-1

Time Stress Questionnaire

Below are several time-related difficulties people sometimes experience. Please indicate how often each is a difficulty for you, using numbers as follows:

    __0__   Seldom or never a difficulty for me

    __5__   Sometimes a difficulty for me

   __10__   Frequently a difficulty for me

_____ My time is controlled by factors beyond my control.

_____ Interruptions

_____ Chronic overload—more to do than time available

_____ Occasional overload

_____ Chronic underload—too little to do in time available

_____ Occasional underload

_____ Alternating periods of overload and underload

_____ Disorganization of my time

_____ Procrastination

_____ Separating home from work

_____ Transition from work to home

_____ Finding time for regular exercise

_____ Finding time for daily periods of relaxation

_____ Finding time for friendships

_____ Finding time for family

_____ Finding time for vacations

_____ Easily bored

_____ Saying "yes" when I later wish I had said "no"

_____ Feeling overwhelmed by large tasks over an extended period of time

_____ Avoiding important tasks by frittering away time on less important ones

_____ Feeling compelled to assume responsibilities in groups

_____ Unable to delegate because distrust quality of others' performance

_____ Unable to delegate because no one to delegate to

_____ My perfectionism creates delays.

_____ I tend to leave tasks unfinished.

_____ I have difficulty living with unfinished tasks.

_____ Too many projects going at one time

_____ Get into time binds by trying to please others too often

_____ I tend to hurry even when it's not necessary.

_____ Lose concentration while thinking about other things I have to do

_____   Not enough alone time

_____   Feel compelled to be punctual

_____   Pressure related to deadlines

1. How do you measure up to the following standard?

    0–49   Low difficulty with time-related stressors

    50–99   Moderate difficulty with time-related stressors

    100 or more   High difficulty with time-related stressors

2. How satisfied are you with your time-related difficulties?

    Very satisfied
    Somewhat satisfied
    Not very satisfied

3. Now go back, and underline the five most significant time-related stressors for you.

4. By yourself or with the aid of someone else, determine concrete steps you can take to remedy each of these key time-related stressors. Write them on a separate sheet of paper, in your stress diary, or in a notebook.

5. When will you begin each of these steps?

Application Exercise 16-2

The Challenge of Balance

A challenge in living well is balancing the various parts of our lives that are important to us.
What are the elements of a high *quality of life* for you? Below are several possibilities. Add others to the list, then indicate for you the importance and present balance of each.

YOUR IDEAL: VI = Very Important
SI = Somewhat Important
NVI = Not Very Important

YOUR REALITY: TM = I Have *Too Much* of This.
RA = I Have about the *Right Amount* of This.
TL = I Have *Too Little* of This

YOUR IDEAL	YOUR REALITY	
_____	_____	BASIC HEALTH
_____	_____	PHYSICAL FITNESS
_____	_____	ENJOYMENT OF EACH DAY
_____	_____	PLAY
_____	_____	INTIMACY
_____	_____	FAMILY
_____	_____	FRIENDSHIP
_____	_____	AWARENESS OF BEAUTY IN EVERYDAY LIFE
_____	_____	CHALLENGE AND GROWTH
_____	_____	MAKING A DIFFERENCE
_____	_____	QUALITY IN WHAT I DO
_____	_____	GOOD COMMUNICATION AT WORK
_____	_____	FREE TIME
_____	_____	FAITH
_____	_____	SOLITUDE/ALONE TIME
_____	_____	OTHER

Application Exercise 16-3

Assessing and Applying Strategies for Reducing Chronic Time Urgency

1. Which of the eight strategies you read about for reducing chronic overload would be most useful to you? List below those you believe would be especially helpful.

2. What specific steps will you take to apply these strategies? When?

CHAPTER
17

People need people. And reaching out with care and concern for another heals both the receiver and the giver! Break beyond your boundaries and give yourself to others. They need you.

—DONALD A. TUBESING AND NANCY L. TUBESING

Social Support: Giving and Receiving

Social Support During Crisis

Margaret had been married for 28 years to a prominent attorney. They were parents of two grown sons. Although their marriage was far from perfect, she was nearly devastated when he announced one day he was leaving to marry another woman. For several days, Margaret hardly slept or ate. During ensuing months, she went through a host of changes in her living situation and daily routines. Yet she survived these tough early days. In fact, she went on after several months of pain and mourning to new levels of strength.

Fortunately Margaret had several close friends and a broad social network for support through this period. They listened as she expressed her loss. They helped with details of the adjustment. They cared. In looking back a year later, she marveled at the support she had received from her friends. She felt immensely grateful for the part they played in her survival—indeed, her growth—through this transition.

SOCIAL TIES: A STRESS-RESISTANCE RESOURCE

Margaret's story in the box illustrates the vital role social support often plays as a stress-resistance resource. In Chapter 11, you read that clustering of life events increases the risk of illness. You also read that not everyone gets sick during periods of transition and change. Both theory and research point to the protective influence of social support when people go through stressful events.

Nearly a century ago, the pioneering sociologist Emile Durkheim found that the more integrated individuals are in social systems, the less vulnerable they are to suicide. This finding fits his more general theory that social connection plays a supportive and protective role in individuals' lives (1893).

You also read that Antonovsky (1979, 1987) contends that generalized resistance resources (GRRs) help provide protection through assisting the person in the belief that events are fairly predictable and will turn out reasonably well. That is, social support promotes a sense of coherence. He identifies social connectedness as an important GRR and cites several studies to support his view.

Similarly, Lazarus and Folkman (1984) suggest in their transactional, process-oriented, coping approach to stress that social support can play a vital role as a resource in dealing with difficult life events. They state, "The social environment is not just a major source of stress; it also provides vital resources which the individual can and must draw upon to survive and flourish" (1984, 243).

The importance of social support as a stress-resistance resource is reflected in the entire issue of a major academic journal devoted to "predicting, activating, and facilitating social support" (Hopfoll, 1990).

Dimensions of Social Support

Before going on, it is important to be clear about our terms. **Social network** refers to the "specific set of linkages among a defined set of persons" or a given person (Mitchell, 1969). The larger the social network, the greater the number of **social ties** or person-to-person linkages. Being socially connected is the opposite of being isolated.

A social network can be characterized not only by its scope but also by its composition (e.g., coworkers, friends, relatives, neighbors) and quality (e.g., close or distant, friendly or unfriendly, supportive or indifferent). Stated differently, social ties can vary in two ways: number of ties and intensity or closeness of ties.

Social support refers to relationships that bring positive benefits to the individual. **Perceived social support** means social ties the person perceives or experiences as yielding positive gains. Thus, not all social networks—or persons within those networks—bring social support. Sometimes quite the opposite occurs, as we all know.

Different **types of social support** can be identified. Dean and Lin (1977) identify two main types: expressive (emotional support) and instrumental (task-related support). Weiss (1974) speaks of six functions of social support, all essential for well-being: attachment, social integration, opportunity for nurturance, reassurance of one's worth, a sense of reliable alliance, and obtaining guidance. House defines social support as: "an interpersonal transaction involving one or more of the following:

- **Emotional concern** (liking, love, empathy)
- **Instrumental aid** (goods or services)
- **Information** (about the environment)
- **Appraisal** (information relative to self-evaluation)" (1981, 39).

Greenberg (1980) points out that social support often flows through social support groups. Support groups exist in so many forms and affiliations that it is sometimes confusing to identify what the basic ingredients are. Some of the necessary factors seem to be the following:

1. The same people attend.
2. The group meets regularly, once a week or more.
3. The group has met for an extended period of time—until closeness develops.
4. It provides an opportunity for informality, spontaneity, and incidental contacts.

Greenberg (1980, 144) also maintains that the most important way true social support takes place in groups with these factors is not through the central activity of the group but through informal, incidental contacts, such as the following.

- Driving to and from meetings with someone
- Having dinner together before and after the meeting
- Having a group potluck meal
- Talking during coffee breaks, in the social get-together after the formal meeting
- Chats, separate social get-togethers, and the like
- Solving problems and making decisions together
- Pairing up outside the group with another group member
- Going on a trip together, to a convention, or to a retreat setting

Which of these types of contacts do you engage in? Might you do so in the future?

Men and women differ in the meaning and content of their friendships (Blieszner & Adams, 1992). For example, men tend to trust their best friends more than women do, but men's conversations with friends tend to be more impersonal than women's. Women rank conversation as the most important benefit of their friendships, also valuing talking about relationships and sharing personal information. Men, by contrast, tend to focus on such topics as careers, sports, and politics.

Gains and Costs of Social Ties

Like other areas of social, psychological, and medical research, not all studies confirm the direct and buffering relationship of social support to mental and physical well-being. And

Figure 17-1

Positive and Negative Effects of Social Ties

	Positive Effects	Negative Effects
PREVENTION	Reduce uncertainty and worry Set good example Share problems Calm model Distract	Create uncertainty and worry Set bad example Create new problems Stressed model Distract Germs
COPING	Label beneficial Provide sympathy Give helpful information	Label negative Subject to irritation and resentment Give misleading information
RECOVERY	Maintain regimen Contrast with health (incentive) Create desire to stop being a nuisance	Discourage regimen Contrast with health (depressed) Create power/dependence need

Source: Suls (1982, 264)

like other topics of research and theory, the nature of the linkages are quite complex. In fact, as Lazarus and Folkman point out, social ties are not always positive and beneficial. Indeed, "When we think about the value of social networks, therefore, we must bear in mind that social relationships create problems which comprise a significant share, probably the lion's share of the sources of stress in life. The balance between costs and benefits probably differs among persons, social roles, and stressful encounters" (1984, 248). A recent study of HIV-positive youth illustrates this point in that social connections were sometimes found to be supportive, but not always, as when family, friends, or romantic partners were involved in drugs or unprotected sex (Rotheeraam-Borus et al., 1996). Another study found that the larger the size of social networks, the faster the early progression of HIV, a finding that might have resulted from having to inform so many people about one's HIV, from being associated with so many supportive people that subjects themselves became more inactive and passive, or from being associated with large numbers of associates with poor health habits (Patterson et al., 1996).

Figure 17-1 lists some of the potential positive and negative effects of social ties. The actual balance of gains and costs depends, of course, on the combination of the external reality and the person's perceptions and utilization of those external resources. The point remains: Social support can be an important stress-resistance resource, contributing to mental and physical well-being.

This point is further illustrated by data from my Human Stress students, who were asked to respond to the following social-support statements with answers of "agree," "uncertain," or "disagree."

1. I usually feel pretty lonely.
2. I have close friends to provide me with plenty of emotional support when I need it.
3. When times are tough for me, there is no one available to provide genuine "moral support."

Figure 17-2

Mean Distress-Symptom Score by Social Support

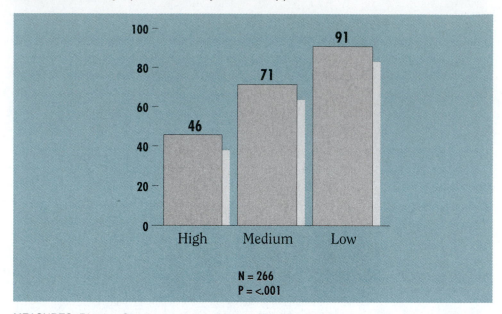

MEASURES: *Distress Symptoms:* 50-Item Distress Symptom Scale
          Social Support: 4-Item Social Support Scale

FINDING: The greater the social support, the lower the distress-symptom score.

4. Generally speaking, I have a pretty good sense of belonging or connectedness to those around me.

Each item separately was associated significantly with respondents' distress-symptom scores: Those agreeing with items 1 and 3 had significantly higher distress-symptom scores; those agreeing with items 2 and 4 had significantly lower distress-symptom scores. Figure 17-2 shows the association between students' total support score, combining the four items, and distress-symptom score. Clearly, the higher the social support, the less the distress. Results also revealed that high social support correlated with sense of coherence (confirming Antonovsky's assertion mentioned earlier), self-reported health and happiness, and having a strong sense of meaning and direction. Clearly, there are important gains from strong support within this class of students.

TWO RELATIONSHIPS OF SOCIAL SUPPORT TO WELL-BEING

Direct Effects

It is important to note that social support can have two different types of relationships to mental and physical well-being. First, it can have a **direct effect.** That is, the greater the social support, the more positive the mental and/or physical health. This type of relationship has been widely studied and widely supported. In a review of these studies, sociologist James House cites one of the classic studies.

Berkman and Syme . . . analyzed data gathered between 1965 and 1974 on 2229 men and 2494 women, aged 30 to 69 in 1965 and randomly sampled from the population of Alameda, California. They assessed whether the presence or absence of four kinds of social ties in 1965—marriage, contacts with friends, church memberships, and informal and formal group associations—affected the likelihood of the person dying over the next nine years. People low or lacking in each type of social tie were 30 percent to 300 percent more likely to die than those who had each type of relationship. Generally, these trends held for both sexes and at all age levels, although marriage had the strongest protective effect for men, while contact with friends was most protective for women. . . . The more intimate ties of marriage and friendships were stronger predictors than were ties of church and group membership. (1981, 39)

The Alameda County study just cited measured only the number of ties. Other studies point to the importance of quality of support for health.

Recently 10,000 married men who were 40 years of age or older were followed for five years in Israel. The researchers, Jack H. Medallie and Yuri Goldbourt, wanted to find out how many new cases of angina pectoris developed. They assessed each man's medical risk factors for heart disease and then asked, among other items, this question: Does your wife show you her love?

The answer turned out to have enormous predictive power. Among high-risk men—men who showed elevated blood cholesterol, electrocardiographic abnormalities, and high risk of anxiety—fewer of those who had loving supportive wives developed angina pectoris than did those whose wives were colder (52 per 1000 versus 93 per 1000). (Pines, 1980, 43)

A study by Oxman and colleagues (1995) found that among 232 older open-heart patients, participation in social or community groups significantly reduced chances of dying within 6 months of surgery. These and other studies strongly suggest that the more the individual is tied into positive, supportive relationships, the more positive one's mental and physical well-being. For reviews of this literature, see, for example, Berkman and Syme (1979); Cohen and Wills, 1985 (1988); Dunkel-Schetter and Skokan (1990); Hobfoll and associates, 1990; House, Landis, and Umberson (1988); Sarason, Pierce, and Sarason (1990); Thoits (1982); and Turner (1981).

Buffering Effects

The second type of relationship between social support and well-being is the **buffering effect.** Here, social support softens the impact of potentially stressful events. Stated differently, it serves as a buffer between difficult life experiences and health outcomes. As Lazarus and Folkman state, "It can help to prevent stress by making harmful or threatening experiences seem less consequential, or provide valuable resources when stress does occur" (1984, 246). This is illustrated, of course, in Margaret's experience (see box, page 439): Given the marital separation, she benefited from friends' support.

An example of a study on the buffering role of social support is that of Lin, Woelfel, and Light (1985). Not surprisingly, they found that depression increased as the importance and undesirability of a major life event also increased in their sample. However, they found that the amount of depression diminished as social support increased, especially when people had strong ties with the subject. Curiously, social support did not help in the case of marital breakup (as it did in Margaret's case). The authors speculate that "marital disengagement may have a substantial disruptive impact on a person's social environment so as to render it, although apparently only temporarily, incapable of providing the necessary support. Such disruption may be due to the transition from old support resources to new ones" (Lin, Woelfel, & Light, 1985, 260).

The key conclusion of this study, therefore, was that social support from close friends provided a buffer against depression, given a major and undesirable life event other than marital separation.

Marriage, even with its ups and downs, repeatedly has been shown to play an especially powerful protective role. For example, Pearlin and Lieberman (1977) found that when stressful life events were relatively infrequent or minor, marrieds and unmarrieds had similar levels of depression. But when social and economic circumstances became more trying, marrieds experienced substantially less depression than unmarrieds. "The combination most productive of psychological distress is to be simultaneously single, poor, isolated, and exposed to burdensome parental obligations." They conclude:

> What we have learned suggests that marriage can function as a protective barrier against the distressful consequences of external threats. Marriage does not prevent economic and social problems from invading life but it can apparently help people fend off the psychological assaults that such problems otherwise create. Even in an era when marriage is an increasingly fragile arrangement, this protective function may contribute to its viability, at least in the absence of alternative relations providing similar functions." (1977, 714)

At the outset, see Application Exercises 17-1 and 17-2. Complete a personal assessment of current social support in your life—giving and receiving.

Lazarus and Folkman (1984) correctly point out that when social support is viewed as a resource available in the social environment, we need to focus on cultivating and using it. Most of all, this means communicating effectively. In this chapter, therefore, we focus on the communication process as a vital part of stress coping. You will note that attention is given to both giving and receiving.

THE CHALLENGE OF BUILDING AND USING SOCIAL SUPPORT

Lazarus and Folkman note that "The basic assumption underlying the current interest in social support is that, other things being equal, people will have better morale and health, and function better, if they receive or believe they will receive social support when it is needed" (1984, 250). As Caplan states, "significant others help an individual mobilize his psychological resources and master his emotional burdens; they share his tasks, and they provide him with extra supplies of money, materials, tools, skills and cognitive guidance to improve his handling of the situation" (1974, 6). Thus, building social networks and drawing on social support becomes an important part of the process of coping. In cultivating networks and supports, of course, one must be mindful of giving as well as receiving. And as one learns early in life, giving is the key to receiving. The more you provide support, the more you have available for yourself when needed.

Entire books have been written, of course, on communication skills for minimizing stress for the self and others. Here we can touch only on a few key facets of the communication process. We begin with Virginia Satir's ideas about communication and well-being.

Satir's Model of Communication

According to psychologist and family therapist Virginia Satir, communication "is the giving and receiving of meaning between any two people" (1976). Key questions about the communication process are these:

Social Support and Self-Talk

An undergraduate student in my Human Stress class wrote the following, used here with her permission.

This past week has been a bit of a stressful and depressing week for me. On Monday, I found out about a problem I have that is somewhat personal. I was depressed and gloomy all day. I went from class to class, not really paying attention to the instructors and not talking to anyone else in class. I moped around all day basically feeling sorry for myself.

Once I got home I did not say much to my roommates, ate dinner and then went to my room. I could not concentrate on anything and felt very worn out. Around 6:30 I laid down and didn't awake until 8:30. I still felt empty inside, lonely and depressed. The nap obviously didn't cure my gloominess.

Well, I then ventured out of my room and began talking to one of my roommates. I hadn't told anyone of my problem yet and wasn't sure if I wanted to or not. Well, sooner than I thought I was babbling the whole story to my roommate. She sat and listened and was very sincere through the whole conversation. Towards the end, she looked at me and said, "Really, Judy [not her real name], it's no big deal. I've had the same problem before and it's really nothing to worry about. It could be worse, you know."

When she said that, the comment we use in class all the time—"Is this truly worth getting upset about?"—hit me, and I realized I was blowing this whole ordeal out of proportion. I suddenly felt a huge burden lifted off my back, and I knew this was something minor that I will get over. In time it shall pass, just like most other problems.

I learned basically that confiding in others helps a great deal with many of our problems. Often these problems are ones that others can hopefully help you with or make you understand that it's not so bad. I also realized that the sayings you give us do have a tremendous amount of relevance to our everyday lives.

- What meaning is made?
- How is it given?
- How is it received?
- What happens to each person as a result, and what happens to the relationship?

The main point to communication, for Satir, is to enhance the self-esteem of the self and others. Effective communication also needs to promote the **Five Freedoms:**

1. *The freedom to see and hear what is here* instead of what should be, was, or will be.
2. *The freedom to say what one feels and thinks* instead of what one should.
3. *The freedom to feel what one feels* instead of what one ought.
4. *The freedom to ask for what one wants* instead of always waiting for permission.
5. *The freedom to take risks in one's own behalf* instead of choosing to be only "secure" and not rocking the boat (1976).

Pets as Social Supports

It has long been known by owners of cats, dogs, horses, and other domesticated animals that pets can be a meaningful personal anchorage. Recently, researchers have begun to study whether pets might also enhance health—and perhaps even extend life. Their findings are indeed noteworthy. Consider the following:

- A British psychologist found a significant increase in health and morale among research subjects who received a parakeet (Ferguson, 1984).
- When children between the ages of 9 and 16 were asked to read aloud, blood pressures invariably went up. However, when a dog was present in the room, blood pressures did not rise as much (Lynch, 1985).
- A group of college students had their blood pressure monitored while interacting with a dog tactually, verbally, and visually (Vormbrock & Grossberg, 1988). Subjects' blood pressures were lowest during dog petting, higher while talking to the dog, and highest while talking to the experimenter.
- When a group of adults communicated in a laboratory with the human experimenter, blood pressures went up. When communicating with their pets, however, blood pressures remained the same or decreased (Lynch, 1985).
- Among 92 heart patients discharged from the University of Maryland's coronary-care unit, 6 percent of pet owners died during the next year, compared with a death rate of 28 percent of non-pet owners—a four and one-half times higher risk to non-pet owners (Friedman, 1980).

Clearly, pets serve as a meaningful personal anchorage and apparently can aid not only in improving the quality of life but also even length of life. As Tom Ferguson of *Medical Self-Care* has stated, "Feeding the cat, bathing the dog, tending the fish tank, taking the parakeet on your finger—these little acts of caring assure the caregiver that he or she is truly needed. Such feelings can at times serve as a literal lifeline" (1984, 32).

Consider the following questions:

1. What are the implications of the above research findings for you?
2. What are the implications for your present or future childrearing?
3. Do you know of older adults without pets who might benefit from one's presence?

According to Satir, a key to good communication is *congruence* within yourself.

The power in congruence comes through the connectedness of your words matching your feelings, your body and facial expressions matching your words, and your actions fitting all. You come from a state of strength because all of your parts have flow with other parts. You are not blocking anything off.

You can easily be believed. Your energy goes to developing trust. You do not cause suspicion. You can be easily understood because you are clear. Other persons feel given to.

You feel open and therefore feel excitement instead of fear.

You can live the Five Freedoms.

You know that you can choose, that you have many choices you can make. (1976)

Satir contends that true communication, or *Making Contact,* can be attained by:

INVITING, first of all, someone to make contact with you. "I have something to tell you, are you ready to hear it? Can you listen now? I would like to talk to you."

"Have you a moment now, I need to share something with you."

"I have a bone to pick with you. Are you ready or will you listen?"

ARRANGING yourself in such a physical position as to be at eye level, arm's length, which usually means being seated because there are so many height differences between people.

BEING PREPARED to take risks for bringing your insides outside.

MAKING YOUR STATEMENTS beginning with "I"; "I am angry" instead of "You make me angry"; "I am worried" instead of "You worry me." In short, you are dealing honestly by owning your statements and the feelings that go with them.

ASKING QUESTIONS, not the kind you ask when your child has his hand in the cookie jar right under your nose and you say, "Are you taking cookies?" Of course you will be lied to. You are not seeking information nor will you get it. Questions are the ways to get information you don't have.

THINKING of all difficulties as opportunities for creating something new instead of the beginning of the toll of funeral bells. Each person can learn and grow from each creative handling of a difficulty. This may include dropping a burden as well as creating a new possibility. (1976)

Satir points out that "Communication is to relationship what breathing is to maintaining life . . ." (1976). She further notes four ways of communicating often used by people with low self-esteem—"those who have not yet learned to live their Five Freedoms." These communication styles can negatively affect physical health. Moreover, "they box in relationships so they become destructive, dead, distant, and frustrating." They limit a person's potential for personal growth and for developing cooperative, satisfying relationships. They promote fear and dependence.

These four styles are:

1. **PLACATING:** talking in an ingratiating way; never disagreeing, no matter what; constantly apologizing.
2. **BLAMING:** fault-finding; dictating; acting superior; putting fault on others.
3. **COMPUTING:** being very correct, very reasonable with no semblance of feeling; acting calm, cool, and collected.
4. **DISTRACTING:** doing or saying whatever is irrelevant to what others are doing or saying; not responding to the point. (1988)

Satir points out that these styles of responding do more than interfere with open and honest communication. They also reinforce the person's feeling of low self-esteem. We now turn to a number of guidelines for achieving the type of congruent communication of which Satir writes.

Research evidence clearly supports the value of friends—and pets—as sources of social support, whatever the age. Studies also show that healthy pleasures such as shown here are vital buffers against distress.

Communication Guidelines for Direct, Honest Communication

A number of guidelines for direct, honest communication follow. They can be useful for making all your face-to-face relationships rich and supportive for you and others. They are adapted from Egan's book, *Encounter* (1970), and from Charles Rossiter's *The Human Potential* (1984).

1. **Own your feelings and thoughts.** Practice speaking in the first person rather than generally. For example, say, "I would like to see a movie tonight," instead of "I hear there are some good movies in town."

2. **Address the other person directly.** Look at the person for whom your remarks are intended, and speak to him or her directly. If you are communicating in a group setting, communicate directly to the person you intend to receive your remarks, rather than abstractly to the group as a whole.

3. **Make statements rather than ask questions,** if you have a point to make. Instead of asking, "Thai menus are usually pretty good, aren't they?," say "I really would like a Thai dinner tonight. Let's go."

4. **Don't sandbag your negative feelings.** This probably is the most common source of relationship-induced distress. When feelings of frustration, resentment, or hurt accumulate, they block energy, cloud one's thinking, and turn into bound physical energy—that is, tension. This is probably the greatest source of stress-related illness. Unexpressed negative feelings also increase chances of blow-ups. In expressing these feelings, be sure to use "I" messages rather than "You" messages. "I feel hurt by what you said," rather than "You make me so mad when you act like that."

5. **When giving feedback, describe the effects of the other's actions rather than be accusatory.** This way, you communicate your awareness of your own experience and avoid putting the other person on the defensive. Say "When you talk to me that way, I feel discounted and not appreciated," rather than "You said that just to put me down."

6. **Be generous in giving positive feedback to others.** It is easy to move through our days with many unexpressed positive feelings and thoughts. Expressing a few more of these can make a real difference in the quality of others' lives—and in how people respond to you. Give a lot; you will get a lot.

7. **Practice active listening.** Genuine listening is one of the most meaningful gifts you can give to others. It feels wonderful to be with someone who expresses interest and caring about you by attending to what you are saying, asking followup questions, and giving honest feedback. The returns to you will far outweigh the effort. Someone once said two kinds of listeners exist: those who genuinely listen and those who wait their turn to speak. Try being a good listener. See the later section on "Active Listening."

8. **Speak only for yourself and not for others.** Husbands and wives, for example, often fall gradually into the habit of speaking for each other. If someone addresses a question to your spouse (friend or lover), do not interrupt and answer yourself instead. Respect your partner by allowing him or her to respond. Speak directly and honestly for yourself—and give others the opportunity to do the same.

Part of congruence, Satir writes, is honest disclosure of inner thoughts and feelings, the topic to which we now turn.

Self-Disclosure

Self-disclosure, the process of revealing authentic, personal thoughts and feelings to others, is to allow oneself to be seen, known, and understood. Self-disclosure entails risk. Normally it is worth risk taking. Yet discretion is needed, as illustrated in the following box by Dorothy's experience.

Self-disclosure helps build the type of relationships that can be vital, not only for ongoing emotional health but especially in times of difficulty. Self-disclosure can promote

---

On Making Time to Care

Writes a family therapist:

> One hot summer afternoon in Ottawa in the mid-1980s, I was sitting in my office listening to a couple. Well, almost listening. As they talked on, I floated in and out of the session, wondering why I hadn't become a hairdresser, as my mother had recommended long ago. The husband, Dan, was a business executive who was coming to terms with the fact that he would never be CEO. He was finding more time for his wife, wanting her to be romantic and wondering why she wasn't there. Judy remained cool and aloof, deftly deflecting Dan's demands without revealing much.
>
> That day, Judy leaned toward him and said, "On Wednesday, November 14, 1982, at six in the afternoon, you let me crash and burn. I was devastated, and you didn't care." After a long day alone with their three children, she explained, she had burst into tears in the kitchen when Dan finally came home, crying out, "I'm so alone." After a few pro forma words of sympathy, he had retired to his den to make "important business calls," leaving her sobbing on the kitchen floor.
>
> "That night changed everything," said Judy, who turned increasingly to her mother and her sister afterward. "I needed you and asked for comfort and you were too busy. Never again. I decided, that's never going to happen again." And it never had.
>
> My spine straightened. Once again a partner in a troubled couple was using life-and-death images to describe the moment when their love bond had ruptured—a moment of abandonment and betrayal that had defined the couple's relationship ever since. *"I needed you and asked for comfort, and you were too busy."*

Source: (Johnson, 1997, 37)

helpful, supportive relationships. When used inappropriately, it can increase, rather than reduce, distress. Tavris notes:

> Self-disclosure occurs through the content of words (revealing or protective), the tone and quality of words spoken (harsh or warm), non-verbal behavior (eye contact, distance from listener, gestures, and facial expressions), and actions taken (reflecting deep love, vulnerability, or animosity, for example). Self-disclosure can take place in breadth (sharing a great deal of information about yourself, but nothing in much detail) or in depth (sharing intimate, deeply personal emotions). (1974, 71)

One book on self-disclosure refers to "the lonely society" to describe the fact that with urbanization, mobility, and the fast pace of life in most modern societies, self-disclosure becomes more difficult, indeed even risky (Derlaga & Chaikin, 1975). Familiarity does not necessarily mean closeness. This is reflected in experiences with **"familiar strangers,"** as described by the social psychologist Stanley Milgram.

For years, I have taken a commuter train to work. I noticed that there were people at my station whom I have seen for many years but never spoken to, people I came to think of as familiar strangers. I found a peculiar tension in this situation,

A Range of Self-Disclosure

Bill R. has trouble making friends. His acquaintances all like him, but no one knows what he is really like.

Dorothy W. also has no close friends. Unlike Bill, however, she is not reluctant to let others know what she is feeling or what her problems are. In fact, she reveals personal things to almost everyone. People regard her as somewhat strange.

Terry is contemplating a divorce from her husband Ken. She now realizes that she has never really known him. For five years, she has lived with him, cooked and cleaned for him, and slept with him. In all that time, they have talked only about day-to-day concerns: what was for dinner, their weekend plans, and so forth. What is he really like? What were his hopes, dreams, and fears? She really doesn't know. (Derlaga & Chaikin, 1975, 1)

when people treat each other as properties of the environment, rather than as individuals to deal with. It happens frequently. Yet there remains a poignancy and discomfort, particularly when there are only two of you at the station; you and someone you have seen daily but never met. A barrier has developed that is not readily broken. (Tavris, 1974, 71)

The "familiar stranger" phenomenon, indeed the absence of self-disclosure in general, is partly the result of a necessary decision to "screen out" most people we meet. We simply cannot give time and energy to be open in a personal way with the dozens or hundreds of people we meet each day. We would be overwhelmed.

Nor is full openness even in everyone's best interest all the time. **"Plungers,"** who too quickly and too completely reveal themselves, often are scorned and avoided. So, too, are those who perpetually engage in **"ego-speak"**—the boosting of their egos by speaking only about what *they* want to talk about. . . . According to Derlago and Chalkin (1975), "Ego-speak is mental masturbation."

Solitude can be golden at times. Insulating yourself from the opportunity to participate in self-disclosure sometimes is healthy and productive. According to Paul Tillich, the theologian, solitude "is the experience of being alone, but not lonely." Henry David Thoreau once said, "I never found a companion that was so companionable as solitude" (1946).

Full self-disclosure is inadvisable in certain circumstances.

- When you clearly would be rebuked or hurt
- When revealing a thought, feeling, or intention would result in harmful reactions toward you
- When the situation clearly calls for completion of a task rather than sharing of feelings
- When the other person clearly is disinterested
- When a feeling or thought is best reserved for intimate partners

You probably can identify other situations in which concealment to some degree is appropriate.

On the other hand, a number of benefits often flow from self-disclosure.

- Expressing inner thoughts and feelings promotes self-awareness and self-understanding. By putting thoughts and feelings into words, they become clear to the sender.

- Communication becomes more complete. Intentions, background information, and associated emotions are better known.
- Emotional pressure is avoided or reduced, lessening the chance of stress buildup.
- Expressing emotions promotes physical health. Unexpressed emotions block energy, get stuck in muscles and joints, help cause high blood pressure and other illnesses, and perhaps even shorten the life span.
- Expressing authentic feelings and thoughts puts the other person at ease, reducing his or her tension.
- The possibility of later depth, warmth, and honesty in a relationship increases.
- You open yourself to caring verbal and action responses.
- You increase the chances of creative problem-solving, both by you and with others.
- You promote expansion of your feelings, ideas, and abilities.

In his lifelong study of self-actualizing persons, Abraham Maslow found that every individual he studied was fully open and disclosing to at least one or two other persons. Maslow concluded that the inability to be honest and revealing to at least a few others blocks growth and prevents fulfillment of potential. He recommends, "when in doubt, be honest rather than not" (1971, 45).

A consistent research finding is that "self-disclosure begets self-disclosure" (Derlaga & Chaikin, 1975, 38). Openness by *A* tends to elicit openness by *B*. On the other hand, a distant communication brings the same thing back. Thus, an important step to bring down unnecessary barriers both for you and for those you interact with is to be open whenever appropriate and possible. You thereby promote your own well-being and that of others around you—and you help build a social climate of support, forthrightness, mutual honesty, and authenticity.

Active Listening

Listening effectively is a basic ingredient in any effort to cope constructively with others. Any exchange between two or more people contains four basic elements.

1. Sender
2. Message
3. Feelings
4. Receiver

Active listening is a simple skill that is too seldom practiced. When used correctly, it can do wonders to ensure that these four elements are in harmony. Clear and crisp exchanges of information and positive feelings between sender and receiver then are possible. Task accomplishment also benefits.

Let us assume the following message at 4 P.M. one day:

Eleven-year-old boy to mother: "I'm sick of school."

At this point, the mother can respond in any number of ways.

Mother to boy:
"You are tired from staying up too late watching TV last night." (Psychologizing)
"Are you saying you don't believe learning is good for you?" (Questioning)
"No, you're not." (Denying)
"Oh, you are always complaining." (Discounting)
"I can tell. I know school is a drag." (Sympathizing)
"You know I have to send you to school every day. The law says so." (Defending)

"You have no business feeling that way. You are only a sixth grader and will have to stay in
   school at least six more years." (Judging)
"You must get to bed earlier, get your homework done on time, and take a better attitude
   towards school. Then you will like it. No more of this." (Ordering)
"Sounds like you're sick of school." (Parroting)
"Let me tell you about one time I was sick of school when I was 9 years old, blah, blah, blah."
   (Flipping to own story)

These are common but defective responses. The boy is likely to feel no better. In fact,
he probably will go away feeling unheard, put-down, intimidated, judged, belittled, attacked, or misunderstood.

Alternative responses, each an example of active listening, might be:

Mother to boy:
"You seem pretty discouraged about school today."
"You sound pretty tired today."
"You sound really pooped."
"You appear really down on school."

Any of these responses is likely to set in motion a fruitful exchange for the following
reasons.

- The initial sender, the son, feels he is being truly heard.
- He will feel he is worthwhile because he is heard.
- The receiver, the mother, checks out the accuracy of what she thinks she has heard.
  She invites him to say more, lowering his stress level by letting off steam and
  further reinforcing his sense of worth.
- She withholds her feelings, at least until she is clear about what he is saying.
- He is given the chance to search for solutions himself, thereby promoting his own
  responsibility for his actions.
- Warmth and understanding are promoted between mother and son.

The basic format for active listening is simple:

"You sound _____ about _____."

The words cannot be mechanical or stilted, of course, but must flow naturally within
the context of the person's own vocabulary and communication style.

The active listener is noncritical and noncontrolling, at least in the early stages of
the exchange. Sometimes it is appropriate, of course, to respond with an order, command, or judgment—but usually only after the sender has been fully heard. In most common daily interchanges at work and at home, active listening is entirely appropriate and
beneficial. Chances are reduced that the sender or receiver will unnecessarily build up
tension or resentment.

In short, active listening includes the following.

- Showing attentiveness
- Clarifying the content of sender's spoken message
- Verifying nonverbal messages
- Inviting more information and expression of feelings
- Providing a genuine personal response
- Promoting joint problem-solving or problem-solving by the sender alone

Active listening is useful because it promotes the following:

See Application Exercise 17-3 for a plan to observe listening behavior by you and others.

- • Accuracy of communication
- • Warmth and acceptance between sender and receiver
- • Self-worth of the sender
- • Elaboration of content
- • Full expression of feelings
- • Equality
- • Openness
- • Faith in sender's ability to solve problems

The most important features of active listening can be summarized in three simple dos and three simple don'ts:

Dos	Don'ts
1. Be and appear attentive	1. Interrupt.
2. Ask follow-up questions.	2. Give immediate judgments or solutions.
3. Rephrase what you have heard.	3. Divert the conversation to yourself.

Active listening, then, is a vitally important skill for minimizing distress for both the self and others.

Listening Tips

Today's Supervisor notes that 80 percent of the typical workday is spent communicating with others. Of that time, nearly half is spent listening. Yet the typical person remembers only one-quarter to one-half of what was heard. Viewed this way, poor listening is very expensive because of lost information and damaged relationships.

Today's Supervisor has identified some of the most common and harmful habits associated with poor listening.

1. **Faking:** Putting on a good show of listening by nodding and giving verbal cues, but not listening at all.
2. **Interrupting:** Breaking in while the other is talking.
3. **Dominating:** Waiting your turn to talk, gathering your thoughts together, then cutting others short.
4. **Correcting:** Lying in wait for factual errors, then immediately correcting these errors in the other's remarks.
5. **Criticizing:** Rather than listening, passing judgment on the other person while he or she is talking—on criticizing voice, mannerisms, appearance, point of view, and attitude.

On the positive side, *Today's Supervisor* suggests several simple methods for better listening:

1. Stop talking.
2. Focus your attention and actions.
3. Notice how things are said.
4. Notice what isn't said.
5. Stop for "clarity checks."

Source: Today's Supervisor (1989, 12)

Giving and Getting Negative Feedback

Among the most volatile interchanges between one person and another is giving and receiving negative feedback. If bungled, stress created by the original unhappiness is multiplied many times. Thus, an ensuing stress buildup mounts for both.

Assume you are under a time deadline at work. The deadline is tomorrow at noon, when you and your work team must turn in a report to management. Also assume that at 3:00 P.M. a member of the team has just produced a rather deficient segment that clearly needs more work and will require you as a team leader to stay up late tonight and revise it. You are quite angry and disappointed. This is not the first time he has come up short. Your patience is wearing thin. How can you best give negative feedback? You want to accomplish several things through this feedback: Make known your own disappointment and frustration and let him know specifically what is deficient; let him know what the consequences may be for

---

Four Keys to Attentive Listening

1. **Ask for clarification:** Asking friendly questions when something is unclear allows you to get more information and demonstrates your interest and concern. "Please tell me more about that." "Can you give me an example?" Even a simple "mm-hmm" will encourage the speaker. Some people feel threatened by questions, so make your probing gentle and supportive. Be especially judicious with "why" questions. "Why do you want to take a night course?" Try instead, "Is there something special you want to learn?"

2. **Reflect content:** This is not the same as parroting. It is offering your own creative summary of what you have heard. "So, even though it's expensive, you think a night course in desktop publishing will help your career." It may be off base, but the purpose of paraphrasing is to correct misunderstandings.

3. **Reflect feelings:** Let the other person know that you heard the emotional content. Listen between the lines. What is the person feeling but not saying? Asking for but not directly? Try empathy. "If I were having that experience, what would I be feeling?" Watch body language; posture, facial expression, and gestures often reveal underlying emotions. Then check out your guesses. "You seem very disappointed; is that true?"

4. **Reflect meanings:** The combination of feelings, facts, and interpretations result in meaning. As you listen attentively, you may begin to sense links between feelings and facts. Offer these tentative interpretations as feedback in an accepting, nonjudgmental way. "You feel scared because it is something you've never done. Does this make sense?" This type of communication helps you both gain understanding and insight.

Source: Sobel & Ornstein (1994, 4)

him, the team, and you; and indicate that in the future his performance must improve in specific ways. (Steinmetz, 1980, 81)

Here is an approach for the situation just described as developed by Steinmetz (1980) both for you as the boss in giving the negative feedback and for your subordinate in receiving it.

1. Describe the situation and the deficiencies in specific and objective terms. Limit your remarks to the present, excluding, for now, the past. Give only what is directly useful, and avoid overloading the recipient with unnecessary details or irrelevant points. Avoid sarcasm. Remain objective in order to minimize chances of defensiveness by the recipient. For example, "You had time available to work on this. We badly need it. It does not include these specific bits of information, which are vital to the overall report. Further, it is not written clearly."

2. Express your own feelings, using **"I feel"** messages. Share these feelings, rather than denying them. Avoid put-downs, attacks, or accusations. For example, "I feel disappointed and frustrated."

3. Give the recipient a chance to respond here. If he or she agrees, you need not proceed further. An interchange with active listening both ways can be very productive.

4. Specify changes you want in specific terms. Be objective and firm. For example, "I will want such and such data by 6 this evening, though it may require staying overtime. Then I want to meet you at 8 A.M. to go over what I have rewritten tonight."

5. Avoid being demanding, authoritarian, or patronizing. Simply be firm. "In the future, I would like you to ask if you are unclear about what is needed and to do a complete, thorough job."

6. Share your perception of the possible or likely outcome of the changes you request. Use positive terms, avoiding "you had better do it, or else" remarks. A threat of punishment muddies the waters. For example, "If you do, we all can be proud of our work, have better feelings as a team, and help out management."

A four-step format also applies in receiving negative feedback. Your goal is to focus objectively on the message being sent in order to remedy the situation through effective individual or joint problem-solving.

1. Describe the situation as you perceive it in objective and specific language.
2. Express your perception of the other person's feelings.
3. State in your own words the changes you think he or she wants.
4. State your perception of the likely consequences of the changes objectively, candidly, and specifically.

These formats must be adapted, of course, to specific people and situations. They can be effective for minimizing further negative feelings and for getting the job done well. The more these techniques are practiced and used, the easier and more natural they become.

My own list of suggested dos and don'ts for giving and getting criticism follows.

Giving Criticism

Dos	Don'ts
1. Know the facts.	1. Attack the person.
2. Pinpoint specific behavior.	2. Criticize past behavior without linking to desired future behavior.
3. Criticize in order to change future attitude or behavior.	3. Overgeneralize.
4. Be sure criticism is understood.	4. Dump your own frustration or anger

5. Show empathy—how would you take it?
6. Think before speaking—organize facts and approach.
7. Criticize only if change is possible.
8. Use good timing—other's mood, your mood, and context.
9. Maintain calm in your body.

through criticism.
5. Criticize without having facts.
6. Criticize and run.
7. Criticize, then punish through silence.
8. Publicly humiliate.
9. Heap on too much at one time.

Getting Criticism

Dos	Don'ts
1. Take criticism as opportunity rather than threat.	1. Overgeneralize by taking criticism as negative reflection on your total performance or your character.
2. Be thick-skinned.	
3. Listen attentively.	2. Allow defensiveness to prevent accurate listening.
4. Understand fully.	
5. Ask for more information.	3. Believe you must always defend yourself.
6. Watch for patterns.	
7. Look for grain of truth.	4. Be thin-skinned.
8. Acknowledge grain of truth.	5. Automatically discount criticism.
9. Assess the source.	6. Attack back.
10. Relax—use a 6-Second Quieting Response.	
11. Repeat back what you are hearing.	

Assertiveness

Our framework of stress and stress management assumes that a stressor is perceived and appraised by the individual. Throughout this chapter, we have focused on constructive options for coping with people-stressors, active listening, appropriate self-disclosure, dealing with angry feelings, and giving and receiving negative feedback. Another useful approach to coping effectively (that is, responding so you get what you want but not at others' expense) is **assertiveness.**

Passive	Assertive	Aggressive
This person is:	This person is:	This person is:
Shy	Usually more extroverted	Somewhat hostile
Withdrawing		
Reluctant to assert rights and privileges	Aware of rights and privileges and uses them constructively	A vehement defender of own rights yet often violates or usurps the rights of others
		Unmindful of where own rights end and of where the violation of others' begins
Socially inhibited	Socially productive	Socially destructive

Source: Girdano & Everly (1979, 148)

Generally, assertiveness is desirable behavior for reducing tension in situations where there is potential buildup of resentment or anger, or when strength must be used to get what you want or to prevent someone else from imposing on you unnecessarily. Yet we must retain options. Aggressiveness is seldom called for, except perhaps in situations of physical attack or danger. Passive behavior sometimes is appropriate. Certainly, *temporary,* timely passivity represents simple good judgment in certain circumstances. Being quiet sometimes is best. Assertive behavior must be exercised with discretion and perceptiveness.

What are the specific characteristics of assertiveness? Steinmetz suggests the following.

1. Eye contact: Steady, eye-to-eye contact while speaking. Not staring or glaring, but firm and unyielding.
2. Hand gestures: Use strong gestures to emphasize important points. Loses effectiveness if overdone.
3. Posture: Standing or sitting tall and straight, rather than slouching, slumping, or hiding.
4. Voice firmness: Maintaining a steady, firm volume, tone, and pace through out, without imposing too much volume. Avoid yelling as well as weak trail-offs through drop of volume or "you-knows."
5. "I" statements: Just as with expressing disappointment, assertiveness calls for such openers as, "I feel," "I want," "I need," "I would appreciate," "I request." By contrast, the passive opener is "Don't you think that," while a common aggressive opener is "You should." "I" statements imply responsibility for what you are feeling and requesting.
6. Short sentences: These are clearly understood and imply firmness. Avoid long, rambling sentences that lose the listener and the potential impact of your message.
7. Pauses for feedback; strategic breaks can both underscore what has just been said and provide an opportunity for clarifying a response. (1980)

Like all other behavior, assertiveness originates from beliefs and self-talk. Butler (1981, 35) suggests the following for before, during, and after challenging encounters. Be an experiment-of-one. Find which ones work for you.

1. **Preparing for self-assertion**
   No negative statements. I'm just going to express my feelings.
   My purpose here is not to be liked and approved of by everyone.
   It isn't awful to make a mistake.
   I'll express my feelings. If I'm honest and direct, then I've been assertive.
   I'm not going to apologize for where I am now.
   Stop catastrophizing. I'm doing them a favor by letting them know what I feel.
2. **Handling an assertive encounter**
   I'll go at my own rate. I can back up if I'm feeling overwhelmed.
   I have a perfect right to express my feelings.
   Everyone doesn't have to agree with me for me to be okay.
   It's okay to feel nervous. That's part of entering new territory.
   There is no perfect way of saying this.
   I can think of something to say if I just express my feelings.
   If my mind goes blank, it's okay to say, "My mind has just gone blank."
3. **Giving yourself credit**
   I'm really glad that I was honest.
   I'm really pleased. That was hard for me to say.

I'm still feeling a little shaky, but I did it. I deserve a lot of credit.
I was terrific.
Hey, the roof didn't fall in. I'm getting better every time.
They didn't respond as I would have liked, but that's not important. The important thing is that I asserted myself.

Communication Style and Stress

In Chapter 4 we noted that many people are distress provokers, sometimes intentionally and with full awareness, other times quite unintentionally. In this chapter, we have reviewed a number of means whereby you can keep your stress at a reasonable level without causing undue distress for others and while getting what you want.

Viewing your communication as a whole, do you give a preponderance of positive strokes (communication messages that add to others' self-worth or reduce tension) or negative strokes (acts that add to stress and lessen self-worth, comfort, and emotional well-being)? Of course, the communication process is never clearly one way or the other, but rather a mixture of the two. Most of us are somewhat in the middle. Yet the following principles generally are valid.

- Positive strokes prevent and reduce distress for others and, through a loop-back effect, for the self.
- Negative strokes cause or add to distress for others and, through the same loop-back effect, for the self.

Karl Albrecht, in *Stress and the Manager* (1979, 265), has presented a list of positive and negative behaviors. We will relabel them "distress-provoking" and "stress-reducing."

1. **Distress-provoking (punishing) actions include:**
   Monopolizing the conversation
   Interrupting
   Showing obvious disinterest
   Keeping a sour facial expression
   Withholding customary social cues such as greetings, nods, "uh-huh," and the like
   Throwing verbal barbs at others
   Using nonverbal put-downs
   Insulting or otherwise verbally abusing others
   Speaking dogmatically; not respecting others' opinions
   Complaining or whining excessively
   Criticizing excessively; fault finding
   Demanding one's own way; refusing to negotiate or compromise
   Ridiculing others
   Patronizing or talking down to others
   Making others feel guilty
   Soliciting approval from others excessively
   Losing one's temper frequently and easily
   Playing "games" with people; manipulating or competing in subtle ways
   Throwing "gotchas" at others; embarrassing or belittling others
   Telling lies; evading honest questions; refusing to level with others
   Overusing "should" language; pushing others with words
   Displaying frustration frequently
   Making aggressive demands on others
   Diverting conversation capriciously; breaking others' trains of thought

Disagreeing routinely
Restating others' ideas for them
Asking loaded or accusing questions
Overusing "why" questions
Breaking confidences; failing to keep important promises
Flattering others insincerely
Joking at inappropriate times
Bragging; showing off; talking only about oneself

2. **Stress-reducing (rewarding) behaviors include:**
    Giving others a chance to express views or share information
    Listening attentively; hearing other person out
    Sharing oneself with others; smiling; greeting others
    Giving positive nonverbal messages of acceptance and respect for others
    Praising and complimenting others sincerely
    Expressing respect for values and opinions of others
    Giving suggestions constructively
    Compromising; negotiating; helping others succeed
    Talking positively and constructively
    Affirming feelings and needs of others
    Treating others as equals whenever possible
    Stating one's needs and desires honestly
    Delaying automatic reactions; not flying off the handle easily
    Leveling with others; sharing information and opinions openly and honestly
    Confronting others constructively on difficult issues
    Staying on the conversational topic until others have been heard
    Stating agreement with others when possible
    Questioning others openly and honestly; asking straightforward, nonloaded
        questions
    Keeping the confidences of others
    Giving one's word sparingly and keeping it
    Joking constructively and in good humor
    Expressing genuine interest in the other person

As we have noted throughout the book, personal stress does not occur in isolation. Rather, we are imbedded in a network of relationships, groups, and larger social environments. Effective management of stress calls for not only regulating how we respond internally to external stressors but how we interact with others. In this chapter you have read illustrations of communication habits that can either minimize or create distress for others—and ultimately for yourself, including those just listed. In the final chapter, we examine the challenge of blending personal wellness with social commitment.

References

Albrecht, K. (1979). Stress and the manager. Englewood Cliffs, NJ: Prentice-Hall.

Antonovsky, A. (1979). *Health, stress and coping.* San Francisco: Jossey-Bass.

Antonovsky, A. (1987). *Unravelling the mystery of health: How people manage stress and stay well.* San Francisco: Jossey-Bass.

Berkman, L., & Syme, S. L. (1979). Social networks, host resistance, and mortality: A nine-year follow-up study of Alameda County residents. *American Journal of Epidemiology, 109,* 186–204.

Blieszner, R., & Adams, R. G. (1992). *Adult friendship.* Thousand Oaks, CA: Sage Publications.

Butler, P. E. (1981). *Self-assertion for women.* San Francisco: Harper & Row.

Caplan, G. (1974). *Support systems and community mental health.* New York: Behavioral Publications.

Cohen, S., & Wills, T. A. (1985). Stress, social support, and the buffering hypothesis. *Psychological Bulletin, 98,* 340–355.

Dean, A., & Lin, N. (1977). The stress-buffering role of social support. *Journal of Nervous and Mental Disease, 169,* 403–417.

Derlaga, V. J., & Chaikin, A. C. (1975). *Sharing intimacy.* Englewood Cliffs, NJ: Prentice-Hall.

Dunkel-Schetter, C., & Skokan, L. A. (1990). Determinants of social support provision in personal relationships. *Journal of Social and Personal Relationships, 7,* 437–450.

Durkheim, E. (1951, 1897). *Suicide.* Glencoe, IL: Free Press.

Egan, G. (1977). *You and me: The skills of communicating and relating to others.* Monterey: Brooks/Cole.

Ferguson, T. (1984). Pets. *Medical Self-Care, 27,* 29–32.

Friedman, E. (1980). Animal companions and one-year survival of patients after discharge from a coronary care unit. *Public Health Reports, 95.4,* 307–312.

Greenberg, H. M. (1980). *Coping with job stress.* Englewood Cliffs, NJ: Prentice-Hall.

Hobfoll, S. E. (Ed.). (1990). *Predicting, activating and facilitating social support.* Special Issue of *Journal of Social and Personal Relationships.*

Hobfoll, S. E., Freedy, J., Lane, C., & Geller, P. (1990). Conservation of social resources: Social support resource theory. *Journal of Social and Personal Relationships, 7,* 465–478.

House, J. S. (1981). *Work stress and social support.* Reading, MA: Addison-Wesley.

House, J. S., Landis, K. R., & Umberson, D. (1988). Social relationships and health. *Science, 241,* 540–544.

Johnson, S. (1997). Grown-up Love. *Networker,* September/October, 37–41.

Lazarus, R. S., & Folkman, S. (1984). *Stress, appraisal and coping.* New York: Springer.

Lin, N., Woelfel, M. W., & Light, S. C. (1985). The buffering effect of social support subsequent to an important life event. *Journal of Health and Social Behavior, 26,* 247–263.

Lynch, J. J. (1985). *The language of the heart.* New York: Basic Books.

Maslow, A. (1971). *The farther reaches of human nature.* New York: Viking.

Mitchell, J. S. (Ed.). (1969). *Social networks in urban situations.* England: Manchester University Press.

Ornstein, R., & Sobel, D. (1985). The healing brain. *Psychology Today, 21,* 48–52.

Ornstein, R., & Sobel, D. (1989). *Healthy pleasures.* Reading, MA: Addison-Wesley.

Oxman, T.E., Freeman, D. H. Jr., Manheimer, E.D. (1995). Lack of social participation or religious strength and comfort as risk factors for death after cardiac surgery in the elderly. *Psychosomatic Medicine, 57,* 5–15.

Pagel, M. D., Erdly, W. W., & Becker, J. (1987). Social networks: We get by with (and in spite of) a little help from our friends. *Journal of Personality and Social Psychology, 53,* 793–804.

Patterson, T. L., Shaw, W. S., Semple, S. J., Cherner, M., McCutchan, J. A., Atkinson, J. H., Grant, I., & Nannis, E. (1996). Relationship of psychosocial factors in HIV disease progression. *Annals of Behavioral Medicine, 18,* 30–39.

Pearlin, L. I., & Lieberman, M. A. (1977). Marital status, life-strains and depression. *American Sociological Review, 42,* 704–715.

Pines, M. (1980). Psychological hardiness: The role of challenge in health. *Psychology Today, 14,* 43–45.

Rotheram-Borus, M. J., Murphy, D. A., Reid, H. M., & Coleman, C. L. (1996). Correlates of emotional distress among HIV+ youth: Health status, stress, and personal resources. *Annals of Behavioral Medicine, 18,* 16–23.

Rossiter, C. (1984). *The human potential.* Alexandria, VA: Human Potential.

Sarason, I. G., Pierce, G. R., & Sarason, B. R. (1990). Social support and interactional processes: A triadic conceptualization. *Journal of Social and Personal Relationships, 7,* 495–506.

Satir, V. (1976). *Making contact.* Berkeley: Celestial Arts.

Satir, V. (1988). *The new peoplemaking.* Mountain View, CA: Science and Behavior Books.

Sobel, D., & Ornstein, R. (1994). 4 keys to attentive listening. *Mental Medicine Update, III,* 2, 4.

Steinmetz, J. (1980). *Managing stress before it manages you.* Palo Alto: Bull.

Suls, J. (1982). Social support, interpersonal relations, and health: Benefits and liabilities. In G. Sanders, & J. Suls (Eds.), *Social psychology of health and illness.* Hillsdale, NJ: Erlbaum, 220–229.

Tavris, C. (1974). The frozen world of the familiar stranger: A conversation with Stanley Milgram. *Psychology Today, 8,* 70–80.

Thoits, P. A. (1982). Conceptual, methodological, and theoretical problems in studying social support as a buffer against life stress. *Journal of Health and Social Behavior, 23,* 145–159.

Thoreau, H. D. (1946). *Walden.* New York: Random House.

Today's Supervisor (1989). Listening better, March, 12.

Turner, R. J. (1981). Social support as a contingency in psychological well-being. *Journal of Health and Social Behavior, 22,* 357–367.

Vormbrock, J. K., & Grossberg, J. M. (1988). Cardiovascular effects of human-pet dog interactions. *Journal of Behavioral Medicine, 11,* 509–518.

Weiss, R. S. (1974). The provisions of social relationships. In Z. Rubin (Ed.), *Doing unto others.* Englewood Cliffs, NJ: Prentice-Hall, 83–89.

Application Exercise 17-1

Social Support Networks From Which You Draw

1. The person(s) I count on for day-to-day support include(s):

2. Agree or disagree? For the most part, my current social support network is quite sufficient for meeting my day-to-day needs. My needs during difficult times? Explain.

3. I wish the following were different in my relationships with my social support network from which I draw:

4. Steps I will take to make this happen include:

Application Exercise 17-2

Networks Through Which You Give Social Support

1. Those to whom I give support daily include:

2. Agree or disagree? I am satisfied with the amount and quality of support I give to others daily. When times are difficult for others? Explain.

3. I wish the following were different in my giving of support to others:

4. Steps I will take to make this happen include:

Application Exercise 17-3

Observing Listening Behavior by You and Others

For the next day or two, watch your own listening behavior with particular attention to the instances in which you do and do not match the dos and don'ts of active listening.

1. What did you see and hear? What can you learn?

For the next day or two, watch others' listening behavior with particular attention to the instances in which others do and do not match the dos and don'ts of active listening.

2. What did you see and hear? What can you learn?

CHAPTER 18

Individual efforts are necessary but insufficient for optimal health. We need to create approaches and systems in economics, environment, politics, and in the delivery of medical care, that elicit and sustain individual strategies.

—Kenneth R. Pelletier

Personal Wellness and Social Commitment

Satisfaction From Making a Difference

- Joan Fernandez finds great personal satisfaction through her work as a nurse. She goes home nearly every afternoon with a sense of genuine pride in the knowledge she has made a real difference in patients' lives.
- Fred Rogowskie works as an accountant with a firm that specializes in service to nonprofit and other community service organizations. His career provides him deep meaning and purpose, since he knows that recipients of these organizations ultimately benefit from the financial guidance he provides these organizations.
- Jack Burt's work as a line supervisor in an auto manufacturing plant may seem mundane to some. But to him it offers a special opportunity to make a difference, since he does everything he can to make the work process humane and healthy for his supervisees.

This book has largely focused on achieving personal wellness through improved stress management strategies and techniques. Yet another theme has also been maintained: Meaningful stress management and true wellness must include blending *personal wellness* with **social commitment**—concern for the well-being of others and **commitment to the common good.** This means transcending one own's problems to help improve the social environment and to enhance others' wellness. In this final chapter we will focus on successful blending of personal wellness with social commitment.

CONSTRUCTIVE MALADJUSTMENT

The term *adjustment* sometimes is used in discussions of mental and physical health. Well-adjusted persons, it is said, are those who adapt effectively to the world around them. As a result, they experience minimal frustration and tension.

Adjustment, like stress management, can be taken too far. If, by adjusting, individuals passively accept conditions in the world around them that are destructive, unjust, cruel, or unfair, they have done a disservice to themselves and their world.

Constructive maladjustment is being appropriately discontented about conditions in the surrounding social, political, or natural environment that in the judgment of the person are wrong and need to be changed—and being motivated to change those conditions. Here are several real-life examples.

- Candy Lightner lost her 13-year-old daughter to a drunk driver in California. She did not passively accept the loss. She did not simply focus on adjusting to her grief and to the new reality of living without her precious daughter. Instead, she decided to do everything in her power to lobby for tougher drunk driving laws. She founded Mothers Against Drunk Drivers—MADD (Babbie, 1985).
- Curtis Sliwa, a young McDonald's manager, decided to do something constructive about urban violence. Rather than stopping with the usual individualistic (and necessary) steps of taking care of his own safety, he persuaded 12 friends to join him in riding subways together in New York City to head off crime. The group expanded to become the Guardian Angels, promising to break up muggings, rapes,

and other acts of violence. It was not long before several thousand Guardian Angels were active in many American cities (Babbie, 1985).

- Monique Grodski was a 9-year-old in 1979 living in suburban New York when by chance she watched a television documentary on the plight of Cambodian refugees. She was moved by these people's strong spirit. "I found it amazing that they were still singing and had the hope and strength to go on. After I saw that, I actually cried. I really had to do something about it" (Babbie, 1985, 113). She was especially disturbed by the plight of the children. Monique made a personal decision to do something to enable the children to have a greater say in this and other world problems. She was instrumental as a youngster in forming the Children's Peace Committee, which went on to circulate petitions, raise funds for several causes, and speak to community groups.

You may recall from Chapters 1 and 11 the idea that personal problems and public issues often are closely linked (Mills, 1956). Individual unhappiness, depression, anxiety, even ill health are tied to public spending priorities, unemployment, community crime rates, the work climate, war and peace, social density, the rate of community growth, and more. These influences of society on the self are one reflection that "no man is an island entire and of itself."

What is needed, then, is **sociological imagination**—the ability to understand that personal experience is influenced by larger social forces (Mills, 1956). Mills correctly maintained that we need not only to pursue our personal solutions to personal problems, but also to do what we can to modify positively those surrounding conditions that help cause the problems. This may take the form, for example, of getting involved in the political process, contributing to a favorite candidate's campaign, writing or calling an officeholder, getting involved in a local committee or commission, or participating in a task force to work on a problem in the workplace. Unfortunately, a recent study (Greene, 1998) reported that political interest has reached its lowest level in 30 years among college freshmen.

In short, truly effective and holistic stress management for wellness includes constructive maladjustment, based on the sociological imagination and the ability to link personal problems with public issues.

At a more personal level, we need to balance self-care with care for those in our immediate environment.

ALTRUISTIC EGOISM AND EGOISTIC ALTRUISM

Selye's Altruistic Egoism

After several decades of physiological research on the nature of the stress response, Hans Selye was frequently asked about the implications of his studies for how to live a healthy and worthwhile life.

At first, he was quite uncomfortable in this realm of prescriptive philosophy. After all, his life's work had been devoted entirely to the realm of objective science. After further thought, however, he found it was possible after all to remain true to scientific principles, on the one hand, and to provide a fundamental guideline for "the good life," on the other hand.

This guideline is captured in the term **altruistic egoism**—"to earn thy neighbor's love" (Selye, 1974, 5). While expressing appropriate caution about telling others how to live or passing judgment on others' lifestyle, Selye did believe it was possible to draw on basic biological laws to arrive at two conclusions. First, humans historically have been and continue to be self-interested. That is, each living creature possesses a fundamental life force that impels it to take care of itself in ways that ensure its growth, well-being, and survival.

Yet, second, the human species has survived only through cooperation and commitment to the welfare of the whole. Thus, it is biologically natural that humans balance concern with the self with consideration for others.

As a guideline for individual motivation and behavior, altruistic egoism incorporates that necessary balance. That is, the individual ought to work hard, even sometimes to the edge of personal stress, in order to contribute to the common good, thereby earning others' affection and esteem. Both the person and the society stand to gain.

The person benefits through ensuring "his own homeostasis and happiness by accumulating the treasure of other people's benevolence towards him." Altruistic egoism, the "hoarding of the goodwill, respect, esteem, support, and love of our neighbor, is the most efficient way to give vent to our pent-up energy and to create enjoyable, beautiful, or useful things" (Selye, 1976, 452).

The society gains through individuals' contributions to the well-being of the whole. If enough individuals merge self-satisfaction with social gain in this way, small groups, organizations, communities, and the whole society surely benefit.

As with all good ideas, altruistic egoism has its traps. For example, individuals can focus excessively on whether others in fact appreciate their altruistic actions as much as they deserve. Moreover, they can give so much to the common good that their own spiritual, mental, or physical health goes downhill. This leads to burnout.

My own consideration of values dealing with the self, society, and stress has led me to a variant of Selye's altruistic egoism. I call it egoistic altruism. It is an alternative guideline for merging self-interest and concern for others.

Egoistic Altruism

Each example in the box illustrates **egoistic altruism**—self-fulfillment through contributing to others' well-being. Contributing to others' well-being can occur in many ways and does not depend on a career of social or public service.

- A college student can facilitate the study habits and fitness routine of his roommate through encouragement and cooperation with household chores.
- Mothers and fathers can contribute to the well-being of their children in a host of small ways.
- Neighbors can enhance the well-being of each other through sharing when needed and by being considerate of noise and air pollution.
- Coworkers can contribute to the well-being of one another by providing support and encouragement.
- An attorney can make the world a better place by providing sound advice and counsel to clients in time of need.
- A full-time mother and homemaker can make a difference by getting involved in the neighborhood school's Parent-Teacher Association as a way of working with others to improve street safety for children walking to and from school.
- Parents in a crime-ridden public housing project can enhance their own self-fulfillment by joining with others in the project to work with police to reduce drug sales in local playgrounds.

Reflections on Altruism

Altruism is a spontaneous and natural expression of our fundamental relatedness, not a form of deviance.

Psychologist Alfie Kohn noted, "Helping may be as dramatic as agreeing to donate a kidney or as mundane as letting another shopper ahead of you in line. . . . Caring about others is as much a part of human nature as caring about ourselves."

Altruism does not necessarily involve self-denial or sacrifice. In acting on behalf of others, both ordinary volunteers and those whose lives are devoted to service report feeling joy and fulfillment. Such joy is a natural consequence of caring.

Being tenderhearted does not mean being softhearted. Those we have recognized as creative altruists work in the most challenging situations. Those they serve—youth at risk, addicts and drug abusers, juvenile delinquents, the mentally ill, the homeless—are unimpressed by do-gooders and bleeding-heart liberals. But their lives are transformed by the pragmatic intelligence and unconditional support they encounter in creative altruists.

While much altruistic behavior is indeed directed at the relief of immediate suffering, creative altruism involves innovative efforts to address the fundamental causes of deeply rooted social inequities. In the words of psychologist Howard Gruber, "Creative altruism, when it goes to the limit, strives to eliminate the cause of suffering, to change the world, to change the fate of the Earth."

Source: Hurley (1990, 33)

As with Selye's concept of altruistic egoism, the notion of egoistic altruism merges self-interest with contributing to the common good. Both the self and others benefit. Like Selye's altruistic egoism, egoistic altruism takes the person outside himself or herself. This is **self-transcendence** (Kohn, 1990).

A key difference between my concept and Selye's is that egoistic altruism brings fulfillment through the knowledge that one has been true to her or his value of enhancing others, whether or not others express their appreciation or indebtedness. In this sense, egoistic altruism promotes self-reliance. The individual thus values but does not depend on others' feedback, acknowledgment, or praise.

As Ray has noted, "Altruism affirms the ultimate value of the existence, or being, of other persons." He notes that this may be why people acting altruistically are truly perplexed when bystanders ask them why they helped others, the implied question being, 'What was in it for you?' Altruists respond, 'It just seemed to be the right thing to do,' or 'It was the human thing to do.' Satisfaction and a sense of personal gratification does not depend on others' praise. It rests on doing the deed (1989, 12).

David Sobel (Ornstein & Sobel, 1989) says this about egoism and altruism:

One thing that really helps is volunteer work, helping those less fortunate than yourself. Volunteer work is an old-time folksy approach to stress management. Put another way, there are a lot of selfish reasons to be altruistic. In addition to the good that comes from the volunteering itself, assisting people in dire straits helps the helpers keep their own problems in perspective. It also boosts self-esteem. (Castleman, 1990, 39)

A study of college students (Winniford et al., 1995) found that volunteers were motivated by altruistic and egoistic factors in their decisions to get involved, as well as to continue. Most important were altruistic values, represented by such statements as these:

- To accomplish something worthwhile/useful for others.
- Because of inner sense of benevolent interest in others.
- It gave me a good feeling or sense of satisfaction to help others.
- I wanted to serve (contribute to) the community.

Next most important were egoistic motives, represented by such statements as these:

- It was an excellent way to show future employers my interest in the community and helping others.
- To broaden by experience.
- For the leadership opportunities it could provide.
- To enrich my personal life.

This study supports the basic point of this section: Contributing to others' well-being brings both altruistic and egoistic gains.

A useful concept for seeking a better balance between self and others is the South African idea of "ubuntu." States Desmond Tutu, former archbishop and Nobel Peace Prize winner and in 1999 chair of the South African Truth and Reconciliation Commission, "Ubuntu is not easy to describe because it has no equivalent in any of the Western languages. Ubuntu speaks to the essence of being human and our understanding that the human person is corporate. The solitary individual is, in our understanding, a contradiction in terms. You are a person through other persons" (Sirotkin, 1997, 7). Ubuntu is both a personal- and community-based way of being. While speaking to the importance of communal harmony, it also "speaks about warmth, compassion, generosity, hospitality, and seeking to embrace others." In his book, *An African Prayer Book,* Tutu warns, "A too highly developed individualism can lead to a debilitating sense of isolation so that you can be lonely and lost in a crowd." According to Sirotkin, who interviewed Tutu, "Ubuntu, he explains, helps us in understanding how the people appearing before the Truth Commission can have suffered such horrendous violations to human dignity and 'still have the capacity to be human.' He smiles, and says, 'This is ubuntu'" (Sirotkin, 1997, 7).

HELPING AND WELLNESS

Helping is healthy. This is the conclusion from a report on several surveys of volunteers throughout the country (Andrews, 1990). For example, a national study of more than 1,800 members of more than 20 volunteer organizations showed that 57 percent of respondents reported increased self-esteem during or after helping others. Fifty-four percent said they experienced a "feeling of warmth." Nearly 1 in 3 reported increased energy, and 1 in 5 noted a "high" feeling—perhaps the result of increased endorphins from the helping experience.

Approximately 95 percent of respondents from several combined samples of volunteers reported feeling good while helping. Eight of 10 said these good feelings kept recurring long afterward, whenever the helping experience was recalled.

The researchers asked respondents about their health—whether it was perceived to be excellent, good, fair, or poor. They found that volunteers in excellent health were significantly more likely to report four or more positive effects of helping. Those whose helping was direct reported better health than those who helped indirectly; that is, not face-to-face. The more frequent the helping, the better the health—and the fewer the visits to a doctor.

Helping others through a group was found to relate more strongly to health outcomes than helping through individual effort. Finally, helping strangers was more positively associated with health than helping family or friends.

Many of the respondents reported feeling greater calmness during and after helping. One woman reported that doing something nice for someone actually snapped her out of bouts of depression. Another reported she treated her stress-related headaches by shopping for clothing for needy children.

More recently, Musick, House, and Herzog (1999) found that among 1,211 adults 65 and older who were followed for 8 years, those who volunteered up to 40 hours per year were significantly less likely to die than those who did not volunteer at all. Stated Musick, "We are social animals, and if you think of volunteering as a type of social interaction, it can make a big difference for older people, particularly those who might otherwise be largely isolated." Volunteering was most likely to affect the longevity of older men and women who otherwise had little social interaction with a roommate or spouse (Bowman, 1999, 1B). However, volunteering more than 40 hours per year slightly increased risk of death. According to Musick, "For older adults, taking on too much volunteer activity may incur just enough detriments to offset the potential beneficial effects of volunteering."

Flacks and Thomas (1998) recently reported that among university students, involvement in community service activities is associated with less alcohol consumption, greater academic involvement, and higher grades. Those who are uninvolved are part of a broader "culture of disengagement."

Herbert Benson, noted expert on the relaxation response, states, "For millennia, people have been describing techniques on how to forget oneself, to experience decreased metabolic rates and blood pressure, heart rate and other health benefits. Altruism works this way, just as do yoga, spirituality and meditation" (Luks, 1988, 42).

These studies did not prove, of course, that helping causes good mental and physical health. The causal influence could be reversed. That is, healthier people might simply help more often than unhealthy people, accounting for the positive associations found in these surveys.

Yet Andrews correctly concludes that the results "provide strong support for the hypothesis that there is a relationship between helping others and a number of health-related factors." He continues:

> In summary, the results of this study suggest that volunteer activity, particularly when performed frequently and directed toward strangers, can be added to the growing list of lifestyle and social network factors associated with physical and mental well-being. More research is required to establish a causal relationship between helping and health and to determine whether the perception of superior health reflects the individual's actual medical condition. However, the findings reported here are consistent with the view that volunteer activity produces real benefits for the provider as well as for the recipient. (1990, 32)

What is needed to demonstrate fully that helping actually causes better health is a longitudinal study in which the mental and physical health of a large group of nonvolunteers is measured initially, and then later comparisons are made between those who go on to volunteer and those who do not. Meanwhile, it is reasonable to suggest that helping others through volunteer activities may be one way to practice egoistic altruism—to heighten one's own self-fulfillment and well-being through contributing to the well-being of others. Many colleges now build community service into the curriculum (Cotter et al., 1995).

The Carter Ethic

Jimmy Carter and Rosalynn Carter live out their lives in headlines. During his presidency, Jimmy Carter informed the nation that ecological conservation, human rights, and conflict resolution based on mutual understanding were immediate global issues. He established a comprehensive energy policy based on the National Energy Act of 1978 and plowed windfall profits from decontrolled domestic oil prices into conservation. Tax incentives were enacted for the use of solar and other alternative energies. He said he would never lie to us. Then, in a resounding defeat over the hostage crisis, Carter lost the election to Ronald Reagan for what would have been his second term. The Carters returned to their farm in Plains, Georgia, to find the business in ruins, themselves nearly bankrupt, and their hopes and plans shattered.

Much has happened to the Carter family since. Above all, they have not only survived but also prevailed. A *Washingtonian* article lists Jimmy Carter (with former Surgeon General C. Everett Koop and [former President] George Bush) as one of the capital's three most-admired men.

Christopher Matthews, the *San Francisco Examiner's* Washington bureau chief and former Carter speechwriter, attributes this comeback in public esteem to changing values in the nation. He goes on to say, "The stands he took as president, together with the things he did afterward, have finally paid off."

The September 1989 issue of *The Economist* says, "His opinions of what is right and necessary for the world have not changed much since he was president, and in that sense he can be said to be using the Center (The Carter Presidential Library and Center) to pursue the unfinished business of the Carter administration, so abruptly interrupted by his electoral defeat in 1980. Conflicts, denials of human rights, hunger, disease, military competition, unproductive agriculture, economic error: Mr. Carter . . . takes off to Panama, Beijing, Khartoum, or Addis Ababa, meanwhile convening conferences on the Middle East, on Latin American debt, on the weaknesses of government in Africa and on the means of combating avoidable disease. The level of quality at these conferences has been high. Good people turn up for Mr. Carter."

The **Carter ethic** is gaining popularity not only in the United States but elsewhere around the world. Casimir Yost, president of the World Affairs Council of Northern California, noted: "The invitation [to be a neutral observer and mediator for the Dominican Republic's recent presidential election] illustrates his very considerable popularity and prestige in Latin America as the man who concluded the Panama Canal treaties and pressed for human rights and democracy. Indeed, as Carter toured voting sites around Santo Domingo last week, voters waiting in lines spontaneously broke into cheers."

"Carter is like the patient investor who sits on the same portfolio for years and suddenly finds himself rich," adds Christopher Matthews. The Carters, no longer constrained by the demands of the "please everybody" political arena, have continued to follow their hearts.

Source: Miller (1990, 32)

Luks points out:

> Taking time to help, then, may be a basic step to protect health. Stress assaults us: Seventy percent of Americans say there is a lot or some stress in their lives, and 40 percent believe stress has made them sick. Yet only 25 percent volunteer regularly. Those who don't say they are too busy and don't want to neglect important responsibilities. The health benefits they're passing up may turn out to be only part of their loss. At this early stage of altruism research, all those selfless people seem to have found ways into a wonderful glow. (1988, 42)

Unfortunately, some data (Putnam, 1995) suggest that American adults are becoming less rather than more involved in civic and volunteer activities. Still, a recent study (Broder, 1997) shows the average American holds membership in four organizations. Only 1 in 7 has no formal links outside family or work. Almost half the adults reported they volunteered during the past year, many with contributions of substantial time. States one of the investigators, "We're not a nation of civic slugs. Despite their lack of trust in government, most Americans have not lost their sense of what they can do individually or collectively in their communities" (Broder, 1997, B7). Also on the positive, a recent survey of more than a quarter million college freshmen found volunteerism at an all-time high, with 73 percent saying they did volunteer work during their senior year in high school (Hayward, 1998).

A continuing challenge, then, is to find your own optimal balance between giving to community groups and other organizations, on one hand, and meeting personal and family needs on the other. Like other good things, giving to others can turn sour if your own health suffers or if your children, lover, or spouse are seriously neglected. For brief periods, of course, intense commitment to a cause or activity is fully warranted. Over the long haul, the key is balance.

HEROISM AND SOCIAL RESPONSIBILITY

The New Heroes

In his inspiring and informative little book, *You Can Make a Difference,* sociologist Earl Babbie contends, "You and I are the heroes who will save America and the world" (1985, 18).

In the past, the term "hero" typically was applied to a select few—those who stood apart from the rest by performing extraordinary feats. Examples of this classic view of heroism were Beowolf, Robin Hood, Joan of Arc, and David. Contemporary fictional heroes of this type persist in comics and films: Batman, Superman, the Marvels, Sky King, John Wayne characters, and Rocky.

What sets heroes apart? Babbie maintains that the essential core of heroism remains the same, namely, **social responsibility**—willingness to assume personal responsibility for public problems (1985, 26). Assuming social responsibility is to devote one's energies to improving something in the social environment—in the absence of personal gain from doing so. In other words, persons who assume responsibility for a wrong or deficiency in a small group, organization, community, or society do so because they believe to do so is the right thing to do, not because they stand to gain in any direct way. Babbie notes that social responsibility "is assumed, not assigned, undertaken rather than imposed" (1985, 27). It is a matter of declaration, rather than duty with a total absence of guilt, burden, or blame.

Beyond Self

There seems to be a growing disillusionment and backlash against narcissism in the name of health. In his article entitled "Through a Glass, Darkly," published in *Newsweek* in December 1991, the playwright and bartender Jeff Morris gave some "bartenderly advice": "Jogging, Stairmasters, aerobics classes and diets are not the answer. They only relieve the symptoms: stress, anxiety, poor physical condition. They do nothing to effect change or to alleviate the causes of our problems. All the effort that goes into focusing on one's self can be detrimental in the long run. All the energy we exert in the name of health and the glorification of the self is diverting and sapping us of the energy we need to come to terms with what our real problems are: the economy, AIDS, human rights, the environment, education—these things can't be fixed unless people think more about other people and less about themselves."

Source: Pelletier (1994, 16)

Barriers to Assuming Social Responsibility

Social Barriers

Assuming social responsibility is not easy. The sheer size of organizations in which problems develop—and must be solved—often intimidates potential ordinary heroes like you and me. At the same time, specialization structures responsibility. We readily assume that someone must have been assigned a given task. Thus, it becomes very easy to walk by a piece of litter on the sidewalk, passing by this small opportunity for assuming social responsibility by telling oneself that the city government hires people to pick up litter. It is most certainly not my job—or my responsibility.

> See Application Exercise 18-1 to write about your own heroes.

It is only a small step next to convince yourself that it is not your responsibility to pick up the phone and call for help when a neighbor is being robbed, beaten, or even murdered, as was Kitty Genovese a number of years ago in New York—while 38 of her neighbors silently watched. None wanted to get involved.

Another less obvious social influence to avoiding responsibility is the high rate of cynicism, apathy, and alienation in America (Babbie, 1985). When surrounded by apathy and cynicism, when in fact this attitude seems the normal way to be, it becomes easy to remain detached, concerned only with self-gain.

Charles Simpkinson, in a fascinating and useful article on "compassionate living," observes that empathy is an essential ingredient in altruism and that self-love is needed for empathy. "Since it is impossible to truly love others unless one loves oneself, our strong cultural bias against any overt form of self-love is one of the biggest blocks against empathy and, therefore, altruism" (1990). "Healthy narcissism," on the other hand, is healthy not only for the self but for our ability to love others.

Personal Barriers

According to Babbie (1985, Chapter 9), several self-talk barriers are commonly used to prevent assumption of social responsibility for public problems.

- I'll seem "goody-goody."
- I'll seem holier than thou.
- My motives will be suspect.

> ## How To Be Rich
>
> The concept of synergy has fascinated me as perhaps the most pure expression of the "right relationship" between people in the act of service. Ruth Benedict, an anthropologist who sought to find ways to compare societies across very different cultures and environments, concluded that there were two kinds of societies, low-synergy and high-synergy. In a low-synergy society, a win-lose paradigm is followed in which the rich get richer and the poor get poorer; this is called funneling of wealth. A high-synergy society is based on a win-win structure in which there is a "siphoning of wealth," in which wealth goes from the rich to the poor rather from the poor to the rich.
>
> For example, during the annual Sun Dance ceremony of the Northern Blackfoot Indians, the richest men of the tribe give away all the possessions which they have accumulated throughout the year to widows, orphaned children, and the blind and diseased. He who gives away the most is considered the riches man. In this synergistic way (neither selfishly nor unselfishly because the polarity has been transcended), the richest man demonstrates how capable, intelligent, strong, hard-working , generous *and therefore how wealthy he is* , since wealth in this society is determined by the possession of these character attributes. These were the most admired, respected and loved men in the tribe; those who actually had the most possessions were not regarded as wealthy if they kept their wealth.

Source: Glover, (1997, 6).

- It's not my responsibility.
- I don't know what to do.
- I may make things worse.
- I may look stupid.
  - Nothing I could do would make a difference.

See Application Exercise 18-2 for a plan to personally get involved in solving a social problem.

True heroes do not let such self-talk (excuses) stand in their way. They hold values that impel them to see a need and respond, regardless of what others might think.

At a broader level, Etzioni and others maintain, we are in an era of "radical individualism" in which individuals are motivated by extreme self-interest with an overabundance of concern for "me" and a paucity of concern for "we." In an important book, *The Spirit of Community,* Etzioni (1993) contends there is excessive concern with individual rights and too little concern for social responsibility. He observes that we seem to be far more committed to self-gain than to the common good and argues for a renewed social and political ethic with this question at its core: What is good for *us,* not just for *me?* By "us" he means family, neighborhood, community, and society. This idea is embodied in the theme of a nearly 90-year-old service organization, Rotary Club: *Service Beyond Self.* As a result of translation of this idea into action among millions of international Rotarians, polio has recently been totally eliminated in the Americas (Neal, 1994). For too many Americans, self-interest predominates over concern for the well-being of others.

Opportunities Are Everywhere

Several years ago while teaching at the University of Hawaii, Earl Babbie gave his undergraduate students in a social problems class an unusual assignment: Find a social problem and fix it. Credit would not be given for finding out who was to blame for the problem, only for solving it. Nor would credit be given for "bitching about how bad things are" (1985, 145). They could only solve a problem others, as well as themselves, were concerned about. And they had to do more than make a mere dent on the problem or give it the "good ol' college try." They had to solve it. Thus, tackling the nuclear arms race, world hunger, or racism in America was discouraged.

During the rest of the summer, Babbie was amazed—and rewarded beyond his expectations. All the social problems that were recognized, tackled, and solved were close to home. They included these:

- Potholes in a neighborhood street. A student and 20 neighbors who watched him get started worked together to fill them.
- A student who was acutely aware of widespread loneliness in her dorm organized a dorm cookout.
- Picking up litter
- Cleaning up broken glass that had been left after a vehicle accident
- Moving an errant sprinkler that had been spraying a sidewalk and one lane of auto traffic
- Tying up and supporting a small tree that had been blocking a sidewalk due to roots loosened by a recent rainstorm
- Trimming a bush on public property that had blocked vision on a dangerous corner
- Removing a fallen branch that was a danger to drivers
- Helping push a stalled car out of traffic
- Taking a purse left on a bus seat up to the driver
- Asking a nearby gas station's attendant to help spray with insecticide a bus stop's overflowing trash can that had become infested with bees, endangering awaiting bus passengers
- Cleaning up a mess in a dormitory bathroom
- Purchasing note pads and pencils for each pay telephone on the dormitory floor—along with a placing a note requesting that they not be taken

While these social problems may seem trivial—and they may be in the larger scheme of things—they do illustrate a valuable point: **Opportunities are everywhere** for everybody to make a difference.

Opportunities exist at every level:

- Among friends
- In families
- In apartments and dormitories
- In classrooms
- In the immediate workplace
- In the organizations in which we work
- In our neighborhoods
- In community organizations
- In our communities
- In our regions
- In our states
- In our nation
- In our world, on our planet

Lessons From the Holocaust

For more than 30 years, Samuel Oliner has been a sociology professor at Humboldt State University. When I met him recently during a visit to that campus, I  had no idea what he had been through in his "other life." I later learned his astounding story.

Before dawn on August 14, 1942, German trucks coldly rolled into the walled-in Jewish ghetto of Bobowa, Poland, where he lived as a 12-year-old boy. Nazi soldiers leaped out of the trucks, yelling, "All Jews outside." The horrified people were brutally beaten, then herded into trucks and driven off into the darkness. Their corpses later were found in a pit in a nearby forest. They had been machine-gunned down. Included were Samuel's (then known as Shmulek) parents, grandparents, brother, sister, other relatives, and thousands of others.

Only Samuel survived, hiding on the rooftop of his house, so terrified he was not sure if he was dead or alive.

He managed to climb down the next day. As a blond, blue-eyed boy who looked like a Christian Pole, he hiked to a nearby village where he begged, then was taken in by a benevolent Christian woman. He left the area, fearing he would be recognized.

Later freed by Russian troops, the 15-year-old orphan was sent to England by a refugee committee. He was educated, eventually migrated to the United States, served in the armed forces in Korea, then went on to raise three children and over a period of 20 years to obtain his doctorate in sociology.

In 1978, he began teaching a course, "On Causes and Consequences of the Holocaust." An unexpected result was the unleashing of a flood of painful memories: his teenage sister weeping the night she was raped by Gestapo officers; his grandfather pushed against a hot stove by a Nazi officer, then knocked to the floor; the screaming throughout the ghetto the night his family and others were rounded up and taken away. Oliner was forced to confront his past and attempt to come to terms with it.

Another result was even more unexpected—emergence of a burning desire to learn more about those who, like his rescuer, Balwina Piecuch, put themselves at great risk to rescue Jews. Oliner began reading about ordinary people from all over Nazi-occupied Europe who performed these acts of courage. As a social scientist, he wanted to know more about what had created the altruistic nature in these twentieth-century heroes.

He and his staff gathered 600 detailed stories of rescue from aging rescuers in Poland, France, Italy, the Netherlands, Denmark, Norway, and Germany itself. They also interviewed 200 people from the same areas and of similar ages and backgrounds who had done nothing to save the Jews.

They then analyzed differences between the two groups. Their findings cast light on the origins of compassionate behavior.

Rescuers were not especially adventurous, self-confident, or religious. They were more empathic, more caring, and displayed a greater sense of responsibility for others.

Rescuers had developed their compassionate natures in part through having lived among people unlike themselves in terms of faith and background. They had learned to tolerate—even defend—diversity.

Early family experiences set rescuers apart from bystanders. Rescuers' parents were more likely to use reason in disciplining their children, thereby instilling values as well as compassion. Bystanders were more likely to have been beaten and abused by their parents.

Rescuers were more likely to have been raised by parents who themselves were models of caring and kindness.

This research helped heal Oliner. "He found the spark of decency in human beings," states Rabbi Harold Schulweis, a close friend. Oliner now is a man of 60 who has made peace with his past and maintains optimism and hope about his future. He says, "The notion that we are each other's keeper is gaining. Maybe we've reached a point where another Holocaust is unimaginable." After pausing, he adds, "It's because of the people who cared that I'm here. There are such people in the world—and we can teach our children to be like them."

Source: Hunt (1990a; 1990b); Oliner (1986); Oliner & Oliner (1988)

As mentioned earlier, egoistic altruism—self-fulfillment through enhancing the well-being of others—has one other virtue: It leads to self-transcendence. It takes us outside ourselves and our own problems. Focusing on how we can contribute to the well-being of others is one of the best ways to prevent and cope with our own distress (Ornstein & Sobel, 1989). Working together, individuals can make a difference in improving the social conditions out of which widespread distress arises. We will next examine some of the social approaches needed to minimize unnecessary distress.

LOOKING AHEAD

The Best of Times and the Worst of Times

We live in the best of times and the worst of times. Through technology, we are able to leave behind most of the struggles of daily existence that in the past burdened humankind. We are gifted with options. We are not bound by space, by the vagaries of climate, or by the rampages of pestilence. We have no apparent limits to what we can discover and do.

Yet technology has brought unintended traps—too much change in too short a time, an ever-faster pace of daily life, a never-ending quest for material goods, loss of anchorages, uprootedness, transience, isolation, and neglect of our bodies. Most of all, technology has brought something entirely new to human history: humankind's ability to destroy civilization, indeed life itself on this planet, if not through planetary pollution then by nuclear catastrophe.

What have changed more slowly are our ideas about how to adapt our way of life to technology. Sociologists refer to this as **cultural lag.** One result has been the rise of new types of distress—the distresses and diseases of "civilization." Relationships are strained; families break up more quickly and more often. Chronic fatigue has become an epidemic in American life.

Yet we have reason for optimism, certainly at the personal level and, perhaps, collectively. The medical and behavioral sciences have made great strides in providing guidelines on how we can face the inevitable, incessant stressors of daily life, yet survive—even thrive.

George Sheehan (1978), the late cardiologist who ran and wrote, stated that we live in a society where the body is a second-class citizen. He correctly maintains that, first of all, we need to be "good animals." What is needed is to treat your body as a first-class citizen, providing the basis for emotional and spiritual health, satisfying relationships, and a productive life.

Wellness and Environmentalism

We usually think of wellness as an individual thing—healthy personal habits for enhancing quality and length of life. **Environmentalism** typically is seen as a social movement focusing on the earth and its precious resources.

A legacy of Earth Day is recognition that wellness and environmentalism overlap. Wellness is the process of promoting environmental as well as personal health. You read in Chapter 3 that environmental wellness habits are included in a whole-person wellness lifestyle.

Personal wellness cannot flourish in a polluted natural environment or on a globe headed toward depletion of nonrenewable resources.

In short, a wellness lifestyle at once benefits the self and the environment.

For example, the U.S. Department of Energy reminds us that the average family can save $70 to $100 per year through energy-conscious driving and good car maintenance—while saving energy and contributing to clean air.

Below are several specific tips for practicing conservation on the roads, as suggested by the Department of Energy.

1. Use public transportation, try biking, or walk if you can.
2. Share your ride.
3. Eliminate unnecessary trips.
4. Vacation at home or nearby this year.
5. Travel by train or bus instead of by car.
6. Rediscover the pleasures of walking and biking during your vacation.
7. Observe speed limits.
8. When driving, accelerate smoothly and moderately, drive at a steady pace, and minimize braking.

Wellness means caring about the earth as well as your own mind-body. Energy-saving habits on the road are one practical way to unite wellness and environmentalism in your own life. Think about it.

Managing Stress in a Challenging World

This book has set forth a framework for understanding stress and its effects, positive and harmful. Within this framework, we have examined a wide variety of specific techniques for monitoring and managing stress. These stress-management methods have been presented within several categories:

- Monitoring early warning signs of distress (Chapter 6)
- Practicing constructive coping responses in dealing with challenging stressors and with your own temporary distress (Chapter 12)
- Managing your perspectives and interpretations of stressful events (Chapter 14)
- Maintaining good health buffers—exercise, nutrition, sleep, and healthy pleasures (Chapter 13)
- Using effective relaxation methods, including on-the-spot tension reducers and deep relaxation methods (Chapter 15)

Quality Living

To live content with small means,
to seek elegance rather than luxury,
and refinement rather than fashion;
to be worthy, not respectable,
and wealthy not rich;
to listen to stars and birds, babes and sages
with open heart;
to study hard;
to think quietly, act frankly, talk gently,
await occasions, hurry never;
in a word, to let the spiritual,
unbidden and unconscious,
grow up through the common—
this is my symphony.
—*William Henry Channing*

Source: Channing (1989, 48)

- Applying effective steps for pacing and balancing time, for making transitions, and for dealing with change (Chapters 11 and 16)
- Using effective communication skills to relate effectively with others around you and participate in caring networks of social support (Chapter 17)
- Properly balancing self-care with social commitment in order to help modify the social context of personal stress and to contribute to the well-being of others (Chapter 18)

In Chapter 1 we identified several assumptions that need to guide your quest for effective stress-management approaches that will work for you over the long run:

Personal responsibility	Balance	Action
Holism	Rhythm	Experiment-of-one
Gradualism	Awareness	Lifelong process

Perhaps most important of all personal qualities for implementing suggestions in this textbook is a strong sense of internal control. As noted previously, the opposite of internal control is helplessness—the sense that one's life is controlled entirely by external forces, by one's inner drives or needs, by fate, or simply by inertia.

The best path to confidence for turning adversity into challenges is the belief that you can make things happen, that you control your own destiny.

In his excellent book, *Control Theory,* William Glasser puts it succinctly.

If I believe that the motivation for all I do, good or bad, comes from within me, not from the outside world, then, when I am miserable, I cannot claim that my misery is caused by uncaring parents, a boorish spouse, an ungrateful child, or a miserable job. If I were a machine, this claim might be valid. I could be programmed to "feel good" only if those I "needed" treated me well. But I am not a machine, and although I strongly desire good treatment from everyone in my life, if I don't get what I want, it is my choice whether or not to be miserable. (1984, 2)

Glasser is correct in noting that it is totally warranted sometimes to be discontented with present circumstances. We referred to this in Chapter 5 as positive anger or indignation. It is our dissatisfaction that motivates us to improve reality within or around us. Dissatisfaction with aspects of work, with community growth patterns, or with national medical-care policies will motivate you to take constructive, corrective action as an employee or citizen. Dissatisfaction does not always feel good. Yet it is vital to improving our existence.

You read about hardiness as a cluster of attitudes and beliefs—including internal control—that can help you survive, even thrive under the pressure of change and adversity. Hardiness will enable you to become involved in making the world a better place, as well as to enjoy it more and stay healthy. Using hardiness to leave this planet in better shape for your children means attending to the social context of stress, as well as to your personal existence.

You have read that there is an upside to stress as well as a downside. Managed effectively, stress can be turned into a positive force to help you reach your highest possible level of well-being and performance.

Stress Management for What?

The primary goal of stress management is *wellness—living at one's highest possible level as a whole person and promoting the same in others.* We noted that wellness, or optimal well-being, includes:

- Absence of illness
- Low illness risk
- Maximum energy for daily living
- Enjoyment of daily life
- Continuous development of one's abilities
- Commitment to the common good

Stated differently, wellness takes you beyond normal health to a higher plane. The effect of wellness is to maximize your potentials while enjoying the process and maintaining optimal health along the way.

You read that wellness is attained through positive habits in the following areas:

Environmental
Intellectual
Emotional
Spiritual
Physical
Social
Time

A Guiding Philosophy

See Application Exercise 18-3 to write about your reactions to the guiding philosophy proposed here.

We have ended the book by noting that a continuing challenge is not only to maximize personal wellness but to balance self-care with social responsibility. In closing, I want to share my own four-part philosophy that provides the guidance and coherence I need to balance self-care with my desire to make a difference. I invite you to consider this for yourself.

1. Continually have visions and dreams, some of which have social significance—that will benefit others.

2. Work hard, at least partly with others, to bring these dreams and visions to reality.
3. Balance that hard work with play, care of body and spirit, intimacy, friendship, and healthy pleasures.
4. Enjoy the process.

I wish you well.

References

Andrews, H. F. (1990). Helping and health. *Advances: The Journal for Mind-Body Health, 7,* 25–34.

Babbie, E. (1985). *You can make a difference.* Anaheim Hills, CA: Opening Books.

Bowman, L. (1999). Volunteering may be good for health. *Chico Enterprise-Record,* March 19, 1B.

Broder, D. (1997). Poll: Distrust of government, but support for commonwealth. *Sacramento Bee,* December 17, B7.

Castleman, M. (1990). How the stress experts deal with theirs. *Medical Self-Care, 56,* 35–40.

Channing, W. H. (1989). Unnamed poem. *Noetic Sciences Review, 13,* 48.

Childs. C. (1997. Deep seeing: Guiding activism through grace. *Noetic Sciences Review, 42,* 18–25.

Cotter, D., Ender, J. G., Gindoff, P., & Kowalewski, B. (1995). Integrating community service into introductory college courses. *Journal of College Student Development, 36,* 87.

Etzioni, A. (1993). *The spirit of community: Rights, responsibilities, and the communitarian agenda.* New York: Crown Publishers.

Flacks, R., & Thomas, S. L. (1998). Among affluent students, a culture of disengagement. *The Chronicle of Higher Education,* November 27, A48.

Greene, R. (1998). Political interest hits new low among freshmen, survey says. *Chico Enterprise-Record,* January 12, 3A.

Glasser, W. (1984). Control theory. New York: Harper & Row.

Glover, J. (1997). How to be rich. *Noetic Sciences Review, 42,* 6.

Hayward, B. (1998). College freshmen show conservative side. *Sacramento Bee,* January 12, A4.

Hunt, M. (1990a). Can goodness be taught? *Parade Magazine,* May 6, 28–29.

Hunt, M. (1990b). *The compassionate beast: What science is discovering about the humane side of humankind.* New York: William Morrow.

Hurley, T. J. (1990). Reflections. *Noetic Sciences Review, 16,* 33.

Kohn, A. (1990). *The brighter side of human nature: Altruism and empathy in everyday life.* New York: Basic Books.

Luks, A. (1988). Helper's high. *Psychology Today, 22,* 39–42.

Miller, J. (1990). Hello, this is Jimmy Carter. *Noetic Sciences Review, 16,* 32.

Mills, C. W. (1956). *The power elite.* New York: Oxford University Press.

Musick, M., House, J. A., & Herzog, R. (1999). Volunteering and health. *Journal of Gerontology: Social Sciences, 54B,* 5173–5177.

Neal, M. (1994). Polio conquered in Western Hemisphere. *The Rotarian, 165:*6, December, 18–21.

Oliner, S. (1986). *Restless memories: Recollections of the Holocaust years.* Berkeley: Judah Magnes Press.

Oliner, S., & Oliner, P. (1988). *The altruistic personality: Rescuers of Jews in Nazi Europe.* New York: Free Press.

Ornstein, R., & Sobel, D. (1989). *Healthy pleasures.* Reading, MA: Addison-Wesley.

Pelletier, K. R. (1994). *Sound mind, sound body.* New York: Simon & Schuster.

Putnam, R. D. (1995). Bowling alone, revisited. *The Responsive Community, 5,* 18–33.

Ray, P. H. (1989). Altruism as value-centered action. *Noetic Sciences Review, 12,* 10–14.

Selye, H. (1974). *Stress without distress.* Philadelphia: Lippincott.

Selye, H. (1976). *The stress of life* (rev. ed.). New York: McGraw-Hill.

Sheehan, G. (1978). *Running and being.* New York: Simon & Schuster.

Simkinson, C. H. (1990). Compassionate living: Can we integrate healthy narcissism and social responsibility? *Common Boundary, 8,* 7–9.

Sirotkin, E. (1997). A word for "Self-through-communion." *Noetic Sciences Review, 42,* 7.

Winniford, J. C., Carpenter, D. S., & Grider, C. (1995). An analysis of the traits and motivations of college students involved in service organizations. *Journal of College Student Development, 36,* 27–38.

Application Exercise 18-1

Your Heroes

1. Identify one or two people in your experience who truly stand out for their kindness or service to others.

2. What differences have they made or are they now making for others around them?

3. Describe their qualities you most admire.

4. What can you learn from these individuals' lives that can help you achieve a desirable balance between personal wellness and social commitment?

Application Exercise 18-2

Committing to an Act of Social Responsibility

This exercise is intended to encourage you to tackle a manageable local social problem. By social problem, I mean any problem outside yourself that involves others well-being. Make a commitment to work on it for at least a period of days or weeks. Afterward, complete the following.

1.   Identify and describe the social problem.

2.   Describe what you did.

3.   Describe the reactions of others who saw you doing it.

4.   Describe your own reactions to the experience.

Application Exercise 18-3

Your Reactions to the Guiding Philosophy for Blending Personal Wellness and Social Commitment

1. What is your personal opinion about the guiding philosophy proposed here? With what do you agree and disagree?

2. How might you modify this guiding philosophy, if at all, to make it more attractive to you?

3. What outcomes might occur if more people followed this philosophy—outcomes at the individual and social levels?

Glossary

AAAABBCC   A framework of coping options including awfulizing about the stressor, altering the stressor, avoiding the stressor, or avoiding the stressor by breathing away tension, building health buffers, changing your interpretation of the stressor, or communicating differently.

ABC-Technique   A time-management technique of designating tasks into high, medium, and low priority.

Absence of Free-Floating Hostility   A Type B characteristic, this refers to a generally trusting attitude toward others and the relative absence of the chronic hostility of the Type A person.

Absence of Time Urgency   A Type B characteristic, this refers to the tendency to be free of chronic hurry, hassle, and urgency with time.

Action   What you do as you manage stress—how you spend your time, the actions you take as you cope, your daily behavior in relation to others and to tasks. The complement to awareness.

Active Listening   An active process of being attentive, taking in information and feelings accurately and completely, and rephrasing what you have heard to check its accuracy.

Adapt to the Stressor   A constructive coping method involving accepting the stressor while using one or more constructive steps to prevent distress.

Adaptation to Stress   Two meanings: Becoming accustomed to progressively more demanding stressors. Becoming accustomed to progressively higher stress levels.

Adaptive Coping   Dealing with stressors in ways that minimize distress for self and others.

Adaptive Reactions to Distress   Reactions that reduce rather than increase one's distress in the long run.

Addiction-Prone Pattern   The addiction-prone pattern is an enduring, compulsive need for a substance or behavior.

Adrenal Cortex   The outer part of the adrenal gland which, in response to ACTH, produces corticoids.

Adrenal Medulla   The inner part of the adrenal gland which, in response to the sympathetic nervous system, produces adrenaline (epinephrine) and noradrenaline (norepinephrine).

Adreno-Corticotropic Hormone (ACTH)   A stress hormone produced by the pituitary gland. Triggers the adrenal cortex during the stress response.

Aerobic Exercise   Physical movement involving sustained elevation of heart rate. To be effective in producing the aerobic training effect, a person must elevate heart rate to 60 percent to 90 percent of maximum heart rate for at least 20 or 30 minutes per session at least three times per week. Illustrated by brisk walking, running, swimming, bicycling, and aerobic dance.

Aerobic Training Effect   The body's adaptation to repeated aerobic exercise. Includes improved ability to take in oxygen (respiration), transport oxygen to the muscles (circulation), and burn oxygen (metabolism).

Affective Learning   Learning about emotions, relationships, and stress.

Afterburn Time   The time needed after an event to complete it behaviorally and emotionally before moving on to the next activity.

Aggressive   A style of relating that includes being hostile, insensitive, angry, or abusive.

AIAI   Anger, irritability, aggravation, and impatience. Central components of Type A behavior.

Alarm Reaction   The first stage of Hans Selye's general adaptation syndrome in which the body is immediately prepared for direct, decisive physical action, largely through activation of the sympathetic nervous system response. During the first part of this phase, the body falls below normal stress level.

Alcohol Abuse   Repeated use of alcohol in physically hazardous situations or continued use in the face of knowledge that doing so worsens a personal problem.

Alcohol Dependence   Presence of symptoms of alcohol abuse, along with the additional symptoms of tolerance and withdrawal.

Alienation   A sense of estrangement or detachment which can take these forms: powerlessness, meaninglessness, self-estrangement, isolation, or normlessness.

Alter the Stressor   A constructive coping method in which efforts are made to change the stressor in order to reduce or prevent future distress.

Altruism   Unselfish concern for the well-being of others.

Altruistic Egoism   Hans Selye's term for doing things others will appreciate and for which they will return their gratitude. Earning others' love.

Anaerobic Exercise   Physical activity in which the body uses more oxygen than is replenished, taking the body into temporary oxygen debt.

Anger   Negative anger is a feeling, expressed or unexpressed, of hostility, aggressiveness, or a desire to hurt. Wanting to punish the source of frustration. Positive anger is the motivation to change or correct the source of frustration. Both are based on wanting something, not getting it, and being frustrated.

Anger as Secondary Emotion   Anger is usually a response to some other emotion such as hurt, rejection, humiliation, self-doubt, or guilt that we keep hidden.

Anorexia Nervosa   An eating disorder involving refusal to maintain minimal normal body weight over time, combined with an intense fear of weight gain or looking fat, and a distorted body image.

Anticipatory Stress   Arousal created by thinking about a forthcoming event or challenge. May be helpful or harmful.

Anxiety   Mental and physical arousal in anticipation of perceived negative future experience. Usually includes fear and tension. May be chronic or acute.

Apathy   Lack of emotion, concern, or interest.

Appraisal   In the context of self-talk, refers to interpretation or assessment of a stressor. In relation to social support, this refers to information relative to self-evaluation.

Arrhythmia   A disturbance in the electrical rhythm of the heart.

Assertive   Communicating in a manner that does not offend or hurt others, yet includes strong statements or actions by the individual to express what he/she wants.

Atherosclerosis   Progressive buildup of plaque on the interior walls of the coronary arteries resulting in reduction of blood flow to the heart muscle.

Autogenic Relaxation   A relaxation technique based on repeated thoughts of warmth and heaviness in specific parts of the body.

Autonomic Nervous System   The peripheral nervous system of the body that sends electrical messages of arousal (sympathetic nervous system) or quieting (parasympathetic nervous system) to muscles, glands, and organs.

Avoid the Stressor   A constructive coping method in which efforts are made to avoid or withdraw from the stressor.

Awareness   Understanding stress and related ideas—and their on-going reality in your daily life. Important as beginning step in effective stress management.

Awfulizing   Turning a difficult situation into something awful, terrible, or intolerable.

Balance   A guideline for managing stress involving effectively balancing such things as rest and activity, risk and safety, change and stability, thought and action.

Banal Life Script   A blueprint for living calling for a life of unhappiness, failure, pity, half-effort, depression, boredom, illness, or loneliness.

Baseline Stress Level   Hour-after-hour arousal level when the person is neither pressed nor experiencing deep relaxation or sleep.

Behavioral Distress Symptoms   Symptoms of distress reflected in one's actions. Illustrations include irritability, withdrawal, attacking someone, or difficulty sitting still.

Being Right   Believing that it is intolerable to be seen as wrong and that one's beliefs or opinions are always right. A negative style of self-talk.

Belief   An enduring assumption.

Benson Method of Relaxation   A type of meditation involving sitting comfortably in a quiet place, relaxing muscles, and then repeating "one" for 10 to 20 minutes once or twice per day.

Big Circle   An active relaxation technique involving large trunk rotations from the waist.

Biofeedback   Use of any device to detect internal physiological processes. Learning to relax by controlling this feedback.

Biphasic Traits   The tendency of the survivor personality to display counterbalanced, seemingly paradoxical traits. This type of person tends to be at various times playful and serious, trusting and cautious, intuitive and logical, impulsive and stable, gentle and strong, easygoing and strong willed, childlike and mature.

Blaming   Attributing responsibility for events, especially negative ones, to someone else, even when such responsibility rightfully belongs to the self.

Blaming the Victim   Unjustifiably placing responsibility on victims for adversity that is caused by factors outside the victim.

Blocked Energy   Energy that is underutilized or stopped by cognitive or emotional causes.

Boredom   Being uninterested, unmotivated, and listless. Ennui.

Bound Energy   Physical tension from unexpressed or unresolved arousal.

Bracing   Chronic muscle tension resulting from prolonged or repeated elicitation of the stress response.

Breathing Away Tension   A relaxation technique in which you imagine tension, upset, or pain leaving your body with each exhalation.

Breathing Countdown   A method of eliciting the relaxation response by counting from 10 backward for 10 to 20 minutes.

Breathing Slowly for Calming Effect   A method of eliciting the relaxation response involving deliberately slowing one's breathing.

Buffering Effects of Social Support   Social support softens the impact of potentially stressful events on mental and/or physical health. Social support serves as a buffer between difficult life experiences and health outcomes.

Bulimia Nervosa   An eating disorder involving a repeated pattern of binging and purging.

Burnout   A condition of mental and physical exhaustion resulting from overstimulation, meaningless, or hopelessness.

C Zone   The zone of positive stress in which the person reaches peak performance. Sometimes known among athletes and other performers as "flow."

Calmness   Mental and physical quiet. One of the 10 C's for thriving under pressure.

Cancer   A life-threatening disease in which cells reproduce uncontrollably.

Cardiovascular Disorders   A category of illnesses involving the heart and/or blood vessels.

Career Choice   One of the developmental tasks and stressors facing college students and other young adults

Career Inopportunity   Lack of opportunity for job advancement.

Career Insecurity   Lack of assurance of continuation of one's job.

Care-Taking   Part of the codependency pattern, this is the tendency to be attracted to needy people, to feel responsible for others' well-being, feelings, wants, and needs, and to feel compelled to help the needy person (usually an addict of one type or another) solve the problem, whether this means fixing feelings, giving advice (even if unwanted), or ignoring one's own needs or desires.

Caring   Giving and receiving social support. One of the 10 C's for thriving under pressure.

Carter Ethic   The commitment of Jimmy and Rosalynn Carter to continually contributing to the well-being of the world through altruistic actions.

Catastrophizing   Expecting that the worst almost certainly will happen. Worrying about perceived impending catastrophe.

Catecholamines   Hormones produced by the adrenal medulla, including adrenaline and noradrenaline (epinephrine and norepinephrine).

Causes of Death   Factors precipitating termination of life.

Centering   Listening to your inner voice of wisdom. Being centered is knowing what you need, want, or believe.

Central Nervous System   The brain and the spinal cord.

Cerebral Cortex   The outer layer of the brain where most thinking occurs.

Challenge   Objective challenge refers to a difficult situation or event. Subjective challenge (a component of hardiness) refers to seeing a change or difficulty as a positive opportunity rather than as a threat.

Cholesterol   A waxy-type lipid used in construction of cell walls and certain hormones. Excessive amounts in the bloodstream contribute to coronary heart disease.

Chronic Stressors   Stressors that are ubiquitous or recurrent.

Chronic Time Urgency   A perpetual sense of hurry and hassle. A common affliction of Americans, especially Type A's.

Circling Shoulders   Rotating the shoulders in a circular fashion to reduce muscle tension.

Clustering of Life Events   Occurrence of many unusual life experiences within a relatively few days, weeks, or months.

Codependency Pattern   Addiction to other people and their problems.

Cognitive Distress Symptoms   Disturbed thinking associated with the chronic or acute excitation of the stress response. Illustrated by difficulty in concentrating, forgetfulness, mental block, and disorganized reasoning.

Commitment   Being positively motivated toward and involved in your daily life (for example, school work, or community groups). A component of hardiness. Opposite is alienation.

Commitment to the Common Good   Individual concern for the well-being of a larger group, community, or society.

Common Stress Difficulties   Problems associated with zones of overload and underload distress.

Competence Under Pressure   The ability of the survivor personality and others to turn adversity and pressure into a positive challenge and to perform very well under this pressure.

Comprehensibility   Part of the sense of coherence, this refers to the person's belief in the degree to which events can be understood or comprehended.

Computing   Being very correct, very reasonable with no semblance of feeling; acting calm, cool, and collected.

Concentration   In relation to time management, refers to working from prioritized lists and doing one thing at a time. In relation to listening, refers to focusing attention on what speaker is saying. In relation to peak performance, refers to focusing attention and energy on accomplishing a task or goal.

Conditioning   One of the 10 C's of thriving under pressure, this refers to physical fitness.

Confidence   Belief in one's ability to master a task or difficulty. A component of hardiness. Opposite is self-doubt.

Conscious Interpretation Pathway   Conscious appraisal of the nature and degree of threat from stressors.

Constructive Maladjustment   Being appropriately discontented about conditions in the surrounding social, political, or natural environment that in the judgment of the person are wrong and need to be changed—and being motivated to change those conditions.

Context of Stress   The larger physical and social environment within which stressors and personal stress occur.

Control   Part of hardiness, this refers to the belief that one can control events and one's reactions to events.

Control Fallacy   The belief that happiness depends on cajoling or coercing others to do what you think they should.

Controlling   The tendency of the codependent, having lived through traumatic events herself that have led to sorrow and disappointment, to compulsively need to keep things under control now. The tendency to control people and events through guilt, coercion, threats, manipulation, helplessness—or whatever else will work.

Coping   Constantly changing cognitive and behavioral efforts to manage specific external and/or internal demands that are appraised as taxing or exceeding the resources of the person.

Coping Constraints   Internal and external factors that impede utilization of coping resources.

Coping Options   A range of potential actions available when dealing with stressors or distressors.

Coping Resources   Internal and external resources that are potentially available to the person in coping with stressors.

Coping-Plus   Methods for not only surviving but thriving under pressure.

Coronary Artery Disease   Partial or complete blockage of one or more coronary arteries with plaque.

Coronary Plaque   A substance consisting of cholesterol, fat, muscle tissue, and other elements that develop along the interior walls of coronary arteries.

Correcting   A habit of poor listening in which the listener lies in wait for factual errors, then pounces on the speaker with the correct facts.

Corticoids   Stress-related hormones preparing the body for direct, immediate, physical action. Produced by the adrenal cortex.

Cost-Benefit Analysis   A time management technique in which you make a list of all the good things that will happen if you stop procrastinating on an important task and review the list regularly, and then list all the miserable results of your procrastination and review that list each night before bed.

Costs of Social Ties   Intended or unintended personal negative effects of one or more social relationships.

Creativity   The tendency of survivor personalities to be inventive in finding solutions to problems and adversities. This results from not being limited by fear of ridicule. The tendency to think spontaneously as the need arises.

Criteria for Effective New Self-Talk   New self-talk is likely to be effective to the degree it is personal, positive, present-tense, practical, and brief.

Criteria for Rational Beliefs   Standards for assessing whether a belief is rational or irrational. To be rational, a belief must be factual, moderate, and helpful.

Critical Judge   A distress-prone personality pattern in which a small inner voice repeatedly tells you what an incompetent person you are and what a stupid thing that was you just said. Continually undermines confidence and self-worth by bombarding you with self-criticism.

Criticizing   Rather than listening attentively, passing silent judgment on the speaker while he or she is talking.

Cultural Lag   When one element in society lags behind in adjusting to change in another element.

Cultural Relativity of Time   The varying interpretations, meanings, and ways to organize time in different cultural settings.

Culture of Wellness   Those features of a group or organization that encourage, reward, and support wellness choices.

Current Stress   Arousal occurring during an event. May be helpful or harmful.

Cynicism   A pervasive negative view of others as untrustworthy, selfish, and not to be trusted.

Daily Hassle Index   A questionnaire that measures irritability.

Daily Hassles   Minor, recurrent, daily events that are experienced as minor distressors.

Daily Uplifts   Minor but meaningful daily positive experiences.

Deep Adaptive Energy   The body's deep chemical and energy reserves that can be depleted by major or recurrent experiences of distress.

Deep Relaxation   Mental and physical relaxation in which metabolism goes below baseline during a relaxation exercise.

Defensivenes   Responding to negative feedback or criticism with efforts to protect your image or opinion.

Deliberate Reactions to Distress   Reactions to your distress that are not scripted by parents but are based on awareness and choice.

Demand-Side Approach to Health Care Reform   Improving the health of population in order to reduce the demand for medical care services.

Denial   Not recognizing or accepting your distress symptoms or life situation. Also a stage in the grieving process following death of a loved one or in anticipation of one's own death.

Dependency   The tendency of the codependent, feeling quite unhappy and discontent, to look for happiness outside herself, most often in the form of desperately seeking love and approval. Feeling very threatened by the loss of anything or anyone she thinks provides her happiness.

Depressants   Drugs such as tranquilizers, alcohol, and barbiturates used to relieve tension. May be prescribed or consumed illegally.

Depression   A multi-faceted experience of lowered energy and motivation, flattened affect, loss of sleep and appetite, and other symptoms.

Deprivational Stress   Stress resulting from understimulation as in sensory deprivation.

Desensitization   A technique for overcoming phobias and fears. Involves progressive exposure to a distressor (such as flying) through such steps as imagery, role playing, and brief practice.

Destructive Coping Response   A response to stressors that contributes to distress for self or others.

Developmental Tasks   Predictable and patterned personal growth challenges facing college students and others entering adulthood.

Diaphragmatic Breathing   Deliberate use of the diaphragm to slow breathing and to elicit the relaxation response.

Diastolic Blood Pressure   The amount of pressure against the walls of blood vessels between heart beats.

Difficult Role Relationships   Troubled or challenging relationships with role partners in such settings as work or family.

Direct Action   A constructive coping approach involving taking direct measures to change a stressor.

Direct Effects of Social Support   The direct impact of social support on mental and/or physical health.

Discounting   Not taking seriously what another person says and putting the speaker down.

Diseases of Civilization   Diseases caused in part by contemporary lifestyle habits such as smoking, high-fat diet, sedentary living, and stress.

Disharmony   When distressed, the sense of dissonance or conflict among wants or needs within the person or between the person's inner wants and needs and outside circumstances.

Disputation   A technique for challenging unreasonable beliefs or negative self-talk.

Distortants   Drugs such as LSD and mescaline that distort perception of reality.

Distracting   Doing or saying whatever is irrelevant to what others are doing or saying; not responding to the point.

Distress   Too much or too little arousal resulting in harm to mind or body.

Distress-Avoiding   Thriving on health, contentment, and involvement. Doing all possible to avoid and reduce personal distress.

Distressor   Any demand resulting in harm to mind or body.

Distress-Preventing Social Influences   Social circumstances and forces that minimize risk of distress among people in those settings.

Distress-Prone Conditions in the Workplace   Social or physical work conditions that tend to produce a high rate of distress among workers.

Distress-Prone Personality Pattern   Enduring habits of thinking, feeling, and acting that result in a pattern of personal distress.

Distress-Prone Social Influences   Social circumstances and forces that contribute to distress among people in those settings.

Distress-Provoking   Thriving intentionally or unintentionally on creating misery, disharmony, illness, or upset for others.

Distress-Reducing   Thriving on doing all possible to promote health, happiness, and growth in others.

Distress-Seeking   Thriving on challenge, risk and sensation.

Dominating   Waiting your turn to talk, gathering your thoughts together, then cutting the speaker short. A habit of poor listening.

Double-Whammy Transitions   Two major simultaneous transitions.

Drive to Self-Destruction   The tendency of Type A persons to behave in ways that seem justified at the time but that undermine one's long-term self-interest and well-being.

Drone Zone   Part of the Type C framework. This refers to the zone of underload distress associated with boredom, understimulation, or too little challenge.

EEG   Electrical encephalograph. A tool for measuring brain waves, sometimes used in biofeedback.

Egoistic Altruism   Self-fulfillment through contributing to the well-being of others.

Ego-Speak   Talking about oneself excessively and inappropriately.

Elected Transitions   Transitions brought about by deliberate choice.

EMG   Electromyograph. A tool for measuring muscle activity, sometimes used in biofeedback.

Emotional Concern   One type of interpersonal transaction in relationships of social support. Refers to liking, loving, or empathy.

Emotional Distress Symptoms   Symptoms of distress reflected in emotions or feelings. Illustrated by depression, hopelessness, anxiety, fear, and joylessness.

Emotional Wellness Habits   Awareness of one's emotions at any given time; the ability to maintain a relatively even emotional state with moderate emotional responses to the flow of life events; the ability to maintain relative control over emotional states; and the ability to experience a preponderance of positive over negative emotional states.

Emotion-Focused Coping   A coping approach in which individuals focus on dealing with their own fears, anger, guilt, or other emotions, rather than on the stressful situation.

Endocrine System   The network of glands that secrete hormones directly into the bloodstream.

Energy   The individual's perception at any given moment of his or her potential for action. One's sense of what you could do if you chose to.

Energy Qualities   Variations in personal energy along four dimensions: natural versus nervous, satisfying versus unsatisfying, helpful versus harmful, directed versus wasted.

Energy Rhythm   The pattern of stability or variability in a person's energy level throughout a day, week, or longer period.

Environmental Wellness Habits   Awareness of the precarious state of the global environment and of the effects of one's daily habits on the physical environment; maintaining a way of life that minimizes harm to the environment; and being involved in socially responsible activities to protect the environment.

Environmentalism   A social movement focusing on preserving and protecting the earth and its resources.

Epinephrine   See *Adrenaline.*

Episodic Stressor   A stressor that occurs irregularly or only once.

Escapism   A destructive reaction to distress in which you escape the situation or deny your feelings of disharmony by immersing yourself into television, books, fantasy, drugs, or flight. Not the same as temporary, constructive withdrawal.

Eustress   Helpful arousal. Same as positive stress.

Experience Continuum   A chart developed by Hans Selye showing that stress can increase with either increases or decreases in stimulation.

Experiment-of-One   Discovering through trial and error which stress management techniques work best for you.

Explanatory Style   Pattern of interpreting positive and negative events. The three dimensions of explanatory style are

personalization, permanence, and pervasiveness. Part of learned optimism and learned pessimism.

External Perfectionism Impossibly demanding expectations of others.

Face Loosener A passive method of deliberately concentrating on allowing facial muscles to loosen.

Faking Putting on a good show of listening by nodding and giving verbal cues while not listening at all.

Fallacy of Fairness The belief that it is impossible to achieve any degree of personal happiness because of perceived unfairness in the world.

Familiar Stranger Someone you regularly see but do not know, such as a student in the same college classroom.

Faulty Interpretations Irrational or distorted interpretation of events.

Fear A feeling of fright, apprehension, or dread based on perceived threat or danger.

Fear of Failure Apprehension about failing based on the belief that to fail is to risk unacceptable rejection by others or severe damage to self-esteem.

Fear of Success Apprehension about achieving based on the belief that to succeed will result in escalation of others' future expectations beyond one's ability to perform.

FHB Fallible human being.

Fight-or-Flight Response A multi-faceted, genetically programmed response of the body preparing the person for immediate action in response to a perceived threat.

Financial Uncertainty A major stressor facing a growing number of college students.

F.I.T. Frequency, intensity, and time as applied to physical exercise. These are the criteria used to determine minimal standards of aerobic exercise.

Five Freedoms A term from Virginia Satir, refers to freedoms promoted by effective communication.

Five-Minute-Plan A time-management technique in which you take a task you've been procrastinating at and work a minimum of five minutes on it. Once you've finished five minutes, then you can set yourself another five minutes and then another.

Flexibility The ability to imagine complex or multiple solutions to problems and many sides to an issue.

Floppy Doll An active relaxation method in which the person stands and rotates the upper trunk with arms dangling and swinging at the side.

Flow of Experience The movement of experiences through a person's life.

Flow of Situations The movement of situations and events through a person's life.

Focus Attention on Breathing A method of eliciting the relaxation response by dwelling on one's breathing.

Food Guide Pyramid A model for communicating the recommended nutritional guidelines for Americans.

Food Scripting A blueprint for relating to food, usually developed in childhood through early messages and early decisions about food. A subtype of life script.

Foresight Perceiving and sometimes stopping an action or thought before it occurs, as in foreseeing and catching one's anger response when his or her public image is threatened.

Frustration A feeling of disappointment or irritation at being thwarted from one's goals or wants.

Future Shock Physical and mental distress from too much change in too short a time.

Game Interpersonal exchanges, usually with underlying or implicit messages, which people use to make themselves or others feel bad.

Gastrointestinal Disorders A category of illnesses of the intestinal track.

General Adaptation Syndrome Hans Selye's theoretical model of the body's response to sustained stress, which includes a sequence of three stages: alarm, resistance, and exhaustion.

Generalized Resistance Resources Any characteristic of the person, the group, or the environment that can facilitate effective tension management.

Geographic Mobility Moving from one place of residence to another.

Glucocorticoids A hormone released by the adrenal cortex that stimulates the liver to produce more blood sugar.

Grade Pressure Internal and/or external pressure to achieve highest possible grades.

Gradualism Incorporating new stress-management techniques into your life gradually and one or two at a time rather than precipitously or in larger clusters.

GSR Galvanic skin response, a biofeedback tool.

Guiding Philosophy One's principles for blending social commitment and personal wellness.

Hair-Trigger Stress Response Frequently and easily triggered defensiveness, hostility, or anger.

Hardiness Personal strength. As used by Maddi and Kobasa, includes challenge, commitment, and control.

Headache Disorders A category of illnesses involving pain in the head.

Head Roll Gently rotating your head from side to side and from front to back in a full circular motion. Repeating several times in opposite directions.

Health Buffers Health habits, especially related to exercise, nutrition, sleep, and healthy pleasures, that help build resistance against distress.

Healthy Pleasures Activities, usually during leisure time, that are at once healthy and pleasurable.

Heart Attack See *Myocardial Infarction.*

Helping Contributing to the well-being of others.

High Blood Pressure A higher than normal amount of pressure (repeated readings higher than 140/90) against the inner walls of arteries and capillaries. Also known as hypertension.

High Density Lipoprotein Protein substances in the blood that act as scavengers by picking up excess cholesterol from artery walls and transporting it back to the liver where it is converted into bile acid and discharged through the stool.

High-Level Wellness   A goal of stress management includes good health (absence of illness and maximum energy), life satisfaction, productivity, and self-development.

High Role Expectations—Low Control   High work demands combined with a low sense of personal control over how tasks are accomplished. This combination carries a high risk of work-related distress.

Hindsight   Becoming aware of or understanding an event or experience after it has occurred.

Holism   The assumption that since the human is a multi-dimensional being, a number of complementary approaches to managing stress are needed involving mind, body, and behavior.

Homeostasis   An equilibrium state of the body in which neuromuscular, cardiovascular, and chemical conditions are relatively constant.

Hostility   Cynicism toward others' motives and values, easily and frequently aroused anger, and a tendency to express that anger toward others.

Hot Reaction   A hyper-response of the cardiovascular system during the stress response.

Humor   The ability of the survivor personality and others to laugh at what has happened and to find something amusing even in the midst of difficult events.

Hurry Sickness   Being addicted to chronic time urgency.

Hydrotherapy   Relaxation through immersion in warm water as in a shower, hot tub, or flotation tank.

Hyperaggressiveness   Being thin-skinned and overly sensitive, resulting in frequently and easily aroused anger.

Hypermetabolic Stress Control   Active relaxation methods, such as aerobic exercise, in which metabolism is temporarily elevated.

Hypertension   See *High Blood Pressure.*

Hypnosis   A condition of very deep relaxation, induced by self or another person, in which the person is especially open to suggestion.

Hypometabolic Stress Control   Passive relaxation methods, such as meditation or autogenic relaxation, in which metabolism temporarily drops below normal.

Hypothalamus   Portion of the lower brain which, in response to perceived threat, sends a chemical message to the nearby pituitary gland to prepare for fight-or-flight.

Identity Formation   The process during childhood and adolescence of formulating answers to the questions, Who am I? Whom will I become?

"I Feel"-Messages   An assertive communication strategy in which the person begins the statement with "I" rather than "you."

Immune System   The body's surveillance system which guards against allergens, infection, cancer, viruses, and bacteria.

Immune System Disorders   A category of illnesses involving the body's surveillance system.

Immunocompetence   The body's ability to defend successfully against a microbial invader.

Implementing   One of the three main categories of time-management techniques.

Inappropriate Response to Stressors   Coping responses in which the person reacts to stimuli in inappropriate ways. Illustrated by rebellion, rescuing, or drinking.

Infectious Illnesses   A category of illnesses caused by microbes (bacteria and viruses).

Information   One element in any transaction of social support. Refers to knowledge about the social environment.

Information-Seeking   A constructive coping method in which the person seeks out as much information as possible in deciding how to respond to a stressful situation.

Inhibition of Action   Coping by controlling the urge to strike out at or harm the source of the distress.

Insecurity of Status   Personal feelings of low standing in others' eyes.

Insomnia   Difficulty sleeping. May refer to disturbed sleep onset or to interrupted sleep.

Instant Replay   A method for managing situational self-talk. Includes three steps: catching negative self-talk, challenging it, and changing it.

Instrumental Aid   One element in interpersonal transactions of social support. Refers to exchange of goods or services.

Instrumentalism   The belief that you make things happen and get things done, that outcomes depend on your own choices and actions.

Insulation   A time-management method involving screening and sorting incoming information and tasks one time each day for processing outgoing information.

Intellectual Distress   Disturbed thinking, such as difficulty organizing thoughts, forgetfulness, and mental block, associated with the stress response.

Intellectual Wellness Habits   The ability to engage in clear thinking and recall, with minimal interference from emotional baggage; to think independently and critically; to possess basic skills of reasoning, and to be open to new ideas. Also includes broadest and deepest possible knowledge of cultural heritage.

Internal Con Artist   A distress-prone personality pattern leading to self-defeating behavior such as procrastinating, taking reckless actions, and making impulsive decisions. All the while, these behaviors seem quite reasonable.

Internal Control   A sense of being able to influence events and one's reactions to events. Opposite is helplessness.

Internal Perfectionism   Impossibly demanding expectations toward self.

Internal Time Keeper   The distress-prone personality pattern in which the person feels compelled to do several things at once and to take on more obligations than time available.

Interpretation of Stressor   Thoughts, automatic or deliberate, about the nature of a stressor and its degree of threat.

Interrupting   Breaking in while another person is speaking. A poor listening habit.

Intersender Role Conflict   Incompatible expectations sent from two or more role partners.

Intrapsychic Efforts   Managing one's self-talk, interpretation, or internal dialogue as a means of coping.

Intrasender Role Conflict   Incompatible role expectations sent from a single role partner.

Intuition   The tendency of the survivor personality to sense subtle, even subliminal cues and clues. They are unusually sensitive to feelings and nuances and consider them valuable sources of information.

Irrational Beliefs About Time   Enduring assumptions about time that are distorted, extreme, and/or harmful.

Isolation   When used in the context of time management, refers to finding a place to work without interruption. When used in the context of social relationships more broadly, refers to being alone or without social ties. One form of alienation.

Isometric Arm Reliever   Briefly pushing or pulling each arm against an immovable object, then relaxing.

Jogging in Place   A method of relieving tension through brief elevation of muscular and cardiovascular activity.

Judging   In relation to active listening, refers to passing judgment on the speaker's statement rather than remaining neutral.

Judging Total Human Worth   Evaluating total worth of self or others on the basis of traits or behavior.

Knockout Technique   A time-management technique in which you take the attitude that the harder and more distasteful a task is, the more quickly it should be done: so do it *immediately.*

Labile Hypertension   Blood pressure that is unstable and temporarily high.

Lack of Trust   The tendency of the codependent to lose trust in others over time—except for untrustworthy people.

Lead Time   Time needed to prepare for an event.

Learned Helplessness   A learned tendency to give up prematurely.

Learned Optimism   A basic belief in the viability of the future, in the likelihood that things will turn out well. The tendency to interpret good events as permanent, personal, and pervasive, and to interpret bad events as temporary, external, and specific.

Learned Pessimism   The tendency to interpret bad events as personally caused, part of a permanent pattern and pervasive into all parts of one's life; and the tendency to interpret positive events as caused by luck or external forces, temporary and limited to this one instance.

Leg Loosener   A passive method of deliberately concentrating on allowing leg muscles to loosen.

Lifelong Process   Managing stress is a continuing challenge throughout one's life, rather than something you do once and then forget.

Life-On-Hold Transitions   Transitions in which decisions are delayed or postponed. Transitions waiting to happen.

Life Script   A blueprint for living, usually developed during childhood as a result of early messages from significant others and early decisions by self.

Lifestyle Change   A change in one or more major lifestyle habits.

Lifestyle Diseases   See *Diseases of Civilization.*

Lifestyle Trap   An overloaded lifestyle filled with obligations that were easily made but difficult to leave.

Limbic System   The midlayer of the brain in which emotions are created.

Loss of Community   The disappearance of social connectedness and community consciousness that often accompanies rapid social change.

Loss of Social Attachment   Reduction of social ties that often accompanies geographic mobility and rapid social change.

Love and Sex   A category of stressors and developmental tasks facing college students and other young adults.

Low Density Lipoprotein   Protein substances in the bloodstream that, among other things, transport cholesterol from the liver to be deposited along the inner walls of the arteries and elsewhere in the body.

Low Self-Worth   The codependent's tendency to blame herself for everything and to put herself down for how she thinks, feels, or behaves. She feels she is not quite good enough, takes things personally, and yet fends off compliments or praise.

Macro-Stressor   A stressor experienced as major in nature, resulting in an intense stress response. May be a positive or negative stressor.

Magnifying   Making more of an event than it actually is. Also known as making mountains out of molehills.

Maintaining Balance   Sustaining a satisfying and healthy balance among valued activity sectors of a person's life. A continuing challenge of time management.

Maladaptive Coping   Coping methods that fail to prevent distress or that make distress worse for self and/or others.

Maladaptive Reactions to Distress   Reactions to personal distress that increase distress for self or others in the long-run if not immediately.

Manageability   Part of the sense of coherence, this refers to the person's belief in the degree to which events can be effectively managed.

Marker Event   A significant, predictable event in the life cycle, such as graduating from high school, marrying, or starting one's first full-time job.

Martyrdom   Seeking out misery, usually because of the repetition compulsion. Common among distress seekers.

Massage   A relaxation technique in which one person uses touch to loosen muscle, joint, or connective tissue tightness in another person.

Maxi-Fight-or-Flight Response   Major arousal of the stress response during an intense, temporary stressor.

Meaning and Purpose   One's sense of value, importance, direction, and/or significance of life.

Meaningfulness   Part of the sense of coherence, this refers to the person's belief in the degree to which events have meaning or significance.

Meaninglessness   Lack of direction or sense of significance in one's life. A risk factor for boredom and a form of alienation.

Meditation   A relaxation technique in which the person focuses on a mantra, sound, word, or phrase (that is, a repeated mental focus) to quiet the mind, thereby quieting the body.

Mental Diversion   Switching one's thoughts to another subject in order to avoid fear, anger, or another unwanted emotion. Also known as thought switching.

Mental Rehearsal   Using imagery and self-talk to rehearse a forthcoming experience.

Micro-Stressor   A stressor experienced as minor in nature, resulting in a low-intensity stress response. May be positive or negative.

Midsight   Recognizing or understanding an experience while it is occurring, rather than before or afterwards.

Migraine Headache   A recurrent, painful condition in the head associated with alternating constriction and dilation of cerebral blood vessels. Often accompanied by nausea and visual disturbance.

Mind-Body-Behavior Linkages   The ongoing mutual influences of mind, body, and behavior on each other.

Mindful Meditation   A method of achieving deep quiet and peacefulness by simply listening to internal thoughts and body processes—being mindful of what you are experiencing at each moment in the meditative state.

Mineral Corticoids   Produced by the adrenal cortex, this hormone helps during the stress response to dissipate heat and water generated by increased metabolism, as well as to retain water and raise blood pressure and blood salinity through retention of sodium.

Mini-Fight-or-Flight Response   Low-level elicitation of the stress response in responding to minor daily stressors.

Minimizing   Diminishing the value or importance of something to less than it actually is.

Mismanagement of Time   A category of difficulties with time.

Missing the Mark   An inappropriate coping response in which the person responds to or does what was not asked or vice versa.

Movies of the Mind   See *Visualization*.

Muscle Slapping   A method of reducing one's muscle tension by gently slapping muscles throughout the body.

Muscular-Skeletal System   The body's integrated system of bones and muscles.

Musterbation   Albert Ellis' term referring to the distorted belief that events must turn out precisely as the person wants otherwise they will inevitably be very upsetting. Putting unreasonable "musts" on the world.

Myocardial Infarction   Death of heart tissue resulting from insufficient supply of oxygen. Also known as heart attack.

Neck Press   Briefly reducing neck tension by pressing the head forward or backward against an immovable object such as a wall or bookcase, then relaxing.

Negativizing   Filtering out positive aspects of a situation while focusing only on negatives.

Neustress   Neutral arousal. Stress that is neither helpful nor harmful.

New Heroes   Common people seeking to create a better world.

Nonevent Transitions   When the expected never happens.

Noradrenaline   A stress hormone produced by the adrenal medulla. Also known as norepinephrine.

Normal Health   Being out of the sickbed but not reaching one's highest level of well-being. Avoidance of illness.

Normality   The opposite of normlessness in the framework of alienation.

Normlessness   The belief that socially unapproved behaviors are necessary and justified to achieve one's goals. A form of alienation.

Obsession   The codependent's tendency to worry about small things and to feel overly anxious about other people and their problems. She focuses most of her energy on fixing other people's problems, often interrupting or abandoning her own routines to give energy to others.

On-the-Spot Tension Reducers   Methods of briefly eliciting the relaxation response in the midst of a stressful situation.

Open Meditation   A meditation in which one allows the mind to wander and drift, allowing in whatever comes and focusing on the image, sensation, or thought as it passes through.

Optimal Arousal   That level of arousal resulting in maximum productivity, satisfaction, and good health. Also known as positive stress.

Optimal Health   Absence of illness, low illness risk, and maximum energy for daily living. May not be the same as "normal" health.

Organizational Stressors   Conditions in an organization with a potential to result in distress among those who work there.

Overchoice   The existence of so many options that the person feels overwhelmed.

Overgeneralizing   Generalizing from a single event or piece of information to all such events or facts.

Overload in Daily Pace of Life   Too much to do in too little time on a daily basis.

Overstimulation   Experiencing stimuli so numerous or intense that one feels overwhelmed.

Oxytocin   A hormone released by the pituitary gland that, along with vasopression, contributes to constriction of blood vessels during physiological arousal.

P and Q Method   A method for managing situational self-talk, this includes two steps: pause and question.

Pace of Life   The number, variety, and intensity of stressors per day, week, or year.

Panic Zone   The zone of overload distress in which the person experiences demands exceeding his or her resources for coping with them.

Parasympathetic Nervous System   Part of the autonomic nervous system, which regulates the relaxation response of the body.

Parroting   An ineffective listening response in which you repeat back the exact words you just heard.

Passivity   A style of interacting in which the person does not express genuine wants, needs, or opinions and allows himself or herself to be controlled by others.

Pathophysiological Processes   Physiological processes resulting in disease, as in coronary artery disease.

Peak Arousal   The height of arousal during demanding or challenging events. May be helpful or harmful.

Peak Performance   Attaining a high level of excellence relative to one's abilities.

Peptic Ulcers   A lesion or open sore in the stomach or upper small intestine causing pain and sometimes bleeding. Sometimes caused by stress.

Perfectionism   Impossibly demanding expectations toward self, others, or both.

Permanence   The tendency to interpret events as either permanent or temporary. Part of learned pessimism and learned optimism.

Personal Anchors   Meaningful persons, rituals, or objects that are relatively stable and dependable through time.

Personal Barriers to Assuming Social Responsibility   Internal beliefs and interpretations impeding individuals taking responsibility for social well-being.

Personal Change   Changes within the person's life, such as moving, changing jobs, becoming more assertive, or starting to exercise.

Personality   An enduring set of habits of thinking, feeling, and acting. Personality is the "style" we carry with us through time.

Personalization   The tendency to interpret events as internally or externally caused. Part of learned pessimism and learned optimism.

Personalizing   A style of distorted thinking in which the person believes others' actions or feelings are entirely caused by self.

Personal Responsibility   Assuming control over and accountability for one's behavior, thoughts, feelings, health, and well-being.

Pervasiveness   The tendency to interpret events as universal or specific. Part of learned pessimism and learned optimism.

Physical Distress Symptoms   Distress symptoms reflected in the body. Illustrated by neck pain, fatigue, stomach upset, and headache.

Physical Wellness Habits   Sound nutritional practices; regular exercise, including aerobic exercise several times a week; consistent and adequate sleep; nonabuse of alcohol, drugs, and tobacco; use of seat belts and cycle helmets and practice of other safe traffic practices; and, if sexually active, practice of safe sex.

Pituitary Gland   Endocrine gland located at the base of the brain below the hypothalamus. Considered the master gland. Secretes ACTH and TTH during the stress response.

Placating   Talking in an ingratiating way; never disagreeing, no matter what; constantly apologizing.

Placebo Power   Occurs when the belief in the effectiveness of a treatment such as a pill produces the expected outcome, even though the treatment has no potency in and of itself, as in a harmless preparation given to control group patients during a drug experiment.

Pleaser   The distress-prone personality pattern wearing an ever-present smile, having great difficulty saying no, and feeling terrible guilt when doing so. She/he tends to do more for others than self and is intimidated by authority.

Plunger   Someone who too quickly and too completely reveals himself or herself in social situations.

Polarized Thinking   The tendency to think in terms of black-white, good-bad, perfection-failure. No middle ground.

Poor Communication   The tendency of the co-dependent to not say what she means or to mean what she says— and in fact to not even know what she means. To get what she wants or to be taken seriously, she blames, threatens, coerces, begs, bribes, and lies.

Positive Addiction   An addiction such as running and meditation with positive, healthy effects on mind or body.

Positive Affirmations   Positive self-talk statements intended to elevate self-esteem or confidence.

Positive Mental Image   A positive picture in the mind of a forthcoming event or challenge.

Positive Stress   Arousal that contributes to health, satisfaction, or productivity.

Powerlessness   The belief that one has little influence over events, which are perceived as occurring mainly due to luck, chance, fate, or others' decisions.

Preventing Distress   Maintaining wellness lifestyle habits and a coping style that minimize the frequency, duration, and intensity of distress.

Primary Appraisal   Determining, given your knowledge of the stressor, whether you are potentially threatened or are in jeopardy.

Prioritizing   A time-management technique involving arranging tasks in rank order in which you decide to do them.

Problem-Focused Coping   The focus of coping is attempting to deal constructively with the stressor or circumstance itself.

Procrastinating Self-Talk   Internal dialogue justifying procrastination.

Procrastination   The tendency to put off doing something until a future time because it is perceived as being too onerous, unpleasant, or unappealing.

Procrastinator's Code   A set of irrational beliefs of the chronic procrastinator.

Prodrome   The first stage of a migraine headache in which cerebral blood vessels constrict, resulting in such symptoms as dizziness, flushness, visual static, or a generalized sense of uneasiness.

Progressive Relaxation   An active relaxation technique in which specific muscles are tensed, then relaxed.

Promoting Wellness   Maintaining wellness lifestyle habits and a coping style that promote the well-being of others.

Psychologizing   An ineffective listening response in which the listener inappropriately or inaccurately attributes thoughts or feelings to the speaker.

Psychoneuroimmunology   An interdisciplinary science focusing on the mutual influences of the mind, nervous system, and immune system.

Psychosomatic Illness   An illness in which the mind plays a significant etiological role.

Pushing Your Limits   Leaving your comfort zone and entering a zone of temporary distress in order to become more competent and confident in an activity.

Qualitative Overload   Feeling overwhelmed by the difficulty of one or more tasks.

Quantitative Overload   Feeling overwhelmed by a large number of tasks or stimuli.

Race Horse   Hans Selye's term for a person with high energy and a high zone of positive stress.

Rackets   Patterns of thinking in which the person keeps himself or herself miserable, for example, anxious, afraid, or angry. Often practiced by distress-seekers.

Radical Individualism   The tendency in American life to glorify individual interests and rights at the expense of personal responsibility and concern for the common good.

Range of Stress Tolerance   The zone of stress in which the individual is healthy, productive, and satisfied.

Reactions to Distress   Mental and/or behavioral ways of handling acute or chronic distress. May be deliberate or scripted, adaptive or maladaptive.

Realistic Self-Talk   Self-talk or internal dialogue about events or persons that is based on a realistic assessment of the situation rather than on distorted or irrational thinking.

Reasonable Belief   An enduring assumption that is factual, moderate, and helpful.

Regressive Coping   Coping by thinking pessimistically or by avoiding the stressor when it might be better to deal with it directly.

Reintegration   The process of building new relationships during the college years as young adults move away from home.

Relaxation Response   Quieting of mind and body.

Remember-Forgetting Technique   A time-management technique in which, whenever you remember a task that you keep forgetting to do, do it—or at least some of it—*immediately.*

Repetition Compulsion   The drive to repeat that which is familiar. The force of habit.

Repression   The tendency of the codependent to repress her own thoughts and feelings out of fear and guilt.

Reprogramming   A method for changing a pattern of negative self-talk to a pattern of realistic or positive self-talk. Steps include deliberate use of new self-talk, repetition and practice, and making the new self-talk part of one's natural thinking.

Residual Stress   Mental and/or physical arousal that remains after an experience. May be positive or negative.

Reticular Activating System   Complex network of nerve fibers through which nerve messages are sent among layers of the brain.

Rewriting Irrational Beliefs   A writing and thinking process for changing beliefs from irrational to rational.

Rheumatoid Arthritis   A chronic disease of unknown origin in which joints become inflamed, swollen, and painful. May be aggravated by stress.

Rhythm   In relation to assumptions about stress management, refers to recognition that stress and distress come and go in rhythms and stages. In relation to the heart and heart disease, refers to repeated electrical stimulation of the heart muscle resulting in heart beats.

Risk Factors for Boredom   Experiences carrying a high risk of boredom: not enough challenge, too much isolation, too much routine, and meaninglessness.

Risk Factors for Heart Disease   Personal characteristics and habits that increase chances of coronary artery disease and myocardial infarction.

Risk Factors for the Hot Reaction   Personal characteristics and habits that increase chances of a hyper-response of the cardiovascular system during the stress response.

Risk-Taking   Engaging in actions that are new, dangerous, or have potential for failure. Moderate amounts needed for personal growth.

Role Ambiguity   Unclear expectations associated with a social position, such as student, employee, or mother.

Role Conflict   Incompatible expectations associated with a social position, such as student, employee, or mother.

Role Difficulties   See *Role-Related Stressors.*

Role of Behavior   The part played by action in the stress response.

Role Overload   Expectations associated with a social position call for more activity than time allows, as experienced by the role occupant.

Role-Related Stressors   Stressors associated with social roles, which are social positions with clustered expectations.

Role Strain   Conflict between personal desires and others' expectations.

Role Transition   Movement of an individual from one social position to another. Illustrated by graduation, marriage, divorce, becoming a parent, a job transfer.

Role Underload   Expectations associated with a social position that call for too little activity, resulting in boredom, understimulation, or lethargy.

Sabertooth   A distress-prone personality pattern in which the person often expresses feelings through sarcasm, chronic irritation, or trivial arguments. Quite unpredictable, this tendency might express itself with an outburst over a cup of spilled milk, a driver on the freeway, a noisy neighbor, or even something a loved one does or says.

Sadness   The dreary, dark feeling associated with a real, imagined, or anticipated loss.

Schafer Coping Model   A set of coping options including three broad alternatives: Altering the stressor, adapting to the stressor, and avoiding the stressor.

Scheduling   One of the three main categories of time-management methods.

Scripted Coping Responses   Coping methods that were developed in childhood and adolescence as part of one's broader life script. A blueprint for how to cope.

Scripted Reactions to Distress   Reactions to distress that are embedded in one's life script as a result of early messages and early decisions about how to handle distress.

Secondary Appraisal   Assessment of resources for dealing with the stressor.

Self-Actualization   State of highest possible human functioning, usually reached only in later years. Being fully human. Includes the full use and exploitation of talent, capacities, potentialities, personalities, etc.

Self-Disclosure   Communicating one's authentic feelings or thoughts. Allowing oneself to be known, seen, understood.

Self-Esteem   Appreciation of a person's own worth and importance.

Self-Estrangement   One form of alienation, this is the sense of being separate from one's thoughts, actions, and experiences which seem to be controlled by others. The sense of one's work being foreign to oneself rather than an expression of oneself.

Self-Hypnosis   A method of producing deep relaxation in which one silently repeats self-suggestive statements, thereby quieting the mind and quieting the body.

Self-Massage   Using your fingertips or palms to massage the face or other areas that might be tense.

Self-Monitoring   Becoming aware of one's thoughts, feelings, and action patterns.

Self-Reward   Rewarding yourself with something pleasant when you've finished any difficult or onerous task. A method of avoiding procrastination.

Self-Punishment   Penalizing yourself by depriving yourself or forcing yourself to do something you don't like until you finish the task. A method for avoiding procrastination.

Self-Talk   Internal dialogue; conversation with self; includes interpretations of events.

Self-Transcendence   Devoting energy to goals beyond yourself.

Sensation-Seeker   A person who generates a high level of stimulation in order to maintain a high level of stress.

Sense of Coherence   A pervasive, enduring though dynamic feeling of confidence that one's internal and external environments are predictable and that there is a high probability that things will work out as well as can reasonably be expected.

Sensory Deprivation   The experience of being deprived of most or all external stimuli. When prolonged, can result in extreme distress.

cmSeparation from Parents   The process of decreasing the frequency and/or intensity of connection with parents as youth or young adults move away.

Serendipity   The ability of the survivor personality to find seemingly fortuitous answers and solutions during adversity.

Sexual Harassment   Unwanted, repeated, and coercive sexual advances.

Shoulding   Constant imposition of "shoulds" and "should haves" on self, others, or both.

Simplification   When used in context of time management, refers to grouping of similar tasks into time blocks.

Simulation Control   A time-management technique in which you make as many changes in your environment as necessary to remove distractions, insure privacy, become neater, and have important materials on hand.

Situational Self-Talk   Self-talk or internal dialogue that occurs at the moment one deals with a stressor.

Six-Second Quieting Response   A brief, on-the-spot tension reliever involving inhaling, holding, exhaling, and allowing the jaws and shoulders to drop.

Sleeper Transitions   Transitions that are so gradual they are hardly noticeable.

Slow-Motion Suicide   Destructive, health-harming habits such as smoking, overeating, excessive drinking, and drug-taking.

Small Sequential Steps   When you procrastinate on a task, break it down into smaller, manageable parts and set yourself the goal of doing a small step by a specific deadline. Once you have finished one step, do the next one.

Social Approaches to Managing Stress   Group efforts to reduce social forces that create distress and to assist people in distress.

Social Barriers to Assuming Social Responsibility   Factors in the social environment that impede individuals taking responsibility for social well-being.

Social Change   Change in the environment surrounding the person.

Social Commitment   Sustained motivation and action to improve social conditions.

Social Inequality   The presence of social ranking of individuals and groups by such criteria as wealth, power, and prestige.

Social Network   The specific set of linkages among a defined set of persons or a given person.

Social Responsibility   Willingness to assume personal responsibility for public problems.

Social Support   An interpersonal transaction involving sharing of one or more of the following: liking, love, empathy, information, goods, or services.

Social Tie   An on-going relationship with another person.

Social Wellness Habits   Sharing intimacy, friendships, and group memberships; practicing empathy and active listening; caring for others; being open to others' caring; and demonstrating an ongoing commitment to the common good of the community, the state, and the nation.

Sociological Imagination   The ability to understand that personal experience is influenced by larger social forces.

Solitude   Being alone, secluded, or isolated. Usually means the person experiences aloneness positively.

Spiritual Wellness Habits   Concern with issues of meaning, value, and purpose; if not clarity or certainty in these respects, at least attentiveness to their importance and a continuing quest for clarity.

Stage of Exhaustion   The third stage of the general adaptation syndrome in which the body's reserves begin to become depleted in defending against a stressor.

Stage of Resistance   The second stage of the general adaptation syndrome in which physiological arousal above baseline assists the body in defending against a stressor.

Stages in Reaction to Loss   Patterned responses to loss through distinguishable phases.

Stages of Coping   This refers to primary appraisal, secondary appraisal, and coping response.

Stages of Sleep   Several levels of sleep that are usually experienced by most people.

Stimulants   Drugs, such as caffeine and amphetamines, that arouse mind and body.

Stress   Arousal of mind and body in response to demands made upon them.

Stress-Avoiding   Thriving on security and familiarity and avoiding challenge, sensation, and risk.

Stress Buildup   Progressively higher arousal during a period of sustained challenge or pressure.

Stressor   Any demand on mind or body.

Stress Personalities   Used by Dempcy and Tihista, this means the same as distress-prone personality patterns.

Stress Recovery   Return of arousal level to baseline.

Stress-Related Illnesses   A category of illnesses in which stress plays a causative role.

Stress Response   Physiological and mental arousal in response to a perceived stressor.

Stress-Seeking   Thriving on challenge, risk, and sensation.

Stretching   An active method for relaxing muscle tension, done standing, or sitting.

Striver   A distress-prone personality pattern that leads to endless struggle to achieve, produce, and accomplish.

Styles of Negative Self-Talk   Patterns of negative or distorted thinking through which people sometimes make themselves miserable—or miserable to be around.

Substance Abuse   Use of illegal drugs or misuse of legal substances.

Sudden Death   Sudden termination of life, usually caused by a malfunction of the heart.

Superficial Adaptive Energy   Energy for coping with life that can be replaced through rest, exercise, good nutrition, and other good health habits.

Supply-Side Approach to Health Care Reform   Expanding medical care services to include a greater proportion of the population in need of such services, developing new approaches to paying for those services, and finding new ways of paying for those services.

Surprise Transitions   When the unexpected happens.

Survivor Personality   A personality pattern in which the person copes effectively with adversity, even of a very high order.

Swimmer's Shake   An active relaxation method in which you allow your arms to hang loosely at your sides, then shake each one from fingers to shoulder in a rotary motion.

Swiss-Cheese Method   A time-management method in which you do *anything at all* that's connected to the task you want to accomplish. Gradually eat large chunks or holes in the task until it becomes easier to do.

Sympathetic Nervous System   That part of the peripheral nervous system which regulates the stress response of the body.

Sympathizing   To show understanding, pity, or compassion. An effective interactional style, except in active listening, when remaining neutral may be more effective.

Sympathomimetic Agent   A substance such as caffeine, which stimulates the sympathetic nervous system.

Synergy   The ability of individuals with the survivor personality to make things go well for themselves and others. Their inner "life force" seems to take them in directions that work out, even under enormous pressure and hardship.

Systolic Blood Pressure   Amount of pressure against the inner walls of blood vessels at the moment of heart beat.

T.A.T.T.   Tired all the time.

T'ai Chi Ch'uan   An ancient discipline from China, sometimes called the "softest of the martial arts," brings the mind and body into unity with the *chi* or life force in the natural world around us. Widely acclaimed as a powerful tool for centering, for holding steady and calm under pressure, for flowing with rather than against external threat and resistance.

Tense and Relax Neck and Shoulders   An active method, drawn from progressive relaxation, for reducing muscle tension in the neck and shoulders.

Tension Headache   Head pain caused by constriction of blood vessels during or after emotional stress.

Thought-Stopping   Using an internal command to stop an unwanted stream of thinking.

Three-Breath Release   A method of relaxing mind and body in which, during each of three long and deep exhalations, specific muscles are relaxed.

Thriving Under Pressure   Not only preventing distress but reaching one's highest possible level of performance under pressure.

Thyroid Gland   Endocrine gland, located in the neck, which secretes thyroid hormones such as thyroxine.

Thyrotropic Hormone (TTH)   A hormone secreted into the bloodstream by the pituitary gland during the stress response to activate the thyroid gland.

Thyroxine   A hormone produced by the thyroid gland during the stress response. Speeds up metabolism and increases sensitivity of tissues of the body to adrenaline.

Time Blocking   Blocking out several hours on a given day for a category of activity.

Time Demands   Pressures, obligations, and tasks requiring your time.

Time Management   Control and organization of time to produce a satisfying, healthy, and productive life.

Time Supply   The amount of time you have available to complete a given set of tasks.

Time Wellness Habits   Maintaining a pace of life that is within one's comfort zone most of the time; maintaining relative control over one's time; minimizing chronic hurry and hassle, on one hand, and boredom and stagnation, on the other; balancing activity and rest, work and play, solitude and relationships.

Time Urgency   Feeling chronically hurried, hassled and short of time, even in the absence of external time pressures.

TMJ Syndrome   The temporomandibular joint (TMJ), connecting the upper and lower jawbones, becomes tense or malaligned, creating severe pain in face, neck, head, even throughout the upper body.

Trackdown   A method of tracking down the meaning of specific distress symptoms.

Tragic Life Script   A life script calling for tragedy, such as suicide, imprisonment, alcoholism, or heart attack.

Transcendental Meditation   A deep-relaxation method involving quieting the mind and body for 10 to 20 minutes twice a day by repeating a silent mantra.

Transformational Coping   Constructive action to change the stressor.

Transitions   The movement of the person from one role, setting, or circumstance to another.

Trusting Heart   This is a distress-resistant personality pattern in which the person believes in the basic goodness of humankind and that most people will be fair and kind in relationships with others. Having such beliefs, the trusting heart is slow to anger. Opposite of the hostile heart.

Turning to Others   A constructive coping method involving sharing frustrations, fears, or other stress-related emotions with others who are supportive.

Turtle   A person who thrives on a relatively slow pace of life. Easily overloaded.

Type A   A pattern of thinking, feeling, and acting marked by intense drive, perfectionism, time urgency, and easily aroused hostility and anger.

Type B   A pattern of thinking, feeling, and acting marked by the relative absence of Type A qualities.

Type C   A pattern of thinking, feeling, and acting in which the person thrives and reaches peak performance under pressure. The Type C perspective includes challenge, confidence, and control.

Type E   A distress-prone personality pattern, usually applied to women, in which the person thinks and acts according to one dominating and pervasive principle: everything for everybody.

Type T   A pattern of thrill-seeking.

Ulcer   An open sore on the lining of the stomach or just inside the small intestine.

Unconditional Love   Unyielding love based on a person's existence rather than on his/her actions.

Unconscious Interpretation Pathway   Activation of the stress response without conscious appraisal or interpretation. Illustrated by the body's automatic response to low-grade sound or lighting.

Underload   A level of stimulation below a person's zone of positive stress.

Under-Reactions   Reactions to stressors that are less than called for by the situation.

Understimulation   Stimuli that are too few or not intense enough for the person. Can result in underload distress symptoms.

Unfinished Business   Incomplete tasks or unexpressed feelings.

Unreasonable Belief   A belief that is not based on fact, is extreme, or is harmful.

Value Clarification   A learning process in which the person clarifies his or her beliefs about what is important/unimportant valuable/not valuable, desirable/undesirable.

Vasopressin   Helps the body to increase blood volume through action of the kidneys.

Vicious Cycle   A negative cycle of thinking, feeling, acting, and others' responses, beginning with an unreasonable belief.

Visualization   The process of deliberately creating positive mental pictures for the purpose of mental rehearsal or relaxation.

Vital Cycle   A positive cycle of thinking, feeling, acting, and others' responses, beginning with a reasonable belief.

Voluntary Nervous System   Controls striate, voluntary muscles throughout the body, controlling posture and movement.

Weak Boundaries   The codependent's tendency to increase gradually her tolerance until she tolerates and does things she never thought she would and to keep letting herself get hurt by others.

Well-Adjusted Persons   Individuals who are well-adapted to the surrounding world. Can be taken too far if individuals ignore distress-producing social conditions.

Wellness   The process of living at one's highest possible level as a whole person and promoting the same for others. Maximizing one's potentials while enjoying the process and maintaining optimal health along the way.

Wellness-Worseness Continuum   The range along which people vary from high energy, good health, and high satisfaction to low energy, illness, and low satisfaction.

Wellness Lifestyle   Mutually reinforcing positive habits in the following areas: environmental, intellectual, emotional, spiritual, physical, social, and time.

Whole Person   The individual's full range of qualities and potentials in all the following areas: intellectual, emotional, spiritual, physical, social, environmental, time.

Work-First Technique   A time-management technique in which you identify the most difficult part of the task and do it first.

Worrier   A person who consistently takes concern into over-concern and engages in excessive rumination.

Worry   Concern taken to over-concern, usually including excessive rumination.

Worseness   The process of living at a low level of potential in the various parts of one's life. The opposite of wellness.

Yo-Yo Dieting   Repeatedly losing and regaining weight. Usually results in long-term weight gain.

Yoga   A discipline of relaxation and spiritual growth involving prescribed body postures and movements while carrying on specific breathing and mental exercises.

Zen Meditation   A technique of quieting mind and body through focusing on the breath.

Zone of Overload Distress   On a hypothetical continuum of arousal, this is the zone above a person's upper limit of tolerance in which overload distress symptoms appear.

Zone of Positive Stress   The tolerance range of stress in which a person is healthy, productive, and satisfied.

Zone of Underload Distress   On a hypothetical continuum of arousal, this is the zone below a person's lower limit of tolerance where underload distress symptoms appear.

Zones of Distress   Those zones of arousal outside the comfort zone in which the person experiences too much or too little arousal resulting in harm to mind or body.

Author Index

Subject Index

AAAABBCC, 299
ABC technique, 424
Absence of free-floating hostility, 231
Absence of time urgency, 230
Acid reflux, 164
ACTH, 87
Active listening, 452–455
Adaptation to stress, 95, 96
Addiction-prone pattern, 216–219
Adrenal cortex, 84
Adrenal medulla, 84
Adrenaline, 84
Adrenocorticotropic hormone (ACTH), 87
Aerobic exercise, 325–337
   how much is needed, 330, 331
   physiological changes, 331
   physiological pathways, 332
   psychological pathways, 331, 332
   running, 332–335
   self-talk, 336, 337
   tips, 337
   walking, 334–336
   what is it, 330
Aerobic training effect, 331
African Prayer Book, An (Tutu), 471
Afterburn, 260
AIAI, 183
Alarm reaction, 94
Alcohol abuse, 301–304
Aldosterone, 87
Alice's Adventures in Wonderland (Carroll), 260
Alienation, 268, 269
Altruism, 470
Altruistic egoism, 468, 469
Anaerobic exercise, 330
Anger, 128, 129, 380–383
Anger Kills (Williams/Williams), 197, 235
Anorexia nervosa, 345, 346
Anticipatory stress, 107, 108
Anxiety, 125, 126
Anxiety neurosis, 126
Ardell Wellness Report, 59
Atherosclerosis, 149
Autogenic relaxation, 405, 406
Autonomic nervous system (ANS), 84
Awfulizing, 367

Bad moods, 125
Banal life scripts, 42

Baseline stress level, 114
Behavioral distress symptoms, 132, 133
Benson meditation method, 396
Beyond Survival: Building on The Hard Times–A POW's Inspiring Story (Coffee), 317, 410
Biofeedback, 404, 405
Blaming, 367, 447
Blaming others, 309
Blaming the system, 252
Blaming the victim, 252
Blocked energy, 67
Body truth, 65
Bonfires of the Vanities, The (Wolfe), 364
Boredom, 429
Bound energy, 93
Bracing, 92
Brain, 82–84
Breathing countdown, 394
Breathing techniques, 393–395
Bulimia nervosa, 346

C Zone: Peak Performance Under Pressure, The (Kriegel/Kriegel), 194
Cancer, 157–159
Cardiovascular activity measures, 405
Cardiovascular disorders, 145–154
Cardiovascular system, 87, 88
Carter ethic, 473
Catastrophizing, 367
Causes of death, 140–142
Cell immunity, 89
Centering, 397
Central nervous system (CNS), 84
Cerebral cortex, 83
Cholesterol, 149, 151, 343, 344
Chronic anxiety, 126
Chronic fatigue syndrome, 63
Chronic insomnia, 165
Clustering of life changes, 28, 29
Clustering of life events, 262–266
Codependency pattern, 219–222
Cognitive distress symptoms, 132
College stress, 25–53
   approaches to managing stress, 45–48
   binge drinking, 302
   clustering of life changes, 28, 29
   daily hassles, 34–36
   eating disorders, 347
   financial uncertainty, 36, 37

Copyrights and Acknowledgments